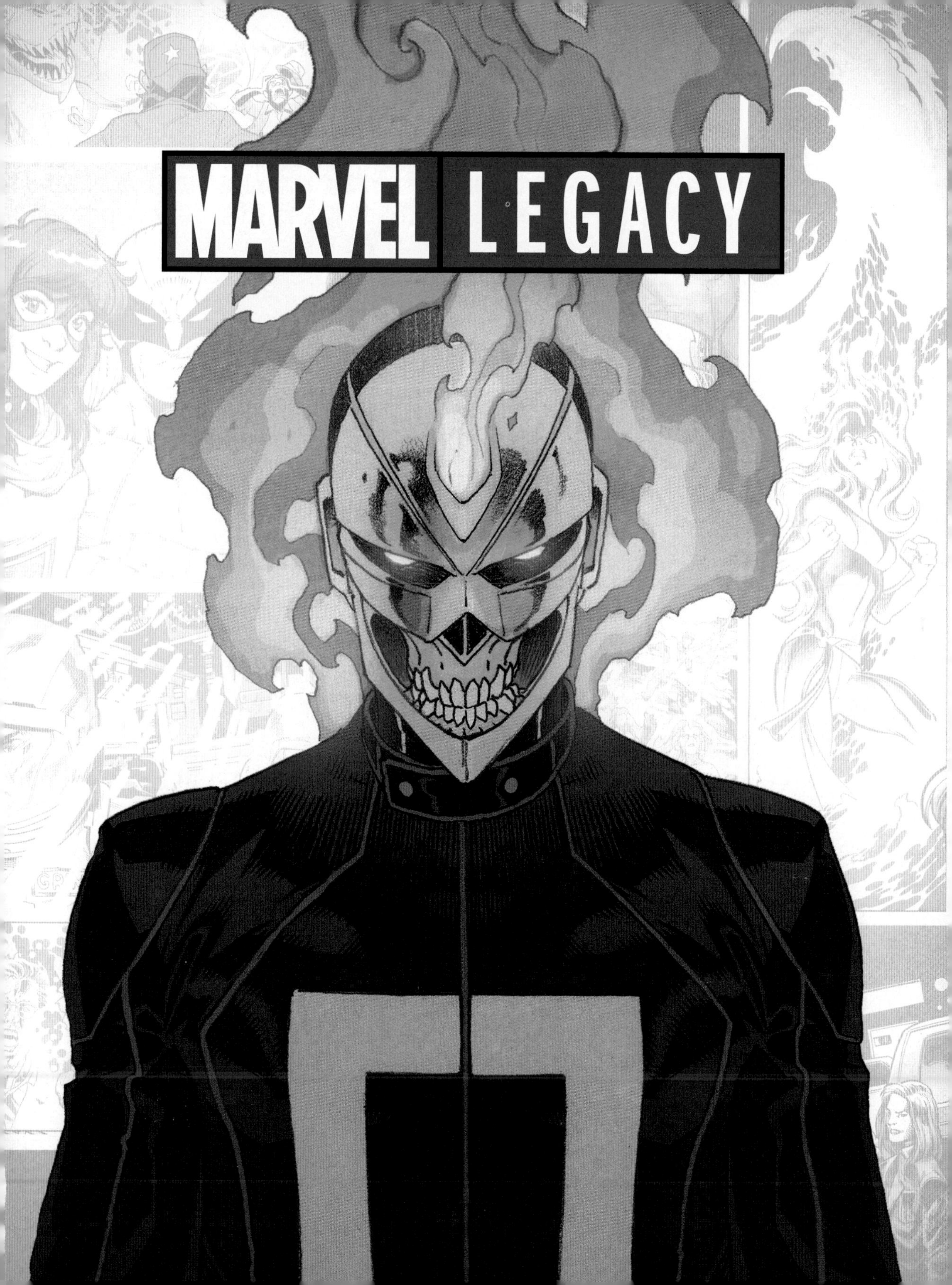
MARVEL LEGACY

MARVEL LEGACY #1

JASON AARON
WRITER

ESAD RIBIĆ WITH STEVE McNIVEN
ARTIST

MATTHEW WILSON
COLOR ARTIST

CHRIS SAMNEE; RUSSELL DAUTERMAN; ALEX MALEEV;
ED McGUINNESS; STUART IMMONEN & WADE VON GRAWBADGER;
PEPE LARRAZ; JIM CHEUNG; DANIEL ACUÑA; GREG LAND
& JAY LEISTEN; MIKE DEODATO JR. AND DAVID MARQUEZ
ADDITIONAL ARTISTS

VC's CORY PETIT
LETTERER

JOE QUESADA, KEVIN NOWLAN & RICHARD ISANOVE
COVER ART

ALANNA SMITH
ASSISTANT EDITOR

TOM BREVOORT
EDITOR

MARVEL PRIMERS

ROBBIE THOMPSON
WRITER

MARK BAGLEY, JOHN DELL, ANDREW HENNESSY, KEVIN LIBRANDA, DANIEL ACUÑA,
EDGAR SALAZAR, ANTHONY PIPER, PERE PÉREZ, ALBERTO ALBURQUERQUE, JOE BENNETT,
BELARDINO BRABO, VALERIO SCHITI, DAVID BALDEÓN, BRENT SCHOONOVER,
WILFREDO TORRES, DAVID LOPEZ, MARCUS TO, TODD NAUCK, GERMÁN PERALTA, ROD REIS,
DALIBOR TALAJIĆ, NIKO HENRICHON, MATT HORAK, MARCO FAILLA,
NATHAN STOCKMAN, RON LIM, MARC DEERING, JORGE COELHO, ANDREA SORRENTINO,
GREG LAND, JAY LEISTEN, VERONICA FISH, IBRAIM ROBERSON, DIEGO OLORTEGUI,
CARLOS PACHECO & RAFAEL FONTEIRZ
ARTISTS

RACHELLE ROSENBERG, CHRIS SOTOMAYOR, DONO SÁNCHEZ-ALMARA, DANIEL ACUÑA,
ANTHONY PIPER, DAN BROWN, ISRAEL SILVA, ANDY TROY, JOSÉ VILLARRUBIA,
RUTH REDMOND, EMILIO LOPEZ, FRANK D'ARMATA, RAIN BEREDO, JORDAN BOYD,
IAN HERRING, JESUS ABURTOV, JIM CAMPBELL, MIROSLAV MRVA, NIKO HENRICHON,
CHRIS O'HALLORAN, MIKE SPICER, ANTONIO FABELA, MARCIO MENYZ, LEE LOUGHRIDGE,
ANDREA SORRENTINO, VERONICA FISH & EDGAR DELGADO
COLOR ARTISTS

VC's CLAYTON COWLES, CORY PETIT, TRAVIS LANHAM,
JOE SABINO & JOE CARAMAGNA
LETTERERS

KATHLEEN WISNESKI
ASSISTANT EDITOR

DARREN SHAN
EDITOR

COLLECTION EDITOR JENNIFER GRÜNWALD ▪ ASSISTANT EDITOR CAITLIN O'CONNELL
ASSOCIATE MANAGING EDITOR KATERI WOODY ▪ EDITOR, SPECIAL PROJECTS MARK D. BEAZLEY
VP PRODUCTION & SPECIAL PROJECTS JEFF YOUNGQUIST ▪ SVP PRINT, SALES & MARKETING DAVID GABRIEL
BOOK DESIGNER JAY BOWEN

EDITOR IN CHIEF C.B. CEBULSKI ▪ CHIEF CREATIVE OFFICER JOE QUESADA
PRESIDENT DAN BUCKLEY ▪ EXECUTIVE PRODUCER ALAN FINE

MARVEL LEGACY. Contains material originally published in magazine form as MARVEL LEGACY #1 and FOOM MAGAZINE. First printing 2018. ISBN 978-1-302-91101-0. Published by MARVEL WORLDWIDE, INC., a subsidiary of MARVEL ENTERTAINMENT, LLC. OFFICE OF PUBLICATION: 135 West 50th Street, New York, NY 10020. Copyright © 2018 MARVEL No similarity between any of the names, characters, persons, and/or institutions in this magazine with those of any living or dead person or institution is intended, and any such similarity which may exist is purely coincidental. **Printed in the U.S.A.** DAN BUCKLEY, President, Marvel Entertainment; JOE QUESADA, Chief Creative Officer; TOM BREVOORT, SVP of Publishing; DAVID BOGART, SVP of Business Affairs & Operations, Publishing & Partnership; DAVID GABRIEL, SVP of Sales & Marketing, Publishing; JEFF YOUNGQUIST, VP of Production & Special Projects; DAN CARR, Executive Director of Publishing Technology; ALEX MORALES, Director of Publishing Operations; SUSAN CRESPI, Production Manager; STAN LEE, Chairman Emeritus. For information regarding advertising in Marvel Comics or on Marvel.com, please contact Vit DeBellis, Custom Solutions & Integrated Advertising Manager, at vdebellis@marvel. com. For Marvel subscription inquiries, please call 888-511-5480. **Manufactured between 12/22/2017 and 1/23/2018 by LSC COMMUNICATIONS INC., KENDALLVILLE, IN, USA.**

10 9 8 7 6 5 4 3 2 1

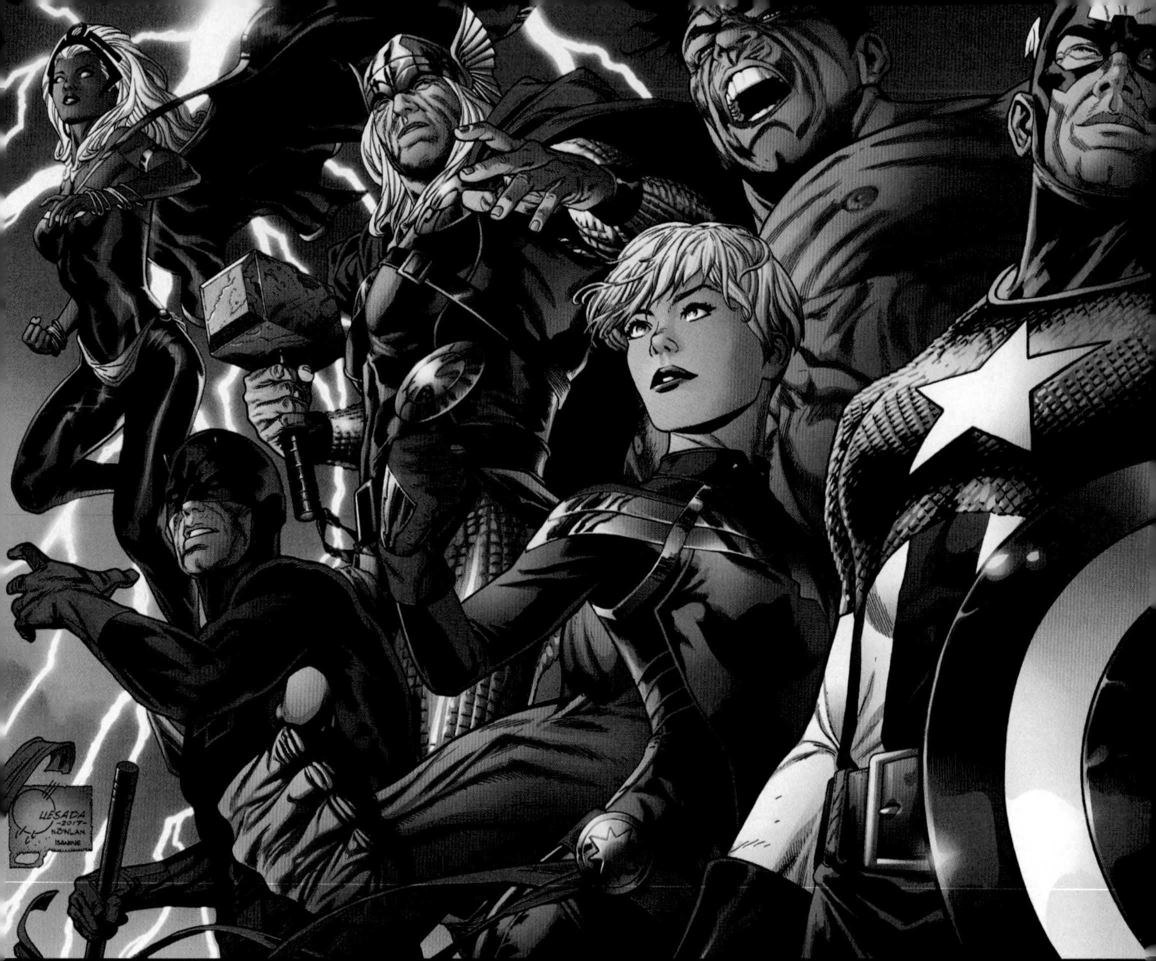

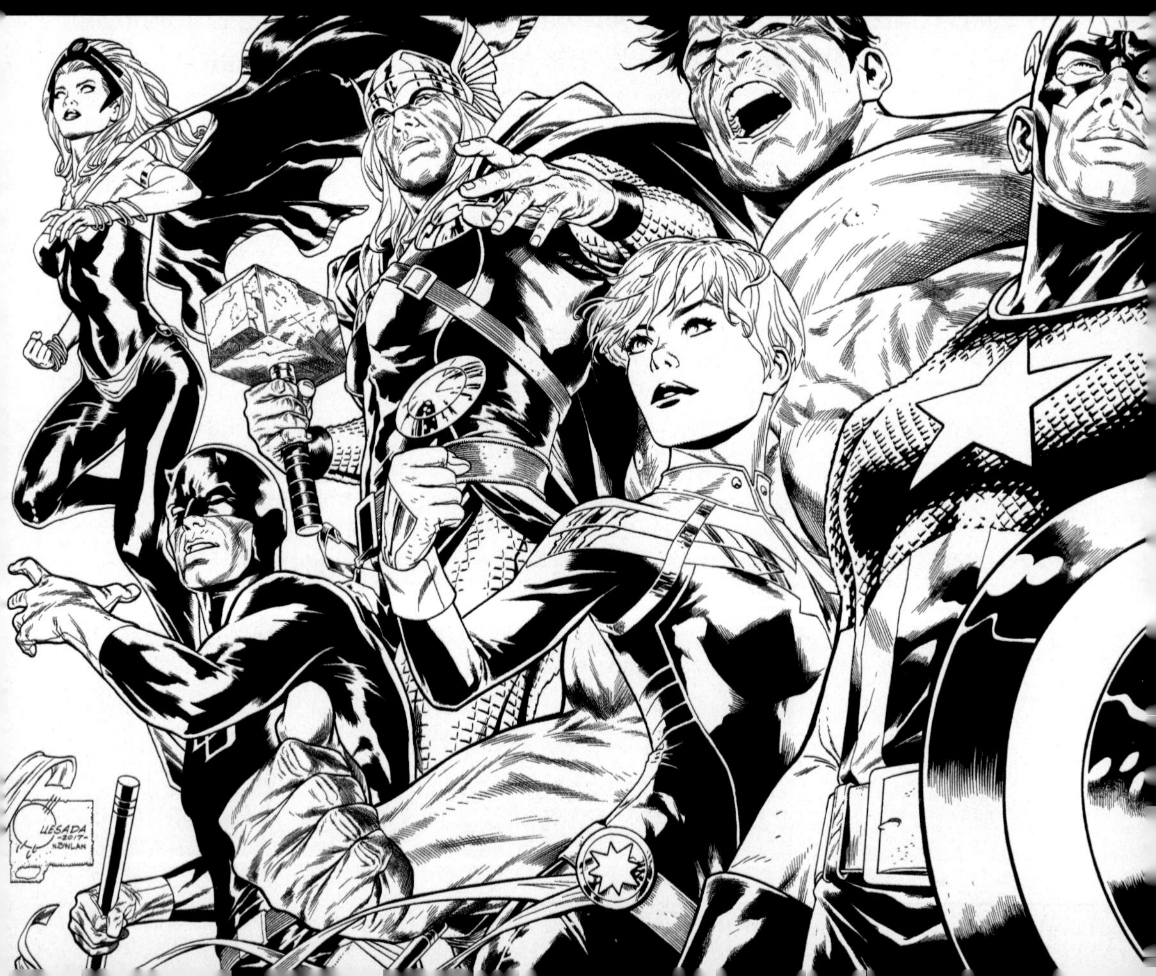

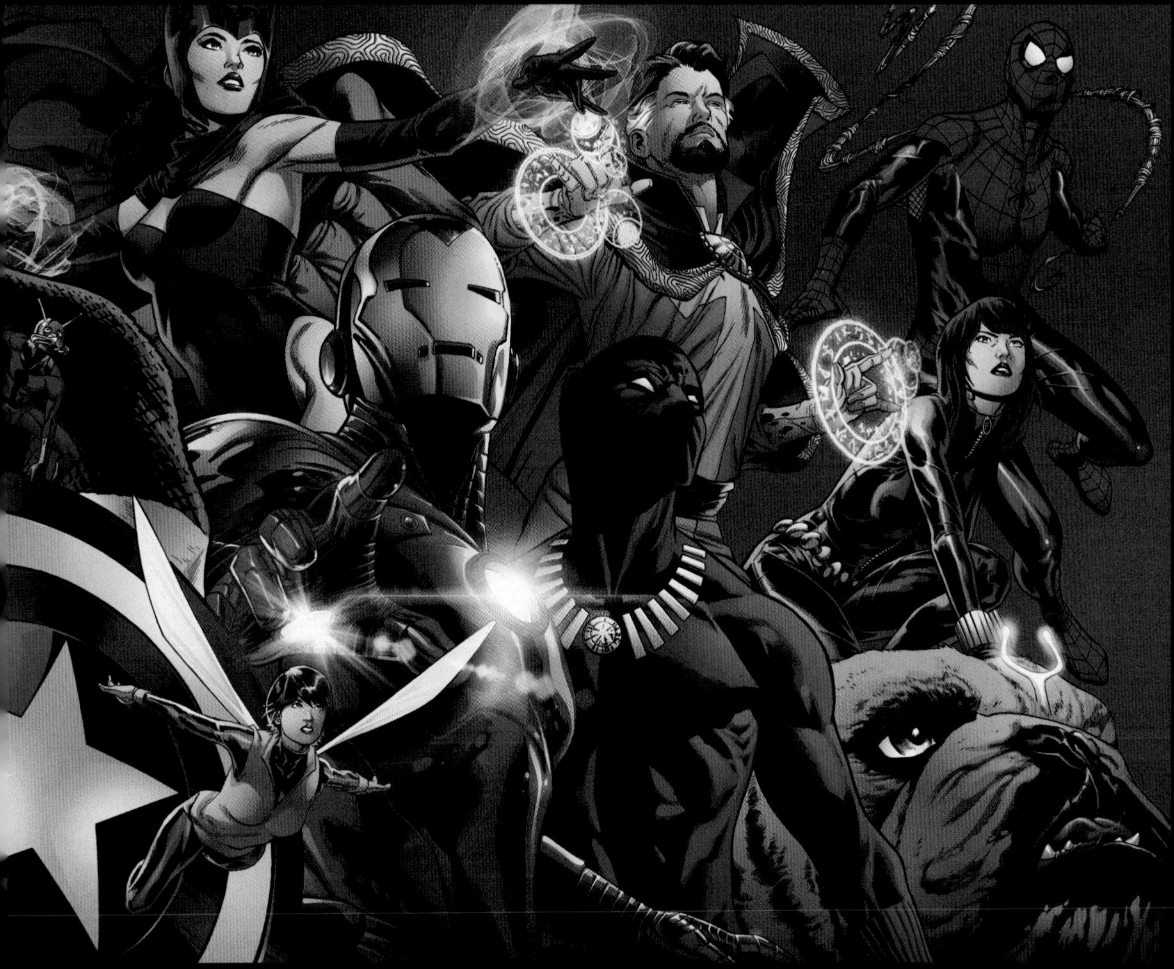

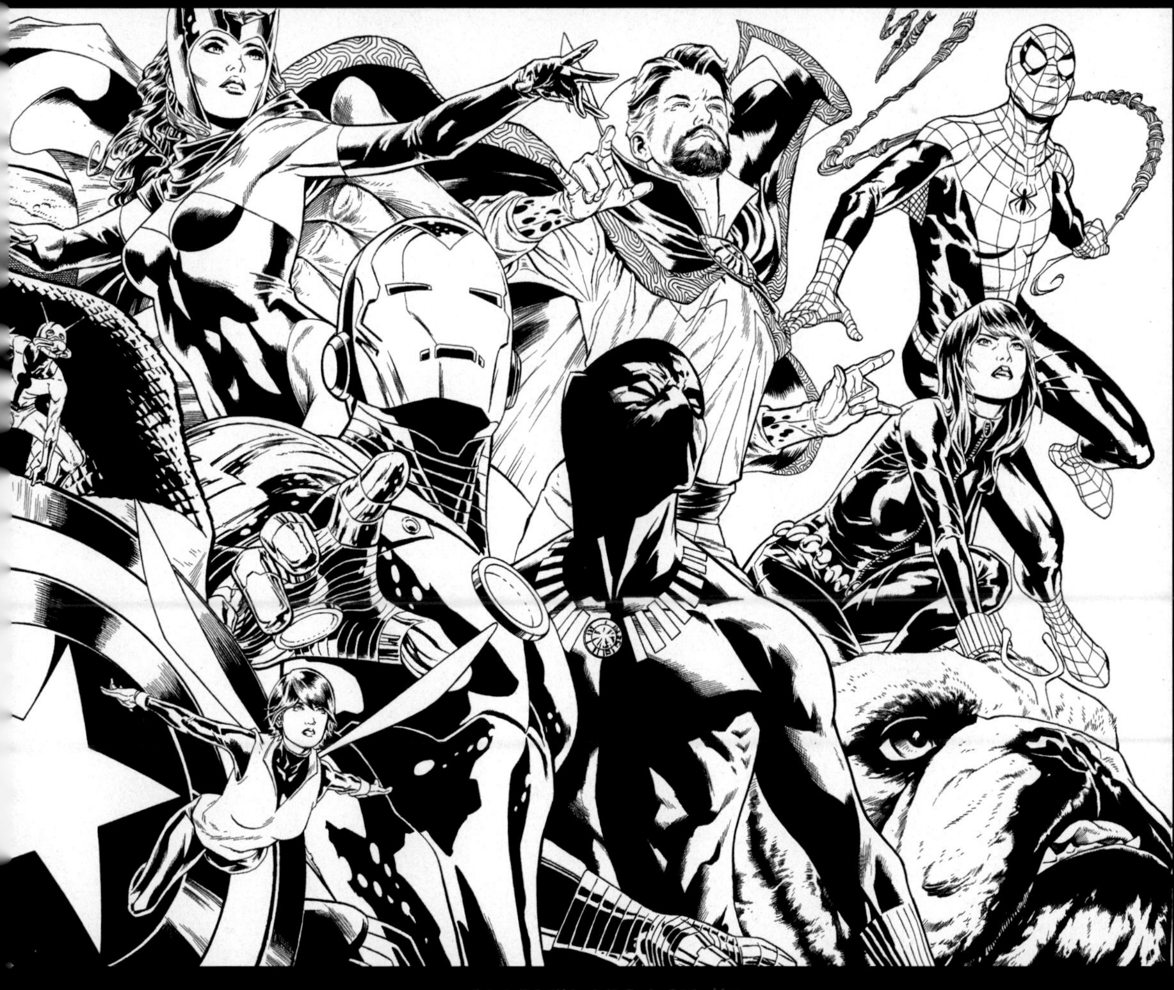

MARVEL LEGACY #1

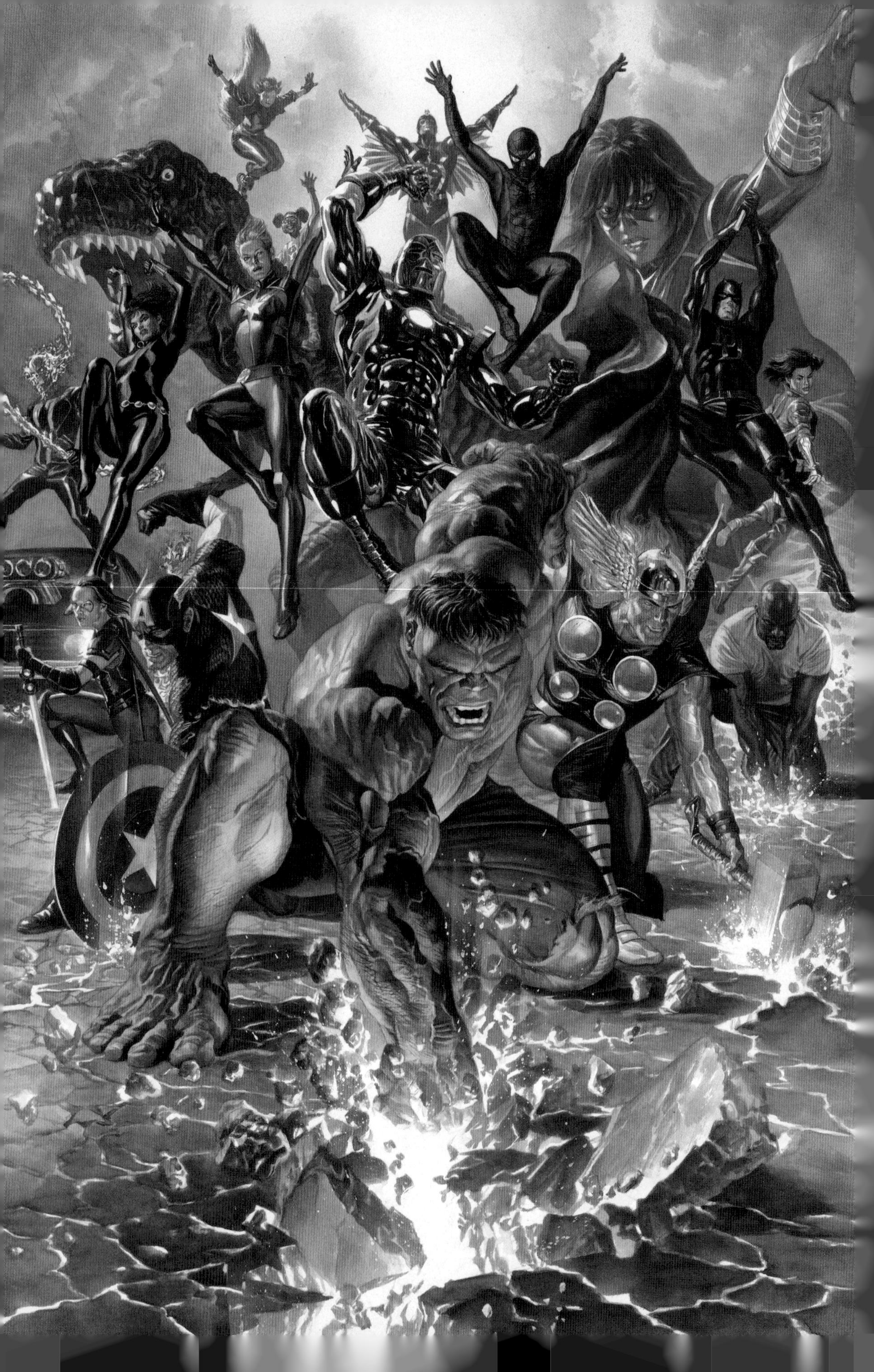

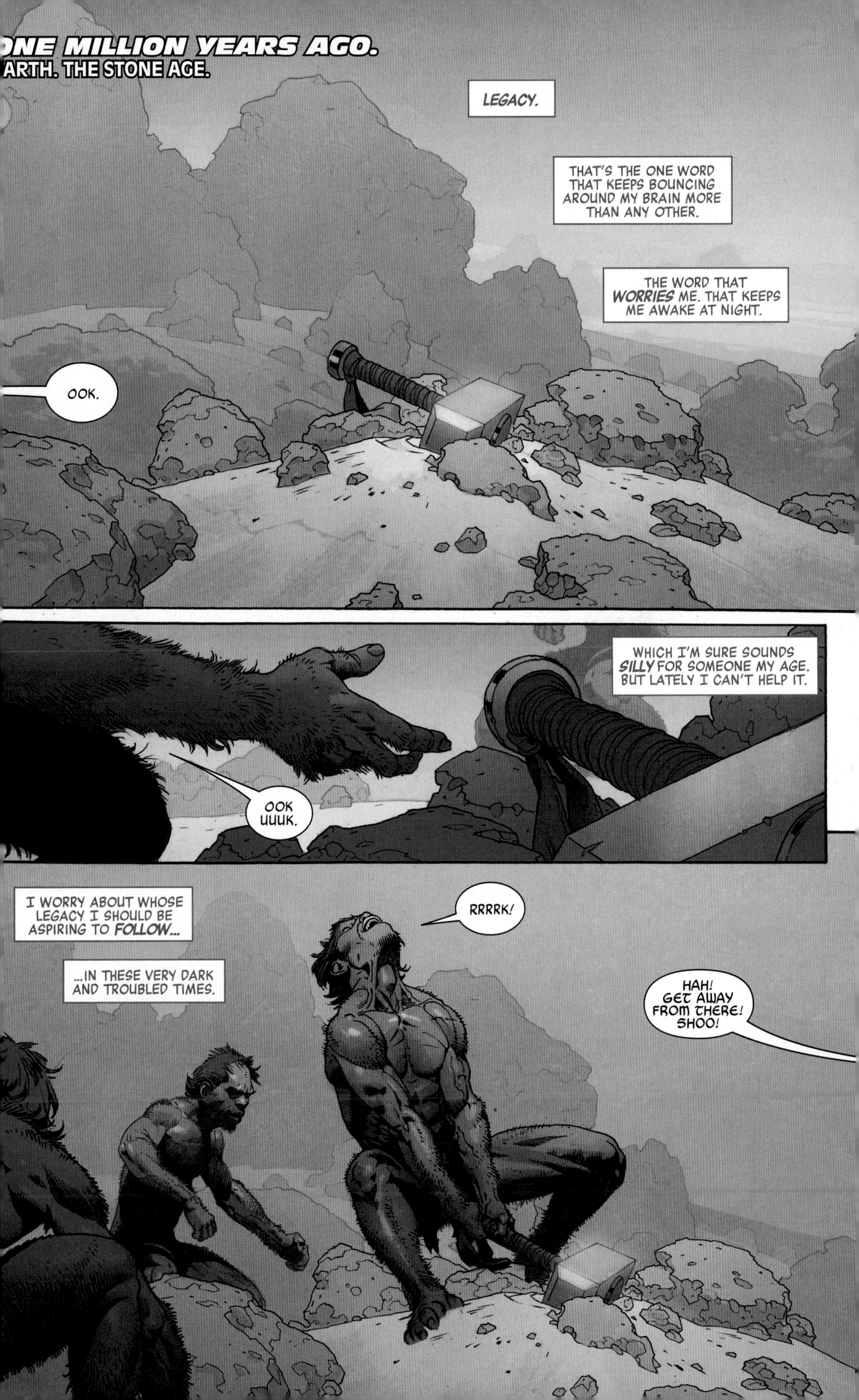
ONE MILLION YEARS AGO.
ARTH. THE STONE AGE.
LEGACY.
THAT'S THE ONE WORD THAT KEEPS BOUNCING AROUND MY BRAIN MORE THAN ANY OTHER.
THE WORD THAT WORRIES ME. THAT KEEPS ME AWAKE AT NIGHT.
OOK.
WHICH I'M SURE SOUNDS SILLY FOR SOMEONE MY AGE. BUT LATELY I CAN'T HELP IT.
OOK UUUK.
I WORRY ABOUT WHOSE LEGACY I SHOULD BE ASPIRING TO FOLLOW...
...IN THESE VERY DARK AND TROUBLED TIMES.
RRRRK!
HAH! GET AWAY FROM THERE! SHOO!

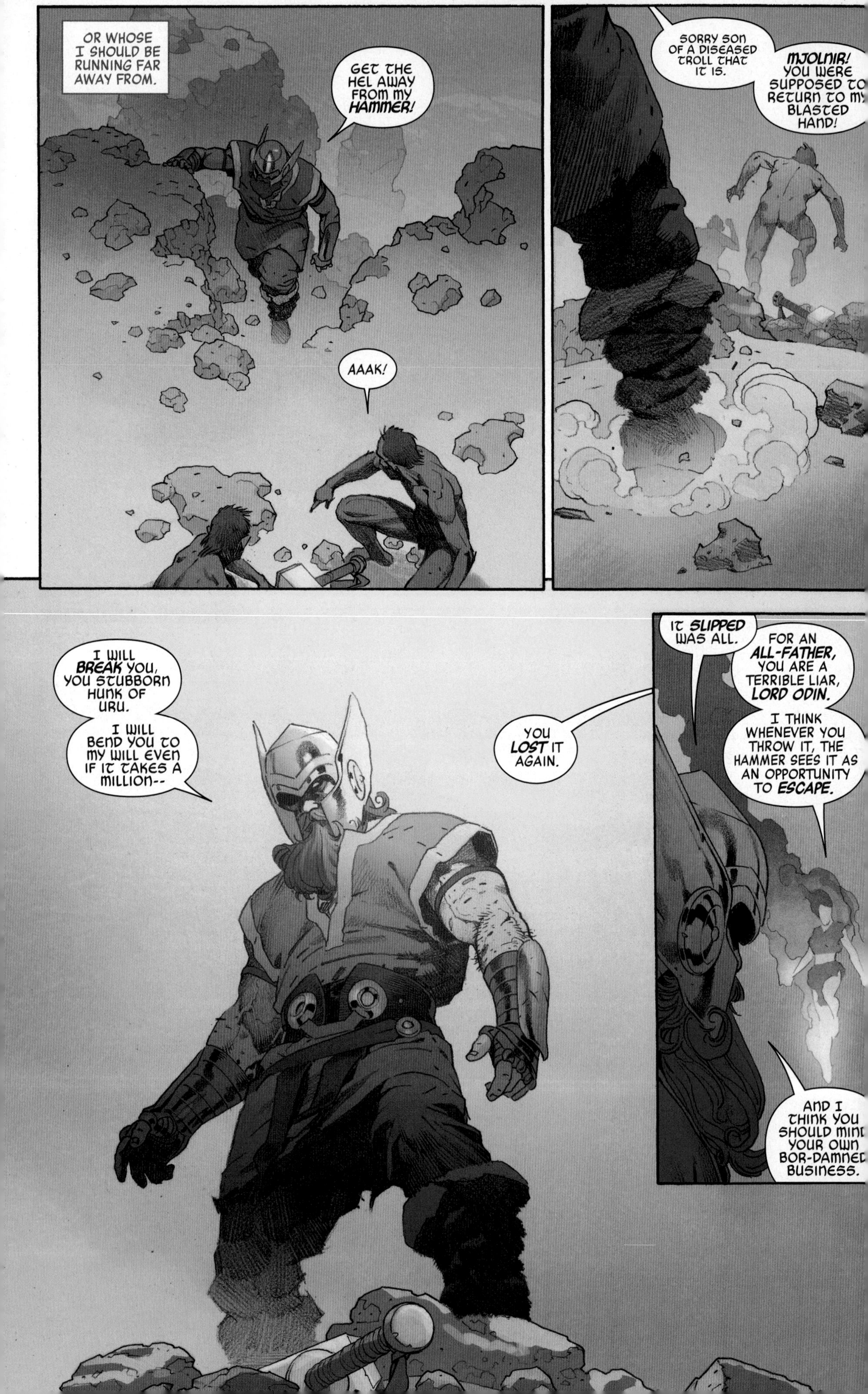
OR WHOSE I SHOULD BE RUNNING FAR AWAY FROM.
GET THE HEL AWAY FROM MY HAMMER!
AAAK!
SORRY SON OF A DISEASED TROLL THAT IT IS.
MJOLNIR! YOU WERE SUPPOSED TO RETURN TO MY BLASTED HAND!
I WILL BREAK YOU, YOU STUBBORN HUNK OF URU.
I WILL BEND YOU TO MY WILL EVEN IF IT TAKES A MILLION--
YOU LOST IT AGAIN.
IT SLIPPED WAS ALL.
FOR AN ALL-FATHER, YOU ARE A TERRIBLE LIAR, LORD ODIN.
I THINK WHENEVER YOU THROW IT, THE HAMMER SEES IT AS AN OPPORTUNITY TO ESCAPE.
AND I THINK YOU SHOULD MIND YOUR OWN BOR-DAMNED BUSINESS.

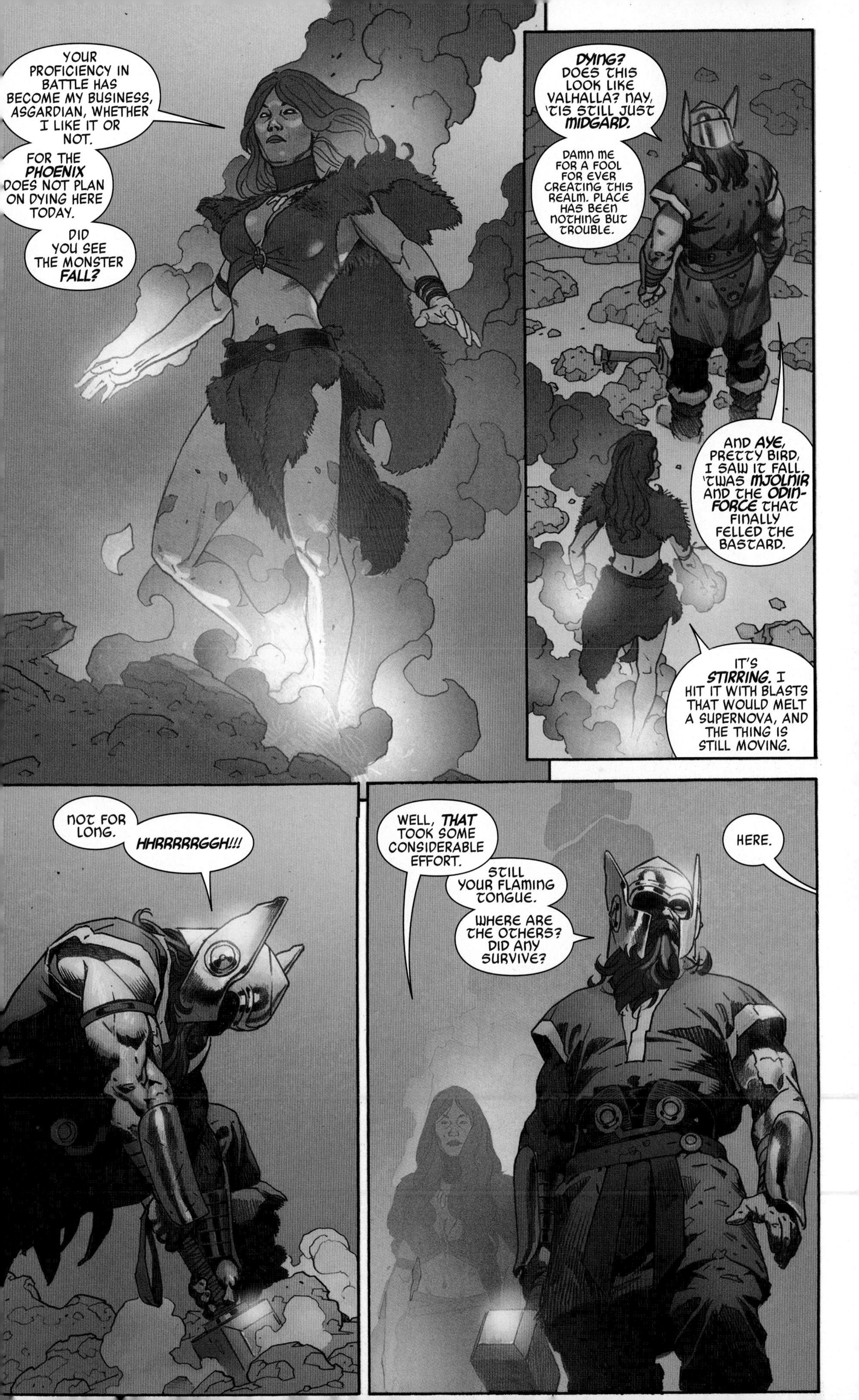

YOUR PROFICIENCY IN BATTLE HAS BECOME MY BUSINESS, ASGARDIAN, WHETHER I LIKE IT OR NOT.
FOR THE PHOENIX DOES NOT PLAN ON DYING HERE TODAY.
DID YOU SEE THE MONSTER FALL?
DYING? DOES THIS LOOK LIKE VALHALLA? NAY, 'TIS STILL JUST MIDGARD.
DAMN ME FOR A FOOL FOR EVER CREATING THIS REALM. PLACE HAS BEEN NOTHING BUT TROUBLE.
AND AYE, PRETTY BIRD, I SAW IT FALL. 'TWAS MJOLNIR AND THE ODIN-FORCE THAT FINALLY FELLED THE BASTARD.
IT'S STIRRING. I HIT IT WITH BLASTS THAT WOULD MELT A SUPERNOVA, AND THE THING IS STILL MOVING.
NOT FOR LONG.
HHRRRRRRGGH!!!
WELL, THAT TOOK SOME CONSIDERABLE EFFORT.
STILL YOUR FLAMING TONGUE.
WHERE ARE THE OTHERS? DID ANY SURVIVE?
HERE.

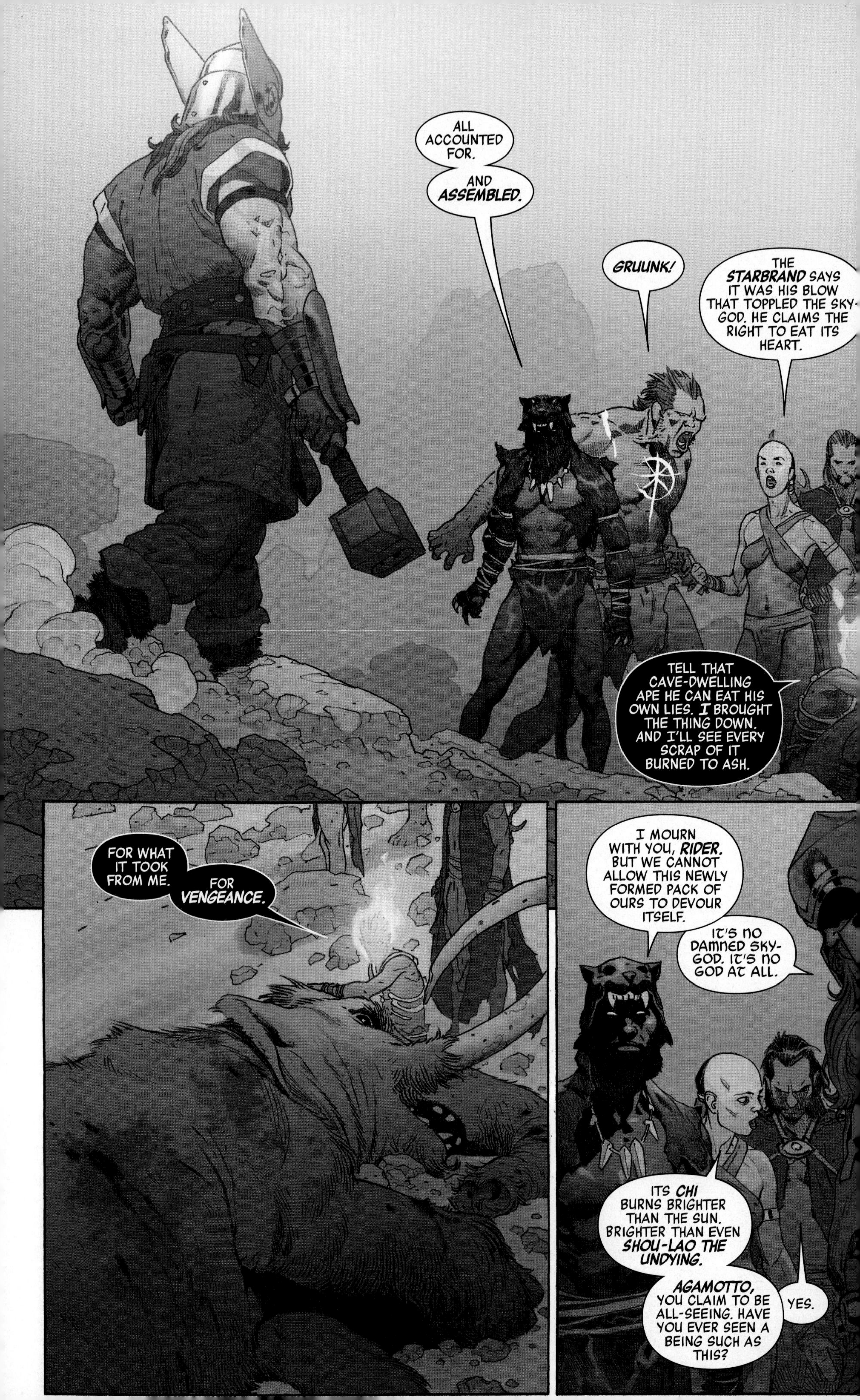
ALL ACCOUNTED FOR.
AND ASSEMBLED.
GRUUNK!
THE STARBRAND SAYS IT WAS HIS BLOW THAT TOPPLED THE SKY-GOD. HE CLAIMS THE RIGHT TO EAT ITS HEART.
TELL THAT CAVE-DWELLING APE HE CAN EAT HIS OWN LIES. I BROUGHT THE THING DOWN. AND I'LL SEE EVERY SCRAP OF IT BURNED TO ASH.
FOR WHAT IT TOOK FROM ME.
FOR VENGEANCE.
I MOURN WITH YOU, RIDER. BUT WE CANNOT ALLOW THIS NEWLY FORMED PACK OF OURS TO DEVOUR ITSELF.
IT'S NO DAMNED SKY-GOD. IT'S NO GOD AT ALL.
ITS CHI BURNS BRIGHTER THAN THE SUN. BRIGHTER THAN EVEN SHOU-LAO THE UNDYING.
AGAMOTTO, YOU CLAIM TO BE ALL-SEEING. HAVE YOU EVER SEEN A BEING SUCH AS THIS?
YES.

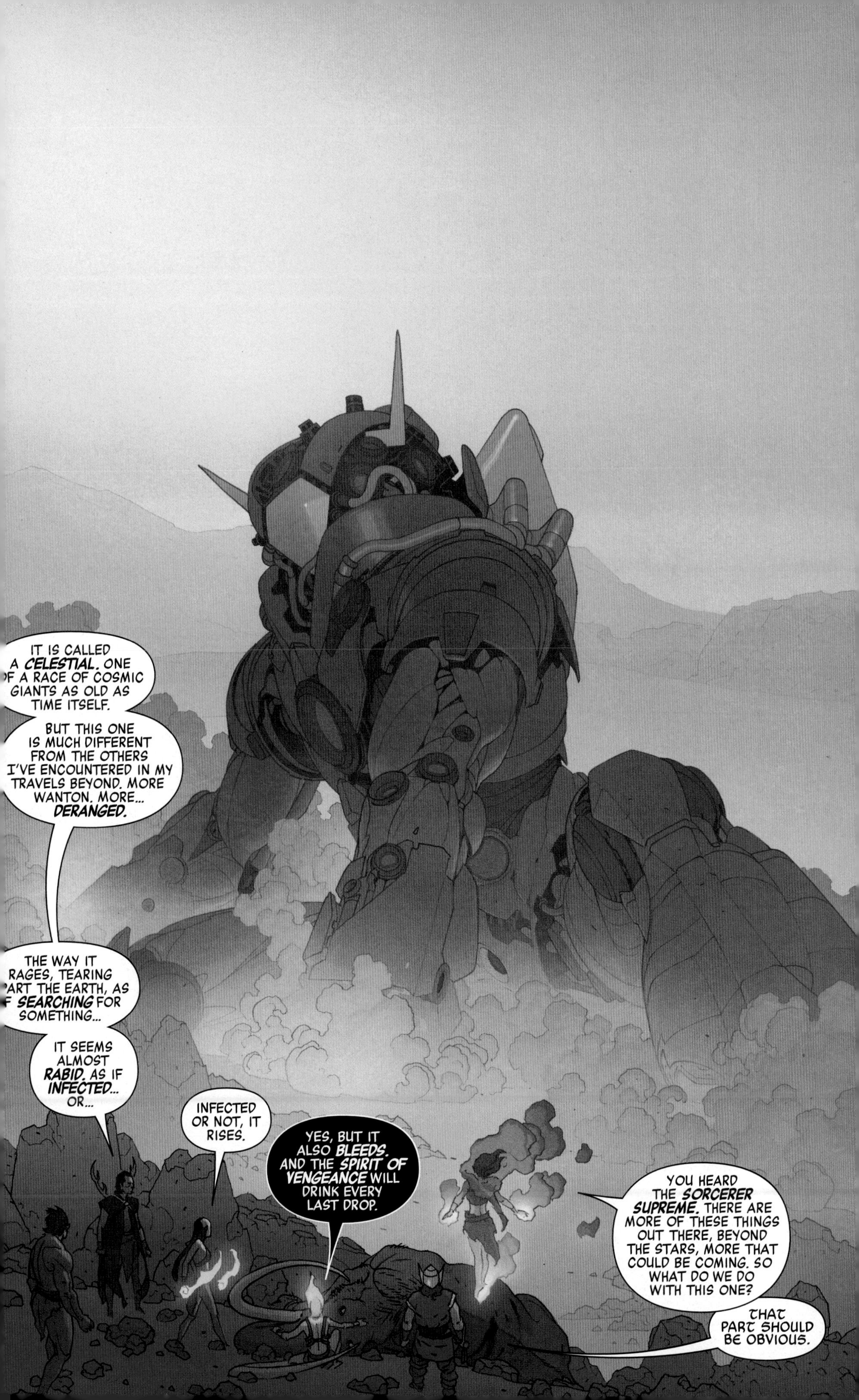
IT IS CALLED A CELESTIAL. ONE OF A RACE OF COSMIC GIANTS AS OLD AS TIME ITSELF.
BUT THIS ONE IS MUCH DIFFERENT FROM THE OTHERS I'VE ENCOUNTERED IN MY TRAVELS BEYOND. MORE WANTON. MORE... DERANGED.
THE WAY IT RAGES, TEARING APART THE EARTH, AS IF SEARCHING FOR SOMETHING...
IT SEEMS ALMOST RABID. AS IF INFECTED... OR...
INFECTED OR NOT, IT RISES.
YES, BUT IT ALSO BLEEDS. AND THE SPIRIT OF VENGEANCE WILL DRINK EVERY LAST DROP.
YOU HEARD THE SORCERER SUPREME. THERE ARE MORE OF THESE THINGS OUT THERE, BEYOND THE STARS, MORE THAT COULD BE COMING. SO WHAT DO WE DO WITH THIS ONE?
THAT PART SHOULD BE OBVIOUS.

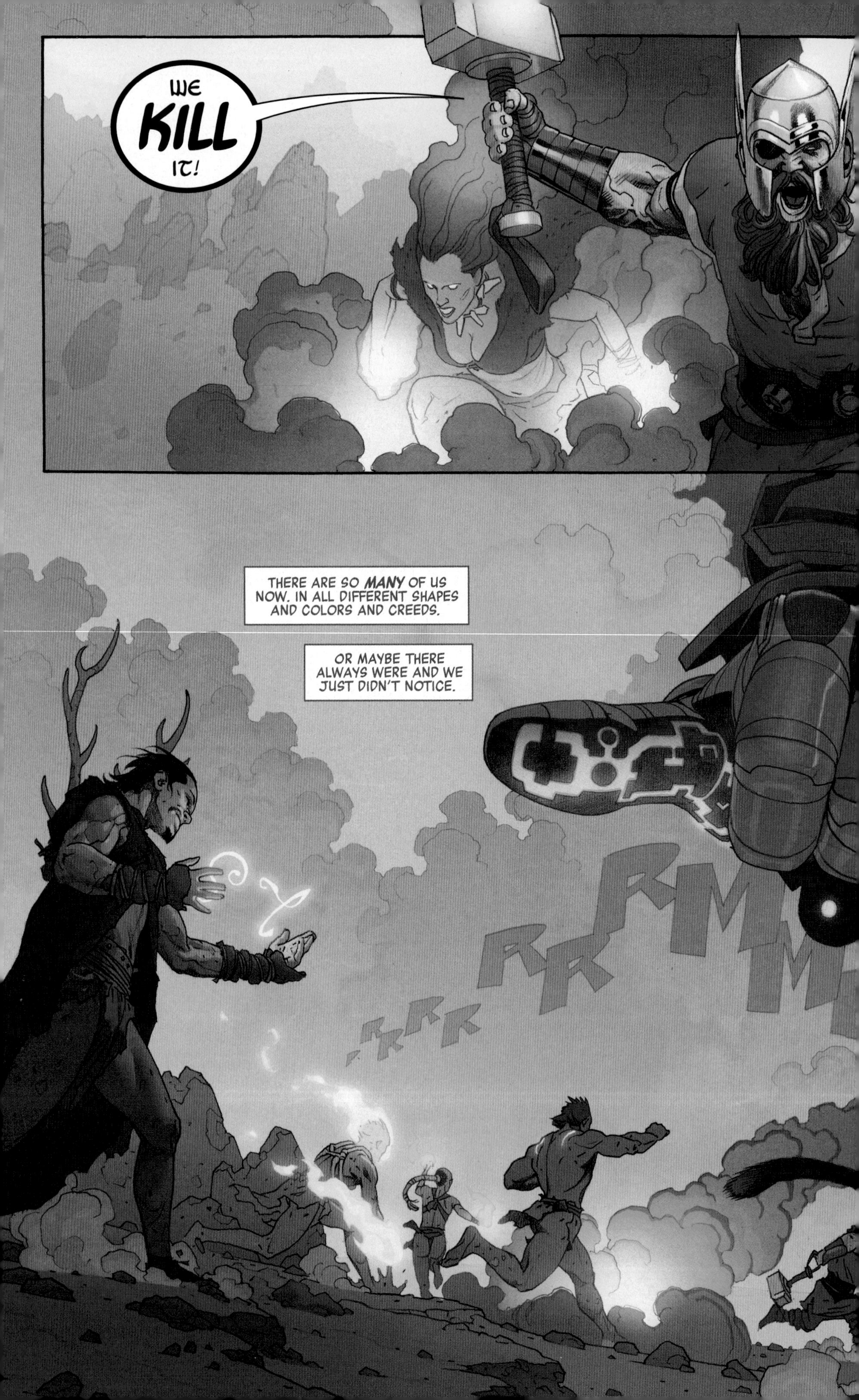
WE KILL IT!
THERE ARE SO MANY OF US NOW. IN ALL DIFFERENT SHAPES AND COLORS AND CREEDS.
OR MAYBE THERE ALWAYS WERE AND WE JUST DIDN'T NOTICE.
RRRRRRMMM

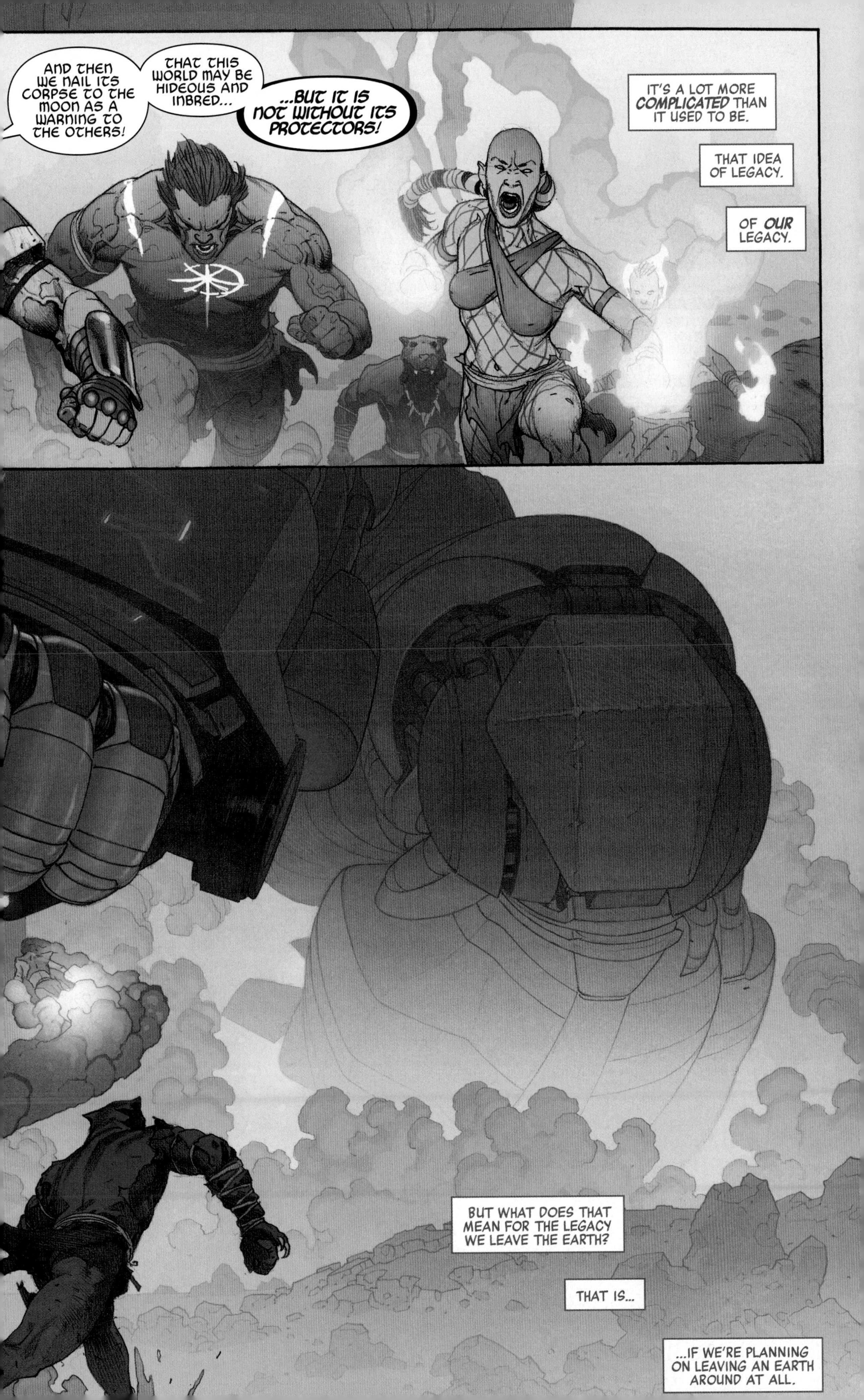
AND THEN WE NAIL ITS CORPSE TO THE MOON AS A WARNING TO THE OTHERS!
THAT THIS WORLD MAY BE HIDEOUS AND INBRED...
...BUT IT IS NOT WITHOUT ITS PROTECTORS!
IT'S A LOT MORE COMPLICATED THAN IT USED TO BE.
THAT IDEA OF LEGACY.
OF OUR LEGACY.
BUT WHAT DOES THAT MEAN FOR THE LEGACY WE LEAVE THE EARTH?
THAT IS...
...IF WE'RE PLANNING ON LEAVING AN EARTH AROUND AT ALL.

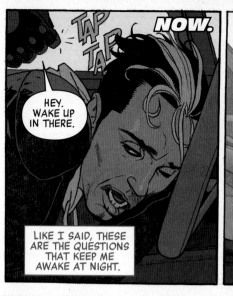

HEY. WAKE UP IN THERE.

LIKE I SAID, THESE ARE THE QUESTIONS THAT KEEP ME AWAKE AT NIGHT.

I GUESS I DON'T MIND NOT SLEEPING. I MEAN, I CAN ALWAYS FIND A WAY TO FILL MORE HOURS IN THE DAY. BUT I DO MISS THE *DREAMS*.

WAAHHH.

DREAMED... I WAS RIDING... A *MASTODON*. AND THERE WAS AN *IRON FIST* AND A *BLACK PANTHER* AND...

OVER HERE, KID.

I USED TO HAVE SOME PRETTY WONDERFUL DREAMS.

I WONDER WHEN I STOPPED.

I'M GOING TO NEED YOU TO STEP OUT OF THE CAR.

AND WHY IT TOOK SO LONG FOR ME TO NOTICE.

UH. WHERE... THE HELL AM I?

LAST THING I REMEMBER, I WAS HOME, WORKING ON THE CAR. MUST'VE DOZED OFF AND...

THIS... THIS DOESN'T LOOK LIKE *EAST L.A.*

ALL RIGHT, *OUT*. LAST WARNING.

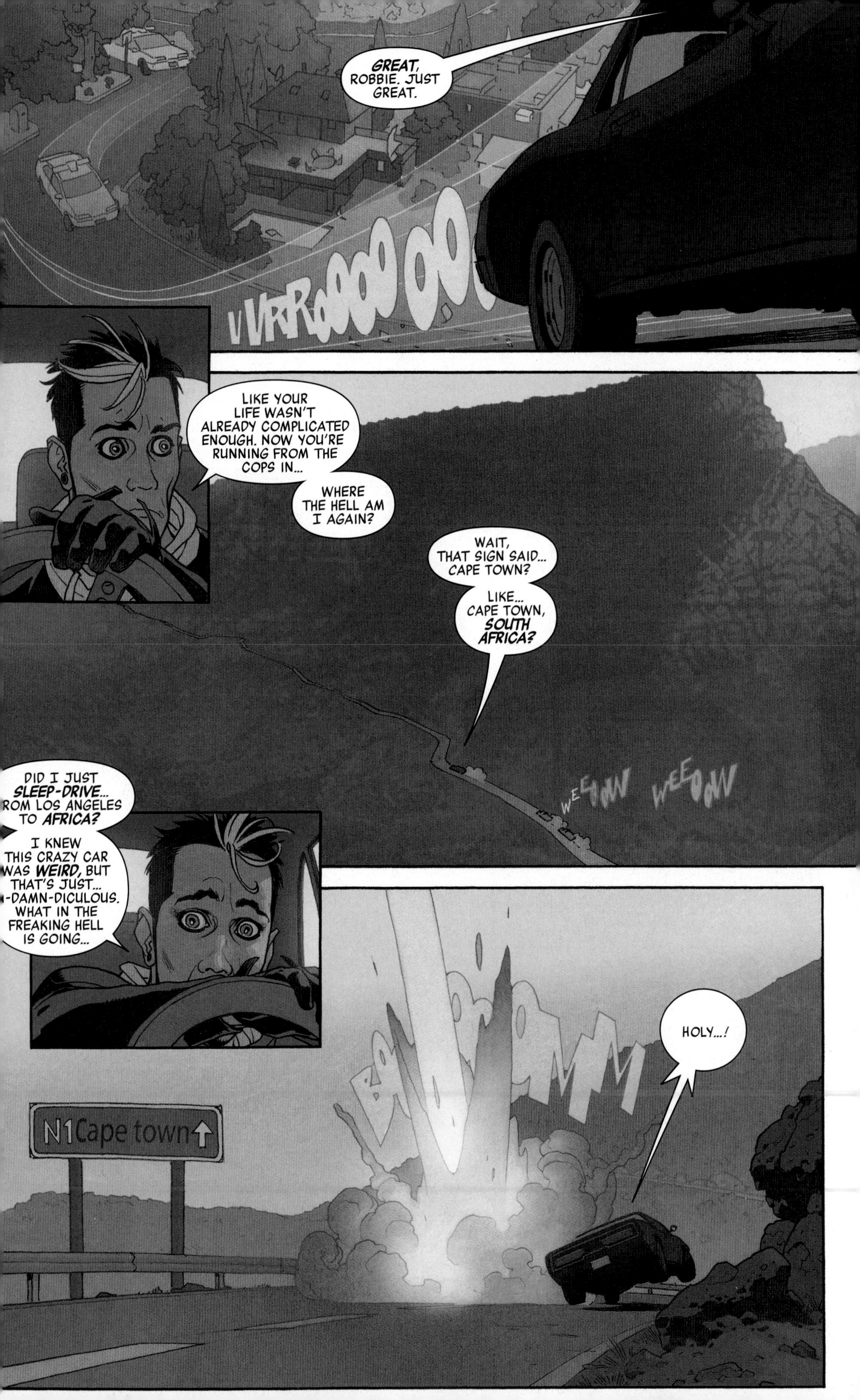

GREAT, ROBBIE. JUST GREAT.
LIKE YOUR LIFE WASN'T ALREADY COMPLICATED ENOUGH. NOW YOU'RE RUNNING FROM THE COPS IN...
WHERE THE HELL AM I AGAIN?
WAIT, THAT SIGN SAID... CAPE TOWN?
LIKE... CAPE TOWN, SOUTH AFRICA?
WEEOOW WEEOOW
DID I JUST SLEEP-DRIVE... ROM LOS ANGELES TO AFRICA?
I KNEW THIS CRAZY CAR WAS WEIRD, BUT THAT'S JUST... -DAMN-DICULOUS. WHAT IN THE FREAKING HELL IS GOING...
N1 Cape town
HOLY...!

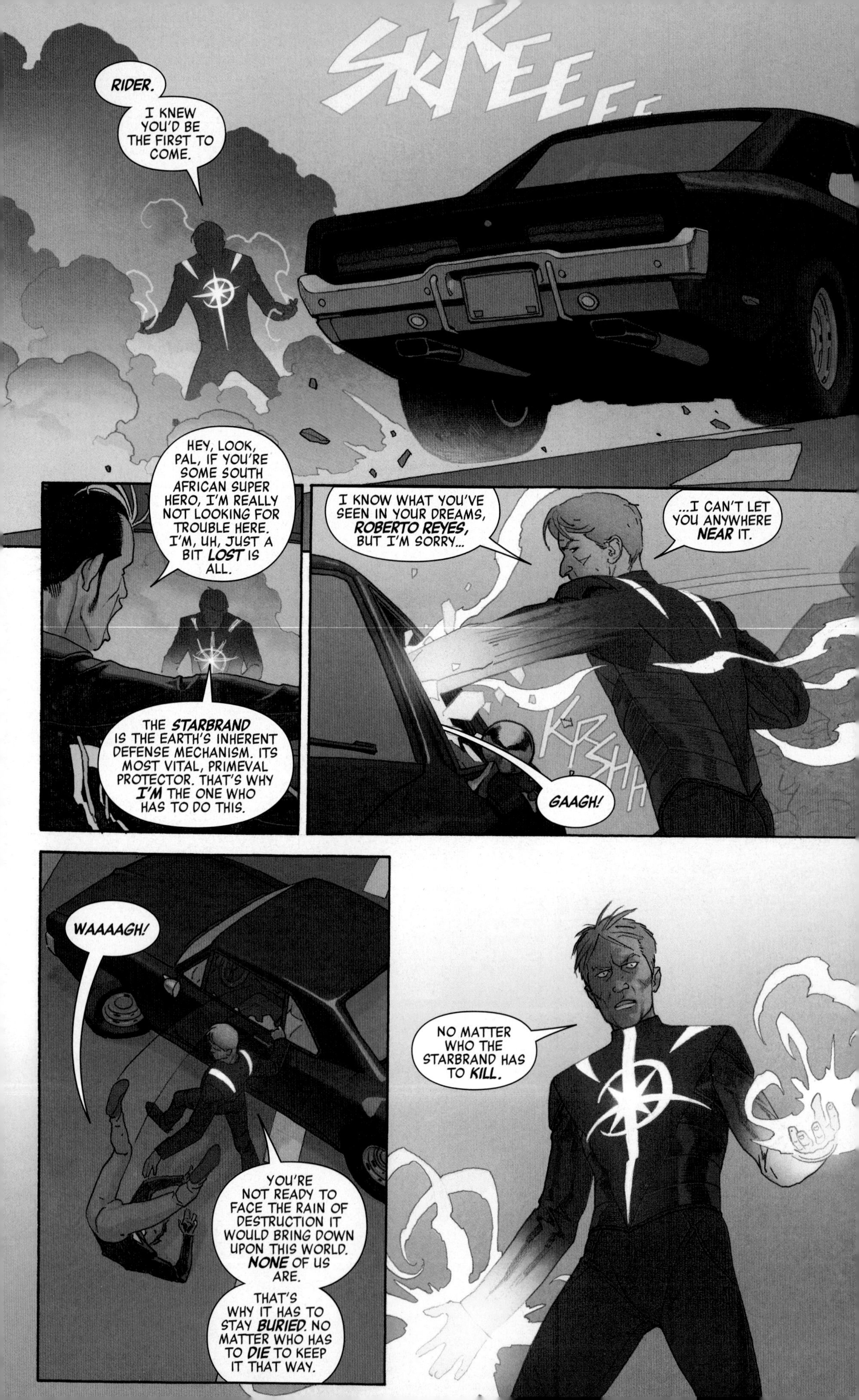
SKREEEE
RIDER.
I KNEW YOU'D BE THE FIRST TO COME.
HEY, LOOK, PAL, IF YOU'RE SOME SOUTH AFRICAN SUPER HERO, I'M REALLY NOT LOOKING FOR TROUBLE HERE. I'M, UH, JUST A BIT LOST IS ALL.
THE STARBRAND IS THE EARTH'S INHERENT DEFENSE MECHANISM. ITS MOST VITAL, PRIMEVAL PROTECTOR. THAT'S WHY I'M THE ONE WHO HAS TO DO THIS.
I KNOW WHAT YOU'VE SEEN IN YOUR DREAMS, ROBERTO REYES, BUT I'M SORRY...
...I CAN'T LET YOU ANYWHERE NEAR IT.
KRSHH
GAAGH!
WAAAAGH!
YOU'RE NOT READY TO FACE THE RAIN OF DESTRUCTION IT WOULD BRING DOWN UPON THIS WORLD. NONE OF US ARE.
THAT'S WHY IT HAS TO STAY BURIED. NO MATTER WHO HAS TO DIE TO KEEP IT THAT WAY.
NO MATTER WHO THE STARBRAND HAS TO KILL.

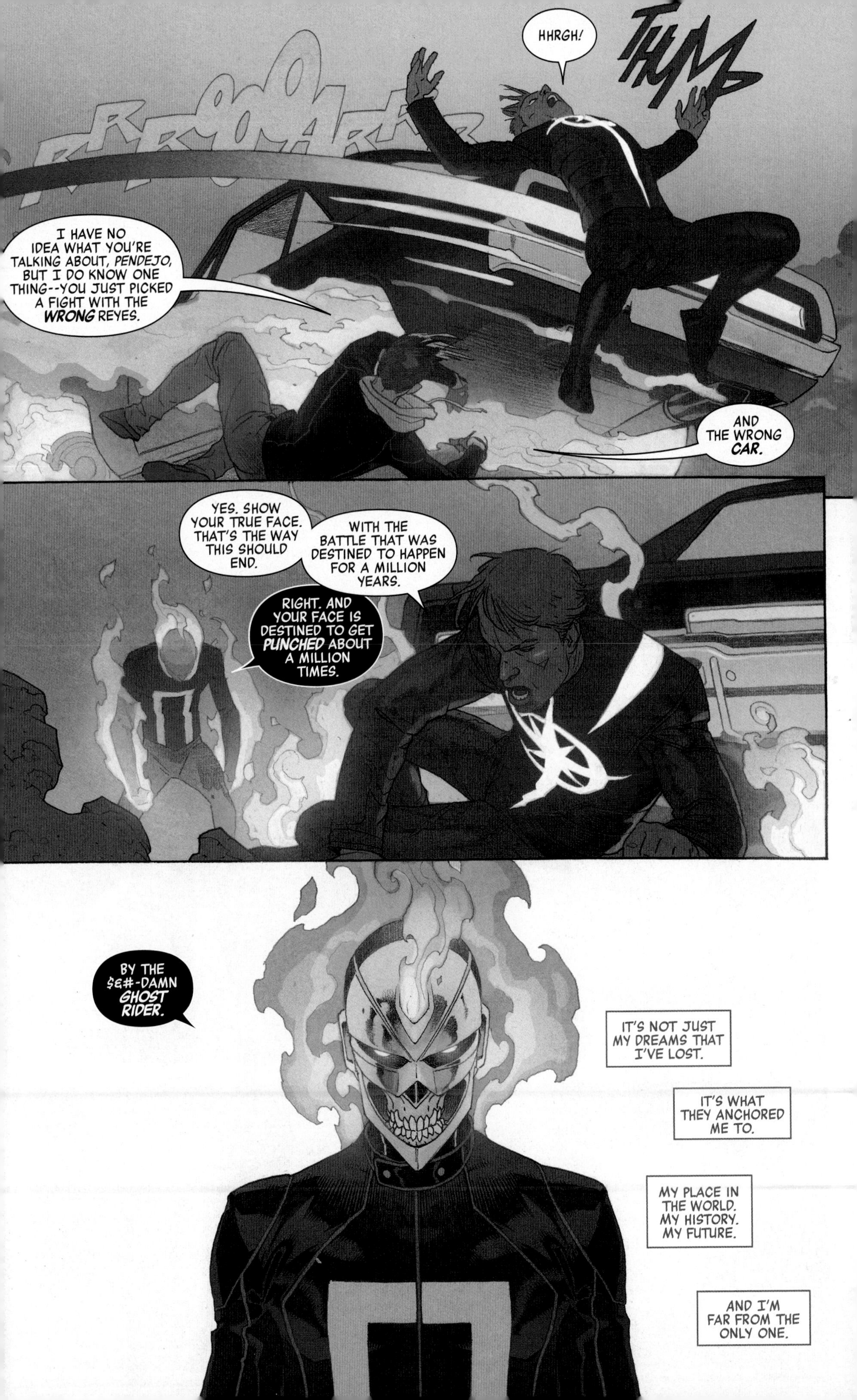
HHRGH!
THUMP
RRROOAARR
I HAVE NO IDEA WHAT YOU'RE TALKING ABOUT, PENDEJO, BUT I DO KNOW ONE THING--YOU JUST PICKED A FIGHT WITH THE WRONG REYES.
AND THE WRONG CAR.
YES. SHOW YOUR TRUE FACE. THAT'S THE WAY THIS SHOULD END.
WITH THE BATTLE THAT WAS DESTINED TO HAPPEN FOR A MILLION YEARS.
RIGHT. AND YOUR FACE IS DESTINED TO GET PUNCHED ABOUT A MILLION TIMES.
BY THE $&#-DAMN GHOST RIDER.
IT'S NOT JUST MY DREAMS THAT I'VE LOST.
IT'S WHAT THEY ANCHORED ME TO.
MY PLACE IN THE WORLD. MY HISTORY. MY FUTURE.
AND I'M FAR FROM THE ONLY ONE.

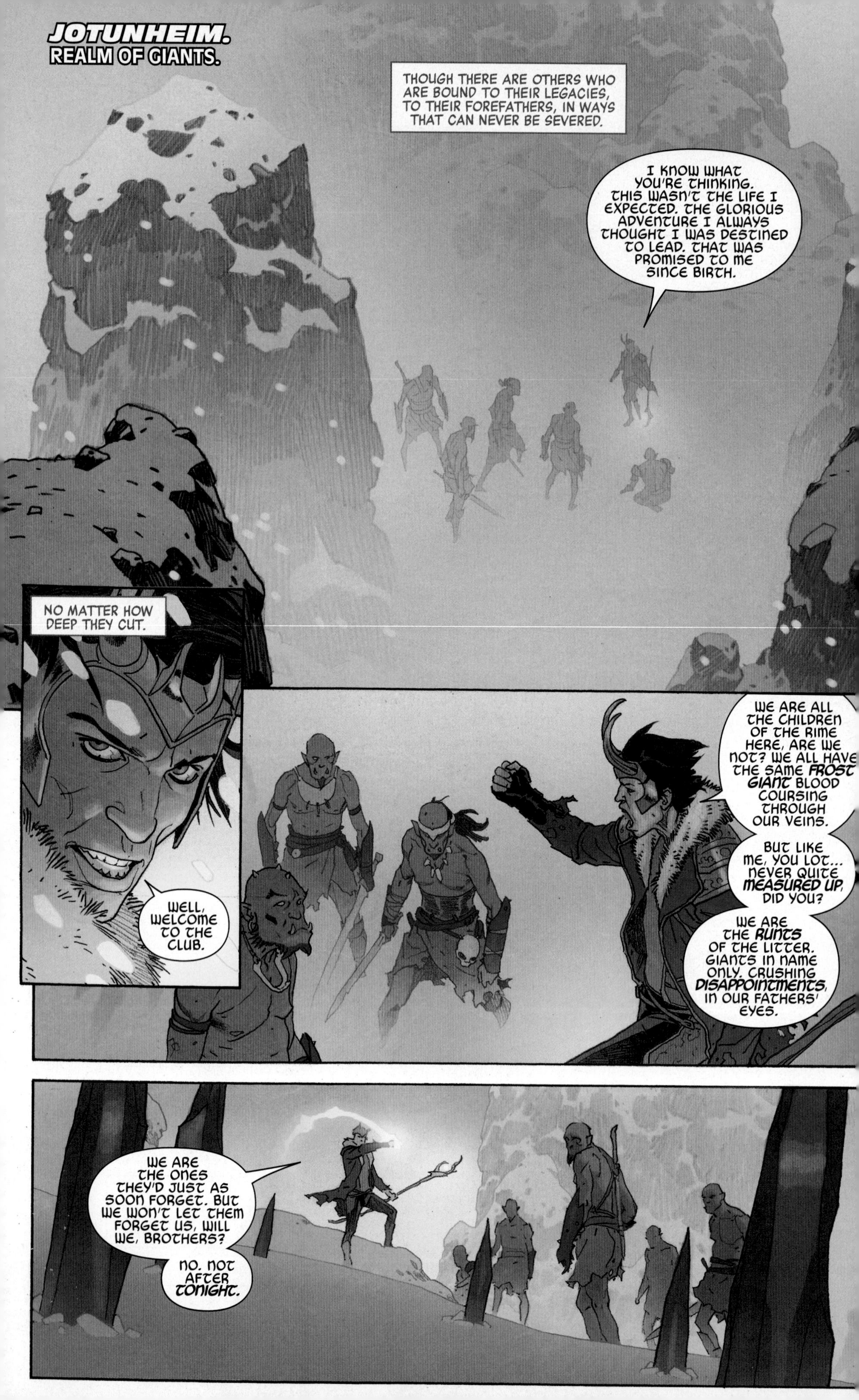
JOTUNHEIM.
REALM OF GIANTS.
THOUGH THERE ARE OTHERS WHO ARE BOUND TO THEIR LEGACIES, TO THEIR FOREFATHERS, IN WAYS THAT CAN NEVER BE SEVERED.
I KNOW WHAT YOU'RE THINKING. THIS WASN'T THE LIFE I EXPECTED. THE GLORIOUS ADVENTURE I ALWAYS THOUGHT I WAS DESTINED TO LEAD. THAT WAS PROMISED TO ME SINCE BIRTH.
NO MATTER HOW DEEP THEY CUT.
WELL, WELCOME TO THE CLUB.
WE ARE ALL THE CHILDREN OF THE RIME HERE, ARE WE NOT? WE ALL HAVE THE SAME FROST GIANT BLOOD COURSING THROUGH OUR VEINS.
BUT LIKE ME, YOU LOT... NEVER QUITE MEASURED UP, DID YOU?
WE ARE THE RUNTS OF THE LITTER. GIANTS IN NAME ONLY. CRUSHING DISAPPOINTMENTS, IN OUR FATHERS' EYES.
WE ARE THE ONES THEY'D JUST AS SOON FORGET. BUT WE WON'T LET THEM FORGET US, WILL WE, BROTHERS?
NO. NOT AFTER TONIGHT.

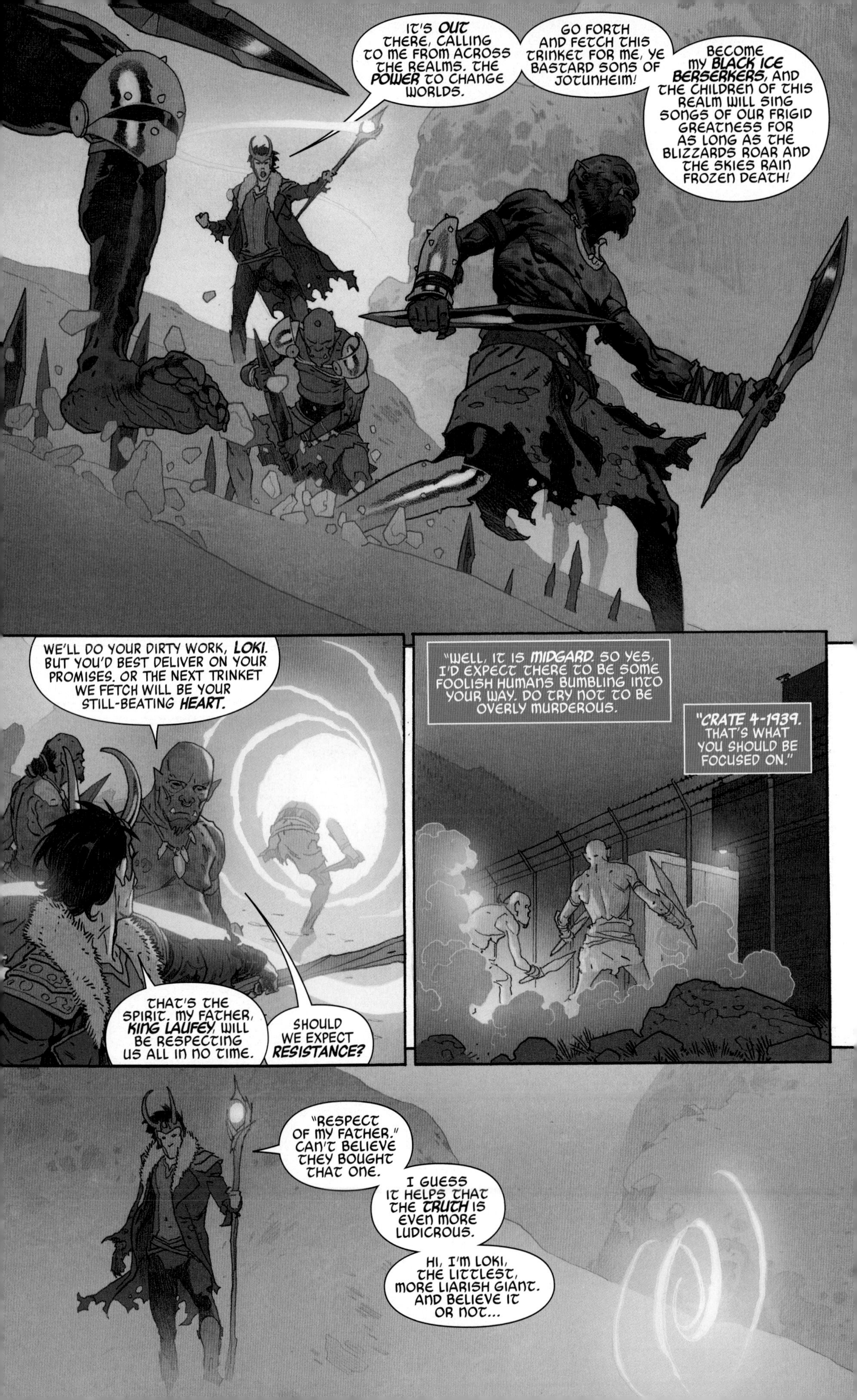
IT'S OUT THERE, CALLING TO ME FROM ACROSS THE REALMS. THE POWER TO CHANGE WORLDS.
GO FORTH AND FETCH THIS TRINKET FOR ME, YE BASTARD SONS OF JOTUNHEIM!
BECOME MY BLACK ICE BERSERKERS, AND THE CHILDREN OF THIS REALM WILL SING SONGS OF OUR FRIGID GREATNESS FOR AS LONG AS THE BLIZZARDS ROAR AND THE SKIES RAIN FROZEN DEATH!
WE'LL DO YOUR DIRTY WORK, LOKI. BUT YOU'D BEST DELIVER ON YOUR PROMISES. OR THE NEXT TRINKET WE FETCH WILL BE YOUR STILL-BEATING HEART.
THAT'S THE SPIRIT. MY FATHER, KING LAUFEY, WILL BE RESPECTING US ALL IN NO TIME.
SHOULD WE EXPECT RESISTANCE?
"WELL, IT IS MIDGARD. SO YES, I'D EXPECT THERE TO BE SOME FOOLISH HUMANS BUMBLING INTO YOUR WAY. DO TRY NOT TO BE OVERLY MURDEROUS.
"CRATE 4-1939. THAT'S WHAT YOU SHOULD BE FOCUSED ON."
"RESPECT OF MY FATHER." CAN'T BELIEVE THEY BOUGHT THAT ONE.
I GUESS IT HELPS THAT THE TRUTH IS EVEN MORE LUDICROUS.
HI, I'M LOKI, THE LITTLEST, MORE LIARISH GIANT. AND BELIEVE IT OR NOT...

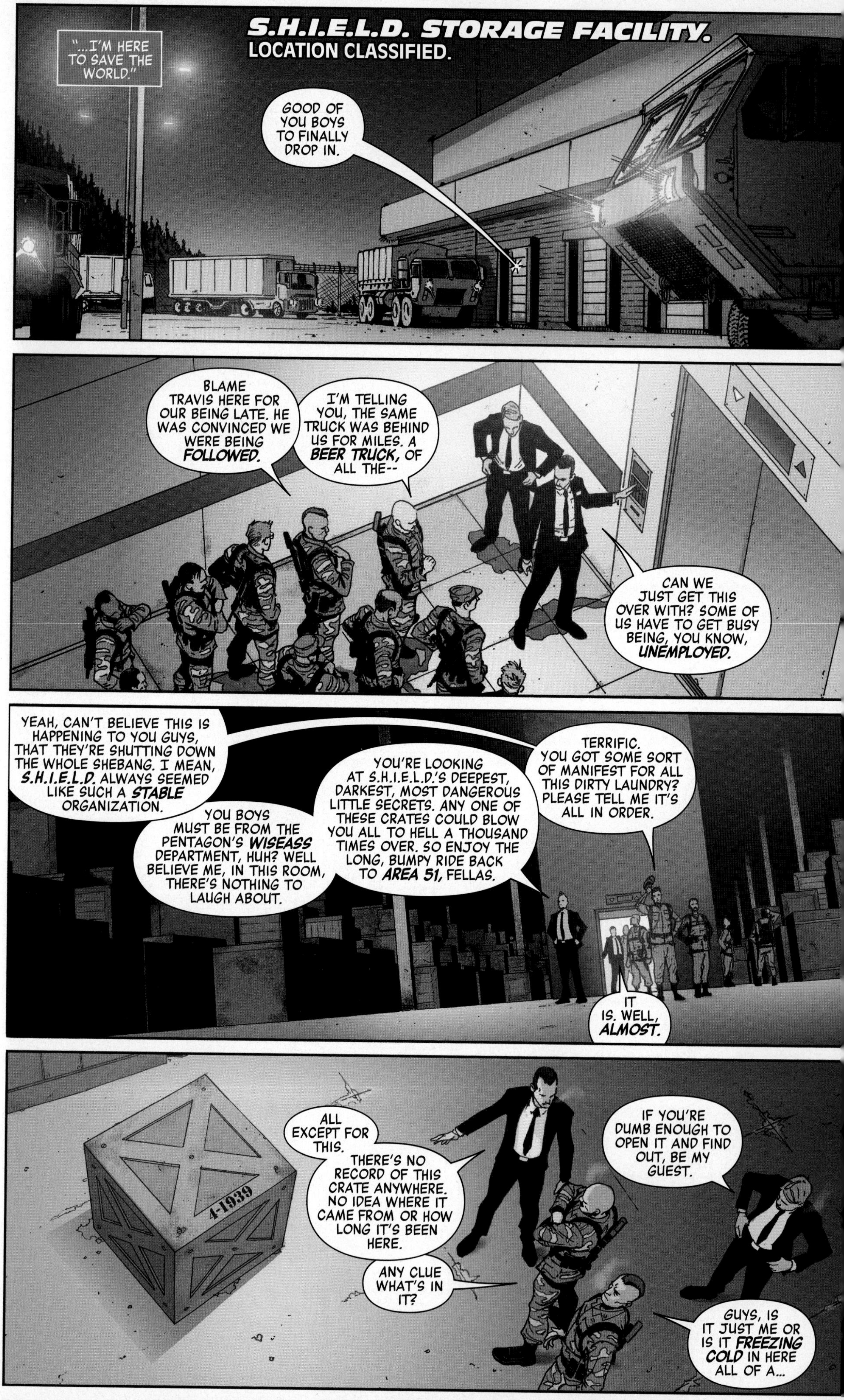
"...I'M HERE TO SAVE THE WORLD."
S.H.I.E.L.D. STORAGE FACILITY.
LOCATION CLASSIFIED.
GOOD OF YOU BOYS TO FINALLY DROP IN.
BLAME TRAVIS HERE FOR OUR BEING LATE. HE WAS CONVINCED WE WERE BEING FOLLOWED.
I'M TELLING YOU, THE SAME TRUCK WAS BEHIND US FOR MILES. A BEER TRUCK, OF ALL THE--
CAN WE JUST GET THIS OVER WITH? SOME OF US HAVE TO GET BUSY BEING, YOU KNOW, UNEMPLOYED.
YEAH, CAN'T BELIEVE THIS IS HAPPENING TO YOU GUYS, THAT THEY'RE SHUTTING DOWN THE WHOLE SHEBANG. I MEAN, S.H.I.E.L.D. ALWAYS SEEMED LIKE SUCH A STABLE ORGANIZATION.
YOU BOYS MUST BE FROM THE PENTAGON'S WISEASS DEPARTMENT, HUH? WELL BELIEVE ME, IN THIS ROOM, THERE'S NOTHING TO LAUGH ABOUT.
YOU'RE LOOKING AT S.H.I.E.L.D.'S DEEPEST, DARKEST, MOST DANGEROUS LITTLE SECRETS. ANY ONE OF THESE CRATES COULD BLOW YOU ALL TO HELL A THOUSAND TIMES OVER. SO ENJOY THE LONG, BUMPY RIDE BACK TO AREA 51, FELLAS.
TERRIFIC. YOU GOT SOME SORT OF MANIFEST FOR ALL THIS DIRTY LAUNDRY? PLEASE TELL ME IT'S ALL IN ORDER.
IT IS. WELL, ALMOST.
4-1939
ALL EXCEPT FOR THIS.
THERE'S NO RECORD OF THIS CRATE ANYWHERE. NO IDEA WHERE IT CAME FROM OR HOW LONG IT'S BEEN HERE.
ANY CLUE WHAT'S IN IT?
IF YOU'RE DUMB ENOUGH TO OPEN IT AND FIND OUT, BE MY GUEST.
GUYS, IS IT JUST ME OR IS IT FREEZING COLD IN HERE ALL OF A...

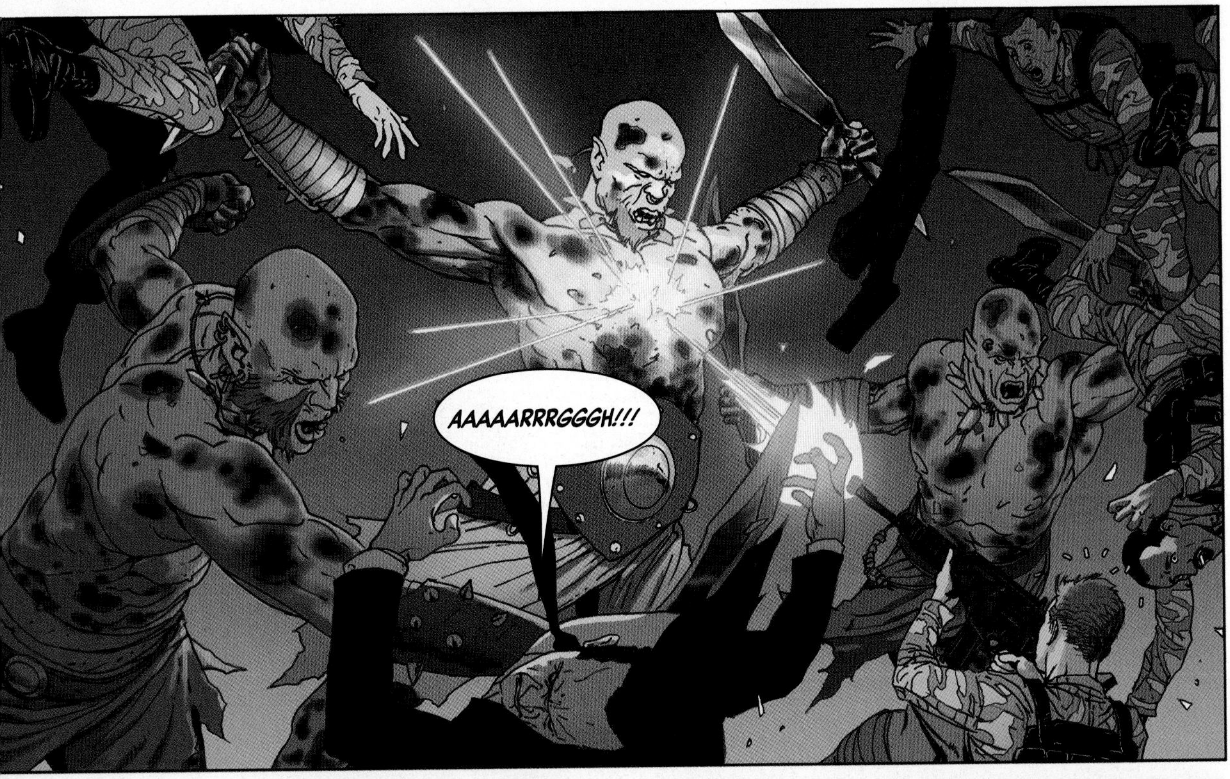
AAAAARRRGGGH!!!

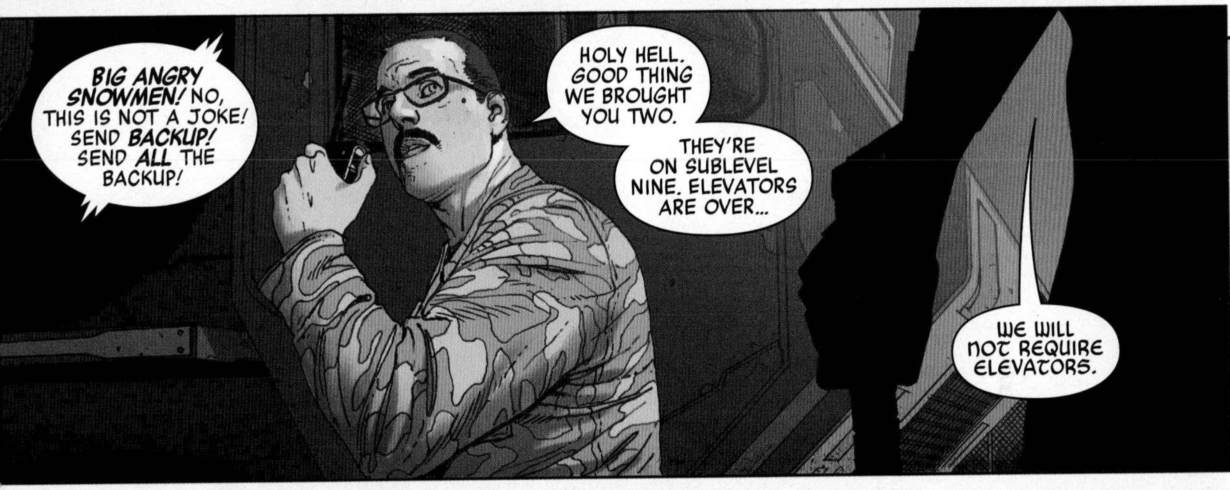
BIG ANGRY SNOWMEN! NO, THIS IS NOT A JOKE! SEND BACKUP! SEND ALL THE BACKUP!
HOLY HELL. GOOD THING WE BROUGHT YOU TWO.
THEY'RE ON SUBLEVEL NINE. ELEVATORS ARE OVER...
WE WILL NOT REQUIRE ELEVATORS.

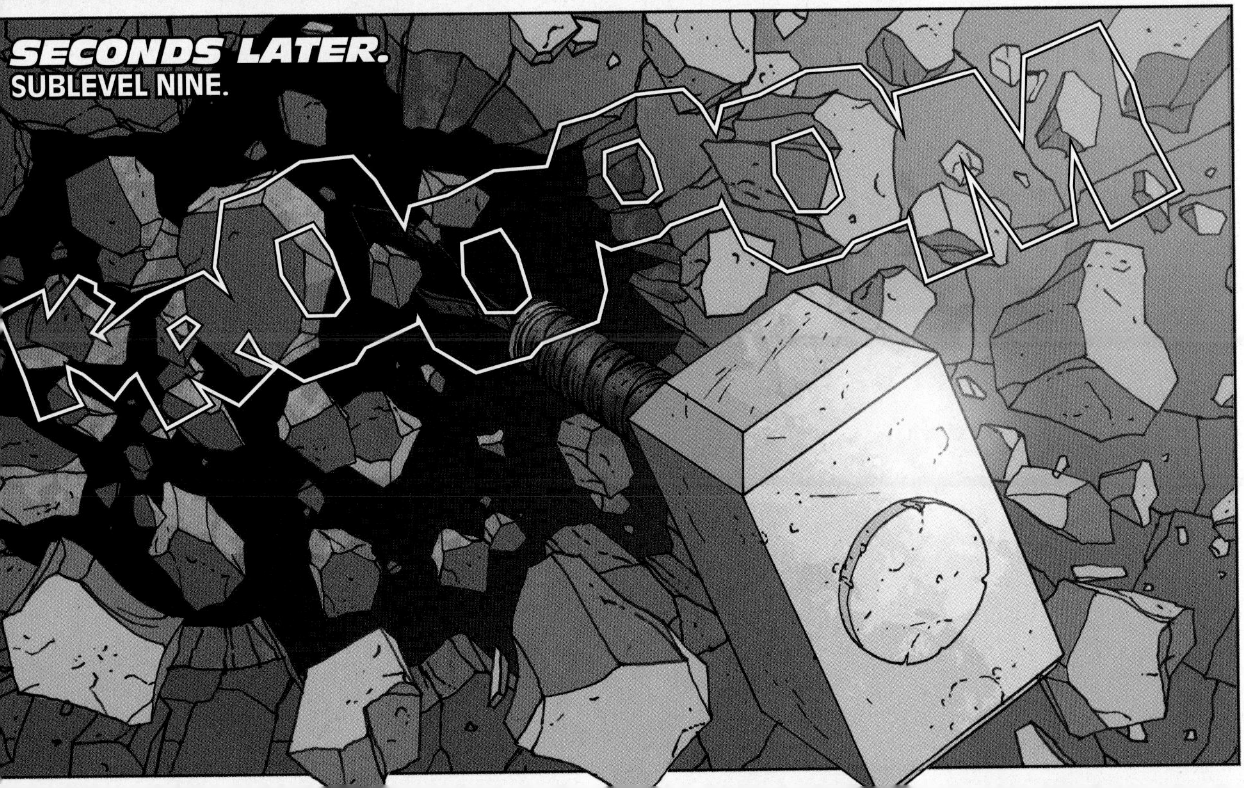
SECONDS LATER.
SUBLEVEL NINE.

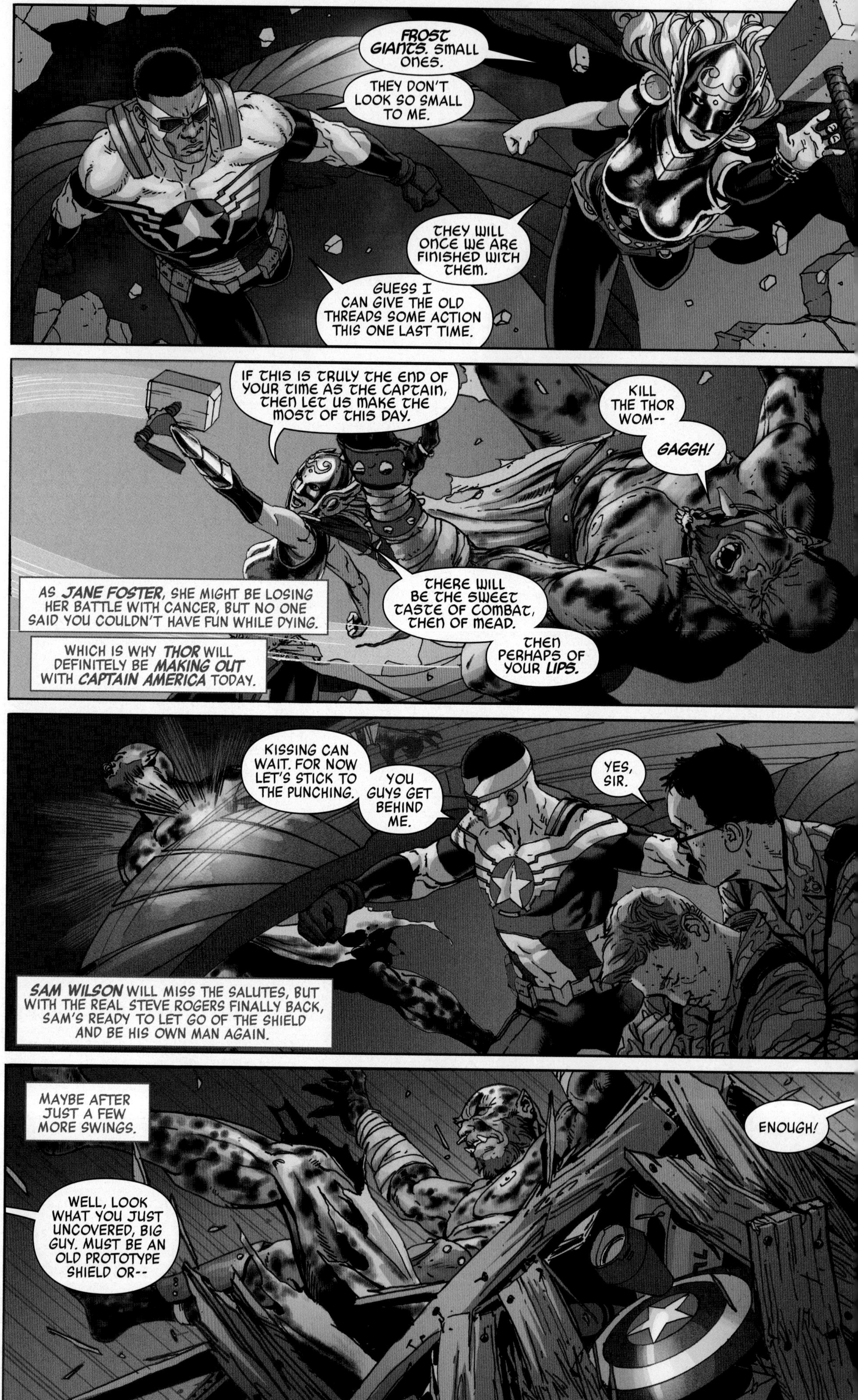
FROST GIANTS. SMALL ONES.
THEY DON'T LOOK SO SMALL TO ME.
THEY WILL ONCE WE ARE FINISHED WITH THEM.
GUESS I CAN GIVE THE OLD THREADS SOME ACTION THIS ONE LAST TIME.
IF THIS IS TRULY THE END OF YOUR TIME AS THE CAPTAIN, THEN LET US MAKE THE MOST OF THIS DAY.
KILL THE THOR WOM--
GAGGH!
AS JANE FOSTER, SHE MIGHT BE LOSING HER BATTLE WITH CANCER, BUT NO ONE SAID YOU COULDN'T HAVE FUN WHILE DYING.
WHICH IS WHY THOR WILL DEFINITELY BE MAKING OUT WITH CAPTAIN AMERICA TODAY.
THERE WILL BE THE SWEET TASTE OF COMBAT, THEN OF MEAD.
THEN PERHAPS OF YOUR LIPS.
KISSING CAN WAIT. FOR NOW LET'S STICK TO THE PUNCHING.
YOU GUYS GET BEHIND ME.
YES, SIR.
SAM WILSON WILL MISS THE SALUTES, BUT WITH THE REAL STEVE ROGERS FINALLY BACK, SAM'S READY TO LET GO OF THE SHIELD AND BE HIS OWN MAN AGAIN.
MAYBE AFTER JUST A FEW MORE SWINGS.
ENOUGH!
WELL, LOOK WHAT YOU JUST UNCOVERED, BIG GUY. MUST BE AN OLD PROTOTYPE SHIELD OR--

LAY DOWN YOUR WEAPONS! OR I TEAR THROUGH THIS MEAT-SACK LIKE A SNOWNADO FULL OF RAZOR SLEET!

NOW, YOU BLITHERING...

GAGGH.

LOOKS LIKE THE BACKUP FOR THE BACKUP JUST ARRIVED.

HEY, SORRY I'M TARDY. GOT A BIT LOST IN SOME...LET'S JUST CALL IT "SUPER SCIENCE" AND MOVE ON.

THOR, MEET IRONHEART. IRONHEART, MEET THE FROST GIANTS.

YEAH, WE JUST MET. THOUGH I'M HAPPY TO MEET A FEW MORE.

IF BY MEET, YOU MEAN BLUDGEON, THEN AYE, LADY OF IRON, THOR CONCURS.

RIGHT. BLUDGEONING IT IS.

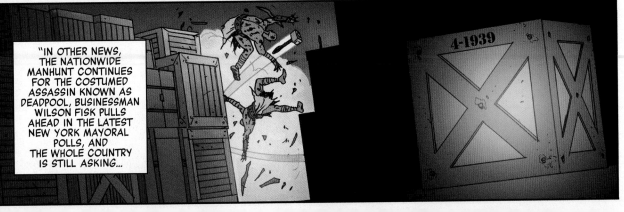

"IN OTHER NEWS, THE NATIONWIDE MANHUNT CONTINUES FOR THE COSTUMED ASSASSIN KNOWN AS DEADPOOL, BUSINESSMAN WILSON FISK PULLS AHEAD IN THE LATEST NEW YORK MAYORAL POLLS, AND THE WHOLE COUNTRY IS STILL ASKING...

4-1939

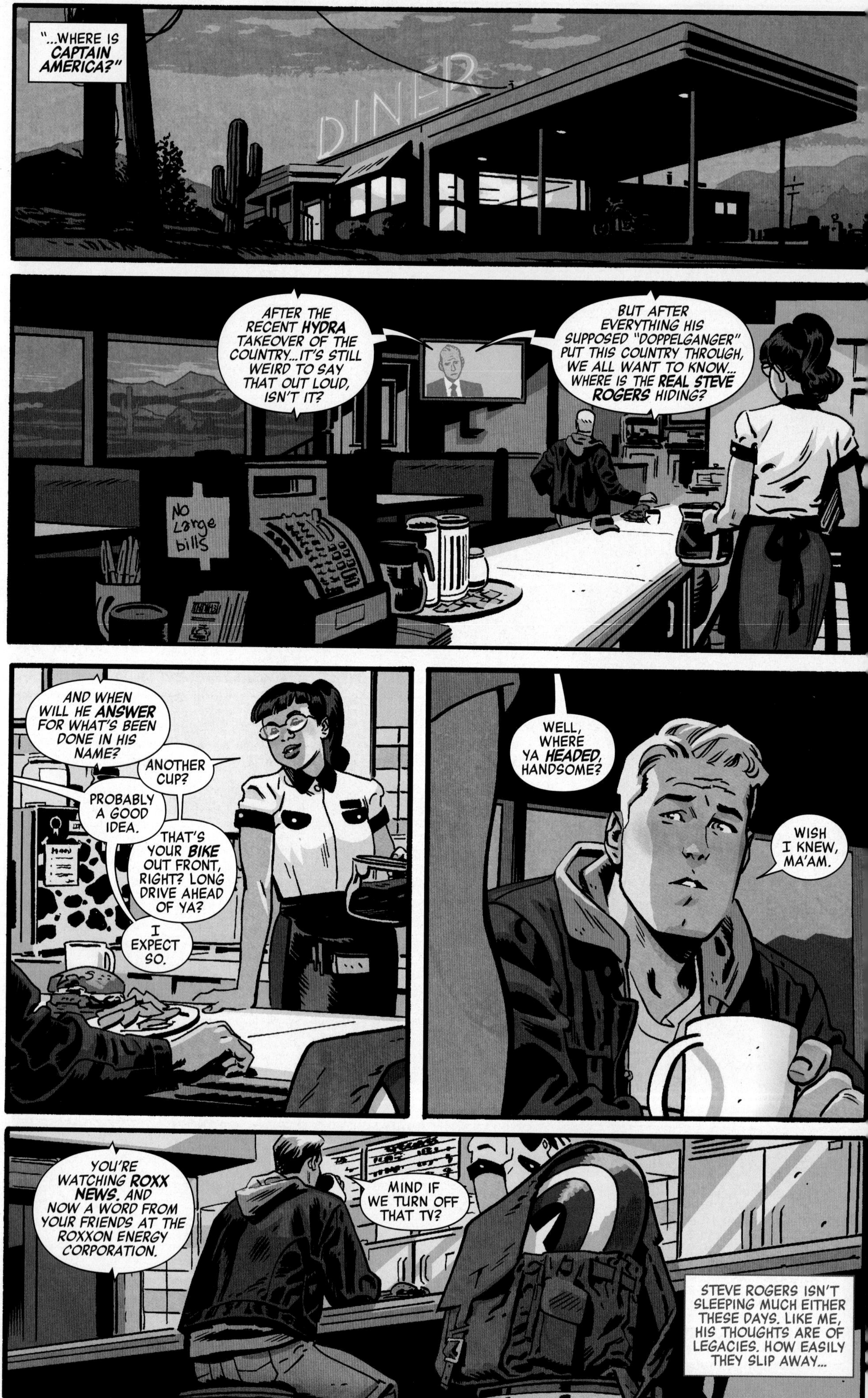
"...WHERE IS CAPTAIN AMERICA?"
DINER
AFTER THE RECENT HYDRA TAKEOVER OF THE COUNTRY...IT'S STILL WEIRD TO SAY THAT OUT LOUD, ISN'T IT?
BUT AFTER EVERYTHING HIS SUPPOSED "DOPPELGANGER" PUT THIS COUNTRY THROUGH, WE ALL WANT TO KNOW... WHERE IS THE REAL STEVE ROGERS HIDING?
No Large bills
AND WHEN WILL HE ANSWER FOR WHAT'S BEEN DONE IN HIS NAME?
ANOTHER CUP?
PROBABLY A GOOD IDEA.
THAT'S YOUR BIKE OUT FRONT, RIGHT? LONG DRIVE AHEAD OF YA?
I EXPECT SO.
WELL, WHERE YA HEADED, HANDSOME?
WISH I KNEW, MA'AM.
YOU'RE WATCHING ROXX NEWS. AND NOW A WORD FROM YOUR FRIENDS AT THE ROXXON ENERGY CORPORATION.
MIND IF WE TURN OFF THAT TV?
STEVE ROGERS ISN'T SLEEPING MUCH EITHER THESE DAYS. LIKE ME, HIS THOUGHTS ARE OF LEGACIES. HOW EASILY THEY SLIP AWAY...

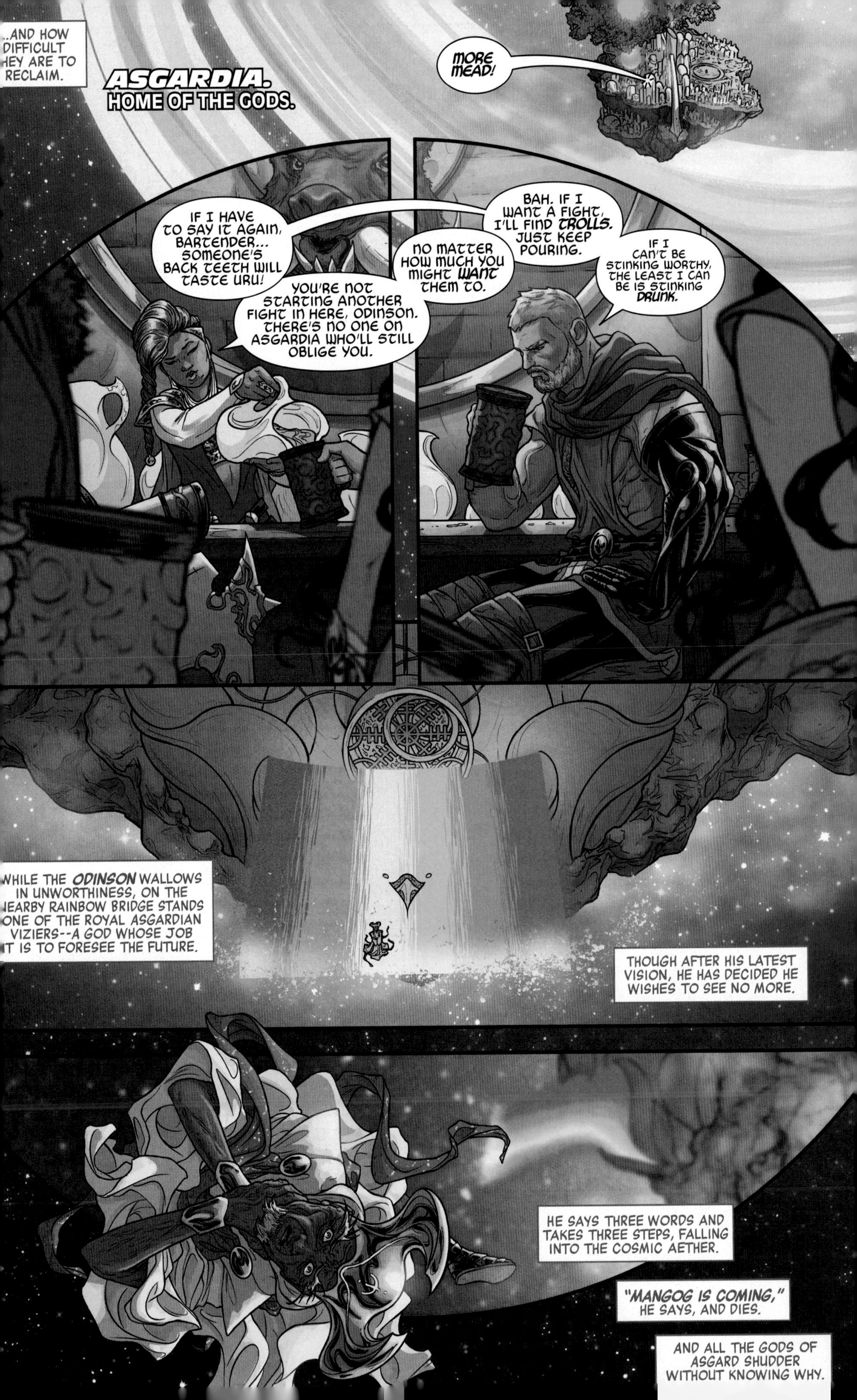

..AND HOW DIFFICULT HEY ARE TO RECLAIM.
ASGARDIA. HOME OF THE GODS.
MORE MEAD!
IF I HAVE TO SAY IT AGAIN, BARTENDER... SOMEONE'S BACK TEETH WILL TASTE URU!
YOU'RE NOT STARTING ANOTHER FIGHT IN HERE, ODINSON. THERE'S NO ONE ON ASGARDIA WHO'LL STILL OBLIGE YOU.
NO MATTER HOW MUCH YOU MIGHT WANT THEM TO.
BAH. IF I WANT A FIGHT, I'LL FIND TROLLS. JUST KEEP POURING.
IF I CAN'T BE STINKING WORTHY, THE LEAST I CAN BE IS STINKING DRUNK.
WHILE THE ODINSON WALLOWS IN UNWORTHINESS, ON THE NEARBY RAINBOW BRIDGE STANDS ONE OF THE ROYAL ASGARDIAN VIZIERS--A GOD WHOSE JOB IT IS TO FORESEE THE FUTURE.
THOUGH AFTER HIS LATEST VISION, HE HAS DECIDED HE WISHES TO SEE NO MORE.
HE SAYS THREE WORDS AND TAKES THREE STEPS, FALLING INTO THE COSMIC AETHER.
"MANGOG IS COMING," HE SAYS, AND DIES.
AND ALL THE GODS OF ASGARD SHUDDER WITHOUT KNOWING WHY.

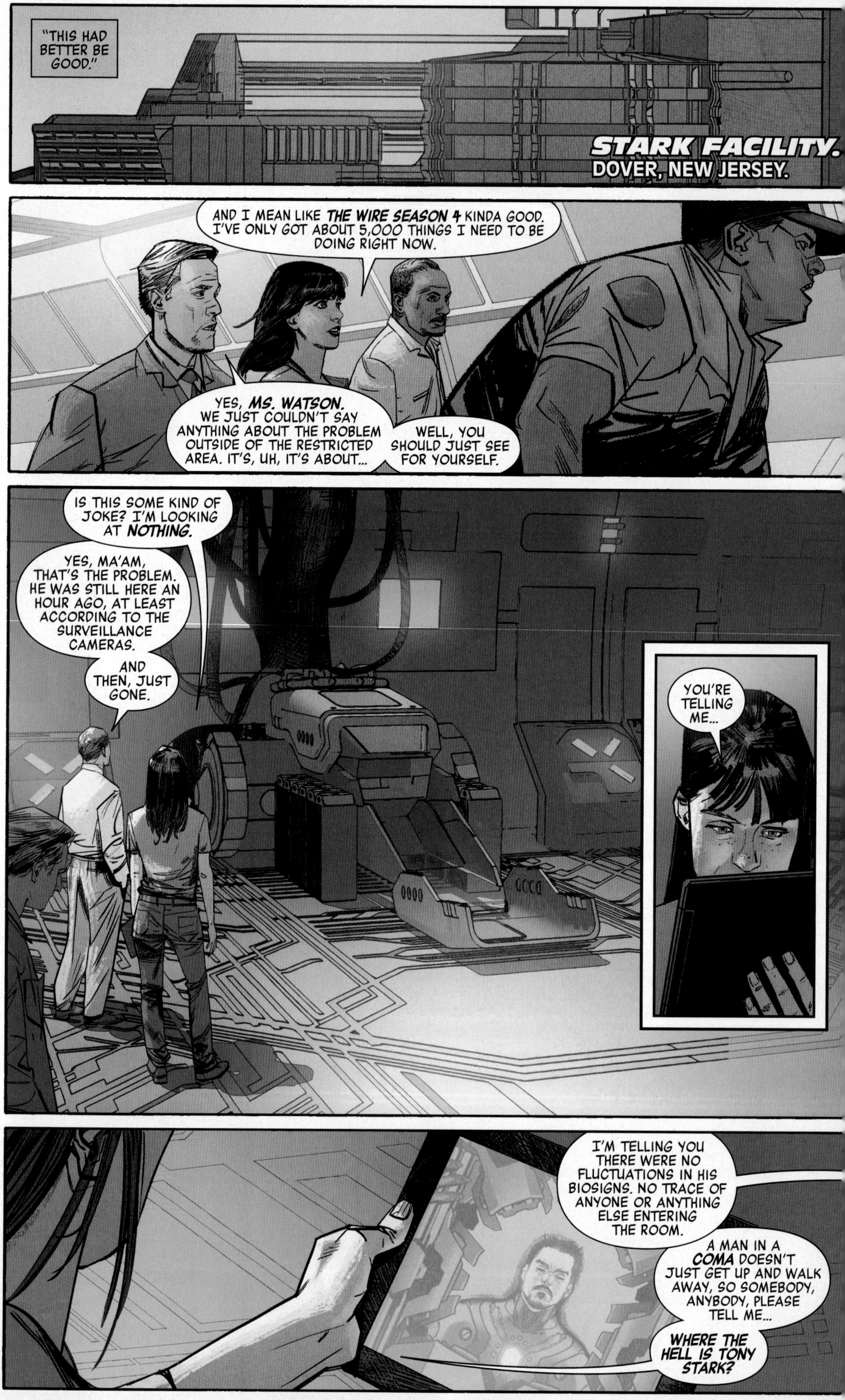
"THIS HAD BETTER BE GOOD."
STARK FACILITY.
DOVER, NEW JERSEY.
AND I MEAN LIKE THE WIRE SEASON 4 KINDA GOOD. I'VE ONLY GOT ABOUT 5,000 THINGS I NEED TO BE DOING RIGHT NOW.
YES, MS. WATSON. WE JUST COULDN'T SAY ANYTHING ABOUT THE PROBLEM OUTSIDE OF THE RESTRICTED AREA. IT'S, UH, IT'S ABOUT...
WELL, YOU SHOULD JUST SEE FOR YOURSELF.
IS THIS SOME KIND OF JOKE? I'M LOOKING AT NOTHING.
YES, MA'AM, THAT'S THE PROBLEM. HE WAS STILL HERE AN HOUR AGO, AT LEAST ACCORDING TO THE SURVEILLANCE CAMERAS.
AND THEN, JUST GONE.
YOU'RE TELLING ME...
I'M TELLING YOU THERE WERE NO FLUCTUATIONS IN HIS BIOSIGNS. NO TRACE OF ANYONE OR ANYTHING ELSE ENTERING THE ROOM.
A MAN IN A COMA DOESN'T JUST GET UP AND WALK AWAY, SO SOMEBODY, ANYBODY, PLEASE TELL ME...
WHERE THE HELL IS TONY STARK?

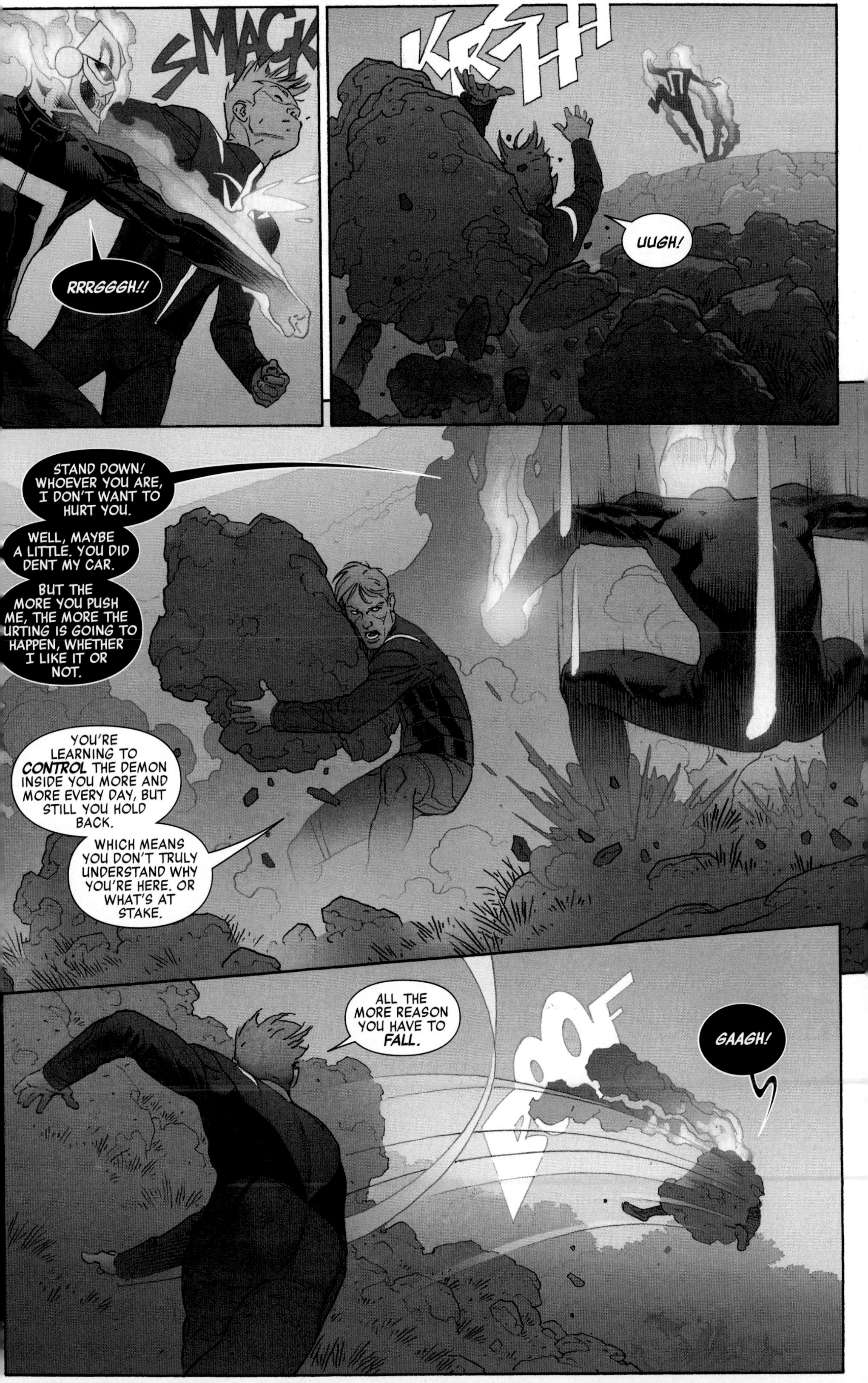
SMACK
RRRGGGH!!
KRSSHH
UUGH!
STAND DOWN! WHOEVER YOU ARE, I DON'T WANT TO HURT YOU.
WELL, MAYBE A LITTLE. YOU DID DENT MY CAR.
BUT THE MORE YOU PUSH ME, THE MORE THE URTING IS GOING TO HAPPEN, WHETHER I LIKE IT OR NOT.
YOU'RE LEARNING TO CONTROL THE DEMON INSIDE YOU MORE AND MORE EVERY DAY, BUT STILL YOU HOLD BACK.
WHICH MEANS YOU DON'T TRULY UNDERSTAND WHY YOU'RE HERE. OR WHAT'S AT STAKE.
ALL THE MORE REASON YOU HAVE TO FALL.
FOOF
GAAGH!

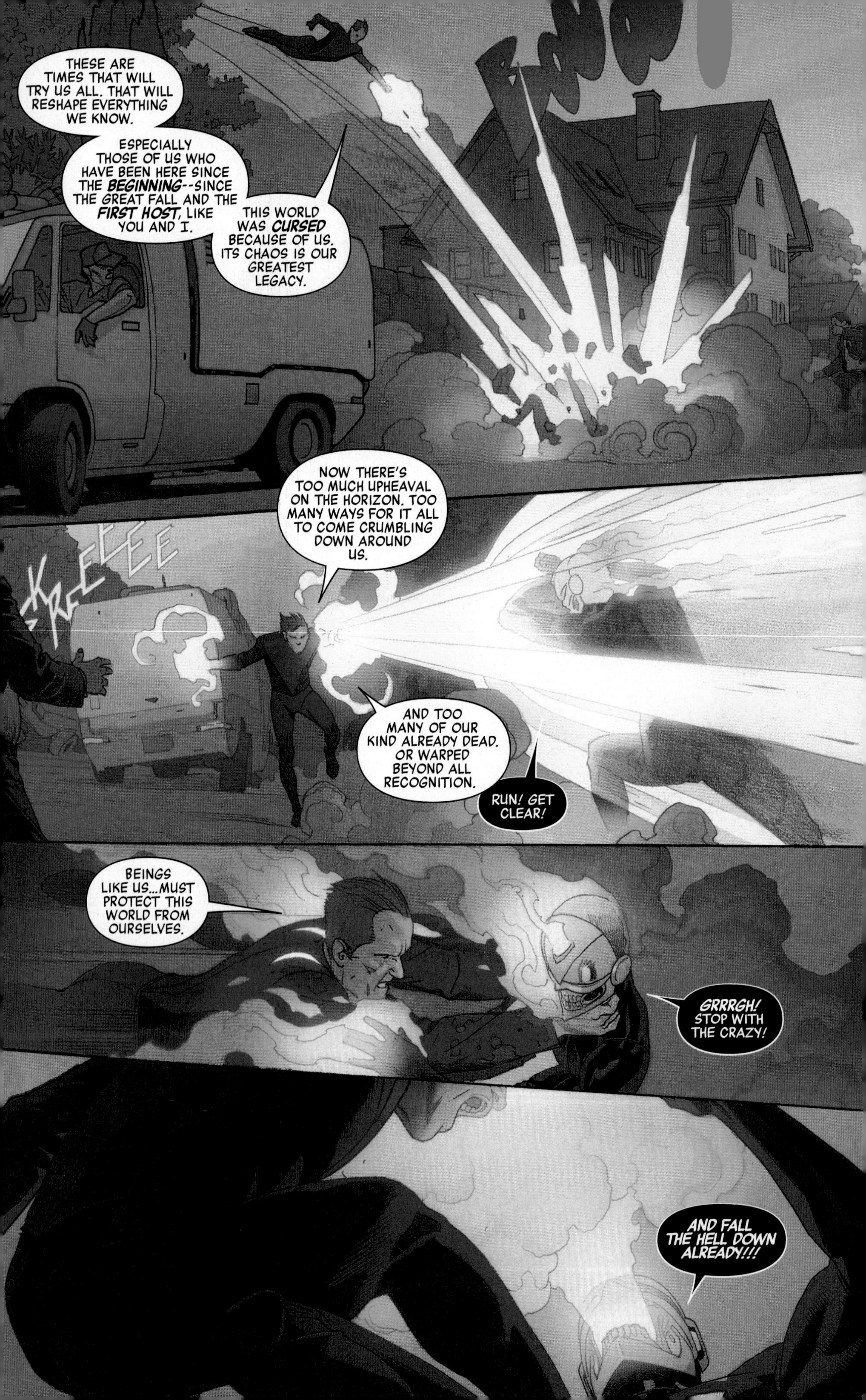
THESE ARE TIMES THAT WILL TRY US ALL. THAT WILL RESHAPE EVERYTHING WE KNOW.
ESPECIALLY THOSE OF US WHO HAVE BEEN HERE SINCE THE BEGINNING--SINCE THE GREAT FALL AND THE FIRST HOST, LIKE YOU AND I.
THIS WORLD WAS CURSED BECAUSE OF US. ITS CHAOS IS OUR GREATEST LEGACY.
NOW THERE'S TOO MUCH UPHEAVAL ON THE HORIZON. TOO MANY WAYS FOR IT ALL TO COME CRUMBLING DOWN AROUND US.
AND TOO MANY OF OUR KIND ALREADY DEAD. OR WARPED BEYOND ALL RECOGNITION.
RUN! GET CLEAR!
BEINGS LIKE US...MUST PROTECT THIS WORLD FROM OURSELVES.
GRRRGH! STOP WITH THE CRAZY!
AND FALL THE HELL DOWN ALREADY!!!

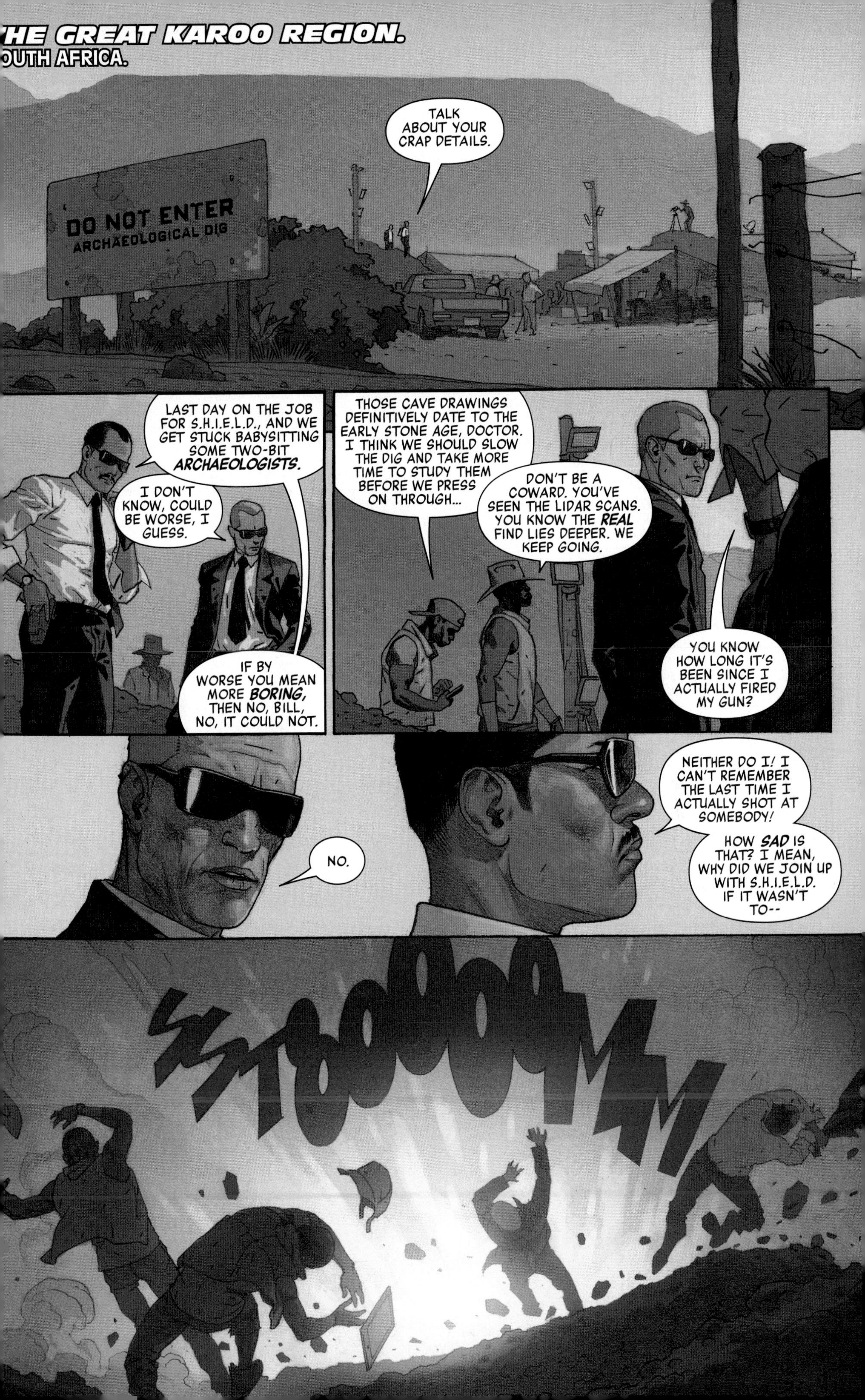
THE GREAT KAROO REGION.
SOUTH AFRICA.
DO NOT ENTER
ARCHAEOLOGICAL DIG
TALK ABOUT YOUR CRAP DETAILS.
LAST DAY ON THE JOB FOR S.H.I.E.L.D., AND WE GET STUCK BABYSITTING SOME TWO-BIT ARCHAEOLOGISTS.
I DON'T KNOW, COULD BE WORSE, I GUESS.
IF BY WORSE YOU MEAN MORE BORING, THEN NO, BILL, NO, IT COULD NOT.
THOSE CAVE DRAWINGS DEFINITIVELY DATE TO THE EARLY STONE AGE, DOCTOR. I THINK WE SHOULD SLOW THE DIG AND TAKE MORE TIME TO STUDY THEM BEFORE WE PRESS ON THROUGH...
DON'T BE A COWARD. YOU'VE SEEN THE LIDAR SCANS. YOU KNOW THE REAL FIND LIES DEEPER. WE KEEP GOING.
YOU KNOW HOW LONG IT'S BEEN SINCE I ACTUALLY FIRED MY GUN?
NO.
NEITHER DO I! I CAN'T REMEMBER THE LAST TIME I ACTUALLY SHOT AT SOMEBODY!
HOW SAD IS THAT? I MEAN, WHY DID WE JOIN UP WITH S.H.I.E.L.D. IF IT WASN'T TO--
STOOOOOM

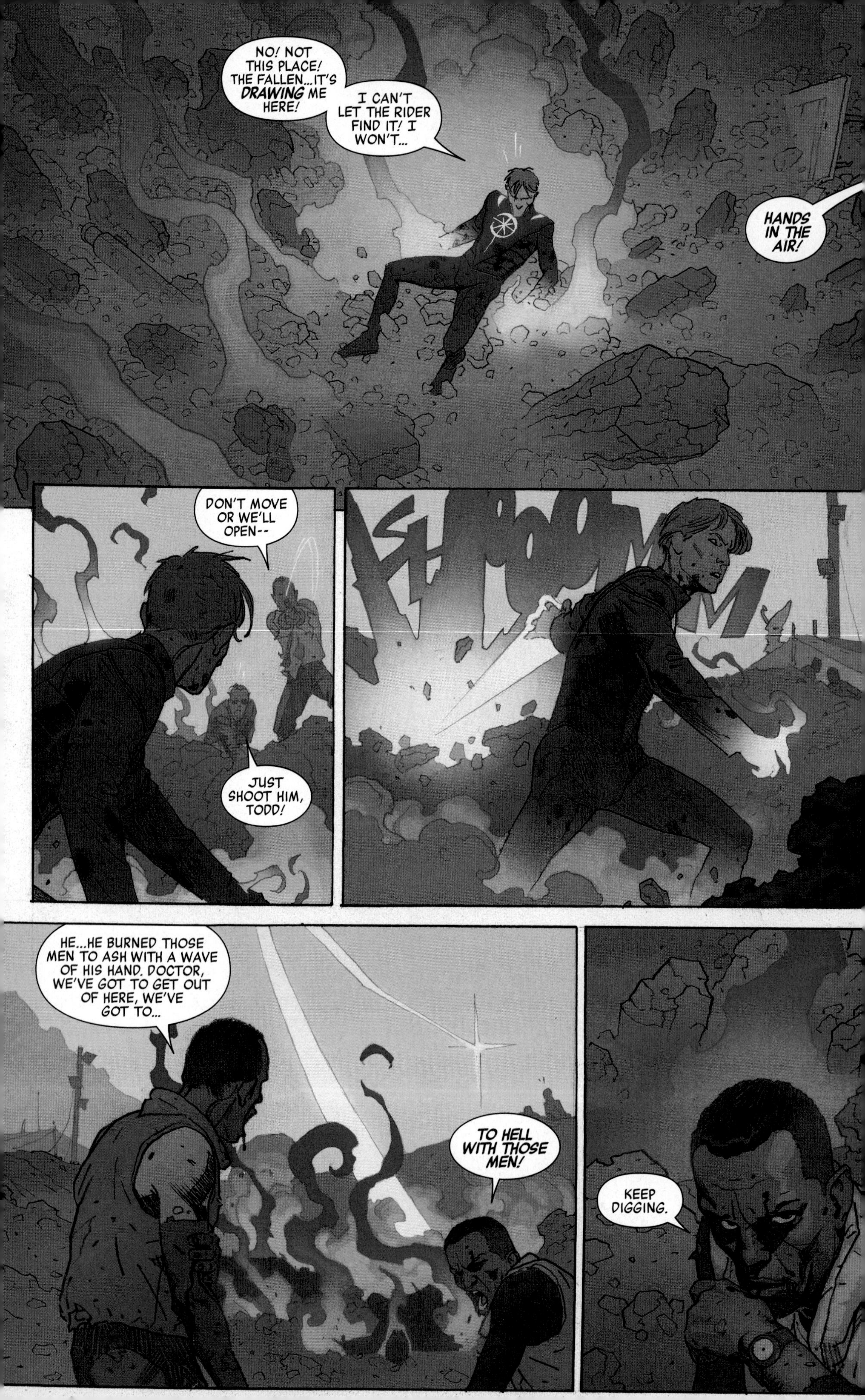

NO! NOT THIS PLACE! THE FALLEN...IT'S *DRAWING* ME HERE!
I CAN'T LET THE RIDER FIND IT! I WON'T...
HANDS IN THE AIR!
DON'T MOVE OR WE'LL OPEN--
JUST SHOOT HIM, TODD!
HE...HE BURNED THOSE MEN TO ASH WITH A WAVE OF HIS HAND. DOCTOR, WE'VE GOT TO GET OUT OF HERE, WE'VE GOT TO...
TO HELL WITH THOSE MEN!
KEEP DIGGING.

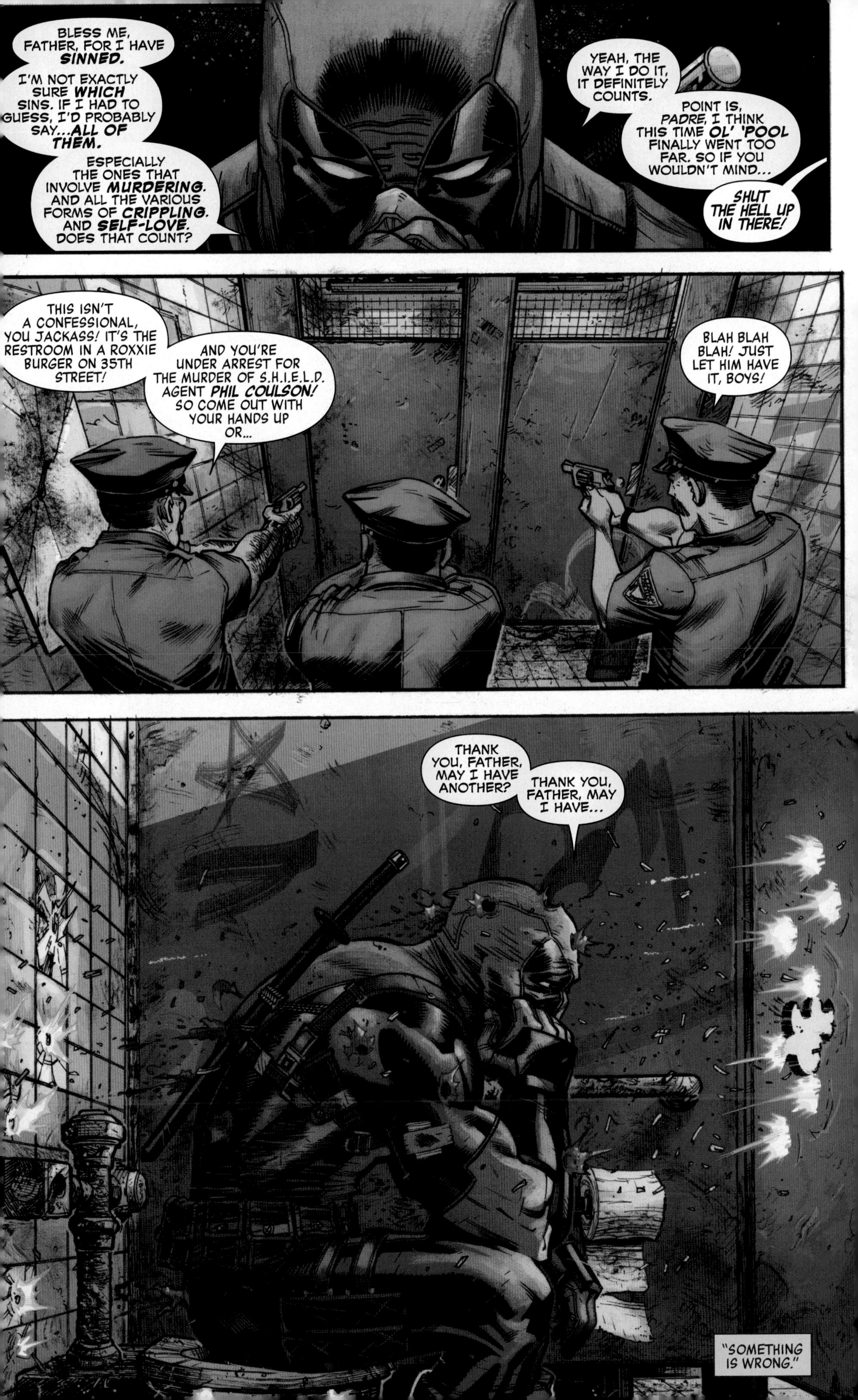
BLESS ME, FATHER, FOR I HAVE SINNED.
I'M NOT EXACTLY SURE WHICH SINS. IF I HAD TO GUESS, I'D PROBABLY SAY...ALL OF THEM.
ESPECIALLY THE ONES THAT INVOLVE MURDERING. AND ALL THE VARIOUS FORMS OF CRIPPLING. AND SELF-LOVE. DOES THAT COUNT?
YEAH, THE WAY I DO IT, IT DEFINITELY COUNTS.
POINT IS, PADRE, I THINK THIS TIME OL' 'POOL FINALLY WENT TOO FAR. SO IF YOU WOULDN'T MIND...
SHUT THE HELL UP IN THERE!
THIS ISN'T A CONFESSIONAL, YOU JACKASS! IT'S THE RESTROOM IN A ROXXIE BURGER ON 35TH STREET!
AND YOU'RE UNDER ARREST FOR THE MURDER OF S.H.I.E.L.D. AGENT PHIL COULSON! SO COME OUT WITH YOUR HANDS UP OR...
BLAH BLAH BLAH! JUST LET HIM HAVE IT, BOYS!
THANK YOU, FATHER, MAY I HAVE ANOTHER?
THANK YOU, FATHER, MAY I HAVE...
"SOMETHING IS WRONG."

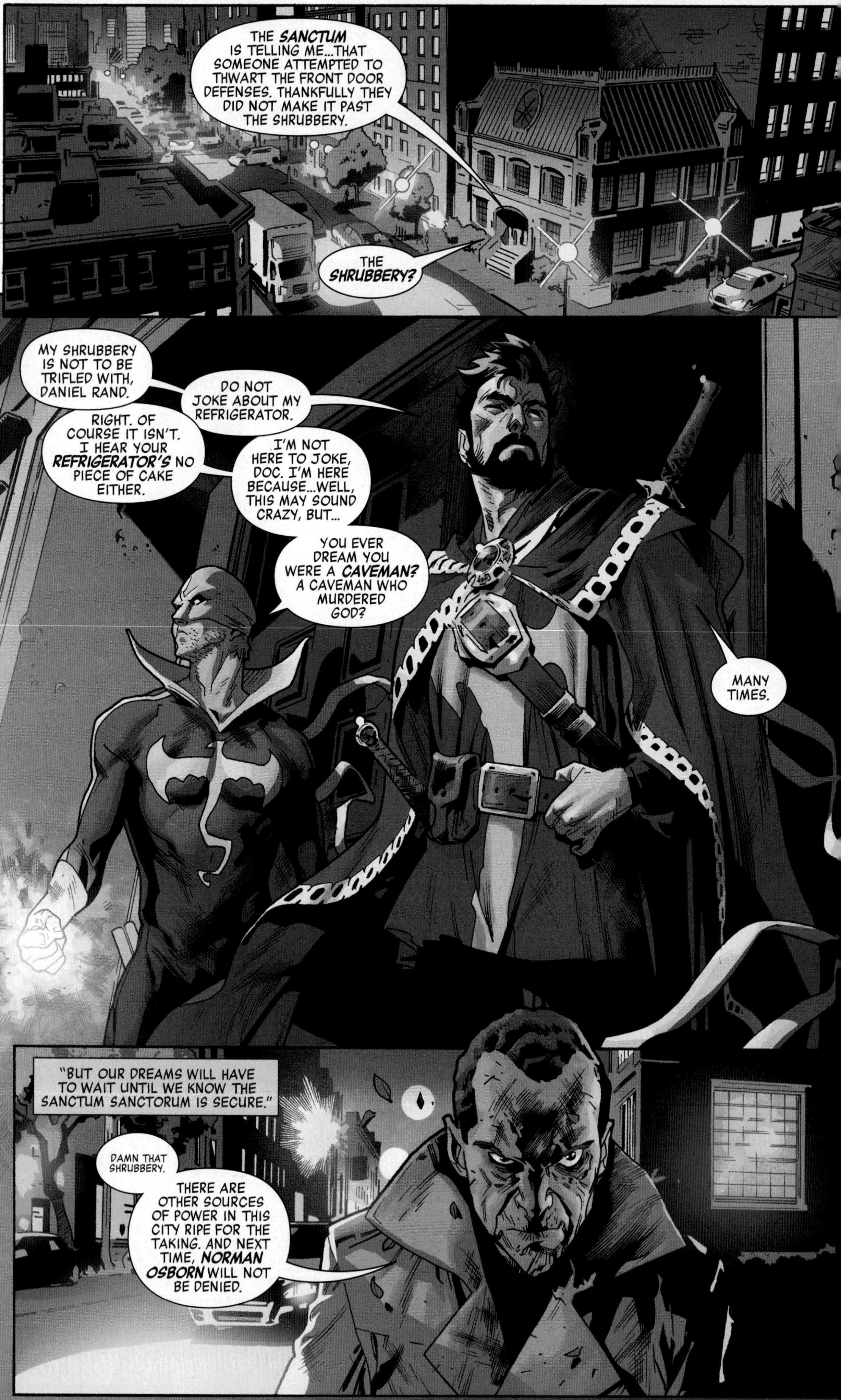
THE SANCTUM IS TELLING ME...THAT SOMEONE ATTEMPTED TO THWART THE FRONT DOOR DEFENSES. THANKFULLY THEY DID NOT MAKE IT PAST THE SHRUBBERY.
THE SHRUBBERY?
MY SHRUBBERY IS NOT TO BE TRIFLED WITH, DANIEL RAND.
RIGHT. OF COURSE IT ISN'T. I HEAR YOUR REFRIGERATOR'S NO PIECE OF CAKE EITHER.
DO NOT JOKE ABOUT MY REFRIGERATOR.
I'M NOT HERE TO JOKE, DOC. I'M HERE BECAUSE...WELL, THIS MAY SOUND CRAZY, BUT...
YOU EVER DREAM YOU WERE A CAVEMAN? A CAVEMAN WHO MURDERED GOD?
MANY TIMES.
"BUT OUR DREAMS WILL HAVE TO WAIT UNTIL WE KNOW THE SANCTUM SANCTORUM IS SECURE."
DAMN THAT SHRUBBERY.
THERE ARE OTHER SOURCES OF POWER IN THIS CITY RIPE FOR THE TAKING. AND NEXT TIME, NORMAN OSBORN WILL NOT BE DENIED.

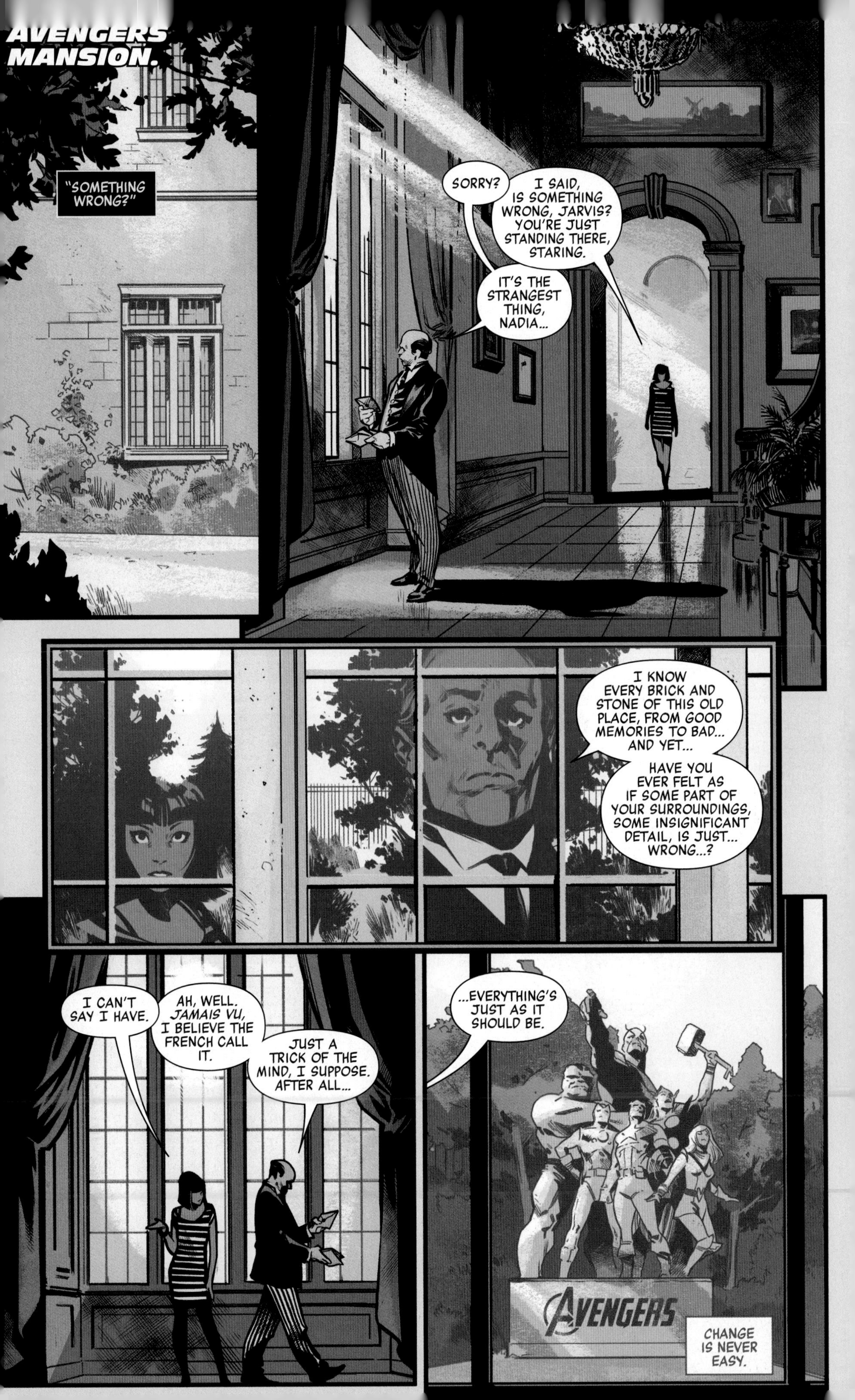
AVENGERS MANSION.
"SOMETHING WRONG?"
SORRY?
I SAID, IS SOMETHING WRONG, JARVIS? YOU'RE JUST STANDING THERE, STARING.
IT'S THE STRANGEST THING, NADIA...
I KNOW EVERY BRICK AND STONE OF THIS OLD PLACE, FROM GOOD MEMORIES TO BAD... AND YET...
HAVE YOU EVER FELT AS IF SOME PART OF YOUR SURROUNDINGS, SOME INSIGNIFICANT DETAIL, IS JUST... WRONG...?
I CAN'T SAY I HAVE.
AH, WELL. *JAMAIS VU*, I BELIEVE THE FRENCH CALL IT.
JUST A TRICK OF THE MIND, I SUPPOSE. AFTER ALL...
...EVERYTHING'S JUST AS IT SHOULD BE.
AVENGERS
CHANGE IS NEVER EASY.

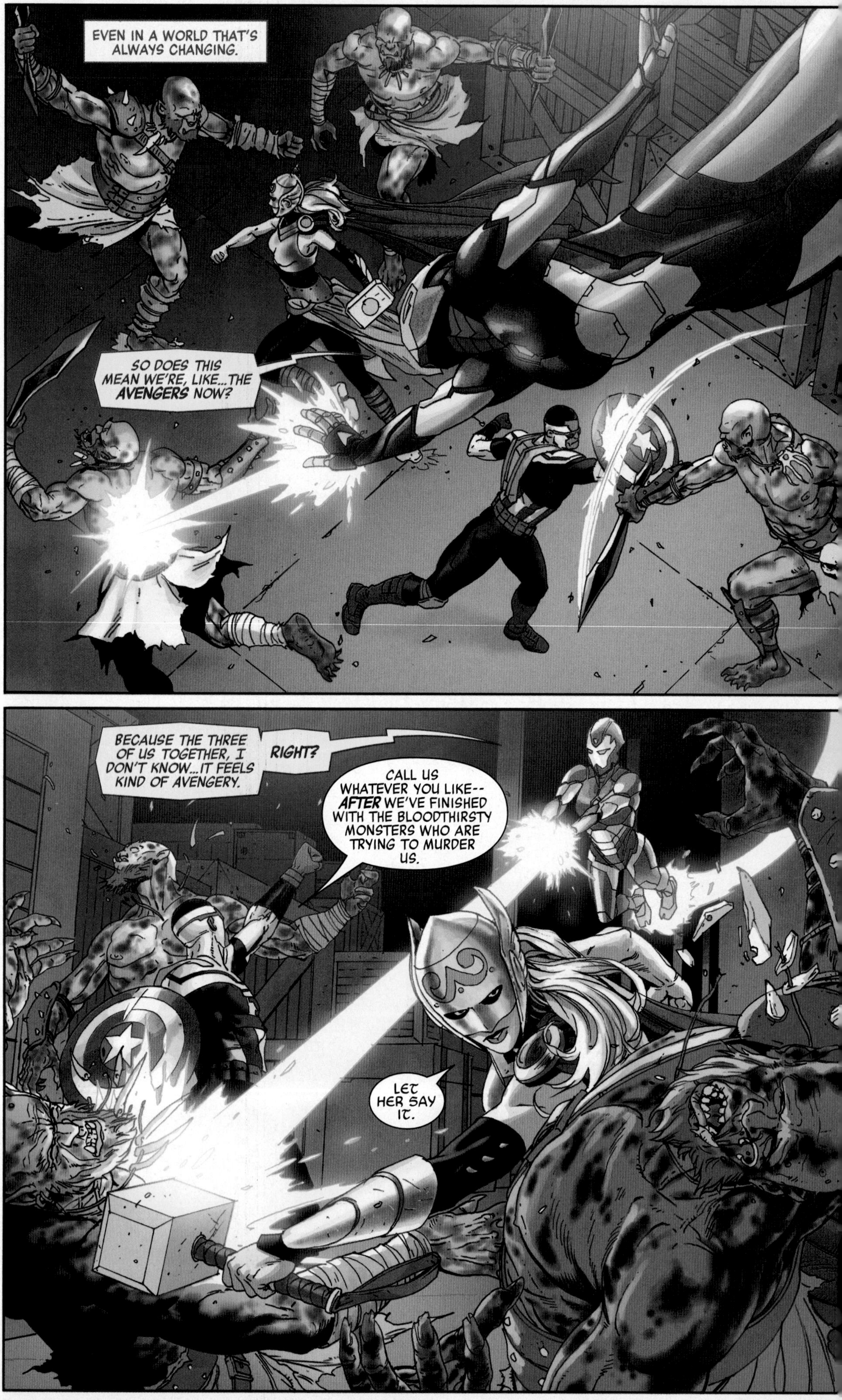
EVEN IN A WORLD THAT'S ALWAYS CHANGING.
SO DOES THIS MEAN WE'RE, LIKE...THE AVENGERS NOW?
BECAUSE THE THREE OF US TOGETHER, I DON'T KNOW...IT FEELS KIND OF AVENGERY.
RIGHT?
CALL US WHATEVER YOU LIKE-- AFTER WE'VE FINISHED WITH THE BLOODTHIRSTY MONSTERS WHO ARE TRYING TO MURDER US.
LET HER SAY IT.

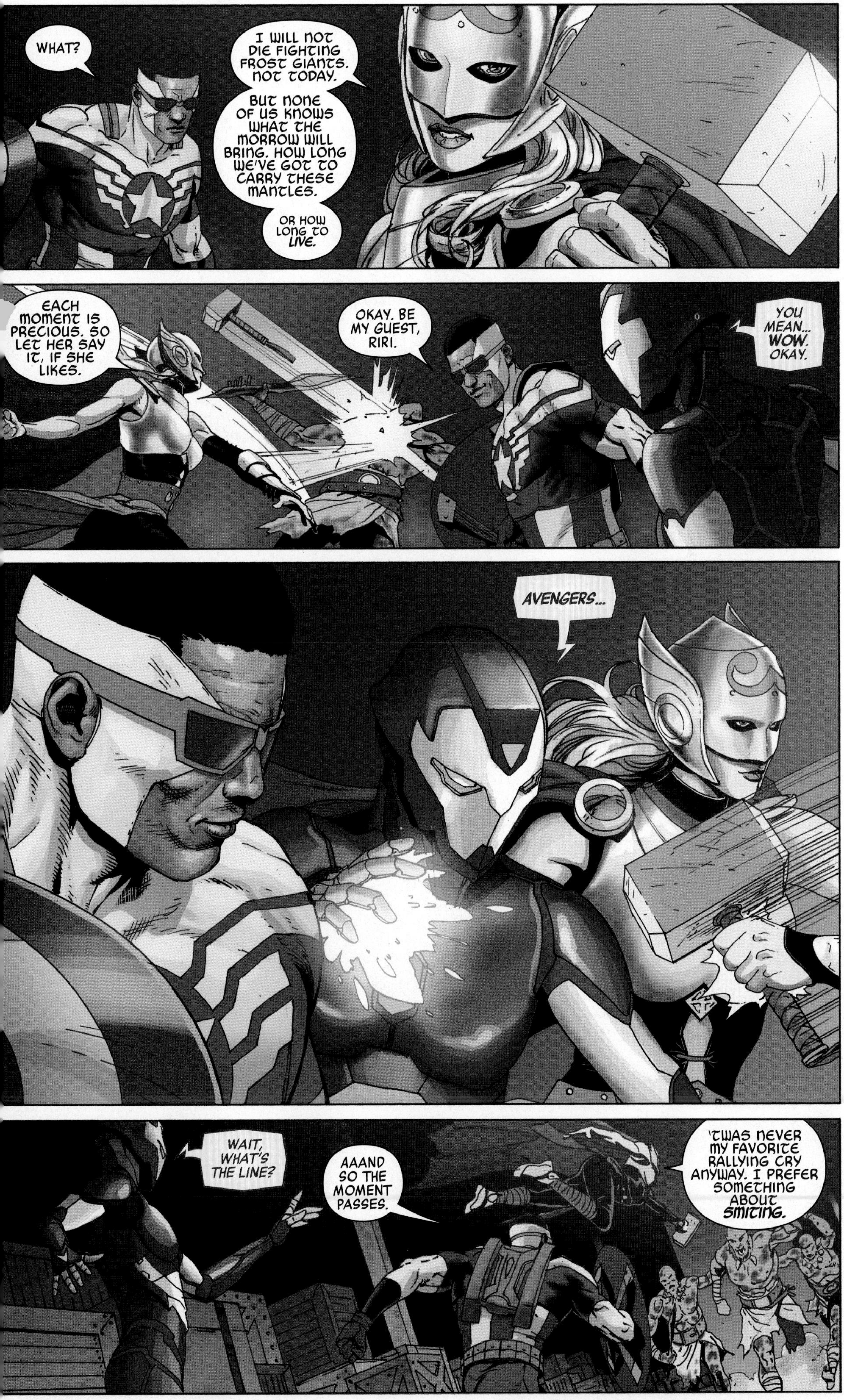
WHAT?
I WILL NOT DIE FIGHTING FROST GIANTS. NOT TODAY.
BUT NONE OF US KNOWS WHAT THE MORROW WILL BRING. HOW LONG WE'VE GOT TO CARRY THESE MANTLES.
OR HOW LONG TO LIVE.
EACH MOMENT IS PRECIOUS. SO LET HER SAY IT, IF SHE LIKES.
OKAY. BE MY GUEST, RIRI.
YOU MEAN... WOW. OKAY.
AVENGERS...
WAIT, WHAT'S THE LINE?
AAAND SO THE MOMENT PASSES.
'TWAS NEVER MY FAVORITE RALLYING CRY ANYWAY. I PREFER SOMETHING ABOUT SMITING.

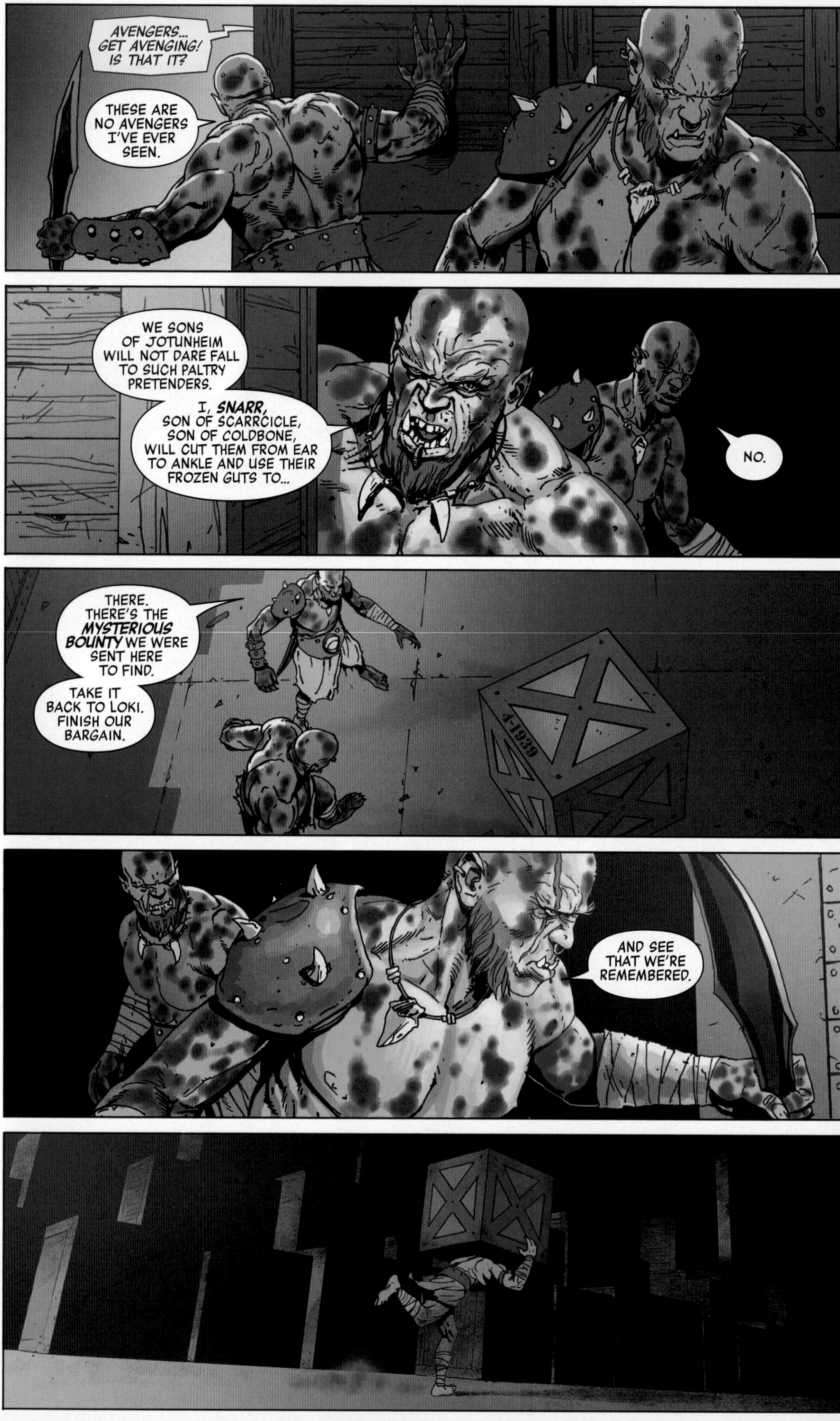
AVENGERS... GET AVENGING! IS THAT IT?
THESE ARE NO AVENGERS I'VE EVER SEEN.
WE SONS OF JOTUNHEIM WILL NOT DARE FALL TO SUCH PALTRY PRETENDERS.
I, SNARR, SON OF SCARRCICLE, SON OF COLDBONE, WILL CUT THEM FROM EAR TO ANKLE AND USE THEIR FROZEN GUTS TO...
NO.
THERE. THERE'S THE MYSTERIOUS BOUNTY WE WERE SENT HERE TO FIND.
TAKE IT BACK TO LOKI. FINISH OUR BARGAIN.
4-1939
AND SEE THAT WE'RE REMEMBERED.

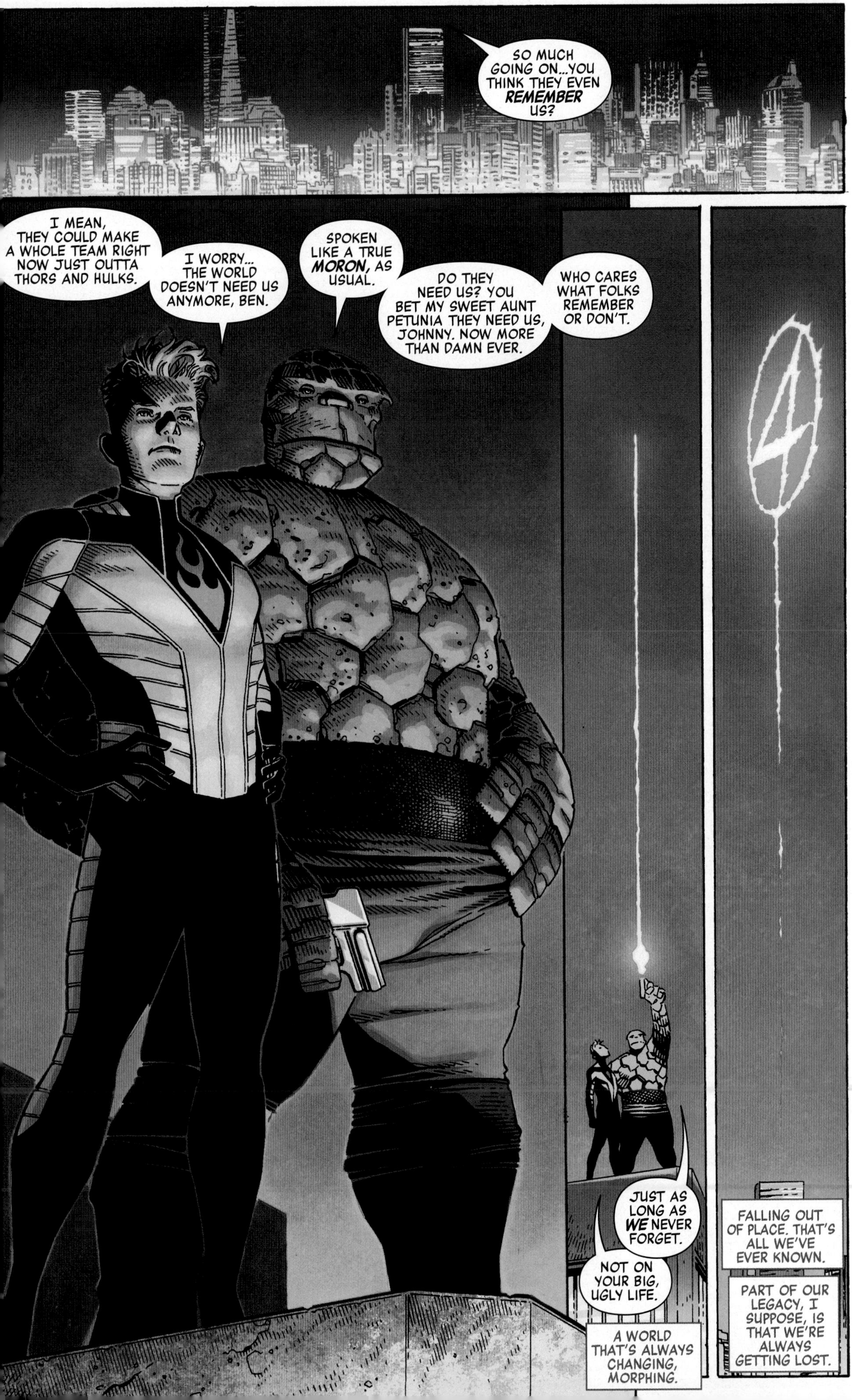
SO MUCH GOING ON...YOU THINK THEY EVEN REMEMBER US?
I MEAN, THEY COULD MAKE A WHOLE TEAM RIGHT NOW JUST OUTTA THORS AND HULKS.
I WORRY... THE WORLD DOESN'T NEED US ANYMORE, BEN.
SPOKEN LIKE A TRUE MORON, AS USUAL.
DO THEY NEED US? YOU BET MY SWEET AUNT PETUNIA THEY NEED US, JOHNNY. NOW MORE THAN DAMN EVER.
WHO CARES WHAT FOLKS REMEMBER OR DON'T.
JUST AS LONG AS WE NEVER FORGET.
NOT ON YOUR BIG, UGLY LIFE.
A WORLD THAT'S ALWAYS CHANGING, MORPHING.
FALLING OUT OF PLACE. THAT'S ALL WE'VE EVER KNOWN.
PART OF OUR LEGACY, I SUPPOSE, IS THAT WE'RE ALWAYS GETTING LOST.

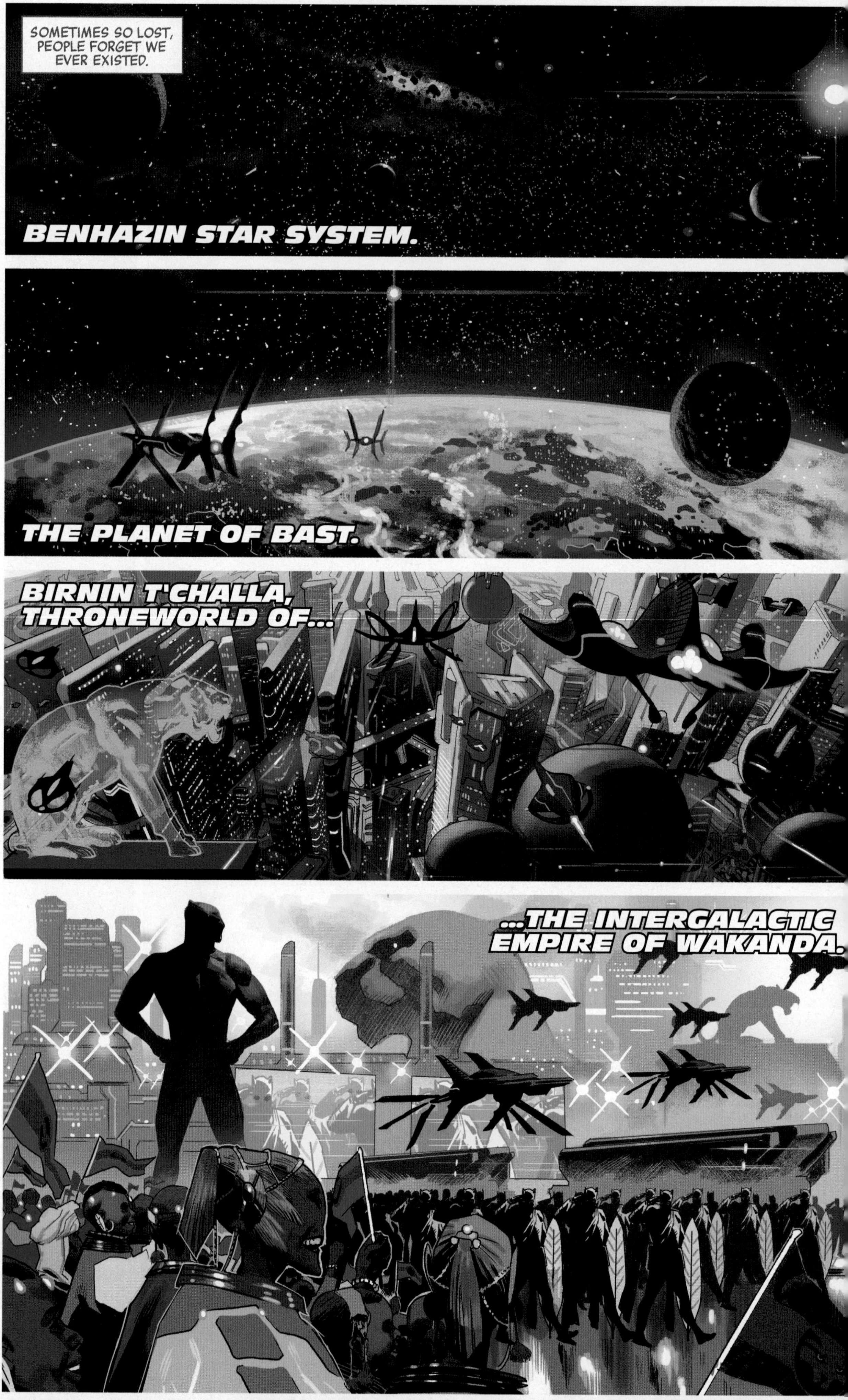
SOMETIMES SO LOST, PEOPLE FORGET WE EVER EXISTED.
BENHAZIN STAR SYSTEM.
THE PLANET OF BAST.
BIRNIN T'CHALLA, THRONEWORLD OF...
...THE INTERGALACTIC EMPIRE OF WAKANDA.

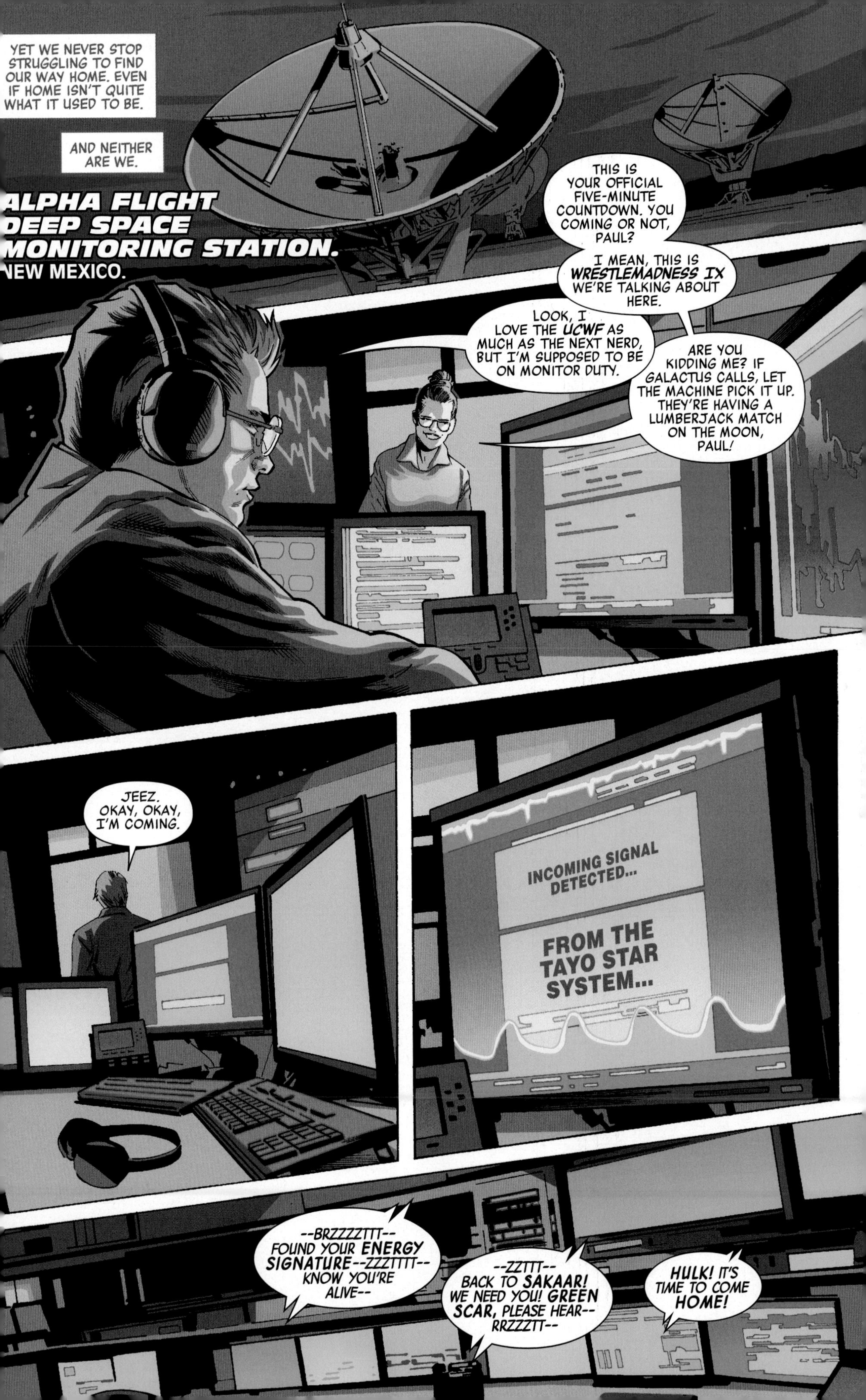
YET WE NEVER STOP STRUGGLING TO FIND OUR WAY HOME. EVEN IF HOME ISN'T QUITE WHAT IT USED TO BE.
AND NEITHER ARE WE.
ALPHA FLIGHT DEEP SPACE MONITORING STATION.
NEW MEXICO.
THIS IS YOUR OFFICIAL FIVE-MINUTE COUNTDOWN. YOU COMING OR NOT, PAUL?
I MEAN, THIS IS WRESTLEMADNESS IX WE'RE TALKING ABOUT HERE.
LOOK, I LOVE THE UCWF AS MUCH AS THE NEXT NERD, BUT I'M SUPPOSED TO BE ON MONITOR DUTY.
ARE YOU KIDDING ME? IF GALACTUS CALLS, LET THE MACHINE PICK IT UP. THEY'RE HAVING A LUMBERJACK MATCH ON THE MOON, PAUL!
JEEZ. OKAY, OKAY, I'M COMING.
INCOMING SIGNAL DETECTED...
FROM THE TAYO STAR SYSTEM...
--BRZZZZTTT-- FOUND YOUR ENERGY SIGNATURE--ZZZTTTT-- KNOW YOU'RE ALIVE--
--ZZTTT-- BACK TO SAKAAR! WE NEED YOU! GREEN SCAR, PLEASE HEAR-- RRZZZTT--
HULK! IT'S TIME TO COME HOME!

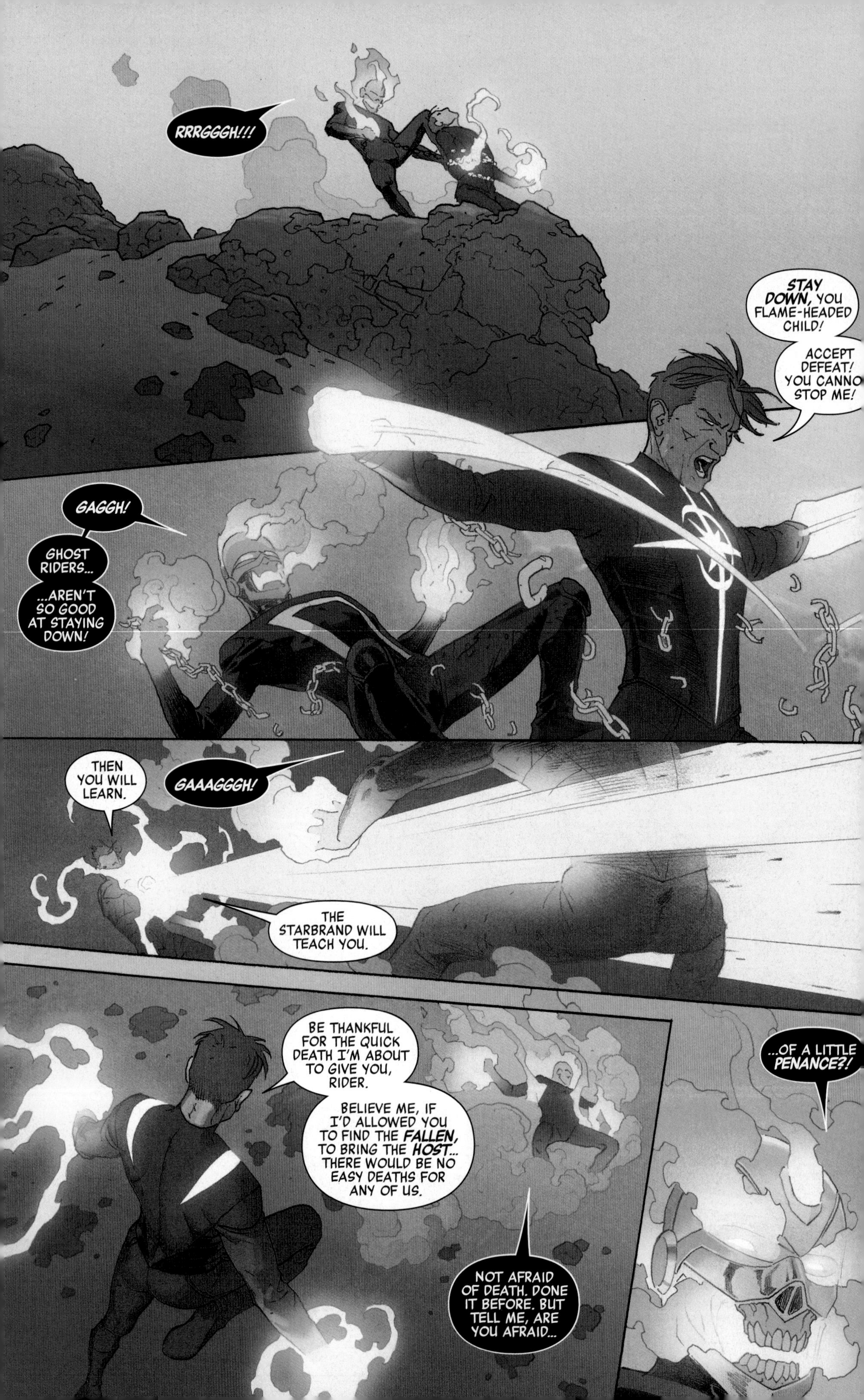
RRRGGGH!!!
STAY DOWN, YOU FLAME-HEADED CHILD!
ACCEPT DEFEAT! YOU CANNO STOP ME!
GAGGH!
GHOST RIDERS...
...AREN'T SO GOOD AT STAYING DOWN!
THEN YOU WILL LEARN.
GAAAGGGH!
THE STARBRAND WILL TEACH YOU.
BE THANKFUL FOR THE QUICK DEATH I'M ABOUT TO GIVE YOU, RIDER.
BELIEVE ME, IF I'D ALLOWED YOU TO FIND THE FALLEN, TO BRING THE HOST... THERE WOULD BE NO EASY DEATHS FOR ANY OF US.
NOT AFRAID OF DEATH. DONE IT BEFORE. BUT TELL ME, ARE YOU AFRAID...
...OF A LITTLE PENANCE?!

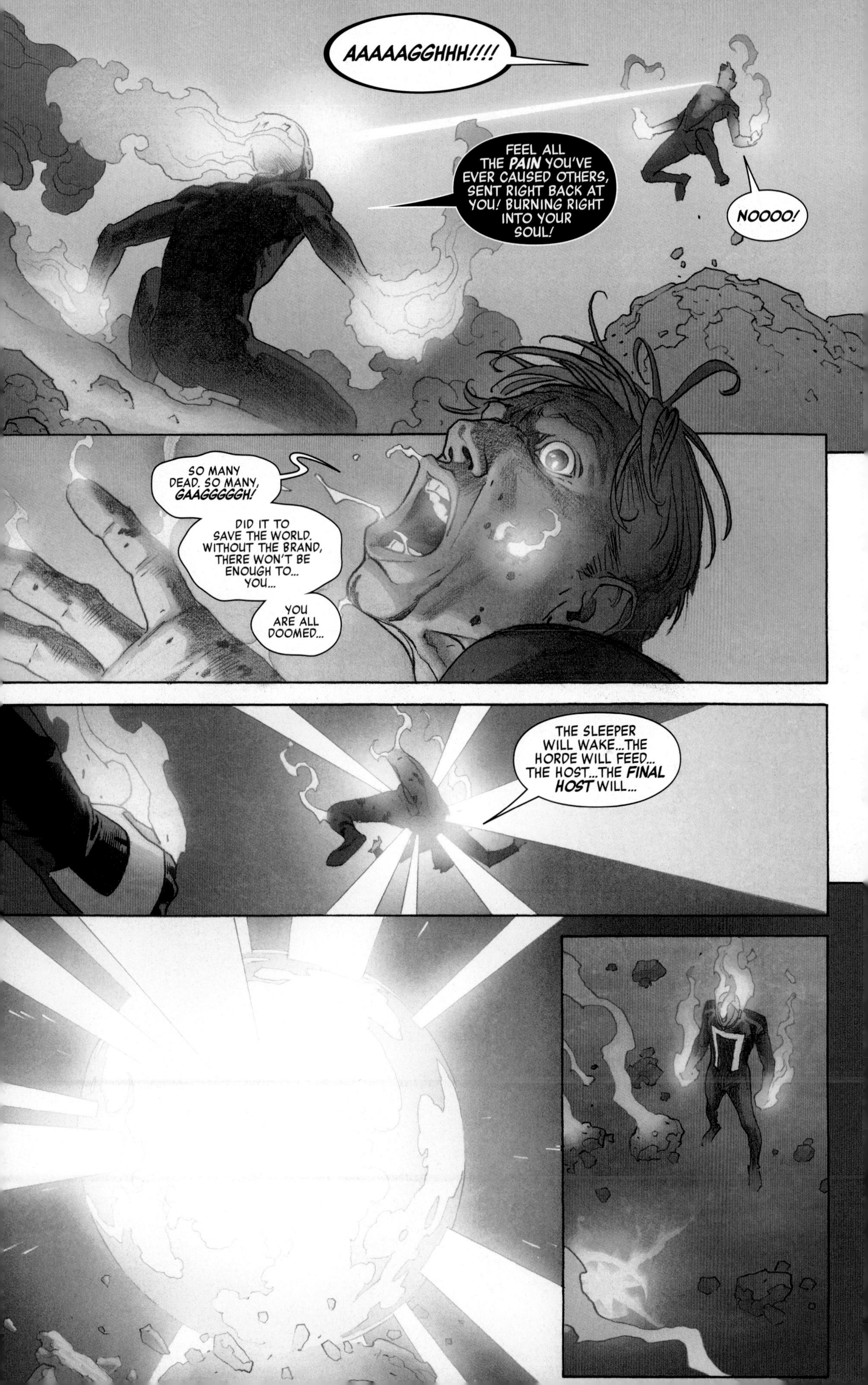
AAAAAGGHHH!!!!
FEEL ALL THE PAIN YOU'VE EVER CAUSED OTHERS, SENT RIGHT BACK AT YOU! BURNING RIGHT INTO YOUR SOUL!
NOOOO!
SO MANY DEAD. SO MANY, GAAGGGGGH!
DID IT TO SAVE THE WORLD. WITHOUT THE BRAND, THERE WON'T BE ENOUGH TO... YOU...
YOU ARE ALL DOOMED...
THE SLEEPER WILL WAKE...THE HORDE WILL FEED... THE HOST...THE FINAL HOST WILL...

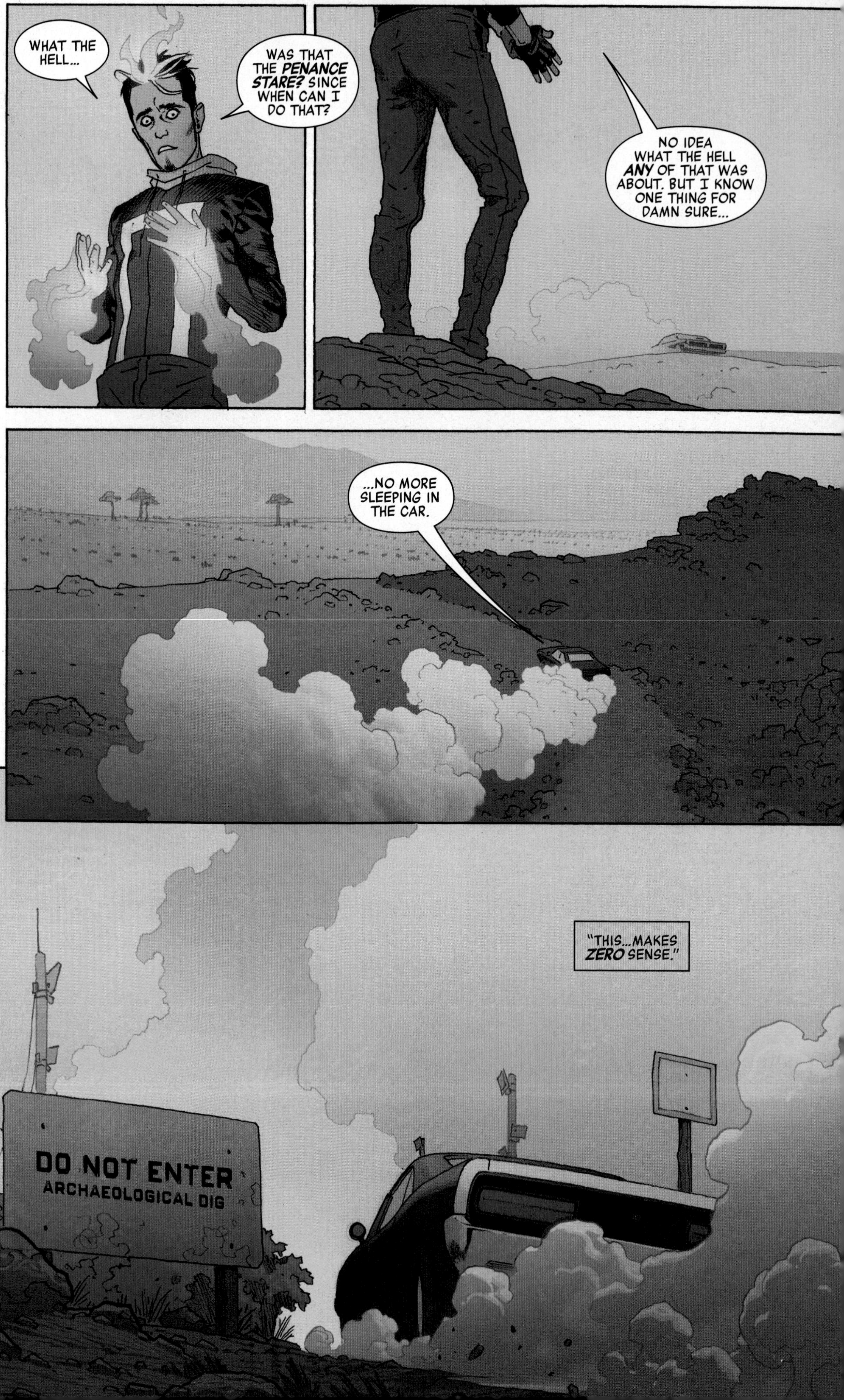
WHAT THE HELL...
WAS THAT THE PENANCE STARE? SINCE WHEN CAN I DO THAT?
NO IDEA WHAT THE HELL ANY OF THAT WAS ABOUT. BUT I KNOW ONE THING FOR DAMN SURE...
...NO MORE SLEEPING IN THE CAR.
"THIS...MAKES ZERO SENSE."
DO NOT ENTER
ARCHAEOLOGICAL DIG

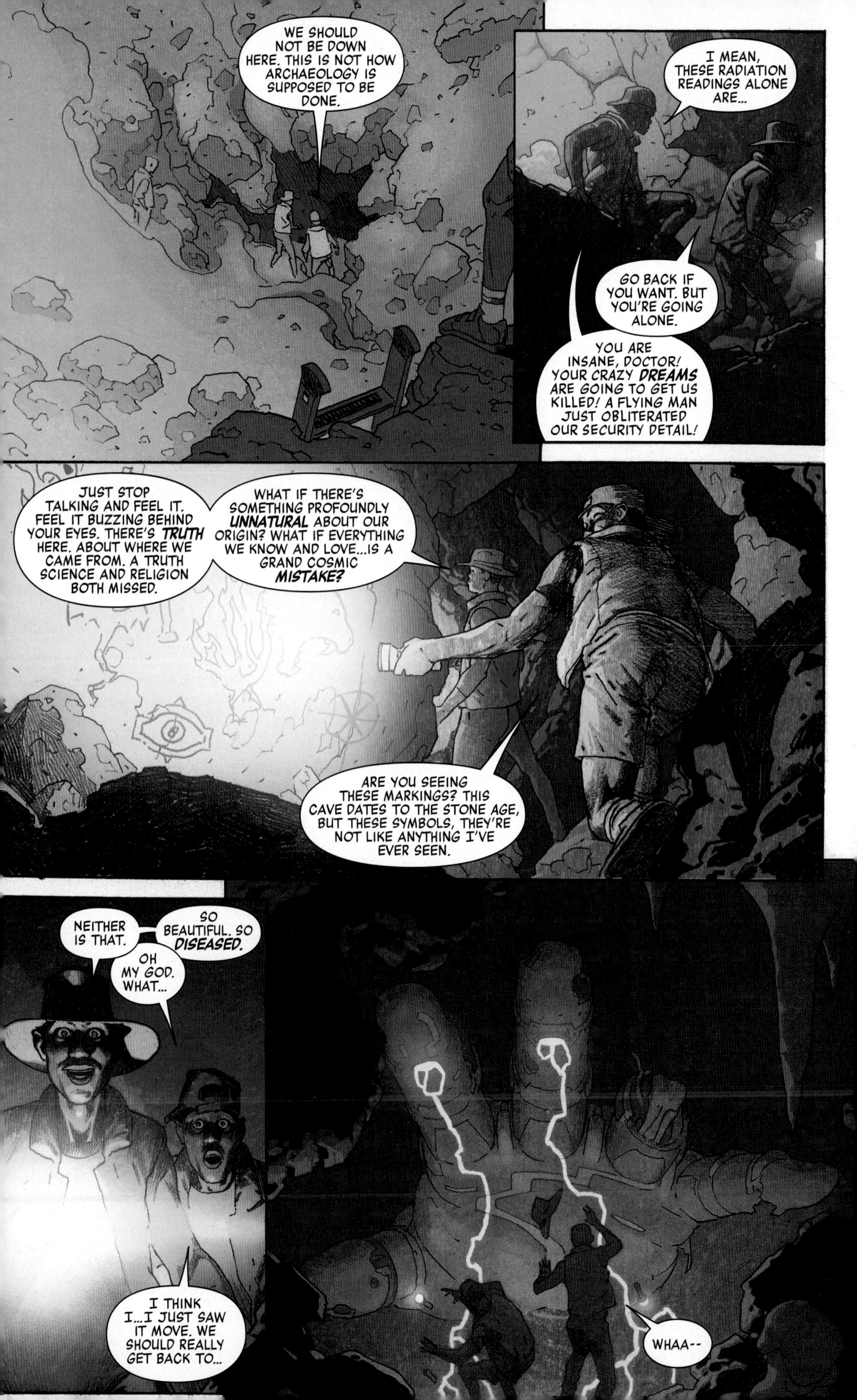

WE SHOULD NOT BE DOWN HERE. THIS IS NOT HOW ARCHAEOLOGY IS SUPPOSED TO BE DONE.
I MEAN, THESE RADIATION READINGS ALONE ARE...
GO BACK IF YOU WANT. BUT YOU'RE GOING ALONE.
YOU ARE INSANE, DOCTOR! YOUR CRAZY DREAMS ARE GOING TO GET US KILLED! A FLYING MAN JUST OBLITERATED OUR SECURITY DETAIL!
JUST STOP TALKING AND FEEL IT. FEEL IT BUZZING BEHIND YOUR EYES. THERE'S TRUTH HERE. ABOUT WHERE WE CAME FROM. A TRUTH SCIENCE AND RELIGION BOTH MISSED.
WHAT IF THERE'S SOMETHING PROFOUNDLY UNNATURAL ABOUT OUR ORIGIN? WHAT IF EVERYTHING WE KNOW AND LOVE...IS A GRAND COSMIC MISTAKE?
ARE YOU SEEING THESE MARKINGS? THIS CAVE DATES TO THE STONE AGE, BUT THESE SYMBOLS, THEY'RE NOT LIKE ANYTHING I'VE EVER SEEN.
NEITHER IS THAT.
SO BEAUTIFUL. SO DISEASED.
OH MY GOD. WHAT...
I THINK I...I JUST SAW IT MOVE. WE SHOULD REALLY GET BACK TO...
WHAA--

SUMMON... THE FINAL HOST.
AAAAH!!!
GAAAGGH!!!

CLEANSE THEM ALL.
AAAARRRRR
RRRRRRRGGH!!!

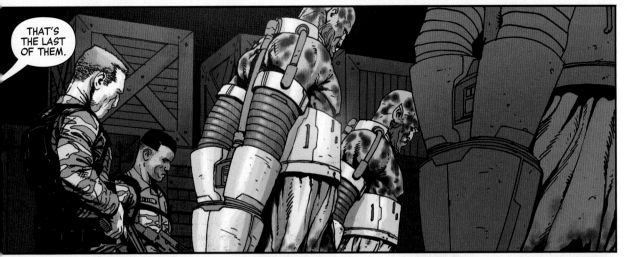

THAT'S THE LAST OF THEM.

THOSE BONDS WILL HOLD?

ACCORDING TO S.H.I.E.L.D., THEY WERE MADE TO RESTRAIN THE HULK.

THOUGH NOW THAT I THINK OF IT, THAT NEVER REALLY WORKED OUT SO WELL, DID IT?

THE TECH'S KIND OF ANTIQUATED. VERY 2015. I COULD MAKE A FEW ADJUSTMENTS, IF YOU LIKE.

THANK YOU.

CAP, THOR AND, UM, IRON MA'AM.

IRONHEART.

THANK YOU. ALL OF YOU. WE... WE LOST SOME GOOD MEN TODAY, BUT WE'D ALL HAVE BEEN DEAD IF IT WEREN'T FOR YOU THREE.

ANY IDEA WHAT THEY WERE AFTER DOWN HERE? OR IF THEY FOUND IT?

GIVE MJOLNIR AND I A MOMENT ALONE WITH ONE OF THEM, AND WE SHALL FIND OUT.

WE'RE SWEEPING NOW, BUT SO FAR, EVERYTHING SEEMS TO BE ACCOUNTED FOR...

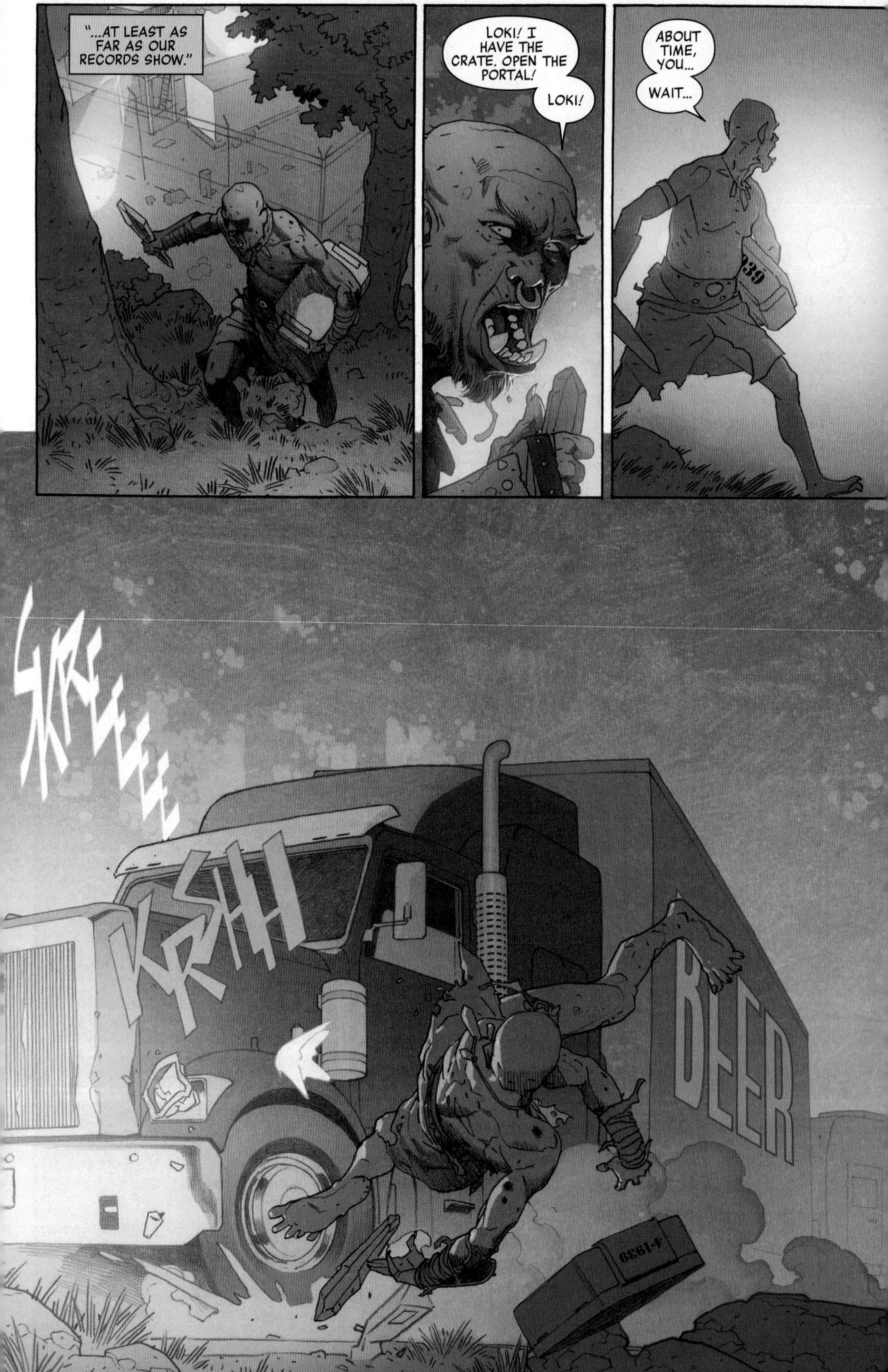
"...AT LEAST AS FAR AS OUR RECORDS SHOW."
LOKI! I HAVE THE CRATE. OPEN THE PORTAL!
LOKI!
ABOUT TIME, YOU...
WAIT...
SKREEEEEE
KRSHH
BEER

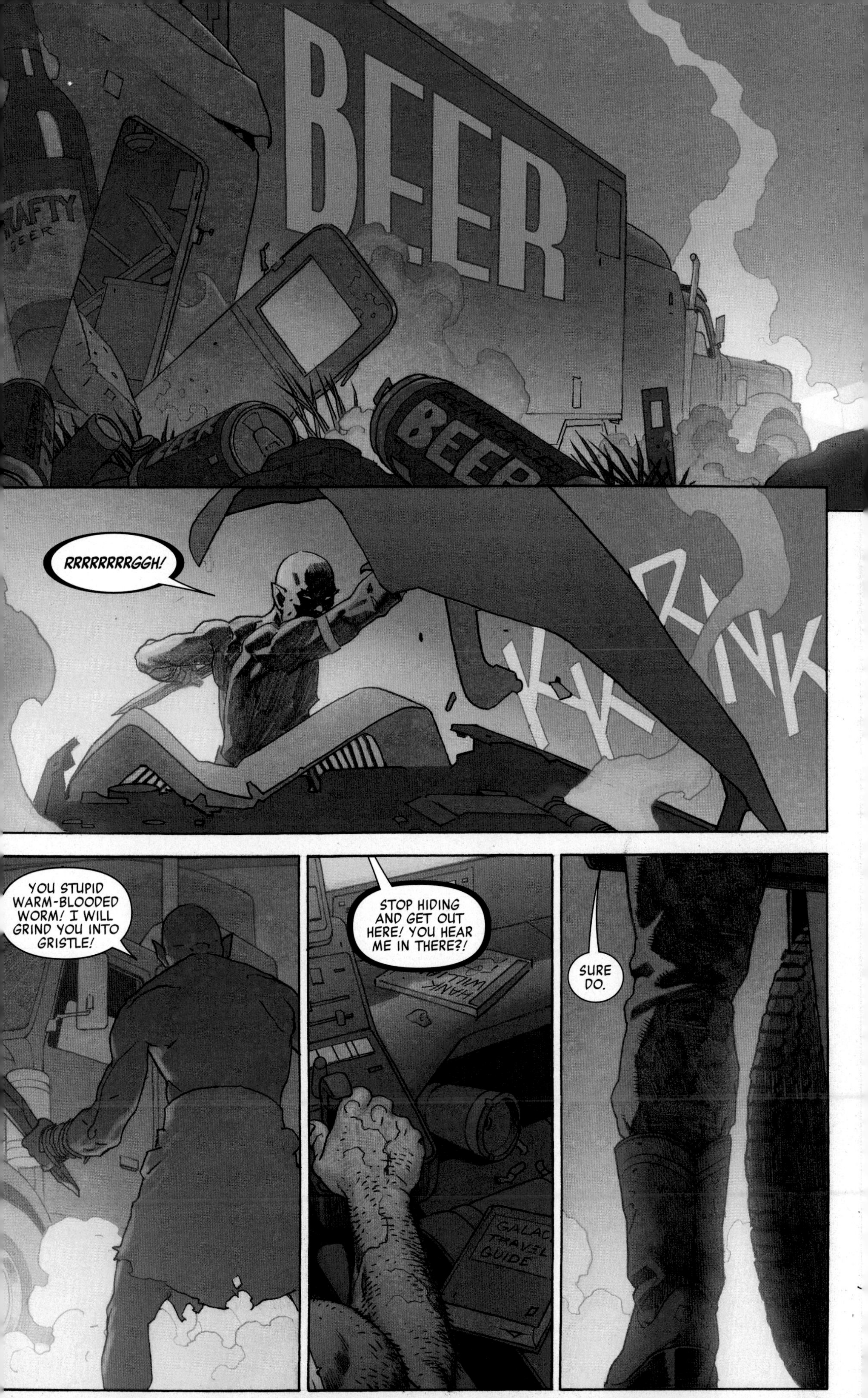
BEER
KRAFTY BEER
BEER
BEER
RRRRRRRRGGH!
KRINK
YOU STUPID WARM-BLOODED WORM! I WILL GRIND YOU INTO GRISTLE!
STOP HIDING AND GET OUT HERE! YOU HEAR ME IN THERE?!
SURE DO.

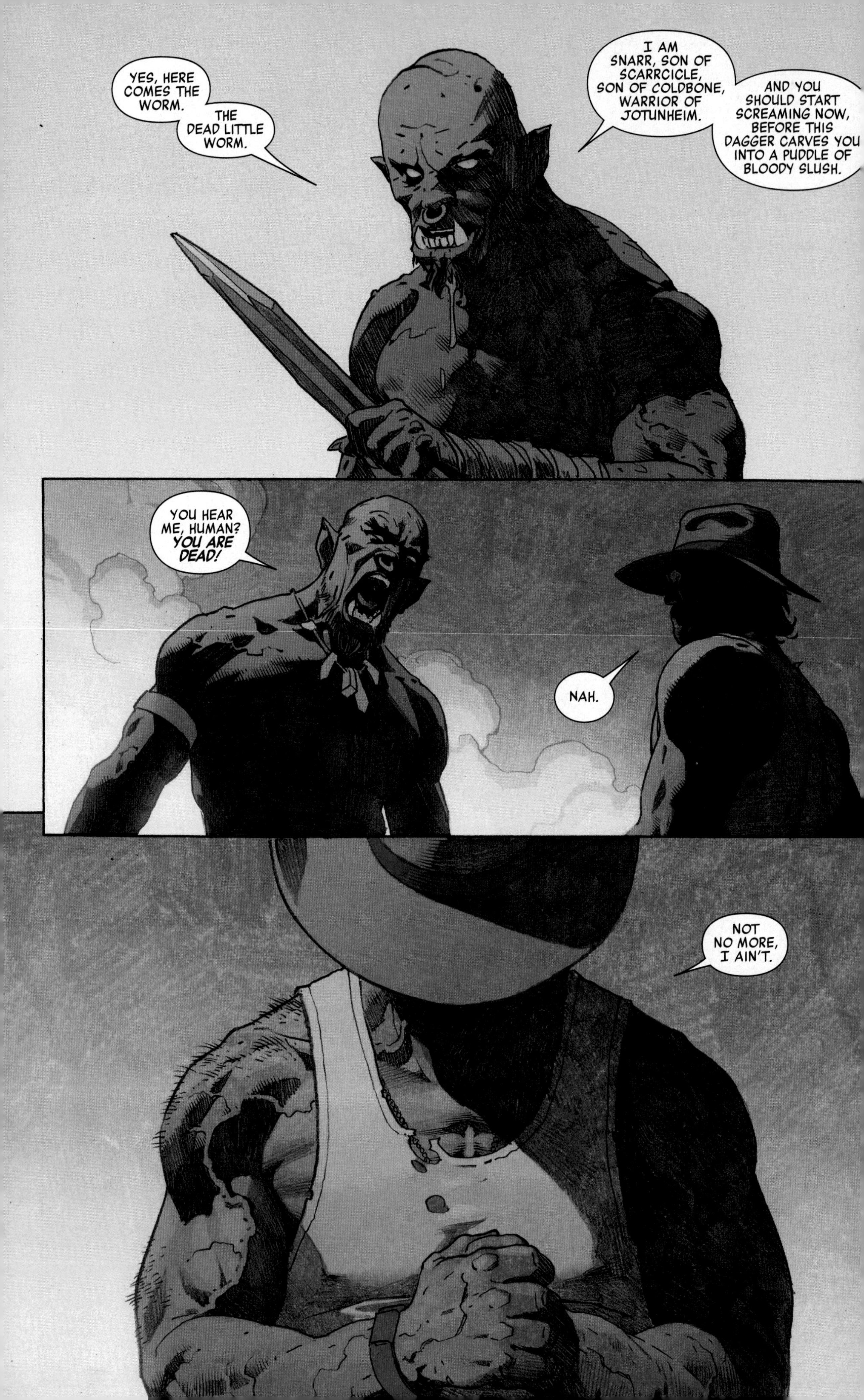
YES, HERE COMES THE WORM.
THE DEAD LITTLE WORM.
I AM SNARR, SON OF SCARRCICLE, SON OF COLDBONE, WARRIOR OF JOTUNHEIM.
AND YOU SHOULD START SCREAMING NOW, BEFORE THIS DAGGER CARVES YOU INTO A PUDDLE OF BLOODY SLUSH.
YOU HEAR ME, HUMAN? *YOU ARE DEAD!*
NAH.
NOT NO MORE, I AIN'T.

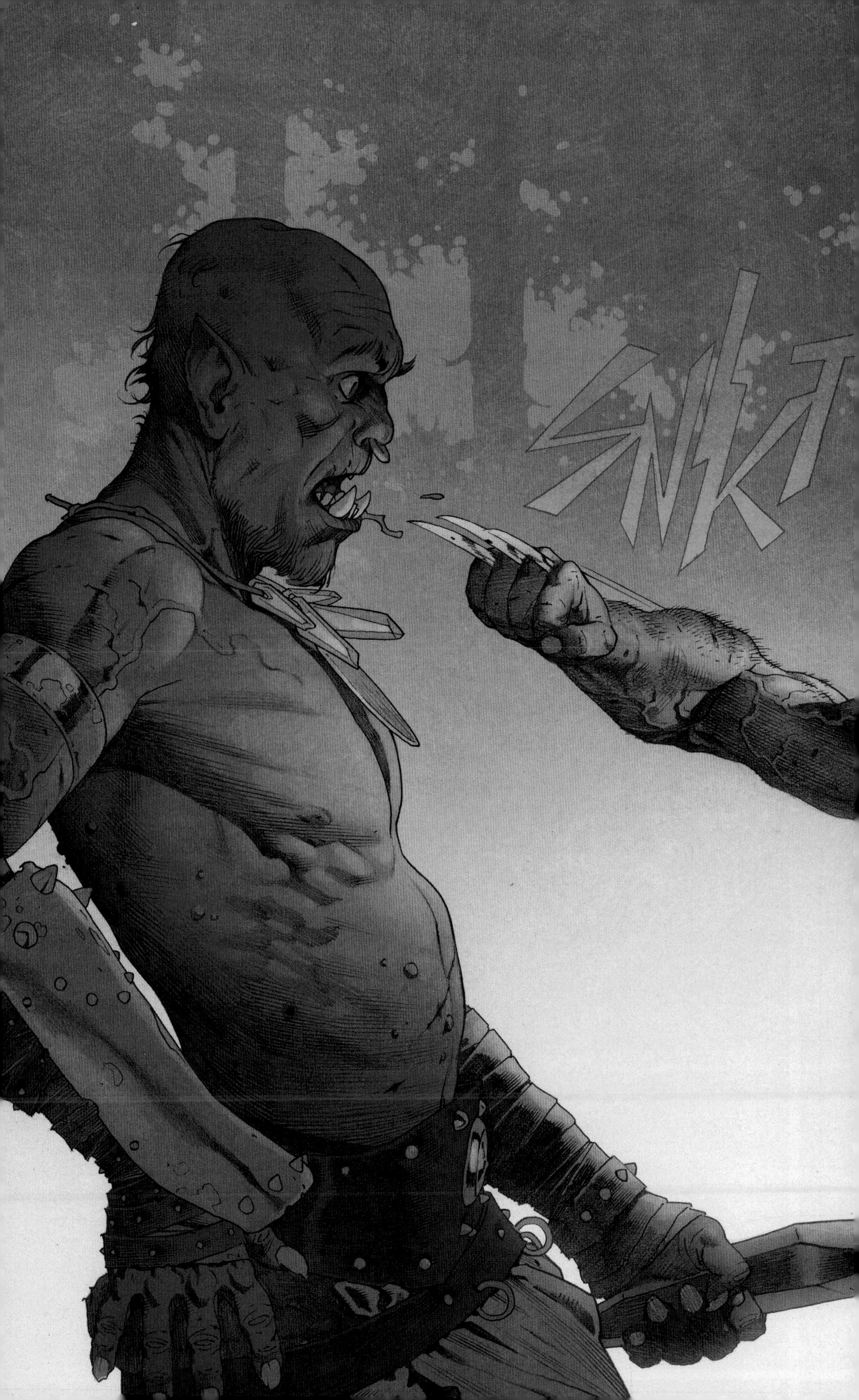
SNIKT

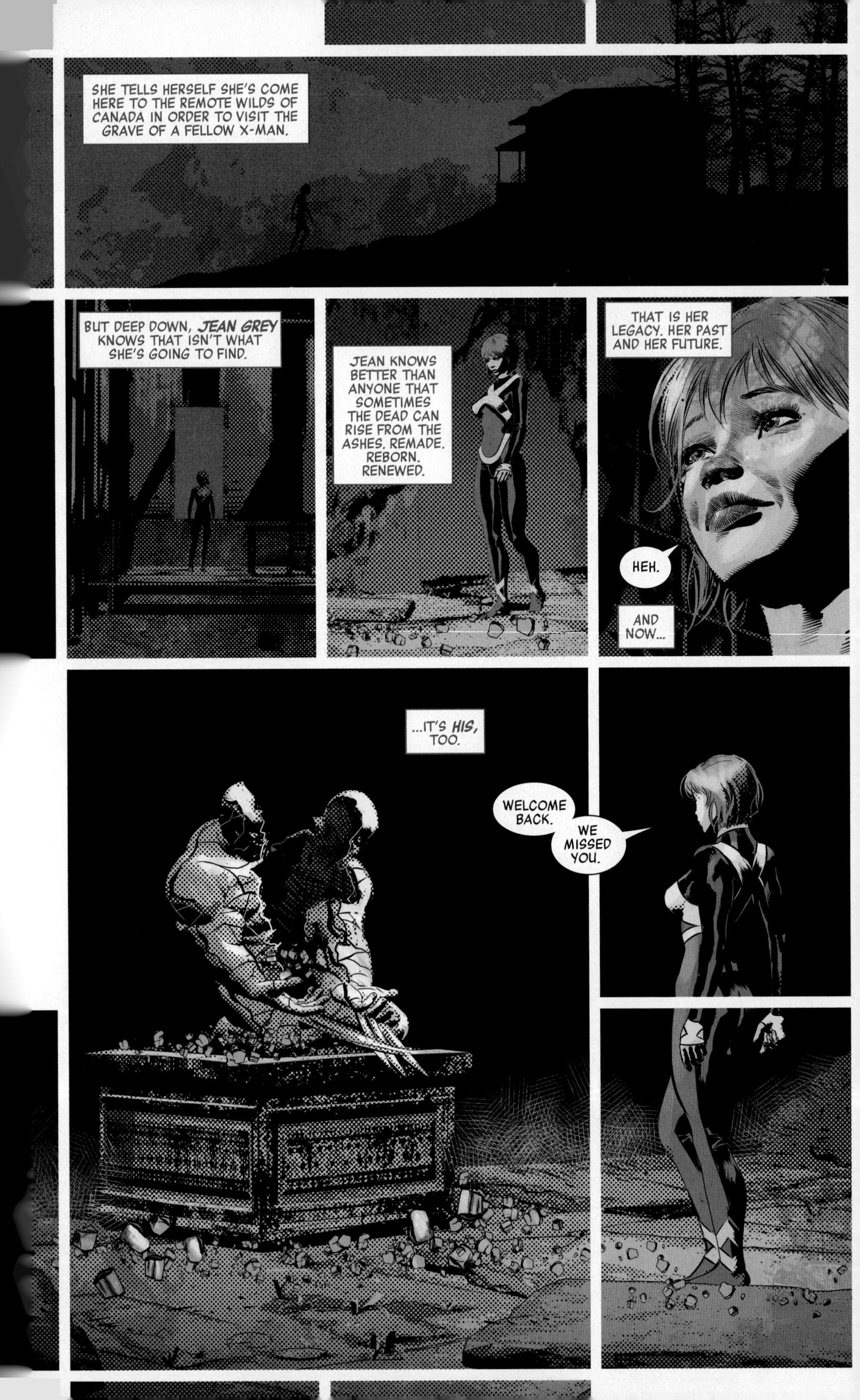
SHE TELLS HERSELF SHE'S COME HERE TO THE REMOTE WILDS OF CANADA IN ORDER TO VISIT THE GRAVE OF A FELLOW X-MAN.
BUT DEEP DOWN, JEAN GREY KNOWS THAT ISN'T WHAT SHE'S GOING TO FIND.
JEAN KNOWS BETTER THAN ANYONE THAT SOMETIMES THE DEAD CAN RISE FROM THE ASHES. REMADE. REBORN. RENEWED.
THAT IS HER LEGACY. HER PAST AND HER FUTURE.
HEH.
AND NOW...
...IT'S HIS, TOO.
WELCOME BACK.
WE MISSED YOU.

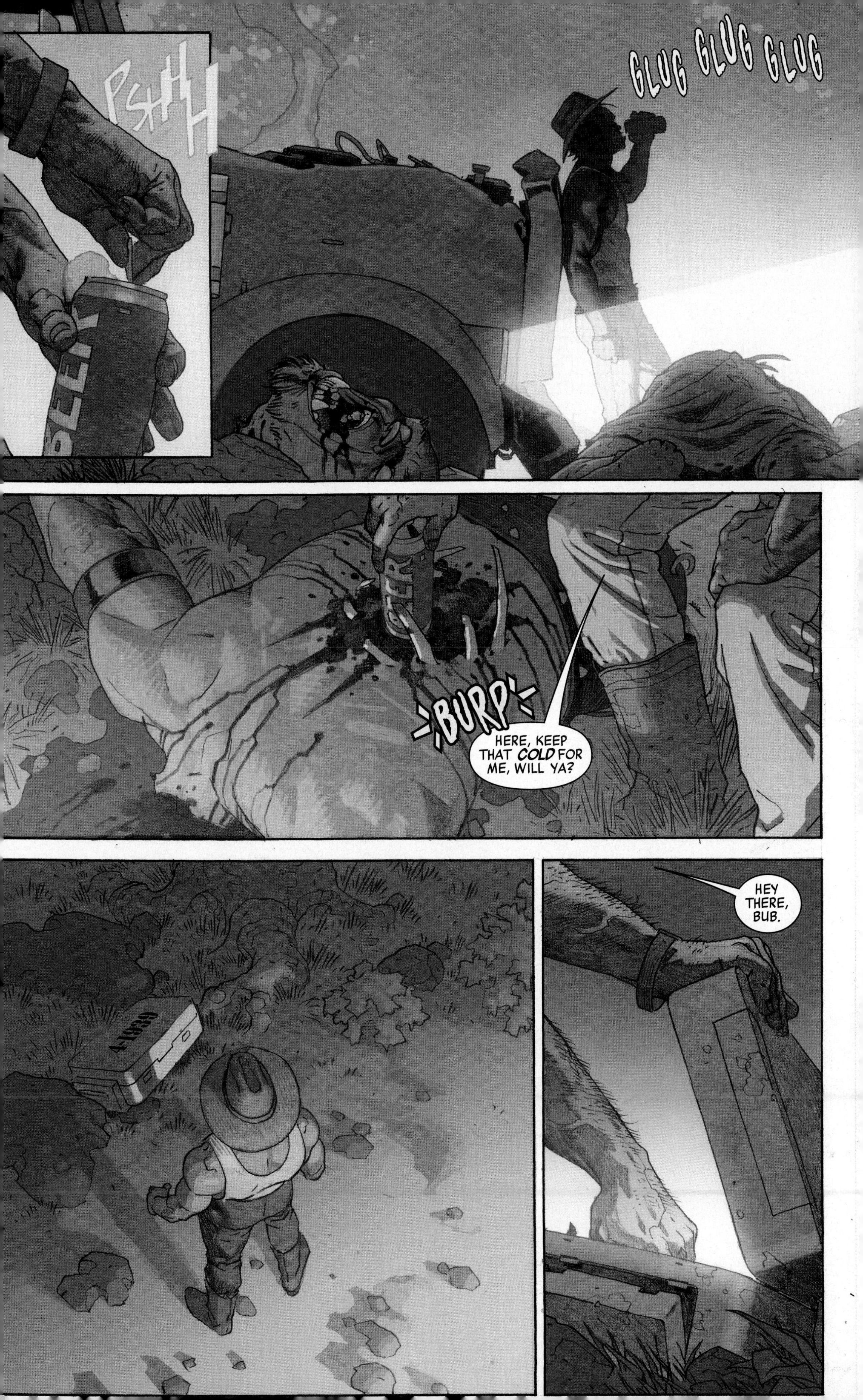
PSHHH
GLUG GLUG GLUG
BURP
HERE, KEEP THAT COLD FOR ME, WILL YA?
4-1999
HEY THERE, BUB.

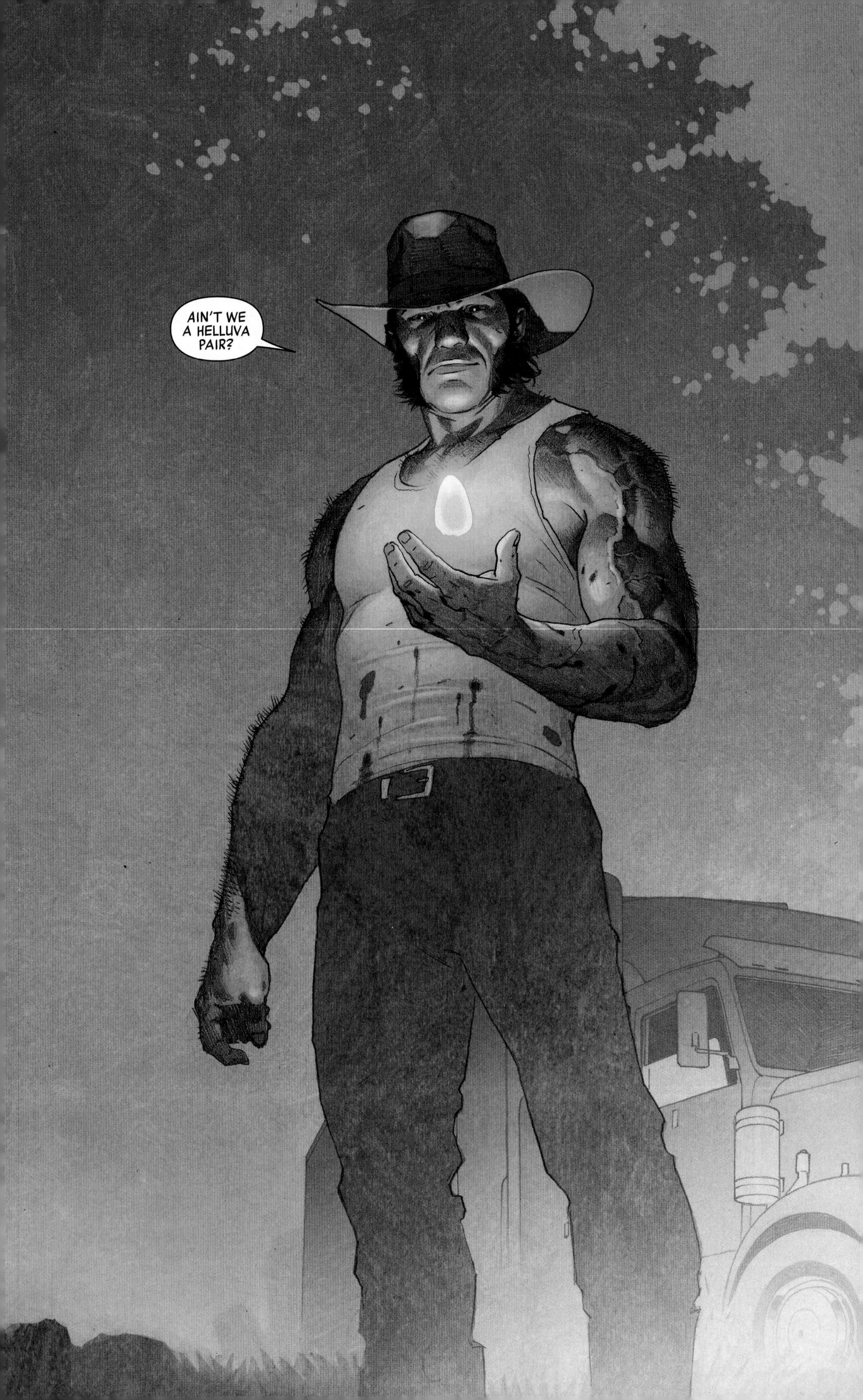
AIN'T WE A HELLUVA PAIR?

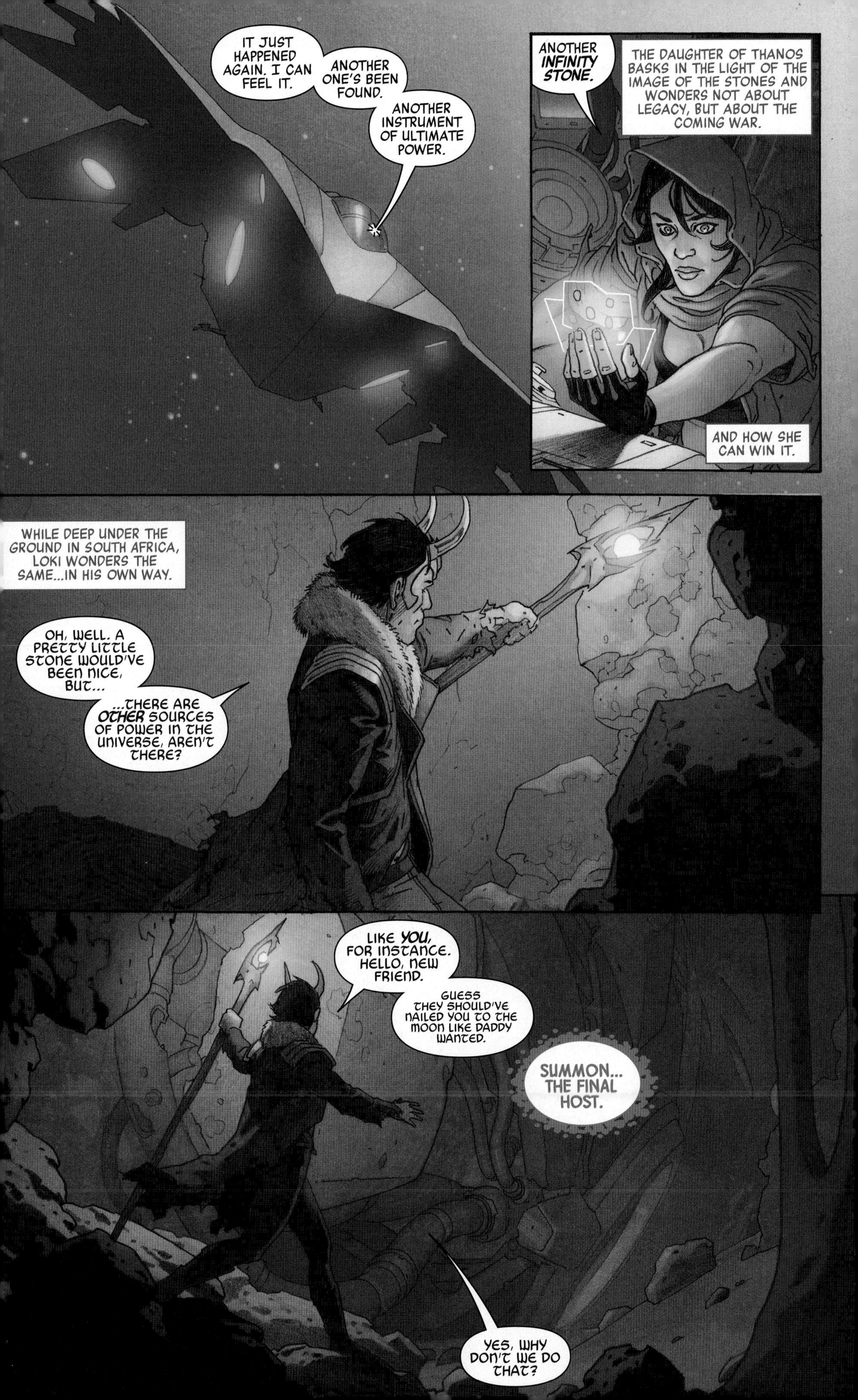
IT JUST HAPPENED AGAIN. I CAN FEEL IT.
ANOTHER ONE'S BEEN FOUND.
ANOTHER INSTRUMENT OF ULTIMATE POWER.
ANOTHER INFINITY STONE.
THE DAUGHTER OF THANOS BASKS IN THE LIGHT OF THE IMAGE OF THE STONES AND WONDERS NOT ABOUT LEGACY, BUT ABOUT THE COMING WAR.
AND HOW SHE CAN WIN IT.
WHILE DEEP UNDER THE GROUND IN SOUTH AFRICA, LOKI WONDERS THE SAME...IN HIS OWN WAY.
OH, WELL. A PRETTY LITTLE STONE WOULD'VE BEEN NICE, BUT...
...THERE ARE OTHER SOURCES OF POWER IN THE UNIVERSE, AREN'T THERE?
LIKE YOU, FOR INSTANCE. HELLO, NEW FRIEND.
GUESS THEY SHOULD'VE NAILED YOU TO THE MOON LIKE DADDY WANTED.
SUMMON... THE FINAL HOST.
YES, WHY DON'T WE DO THAT?

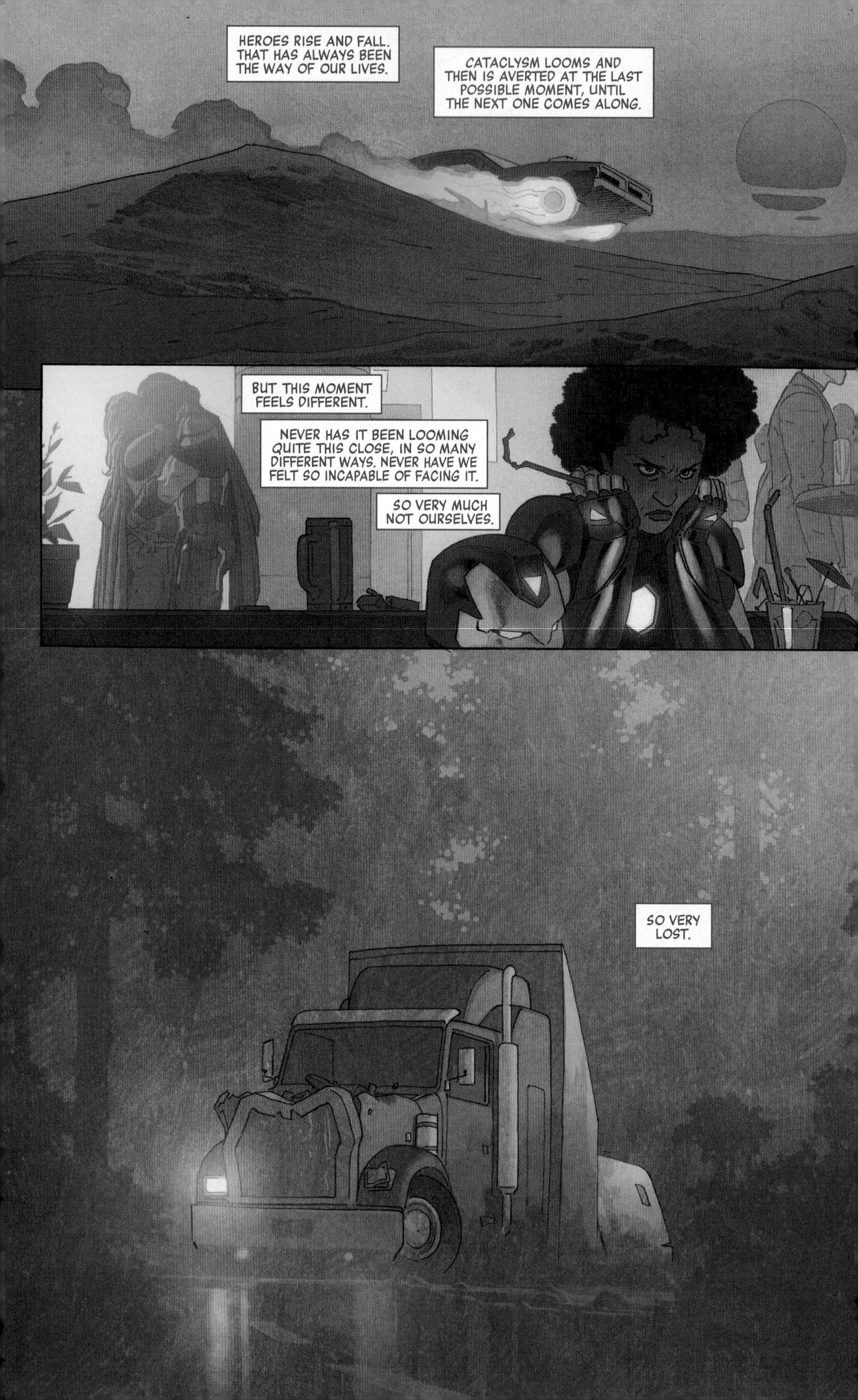
HEROES RISE AND FALL. THAT HAS ALWAYS BEEN THE WAY OF OUR LIVES.
CATACLYSM LOOMS AND THEN IS AVERTED AT THE LAST POSSIBLE MOMENT, UNTIL THE NEXT ONE COMES ALONG.
BUT THIS MOMENT FEELS DIFFERENT.
NEVER HAS IT BEEN LOOMING QUITE THIS CLOSE, IN SO MANY DIFFERENT WAYS. NEVER HAVE WE FELT SO INCAPABLE OF FACING IT.
SO VERY MUCH NOT OURSELVES.
SO VERY LOST.

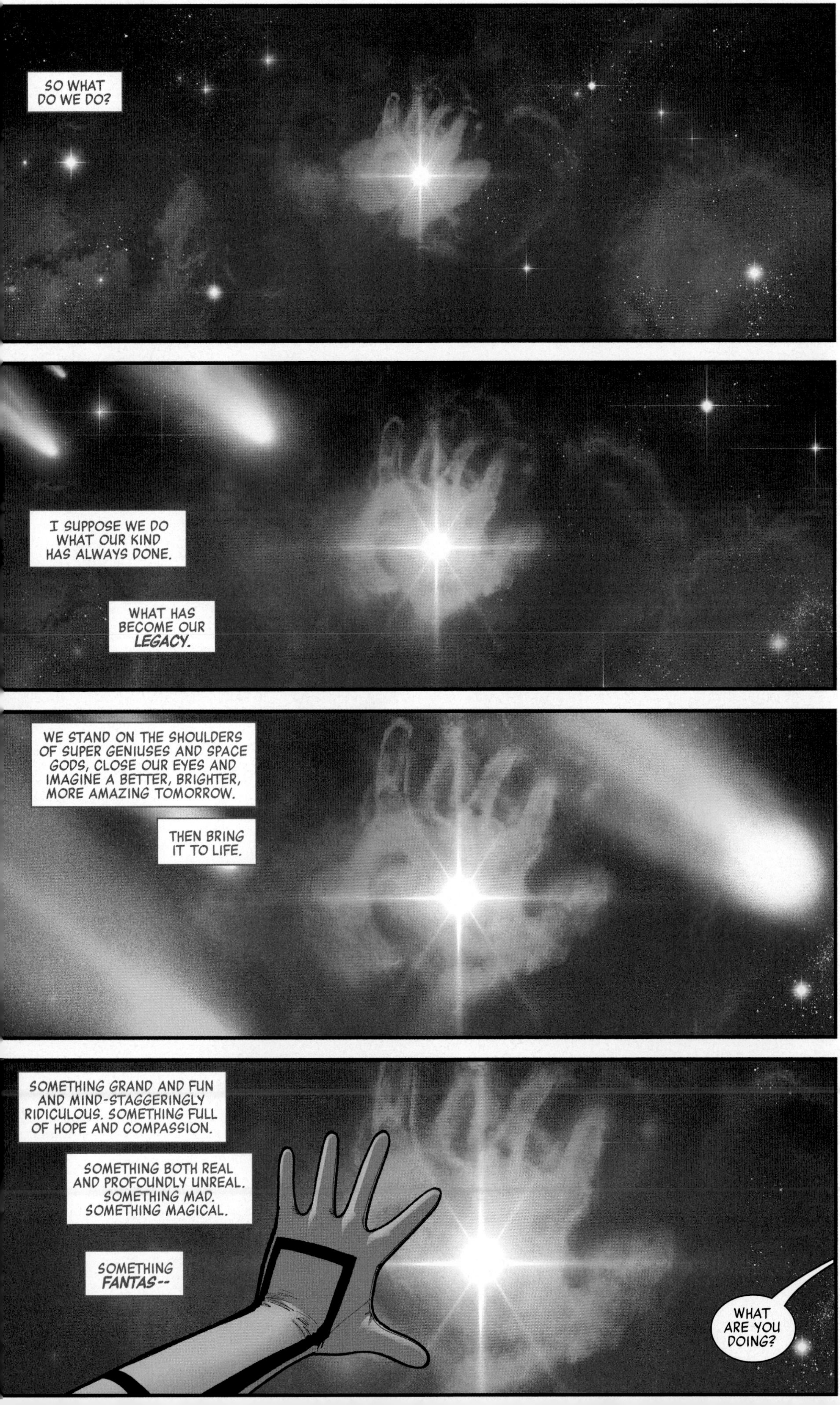
SO WHAT DO WE DO?
I SUPPOSE WE DO WHAT OUR KIND HAS ALWAYS DONE.
WHAT HAS BECOME OUR LEGACY.
WE STAND ON THE SHOULDERS OF SUPER GENIUSES AND SPACE GODS, CLOSE OUR EYES AND IMAGINE A BETTER, BRIGHTER, MORE AMAZING TOMORROW.
THEN BRING IT TO LIFE.
SOMETHING GRAND AND FUN AND MIND-STAGGERINGLY RIDICULOUS. SOMETHING FULL OF HOPE AND COMPASSION.
SOMETHING BOTH REAL AND PROFOUNDLY UNREAL. SOMETHING MAD. SOMETHING MAGICAL.
SOMETHING FANTAS--
WHAT ARE YOU DOING?

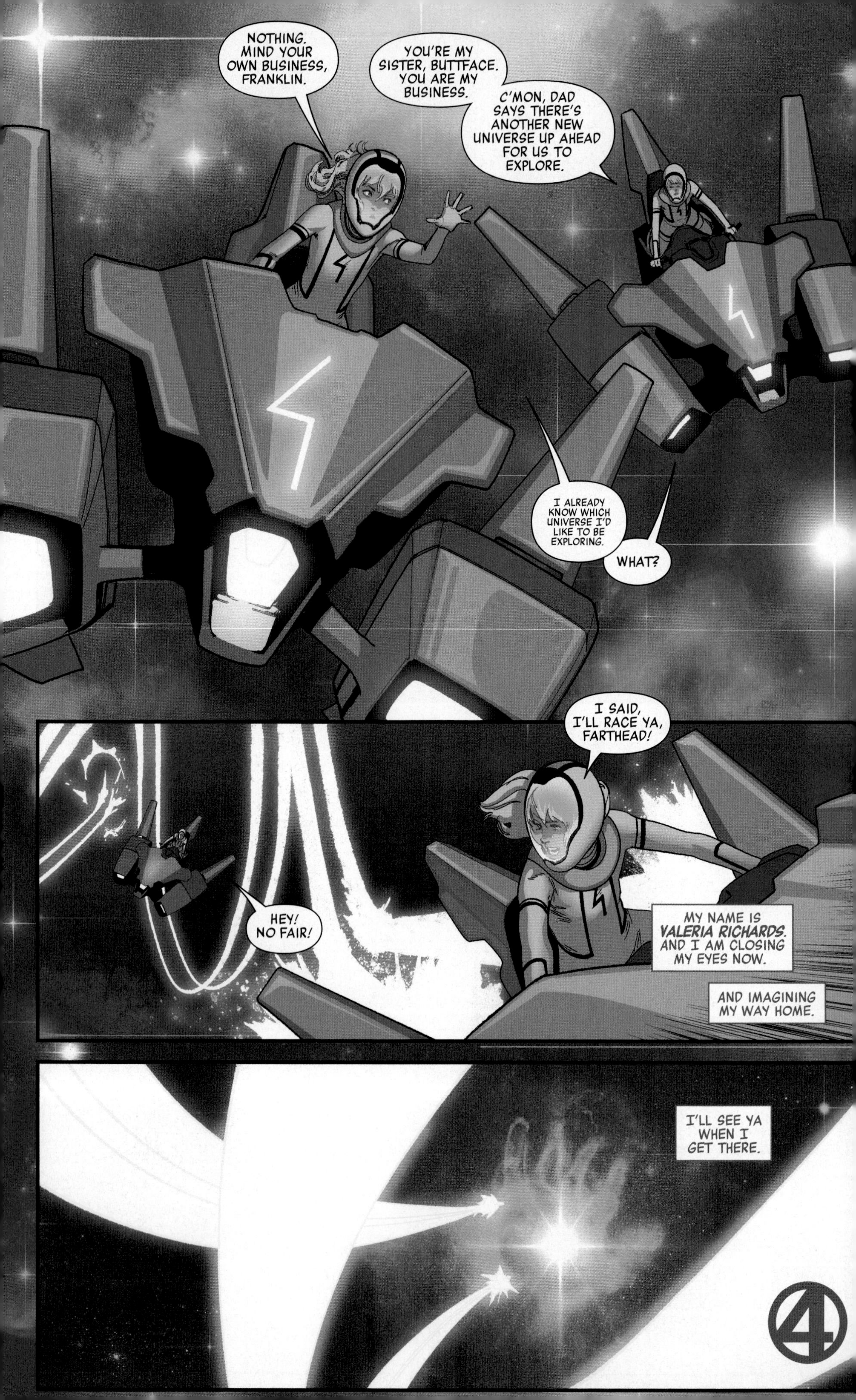

NOTHING. MIND YOUR OWN BUSINESS, FRANKLIN.
YOU'RE MY SISTER, BUTTFACE. YOU ARE MY BUSINESS.
C'MON, DAD SAYS THERE'S ANOTHER NEW UNIVERSE UP AHEAD FOR US TO EXPLORE.
I ALREADY KNOW WHICH UNIVERSE I'D LIKE TO BE EXPLORING.
WHAT?
I SAID, I'LL RACE YA, FARTHEAD!
HEY! NO FAIR!
MY NAME IS VALERIA RICHARDS. AND I AM CLOSING MY EYES NOW.
AND IMAGINING MY WAY HOME.
I'LL SEE YA WHEN I GET THERE.

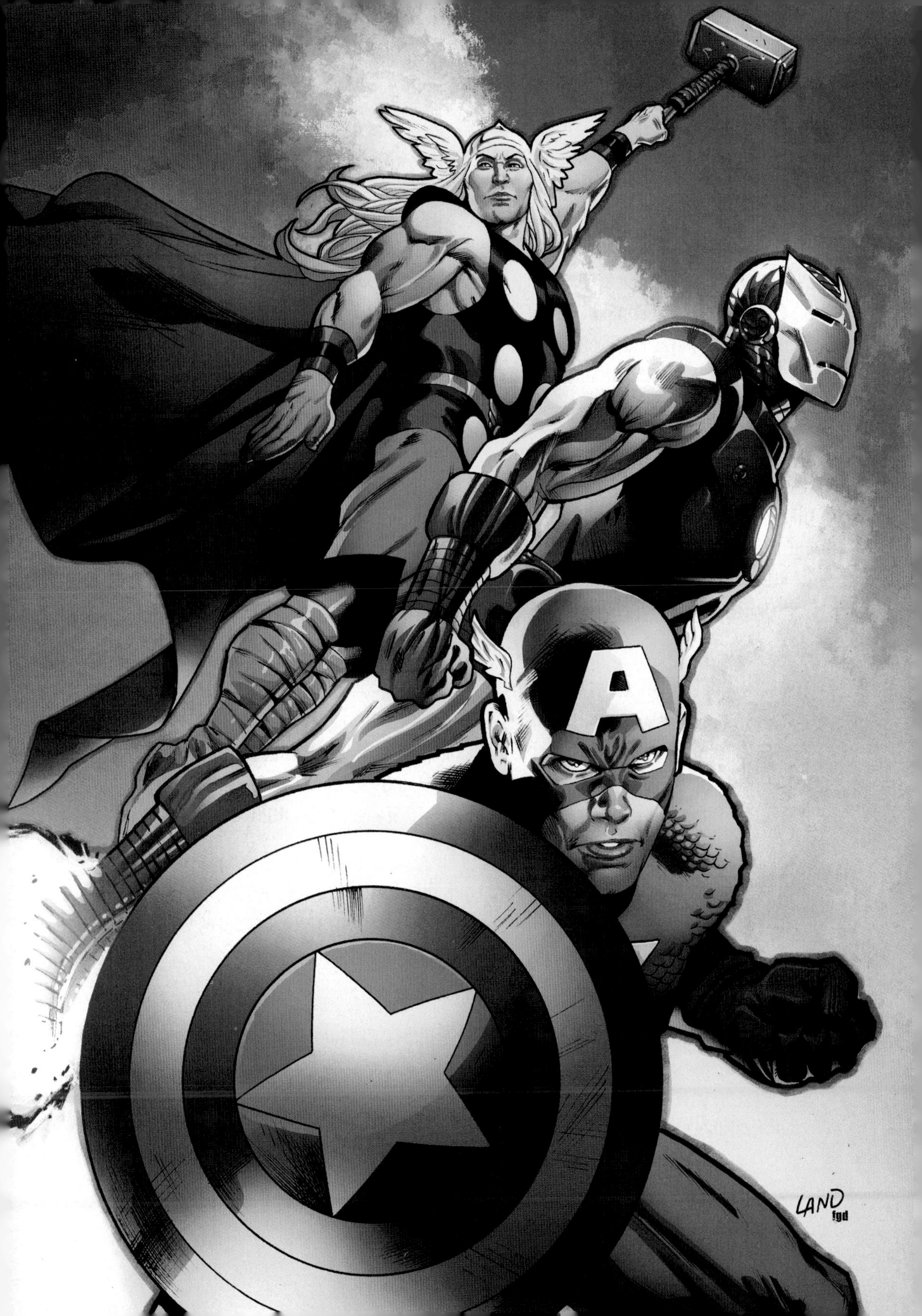
LAND
fgd

MARVEL IS PROUD TO PRESENT MARVEL PRIMER PAGES, THREE ALL-NEW PAGES OF COMIC CONTENT WRITTEN BY ROBBIE THOMPSON (*SILK, DOCTOR STRANGE AND THE SORCERERS SUPREME*) WITH A MAJORITY OF ART FROM ACCLAIMED SUPERSTAR MARK BAGLEY (*AMAZING SPIDER-MAN, ALL-NEW X-MEN, ULTIMATE SPIDER-MAN*). THESE STORIES WILL DRAW READERS INTO THE MARVEL UNIVERSE LIKE NEVER BEFORE. EACH STORY PROVIDES EASY ACCESS INTO THE WORLD OF EACH TITLE CHARACTER, AS WELL AS INTO THE LEGACY STORIES. DESIGNED TO GIVE NEW READERS A HOOK INTO THE SERIES, MARVEL PRIMER PAGES WILL OFFER FANS A SIMPLE JUMPING-ON POINT FOR ALMOST ALL OF MARVEL'S HEROIC AND ICONIC CHARACTERS.

"WHEN I FIRST APPROACHED ROBBIE AND MARK TO DO THESE PRIMER STORIES, I GAVE THEM ONLY ONE EDICT: TO REMIND ALL READERS BOTH WHO THESE CHARACTERS ARE AND WHAT THEY'RE ABOUT IN THREE ALL-NEW PAGES," SAID MARVEL EDITOR DARREN SHAN. "WHAT WE GOT BACK HAS BEEN SOME OF THE MOST FUN ART I'VE EVER SEEN FROM MARK! AND WE COULDN'T BE LUCKIER TO HAVE SOMEONE LIKE ROBBIE TO CHERRY-PICK THE MOST CLASSIC MOMENTS IN MARVEL HISTORY. THEN THE TWO OF THEM TIE THIS ALL UP INTO ONE PERFECT PACKAGE. I THINK EVERYONE WILL LOVE THESE!"

"IT'S BEEN AN ABSOLUTE BLAST WORKING ON THIS PROJECT — IT GIVES ME A GREAT EXCUSE TO RE-READ SO MANY OF MY FAVORITE COMICS!" THOMPSON SAID. I'VE BEEN A FAN OF MARK'S FOR YEARS, SO TO GET TO WORK WITH HIM IS A DREAM COME TRUE. MARK TAKES THE SCRIPTS AND DISTILLS THEM DOWN TO THEIR ESSENCE, FINDING BRILLIANT WAYS TO TELL THESE STORIES WITH TRULY ICONIC IMAGES. I CAN'T WAIT FOR PEOPLE TO SEE WHAT HE'S DONE WITH THESE!"

"THIS LEGACY GIG HAS BEEN A LOT OF FUN TO WORK ON AND A BIT OF AN EDUCATION...EVEN FOR SOMEONE WHO HAS BEEN DRAWING COMICS FOR AS LONG AS I HAVE! I THINK READERS WILL REALLY ENJOY THE STORIES WE'RE REVISITING," BAGLEY ADDED.

MARVEL PRIMER PAGES GIVE EVERY FAN THE OPPORTUNITY TO TRULY "MAKE MINE MARVEL" BY PROVIDING THE MOST ACCESSIBLE WAY TO ENJOY MARVEL COMICS — ENSURING THAT LONGTIME FANS WILL FALL IN LOVE WITH THEIR FAVORITE STORIES ALL OVER AGAIN, AND THAT NEW FANS WILL BE DRAWN INTO MARVEL'S MAGICAL UNIVERSE OF ADVENTURE AND HEROICS.

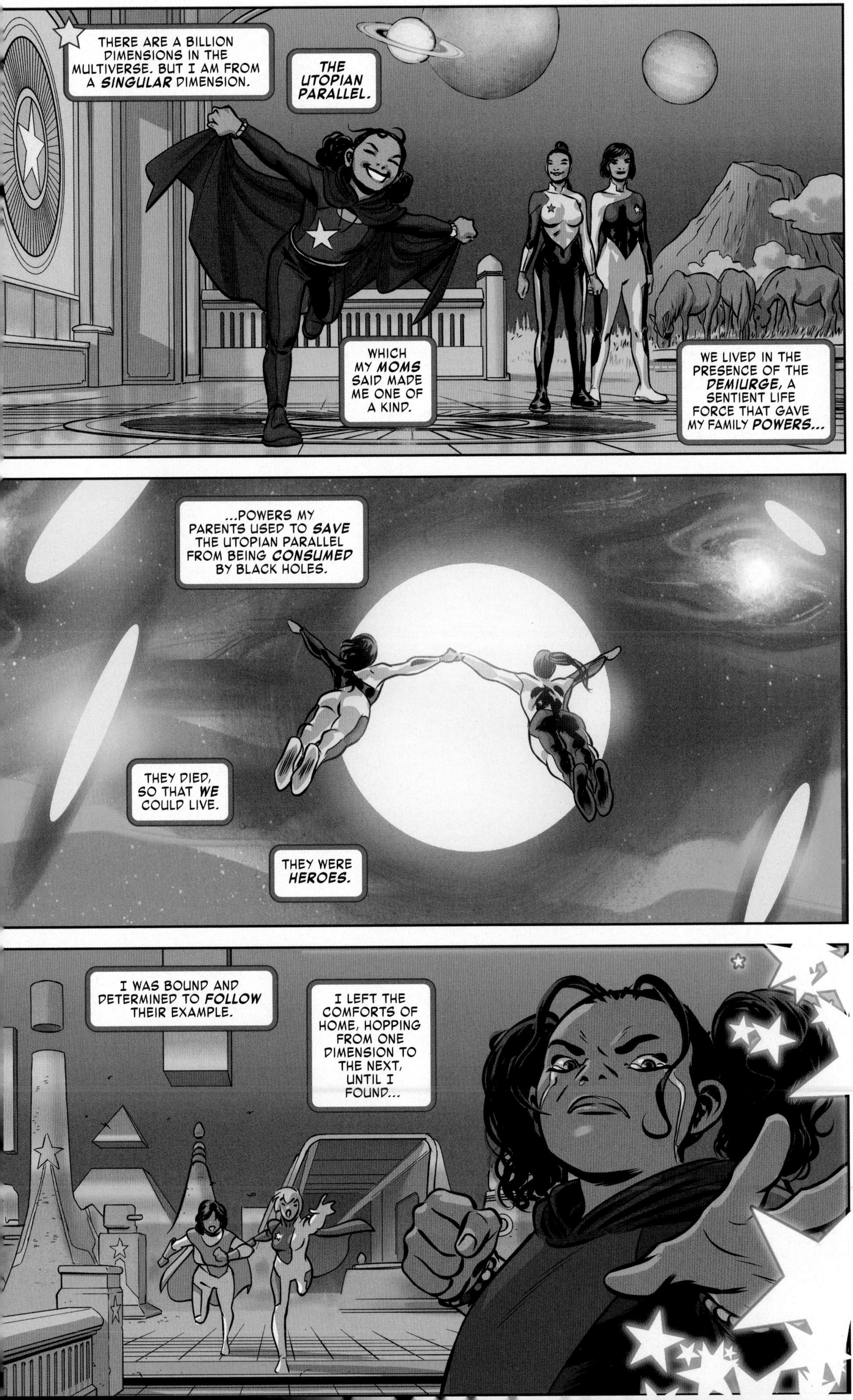
THERE ARE A BILLION DIMENSIONS IN THE MULTIVERSE. BUT I AM FROM A SINGULAR DIMENSION.
THE UTOPIAN PARALLEL.
WHICH MY MOMS SAID MADE ME ONE OF A KIND.
WE LIVED IN THE PRESENCE OF THE DEMIURGE, A SENTIENT LIFE FORCE THAT GAVE MY FAMILY POWERS...
...POWERS MY PARENTS USED TO SAVE THE UTOPIAN PARALLEL FROM BEING CONSUMED BY BLACK HOLES.
THEY DIED, SO THAT WE COULD LIVE.
THEY WERE HEROES.
I WAS BOUND AND DETERMINED TO FOLLOW THEIR EXAMPLE.
I LEFT THE COMFORTS OF HOME, HOPPING FROM ONE DIMENSION TO THE NEXT, UNTIL I FOUND...

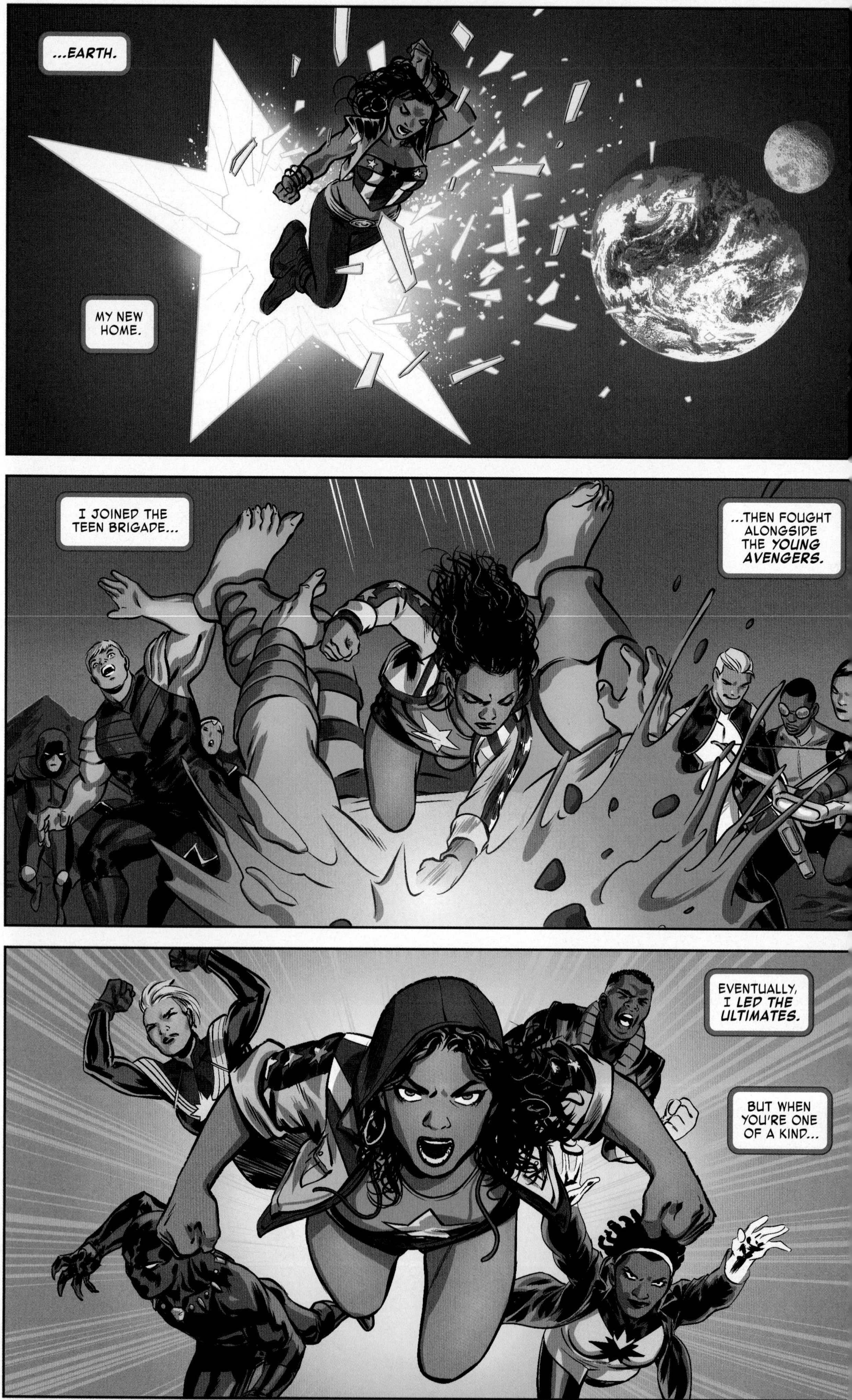
...EARTH.
MY NEW HOME.
I JOINED THE TEEN BRIGADE...
...THEN FOUGHT ALONGSIDE THE *YOUNG AVENGERS.*
EVENTUALLY, I *LED* THE *ULTIMATES.*
BUT WHEN YOU'RE ONE OF A KIND...

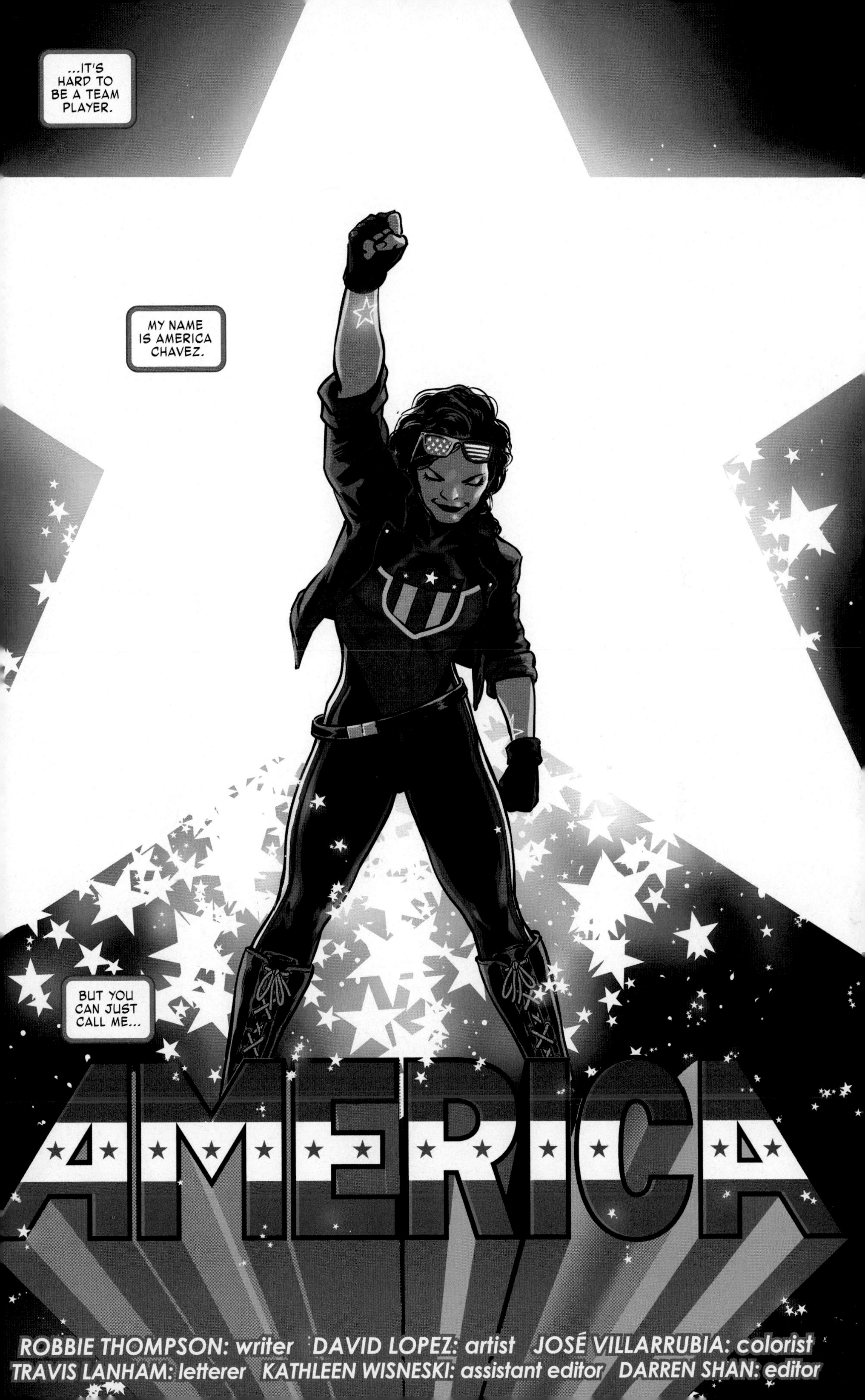
...IT'S HARD TO BE A TEAM PLAYER.
MY NAME IS AMERICA CHAVEZ.
BUT YOU CAN JUST CALL ME...
AMERICA
ROBBIE THOMPSON: writer DAVID LOPEZ: artist JOSÉ VILLARRUBIA: colorist
TRAVIS LANHAM: letterer KATHLEEN WISNESKI: assistant editor DARREN SHAN: editor

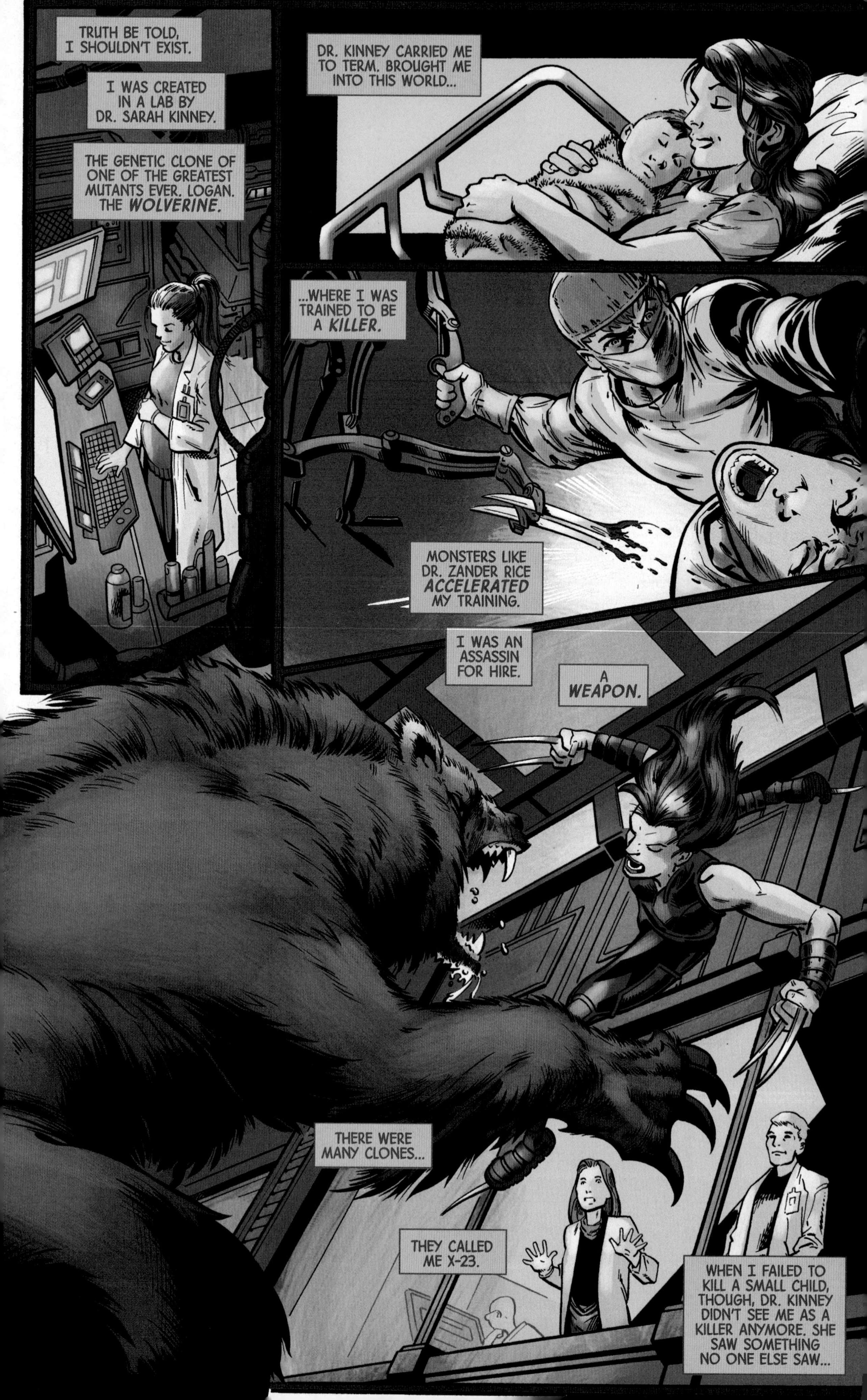
TRUTH BE TOLD, I SHOULDN'T EXIST.
I WAS CREATED IN A LAB BY DR. SARAH KINNEY.
THE GENETIC CLONE OF ONE OF THE GREATEST MUTANTS EVER. LOGAN. THE *WOLVERINE.*
DR. KINNEY CARRIED ME TO TERM. BROUGHT ME INTO THIS WORLD...
...WHERE I WAS TRAINED TO BE A *KILLER.*
MONSTERS LIKE DR. ZANDER RICE *ACCELERATED* MY TRAINING.
I WAS AN ASSASSIN FOR HIRE.
A *WEAPON.*
THERE WERE MANY CLONES...
THEY CALLED ME X-23.
WHEN I FAILED TO KILL A SMALL CHILD, THOUGH, DR. KINNEY DIDN'T SEE ME AS A KILLER ANYMORE. SHE SAW SOMETHING NO ONE ELSE SAW...

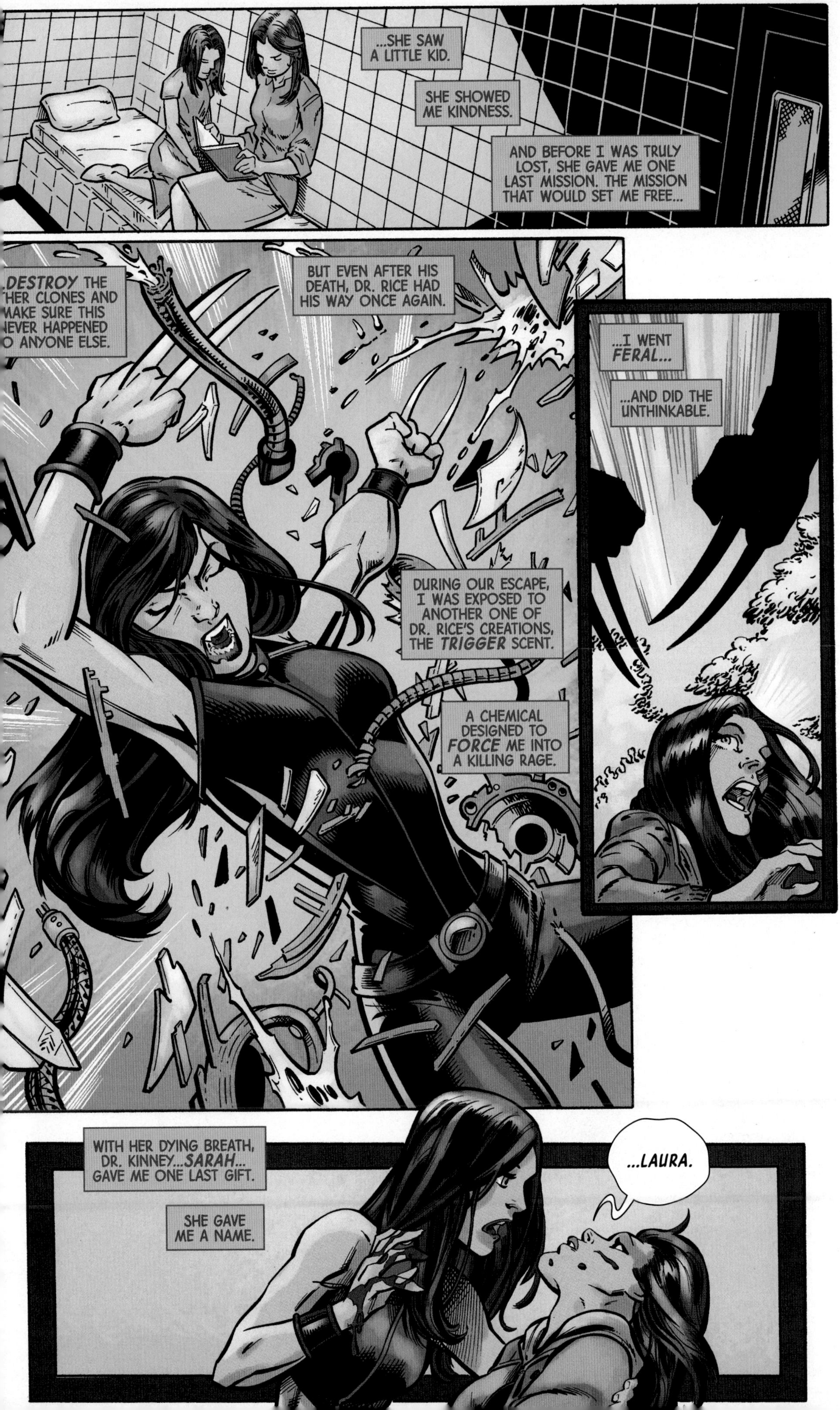

...SHE SAW A LITTLE KID.
SHE SHOWED ME KINDNESS.
AND BEFORE I WAS TRULY LOST, SHE GAVE ME ONE LAST MISSION. THE MISSION THAT WOULD SET ME FREE...
.DESTROY THE THER CLONES AND MAKE SURE THIS NEVER HAPPENED O ANYONE ELSE.
BUT EVEN AFTER HIS DEATH, DR. RICE HAD HIS WAY ONCE AGAIN.
DURING OUR ESCAPE, I WAS EXPOSED TO ANOTHER ONE OF DR. RICE'S CREATIONS, THE TRIGGER SCENT.
A CHEMICAL DESIGNED TO FORCE ME INTO A KILLING RAGE.
...I WENT FERAL...
...AND DID THE UNTHINKABLE.
WITH HER DYING BREATH, DR. KINNEY...SARAH... GAVE ME ONE LAST GIFT.
SHE GAVE ME A NAME.
...LAURA.

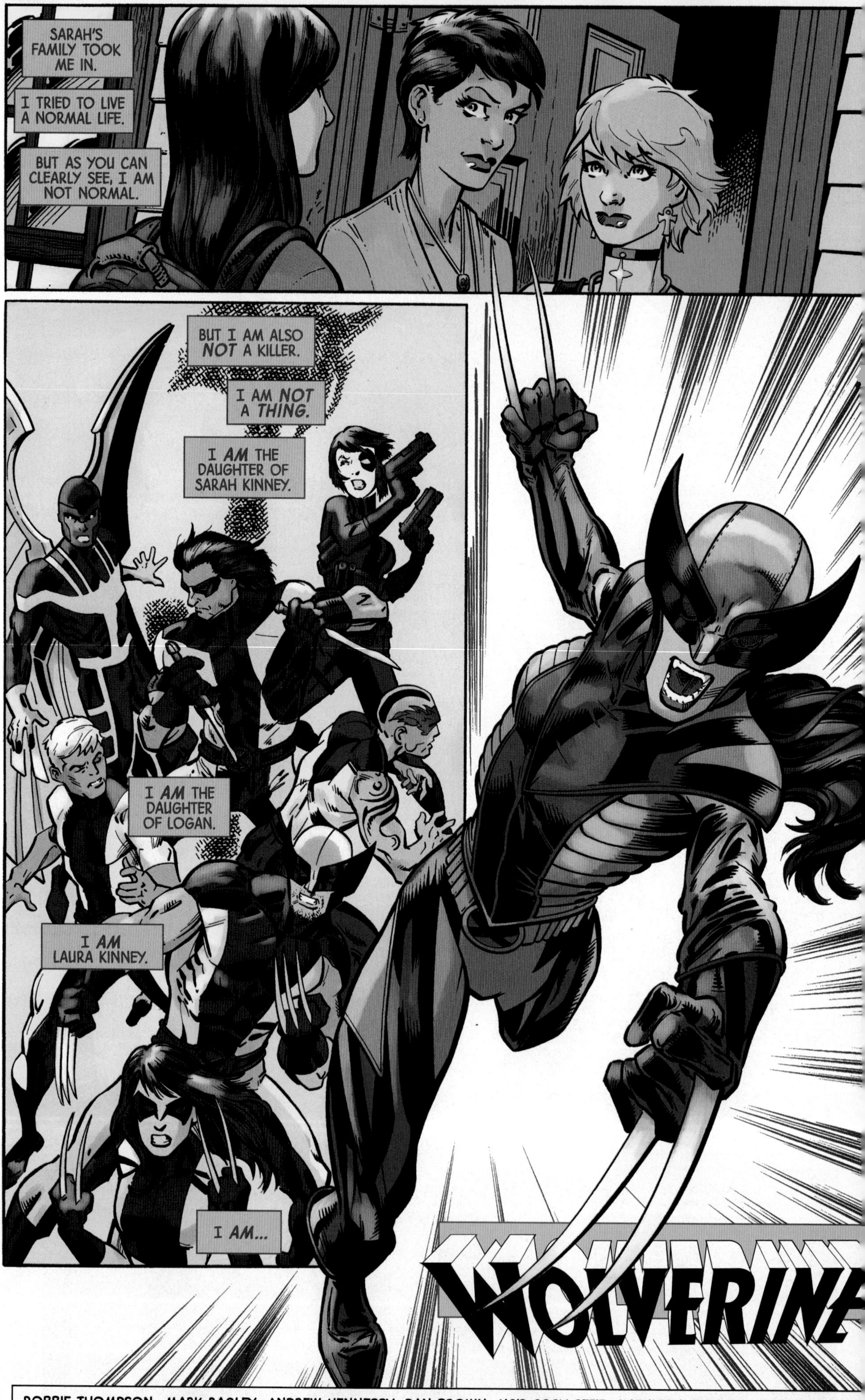
SARAH'S FAMILY TOOK ME IN.
I TRIED TO LIVE A NORMAL LIFE.
BUT AS YOU CAN CLEARLY SEE, I AM NOT NORMAL.
BUT I AM ALSO NOT A KILLER.
I AM NOT A THING.
I AM THE DAUGHTER OF SARAH KINNEY.
I AM THE DAUGHTER OF LOGAN.
I AM LAURA KINNEY.
I AM...
WOLVERINE

ROBBIE THOMPSON WRITER | MARK BAGLEY PENCILER | ANDREW HENNESSY INKER | DAN BROWN COLORIST | VC'S CORY PETIT LETTERER | KATHLEEN WISNESKI ASSISTANT EDITOR | DARREN SHAN EDITOR

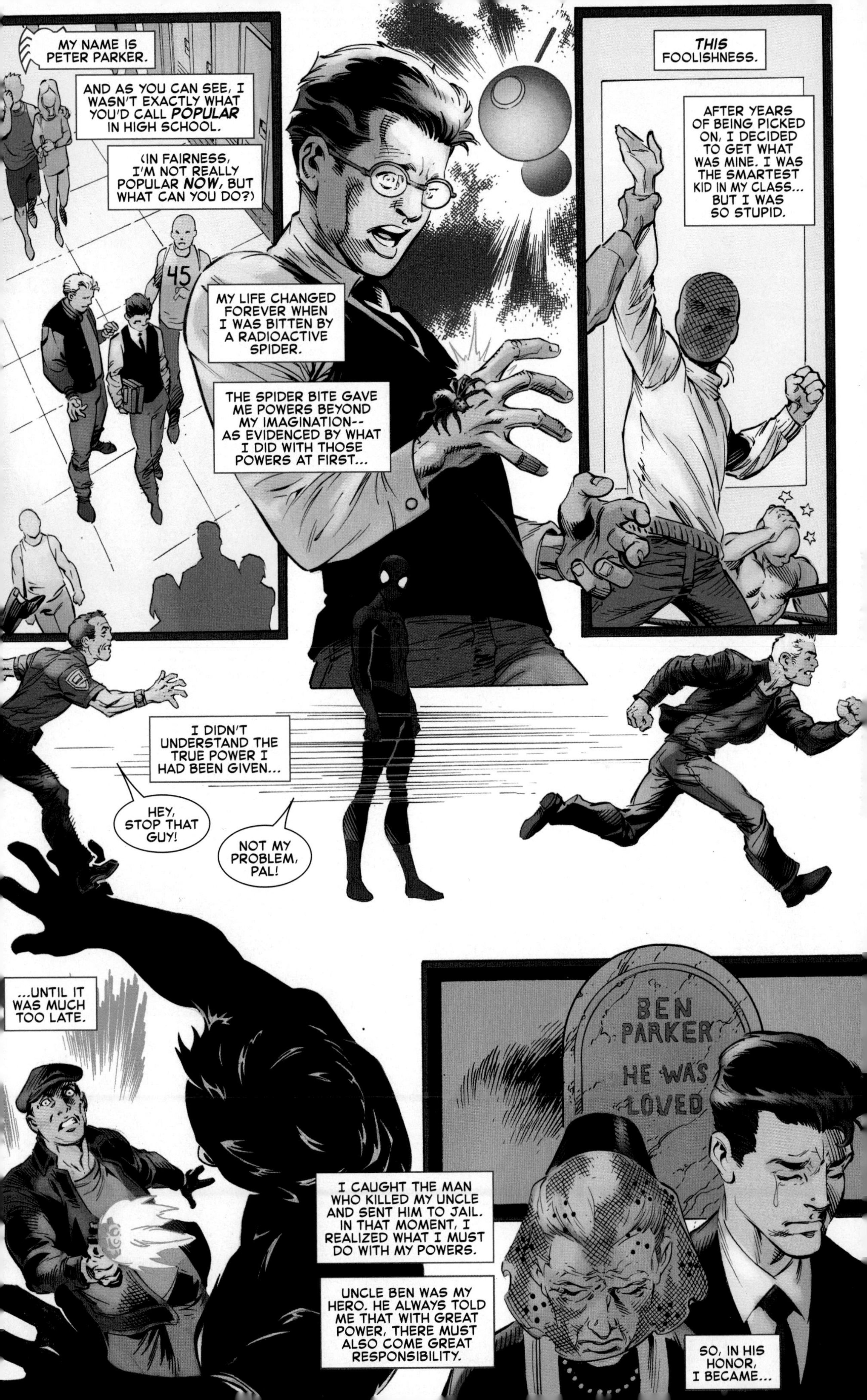
MY NAME IS PETER PARKER.
AND AS YOU CAN SEE, I WASN'T EXACTLY WHAT YOU'D CALL POPULAR IN HIGH SCHOOL.
(IN FAIRNESS, I'M NOT REALLY POPULAR NOW, BUT WHAT CAN YOU DO?)
45
MY LIFE CHANGED FOREVER WHEN I WAS BITTEN BY A RADIOACTIVE SPIDER.
THE SPIDER BITE GAVE ME POWERS BEYOND MY IMAGINATION-- AS EVIDENCED BY WHAT I DID WITH THOSE POWERS AT FIRST...
THIS FOOLISHNESS.
AFTER YEARS OF BEING PICKED ON, I DECIDED TO GET WHAT WAS MINE. I WAS THE SMARTEST KID IN MY CLASS... BUT I WAS SO STUPID.
I DIDN'T UNDERSTAND THE TRUE POWER I HAD BEEN GIVEN...
HEY, STOP THAT GUY!
NOT MY PROBLEM, PAL!
...UNTIL IT WAS MUCH TOO LATE.
BEN PARKER
HE WAS LOVED
I CAUGHT THE MAN WHO KILLED MY UNCLE AND SENT HIM TO JAIL. IN THAT MOMENT, I REALIZED WHAT I MUST DO WITH MY POWERS.
UNCLE BEN WAS MY HERO. HE ALWAYS TOLD ME THAT WITH GREAT POWER, THERE MUST ALSO COME GREAT RESPONSIBILITY.
SO, IN HIS HONOR, I BECAME...

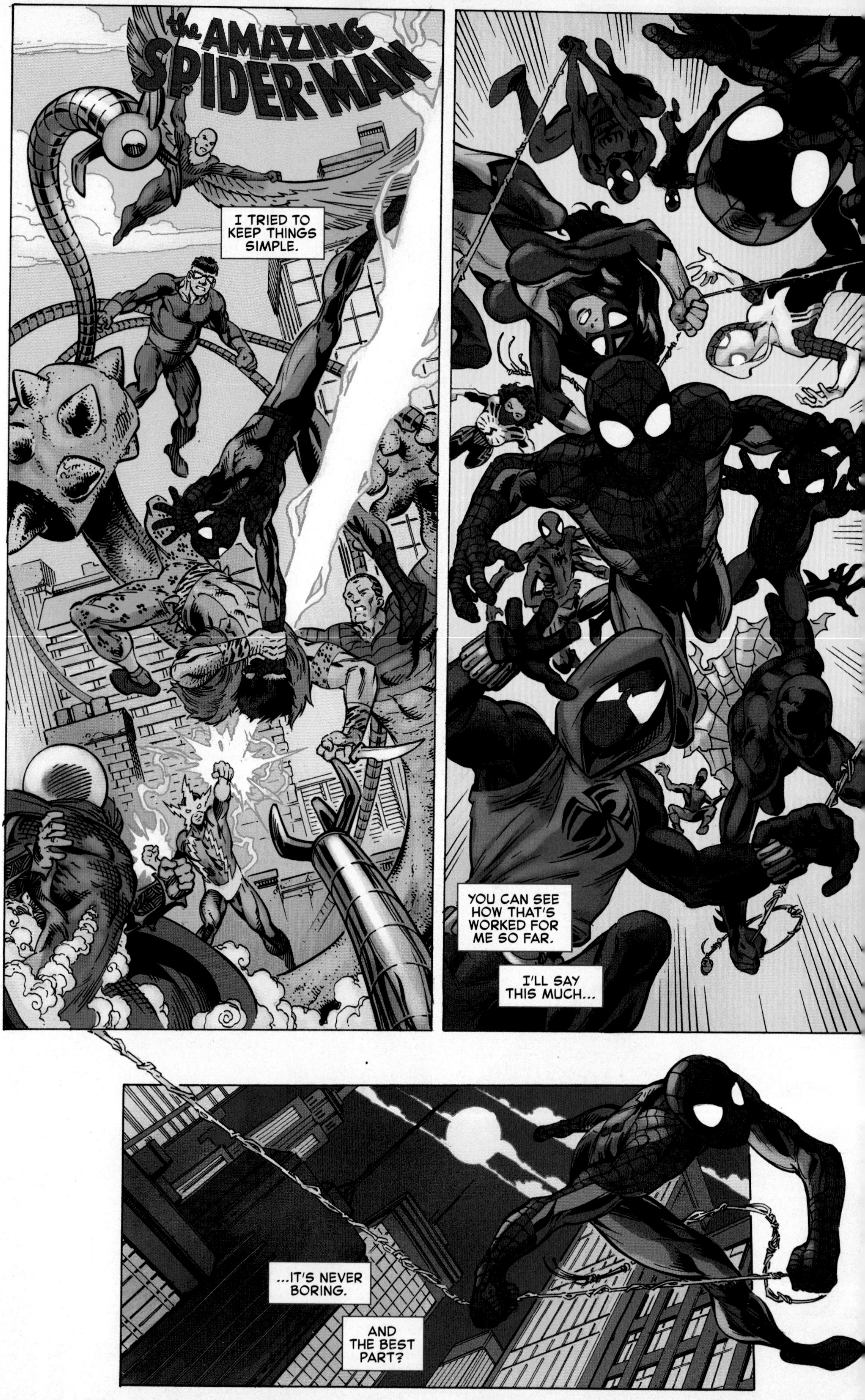
the AMAZING SPIDER-MAN
I TRIED TO KEEP THINGS SIMPLE.
YOU CAN SEE HOW THAT'S WORKED FOR ME SO FAR.
I'LL SAY THIS MUCH...
...IT'S NEVER BORING.
AND THE BEST PART?

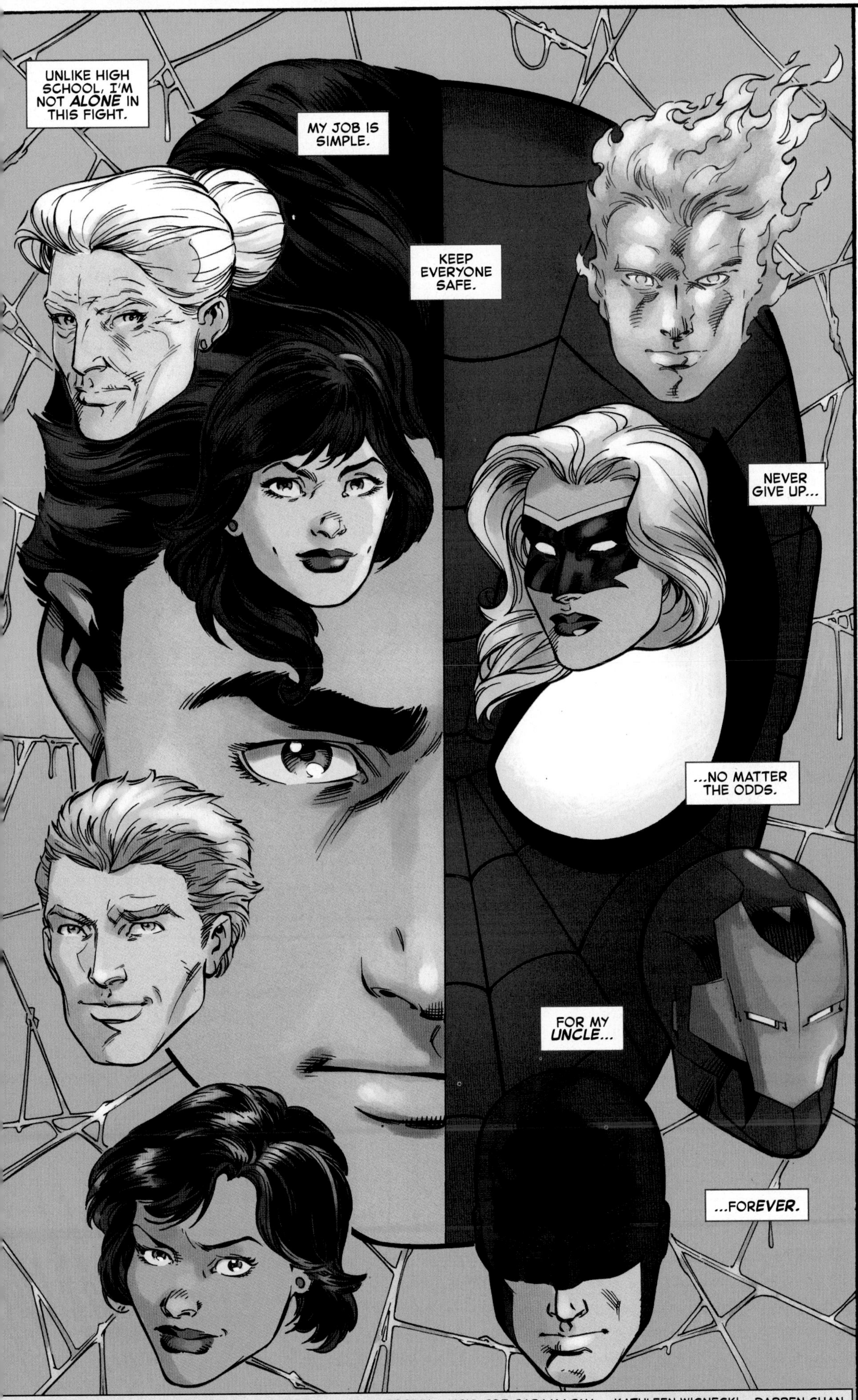
UNLIKE HIGH SCHOOL, I'M NOT ALONE IN THIS FIGHT.
MY JOB IS SIMPLE.
KEEP EVERYONE SAFE.
NEVER GIVE UP...
...NO MATTER THE ODDS.
FOR MY UNCLE...
...FOREVER.

ROBBIE THOMPSON WRITER | MARK BAGLEY PENCILER | JOHN DELL INKER | DAN BROWN COLORIST | VC'S JOE CARAMAGNA LETTERER | KATHLEEN WISNESKI ASSISTANT EDITOR | DARREN SHAN EDITOR

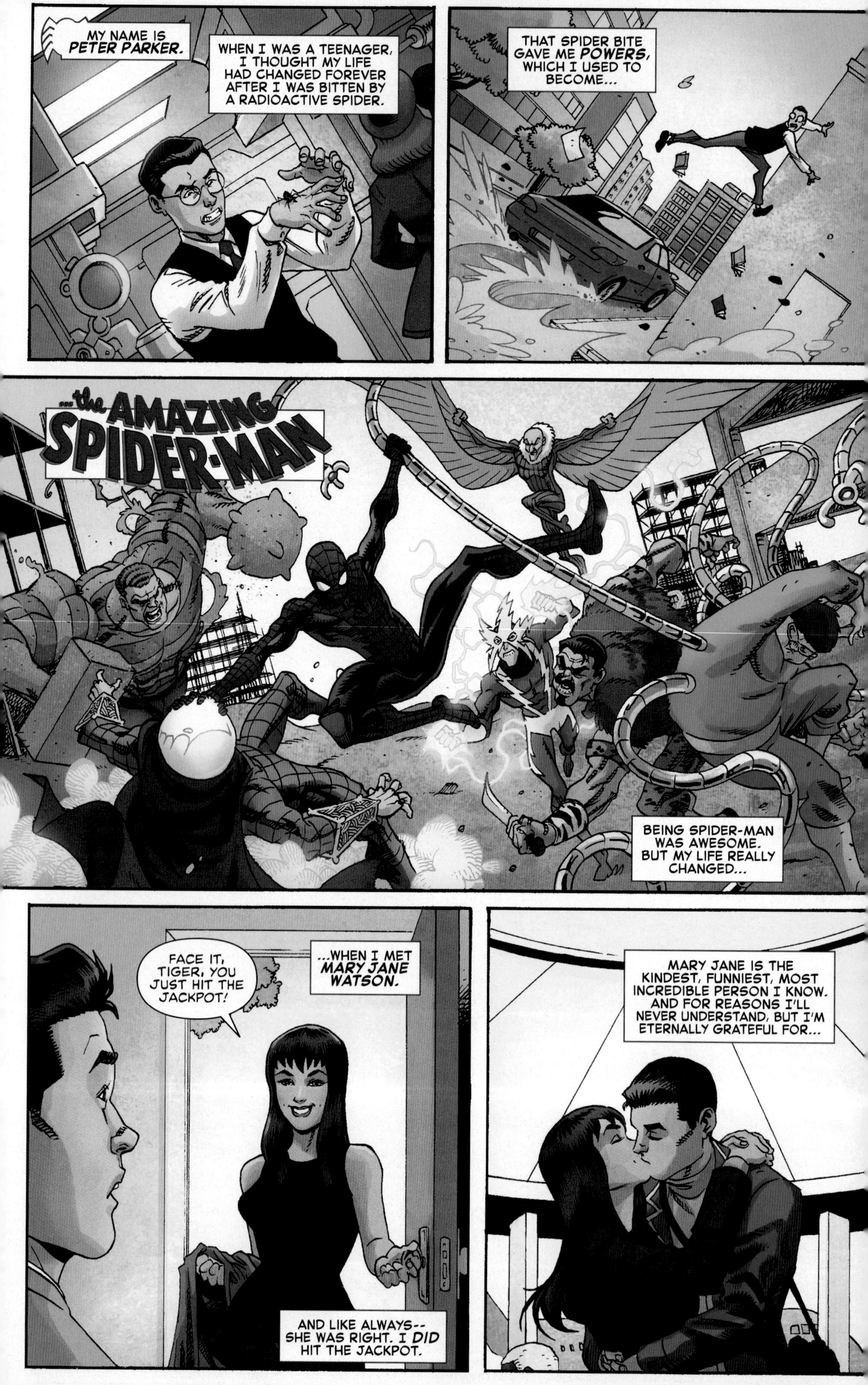
MY NAME IS PETER PARKER.
WHEN I WAS A TEENAGER, I THOUGHT MY LIFE HAD CHANGED FOREVER AFTER I WAS BITTEN BY A RADIOACTIVE SPIDER.
THAT SPIDER BITE GAVE ME POWERS, WHICH I USED TO BECOME...
THE AMAZING SPIDER-MAN
BEING SPIDER-MAN WAS AWESOME. BUT MY LIFE REALLY CHANGED...
FACE IT, TIGER, YOU JUST HIT THE JACKPOT!
...WHEN I MET MARY JANE WATSON.
AND LIKE ALWAYS-- SHE WAS RIGHT. I DID HIT THE JACKPOT.
MARY JANE IS THE KINDEST, FUNNIEST, MOST INCREDIBLE PERSON I KNOW. AND FOR REASONS I'LL NEVER UNDERSTAND, BUT I'M ETERNALLY GRATEFUL FOR...

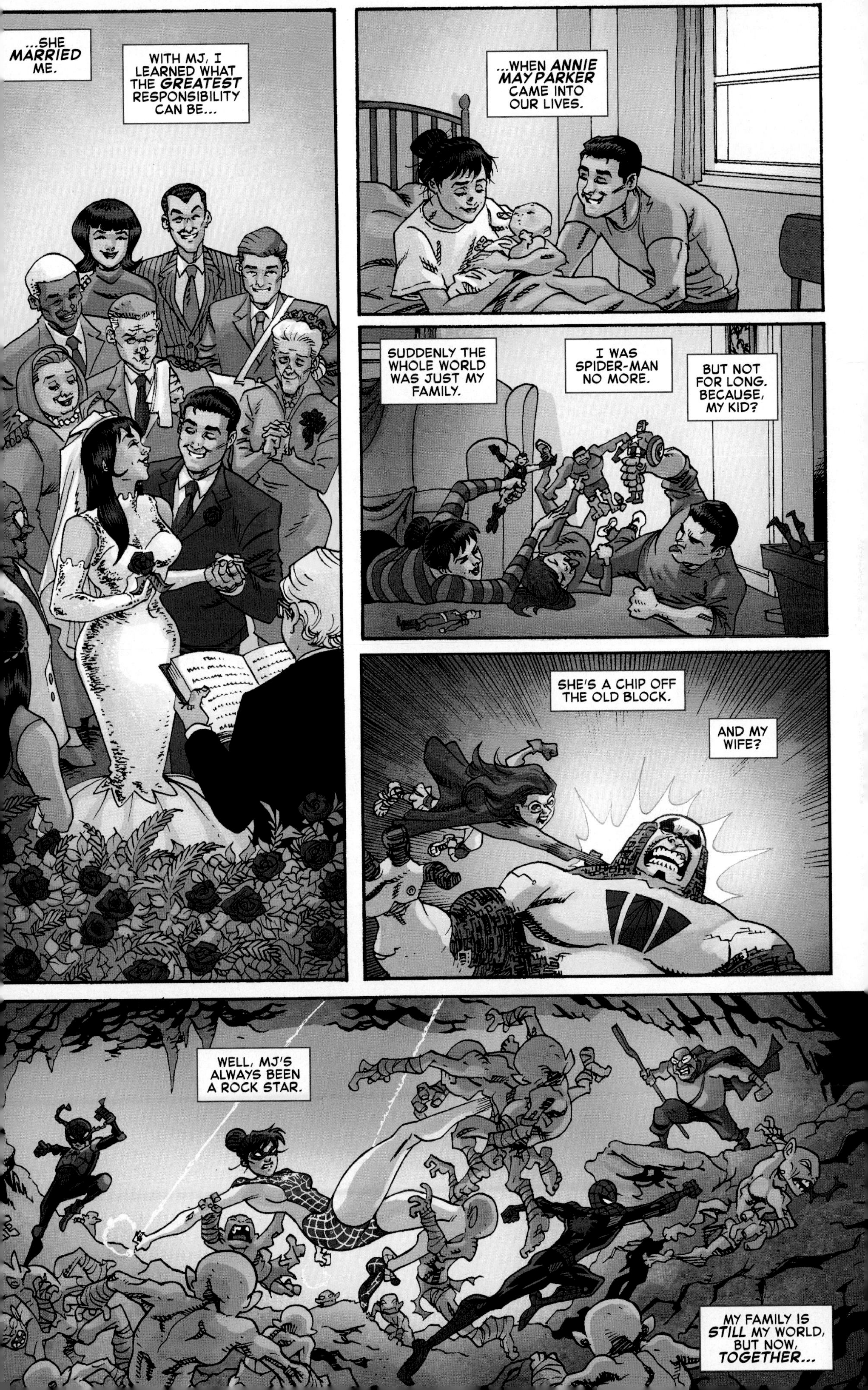

...SHE MARRIED ME.
WITH MJ, I LEARNED WHAT THE GREATEST RESPONSIBILITY CAN BE...
...WHEN ANNIE MAY PARKER CAME INTO OUR LIVES.
SUDDENLY THE WHOLE WORLD WAS JUST MY FAMILY.
I WAS SPIDER-MAN NO MORE.
BUT NOT FOR LONG. BECAUSE, MY KID?
SHE'S A CHIP OFF THE OLD BLOCK.
AND MY WIFE?
WELL, MJ'S ALWAYS BEEN A ROCK STAR.
MY FAMILY IS STILL MY WORLD, BUT NOW, TOGETHER...

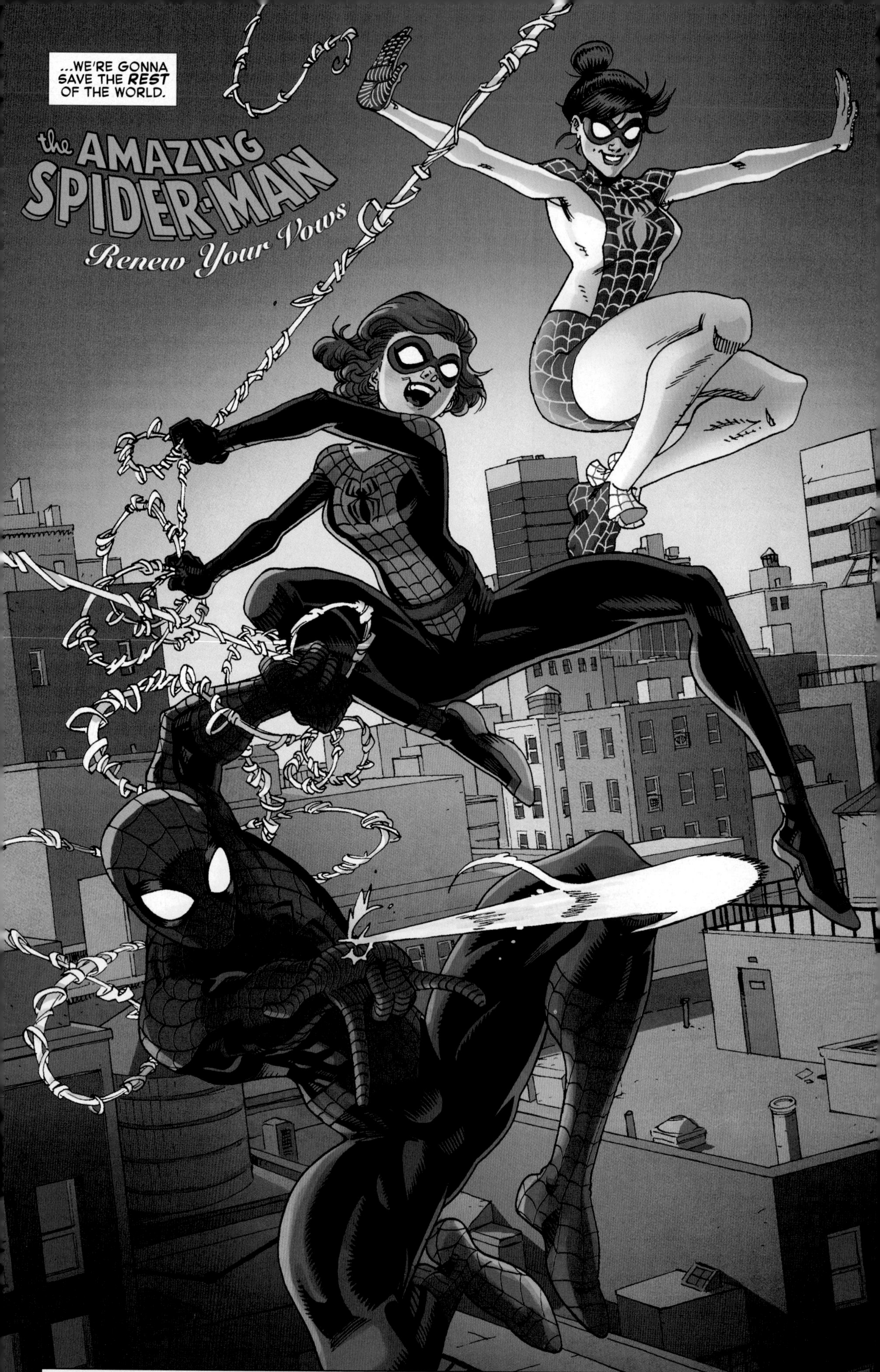

...WE'RE GONNA SAVE THE REST OF THE WORLD.
the AMAZING SPIDER-MAN
Renew Your Vows

ROBBIE THOMPSON WRITER | NATHAN STOCKMAN ARTIST | JIM CAMPBELL COLORIST | VC'S JOE CARAMAGNA LETTERER | KATHLEEN WISNESKI ASSISTANT EDITOR | DARREN SHAN EDITOR

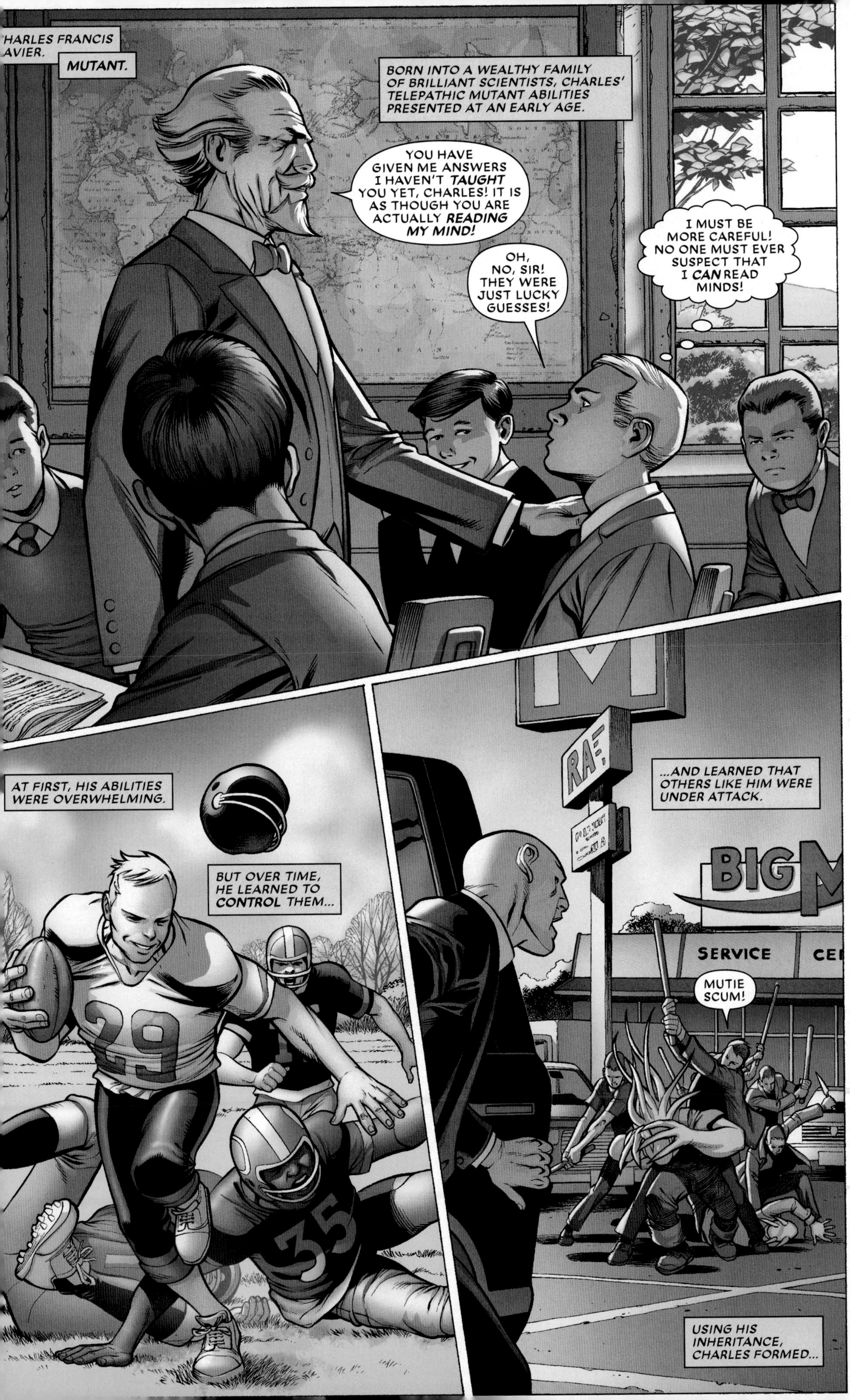

HARLES FRANCIS
AVIER.
MUTANT.
BORN INTO A WEALTHY FAMILY OF BRILLIANT SCIENTISTS, CHARLES' TELEPATHIC MUTANT ABILITIES PRESENTED AT AN EARLY AGE.
YOU HAVE GIVEN ME ANSWERS I HAVEN'T TAUGHT YOU YET, CHARLES! IT IS AS THOUGH YOU ARE ACTUALLY READING MY MIND!
OH, NO, SIR! THEY WERE JUST LUCKY GUESSES!
I MUST BE MORE CAREFUL! NO ONE MUST EVER SUSPECT THAT I CAN READ MINDS!
AT FIRST, HIS ABILITIES WERE OVERWHELMING.
BUT OVER TIME, HE LEARNED TO CONTROL THEM...
29
35
...AND LEARNED THAT OTHERS LIKE HIM WERE UNDER ATTACK.
SERVICE
MUTIE SCUM!
USING HIS INHERITANCE, CHARLES FORMED...

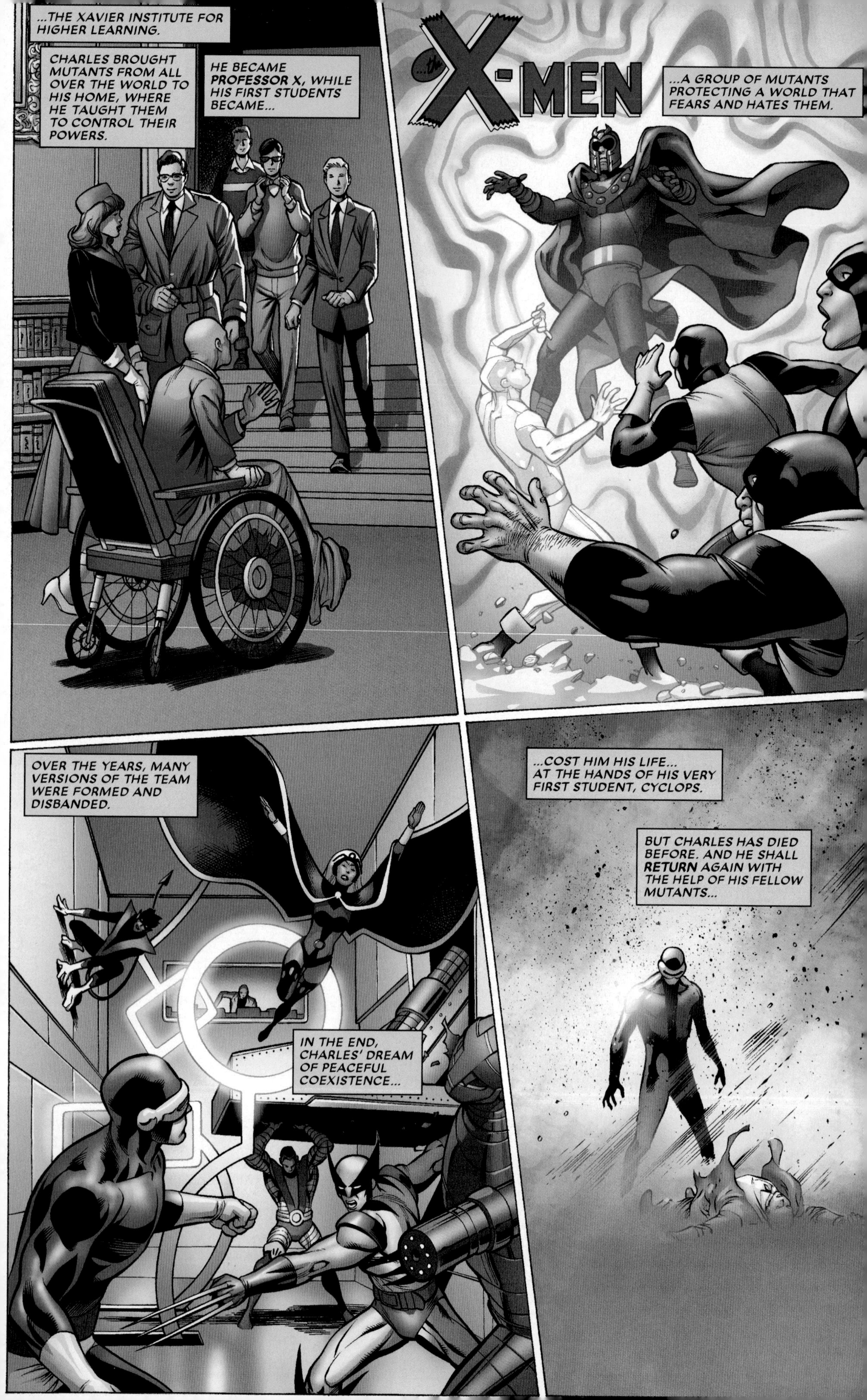
...THE XAVIER INSTITUTE FOR HIGHER LEARNING.
CHARLES BROUGHT MUTANTS FROM ALL OVER THE WORLD TO HIS HOME, WHERE HE TAUGHT THEM TO CONTROL THEIR POWERS.
HE BECAME **PROFESSOR X**, WHILE HIS FIRST STUDENTS BECAME...
...THE X-MEN
...A GROUP OF MUTANTS PROTECTING A WORLD THAT FEARS AND HATES THEM.
OVER THE YEARS, MANY VERSIONS OF THE TEAM WERE FORMED AND DISBANDED.
IN THE END, CHARLES' DREAM OF PEACEFUL COEXISTENCE...
...COST HIM HIS LIFE... AT THE HANDS OF HIS VERY FIRST STUDENT, CYCLOPS.
BUT CHARLES HAS DIED BEFORE. AND HE SHALL **RETURN** AGAIN WITH THE HELP OF HIS FELLOW MUTANTS...

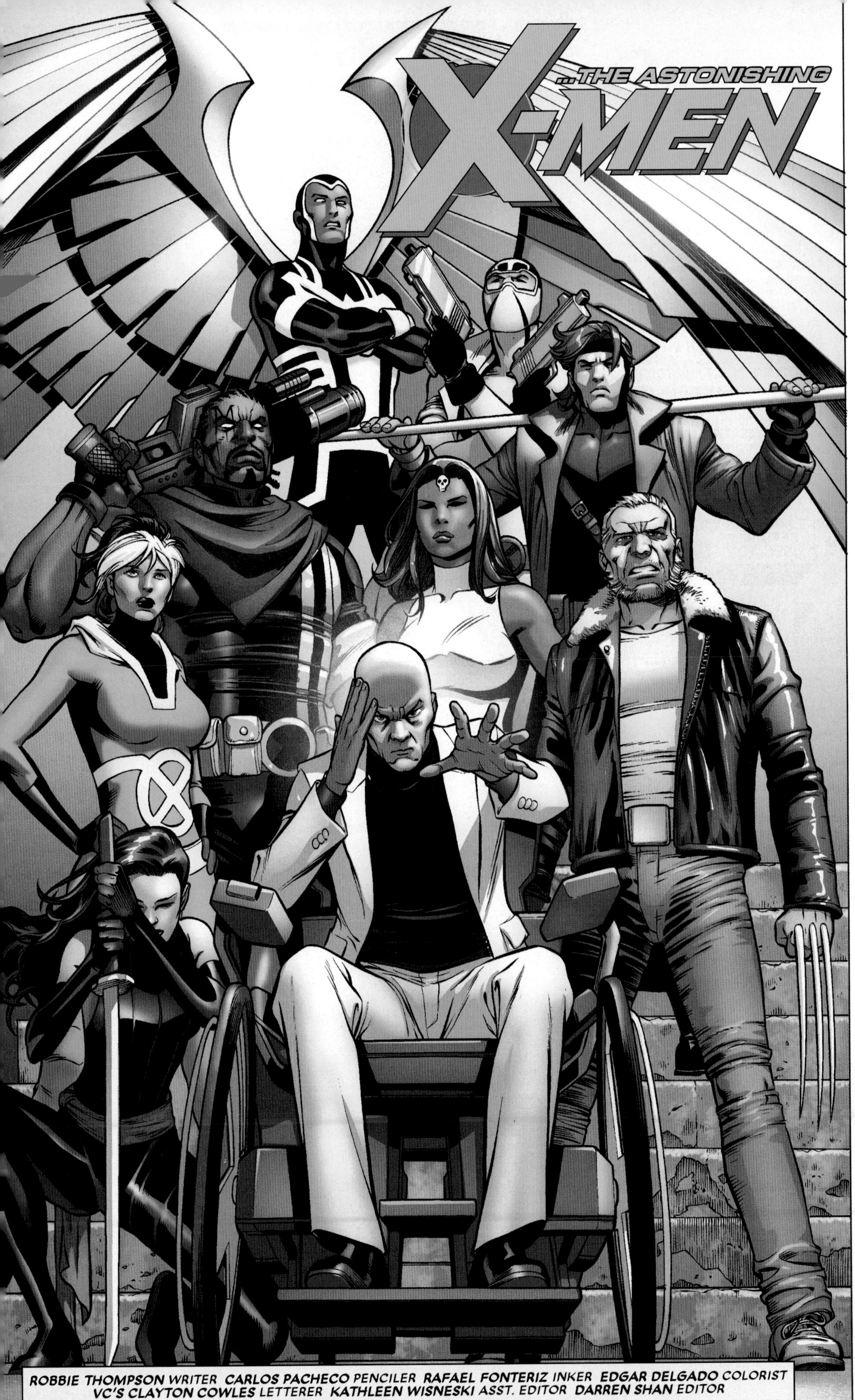
...THE ASTONISHING
X-MEN

ROBBIE THOMPSON WRITER CARLOS PACHECO PENCILER RAFAEL FONTERIZ INKER EDGAR DELGADO COLORIST
VC'S CLAYTON COWLES LETTERER KATHLEEN WISNESKI ASST. EDITOR DARREN SHAN EDITOR

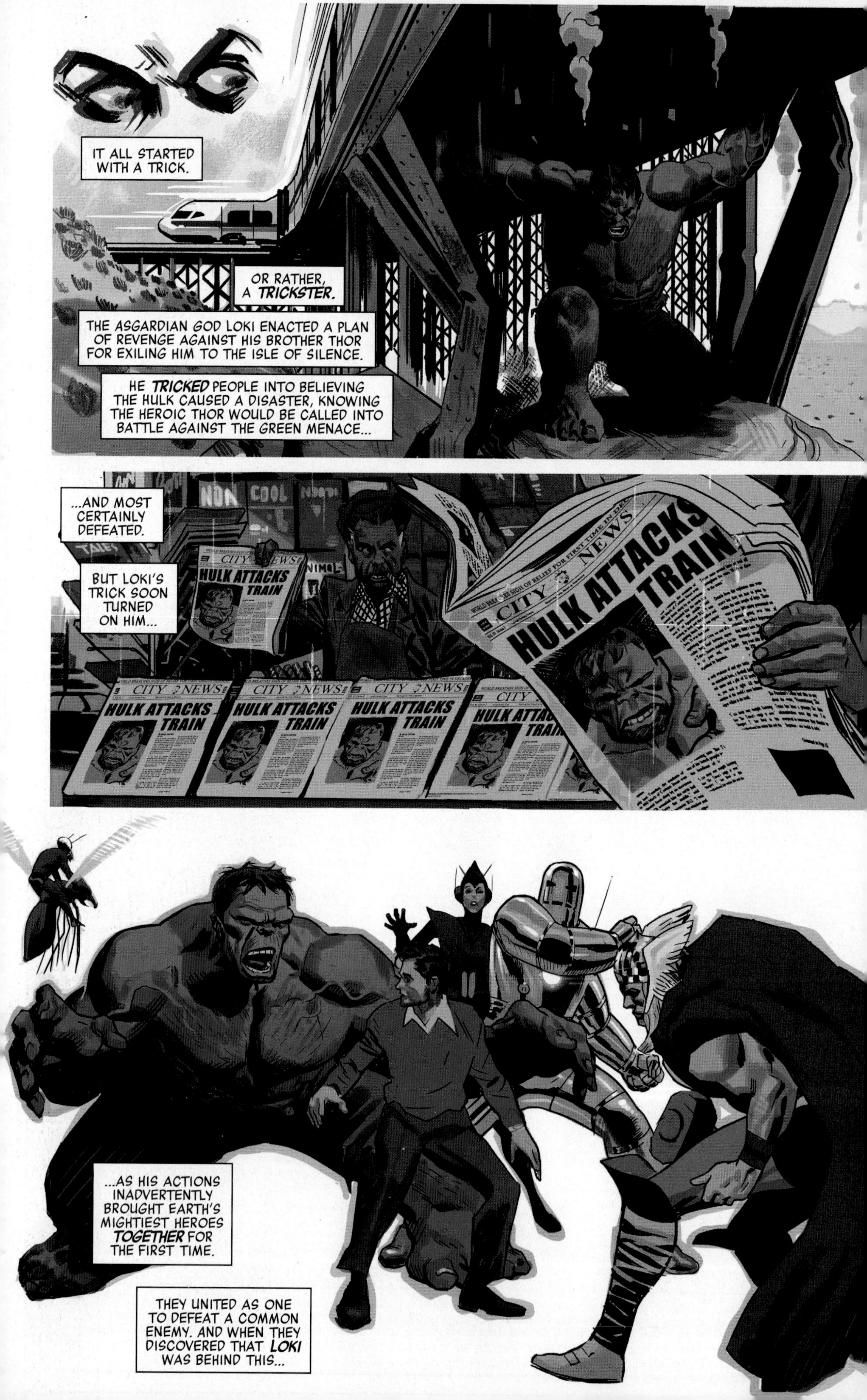
IT ALL STARTED WITH A TRICK.
OR RATHER, A *TRICKSTER.*
THE ASGARDIAN GOD LOKI ENACTED A PLAN OF REVENGE AGAINST HIS BROTHER THOR FOR EXILING HIM TO THE ISLE OF SILENCE.
HE *TRICKED* PEOPLE INTO BELIEVING THE HULK CAUSED A DISASTER, KNOWING THE HEROIC THOR WOULD BE CALLED INTO BATTLE AGAINST THE GREEN MENACE...
...AND MOST CERTAINLY DEFEATED.
BUT LOKI'S TRICK SOON TURNED ON HIM...
CITY NEWS
HULK ATTACKS TRAIN
...AS HIS ACTIONS INADVERTENTLY BROUGHT EARTH'S MIGHTIEST HEROES *TOGETHER* FOR THE FIRST TIME.
THEY UNITED AS ONE TO DEFEAT A COMMON ENEMY. AND WHEN THEY DISCOVERED THAT *LOKI* WAS BEHIND THIS...

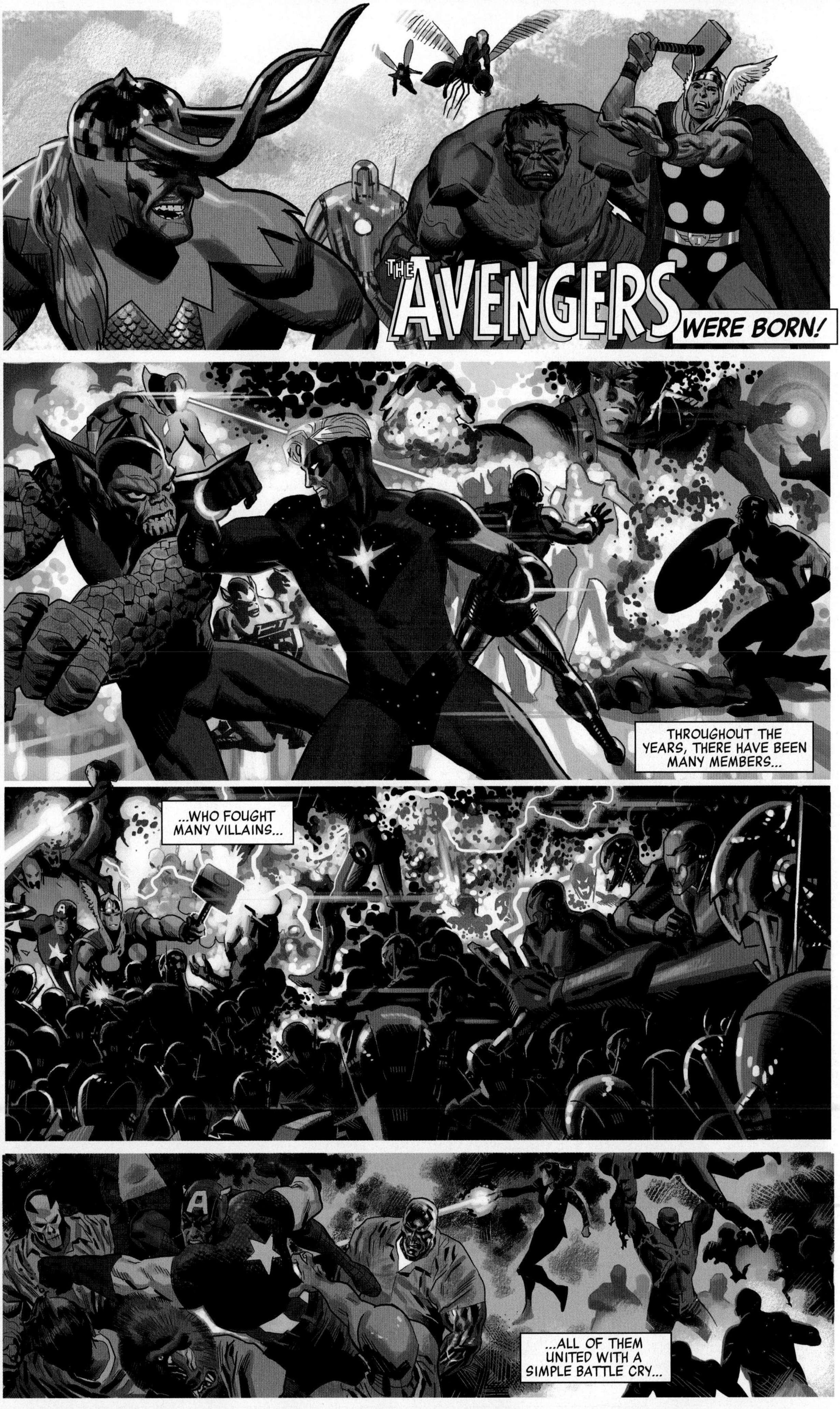

THE AVENGERS WERE BORN!
THROUGHOUT THE YEARS, THERE HAVE BEEN MANY MEMBERS...
...WHO FOUGHT MANY VILLAINS...
...ALL OF THEM UNITED WITH A SIMPLE BATTLE CRY...

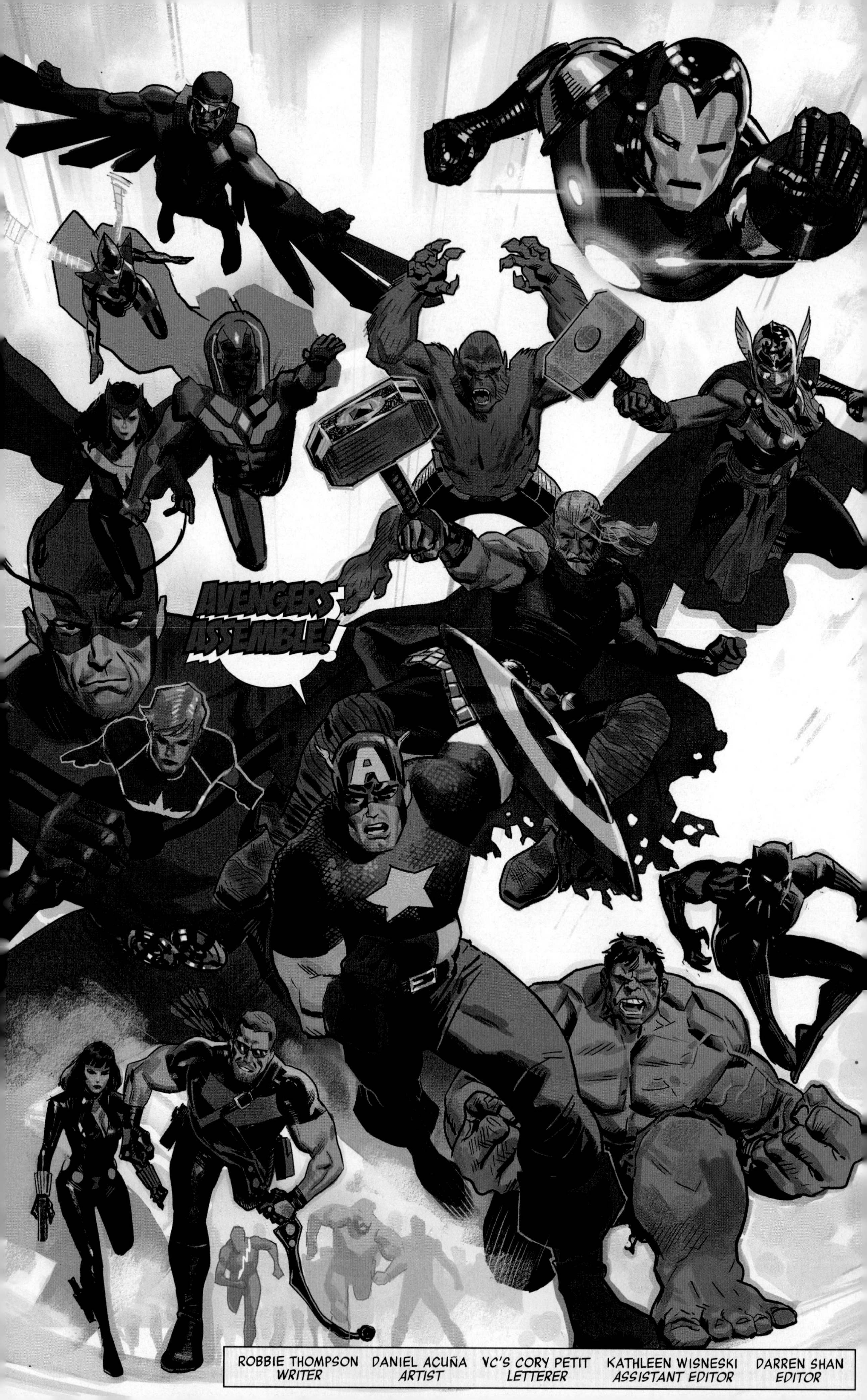
AVENGERS ASSEMBLE!
ROBBIE THOMPSON WRITER
DANIEL ACUÑA ARTIST
VC'S CORY PETIT LETTERER
KATHLEEN WISNESKI ASSISTANT EDITOR
DARREN SHAN EDITOR

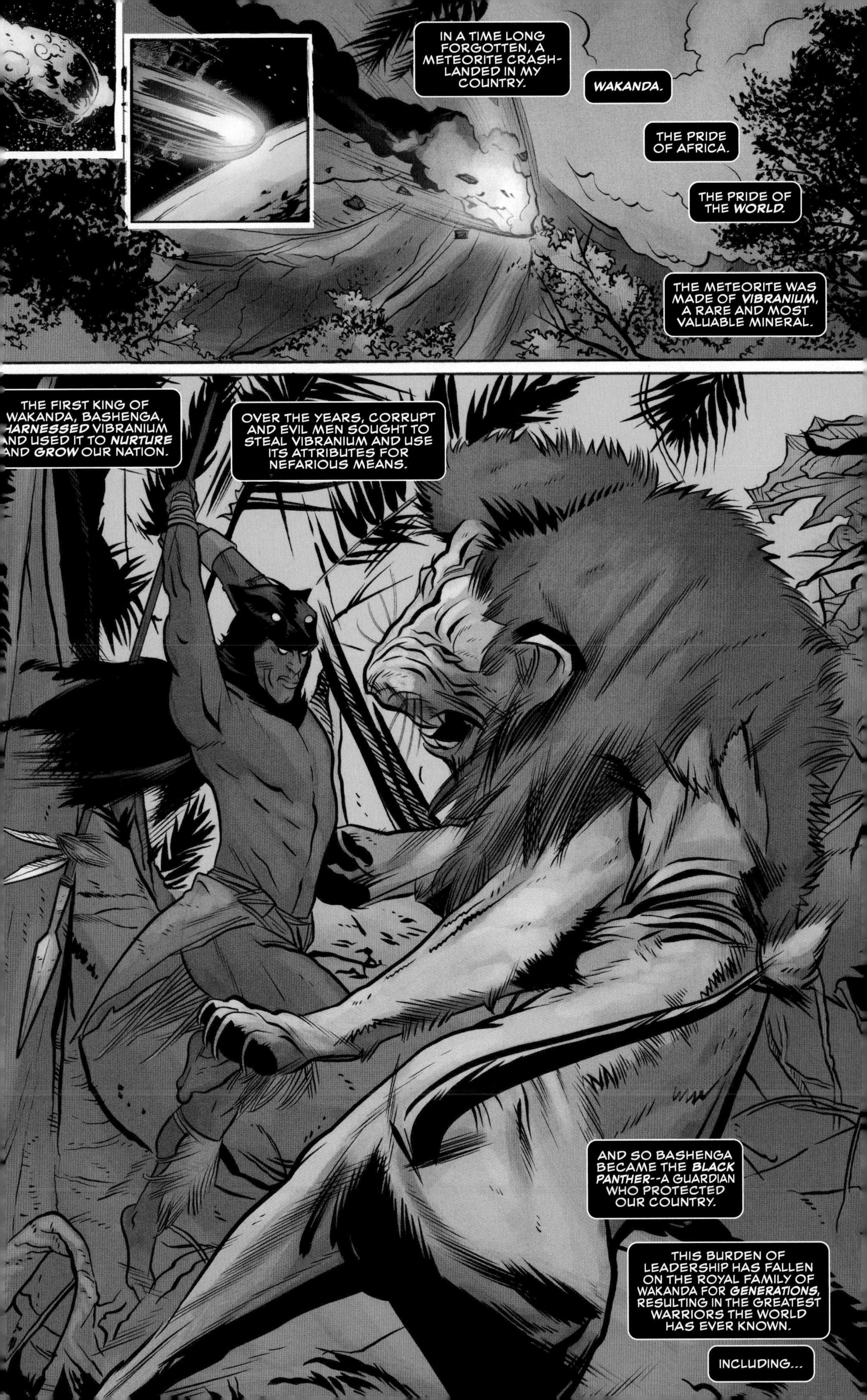
IN A TIME LONG FORGOTTEN, A METEORITE CRASH-LANDED IN MY COUNTRY.
WAKANDA.
THE PRIDE OF AFRICA.
THE PRIDE OF THE WORLD.
THE METEORITE WAS MADE OF VIBRANIUM, A RARE AND MOST VALUABLE MINERAL.
THE FIRST KING OF WAKANDA, BASHENGA, HARNESSED VIBRANIUM AND USED IT TO NURTURE AND GROW OUR NATION.
OVER THE YEARS, CORRUPT AND EVIL MEN SOUGHT TO STEAL VIBRANIUM AND USE ITS ATTRIBUTES FOR NEFARIOUS MEANS.
AND SO BASHENGA BECAME THE BLACK PANTHER--A GUARDIAN WHO PROTECTED OUR COUNTRY.
THIS BURDEN OF LEADERSHIP HAS FALLEN ON THE ROYAL FAMILY OF WAKANDA FOR GENERATIONS, RESULTING IN THE GREATEST WARRIORS THE WORLD HAS EVER KNOWN.
INCLUDING...

...T'CHAKA. MY *FATHER*.

AS KING AND BLACK PANTHER, MY FATHER MADE WAKANDA THE GREATEST AND MOST TECHNOLOGICALLY ADVANCED COUNTRY IN HISTORY.

HE KEPT US *HIDDEN* FROM THE WORLD. IT WAS A PEACEFUL TIME. A HAPPY TIME...

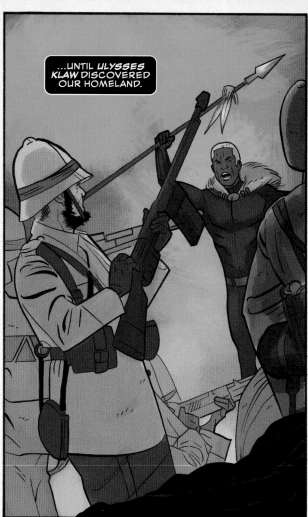

...UNTIL *ULYSSES KLAW* DISCOVERED OUR HOMELAND.

IN HIS RUTHLESS PURSUIT OF VIBRANIUM, HE TOOK MY FATHER'S LIFE.

I *AVENGED* MY FATHER'S DEATH, AND BROUGHT KLAW TO HEEL.

AND IN THAT MOMENT, THE MANTLE WAS PASSED TO ME.

MY NAME IS T'CHALLA...

ZAK

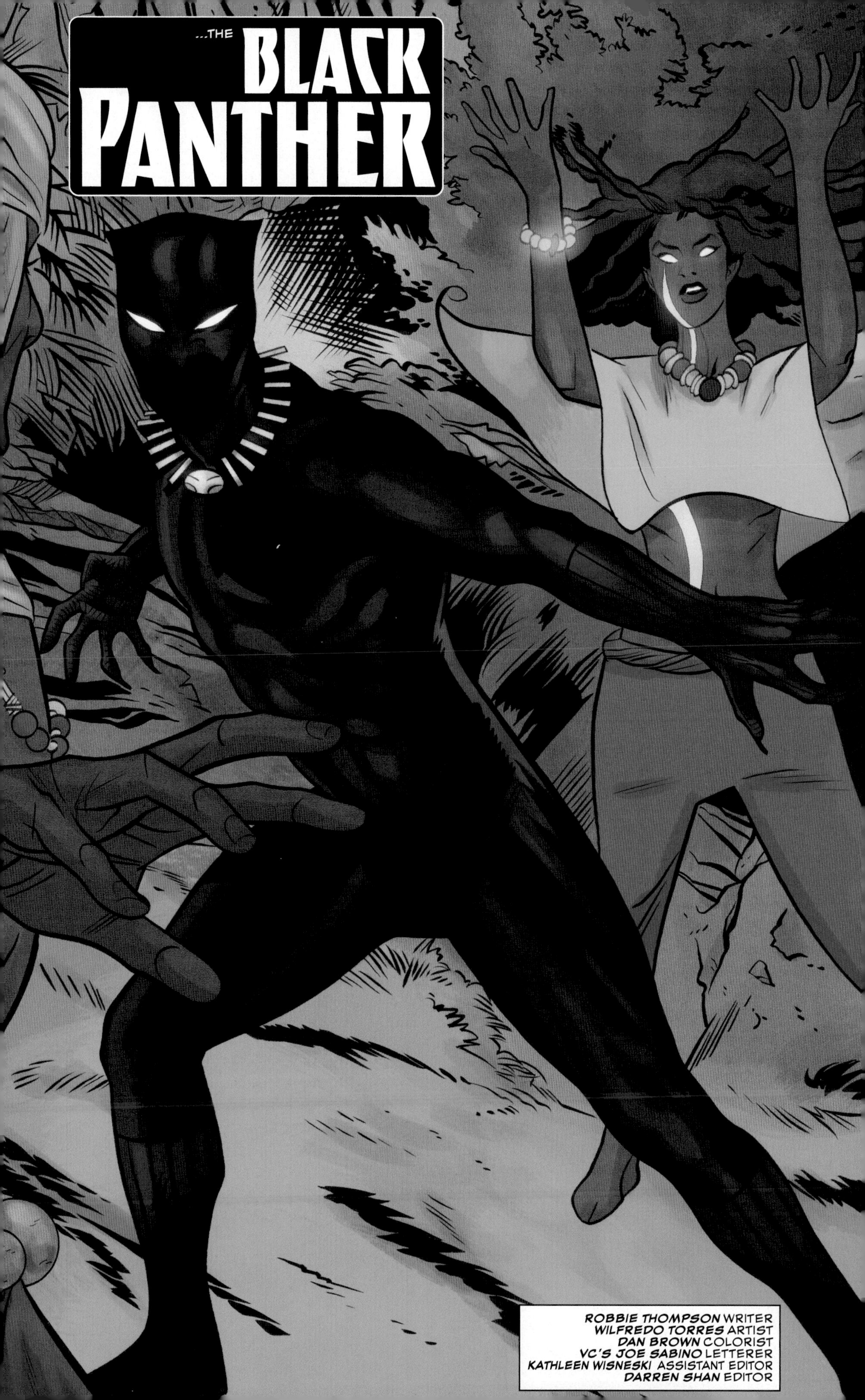
...THE
BLACK PANTHER
ROBBIE THOMPSON WRITER
WILFREDO TORRES ARTIST
DAN BROWN COLORIST
VC'S JOE SABINO LETTERER
KATHLEEN WISNESKI ASSISTANT EDITOR
DARREN SHAN EDITOR

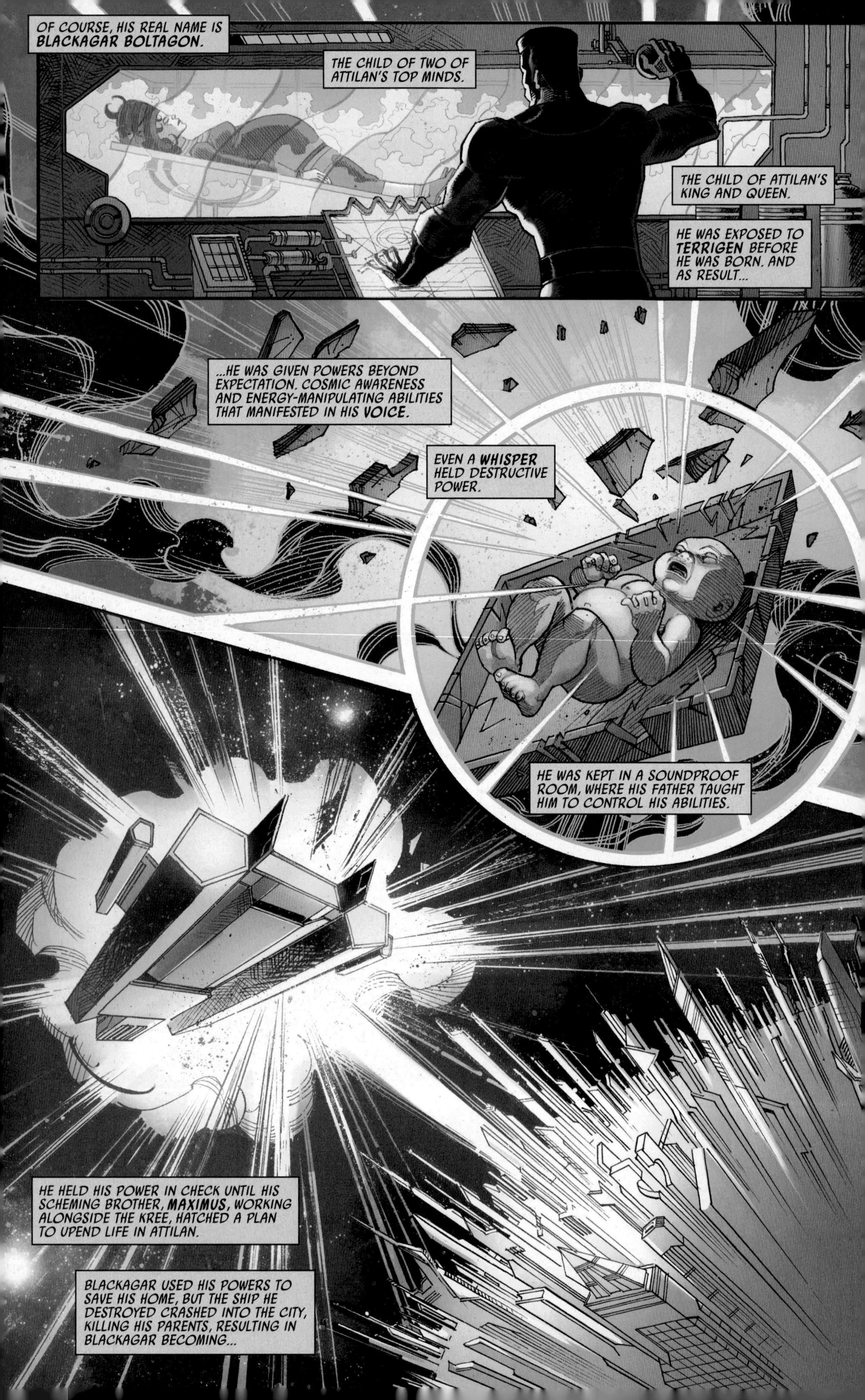
OF COURSE, HIS REAL NAME IS BLACKAGAR BOLTAGON.
THE CHILD OF TWO OF ATTILAN'S TOP MINDS.
THE CHILD OF ATTILAN'S KING AND QUEEN.
HE WAS EXPOSED TO TERRIGEN BEFORE HE WAS BORN. AND AS RESULT...
...HE WAS GIVEN POWERS BEYOND EXPECTATION. COSMIC AWARENESS AND ENERGY-MANIPULATING ABILITIES THAT MANIFESTED IN HIS VOICE.
EVEN A WHISPER HELD DESTRUCTIVE POWER.
HE WAS KEPT IN A SOUNDPROOF ROOM, WHERE HIS FATHER TAUGHT HIM TO CONTROL HIS ABILITIES.
HE HELD HIS POWER IN CHECK UNTIL HIS SCHEMING BROTHER, MAXIMUS, WORKING ALONGSIDE THE KREE, HATCHED A PLAN TO UPEND LIFE IN ATTILAN.
BLACKAGAR USED HIS POWERS TO SAVE HIS HOME, BUT THE SHIP HE DESTROYED CRASHED INTO THE CITY, KILLING HIS PARENTS, RESULTING IN BLACKAGAR BECOMING...

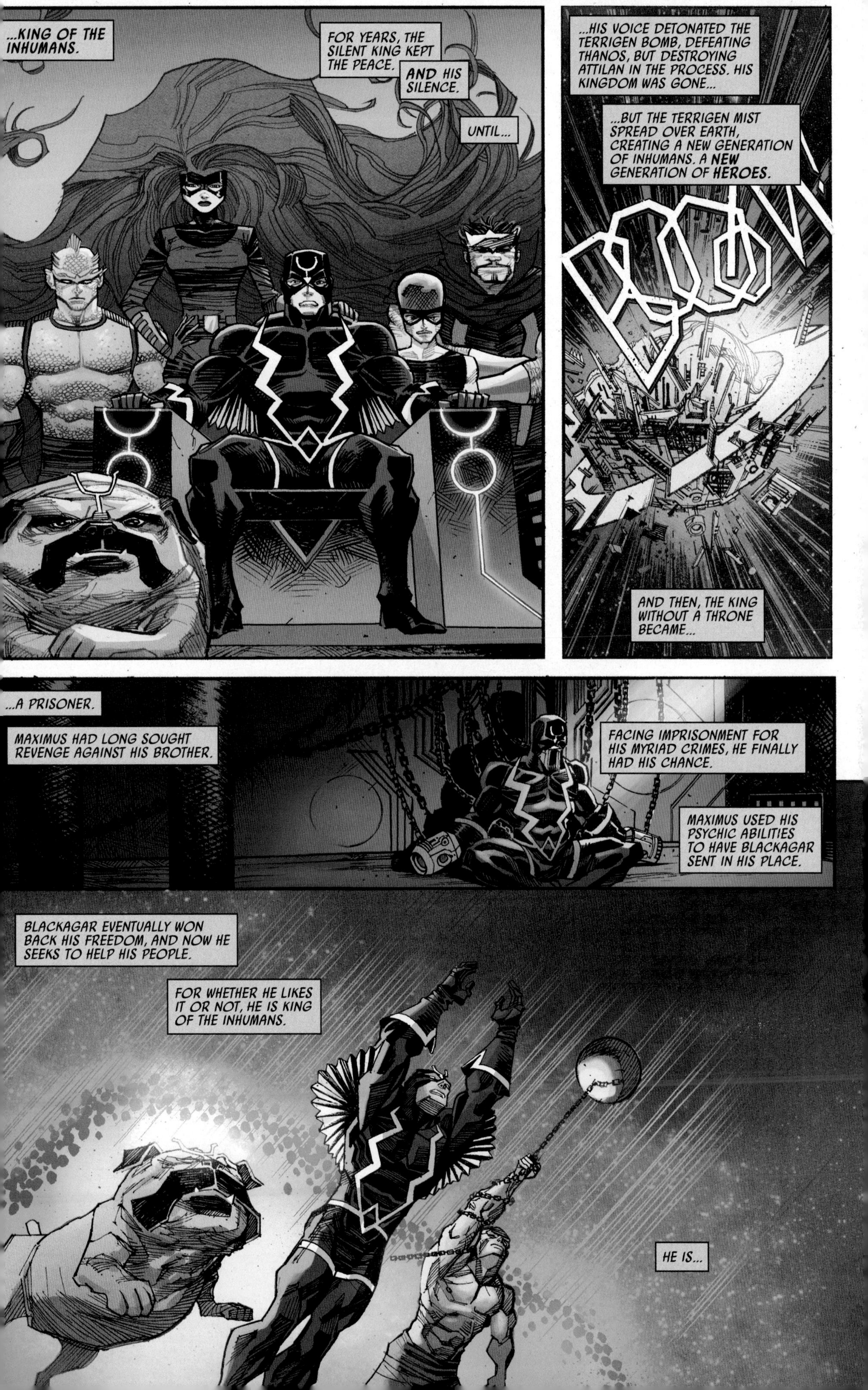
...KING OF THE INHUMANS.
FOR YEARS, THE SILENT KING KEPT THE PEACE.
AND HIS SILENCE.
UNTIL...
...HIS VOICE DETONATED THE TERRIGEN BOMB, DEFEATING THANOS, BUT DESTROYING ATTILAN IN THE PROCESS. HIS KINGDOM WAS GONE...
...BUT THE TERRIGEN MIST SPREAD OVER EARTH, CREATING A NEW GENERATION OF INHUMANS. A NEW GENERATION OF HEROES.
AND THEN, THE KING WITHOUT A THRONE BECAME...
...A PRISONER.
MAXIMUS HAD LONG SOUGHT REVENGE AGAINST HIS BROTHER.
FACING IMPRISONMENT FOR HIS MYRIAD CRIMES, HE FINALLY HAD HIS CHANCE.
MAXIMUS USED HIS PSYCHIC ABILITIES TO HAVE BLACKAGAR SENT IN HIS PLACE.
BLACKAGAR EVENTUALLY WON BACK HIS FREEDOM, AND NOW HE SEEKS TO HELP HIS PEOPLE.
FOR WHETHER HE LIKES IT OR NOT, HE IS KING OF THE INHUMANS.
HE IS...

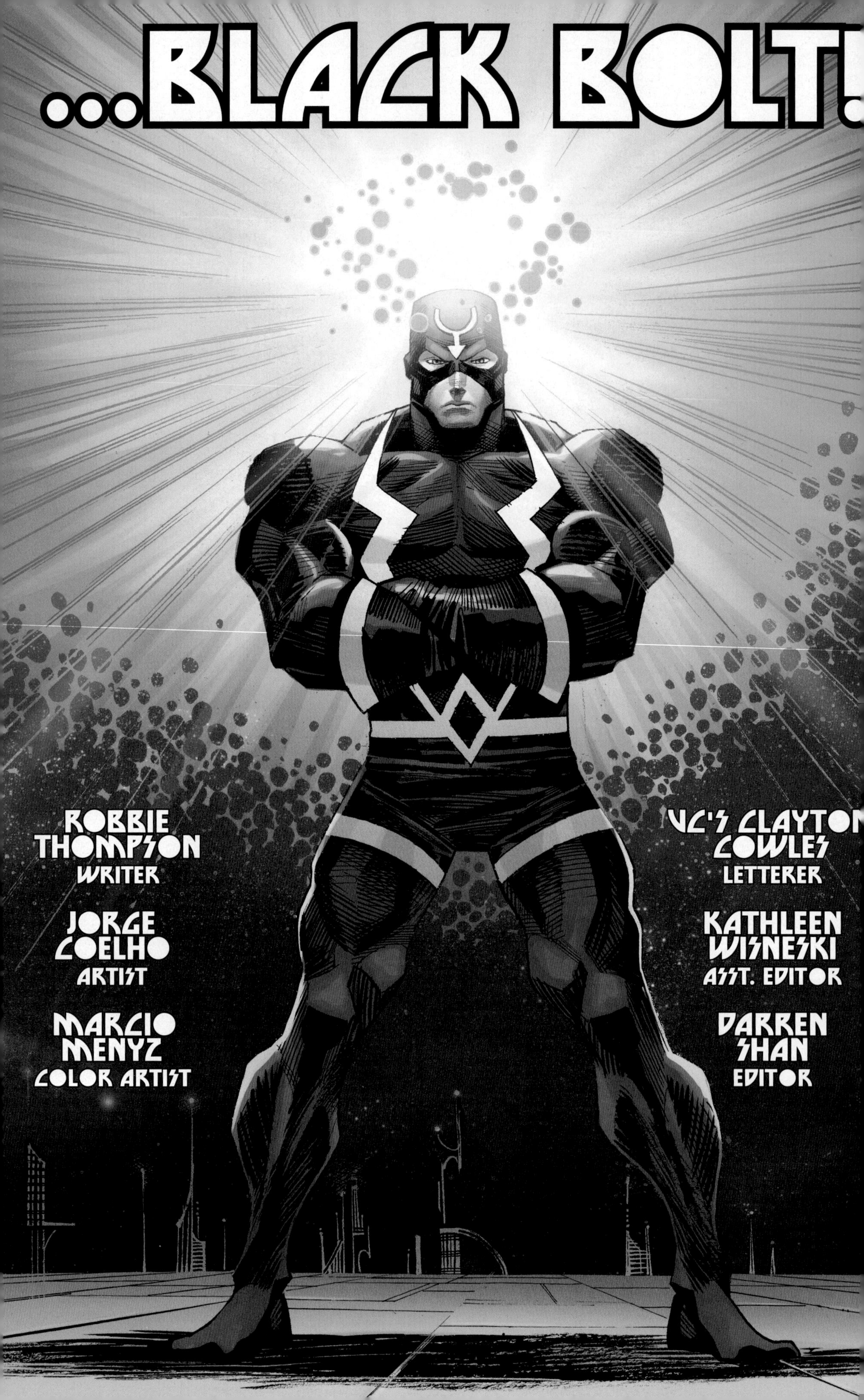

...BLACK BOLT!
ROBBIE THOMPSON WRITER
JORGE COELHO ARTIST
MARCIO MENYZ COLOR ARTIST
VC'S CLAYTON COWLES LETTERER
KATHLEEN WISNESKI ASST. EDITOR
DARREN SHAN EDITOR

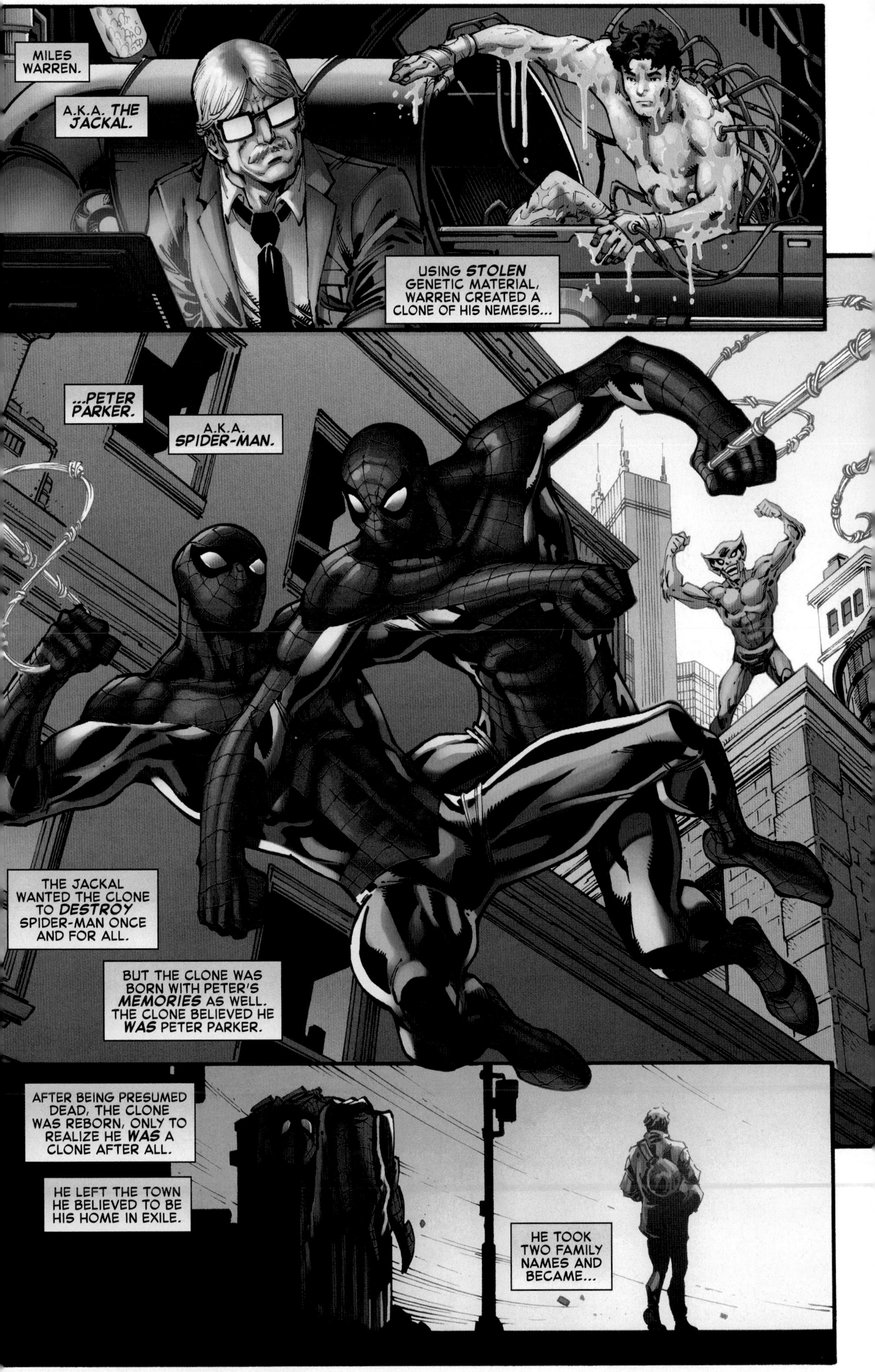
MILES WARREN.
A.K.A. THE JACKAL.
USING STOLEN GENETIC MATERIAL, WARREN CREATED A CLONE OF HIS NEMESIS...
...PETER PARKER.
A.K.A. SPIDER-MAN.
THE JACKAL WANTED THE CLONE TO DESTROY SPIDER-MAN ONCE AND FOR ALL.
BUT THE CLONE WAS BORN WITH PETER'S MEMORIES AS WELL. THE CLONE BELIEVED HE WAS PETER PARKER.
AFTER BEING PRESUMED DEAD, THE CLONE WAS REBORN, ONLY TO REALIZE HE WAS A CLONE AFTER ALL.
HE LEFT THE TOWN HE BELIEVED TO BE HIS HOME IN EXILE.
HE TOOK TWO FAMILY NAMES AND BECAME...

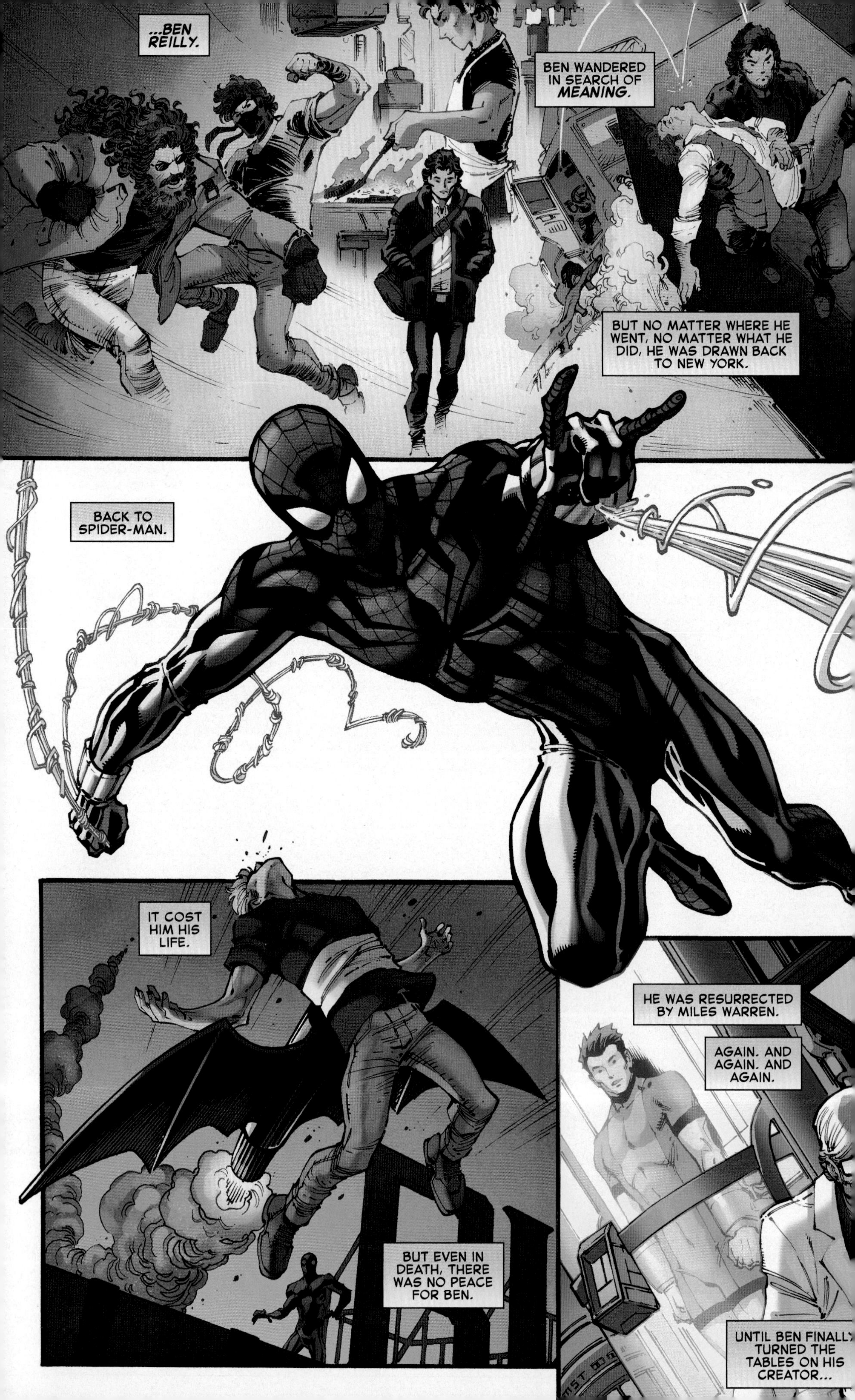
...BEN REILLY.
BEN WANDERED IN SEARCH OF MEANING.
BUT NO MATTER WHERE HE WENT, NO MATTER WHAT HE DID, HE WAS DRAWN BACK TO NEW YORK.
BACK TO SPIDER-MAN.
IT COST HIM HIS LIFE.
BUT EVEN IN DEATH, THERE WAS NO PEACE FOR BEN.
HE WAS RESURRECTED BY MILES WARREN.
AGAIN. AND AGAIN. AND AGAIN.
UNTIL BEN FINALLY TURNED THE TABLES ON HIS CREATOR...

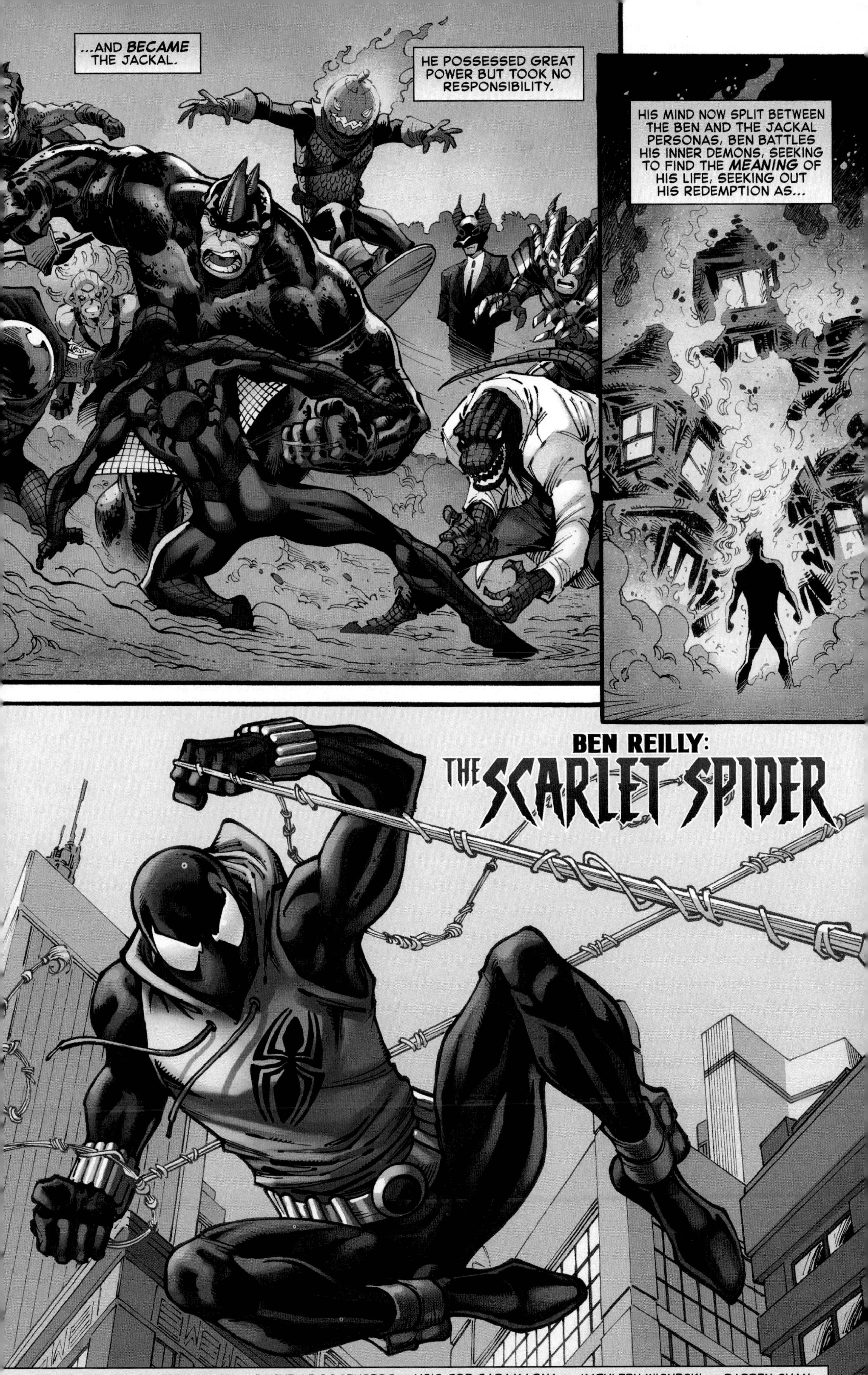
...AND BECAME THE JACKAL.
HE POSSESSED GREAT POWER BUT TOOK NO RESPONSIBILITY.
HIS MIND NOW SPLIT BETWEEN THE BEN AND THE JACKAL PERSONAS, BEN BATTLES HIS INNER DEMONS, SEEKING TO FIND THE MEANING OF HIS LIFE, SEEKING OUT HIS REDEMPTION AS...
BEN REILLY:
THE SCARLET SPIDER

ROBBIE THOMPSON WRITER | TODD NAUCK ARTIST | RACHELLE ROSENBERG COLORIST | VC'S JOE CARAMAGNA LETTERER | KATHLEEN WISNESKI ASSISTANT EDITOR | DARREN SHAN EDITOR

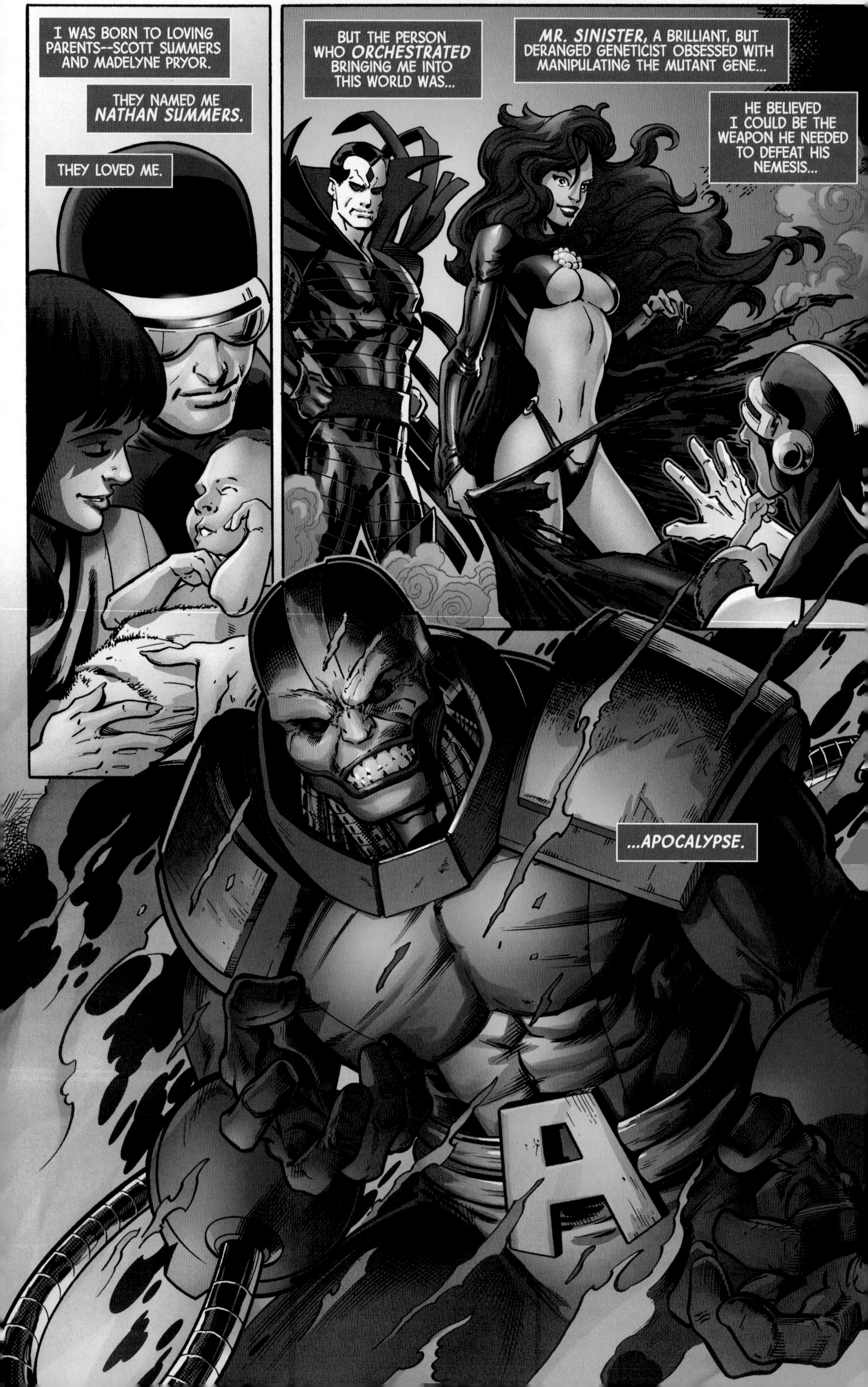
I WAS BORN TO LOVING PARENTS--SCOTT SUMMERS AND MADELYNE PRYOR.
THEY NAMED ME NATHAN SUMMERS.
THEY LOVED ME.
BUT THE PERSON WHO ORCHESTRATED BRINGING ME INTO THIS WORLD WAS...
MR. SINISTER, A BRILLIANT, BUT DERANGED GENETICIST OBSESSED WITH MANIPULATING THE MUTANT GENE...
HE BELIEVED I COULD BE THE WEAPON HE NEEDED TO DEFEAT HIS NEMESIS...
...APOCALYPSE.

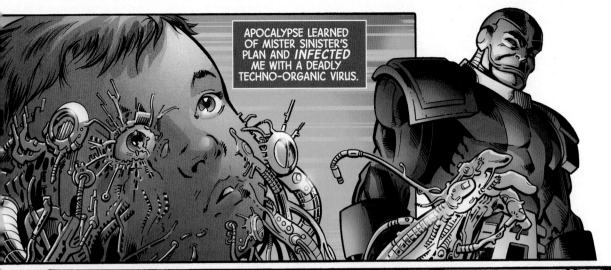

APOCALYPSE LEARNED OF MISTER SINISTER'S PLAN AND *INFECTED* ME WITH A DEADLY TECHNO-ORGANIC VIRUS.

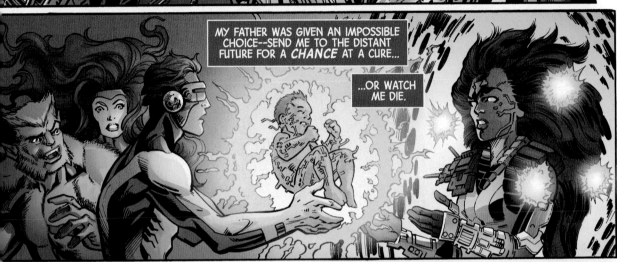

MY FATHER WAS GIVEN AN IMPOSSIBLE CHOICE--SEND ME TO THE DISTANT FUTURE FOR A *CHANCE* AT A CURE...

...OR WATCH ME DIE.

HE SENT ME TO THE FUTURE.

WHERE THE IMPOSSIBLE WAS *POSSIBLE.*

THE PSYCHES OF SCOTT AND JEAN GREY-SUMMERS WERE BROUGHT *FORWARD* IN TIME WITH ME AND *INTO* SLYM AND REDD DAYSPRING. THEY *RAISED* ME...

...*TRAINED* ME TO USE MY MUTANT POWERS TO KEEP THE *VIRUS* AT BAY. I WAS MY OWN CURE, AND IN TIME, I BECAME...

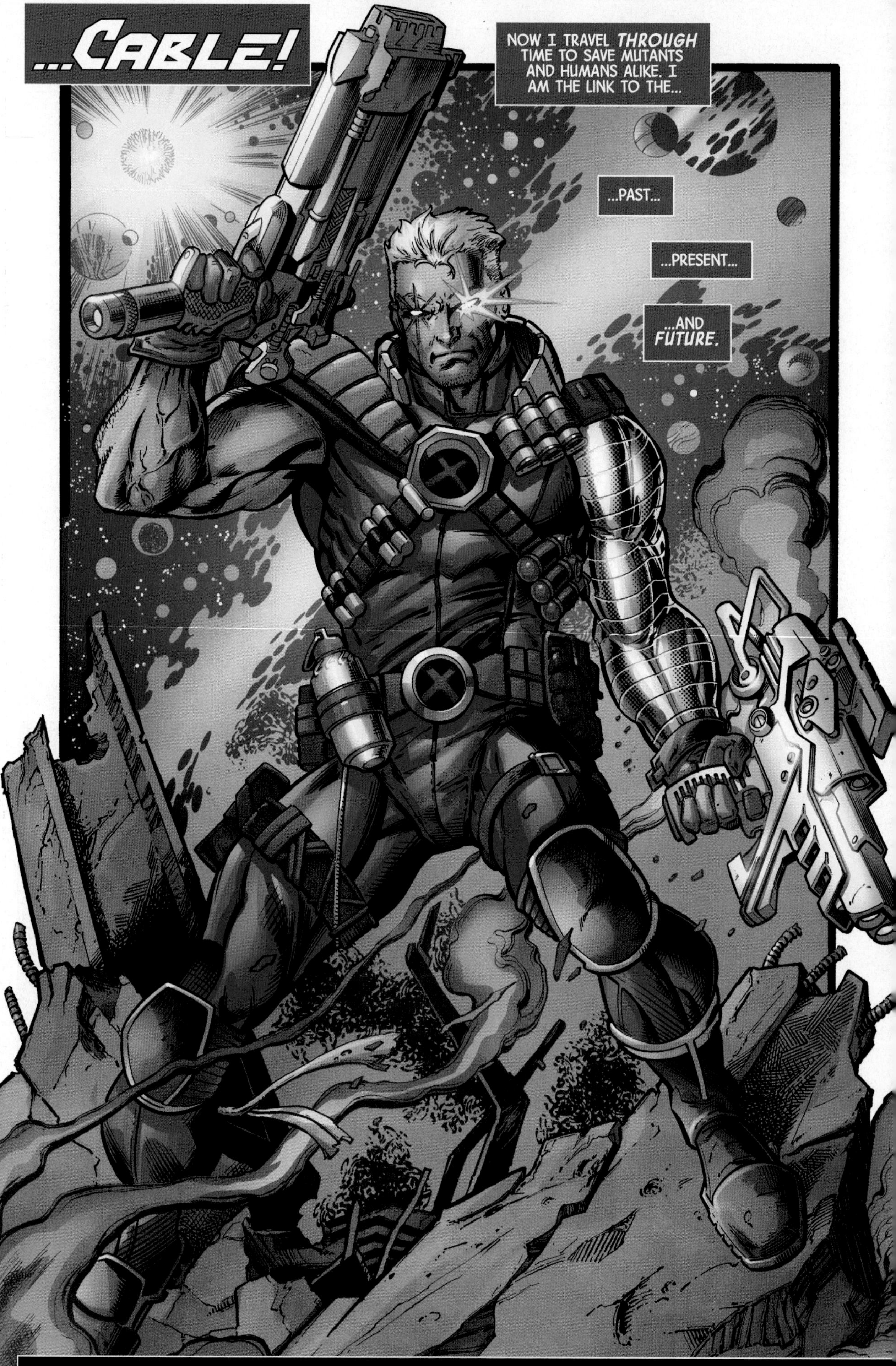
...CABLE!
NOW I TRAVEL THROUGH TIME TO SAVE MUTANTS AND HUMANS ALIKE. I AM THE LINK TO THE...
...PAST...
...PRESENT...
...AND FUTURE.

ROBBIE THOMPSON: WRITER **MARK BAGLEY:** PENCILER **JOHN DELL:** INKER
ANDY TROY: COLORS **VC'S TRAVIS LANHAM:** LETTERING
KATHLEEN WISNESKI: ASSISTANT EDITOR **DARREN SHAN:** EDITOR

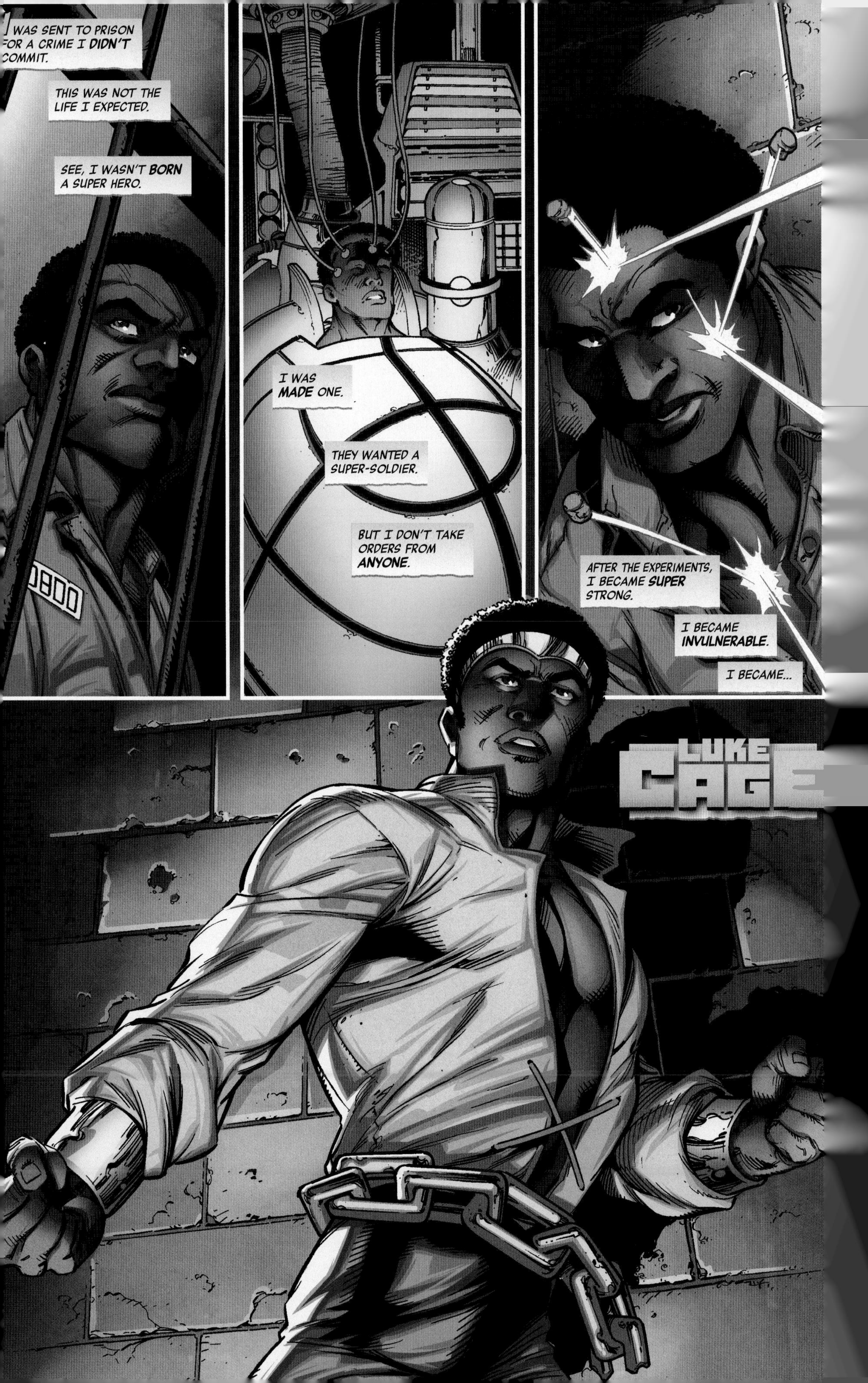
I WAS SENT TO PRISON FOR A CRIME I DIDN'T COMMIT.
THIS WAS NOT THE LIFE I EXPECTED.
SEE, I WASN'T BORN A SUPER HERO.
I WAS MADE ONE.
THEY WANTED A SUPER-SOLDIER.
BUT I DON'T TAKE ORDERS FROM ANYONE.
AFTER THE EXPERIMENTS, I BECAME SUPER STRONG.
I BECAME INVULNERABLE.
I BECAME...
LUKE CAGE

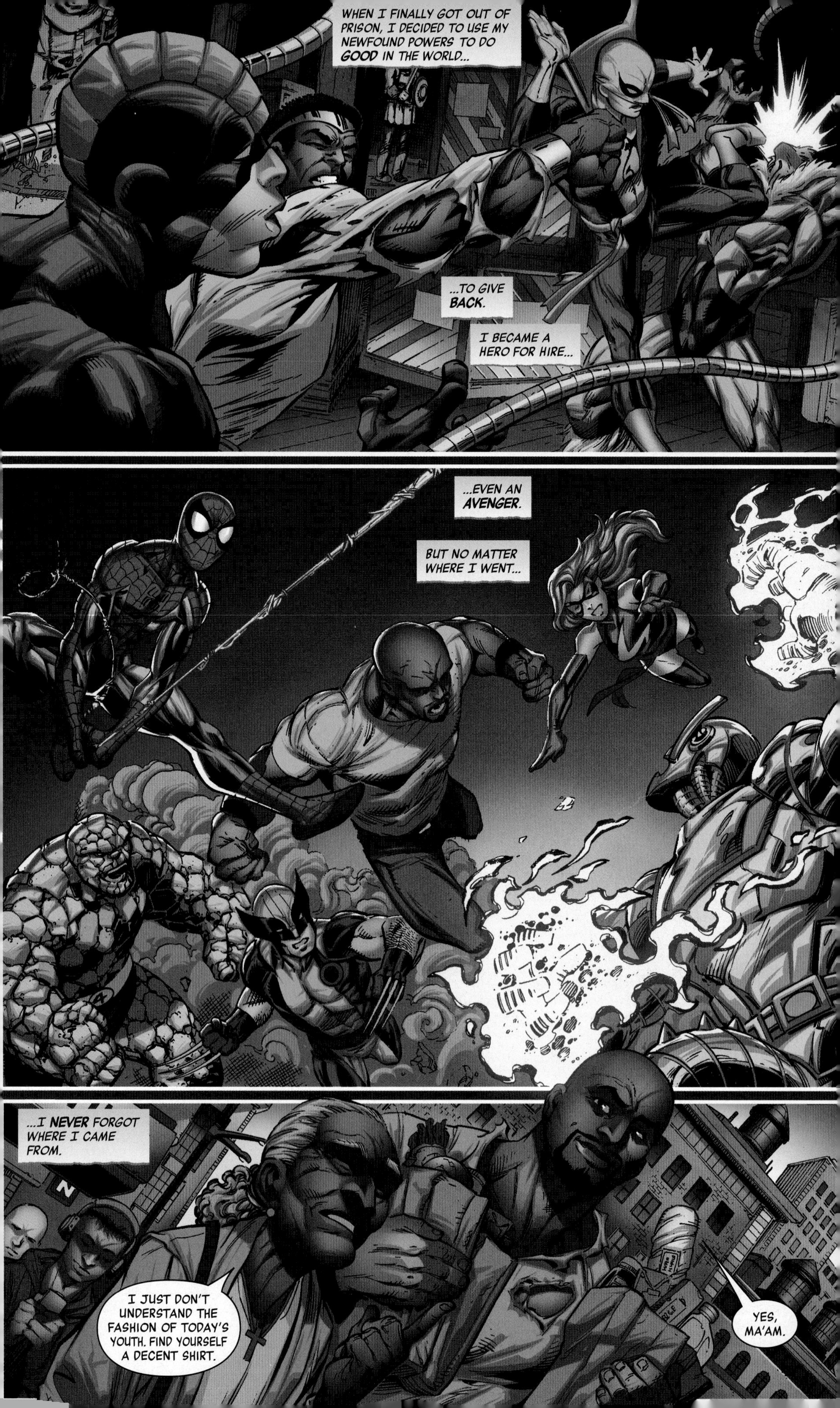
WHEN I FINALLY GOT OUT OF PRISON, I DECIDED TO USE MY NEWFOUND POWERS TO DO GOOD IN THE WORLD...
...TO GIVE BACK.
I BECAME A HERO FOR HIRE...
...EVEN AN AVENGER.
BUT NO MATTER WHERE I WENT...
...I NEVER FORGOT WHERE I CAME FROM.
I JUST DON'T UNDERSTAND THE FASHION OF TODAY'S YOUTH. FIND YOURSELF A DECENT SHIRT.
YES, MA'AM.

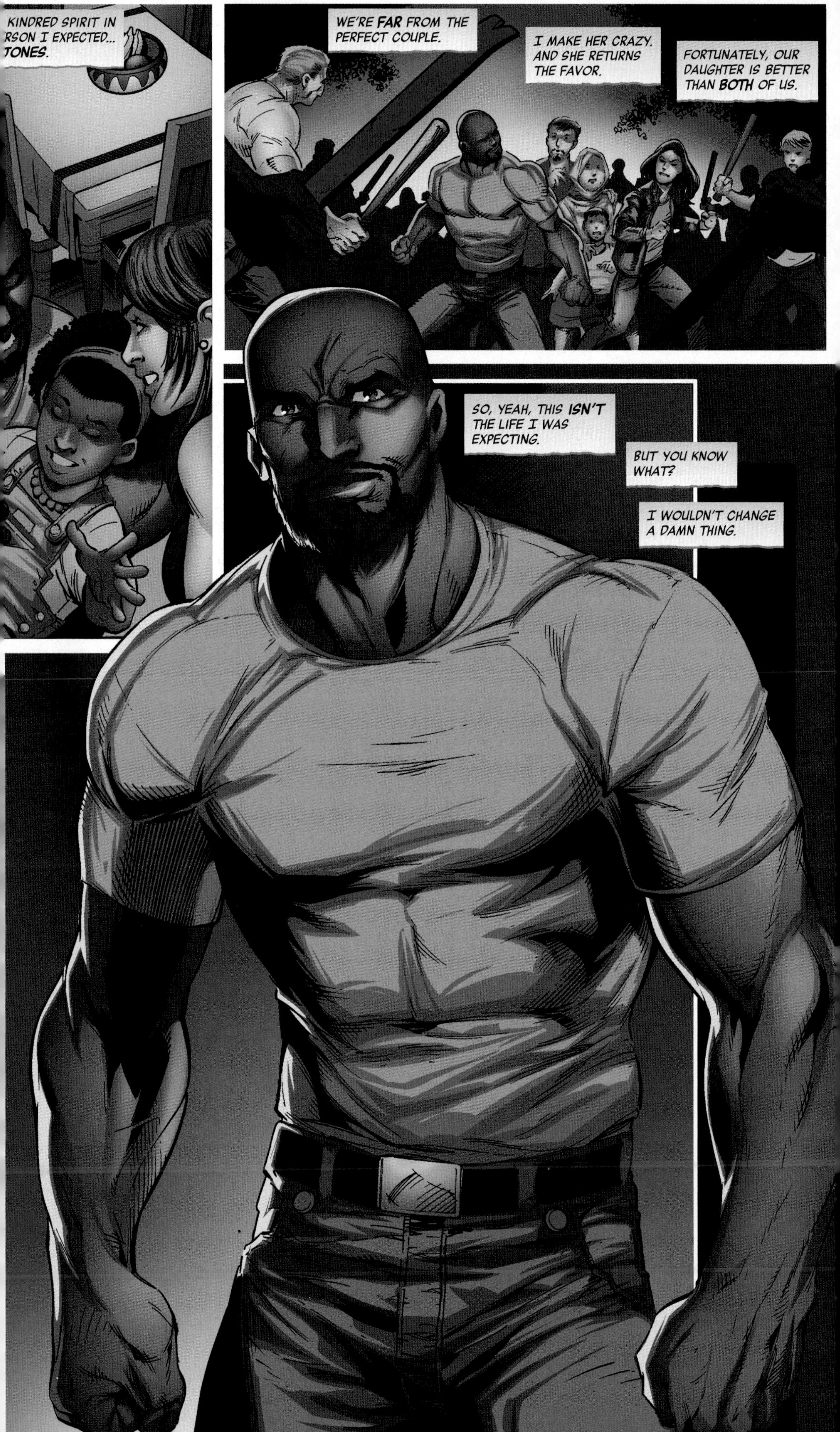
KINDRED SPIRIT IN
RSON I EXPECTED...
JONES.
WE'RE FAR FROM THE PERFECT COUPLE.
I MAKE HER CRAZY. AND SHE RETURNS THE FAVOR.
FORTUNATELY, OUR DAUGHTER IS BETTER THAN BOTH OF US.
SO, YEAH, THIS ISN'T THE LIFE I WAS EXPECTING.
BUT YOU KNOW WHAT?
I WOULDN'T CHANGE A DAMN THING.

ROBBIE THOMPSON WRITER MARK BAGLEY PENCILER JOHN DELL INKER ISRAEL SILVA COLORIST
VC'S JOE SABINO LETTERER KATHLEEN WISNESKI ASSISTANT EDITOR DARREN SHAN EDITOR

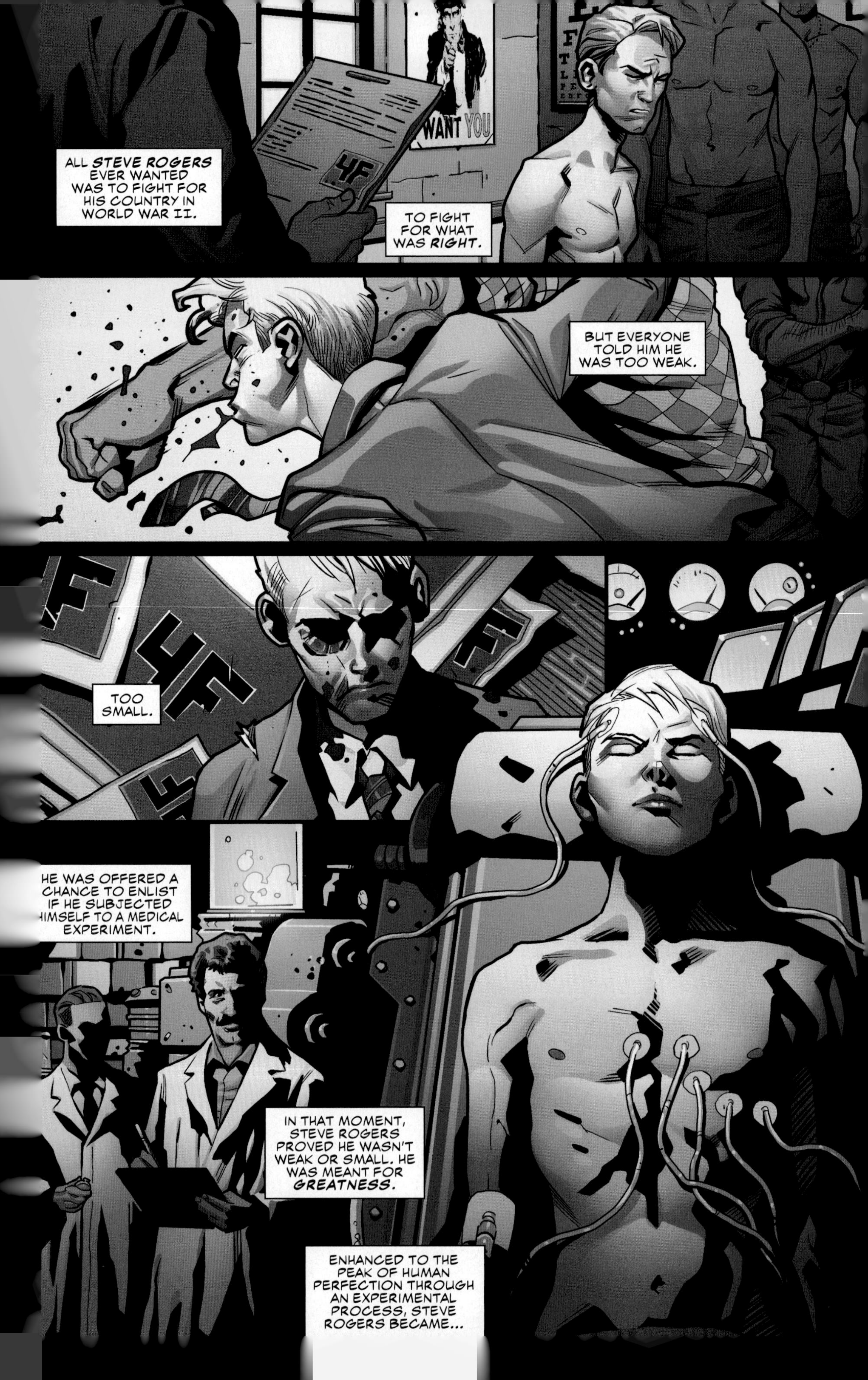
ALL STEVE ROGERS EVER WANTED WAS TO FIGHT FOR HIS COUNTRY IN WORLD WAR II.
I WANT YOU
4F
TO FIGHT FOR WHAT WAS RIGHT.
BUT EVERYONE TOLD HIM HE WAS TOO WEAK.
TOO SMALL.
HE WAS OFFERED A CHANCE TO ENLIST IF HE SUBJECTED HIMSELF TO A MEDICAL EXPERIMENT.
IN THAT MOMENT, STEVE ROGERS PROVED HE WASN'T WEAK OR SMALL. HE WAS MEANT FOR GREATNESS.
ENHANCED TO THE PEAK OF HUMAN PERFECTION THROUGH AN EXPERIMENTAL PROCESS, STEVE ROGERS BECAME...

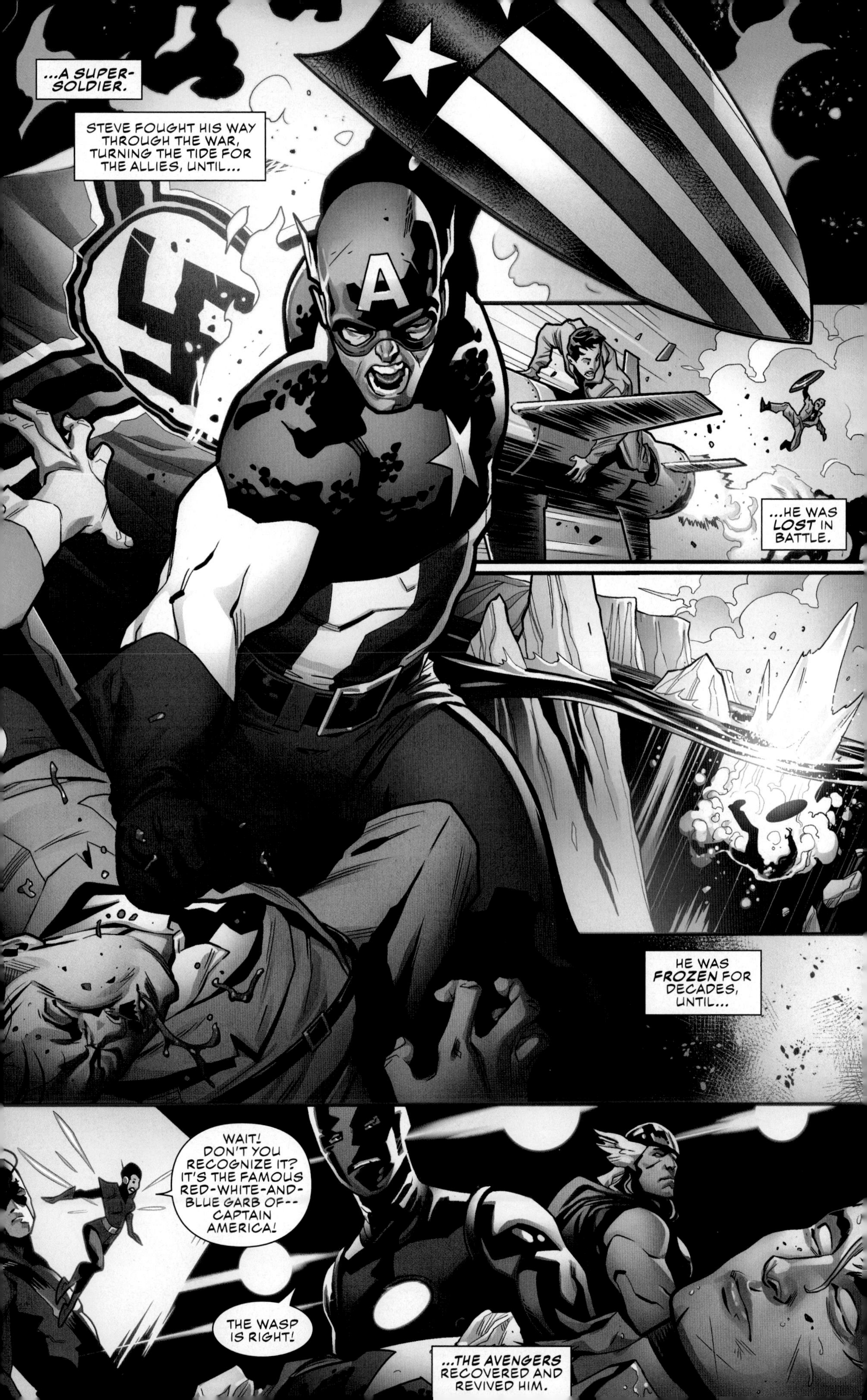
...A SUPER-SOLDIER.
STEVE FOUGHT HIS WAY THROUGH THE WAR, TURNING THE TIDE FOR THE ALLIES, UNTIL...
...HE WAS LOST IN BATTLE.
HE WAS FROZEN FOR DECADES, UNTIL...
WAIT! DON'T YOU RECOGNIZE IT? IT'S THE FAMOUS RED-WHITE-AND-BLUE GARB OF--CAPTAIN AMERICA!
THE WASP IS RIGHT!
...THE AVENGERS RECOVERED AND REVIVED HIM.

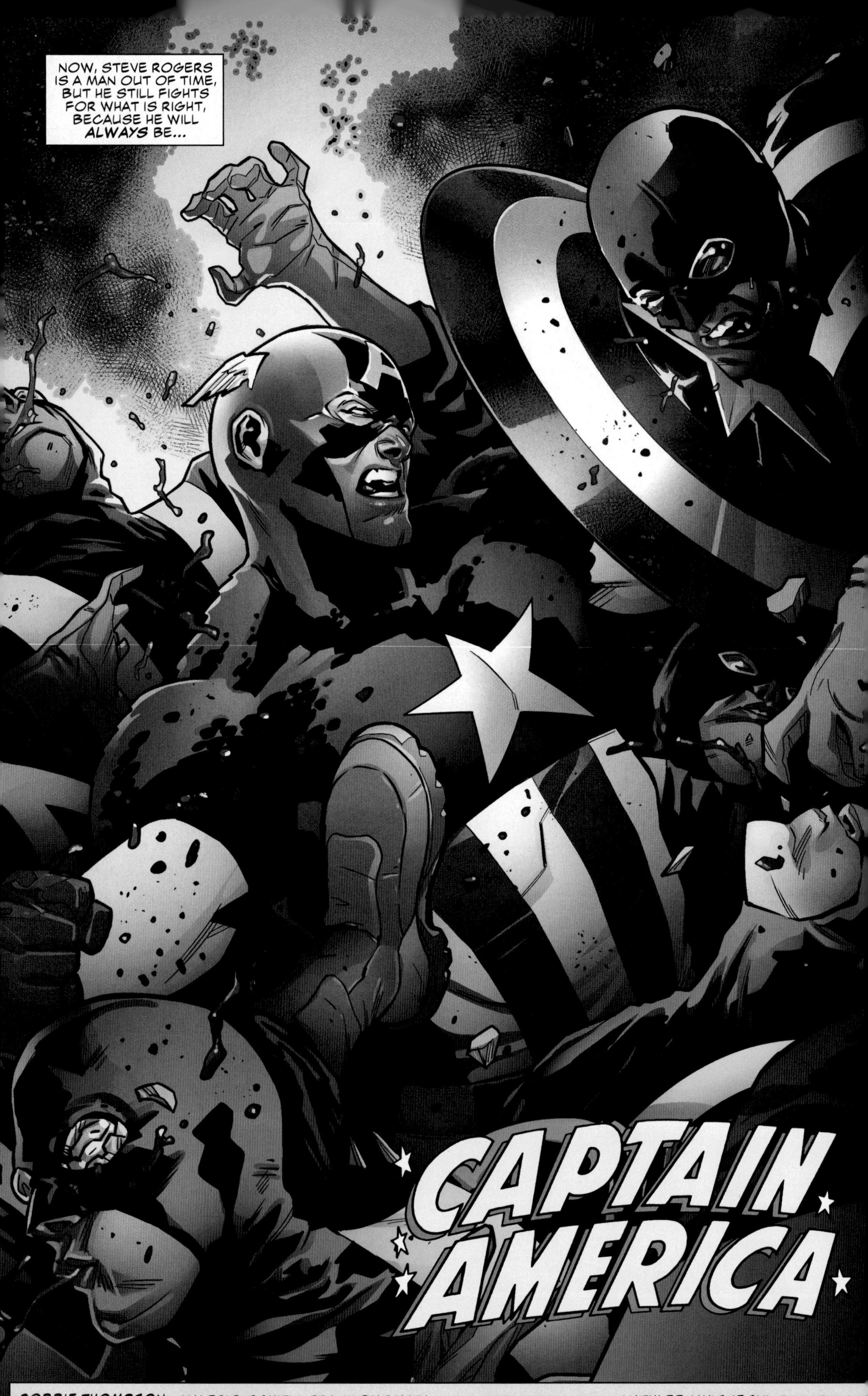
NOW, STEVE ROGERS IS A MAN OUT OF TIME, BUT HE STILL FIGHTS FOR WHAT IS RIGHT, BECAUSE HE WILL ALWAYS BE...
CAPTAIN AMERICA

ROBBIE THOMPSON WRITER | VALERIO SCHITI ARTIST | FRANK D'ARMATA COLORIST | VC'S JOE CARAMAGNA LETTERER | KATHLEEN WISNESKI ASSISTANT EDITOR | DARREN SHA EDITOR

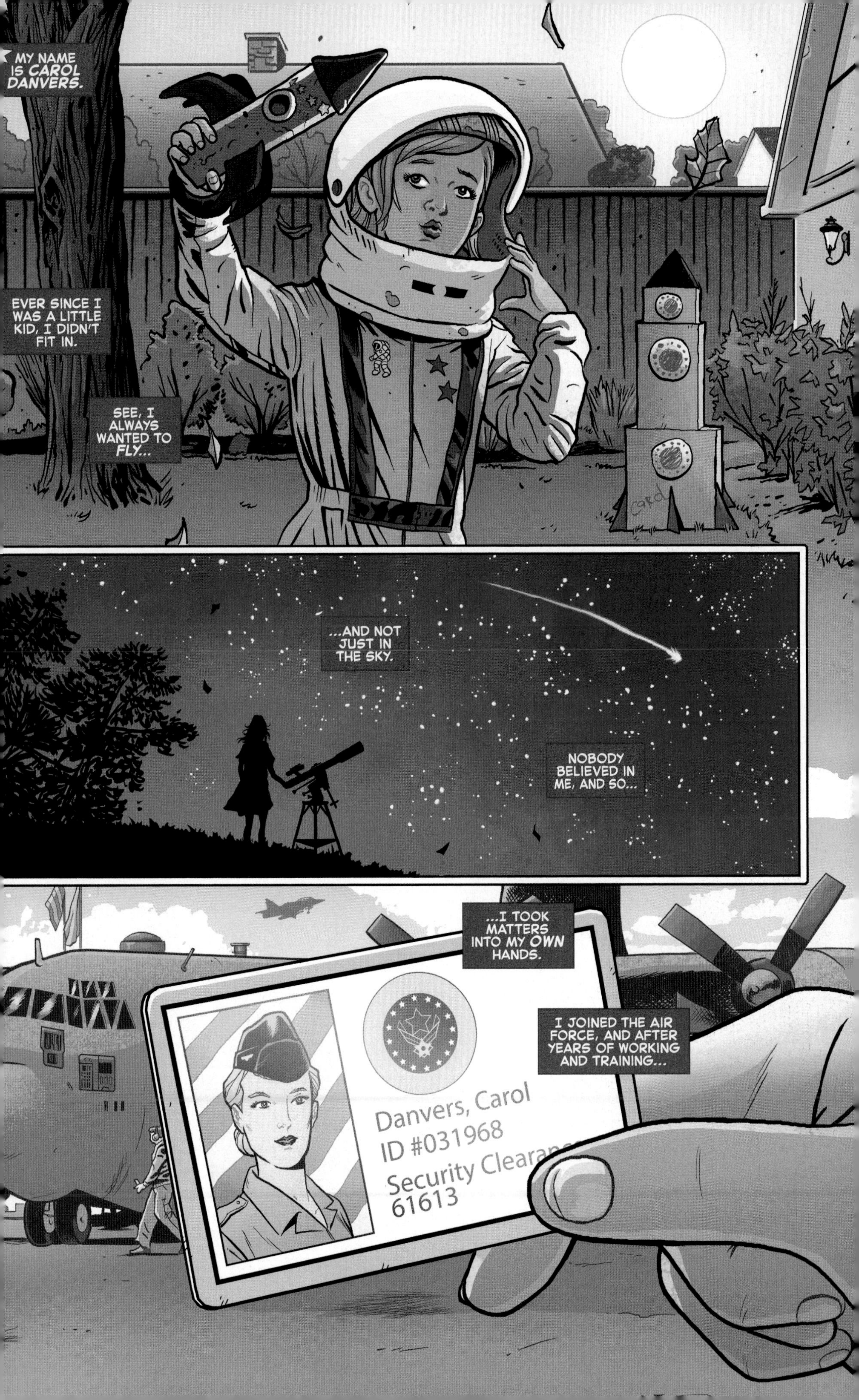
MY NAME IS CAROL DANVERS.
EVER SINCE I WAS A LITTLE KID, I DIDN'T FIT IN.
SEE, I ALWAYS WANTED TO FLY...
CAROL
...AND NOT JUST IN THE SKY.
NOBODY BELIEVED IN ME, AND SO...
...I TOOK MATTERS INTO MY OWN HANDS.
I JOINED THE AIR FORCE, AND AFTER YEARS OF WORKING AND TRAINING...
Danvers, Carol
ID #031968
Security Clearan
61613

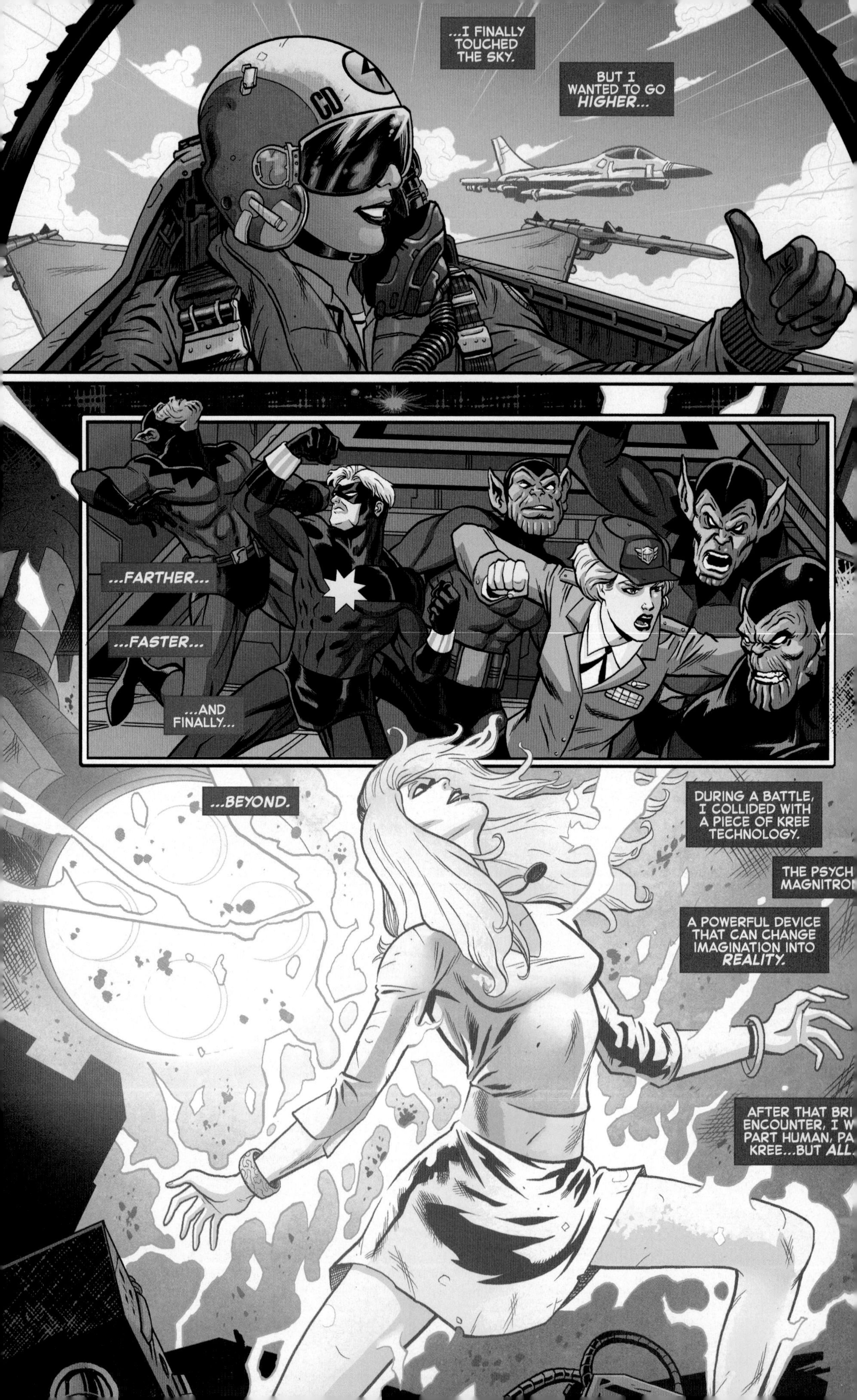
...I FINALLY TOUCHED THE SKY.
BUT I WANTED TO GO *HIGHER*...
...FARTHER...
...FASTER...
...AND FINALLY...
...BEYOND.
DURING A BATTLE, I COLLIDED WITH A PIECE OF KREE TECHNOLOGY.
THE PSYCH MAGNITRO
A POWERFUL DEVICE THAT CAN CHANGE IMAGINATION INTO *REALITY*.
AFTER THAT BRI ENCOUNTER, I W PART HUMAN, PA KREE...BUT *ALL*

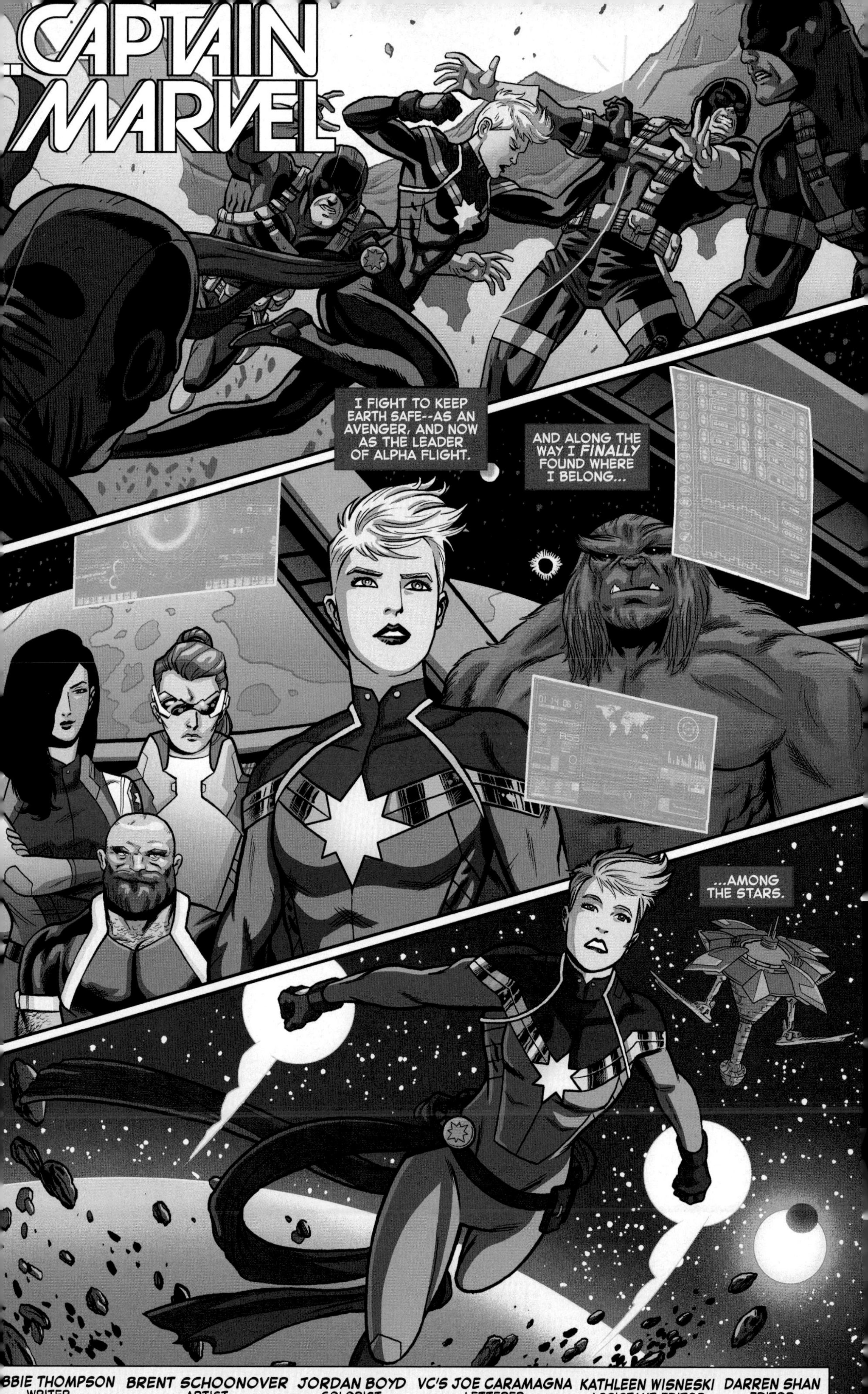
CAPTAIN MARVEL
I FIGHT TO KEEP EARTH SAFE--AS AN AVENGER, AND NOW AS THE LEADER OF ALPHA FLIGHT.
AND ALONG THE WAY I *FINALLY* FOUND WHERE I BELONG...
...AMONG THE STARS.

BBIE THOMPSON WRITER | BRENT SCHOONOVER ARTIST | JORDAN BOYD COLORIST | VC'S JOE CARAMAGNA LETTERER | KATHLEEN WISNESKI ASSISTANT EDITOR | DARREN SHAN EDITOR

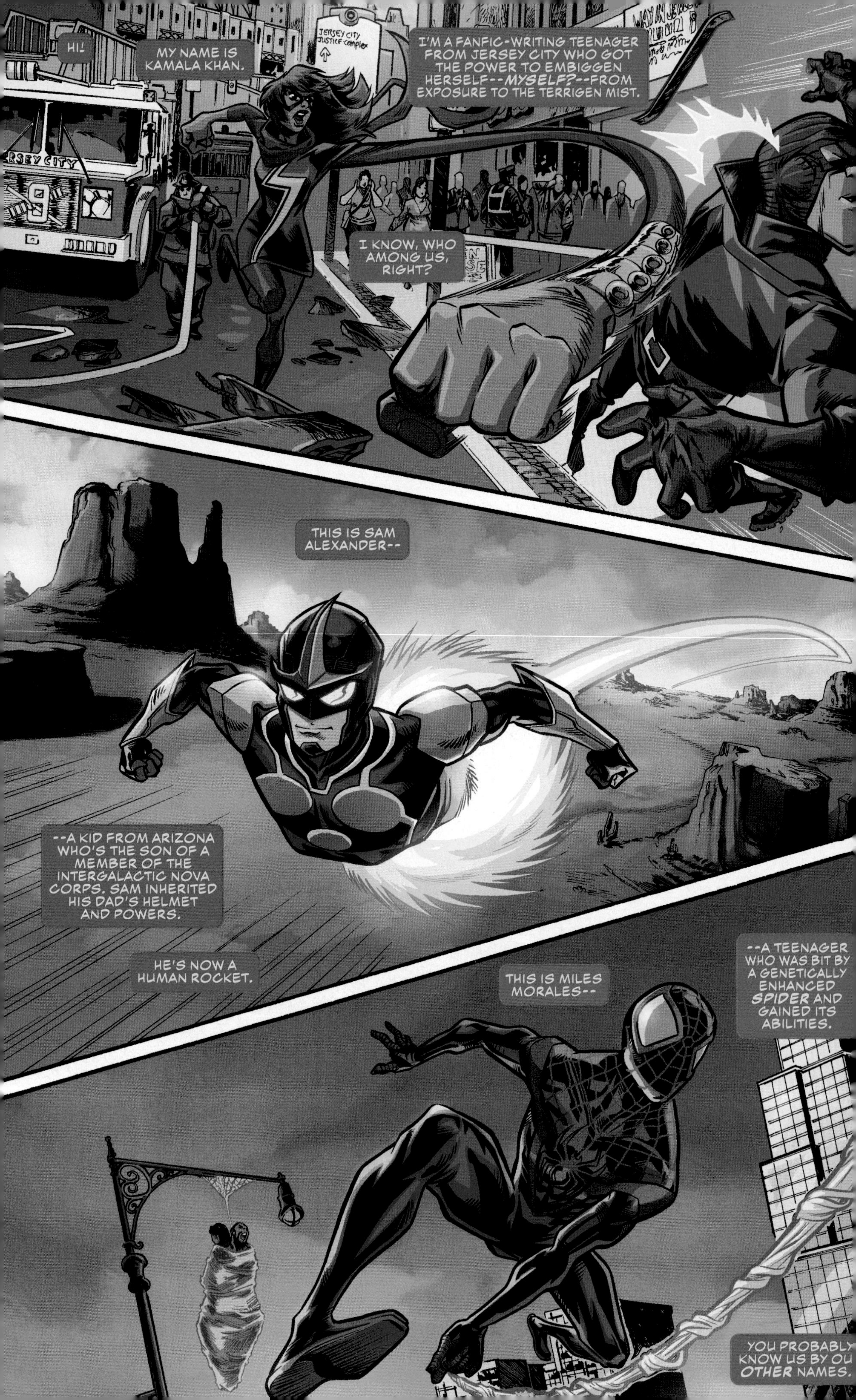
HI!
MY NAME IS KAMALA KHAN.
JERSEY CITY JUSTICE complex
I'M A FANFIC-WRITING TEENAGER FROM JERSEY CITY WHO GOT THE POWER TO EMBIGGEN HERSELF--MYSELF?--FROM EXPOSURE TO THE TERRIGEN MIST.
I KNOW, WHO AMONG US, RIGHT?
THIS IS SAM ALEXANDER--
--A KID FROM ARIZONA WHO'S THE SON OF A MEMBER OF THE INTERGALACTIC NOVA CORPS. SAM INHERITED HIS DAD'S HELMET AND POWERS.
HE'S NOW A HUMAN ROCKET.
THIS IS MILES MORALES--
--A TEENAGER WHO WAS BIT BY A GENETICALLY ENHANCED SPIDER AND GAINED ITS ABILITIES.
YOU PROBABLY KNOW US BY OU OTHER NAMES.

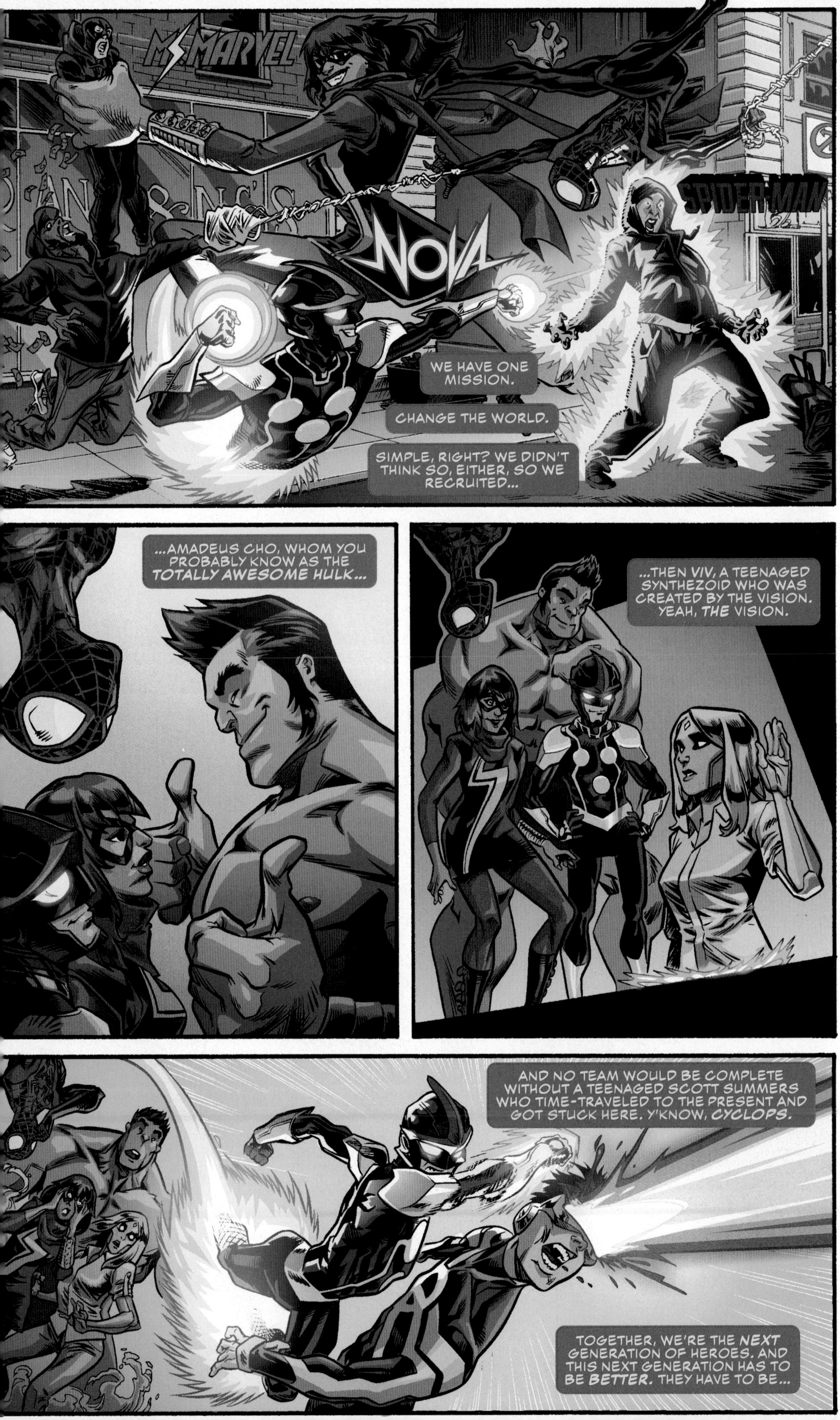
M MARVEL
SPIDER-MAN
NOVA
WE HAVE ONE MISSION.
CHANGE THE WORLD.
SIMPLE, RIGHT? WE DIDN'T THINK SO, EITHER, SO WE RECRUITED...
...AMADEUS CHO, WHOM YOU PROBABLY KNOW AS THE *TOTALLY AWESOME HULK*...
...THEN VIV, A TEENAGED SYNTHEZOID WHO WAS CREATED BY THE VISION. YEAH, *THE* VISION.
AND NO TEAM WOULD BE COMPLETE WITHOUT A TEENAGED SCOTT SUMMERS WHO TIME-TRAVELED TO THE PRESENT AND GOT STUCK HERE. Y'KNOW, *CYCLOPS*.
TOGETHER, WE'RE THE *NEXT* GENERATION OF HEROES. AND THIS NEXT GENERATION HAS TO BE *BETTER*. THEY HAVE TO BE...

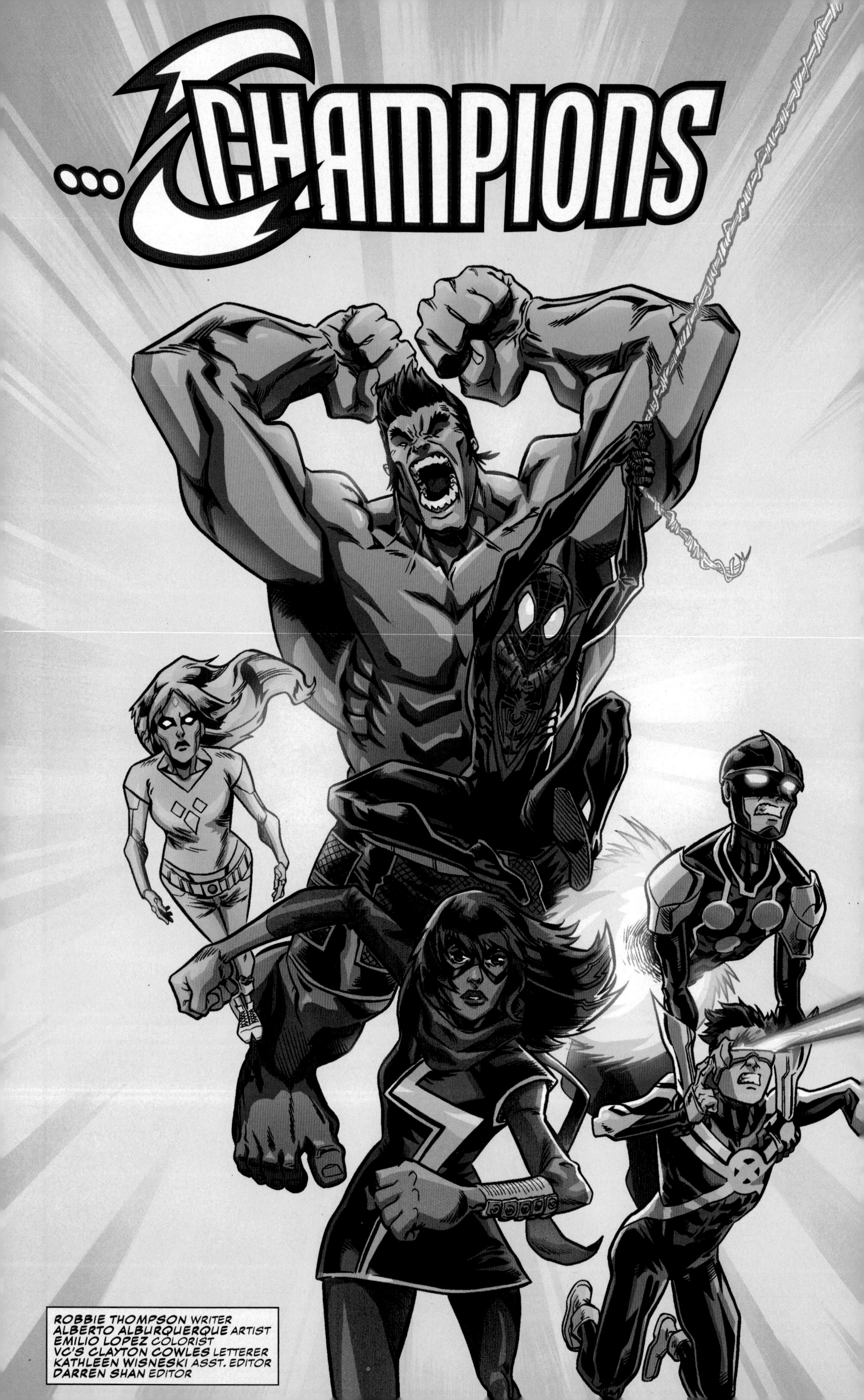
...CHAMPIONS
ROBBIE THOMPSON WRITER
ALBERTO ALBURQUERQUE ARTIST
EMILIO LOPEZ COLORIST
VC'S CLAYTON COWLES LETTERER
KATHLEEN WISNESKI ASST. EDITOR
DARREN SHAN EDITOR

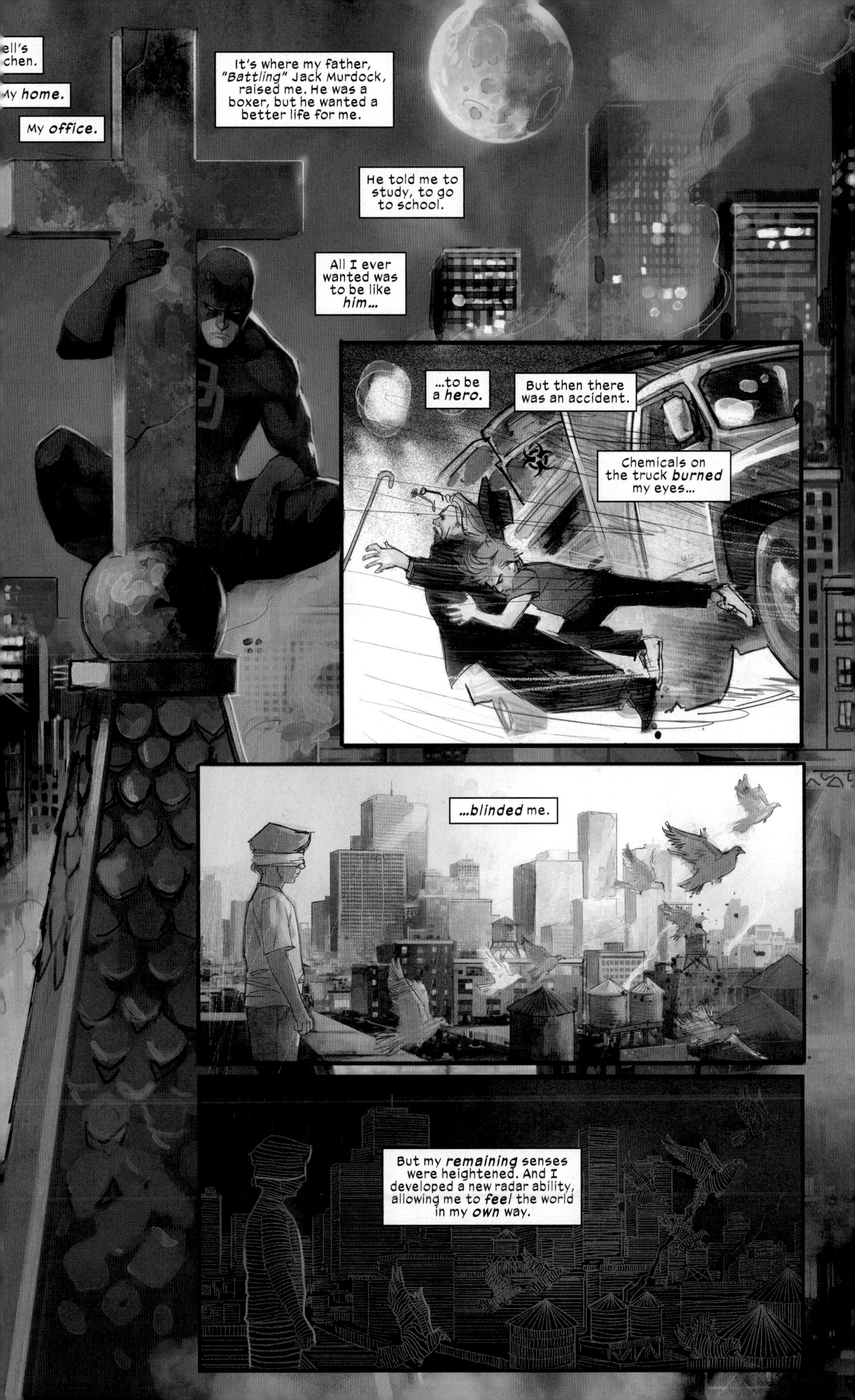
ell's
chen.
My home.
My office.
It's where my father, "Battling" Jack Murdock, raised me. He was a boxer, but he wanted a better life for me.
He told me to study, to go to school.
All I ever wanted was to be like him...
...to be a hero.
But then there was an accident.
Chemicals on the truck burned my eyes...
...blinded me.
But my remaining senses were heightened. And I developed a new radar ability, allowing me to feel the world in my own way.

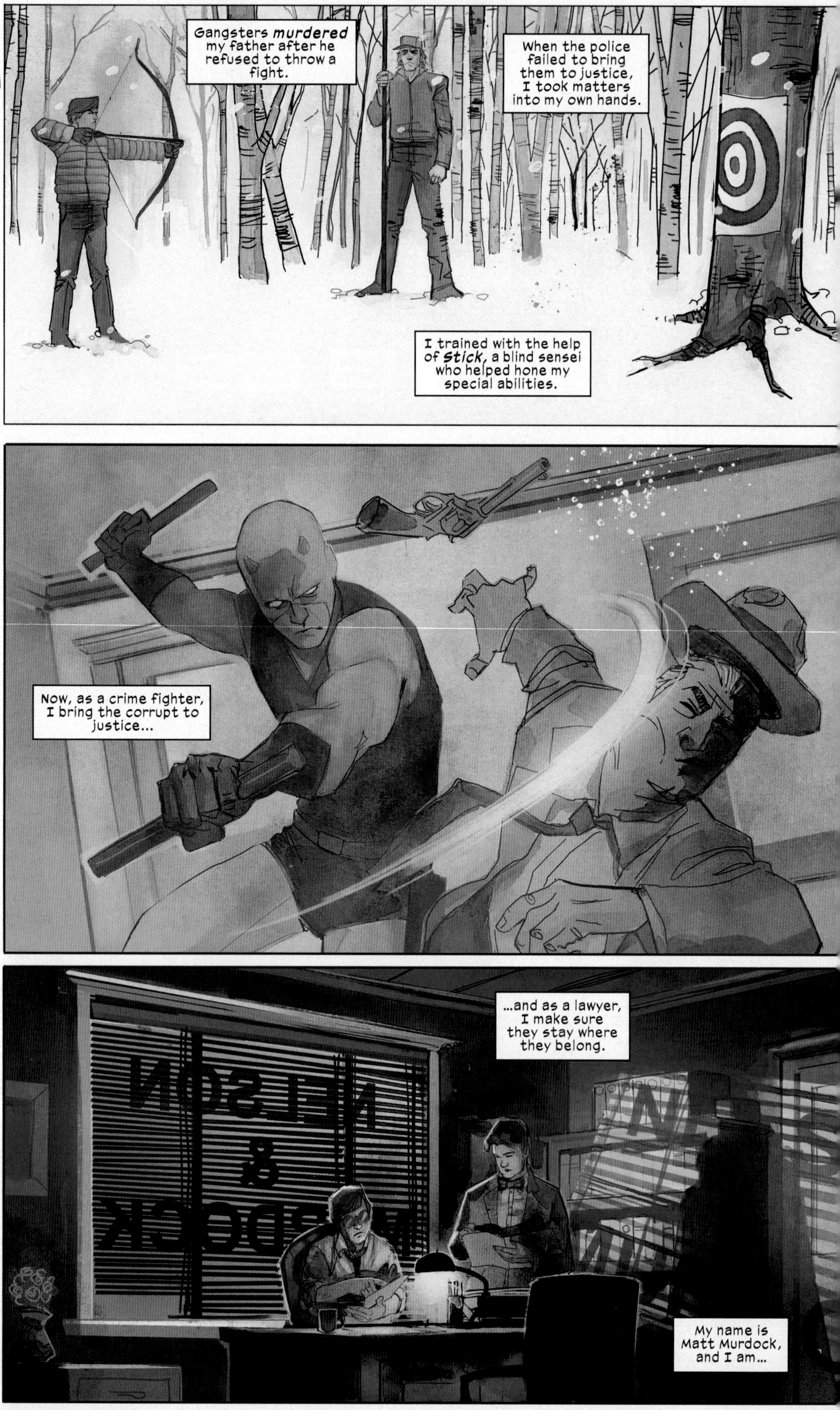
Gangsters *murdered* my father after he refused to throw a fight.
When the police failed to bring them to justice, I took matters into my own hands.
I trained with the help of *Stick*, a blind sensei who helped hone my special abilities.
Now, as a crime fighter, I bring the corrupt to justice...
...and as a lawyer, I make sure they stay where they belong.
My name is Matt Murdock, and I am...

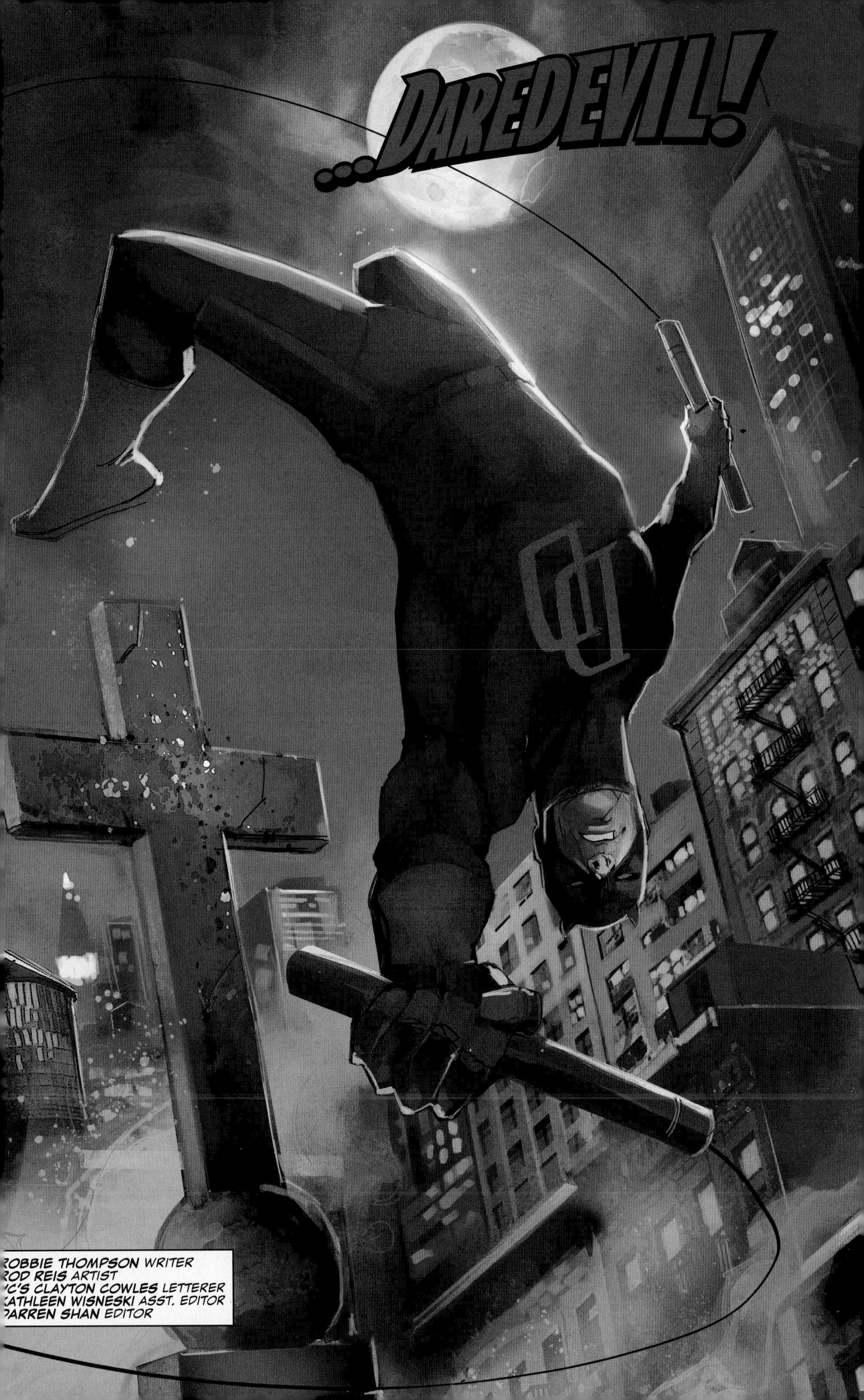
...DAREDEVIL!
ROBBIE THOMPSON WRITER
ROD REIS ARTIST
VC'S CLAYTON COWLES LETTERER
KATHLEEN WISNESKI ASST. EDITOR
DARREN SHAN EDITOR

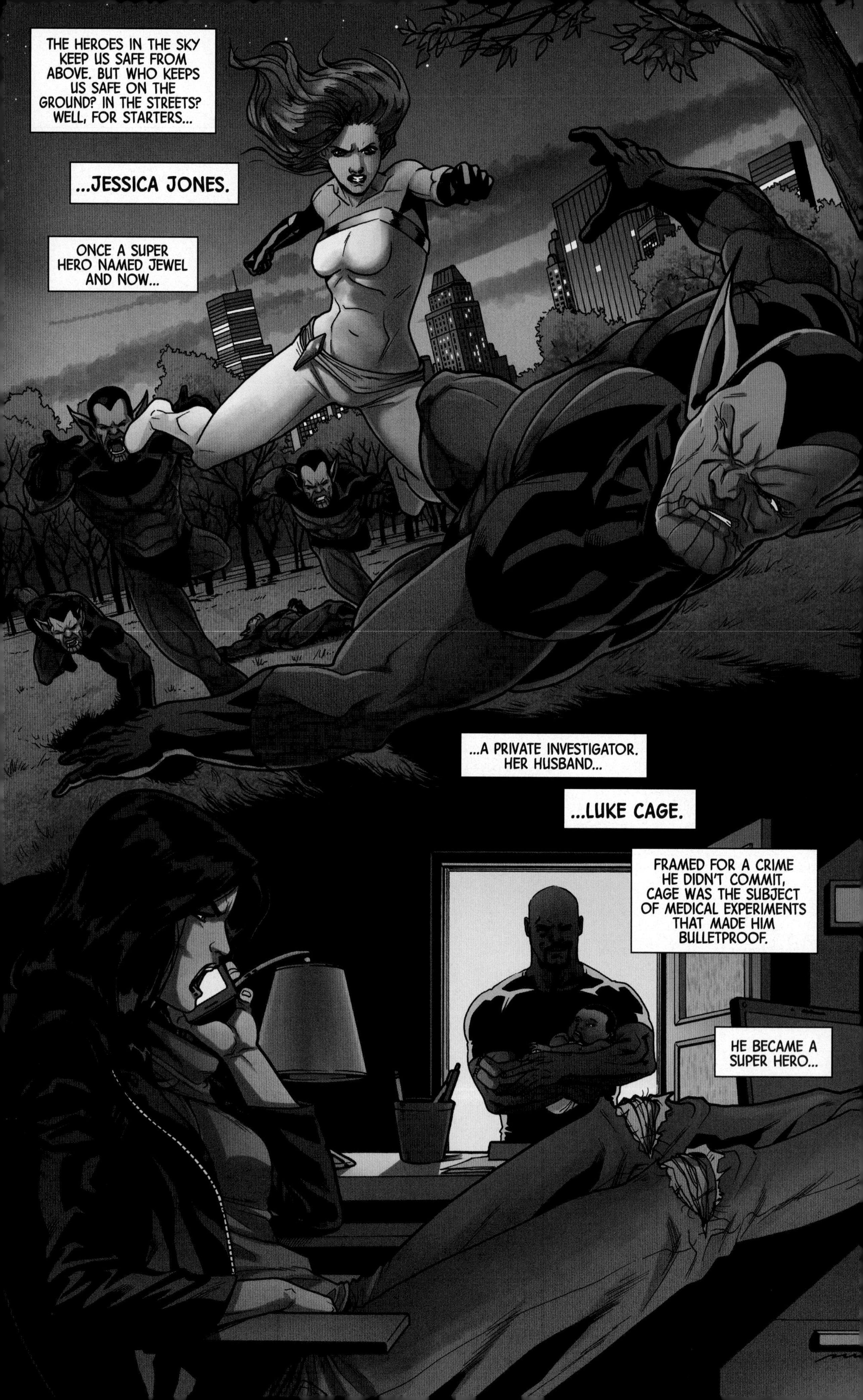
THE HEROES IN THE SKY KEEP US SAFE FROM ABOVE. BUT WHO KEEPS US SAFE ON THE GROUND? IN THE STREETS? WELL, FOR STARTERS...
...JESSICA JONES.
ONCE A SUPER HERO NAMED JEWEL AND NOW...
...A PRIVATE INVESTIGATOR. HER HUSBAND...
...LUKE CAGE.
FRAMED FOR A CRIME HE DIDN'T COMMIT, CAGE WAS THE SUBJECT OF MEDICAL EXPERIMENTS THAT MADE HIM BULLETPROOF.
HE BECAME A SUPER HERO...

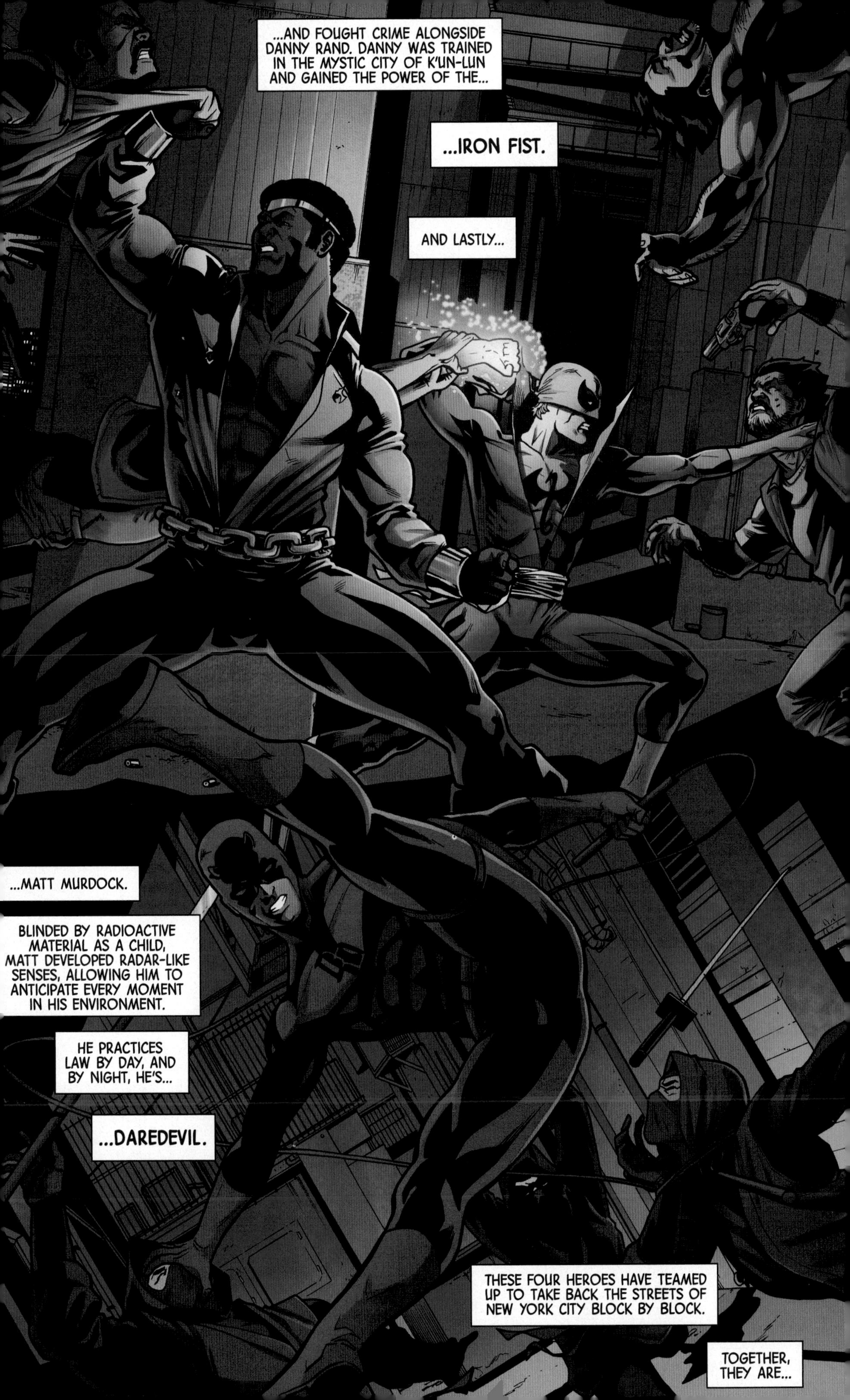
...AND FOUGHT CRIME ALONGSIDE DANNY RAND. DANNY WAS TRAINED IN THE MYSTIC CITY OF K'UN-LUN AND GAINED THE POWER OF THE...
...IRON FIST.
AND LASTLY...
...MATT MURDOCK.
BLINDED BY RADIOACTIVE MATERIAL AS A CHILD, MATT DEVELOPED RADAR-LIKE SENSES, ALLOWING HIM TO ANTICIPATE EVERY MOMENT IN HIS ENVIRONMENT.
HE PRACTICES LAW BY DAY, AND BY NIGHT, HE'S...
...DAREDEVIL.
THESE FOUR HEROES HAVE TEAMED UP TO TAKE BACK THE STREETS OF NEW YORK CITY BLOCK BY BLOCK.
TOGETHER, THEY ARE...

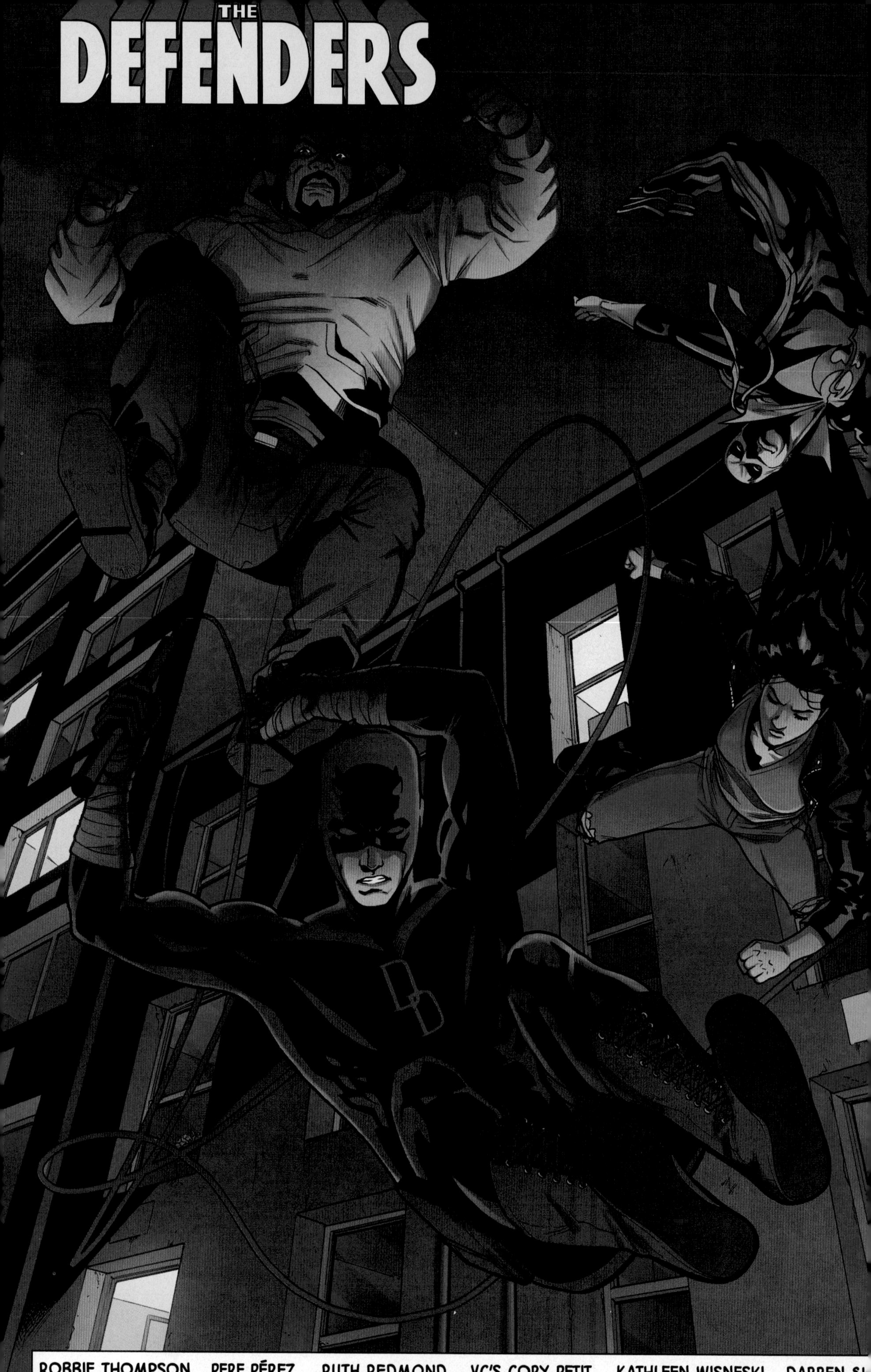
THE DEFENDERS

ROBBIE THOMPSON WRITER | PERE PÉREZ ARTIST | RUTH REDMOND COLOR ARTIST | VC'S CORY PETIT LETTERER | KATHLEEN WISNESKI ASSISTANT EDITOR | DARREN S EDITOR

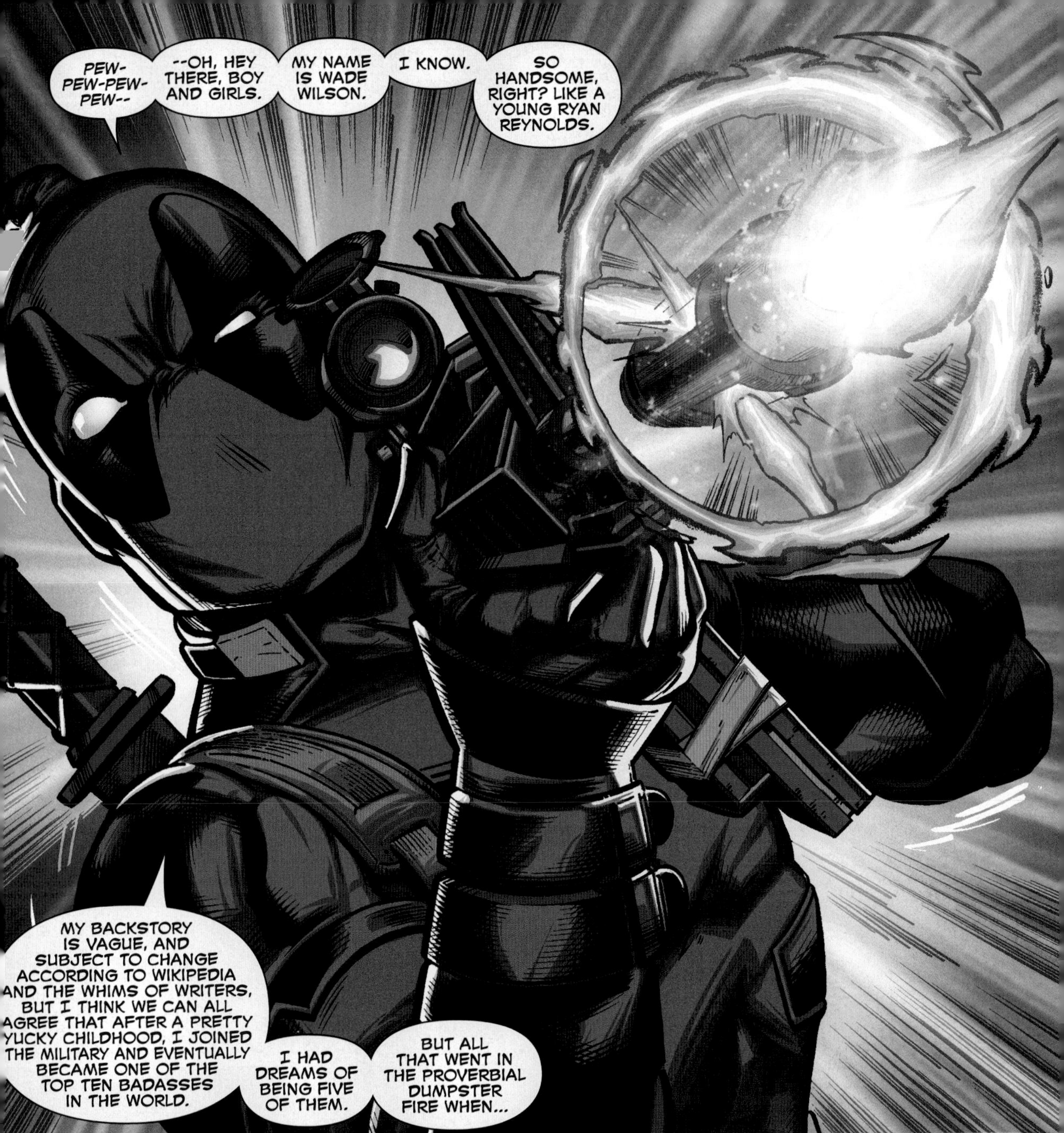
PEW-PEW-PEW-PEW--
--OH, HEY THERE, BOY AND GIRLS.
MY NAME IS WADE WILSON.
I KNOW.
SO HANDSOME, RIGHT? LIKE A YOUNG RYAN REYNOLDS.
MY BACKSTORY IS VAGUE, AND SUBJECT TO CHANGE ACCORDING TO WIKIPEDIA AND THE WHIMS OF WRITERS, BUT I THINK WE CAN ALL AGREE THAT AFTER A PRETTY YUCKY CHILDHOOD, I JOINED THE MILITARY AND EVENTUALLY BECAME ONE OF THE TOP TEN BADASSES IN THE WORLD.
I HAD DREAMS OF BEING FIVE OF THEM.
BUT ALL THAT WENT IN THE PROVERBIAL DUMPSTER FIRE WHEN...

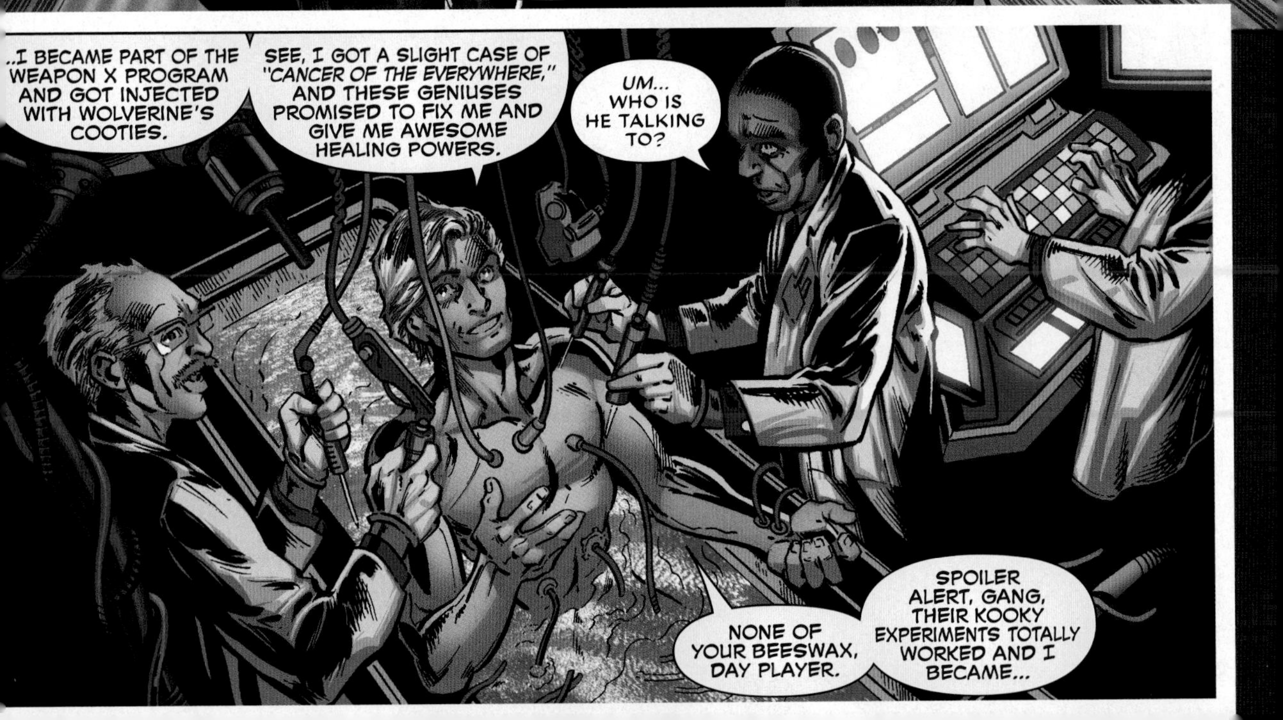
..I BECAME PART OF THE WEAPON X PROGRAM AND GOT INJECTED WITH WOLVERINE'S COOTIES.
SEE, I GOT A SLIGHT CASE OF *"CANCER OF THE EVERYWHERE,"* AND THESE GENIUSES PROMISED TO FIX ME AND GIVE ME AWESOME HEALING POWERS.
UM... WHO IS HE TALKING TO?
NONE OF YOUR BEESWAX, DAY PLAYER.
SPOILER ALERT, GANG, THEIR KOOKY EXPERIMENTS TOTALLY WORKED AND I BECAME...

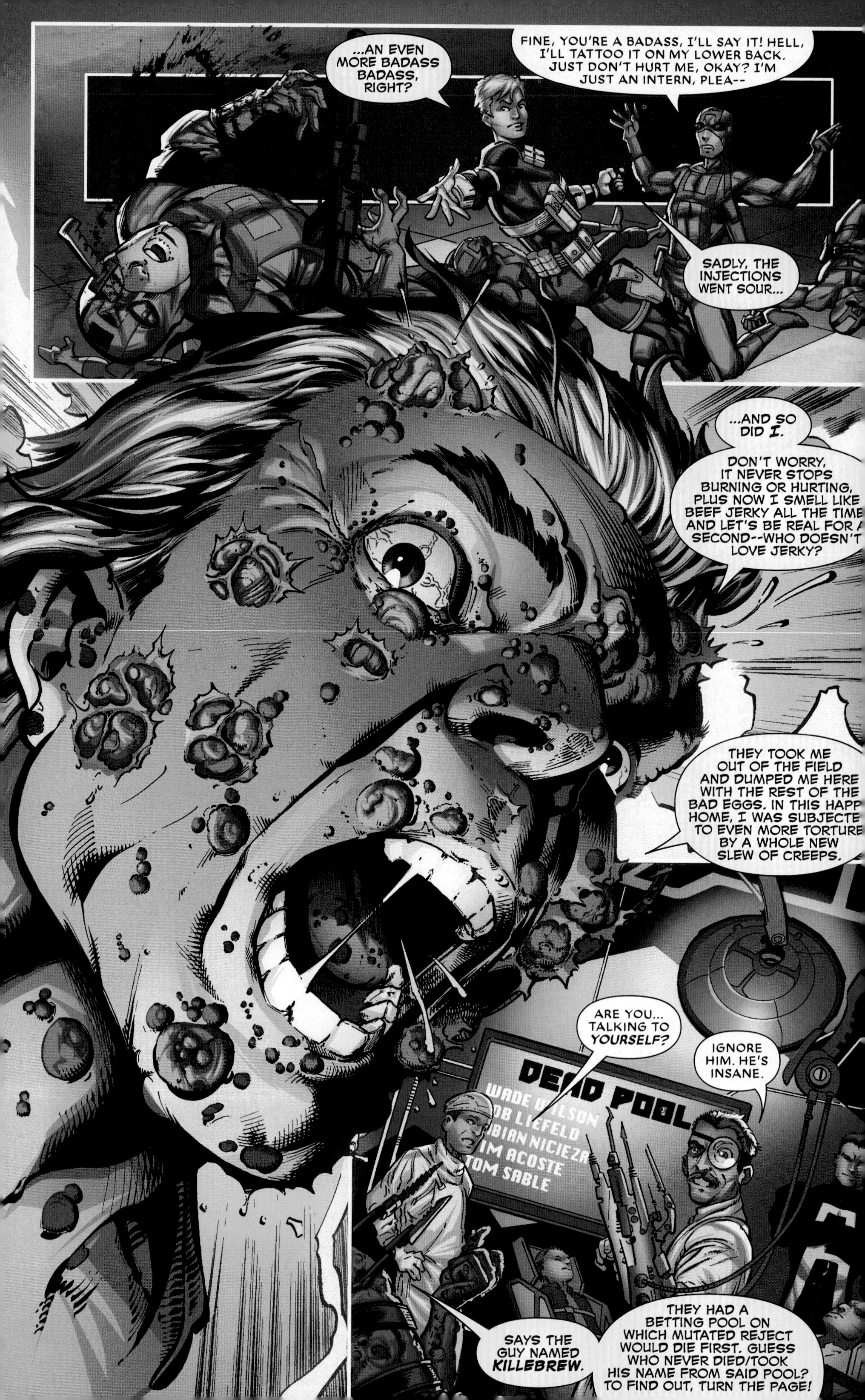
...AN EVEN MORE BADASS BADASS, RIGHT?
FINE, YOU'RE A BADASS, I'LL SAY IT! HELL, I'LL TATTOO IT ON MY LOWER BACK. JUST DON'T HURT ME, OKAY? I'M JUST AN INTERN, PLEA--
SADLY, THE INJECTIONS WENT SOUR...
...AND SO DID I.
DON'T WORRY, IT NEVER STOPS BURNING OR HURTING, PLUS NOW I SMELL LIKE BEEF JERKY ALL THE TIME AND LET'S BE REAL FOR A SECOND--WHO DOESN'T LOVE JERKY?
THEY TOOK ME OUT OF THE FIELD AND DUMPED ME HERE WITH THE REST OF THE BAD EGGS. IN THIS HAPP HOME, I WAS SUBJECTE TO EVEN MORE TORTURE BY A WHOLE NEW SLEW OF CREEPS.
ARE YOU... TALKING TO YOURSELF?
IGNORE HIM. HE'S INSANE.
DEAD POOL
WADE WILSON
OB LIEFELD
BIAN NICIEZA
IM ACOSTE
TOM SABLE
SAYS THE GUY NAMED KILLEBREW.
THEY HAD A BETTING POOL ON WHICH MUTATED REJECT WOULD DIE FIRST. GUESS WHO NEVER DIED/TOOK HIS NAME FROM SAID POOL? TO FIND OUT, TURN THE PAGE!

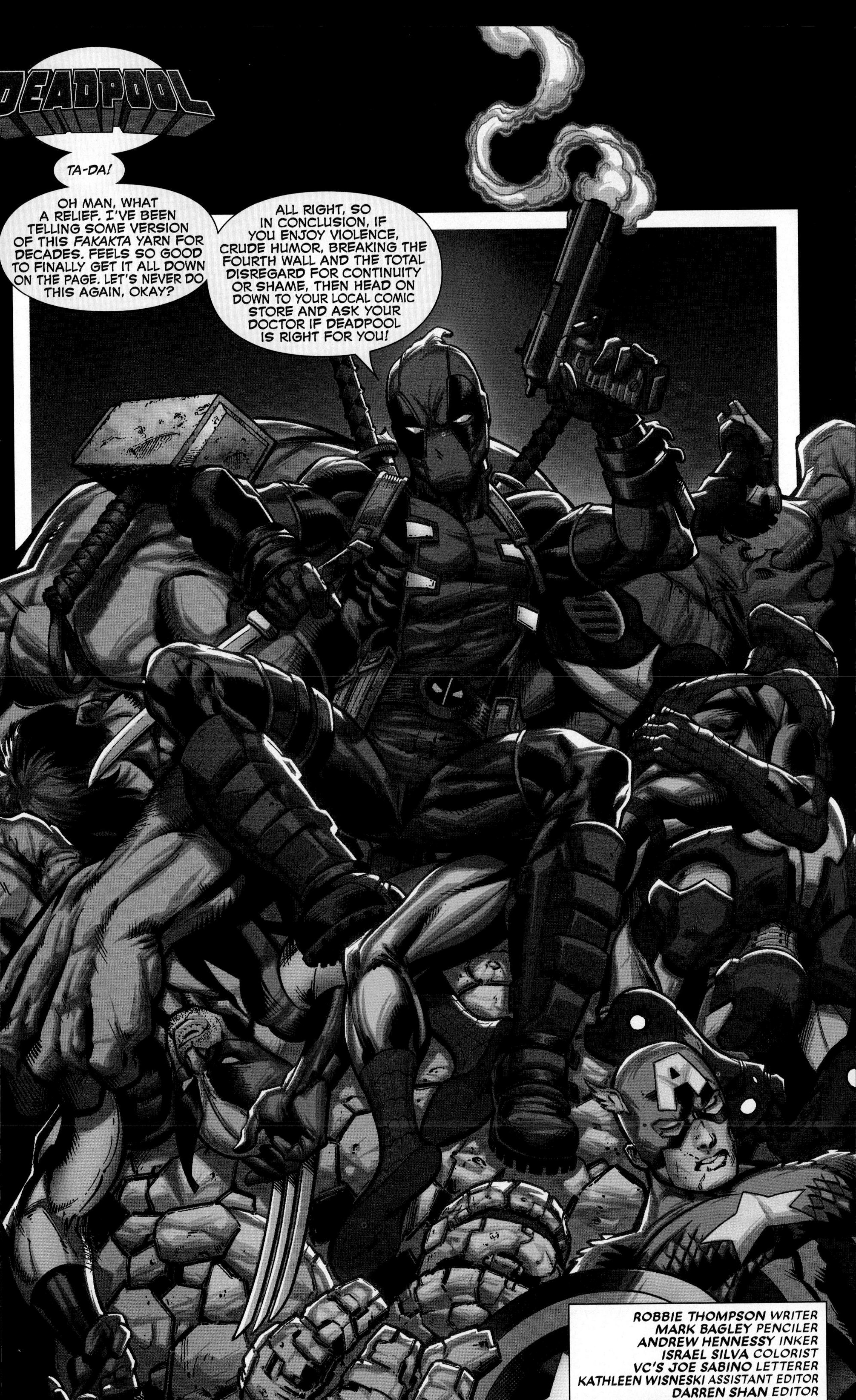
DEADPOOL
TA-DA!
OH MAN, WHAT A RELIEF. I'VE BEEN TELLING SOME VERSION OF THIS FAKAKTA YARN FOR DECADES. FEELS SO GOOD TO FINALLY GET IT ALL DOWN ON THE PAGE. LET'S NEVER DO THIS AGAIN, OKAY?
ALL RIGHT, SO IN CONCLUSION, IF YOU ENJOY VIOLENCE, CRUDE HUMOR, BREAKING THE FOURTH WALL AND THE TOTAL DISREGARD FOR CONTINUITY OR SHAME, THEN HEAD ON DOWN TO YOUR LOCAL COMIC STORE AND ASK YOUR DOCTOR IF DEADPOOL IS RIGHT FOR YOU!
ROBBIE THOMPSON WRITER
MARK BAGLEY PENCILER
ANDREW HENNESSY INKER
ISRAEL SILVA COLORIST
VC'S JOE SABINO LETTERER
KATHLEEN WISNESKI ASSISTANT EDITOR
DARREN SHAN EDITOR

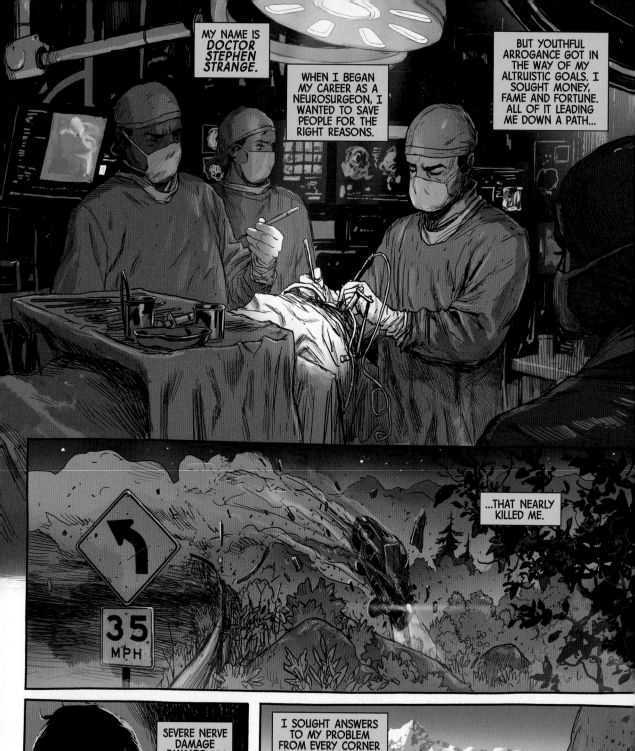

MY NAME IS DOCTOR STEPHEN STRANGE.

WHEN I BEGAN MY CAREER AS A NEUROSURGEON, I WANTED TO SAVE PEOPLE FOR THE RIGHT REASONS.

BUT YOUTHFUL ARROGANCE GOT IN THE WAY OF MY ALTRUISTIC GOALS. I SOUGHT MONEY, FAME AND FORTUNE. ALL OF IT LEADING ME DOWN A PATH...

...THAT NEARLY KILLED ME.

SEVERE NERVE DAMAGE *RUINED* MY HANDS.

I SOUGHT ANSWERS TO MY PROBLEM FROM EVERY CORNER OF THE EARTH.

AND THEN I DISCOVERED A *NEW* PATH, A PATH THAT INVOLVED...

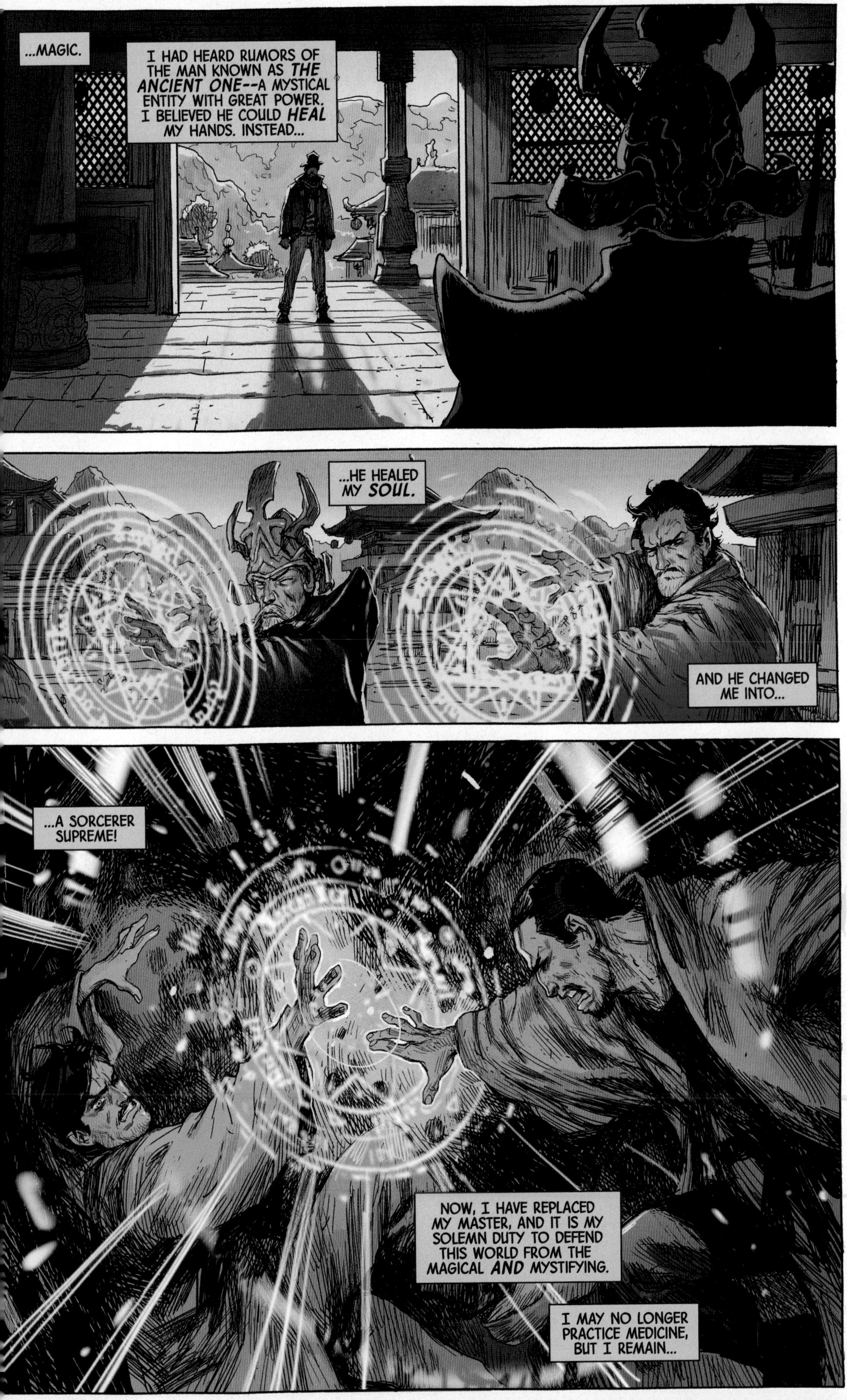
...MAGIC.
I HAD HEARD RUMORS OF THE MAN KNOWN AS THE ANCIENT ONE--A MYSTICAL ENTITY WITH GREAT POWER. I BELIEVED HE COULD HEAL MY HANDS. INSTEAD...
...HE HEALED MY SOUL.
AND HE CHANGED ME INTO...
...A SORCERER SUPREME!
NOW, I HAVE REPLACED MY MASTER, AND IT IS MY SOLEMN DUTY TO DEFEND THIS WORLD FROM THE MAGICAL AND MYSTIFYING.
I MAY NO LONGER PRACTICE MEDICINE, BUT I REMAIN...

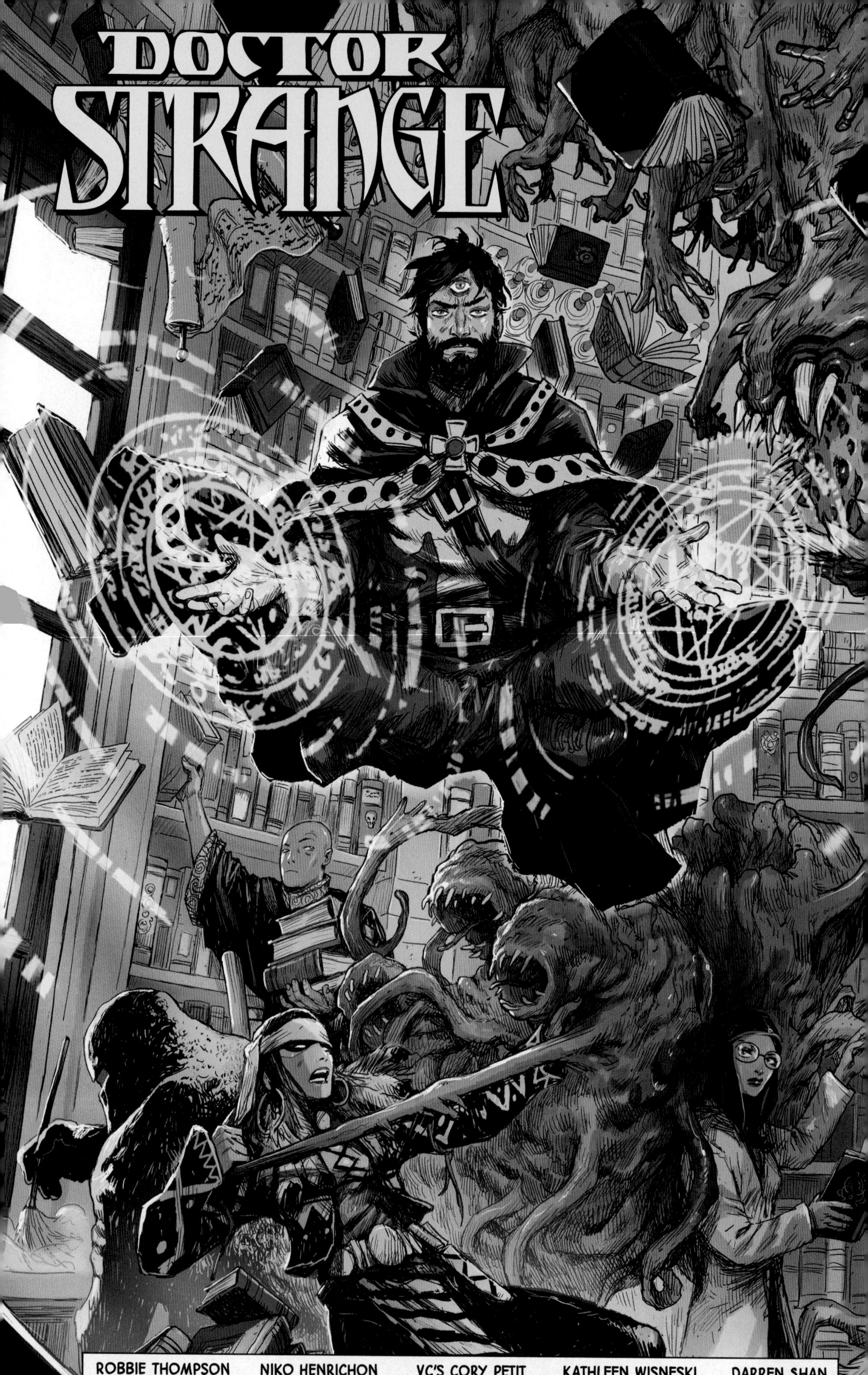
DOCTOR STRANGE

ROBBIE THOMPSON WRITER | NIKO HENRICHON ARTIST | VC'S CORY PETIT LETTERER | KATHLEEN WISNESKI ASSISTANT EDITOR | DARREN SHAN EDITOR

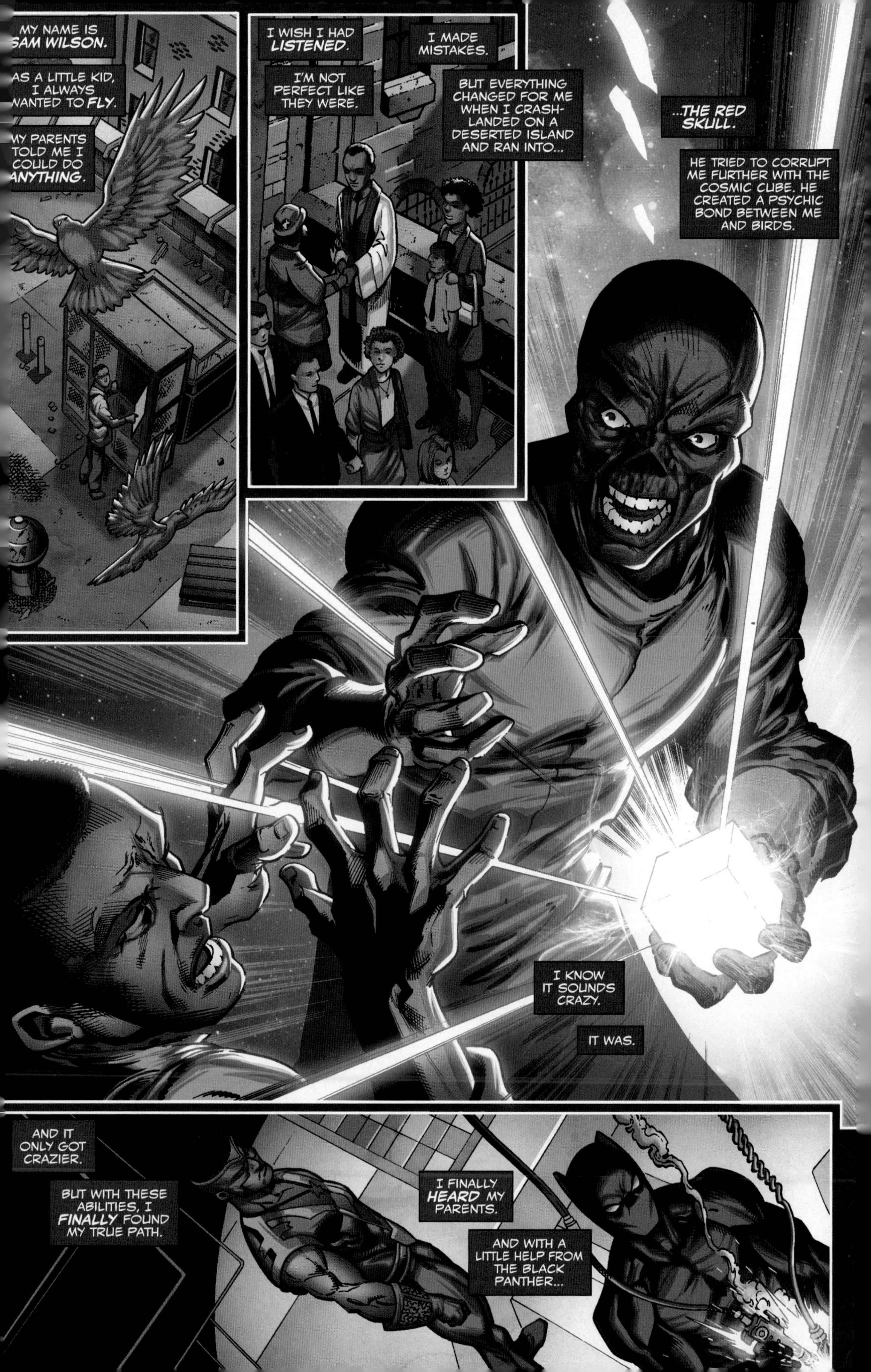
MY NAME IS SAM WILSON.
AS A LITTLE KID, I ALWAYS WANTED TO FLY.
MY PARENTS TOLD ME I COULD DO ANYTHING.
I WISH I HAD LISTENED.
I'M NOT PERFECT LIKE THEY WERE.
I MADE MISTAKES.
BUT EVERYTHING CHANGED FOR ME WHEN I CRASH-LANDED ON A DESERTED ISLAND AND RAN INTO...
...THE RED SKULL.
HE TRIED TO CORRUPT ME FURTHER WITH THE COSMIC CUBE. HE CREATED A PSYCHIC BOND BETWEEN ME AND BIRDS.
I KNOW IT SOUNDS CRAZY.
IT WAS.
AND IT ONLY GOT CRAZIER.
BUT WITH THESE ABILITIES, I FINALLY FOUND MY TRUE PATH.
I FINALLY HEARD MY PARENTS.
AND WITH A LITTLE HELP FROM THE BLACK PANTHER...

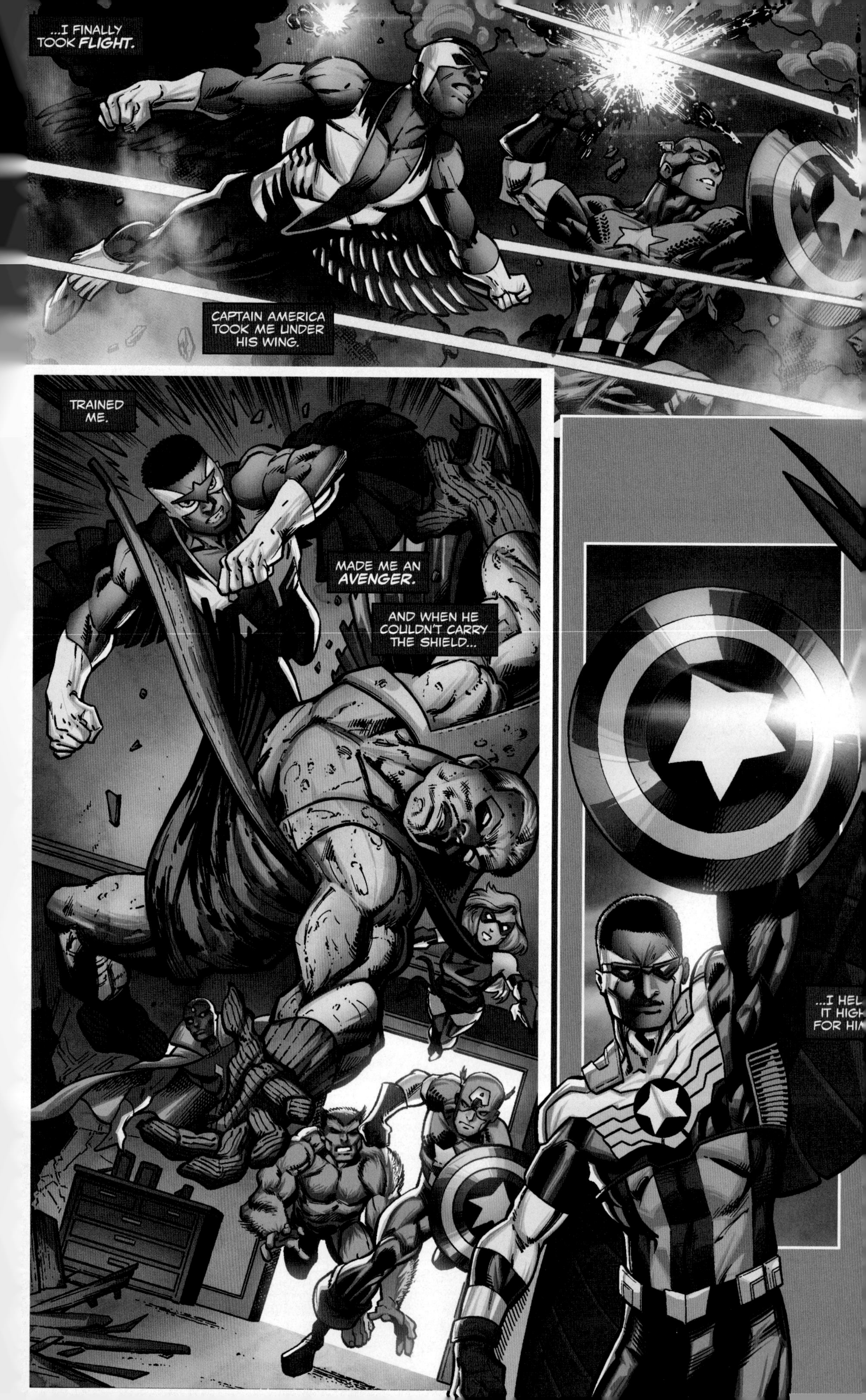
...I FINALLY TOOK FLIGHT.
CAPTAIN AMERICA TOOK ME UNDER HIS WING.
TRAINED ME.
MADE ME AN AVENGER.
AND WHEN HE COULDN'T CARRY THE SHIELD...

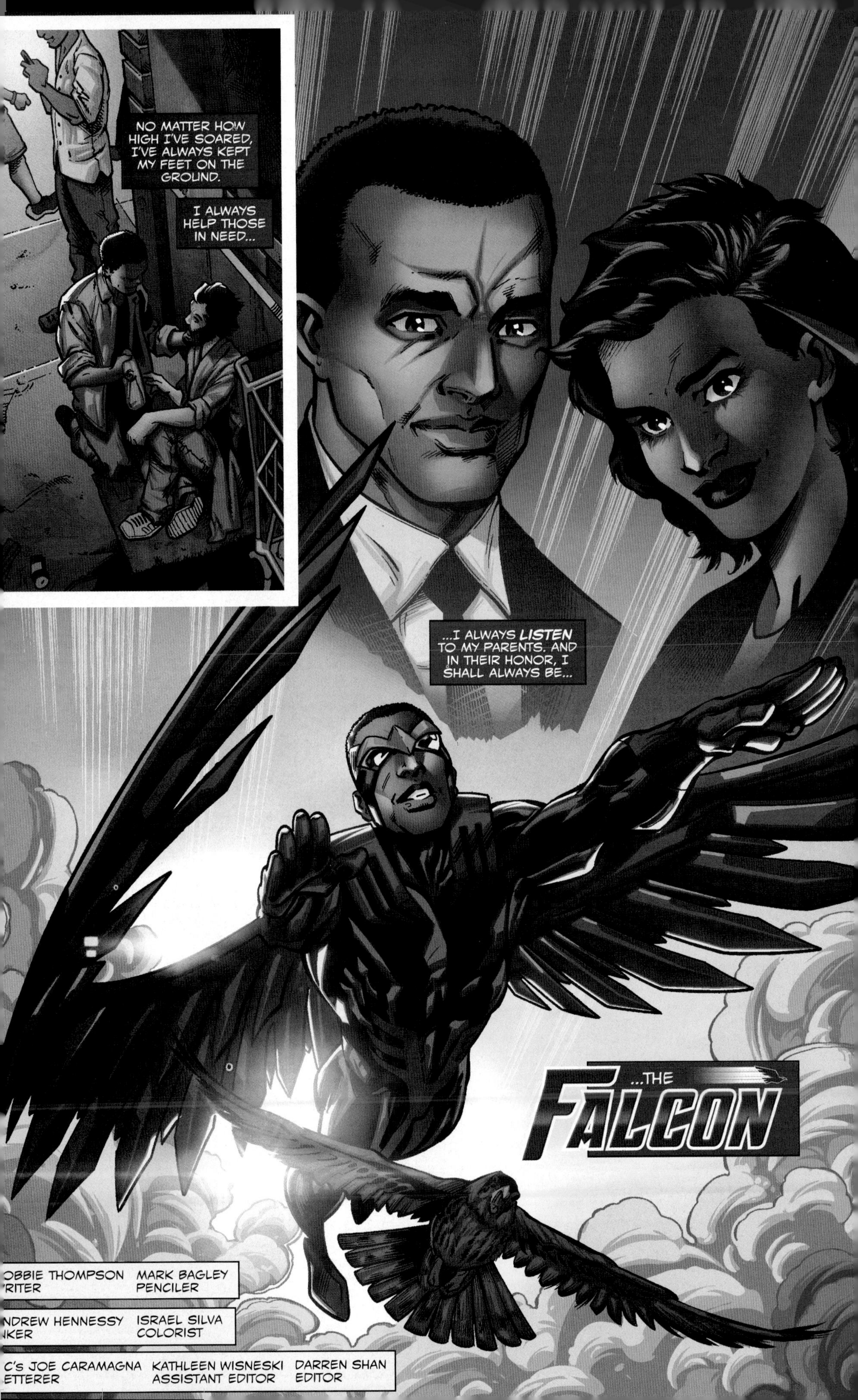

NO MATTER HOW HIGH I'VE SOARED, I'VE ALWAYS KEPT MY FEET ON THE GROUND.
I ALWAYS HELP THOSE IN NEED...
...I ALWAYS LISTEN TO MY PARENTS. AND IN THEIR HONOR, I SHALL ALWAYS BE...
...THE FALCON
OBBIE THOMPSON RITER
MARK BAGLEY PENCILER
NDREW HENNESSY NKER
ISRAEL SILVA COLORIST
C'S JOE CARAMAGNA ETTERER
KATHLEEN WISNESKI ASSISTANT EDITOR
DARREN SHAN EDITOR

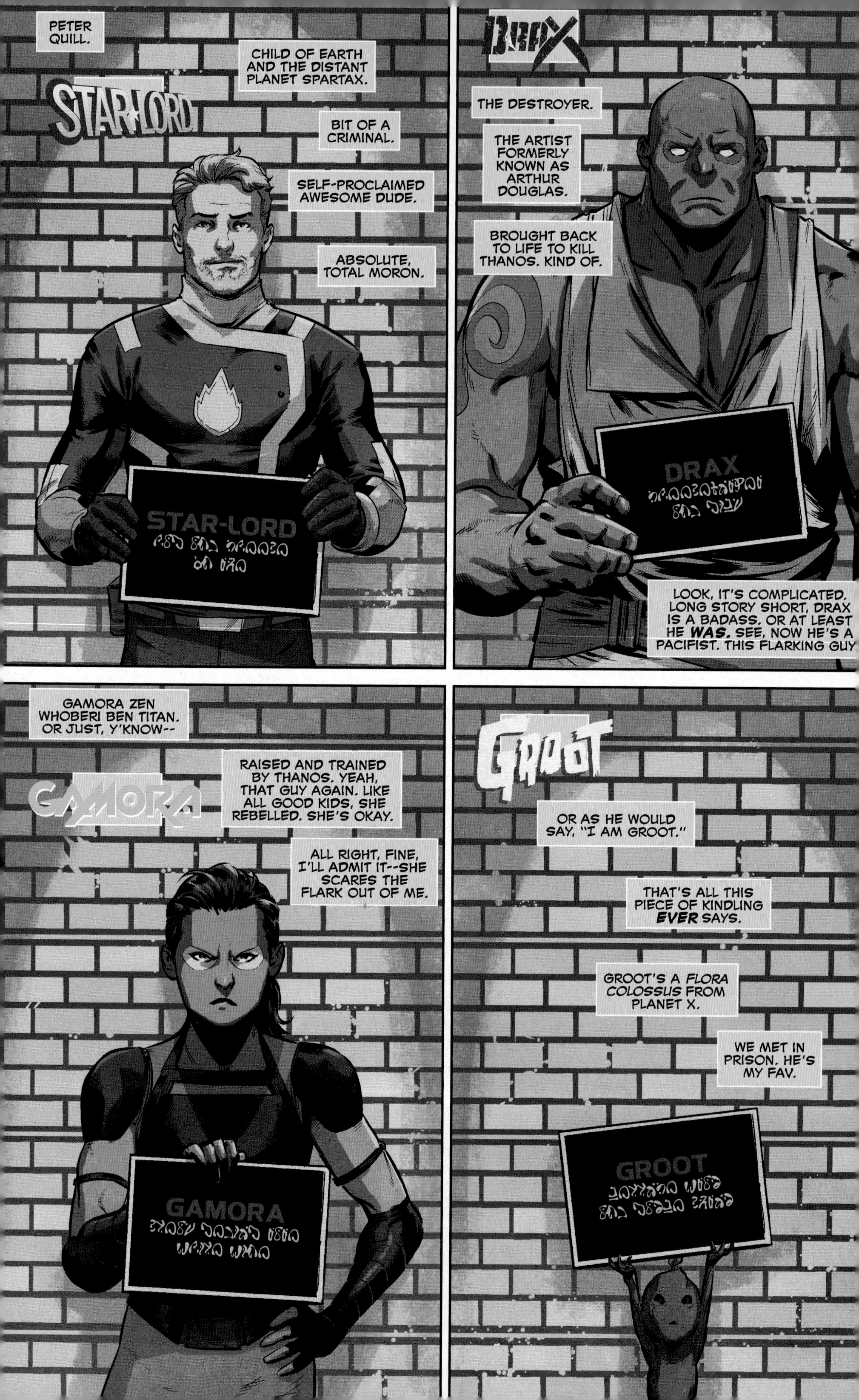

PETER QUILL.
CHILD OF EARTH AND THE DISTANT PLANET SPARTAX.
STAR-LORD
BIT OF A CRIMINAL.
SELF-PROCLAIMED AWESOME DUDE.
ABSOLUTE, TOTAL MORON.
STAR-LORD
DRAX
THE DESTROYER.
THE ARTIST FORMERLY KNOWN AS ARTHUR DOUGLAS.
BROUGHT BACK TO LIFE TO KILL THANOS. KIND OF.
DRAX
LOOK, IT'S COMPLICATED. LONG STORY SHORT, DRAX IS A BADASS. OR AT LEAST HE **WAS.** SEE, NOW HE'S A PACIFIST. THIS FLARKING GUY.
GAMORA ZEN WHOBERI BEN TITAN. OR JUST, Y'KNOW--
GAMORA
RAISED AND TRAINED BY THANOS. YEAH, THAT GUY AGAIN. LIKE ALL GOOD KIDS, SHE REBELLED. SHE'S OKAY.
ALL RIGHT, FINE, I'LL ADMIT IT--SHE SCARES THE FLARK OUT OF ME.
GAMORA
GROOT
OR AS HE WOULD SAY, "I AM GROOT."
THAT'S ALL THIS PIECE OF KINDLING ***EVER*** SAYS.
GROOT'S A *FLORA COLOSSUS* FROM PLANET X.
WE MET IN PRISON. HE'S MY FAV.
GROOT

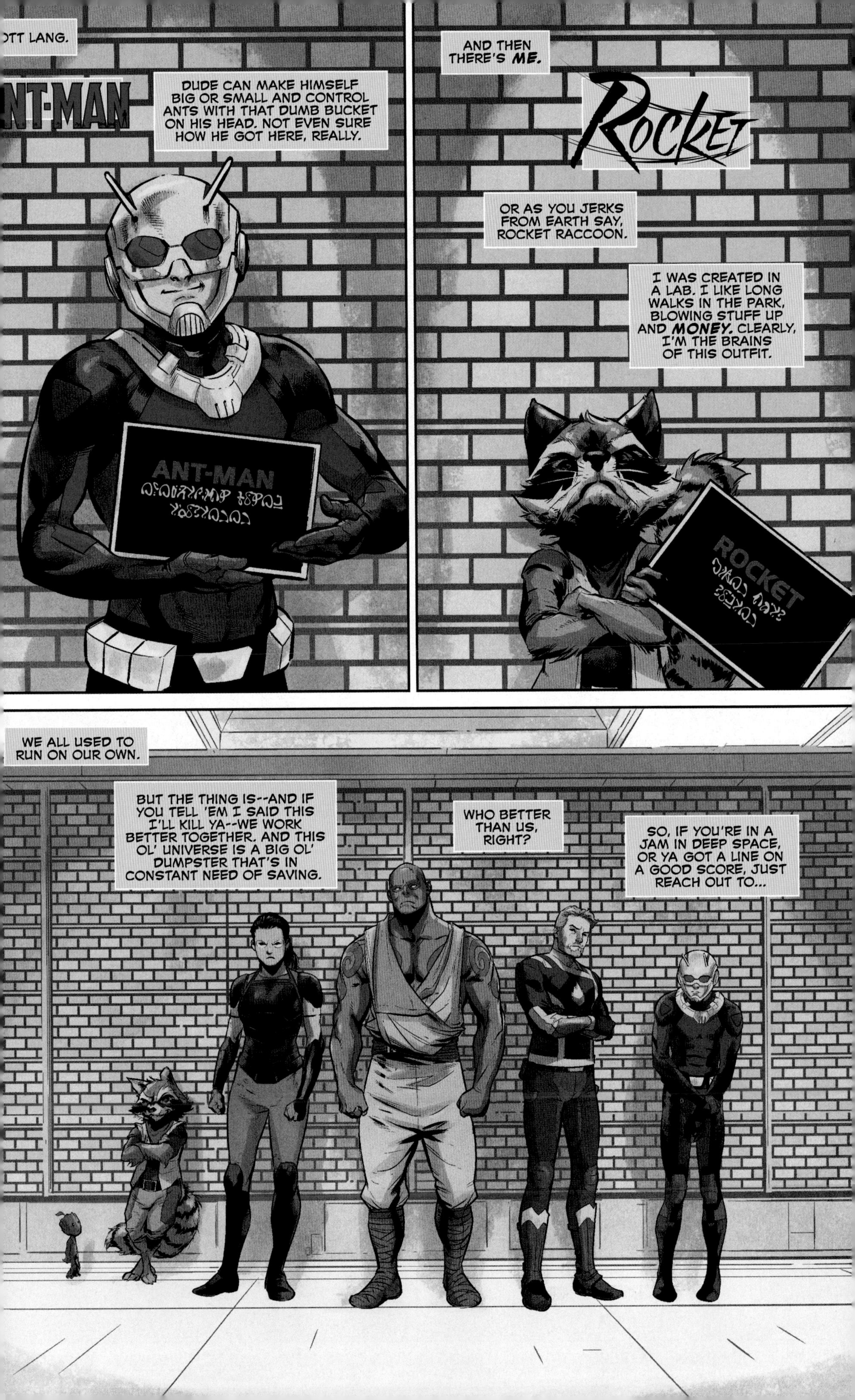
OTT LANG.
ANT-MAN
DUDE CAN MAKE HIMSELF BIG OR SMALL AND CONTROL ANTS WITH THAT DUMB BUCKET ON HIS HEAD. NOT EVEN SURE HOW HE GOT HERE, REALLY.
ANT-MAN
AND THEN THERE'S ME.
ROCKET
OR AS YOU JERKS FROM EARTH SAY, ROCKET RACCOON.
I WAS CREATED IN A LAB. I LIKE LONG WALKS IN THE PARK, BLOWING STUFF UP AND MONEY. CLEARLY, I'M THE BRAINS OF THIS OUTFIT.
ROCKET
WE ALL USED TO RUN ON OUR OWN.
BUT THE THING IS--AND IF YOU TELL 'EM I SAID THIS I'LL KILL YA--WE WORK BETTER TOGETHER. AND THIS OL' UNIVERSE IS A BIG OL' DUMPSTER THAT'S IN CONSTANT NEED OF SAVING.
WHO BETTER THAN US, RIGHT?
SO, IF YOU'RE IN A JAM IN DEEP SPACE, OR YA GOT A LINE ON A GOOD SCORE, JUST REACH OUT TO...

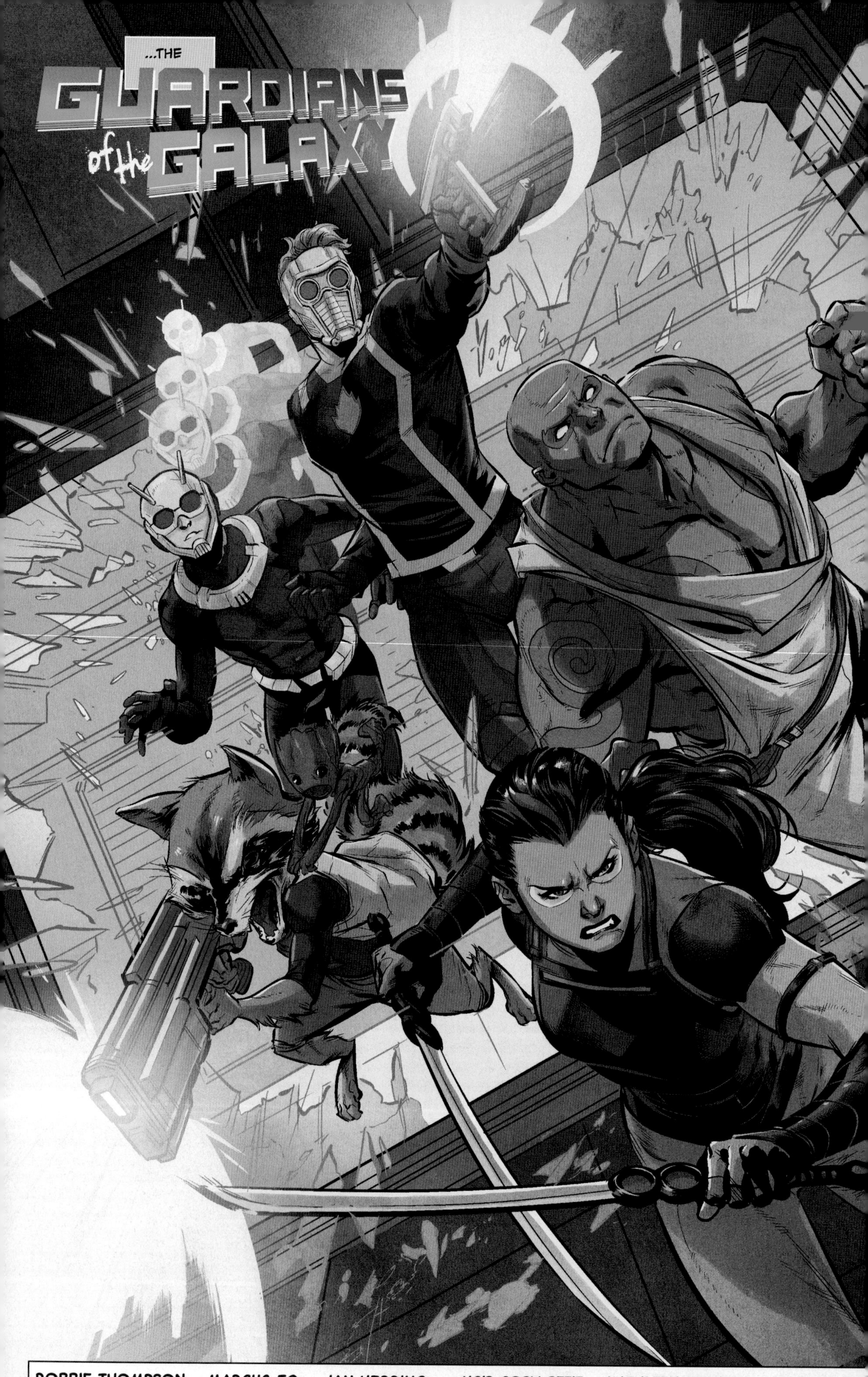
...THE
GUARDIANS of the GALAXY

ROBBIE THOMPSON WRITER | MARCUS TO ARTIST | IAN HERRING COLOR ARTIST | VC'S CORY PETIT LETTERER | KATHLEEN WISNESKI ASSISTANT EDITOR | DARREN SHA EDITOR

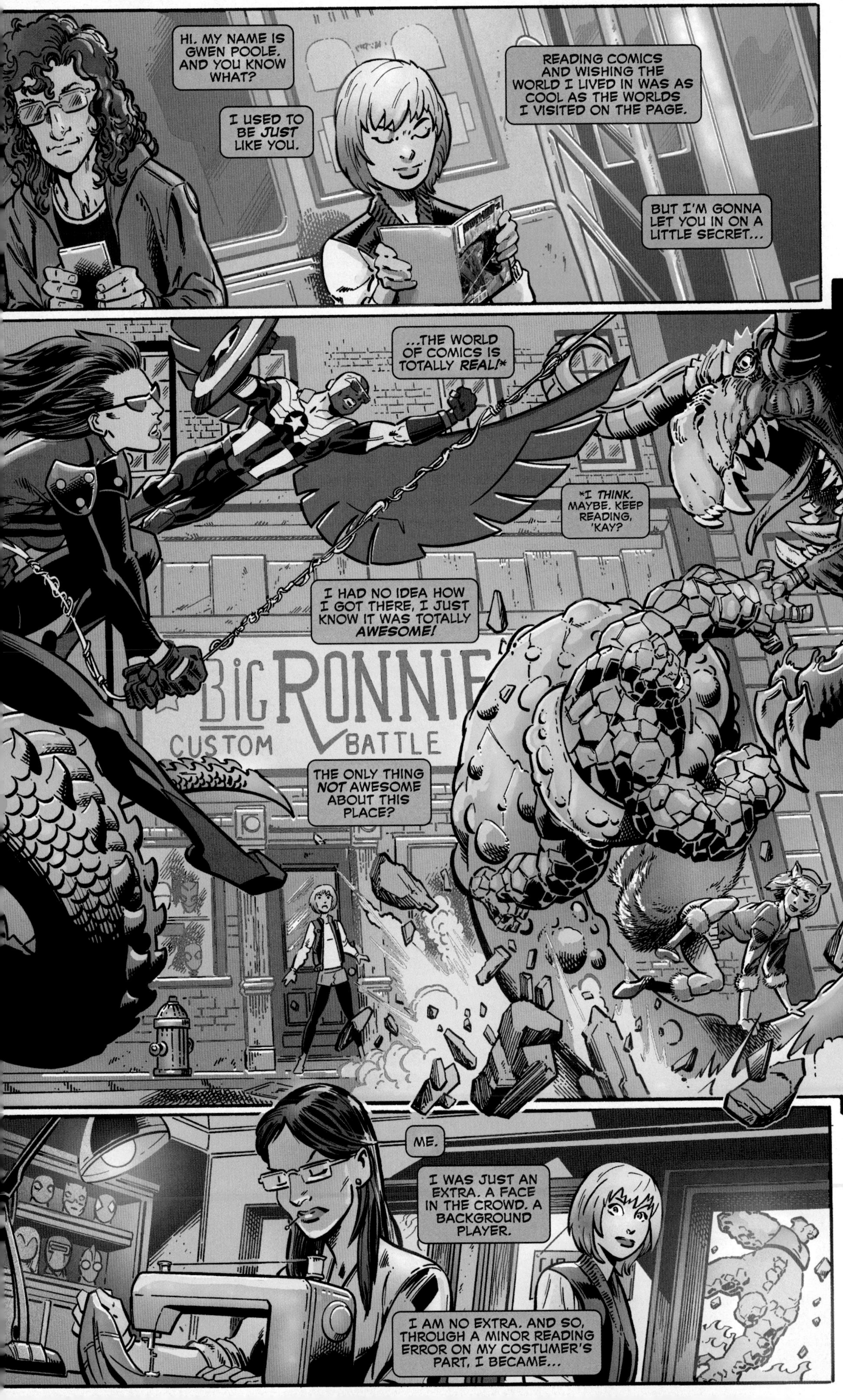
HI. MY NAME IS GWEN POOLE. AND YOU KNOW WHAT?
I USED TO BE JUST LIKE YOU.
READING COMICS AND WISHING THE WORLD I LIVED IN WAS AS COOL AS THE WORLDS I VISITED ON THE PAGE.
BUT I'M GONNA LET YOU IN ON A LITTLE SECRET...
...THE WORLD OF COMICS IS TOTALLY REAL!*
*I THINK. MAYBE. KEEP READING, 'KAY?
I HAD NO IDEA HOW I GOT THERE, I JUST KNOW IT WAS TOTALLY AWESOME!
BIG RONNIE
CUSTOM BATTLE
THE ONLY THING NOT AWESOME ABOUT THIS PLACE?
ME.
I WAS JUST AN EXTRA. A FACE IN THE CROWD. A BACKGROUND PLAYER.
I AM NO EXTRA. AND SO, THROUGH A MINOR READING ERROR ON MY COSTUMER'S PART, I BECAME...

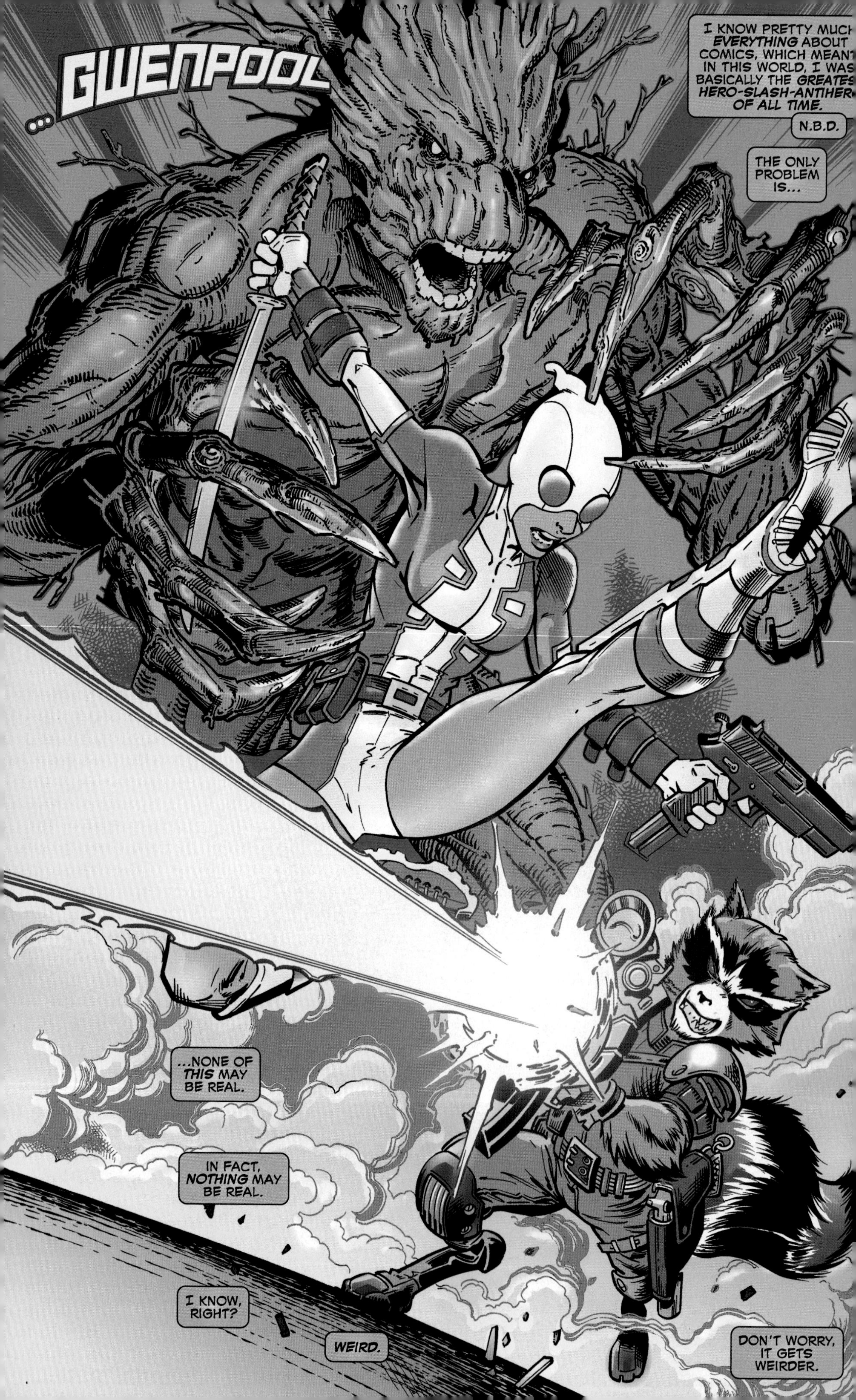

GWENPOOL
...
I KNOW PRETTY MUCH EVERYTHING ABOUT COMICS, WHICH MEANT IN THIS WORLD, I WAS BASICALLY THE GREATEST HERO-SLASH-ANTIHERO OF ALL TIME.
N.B.D.
THE ONLY PROBLEM IS...
...NONE OF THIS MAY BE REAL.
IN FACT, NOTHING MAY BE REAL.
I KNOW, RIGHT?
WEIRD.
DON'T WORRY, IT GETS WEIRDER.

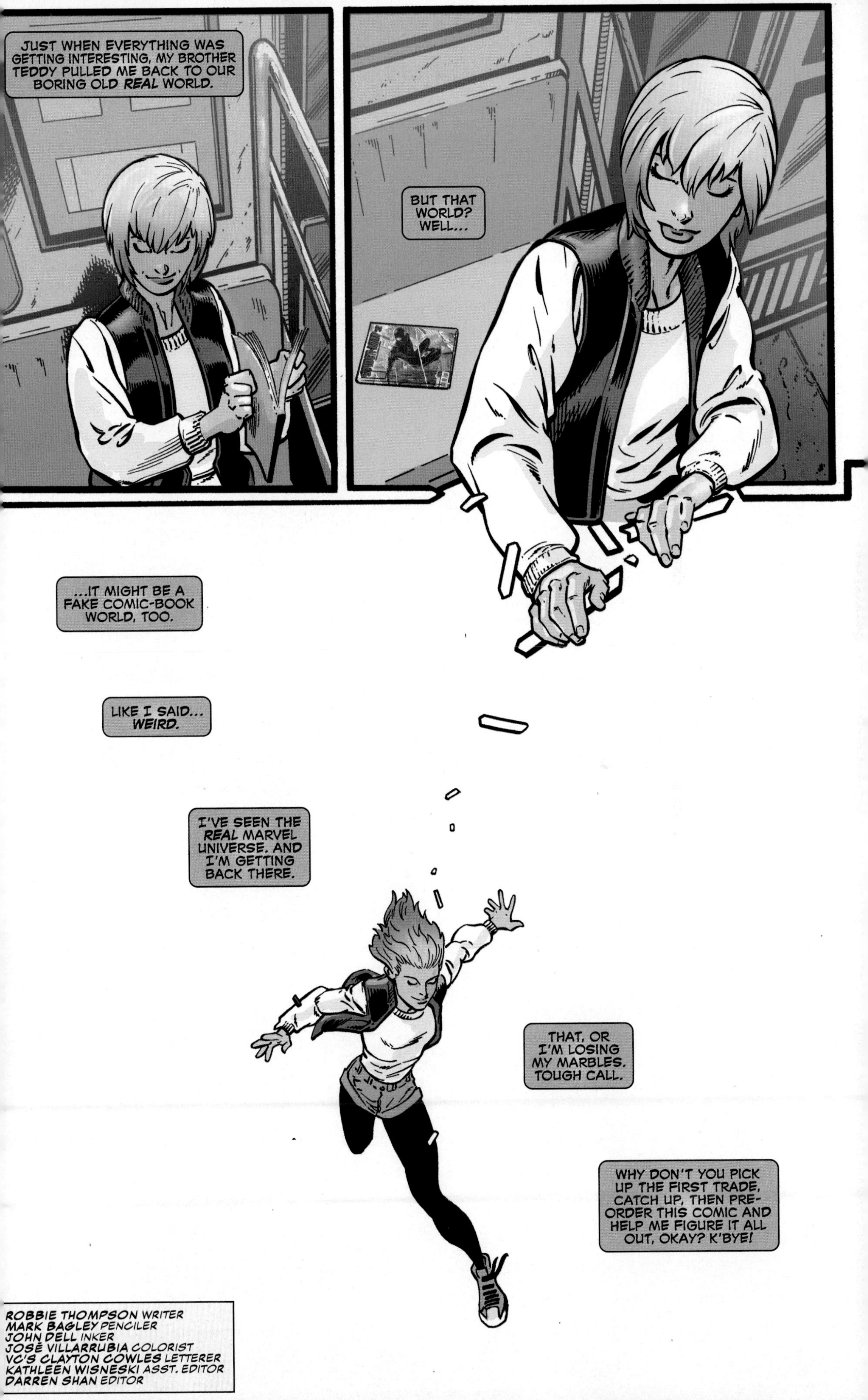
JUST WHEN EVERYTHING WAS GETTING INTERESTING, MY BROTHER TEDDY PULLED ME BACK TO OUR BORING OLD *REAL* WORLD.
BUT THAT WORLD? WELL...
...IT MIGHT BE A FAKE COMIC-BOOK WORLD, TOO.
LIKE I SAID... *WEIRD.*
I'VE SEEN THE *REAL* MARVEL UNIVERSE. AND I'M GETTING BACK THERE.
THAT, OR I'M LOSING MY MARBLES. TOUGH CALL.
WHY DON'T YOU PICK UP THE FIRST TRADE, CATCH UP, THEN PRE-ORDER THIS COMIC AND HELP ME FIGURE IT ALL OUT, OKAY? K'BYE!

ROBBIE THOMPSON WRITER
MARK BAGLEY PENCILER
JOHN DELL INKER
JOSÉ VILLARRUBIA COLORIST
VC'S CLAYTON COWLES LETTERER
KATHLEEN WISNESKI ASST. EDITOR
DARREN SHAN EDITOR

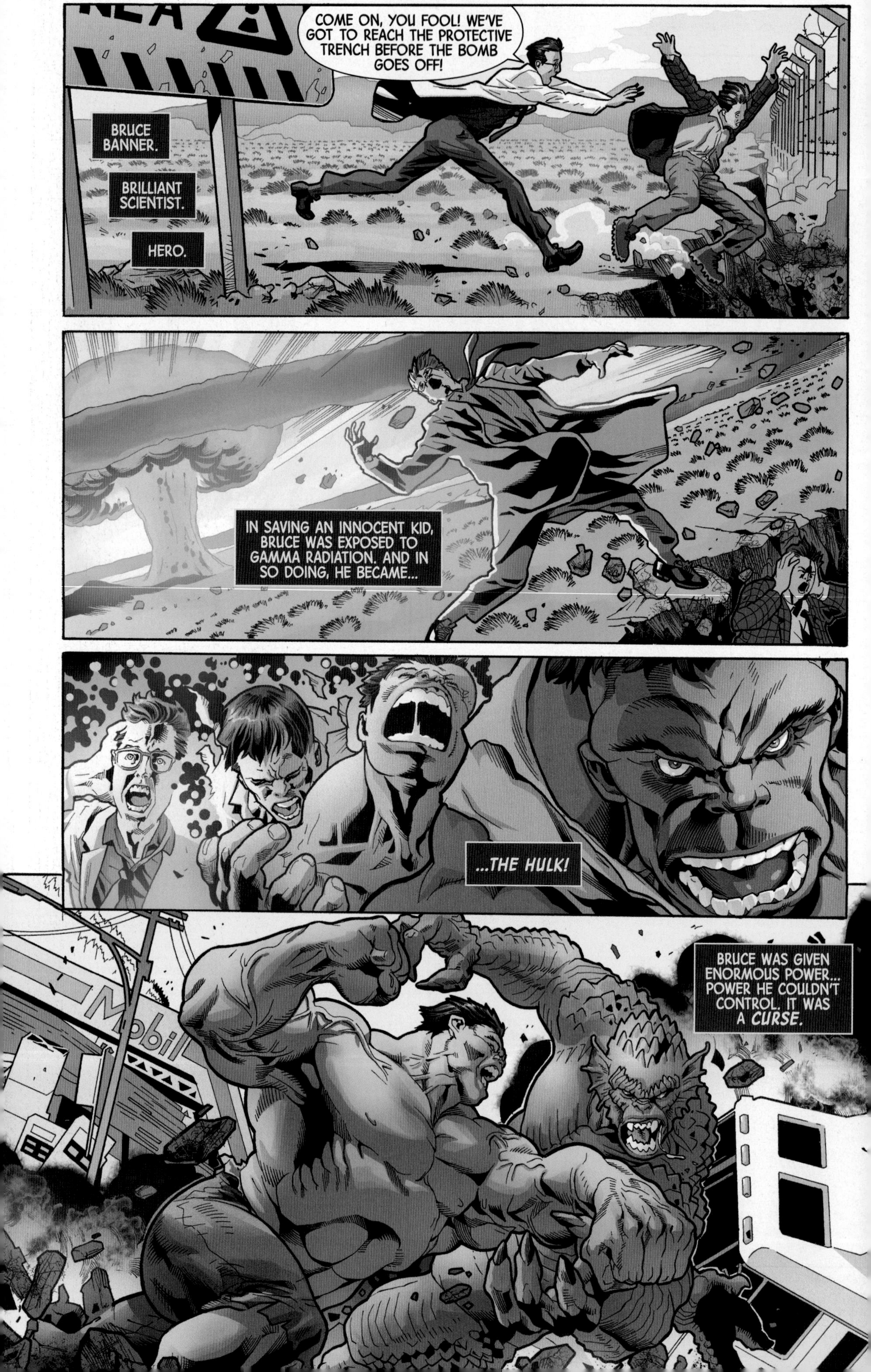
COME ON, YOU FOOL! WE'VE GOT TO REACH THE PROTECTIVE TRENCH BEFORE THE BOMB GOES OFF!
BRUCE BANNER.
BRILLIANT SCIENTIST.
HERO.
IN SAVING AN INNOCENT KID, BRUCE WAS EXPOSED TO GAMMA RADIATION. AND IN SO DOING, HE BECAME...
...THE HULK!
Mobil
BRUCE WAS GIVEN ENORMOUS POWER... POWER HE COULDN'T CONTROL. IT WAS A *CURSE*.

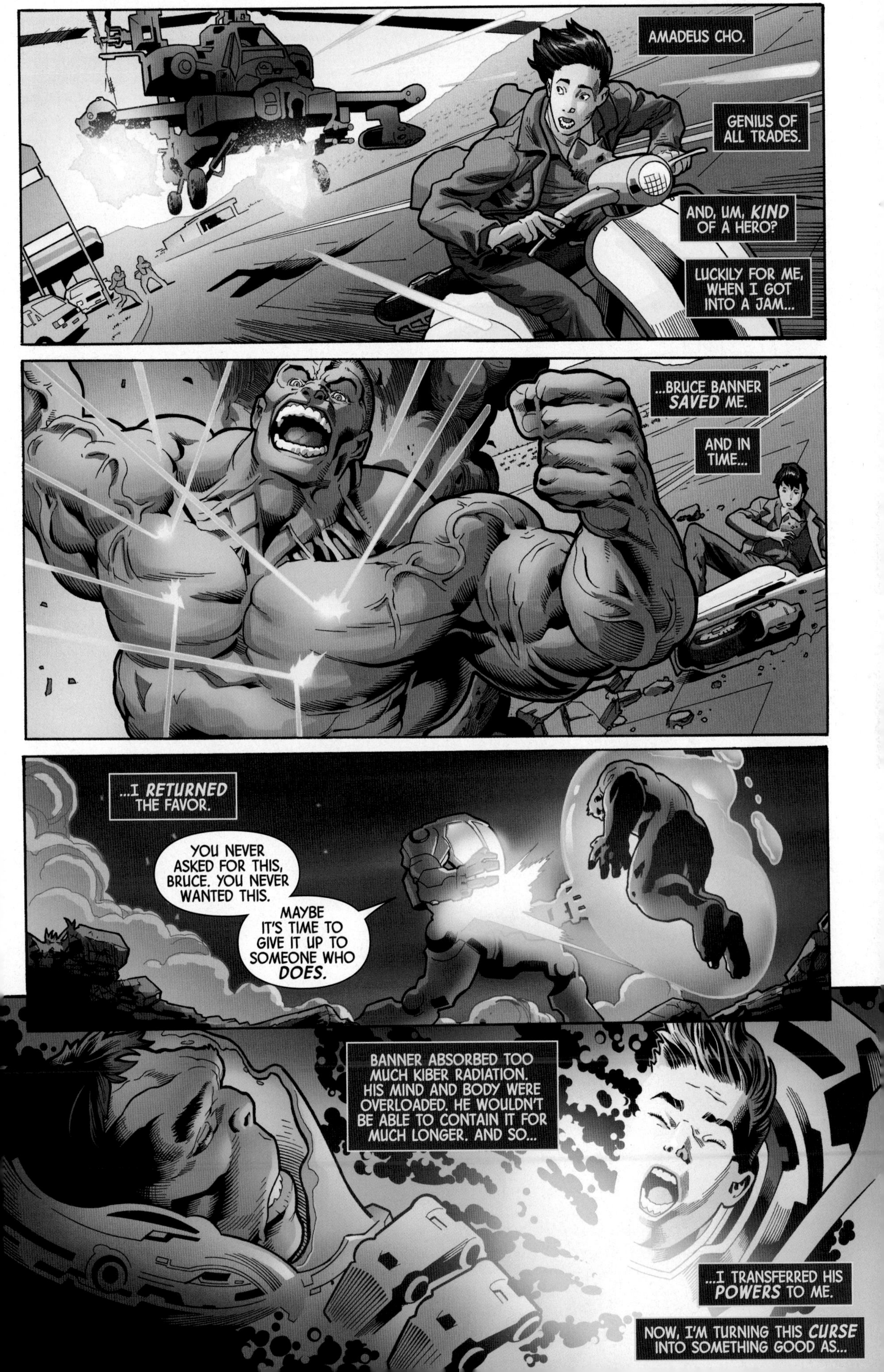
AMADEUS CHO.
GENIUS OF ALL TRADES.
AND, UM, KIND OF A HERO?
LUCKILY FOR ME, WHEN I GOT INTO A JAM...
...BRUCE BANNER SAVED ME.
AND IN TIME...
...I RETURNED THE FAVOR.
YOU NEVER ASKED FOR THIS, BRUCE. YOU NEVER WANTED THIS.
MAYBE IT'S TIME TO GIVE IT UP TO SOMEONE WHO DOES.
BANNER ABSORBED TOO MUCH KIBER RADIATION. HIS MIND AND BODY WERE OVERLOADED. HE WOULDN'T BE ABLE TO CONTAIN IT FOR MUCH LONGER. AND SO...
...I TRANSFERRED HIS POWERS TO ME.
NOW, I'M TURNING THIS CURSE INTO SOMETHING GOOD AS...

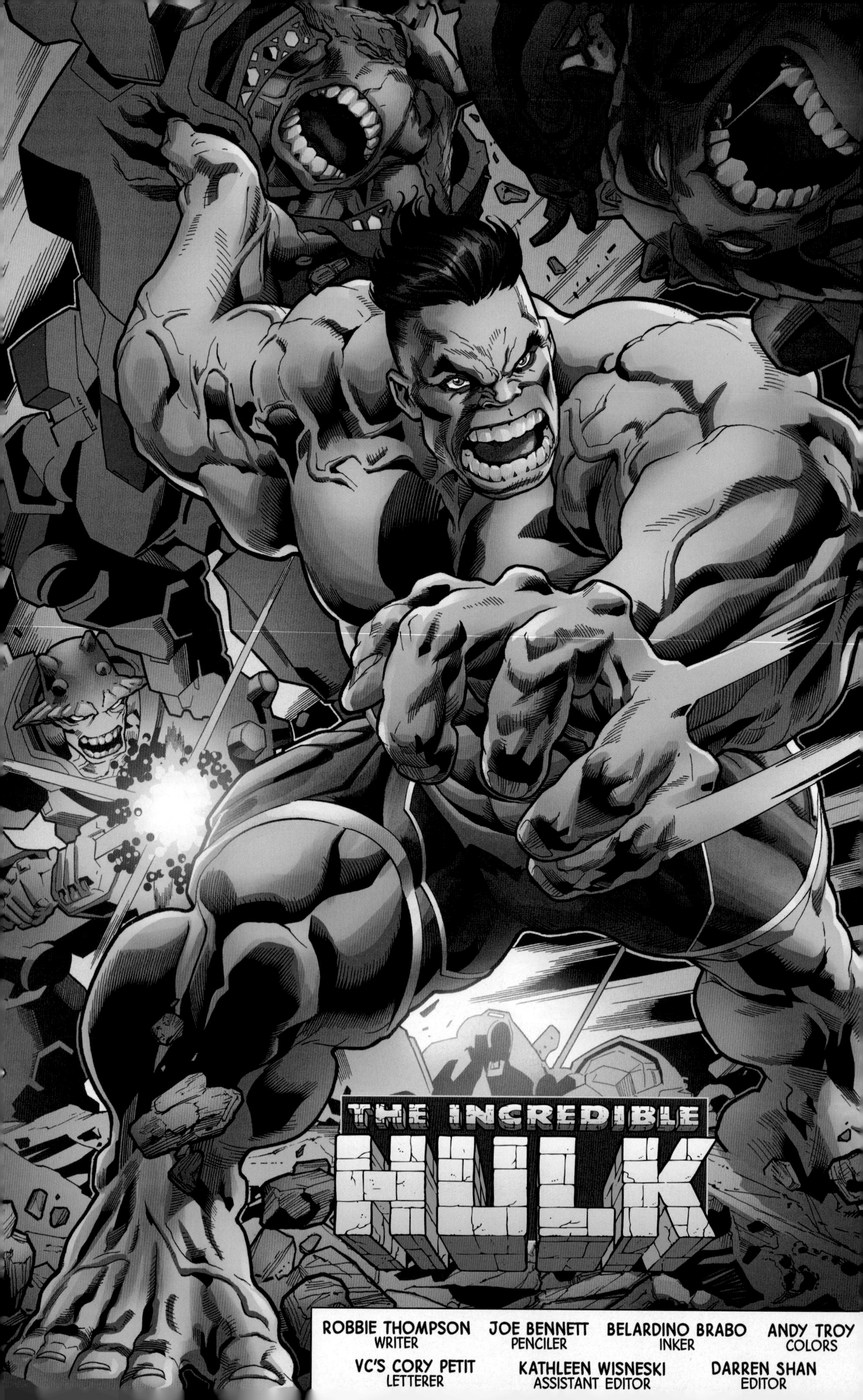
THE INCREDIBLE
HULK
ROBBIE THOMPSON
WRITER
JOE BENNETT
PENCILER
BELARDINO BRABO
INKER
ANDY TROY
COLORS
VC'S CORY PETIT
LETTERER
KATHLEEN WISNESKI
ASSISTANT EDITOR
DARREN SHAN
EDITOR

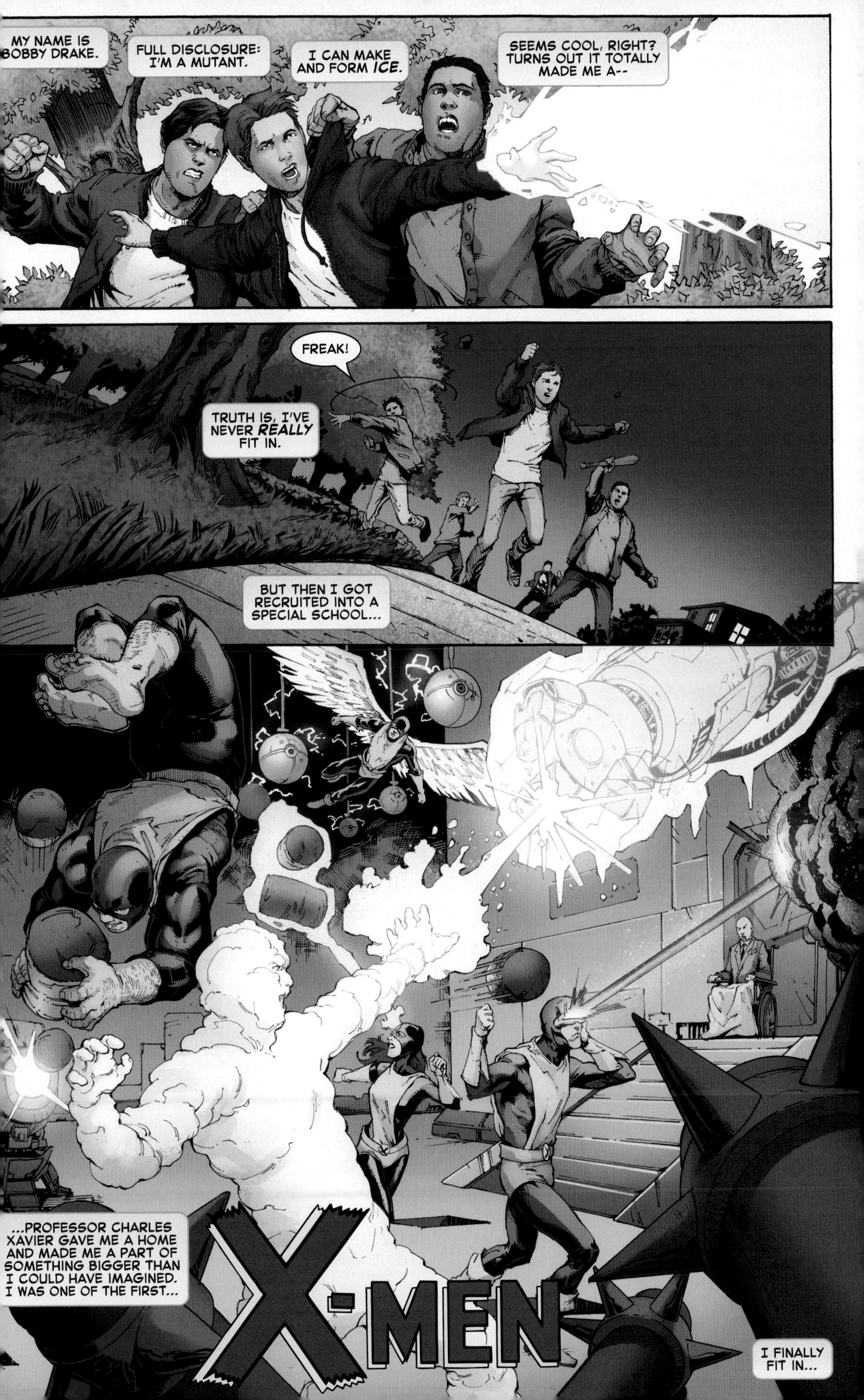

MY NAME IS BOBBY DRAKE.
FULL DISCLOSURE: I'M A MUTANT.
I CAN MAKE AND FORM ICE.
SEEMS COOL, RIGHT? TURNS OUT IT TOTALLY MADE ME A--
FREAK!
TRUTH IS, I'VE NEVER REALLY FIT IN.
BUT THEN I GOT RECRUITED INTO A SPECIAL SCHOOL...
...PROFESSOR CHARLES XAVIER GAVE ME A HOME AND MADE ME A PART OF SOMETHING BIGGER THAN I COULD HAVE IMAGINED. I WAS ONE OF THE FIRST...
X-MEN
I FINALLY FIT IN...

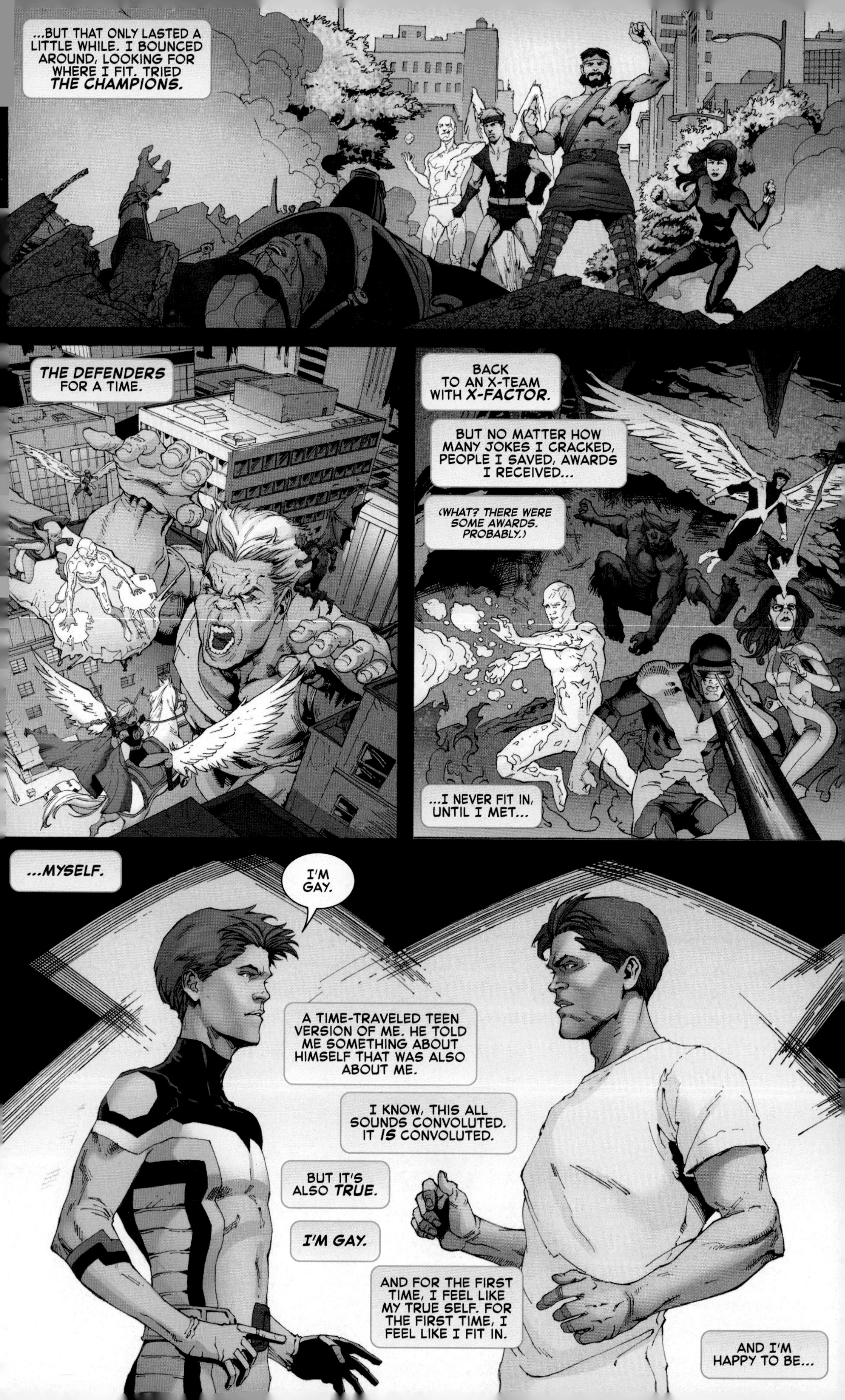
...BUT THAT ONLY LASTED A LITTLE WHILE. I BOUNCED AROUND, LOOKING FOR WHERE I FIT. TRIED THE CHAMPIONS.
THE DEFENDERS FOR A TIME.
BACK TO AN X-TEAM WITH X-FACTOR.
BUT NO MATTER HOW MANY JOKES I CRACKED, PEOPLE I SAVED, AWARDS I RECEIVED...
(WHAT? THERE WERE SOME AWARDS. PROBABLY.)
...I NEVER FIT IN, UNTIL I MET...
...MYSELF.
I'M GAY.
A TIME-TRAVELED TEEN VERSION OF ME. HE TOLD ME SOMETHING ABOUT HIMSELF THAT WAS ALSO ABOUT ME.
I KNOW, THIS ALL SOUNDS CONVOLUTED. IT IS CONVOLUTED.
BUT IT'S ALSO TRUE.
I'M GAY.
AND FOR THE FIRST TIME, I FEEL LIKE MY TRUE SELF. FOR THE FIRST TIME, I FEEL LIKE I FIT IN.
AND I'M HAPPY TO BE...

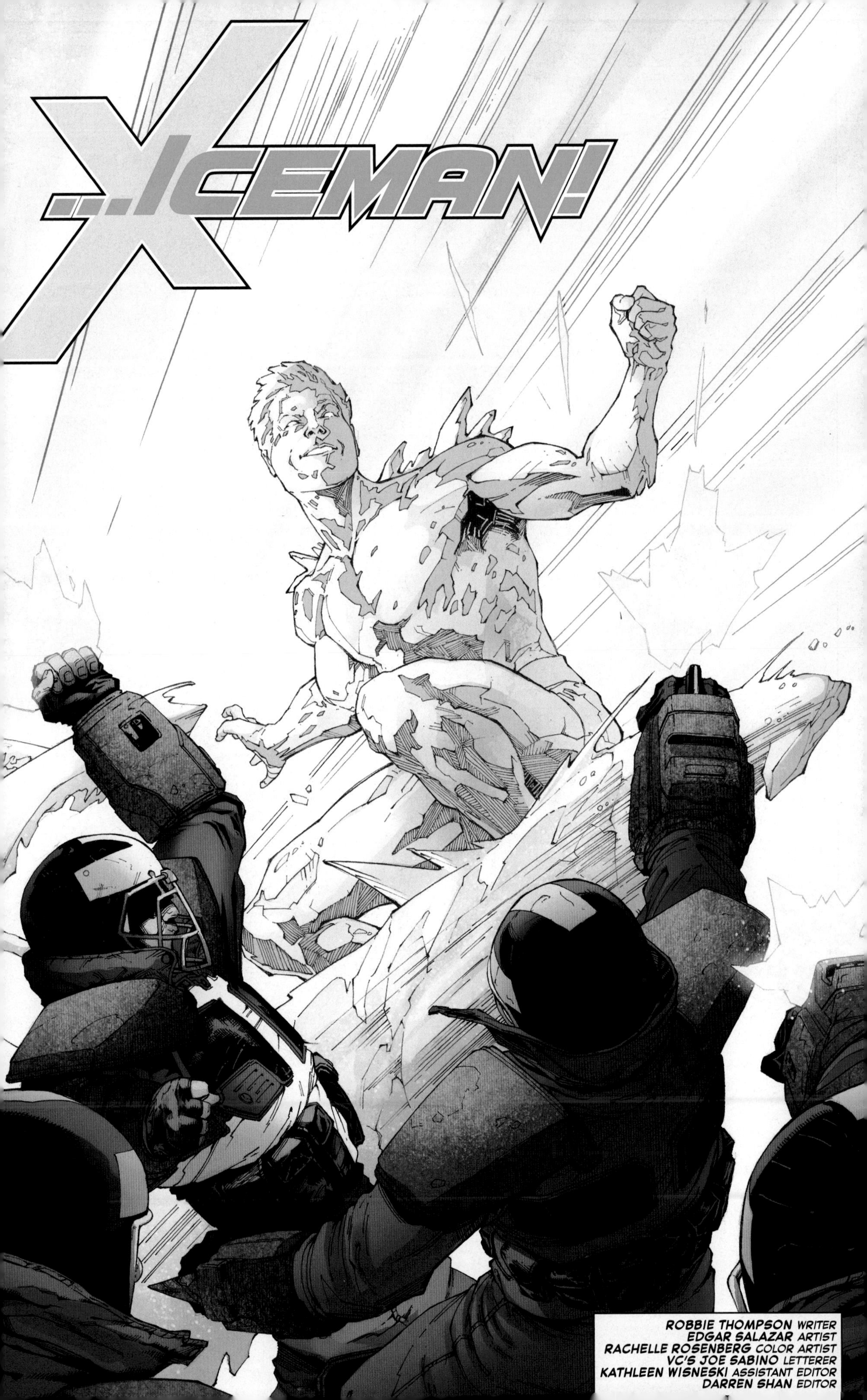

...ICEMAN!
ROBBIE THOMPSON WRITER
EDGAR SALAZAR ARTIST
RACHELLE ROSENBERG COLOR ARTIST
VC'S JOE SABINO LETTERER
KATHLEEN WISNESKI ASSISTANT EDITOR
DARREN SHAN EDITOR

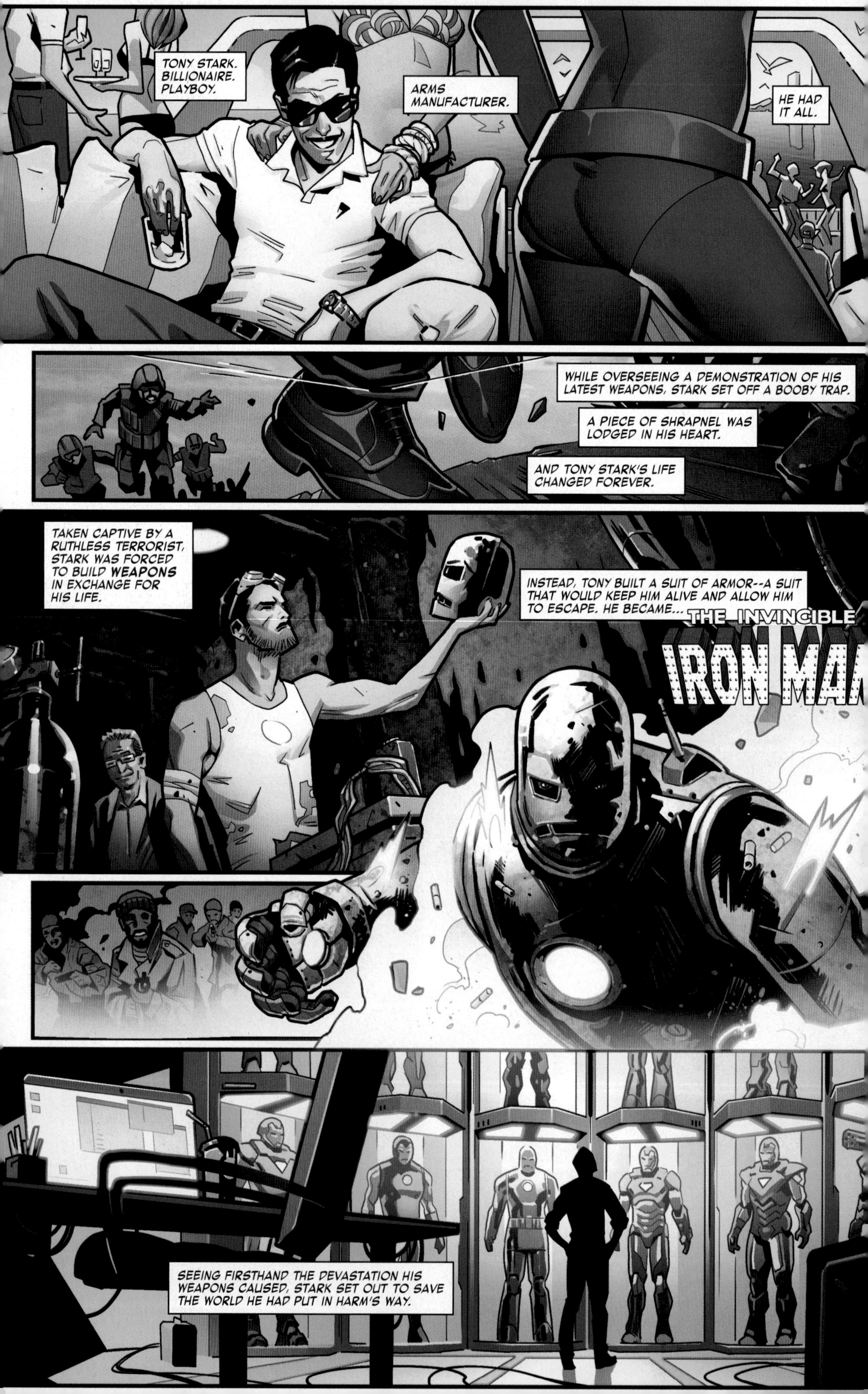
TONY STARK. BILLIONAIRE. PLAYBOY.
ARMS MANUFACTURER.
HE HAD IT ALL.
WHILE OVERSEEING A DEMONSTRATION OF HIS LATEST WEAPONS, STARK SET OFF A BOOBY TRAP.
A PIECE OF SHRAPNEL WAS LODGED IN HIS HEART.
AND TONY STARK'S LIFE CHANGED FOREVER.
TAKEN CAPTIVE BY A RUTHLESS TERRORIST, STARK WAS FORCED TO BUILD WEAPONS IN EXCHANGE FOR HIS LIFE.
INSTEAD, TONY BUILT A SUIT OF ARMOR--A SUIT THAT WOULD KEEP HIM ALIVE AND ALLOW HIM TO ESCAPE. HE BECAME...
THE INVINCIBLE
SEEING FIRSTHAND THE DEVASTATION HIS WEAPONS CAUSED, STARK SET OUT TO SAVE THE WORLD HE HAD PUT IN HARM'S WAY.

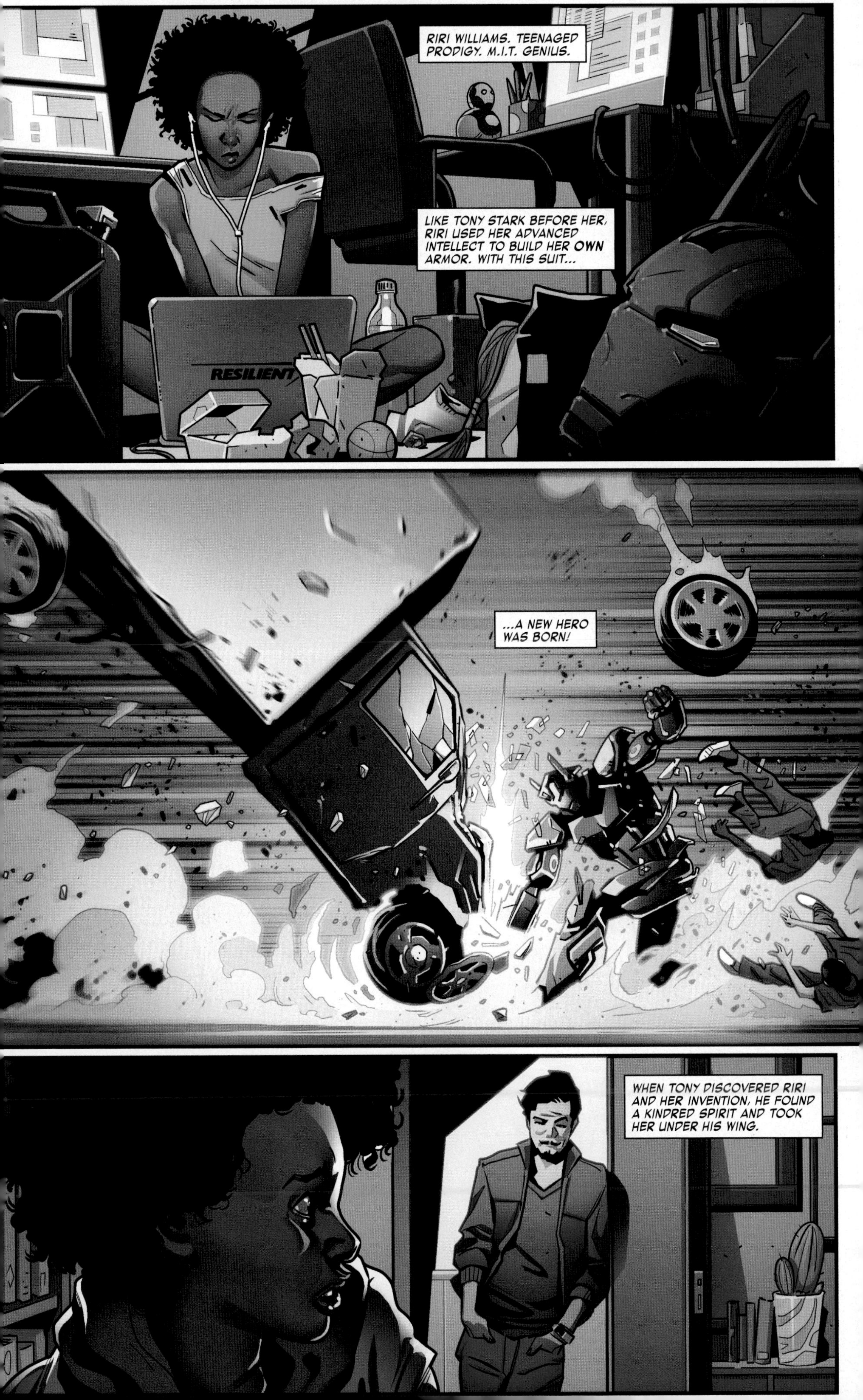
RIRI WILLIAMS. TEENAGED PRODIGY. M.I.T. GENIUS.
LIKE TONY STARK BEFORE HER, RIRI USED HER ADVANCED INTELLECT TO BUILD HER OWN ARMOR. WITH THIS SUIT...
RESILIENT
...A NEW HERO WAS BORN!
WHEN TONY DISCOVERED RIRI AND HER INVENTION, HE FOUND A KINDRED SPIRIT AND TOOK HER UNDER HIS WING.

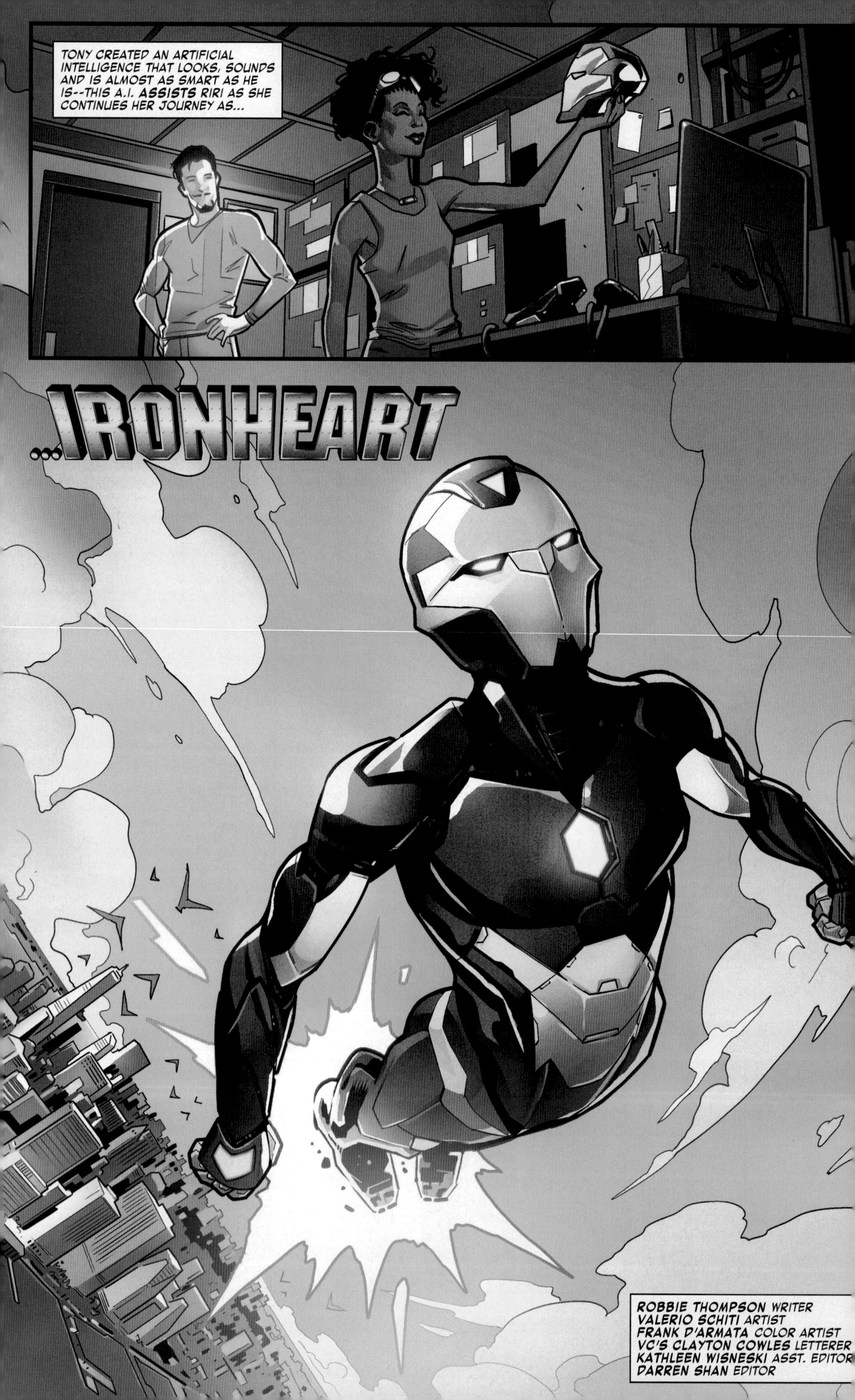

TONY CREATED AN ARTIFICIAL INTELLIGENCE THAT LOOKS, SOUNDS AND IS ALMOST AS SMART AS HE IS--THIS A.I. ASSISTS RIRI AS SHE CONTINUES HER JOURNEY AS...
...IRONHEART
ROBBIE THOMPSON WRITER
VALERIO SCHITI ARTIST
FRANK D'ARMATA COLOR ARTIST
VC'S CLAYTON COWLES LETTERER
KATHLEEN WISNESKI ASST. EDITOR
DARREN SHAN EDITOR

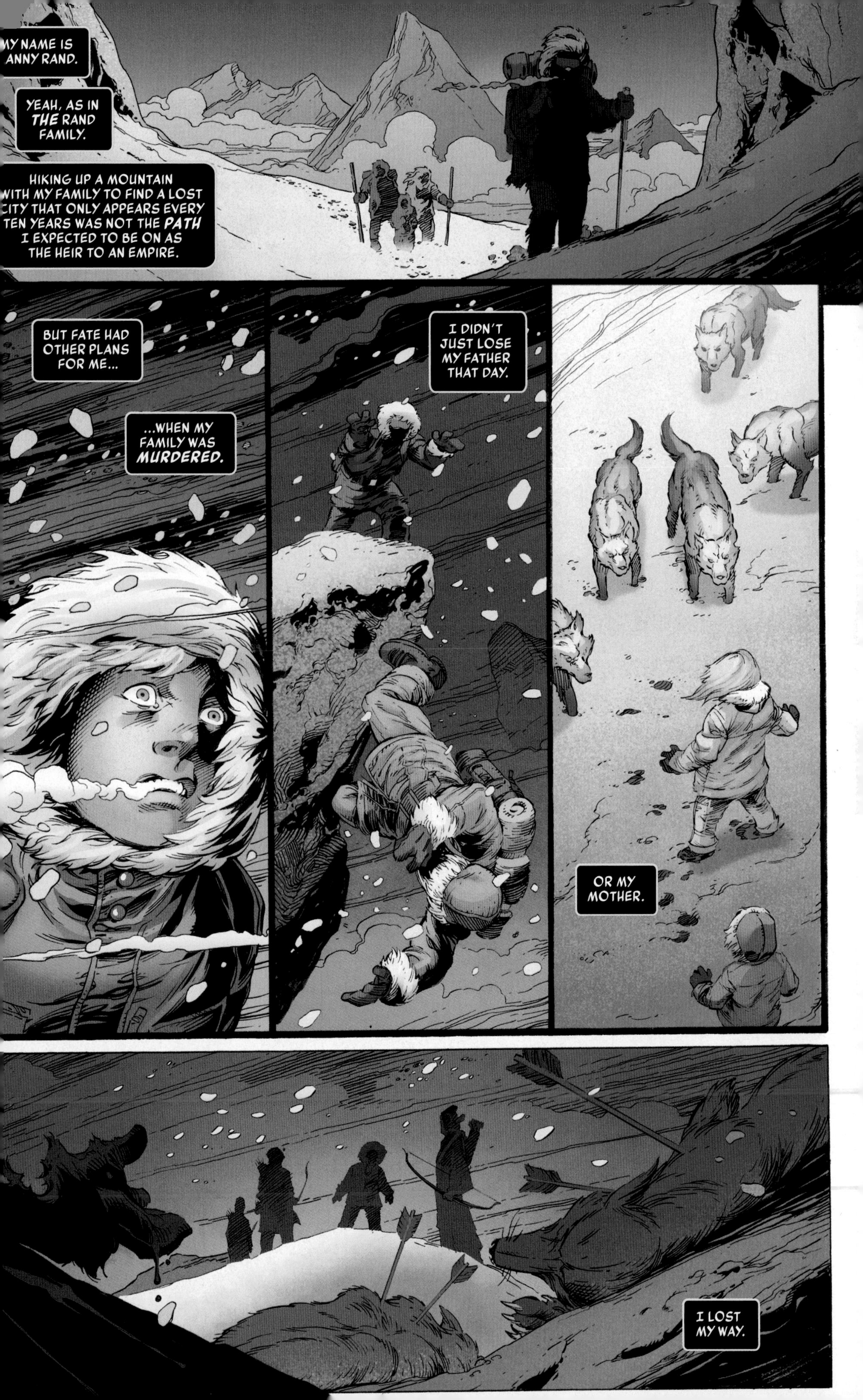
MY NAME IS ANNY RAND.
YEAH, AS IN THE RAND FAMILY.
HIKING UP A MOUNTAIN WITH MY FAMILY TO FIND A LOST CITY THAT ONLY APPEARS EVERY TEN YEARS WAS NOT THE PATH I EXPECTED TO BE ON AS THE HEIR TO AN EMPIRE.
BUT FATE HAD OTHER PLANS FOR ME...
...WHEN MY FAMILY WAS MURDERED.
I DIDN'T JUST LOSE MY FATHER THAT DAY.
OR MY MOTHER.
I LOST MY WAY.

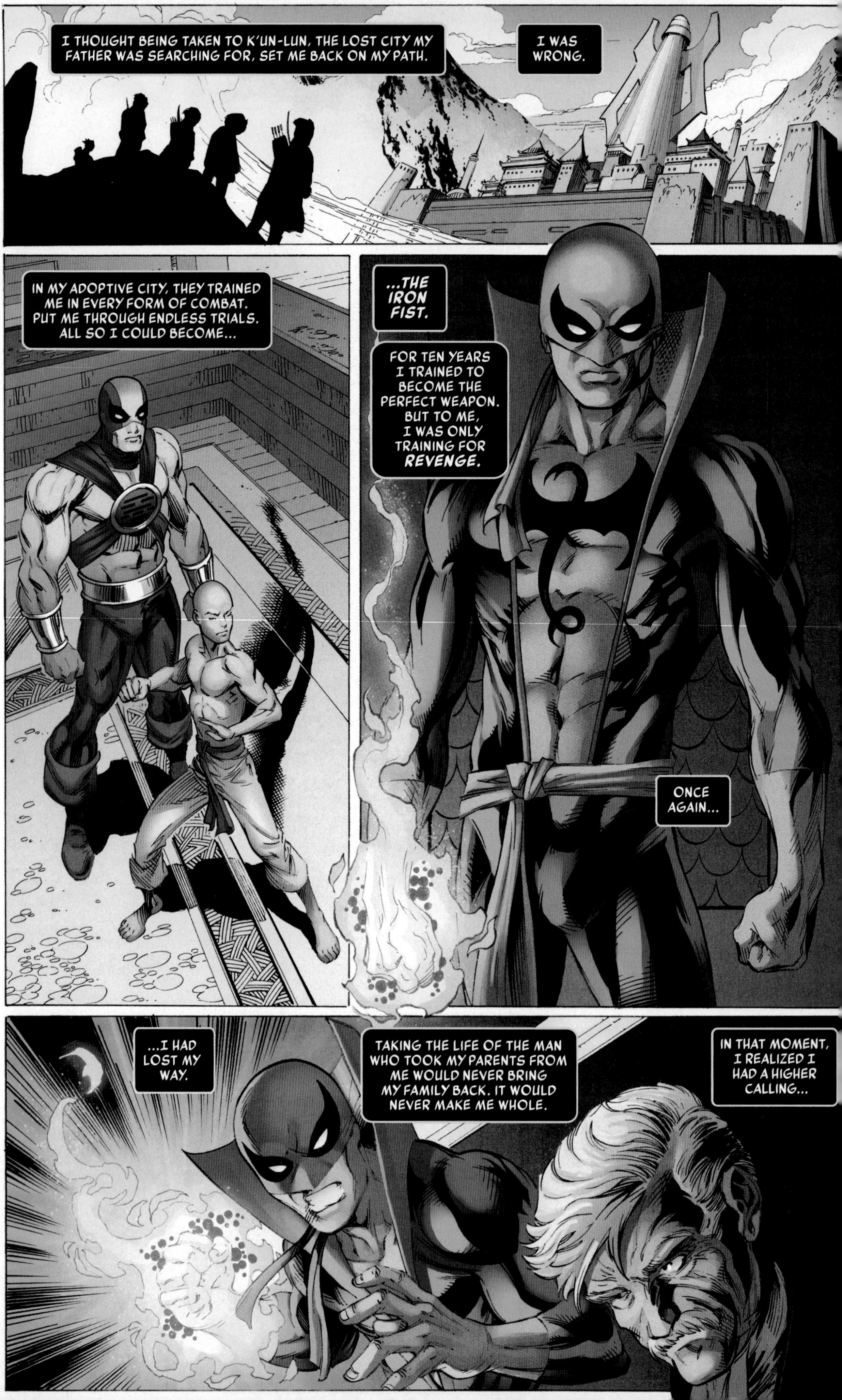
I THOUGHT BEING TAKEN TO K'UN-LUN, THE LOST CITY MY FATHER WAS SEARCHING FOR, SET ME BACK ON MY PATH.
I WAS WRONG.
IN MY ADOPTIVE CITY, THEY TRAINED ME IN EVERY FORM OF COMBAT. PUT ME THROUGH ENDLESS TRIALS. ALL SO I COULD BECOME...
...THE IRON FIST.
FOR TEN YEARS I TRAINED TO BECOME THE PERFECT WEAPON. BUT TO ME, I WAS ONLY TRAINING FOR REVENGE.
ONCE AGAIN...
...I HAD LOST MY WAY.
TAKING THE LIFE OF THE MAN WHO TOOK MY PARENTS FROM ME WOULD NEVER BRING MY FAMILY BACK. IT WOULD NEVER MAKE ME WHOLE.
IN THAT MOMENT, I REALIZED I HAD A HIGHER CALLING...

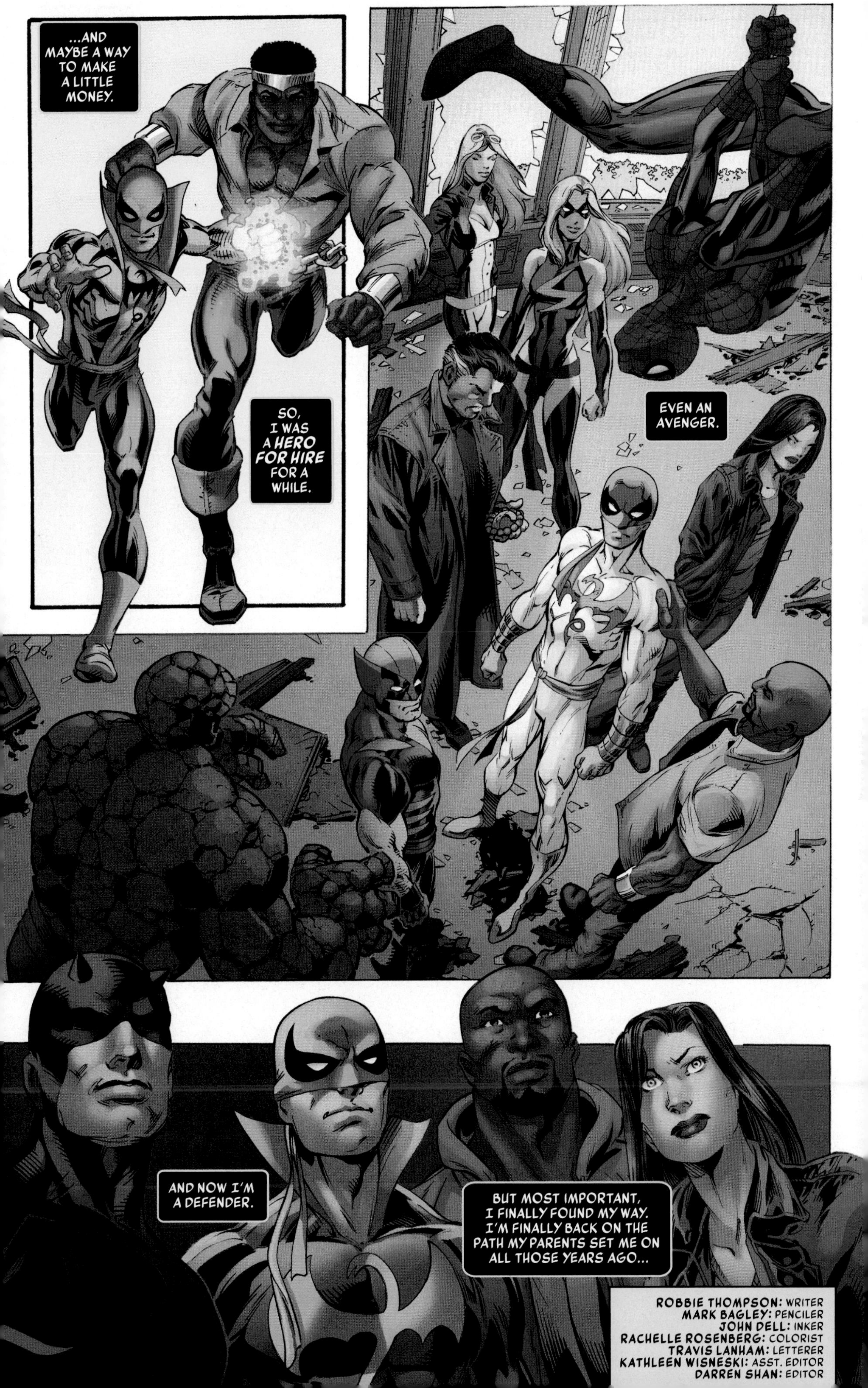
...AND MAYBE A WAY TO MAKE A LITTLE MONEY.
SO, I WAS A HERO FOR HIRE FOR A WHILE.
EVEN AN AVENGER.
AND NOW I'M A DEFENDER.
BUT MOST IMPORTANT, I FINALLY FOUND MY WAY. I'M FINALLY BACK ON THE PATH MY PARENTS SET ME ON ALL THOSE YEARS AGO...
ROBBIE THOMPSON: WRITER
MARK BAGLEY: PENCILER
JOHN DELL: INKER
RACHELLE ROSENBERG: COLORIST
TRAVIS LANHAM: LETTERER
KATHLEEN WISNESKI: ASST. EDITOR
DARREN SHAN: EDITOR

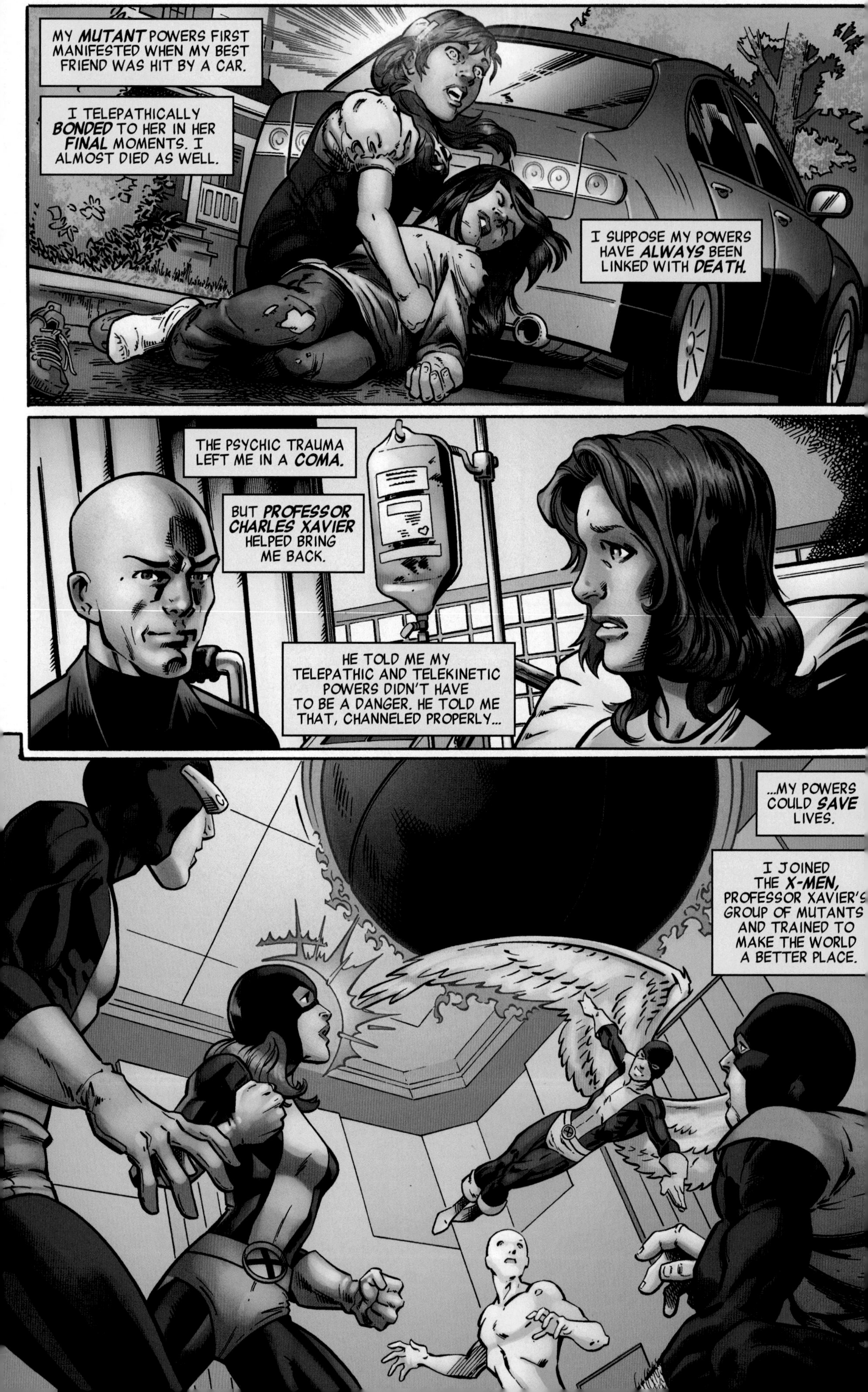
MY MUTANT POWERS FIRST MANIFESTED WHEN MY BEST FRIEND WAS HIT BY A CAR.
I TELEPATHICALLY BONDED TO HER IN HER FINAL MOMENTS. I ALMOST DIED AS WELL.
I SUPPOSE MY POWERS HAVE ALWAYS BEEN LINKED WITH DEATH.
THE PSYCHIC TRAUMA LEFT ME IN A COMA.
BUT PROFESSOR CHARLES XAVIER HELPED BRING ME BACK.
HE TOLD ME MY TELEPATHIC AND TELEKINETIC POWERS DIDN'T HAVE TO BE A DANGER. HE TOLD ME THAT, CHANNELED PROPERLY...
...MY POWERS COULD SAVE LIVES.
I JOINED THE X-MEN, PROFESSOR XAVIER'S GROUP OF MUTANTS AND TRAINED TO MAKE THE WORLD A BETTER PLACE.

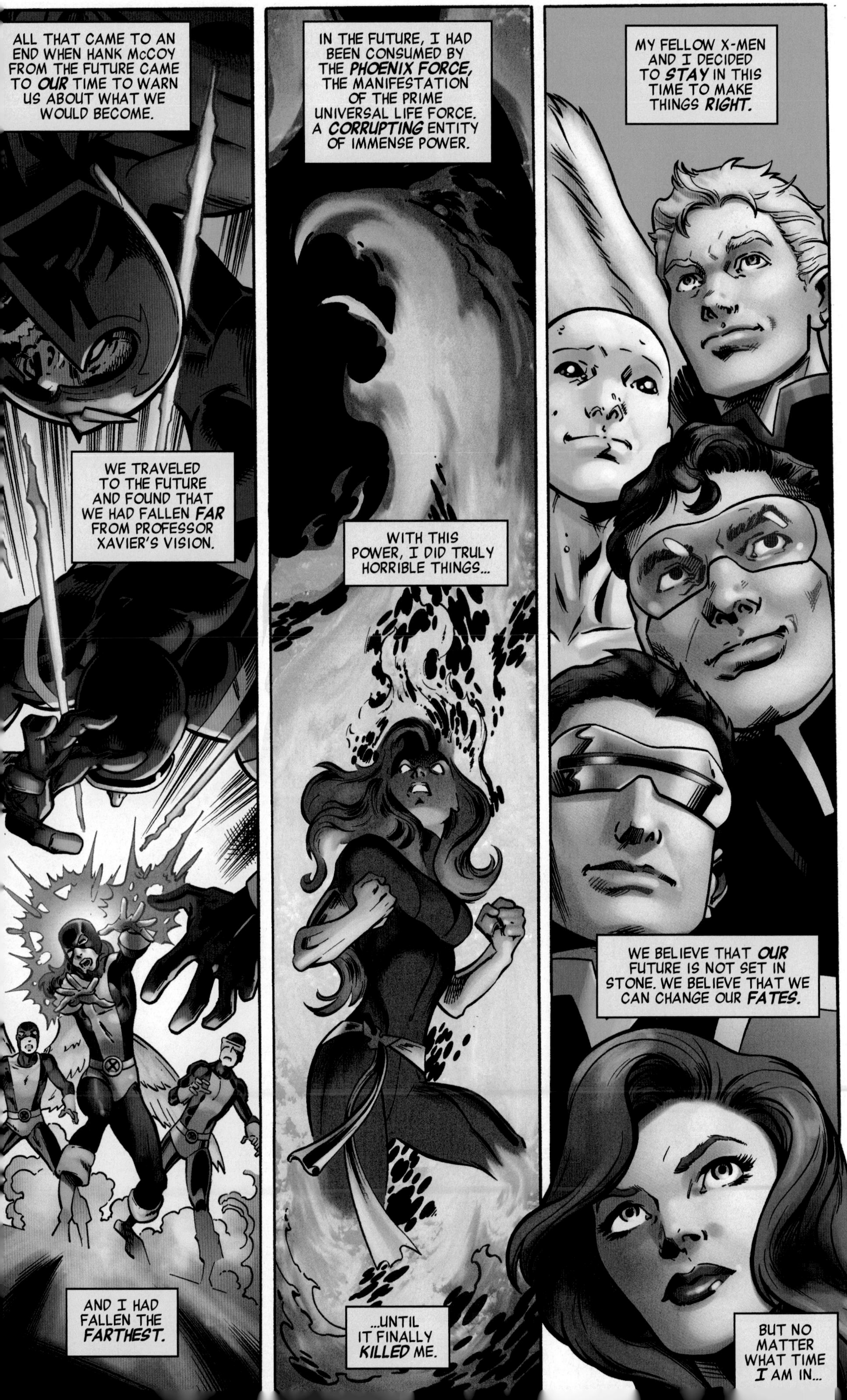
ALL THAT CAME TO AN END WHEN HANK McCOY FROM THE FUTURE CAME TO OUR TIME TO WARN US ABOUT WHAT WE WOULD BECOME.
WE TRAVELED TO THE FUTURE AND FOUND THAT WE HAD FALLEN FAR FROM PROFESSOR XAVIER'S VISION.
AND I HAD FALLEN THE FARTHEST.
IN THE FUTURE, I HAD BEEN CONSUMED BY THE PHOENIX FORCE, THE MANIFESTATION OF THE PRIME UNIVERSAL LIFE FORCE. A CORRUPTING ENTITY OF IMMENSE POWER.
WITH THIS POWER, I DID TRULY HORRIBLE THINGS...
...UNTIL IT FINALLY KILLED ME.
MY FELLOW X-MEN AND I DECIDED TO STAY IN THIS TIME TO MAKE THINGS RIGHT.
WE BELIEVE THAT OUR FUTURE IS NOT SET IN STONE. WE BELIEVE THAT WE CAN CHANGE OUR FATES.
BUT NO MATTER WHAT TIME I AM IN...

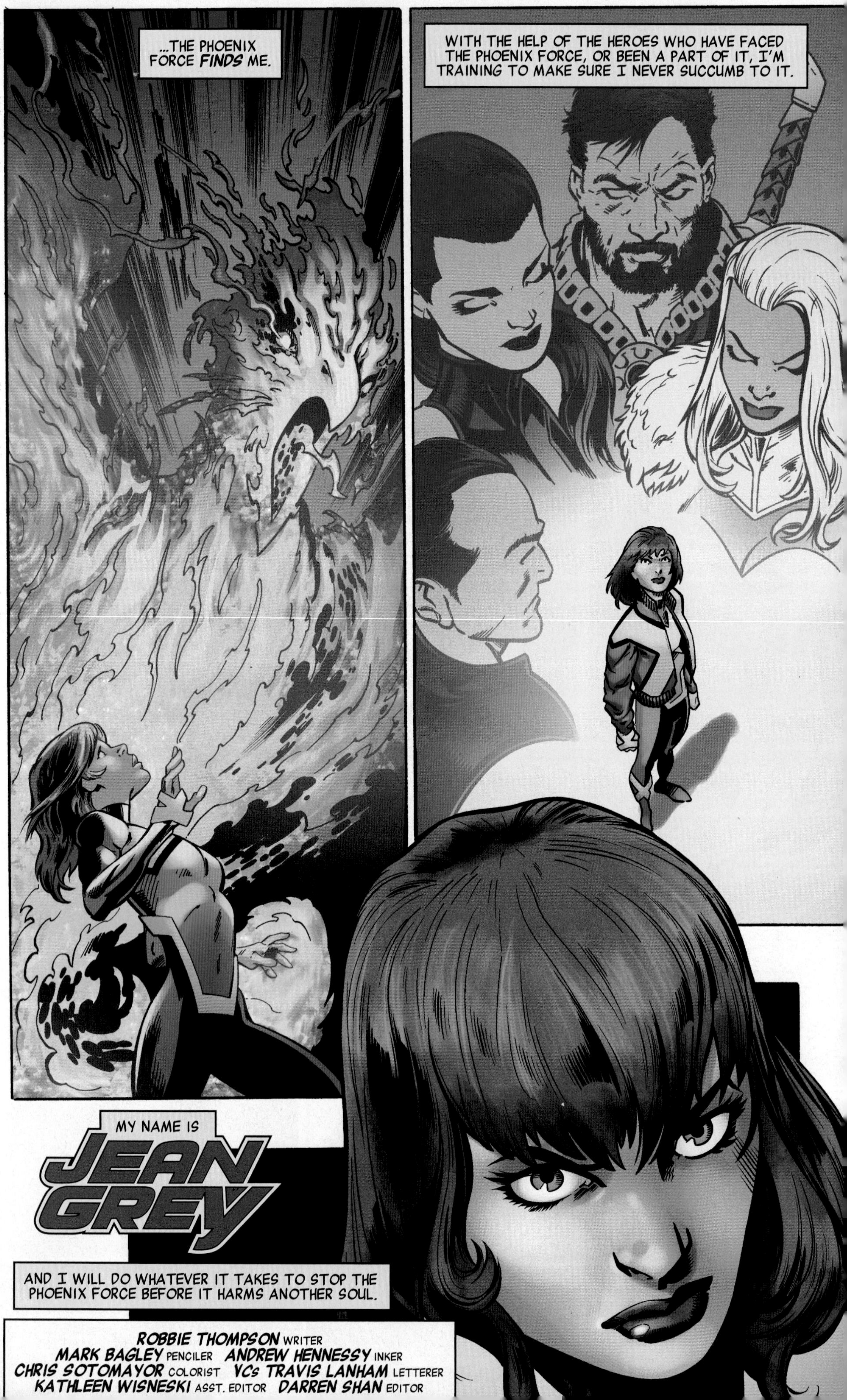

...THE PHOENIX FORCE FINDS ME.
WITH THE HELP OF THE HEROES WHO HAVE FACED THE PHOENIX FORCE, OR BEEN A PART OF IT, I'M TRAINING TO MAKE SURE I NEVER SUCCUMB TO IT.
MY NAME IS
JEAN GREY
AND I WILL DO WHATEVER IT TAKES TO STOP THE PHOENIX FORCE BEFORE IT HARMS ANOTHER SOUL.
ROBBIE THOMPSON WRITER
MARK BAGLEY PENCILER ANDREW HENNESSY INKER
CHRIS SOTOMAYOR COLORIST VC's TRAVIS LANHAM LETTERER
KATHLEEN WISNESKI ASST. EDITOR DARREN SHAN EDITOR

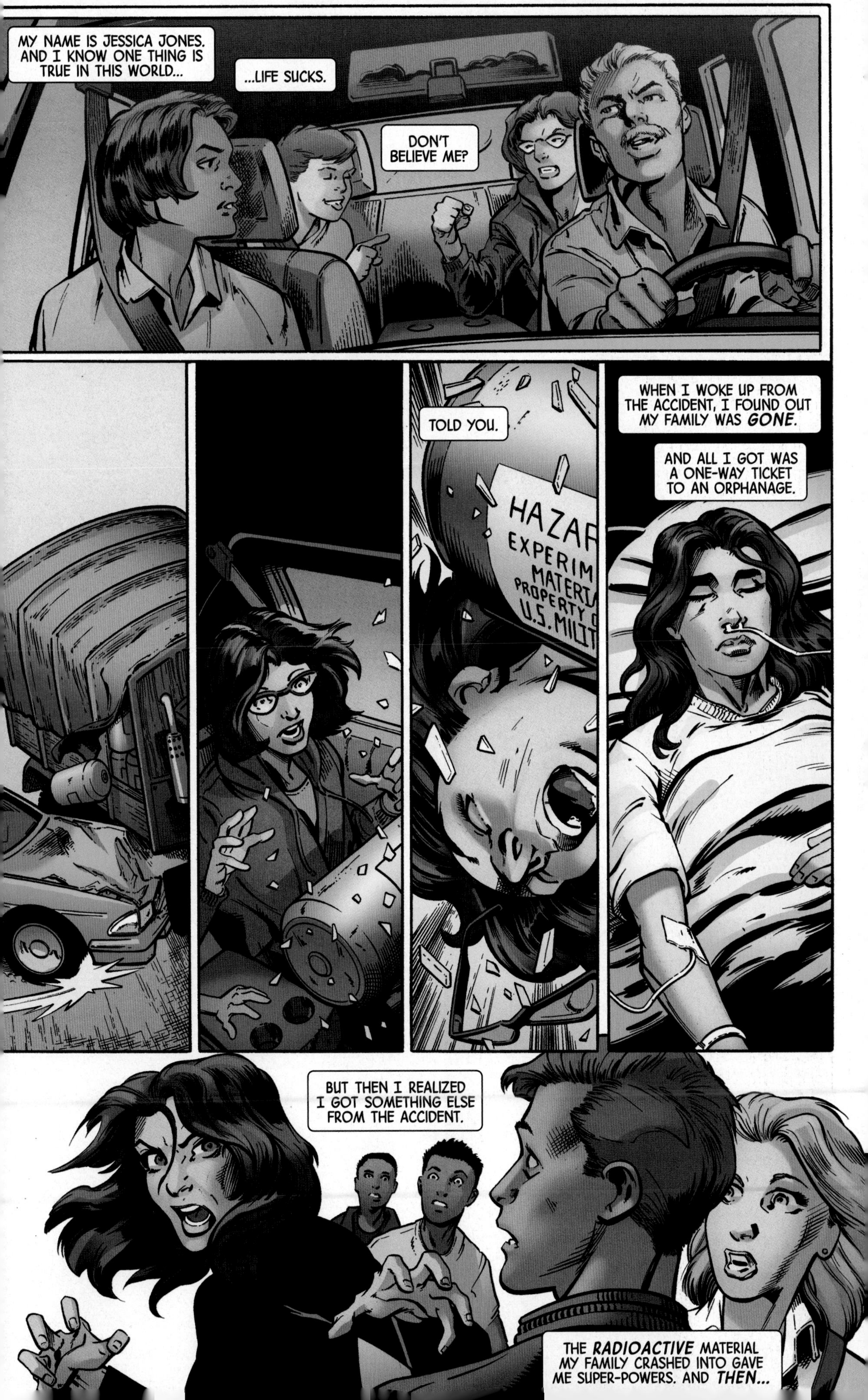
MY NAME IS JESSICA JONES. AND I KNOW ONE THING IS TRUE IN THIS WORLD...
...LIFE SUCKS.
DON'T BELIEVE ME?
TOLD YOU.
HAZAR
EXPERIM
MATERIA
PROPERTY O
U.S. MILIT
WHEN I WOKE UP FROM THE ACCIDENT, I FOUND OUT MY FAMILY WAS *GONE*.
AND ALL I GOT WAS A ONE-WAY TICKET TO AN ORPHANAGE.
BUT THEN I REALIZED I GOT SOMETHING ELSE FROM THE ACCIDENT.
THE *RADIOACTIVE* MATERIAL MY FAMILY CRASHED INTO GAVE ME SUPER-POWERS. AND *THEN*...

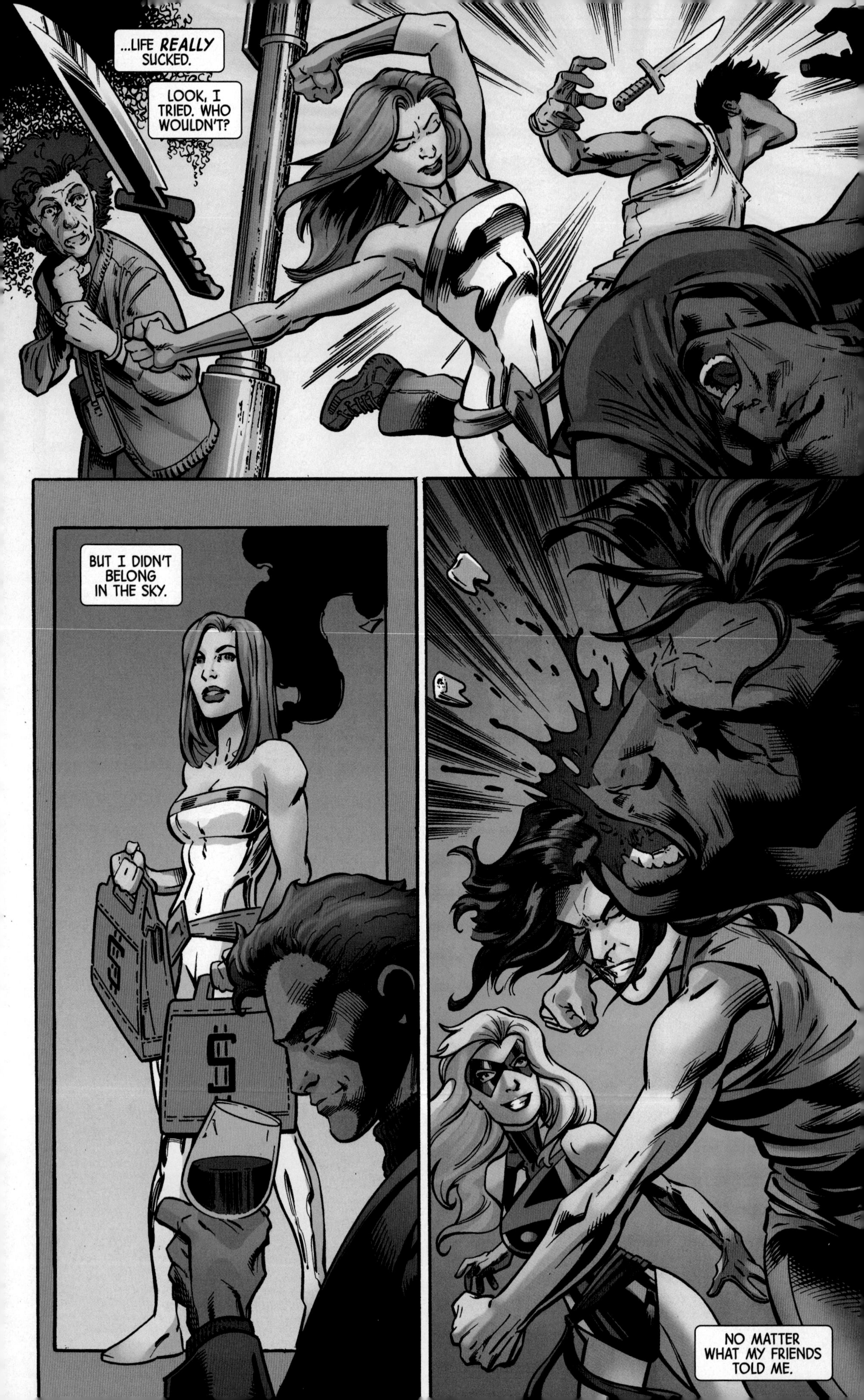
...LIFE *REALLY* SUCKED.
LOOK, I TRIED. WHO WOULDN'T?
BUT I DIDN'T BELONG IN THE SKY.
NO MATTER WHAT MY FRIENDS TOLD ME.

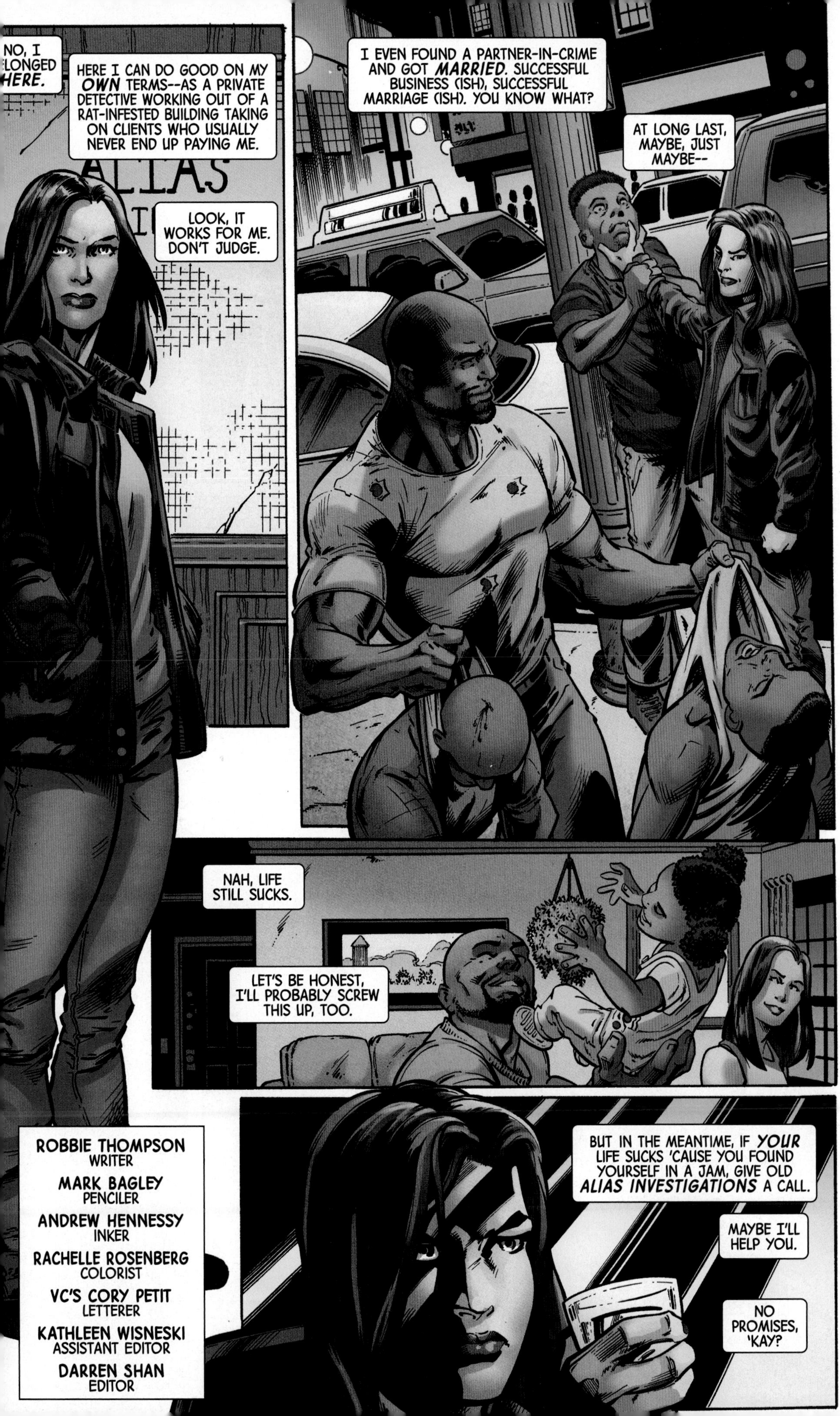
NO, I ELONGED HERE.
HERE I CAN DO GOOD ON MY OWN TERMS--AS A PRIVATE DETECTIVE WORKING OUT OF A RAT-INFESTED BUILDING TAKING ON CLIENTS WHO USUALLY NEVER END UP PAYING ME.
LOOK, IT WORKS FOR ME. DON'T JUDGE.
I EVEN FOUND A PARTNER-IN-CRIME AND GOT MARRIED. SUCCESSFUL BUSINESS (ISH), SUCCESSFUL MARRIAGE (ISH). YOU KNOW WHAT?
AT LONG LAST, MAYBE, JUST MAYBE--
NAH, LIFE STILL SUCKS.
LET'S BE HONEST, I'LL PROBABLY SCREW THIS UP, TOO.
BUT IN THE MEANTIME, IF YOUR LIFE SUCKS 'CAUSE YOU FOUND YOURSELF IN A JAM, GIVE OLD ALIAS INVESTIGATIONS A CALL.
MAYBE I'LL HELP YOU.
NO PROMISES, 'KAY?
ROBBIE THOMPSON
WRITER
MARK BAGLEY
PENCILER
ANDREW HENNESSY
INKER
RACHELLE ROSENBERG
COLORIST
VC'S CORY PETIT
LETTERER
KATHLEEN WISNESKI
ASSISTANT EDITOR
DARREN SHAN
EDITOR

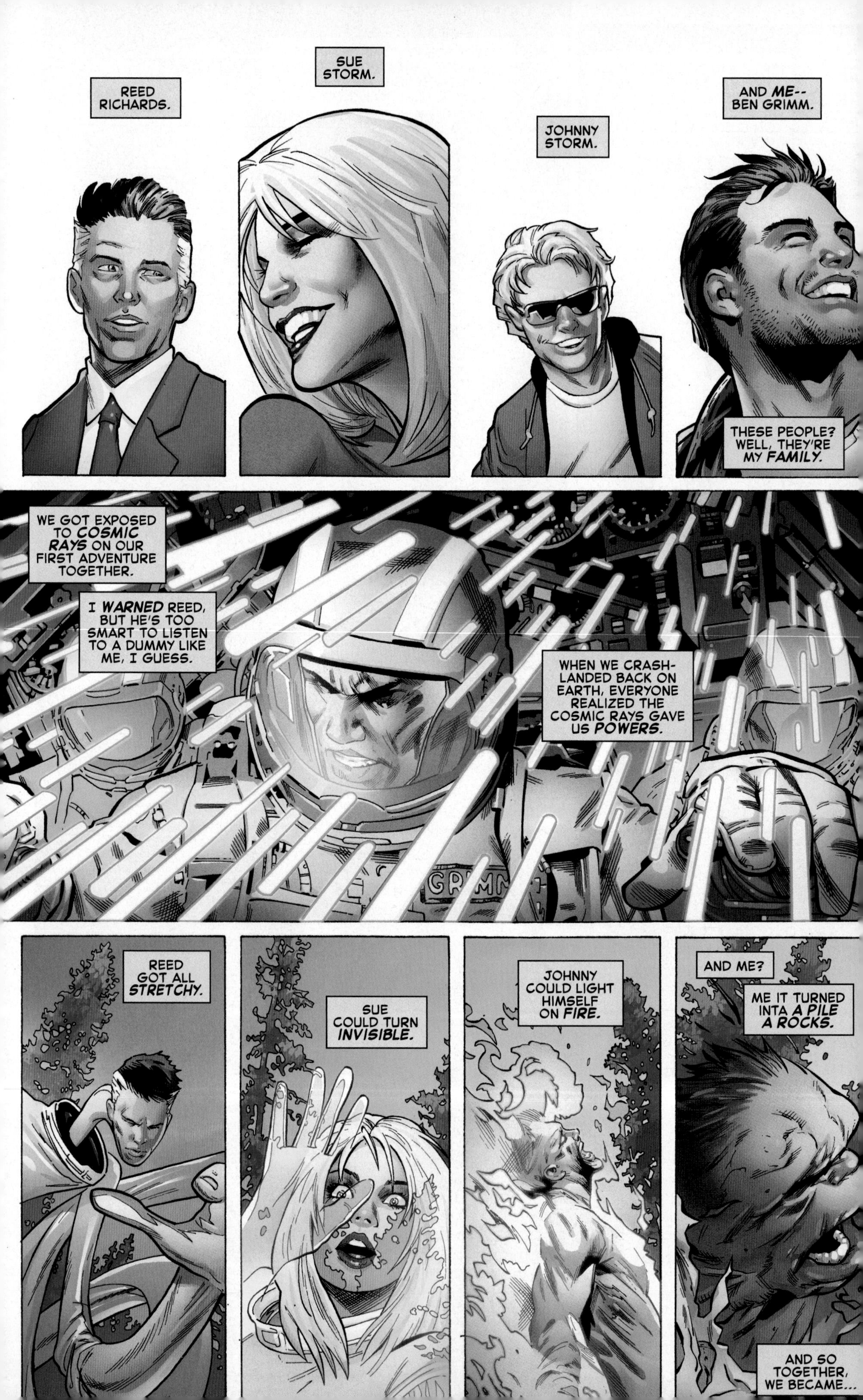
REED RICHARDS.
SUE STORM.
JOHNNY STORM.
AND ME-- BEN GRIMM.
THESE PEOPLE? WELL, THEY'RE MY FAMILY.
WE GOT EXPOSED TO COSMIC RAYS ON OUR FIRST ADVENTURE TOGETHER.
I WARNED REED, BUT HE'S TOO SMART TO LISTEN TO A DUMMY LIKE ME, I GUESS.
WHEN WE CRASH-LANDED BACK ON EARTH, EVERYONE REALIZED THE COSMIC RAYS GAVE US POWERS.
GRIMM
REED GOT ALL STRETCHY.
SUE COULD TURN INVISIBLE.
JOHNNY COULD LIGHT HIMSELF ON FIRE.
AND ME?
ME IT TURNED INTA A PILE A ROCKS.
AND SO TOGETHER, WE BECAME...

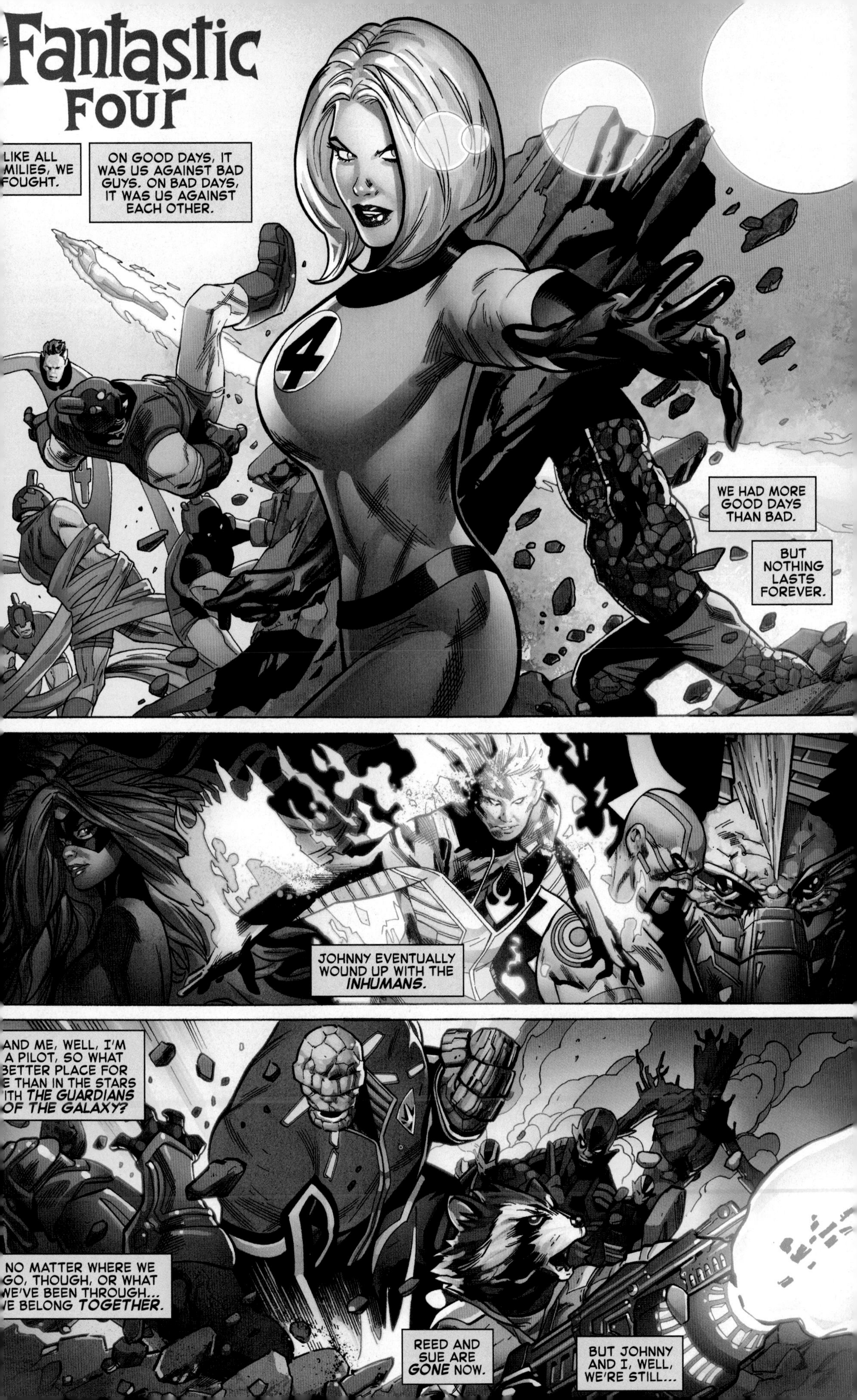
Fantastic Four
LIKE ALL
MILIES, WE
FOUGHT.
ON GOOD DAYS, IT WAS US AGAINST BAD GUYS. ON BAD DAYS, IT WAS US AGAINST EACH OTHER.
WE HAD MORE GOOD DAYS THAN BAD.
BUT NOTHING LASTS FOREVER.
JOHNNY EVENTUALLY WOUND UP WITH THE INHUMANS.
AND ME, WELL, I'M A PILOT, SO WHAT BETTER PLACE FOR E THAN IN THE STARS ITH THE GUARDIANS OF THE GALAXY?
NO MATTER WHERE WE GO, THOUGH, OR WHAT WE'VE BEEN THROUGH... E BELONG TOGETHER.
REED AND SUE ARE GONE NOW.
BUT JOHNNY AND I, WELL, WE'RE STILL...

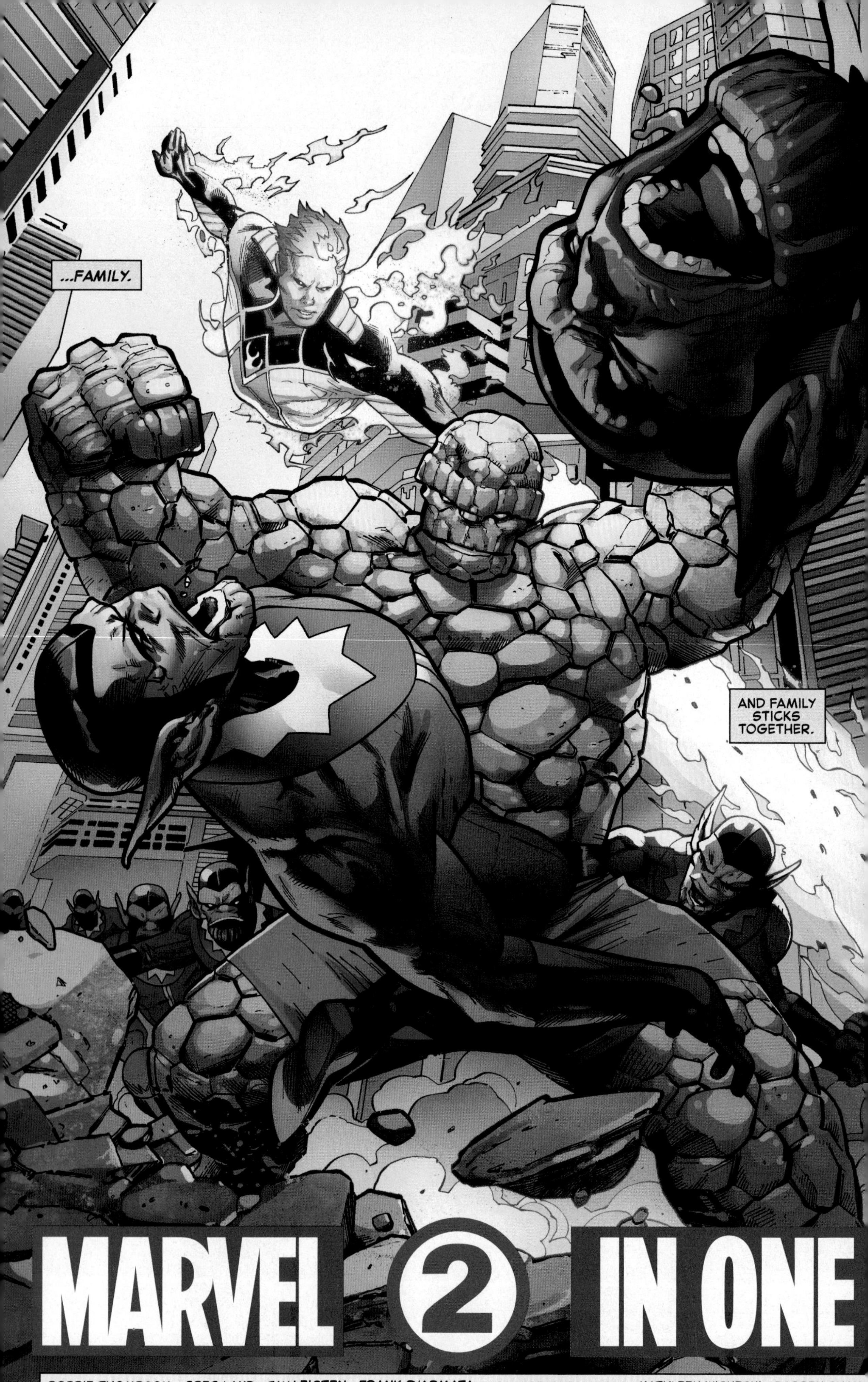
...FAMILY.
AND FAMILY STICKS TOGETHER.
MARVEL 2 IN ONE

ROBBIE THOMPSON WRITER | GREG LAND PENCILER | JAY LEISTEN INKER | FRANK D'ARMATA COLORIST | VC'S JOE CARAMAGNA LETTERER | KATHLEEN WISNESKI ASSISTANT EDITOR | DARREN SHAN EDITOR

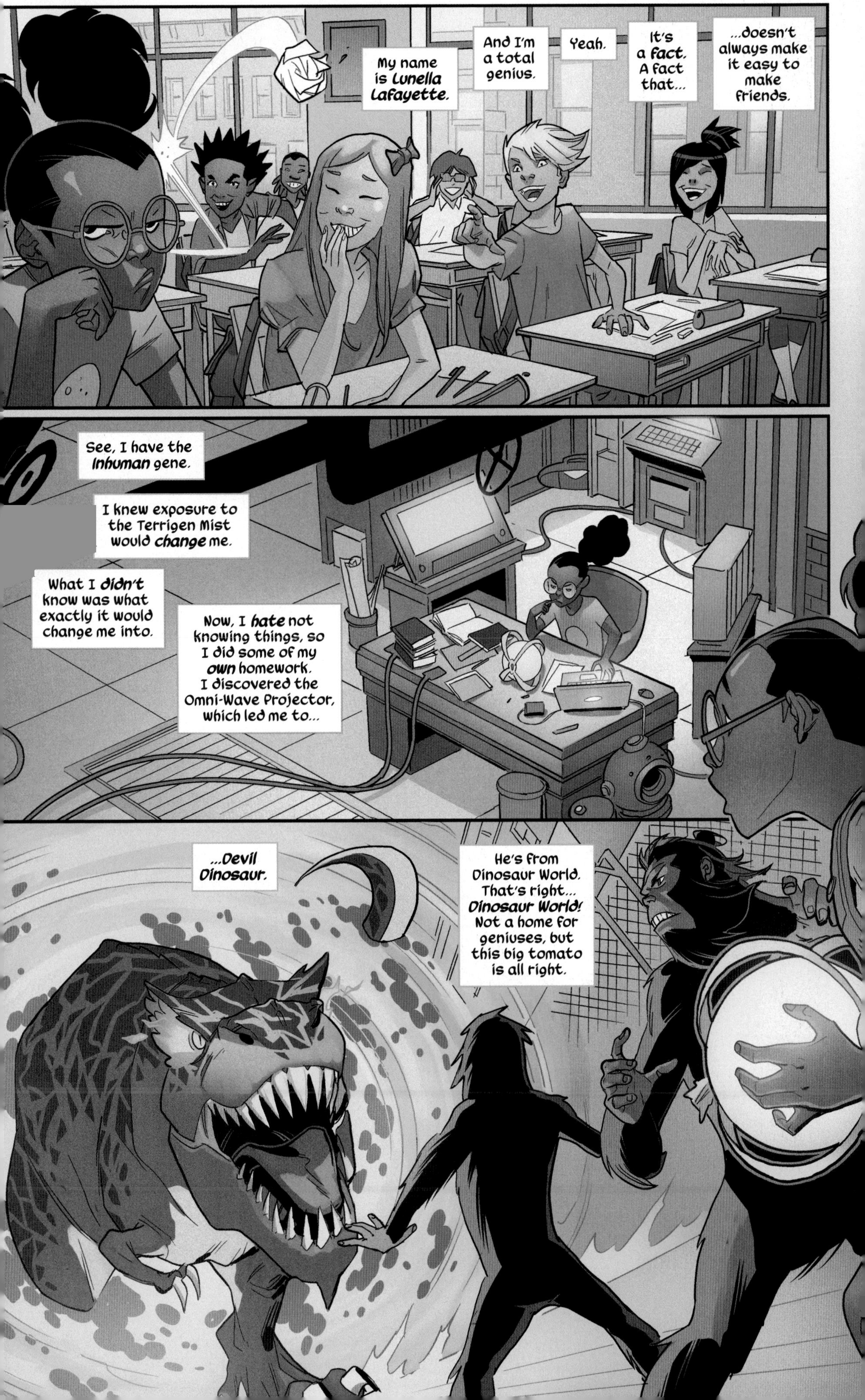
My name is Lunella Lafayette.
And I'm a total genius.
Yeah.
It's a fact. A fact that...
...doesn't always make it easy to make friends.
See, I have the Inhuman gene.
I knew exposure to the Terrigen Mist would change me.
What I didn't know was what exactly it would change me into.
Now, I hate not knowing things, so I did some of my own homework. I discovered the Omni-Wave Projector, which led me to...
...Devil Dinosaur.
He's from Dinosaur World. That's right... Dinosaur World! Not a home for geniuses, but this big tomato is all right.

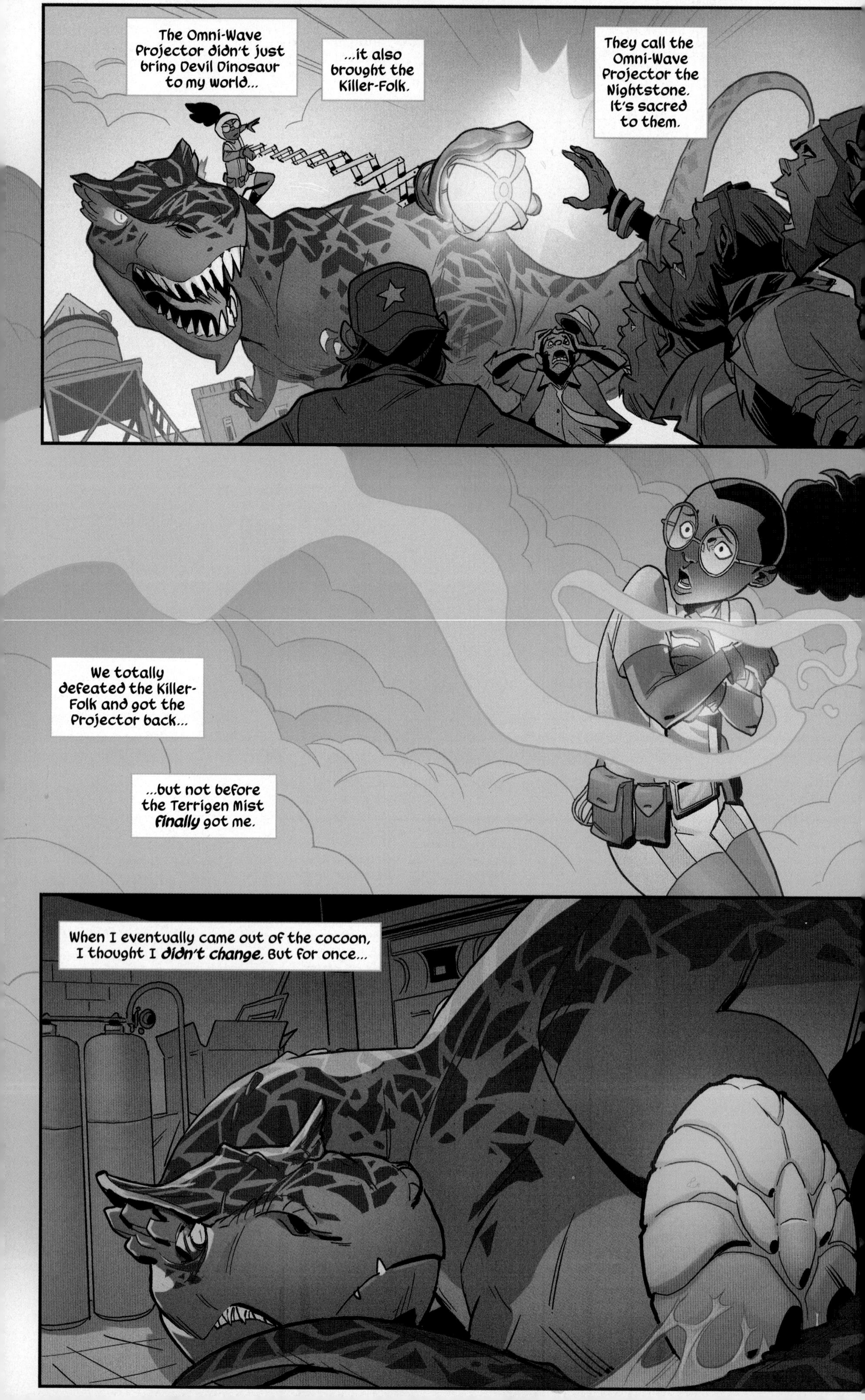
The Omni-Wave Projector didn't just bring Devil Dinosaur to my world...
...it also brought the Killer-Folk.
They call the Omni-Wave Projector the Nightstone. It's sacred to them.
We totally defeated the Killer-Folk and got the Projector back...
...but not before the Terrigen Mist *finally* got me.
When I eventually came out of the cocoon, I thought I *didn't change*. But for once...

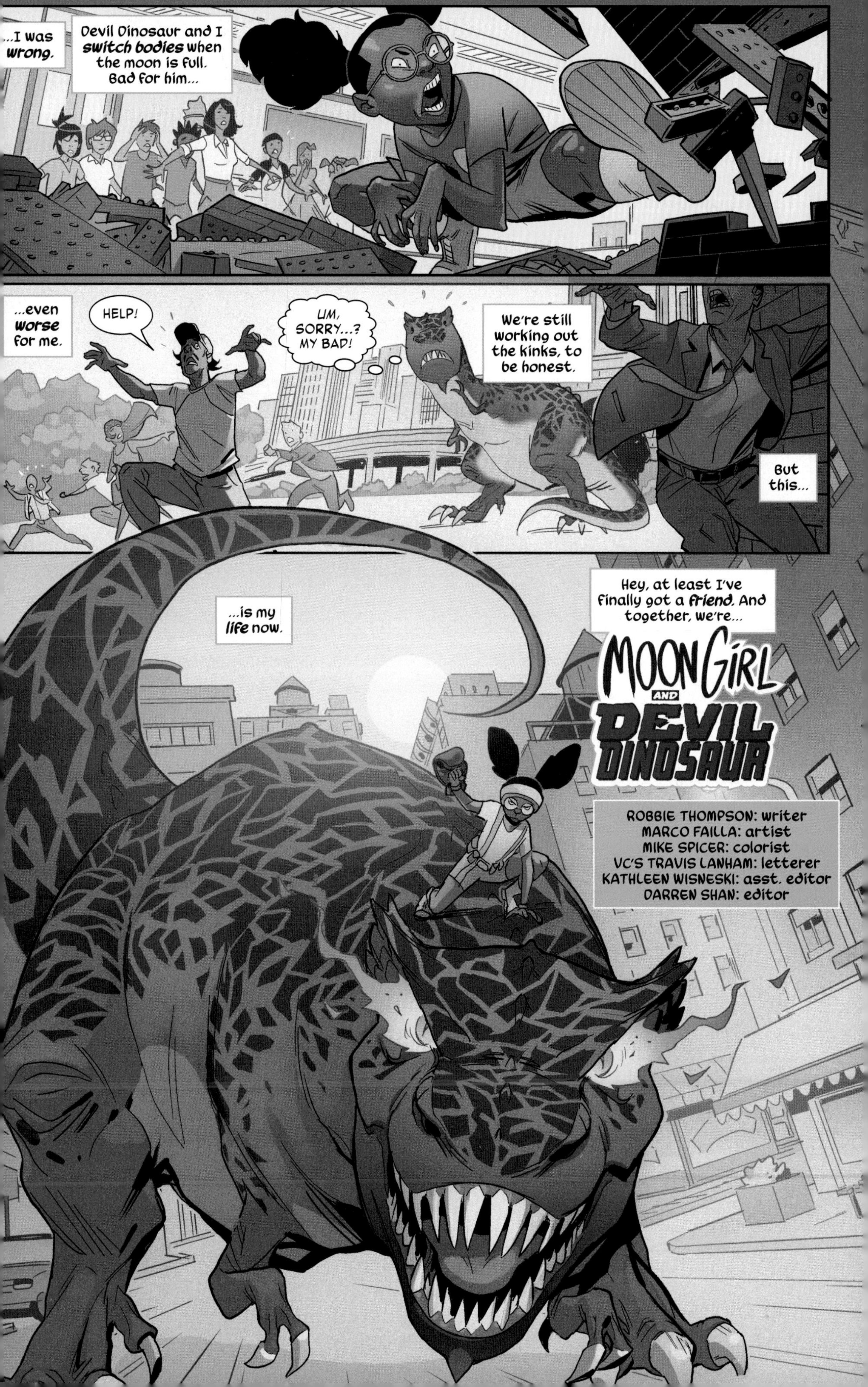

...I was wrong.
Devil Dinosaur and I switch bodies when the moon is full. Bad for him...
...even worse for me.
HELP!
UM, SORRY...? MY BAD!
We're still working out the kinks, to be honest.
But this...
...is my life now.
Hey, at least I've finally got a friend. And together, we're...
MOON GIRL AND DEVIL DINOSAUR
ROBBIE THOMPSON: writer
MARCO FAILLA: artist
MIKE SPICER: colorist
VC'S TRAVIS LANHAM: letterer
KATHLEEN WISNESKI: asst. editor
DARREN SHAN: editor

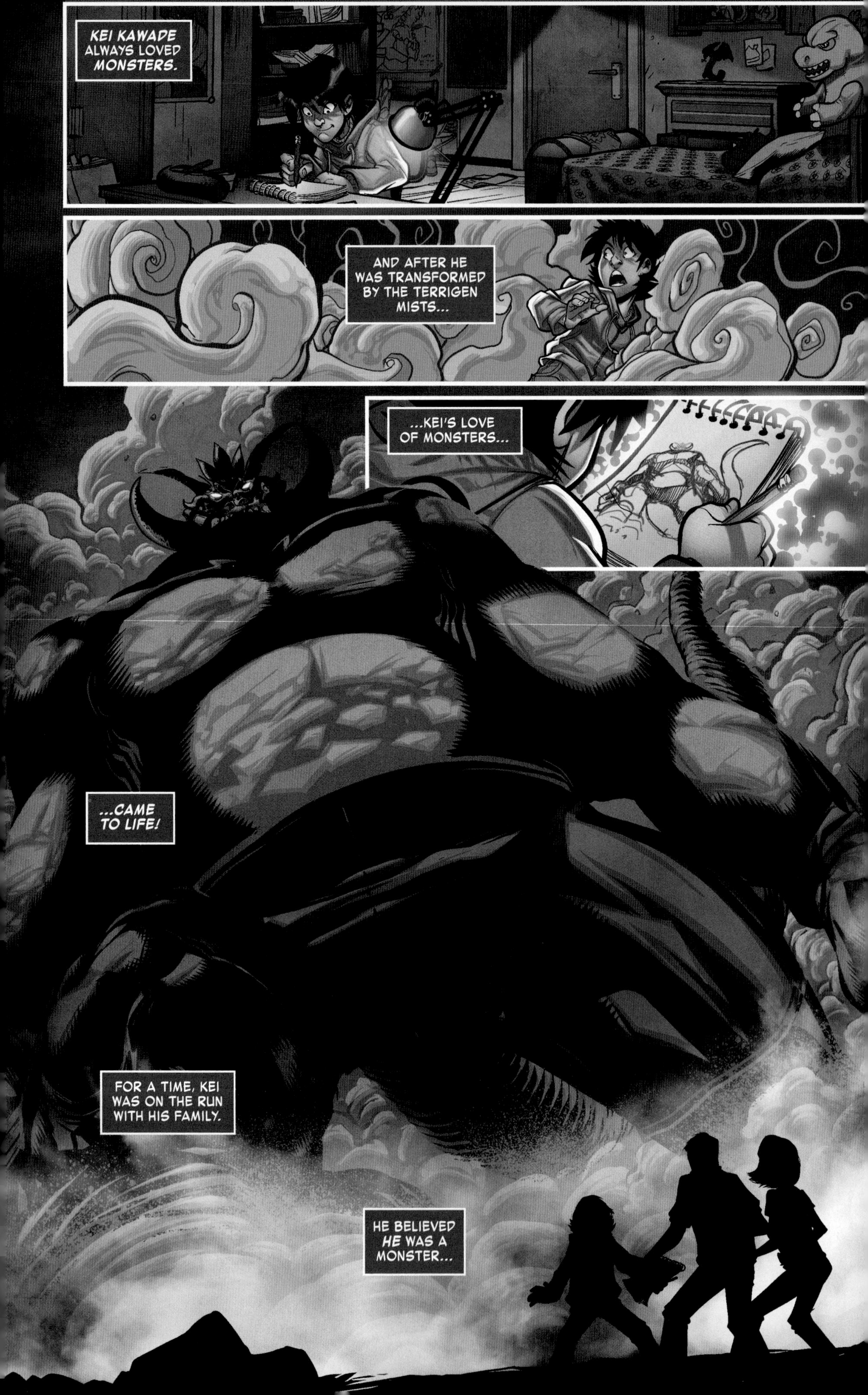
KEI KAWADE ALWAYS LOVED MONSTERS.
AND AFTER HE WAS TRANSFORMED BY THE TERRIGEN MISTS...
...KEI'S LOVE OF MONSTERS...
...CAME TO LIFE!
FOR A TIME, KEI WAS ON THE RUN WITH HIS FAMILY.
HE BELIEVED HE WAS A MONSTER...

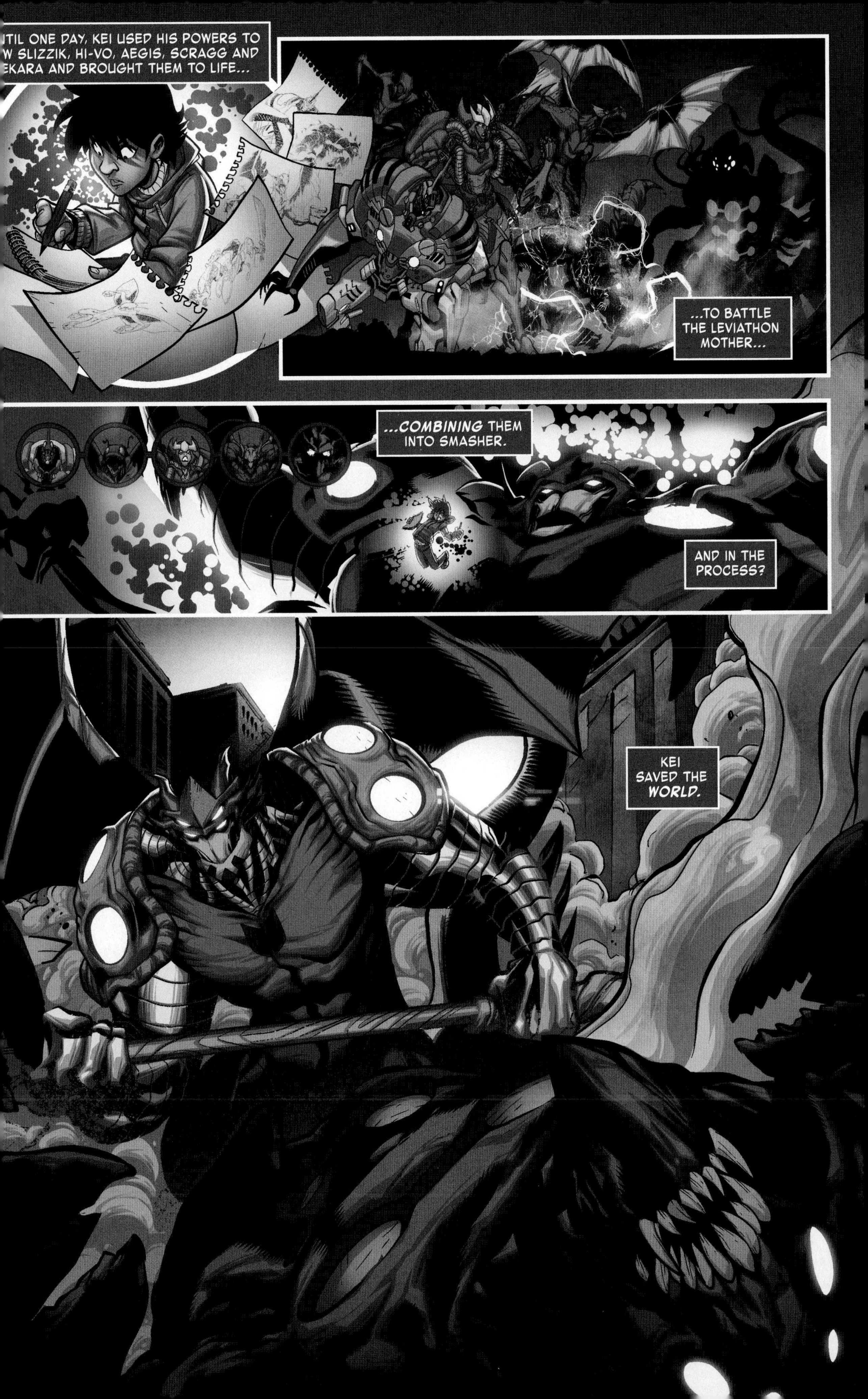

TIL ONE DAY, KEI USED HIS POWERS TO
W SLIZZIK, HI-VO, AEGIS, SCRAGG AND
EKARA AND BROUGHT THEM TO LIFE...
...TO BATTLE THE LEVIATHON MOTHER...
...COMBINING THEM INTO SMASHER.
AND IN THE PROCESS?
KEI SAVED THE WORLD.

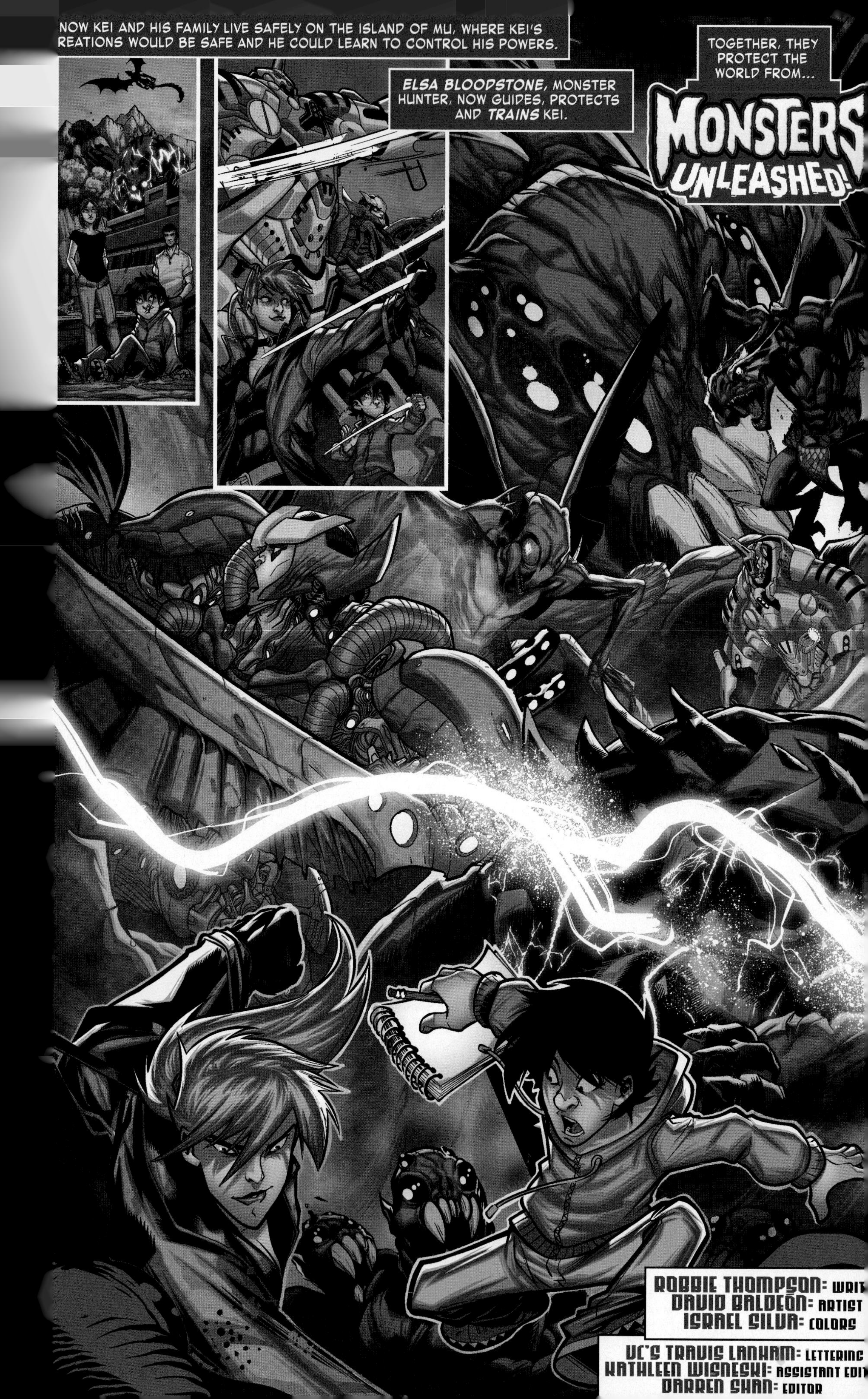
NOW KEI AND HIS FAMILY LIVE SAFELY ON THE ISLAND OF MU, WHERE KEI'S
REATIONS WOULD BE SAFE AND HE COULD LEARN TO CONTROL HIS POWERS.
ELSA BLOODSTONE, MONSTER HUNTER, NOW GUIDES, PROTECTS AND TRAINS KEI.
TOGETHER, THEY PROTECT THE WORLD FROM...
MONSTERS UNLEASHED!
ROBBIE THOMPSON: WRIT
DAVID BALDEÓN: ARTIST
ISRAEL SILVA: COLORS
VC'S TRAVIS LANHAM: LETTERING
KATHLEEN WISNESKI: ASSISTANT EDIT
DARREN SHAN: EDITOR

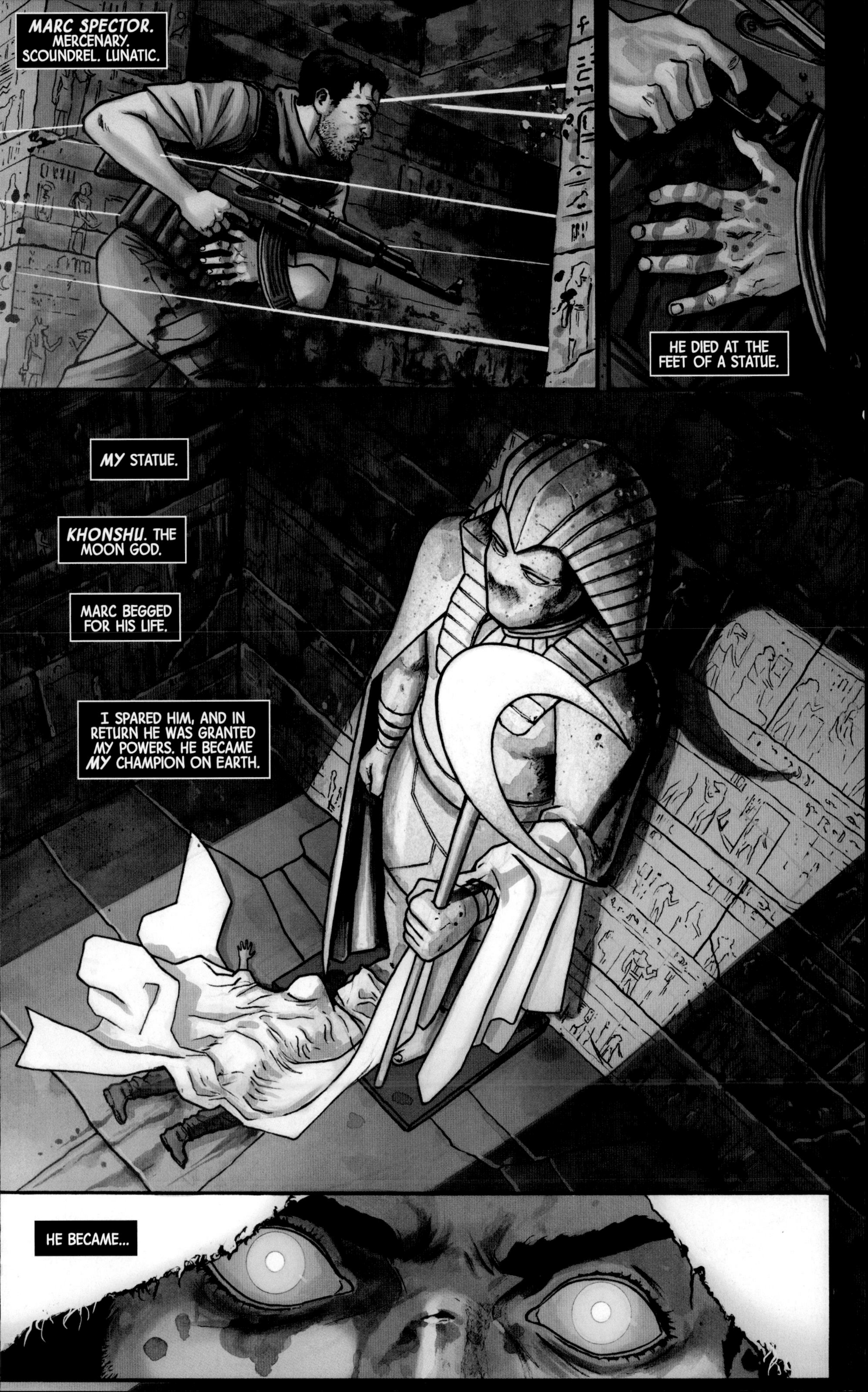
MARC SPECTOR. MERCENARY. SCOUNDREL. LUNATIC.
HE DIED AT THE FEET OF A STATUE.
MY STATUE.
KHONSHU. THE MOON GOD.
MARC BEGGED FOR HIS LIFE.
I SPARED HIM, AND IN RETURN HE WAS GRANTED MY POWERS. HE BECAME MY CHAMPION ON EARTH.
HE BECAME...

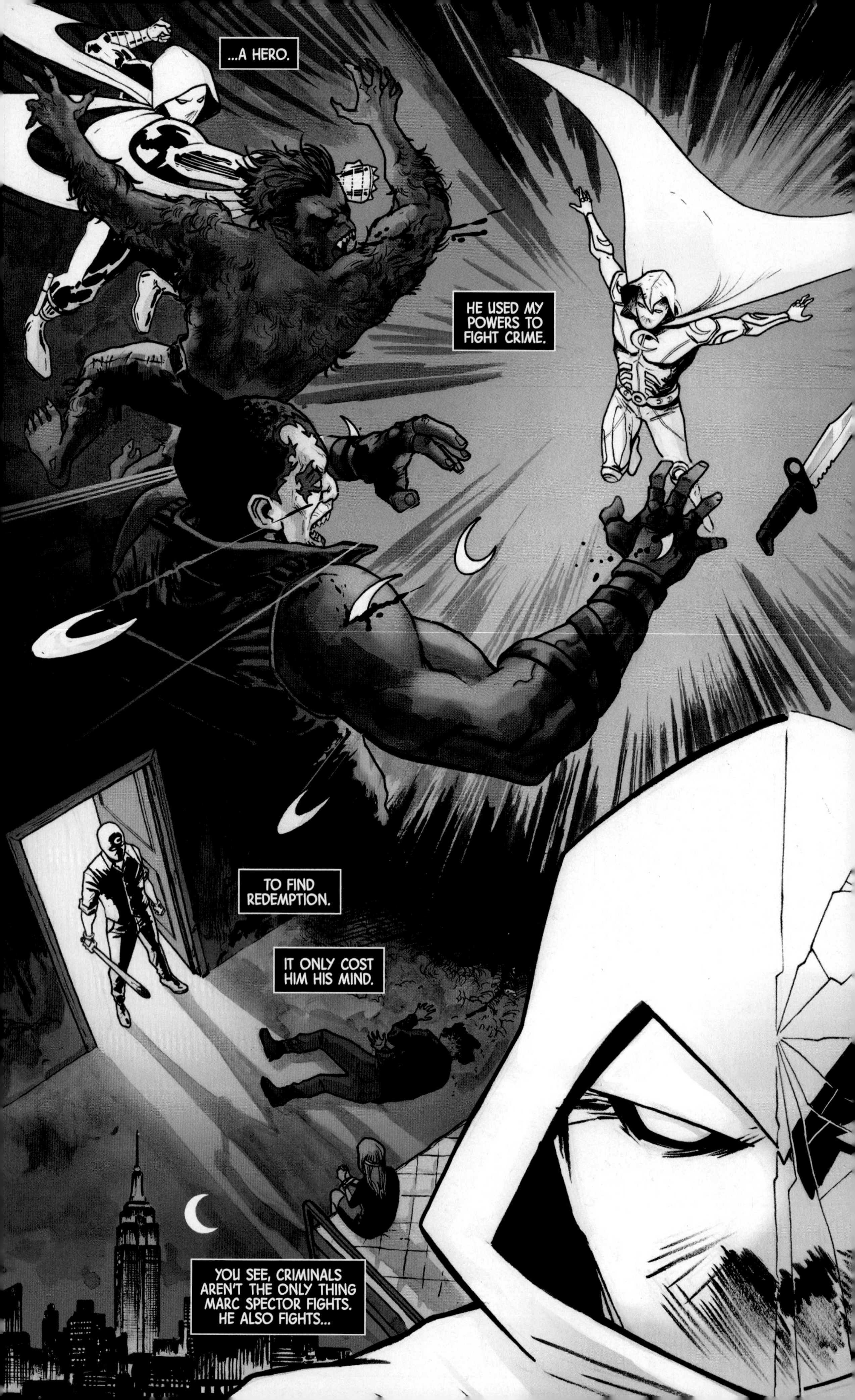
...A HERO.
HE USED MY POWERS TO FIGHT CRIME.
TO FIND REDEMPTION.
IT ONLY COST HIM HIS MIND.
YOU SEE, CRIMINALS AREN'T THE ONLY THING MARC SPECTOR FIGHTS. HE ALSO FIGHTS...

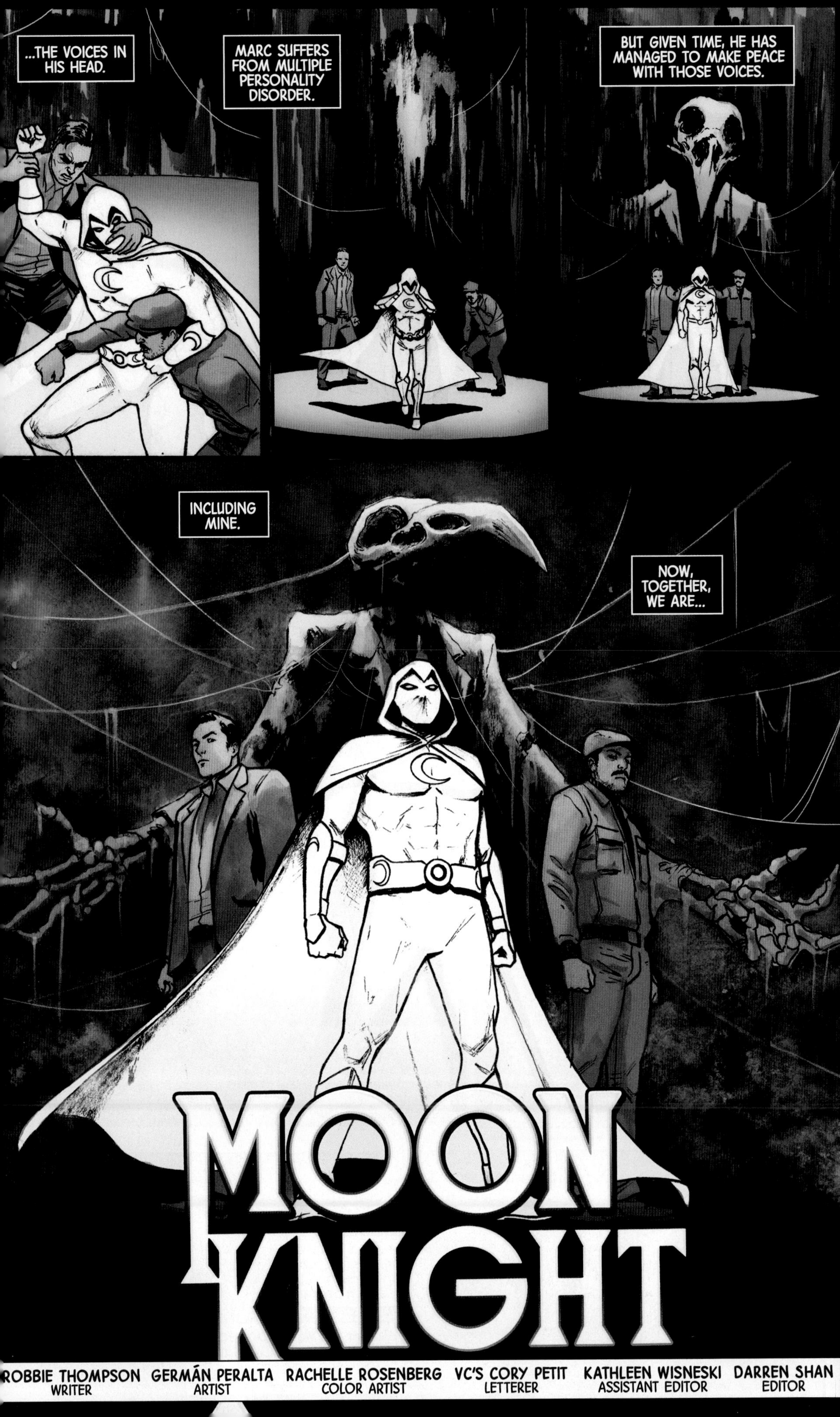
...THE VOICES IN HIS HEAD.
MARC SUFFERS FROM MULTIPLE PERSONALITY DISORDER.
BUT GIVEN TIME, HE HAS MANAGED TO MAKE PEACE WITH THOSE VOICES.
INCLUDING MINE.
NOW, TOGETHER, WE ARE...
MOON KNIGHT
ROBBIE THOMPSON WRITER
GERMÁN PERALTA ARTIST
RACHELLE ROSENBERG COLOR ARTIST
VC'S CORY PETIT LETTERER
KATHLEEN WISNESKI ASSISTANT EDITOR
DARREN SHAN EDITOR

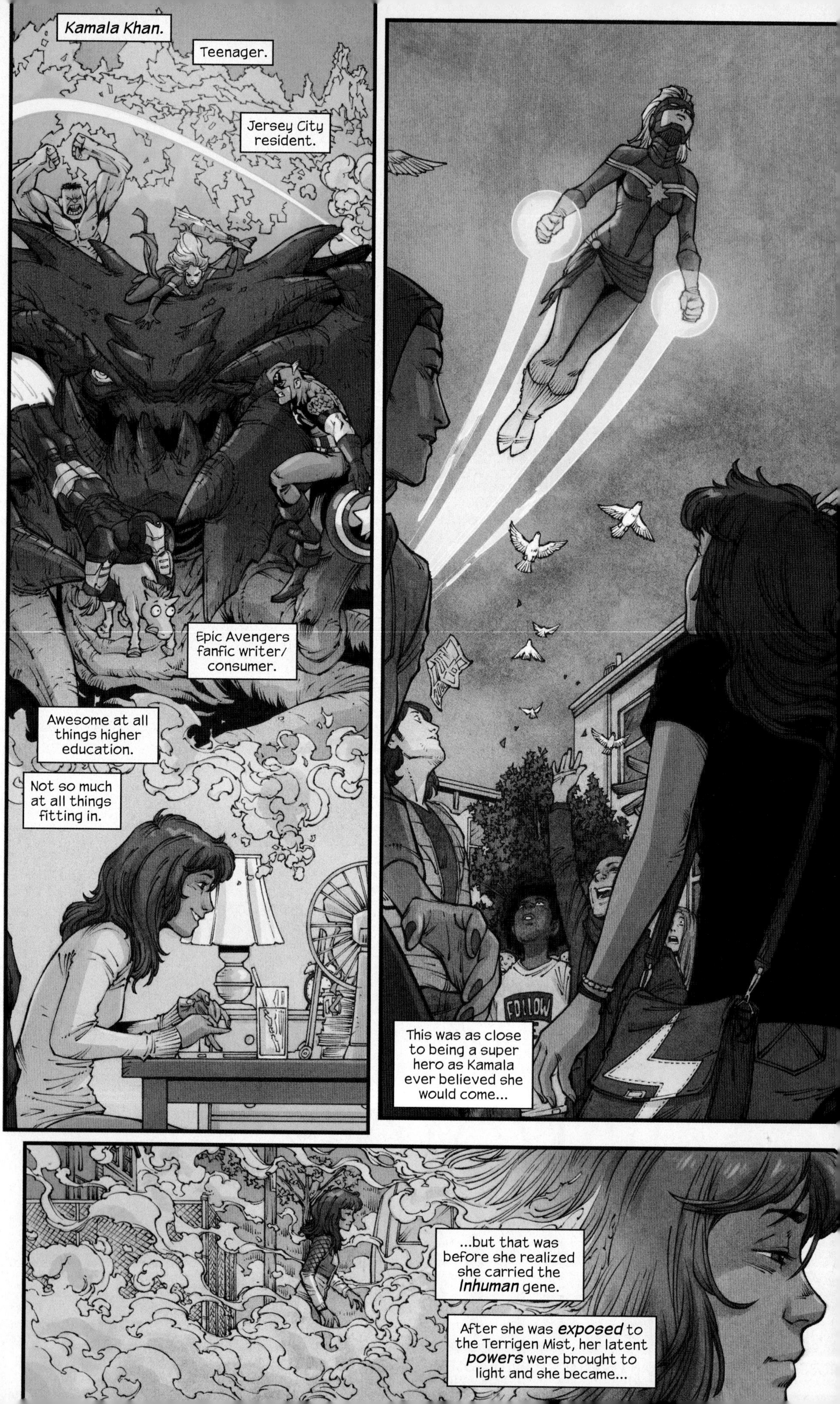
Kamala Khan.
Teenager.
Jersey City resident.
Epic Avengers fanfic writer/ consumer.
Awesome at all things higher education.
Not so much at all things fitting in.
This was as close to being a super hero as Kamala ever believed she would come...
...but that was before she realized she carried the Inhuman gene.
After she was exposed to the Terrigen Mist, her latent powers were brought to light and she became...

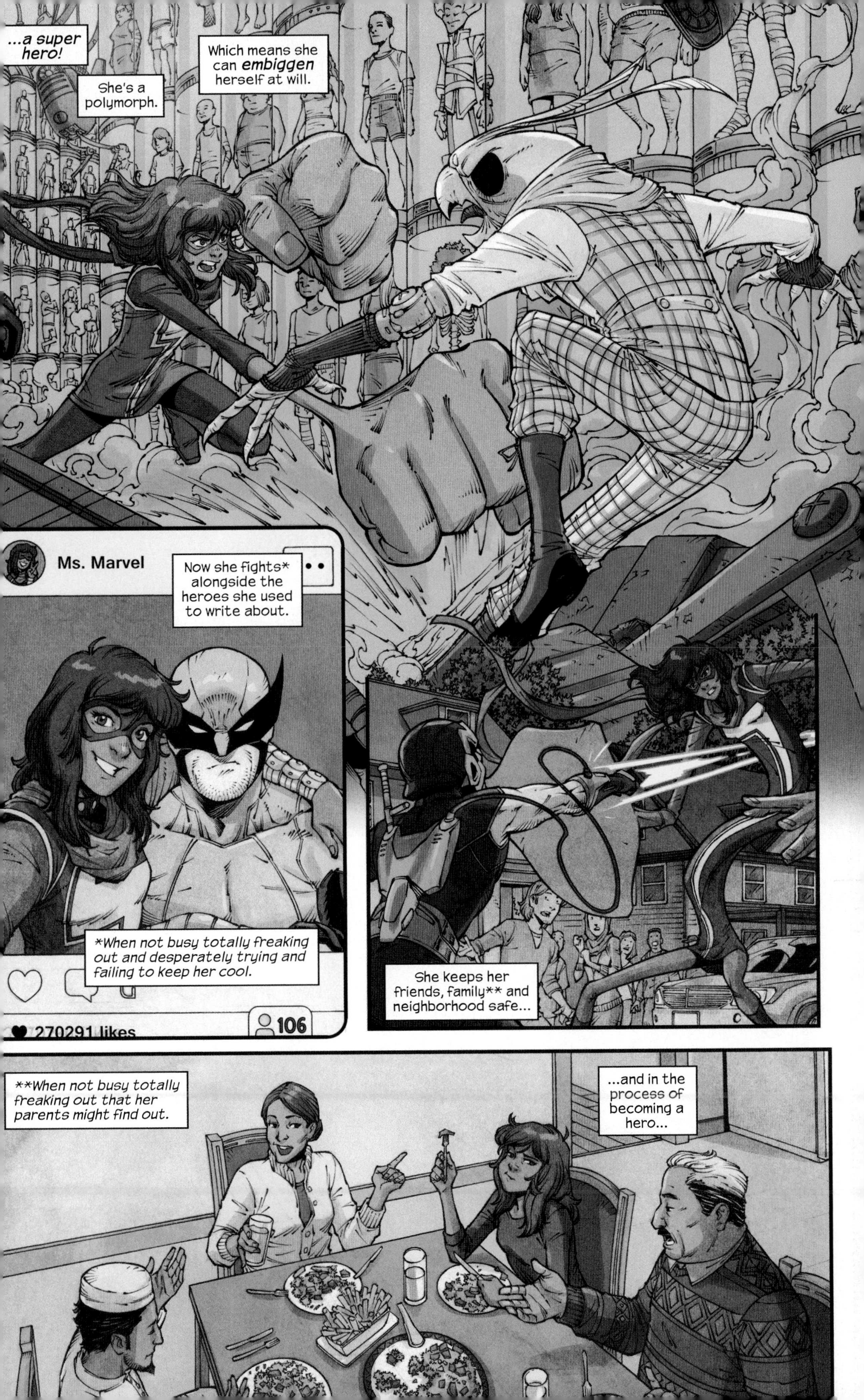

...a super hero!
She's a polymorph.
Which means she can embiggen herself at will.
Ms. Marvel
Now she fights* alongside the heroes she used to write about.
*When not busy totally freaking out and desperately trying and failing to keep her cool.
270291 likes
106
She keeps her friends, family** and neighborhood safe...
**When not busy totally freaking out that her parents might find out.
...and in the process of becoming a hero...

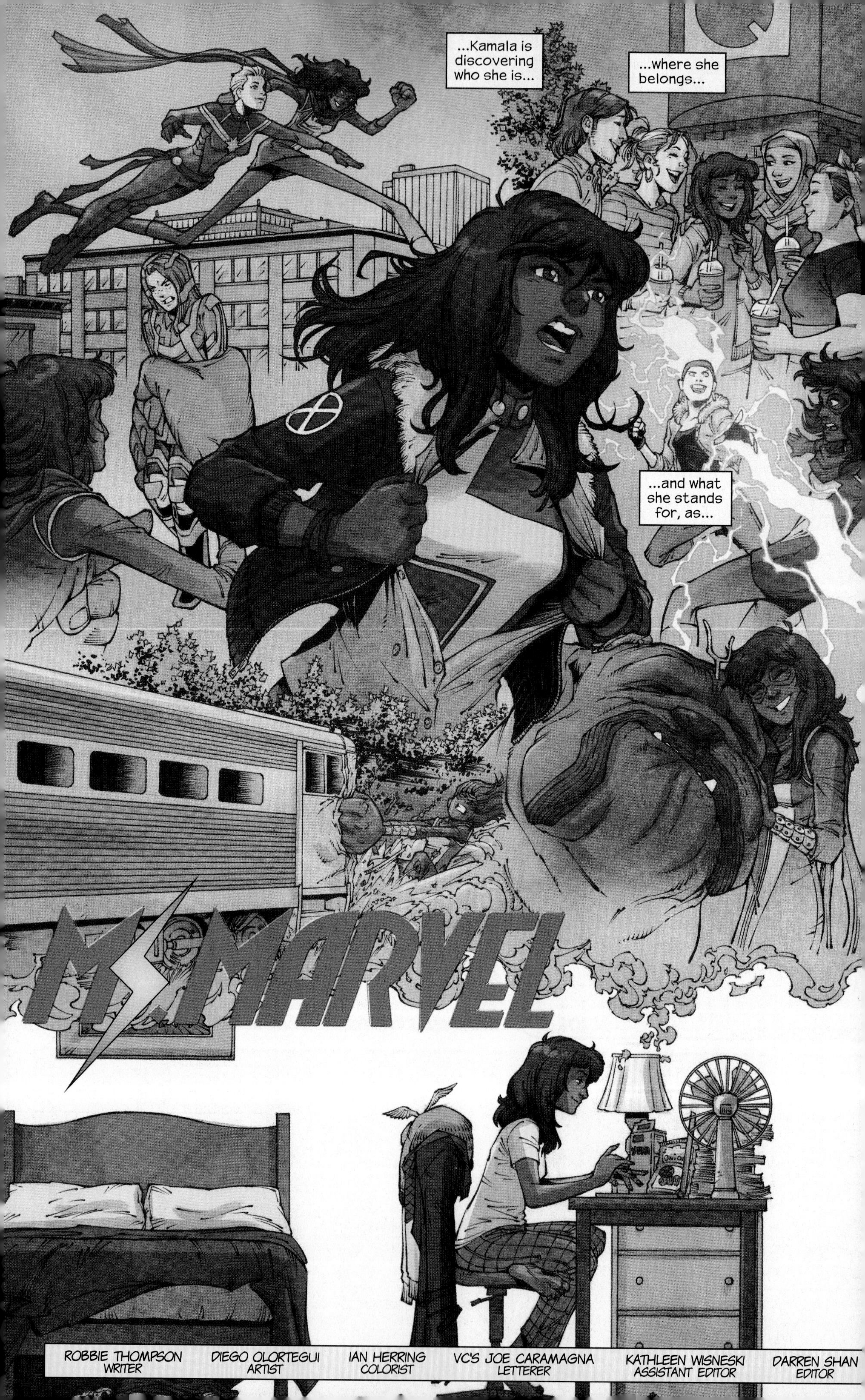
...Kamala is discovering who she is...
...where she belongs...
...and what she stands for, as...
MS. MARVEL
ROBBIE THOMPSON WRITER
DIEGO OLORTEGUI ARTIST
IAN HERRING COLORIST
VC'S JOE CARAMAGNA LETTERER
KATHLEEN WISNESKI ASSISTANT EDITOR
DARREN SHAN EDITOR

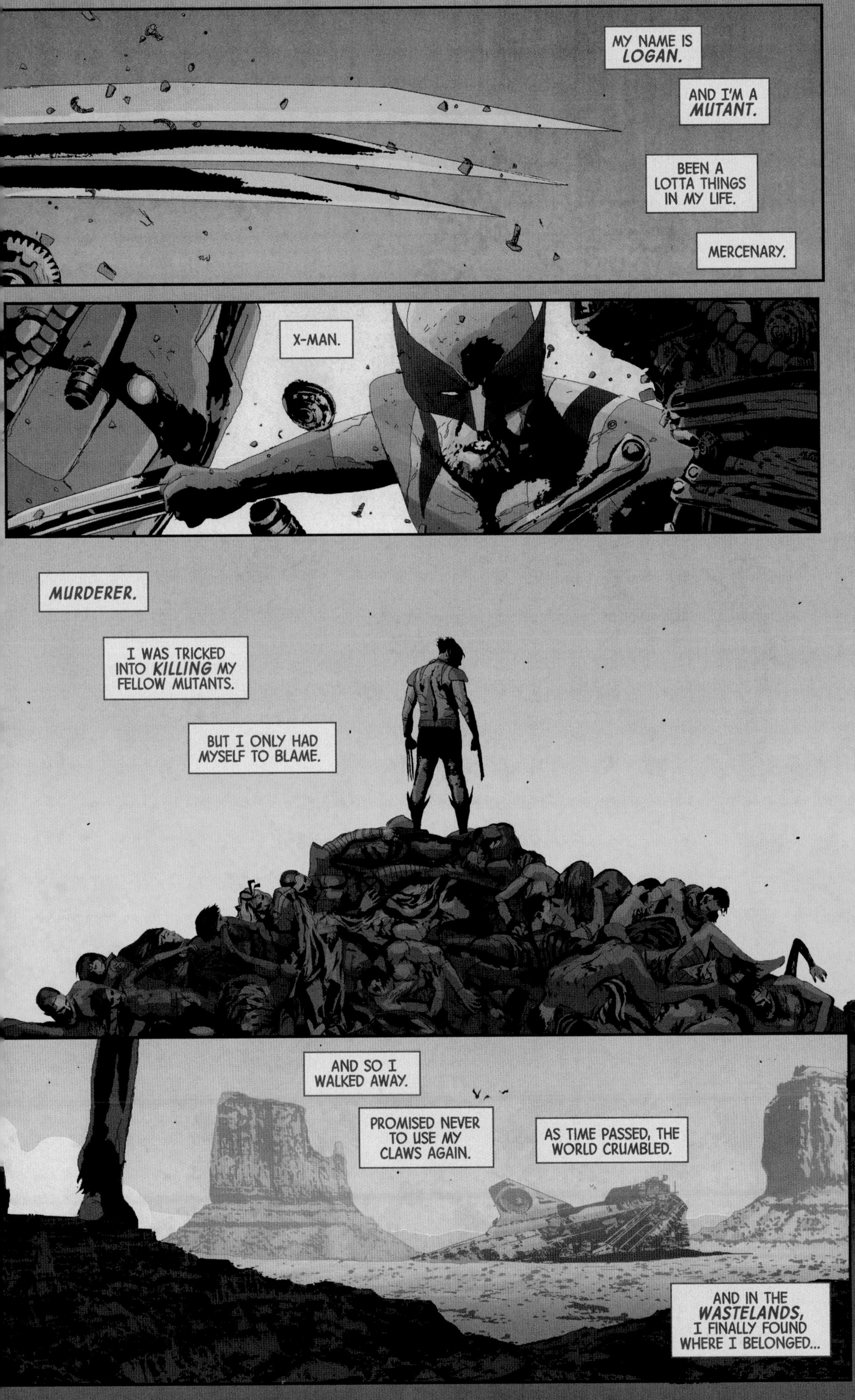
MY NAME IS LOGAN.
AND I'M A MUTANT.
BEEN A LOTTA THINGS IN MY LIFE.
MERCENARY.
X-MAN.
MURDERER.
I WAS TRICKED INTO KILLING MY FELLOW MUTANTS.
BUT I ONLY HAD MYSELF TO BLAME.
AND SO I WALKED AWAY.
PROMISED NEVER TO USE MY CLAWS AGAIN.
AS TIME PASSED, THE WORLD CRUMBLED.
AND IN THE WASTELANDS, I FINALLY FOUND WHERE I BELONGED...

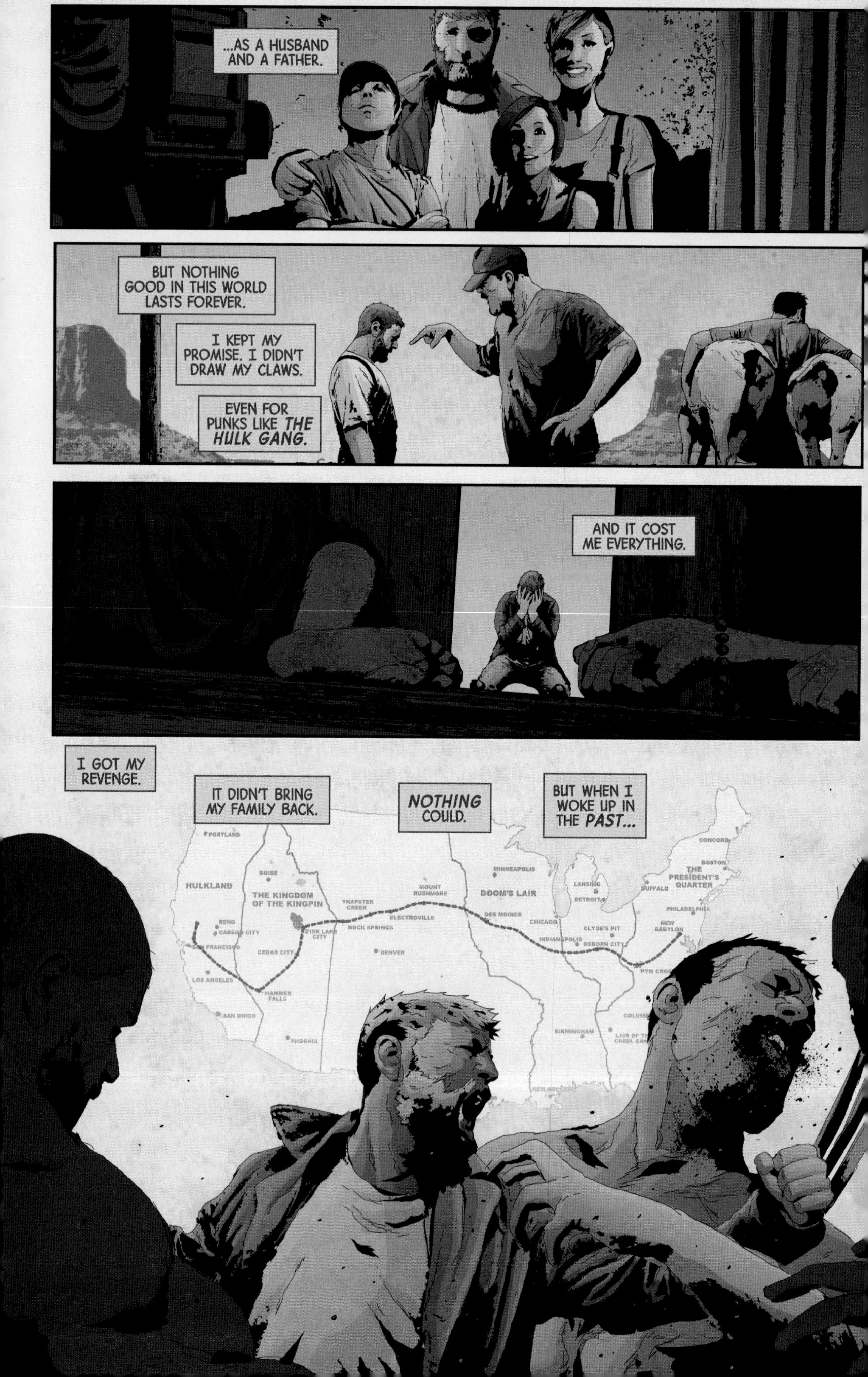
...AS A HUSBAND AND A FATHER.
BUT NOTHING GOOD IN THIS WORLD LASTS FOREVER.
I KEPT MY PROMISE. I DIDN'T DRAW MY CLAWS.
EVEN FOR PUNKS LIKE THE HULK GANG.
AND IT COST ME EVERYTHING.
I GOT MY REVENGE.
IT DIDN'T BRING MY FAMILY BACK.
NOTHING COULD.
BUT WHEN I WOKE UP IN THE PAST...
PORTLAND
HULKLAND
BOISE
THE KINGDOM OF THE KINGPIN
RENO
CARSON CITY
SAN FRANCISCO
CEDAR CITY
LOS ANGELES
HAMMER FALLS
SAN DIEGO
PHOENIX
TRAPSTER CREEK
MOUNT RUSHMORE
ELECTROVILLE
FISK LAKE CITY
ROCK SPRINGS
DENVER
MINNEAPOLIS
DOOM'S LAIR
DES MOINES
CHICAGO
LANSING
DETROIT
INDIANAPOLIS
CLYDE'S PIT
OSBORN CITY
BUFFALO
CONCORD
BOSTON
THE PRESIDENT'S QUARTER
PHILADELPHIA
NEW BABYLON
BIRMINGHAM

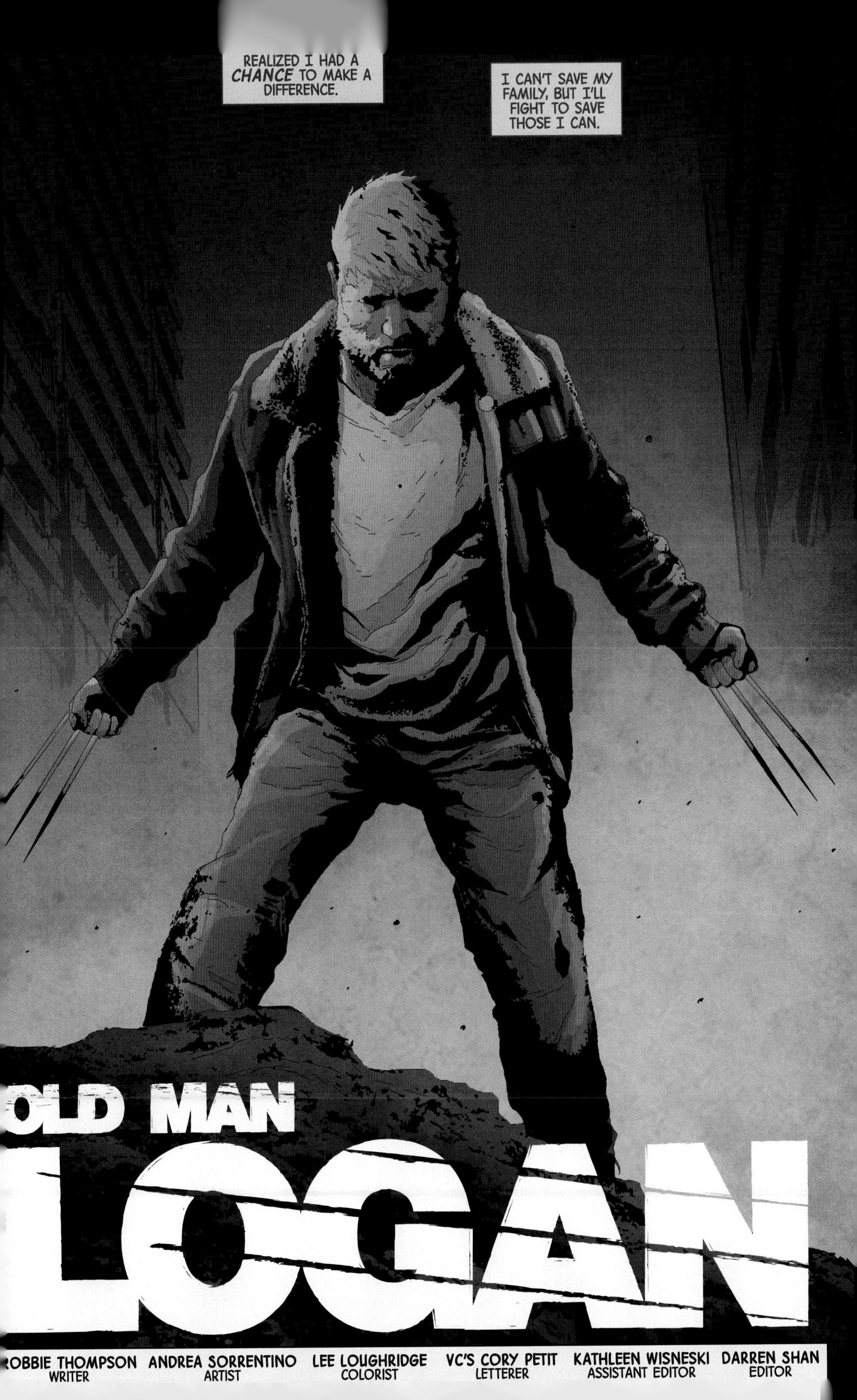
REALIZED I HAD A CHANCE TO MAKE A DIFFERENCE.
I CAN'T SAVE MY FAMILY, BUT I'LL FIGHT TO SAVE THOSE I CAN.
OLD MAN
LOGAN
ROBBIE THOMPSON WRITER
ANDREA SORRENTINO ARTIST
LEE LOUGHRIDGE COLORIST
VC'S CORY PETIT LETTERER
KATHLEEN WISNESKI ASSISTANT EDITOR
DARREN SHAN EDITOR

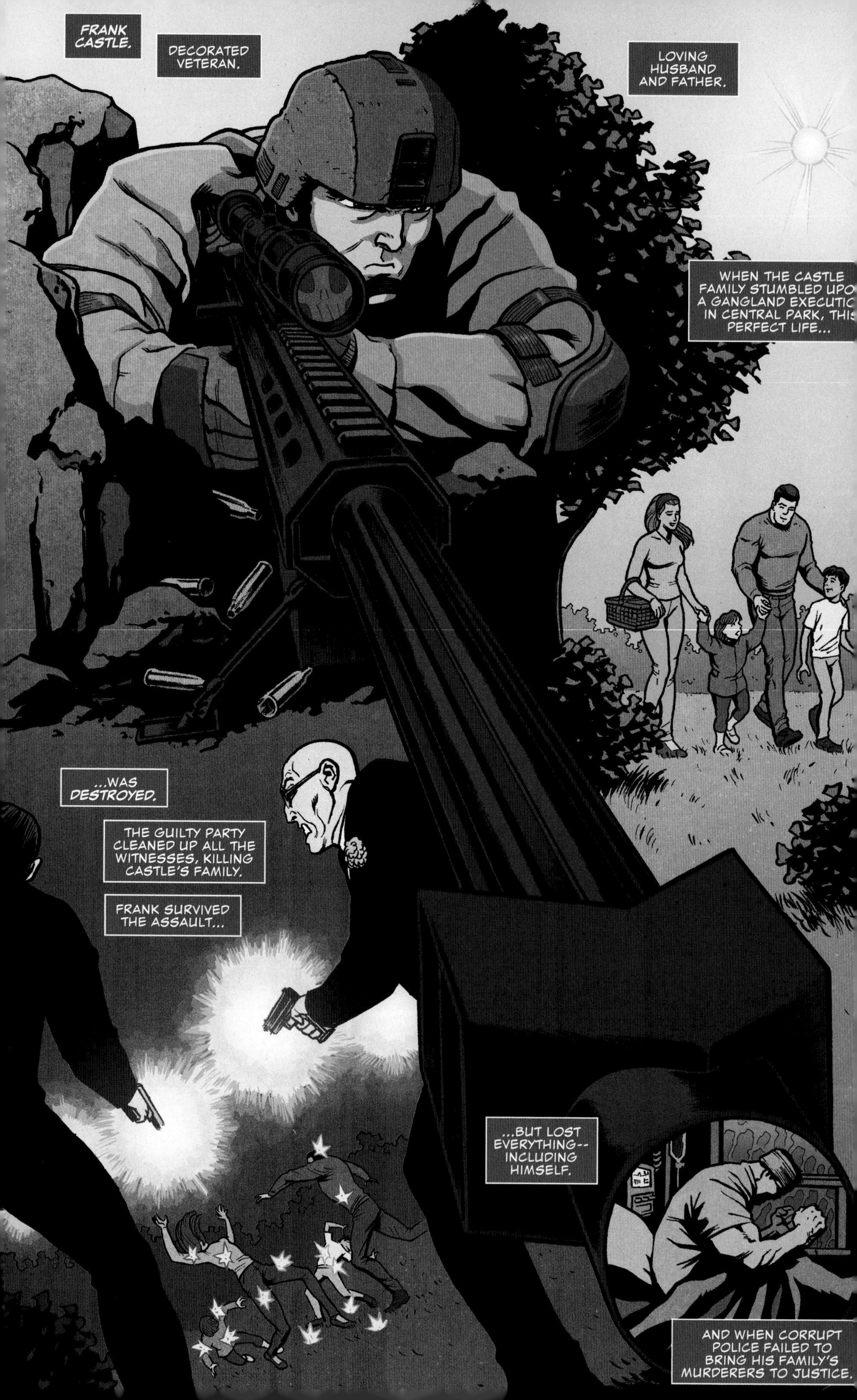
FRANK CASTLE.
DECORATED VETERAN.
LOVING HUSBAND AND FATHER.
WHEN THE CASTLE FAMILY STUMBLED UPO
A GANGLAND EXECUTIC
IN CENTRAL PARK, THIS PERFECT LIFE...
...WAS DESTROYED.
THE GUILTY PARTY CLEANED UP ALL THE WITNESSES, KILLING CASTLE'S FAMILY.
FRANK SURVIVED THE ASSAULT...
...BUT LOST EVERYTHING-- INCLUDING HIMSELF.
AND WHEN CORRUPT POLICE FAILED TO BRING HIS FAMILY'S MURDERERS TO JUSTICE.

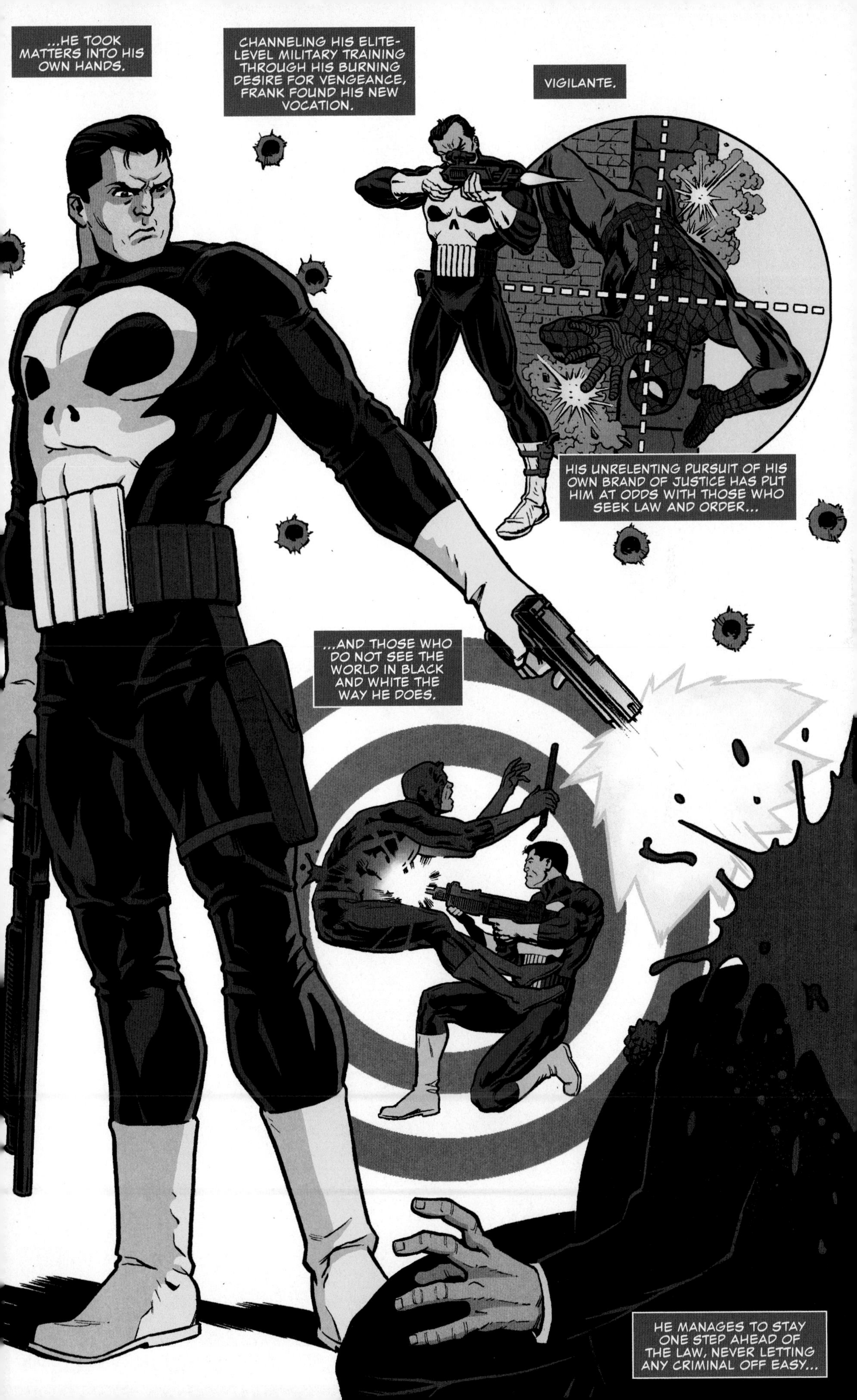
...HE TOOK MATTERS INTO HIS OWN HANDS.
CHANNELING HIS ELITE-LEVEL MILITARY TRAINING THROUGH HIS BURNING DESIRE FOR VENGEANCE, FRANK FOUND HIS NEW VOCATION.
VIGILANTE.
HIS UNRELENTING PURSUIT OF HIS OWN BRAND OF JUSTICE HAS PUT HIM AT ODDS WITH THOSE WHO SEEK LAW AND ORDER...
...AND THOSE WHO DO NOT SEE THE WORLD IN BLACK AND WHITE THE WAY HE DOES.
HE MANAGES TO STAY ONE STEP AHEAD OF THE LAW, NEVER LETTING ANY CRIMINAL OFF EASY...

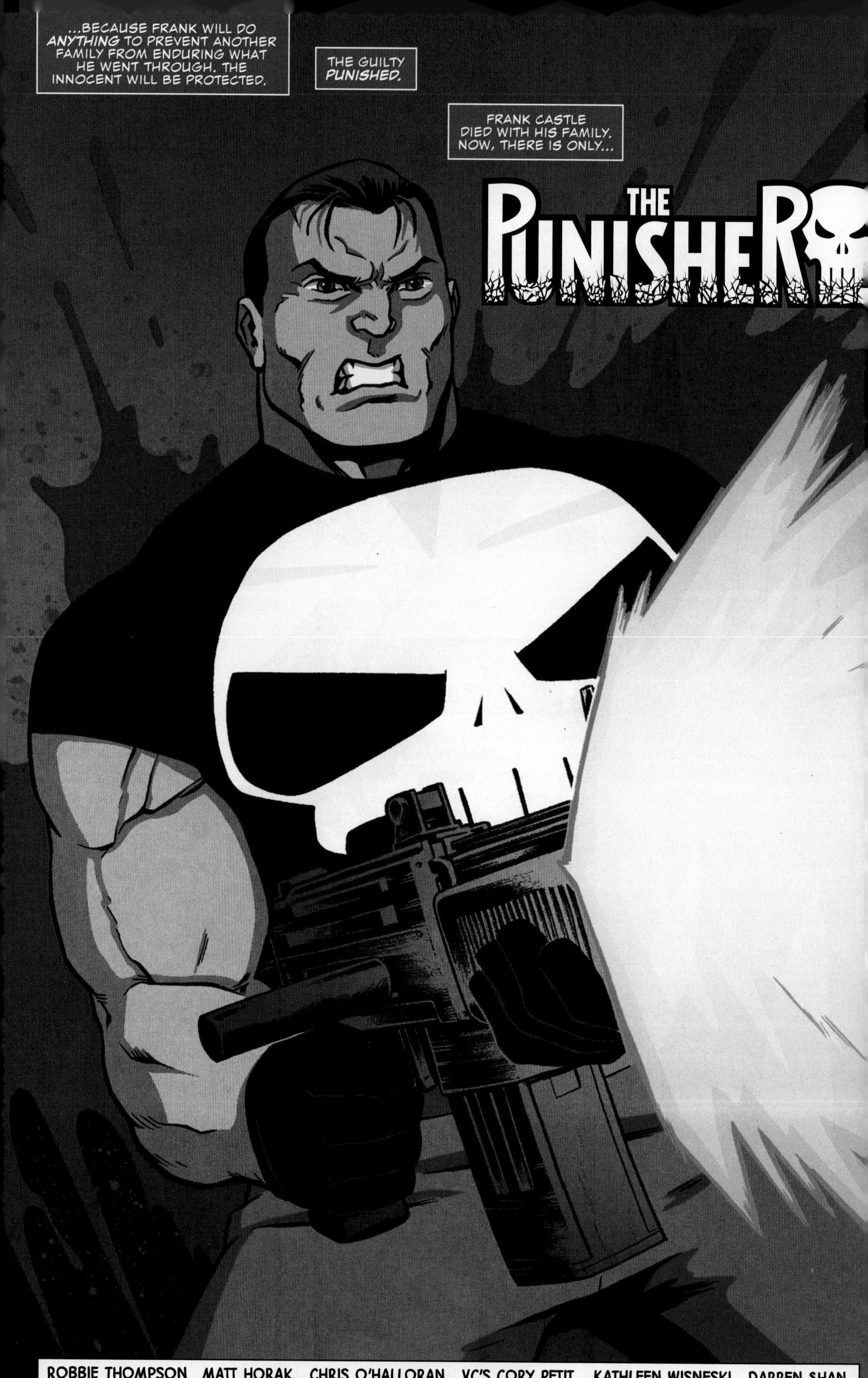
...BECAUSE FRANK WILL DO *ANYTHING* TO PREVENT ANOTHER FAMILY FROM ENDURING WHAT HE WENT THROUGH. THE INNOCENT WILL BE PROTECTED.
THE GUILTY *PUNISHED.*
FRANK CASTLE DIED WITH HIS FAMILY. NOW, THERE IS ONLY...
THE PUNISHER

ROBBIE THOMPSON WRITER | MATT HORAK ARTIST | CHRIS O'HALLORAN COLOR ARTIST | VC'S CORY PETIT LETTERER | KATHLEEN WISNESKI ASSISTANT EDITOR | DARREN SHAN EDITOR

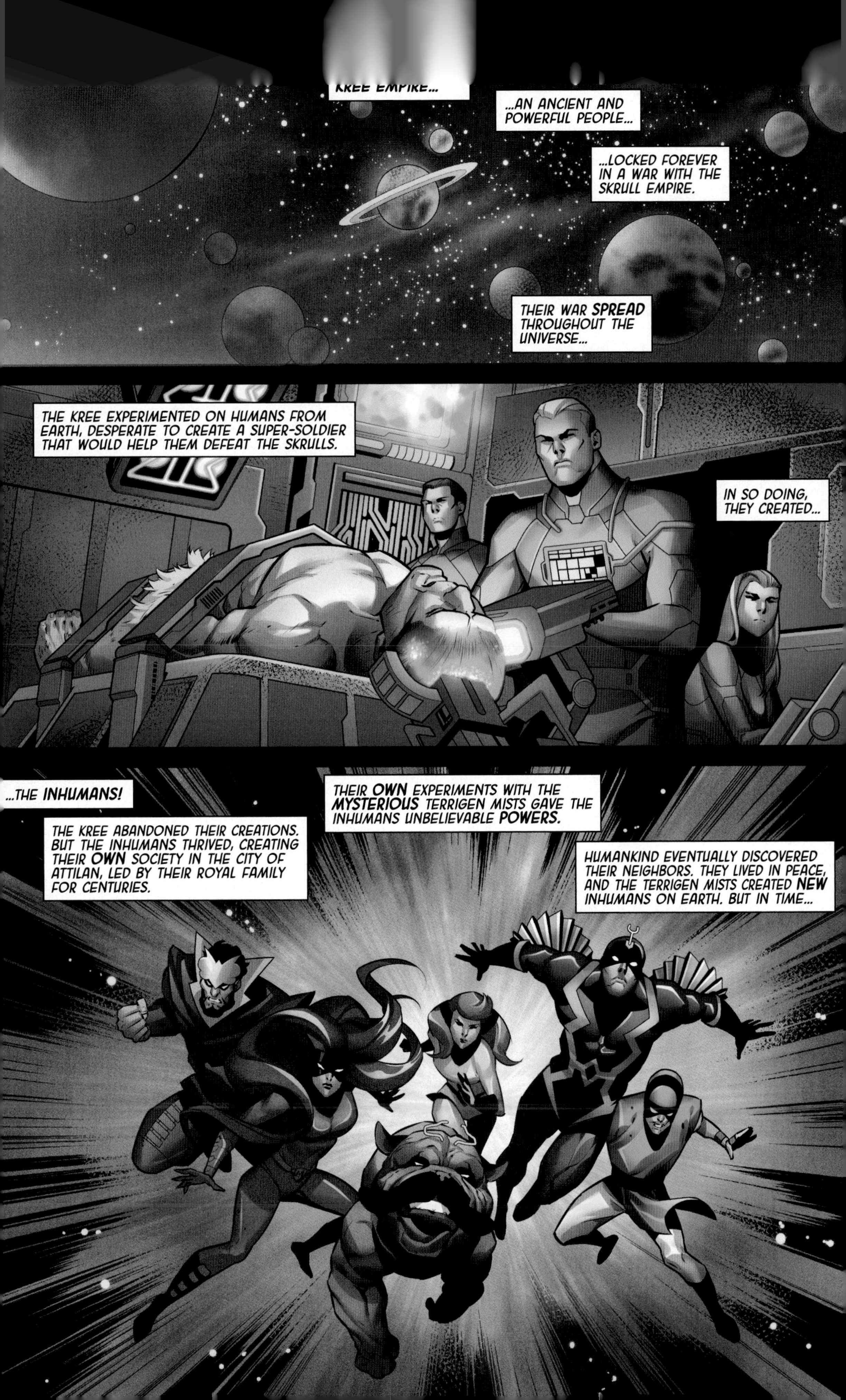
KREE EMPIRE...
...AN ANCIENT AND POWERFUL PEOPLE...
...LOCKED FOREVER IN A WAR WITH THE SKRULL EMPIRE.
THEIR WAR SPREAD THROUGHOUT THE UNIVERSE...
THE KREE EXPERIMENTED ON HUMANS FROM EARTH, DESPERATE TO CREATE A SUPER-SOLDIER THAT WOULD HELP THEM DEFEAT THE SKRULLS.
IN SO DOING, THEY CREATED...
...THE INHUMANS!
THE KREE ABANDONED THEIR CREATIONS. BUT THE INHUMANS THRIVED, CREATING THEIR OWN SOCIETY IN THE CITY OF ATTILAN, LED BY THEIR ROYAL FAMILY FOR CENTURIES.
THEIR OWN EXPERIMENTS WITH THE MYSTERIOUS TERRIGEN MISTS GAVE THE INHUMANS UNBELIEVABLE POWERS.
HUMANKIND EVENTUALLY DISCOVERED THEIR NEIGHBORS. THEY LIVED IN PEACE, AND THE TERRIGEN MISTS CREATED NEW INHUMANS ON EARTH. BUT IN TIME...

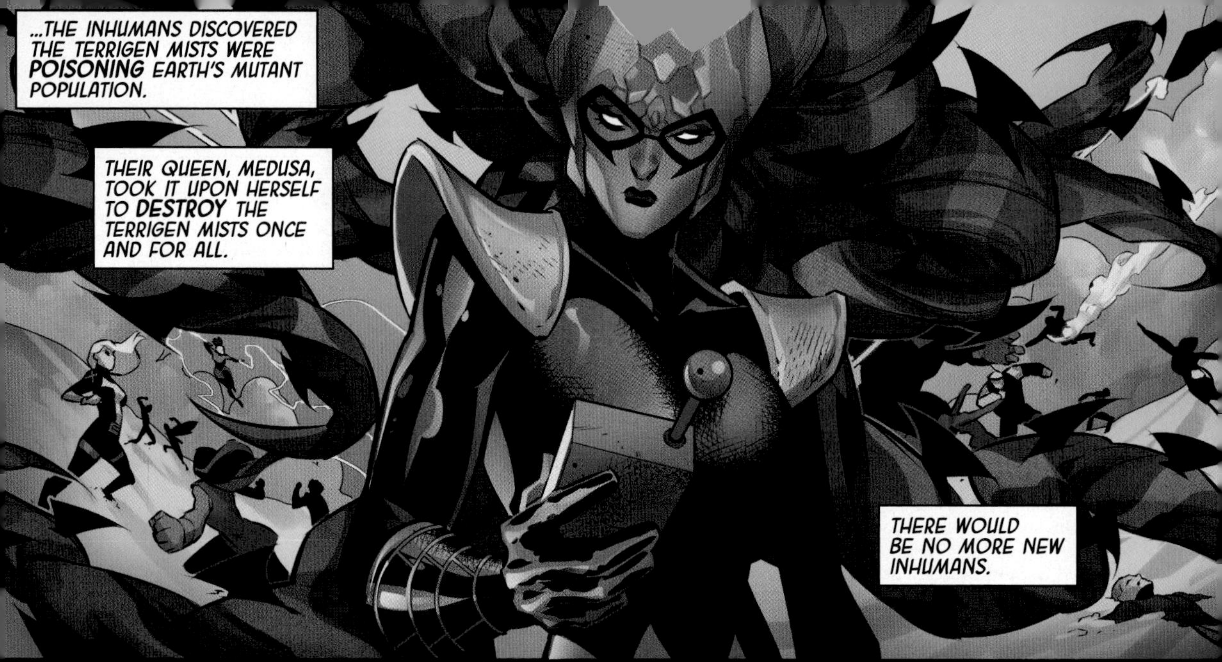
...THE INHUMANS DISCOVERED THE TERRIGEN MISTS WERE **POISONING** EARTH'S MUTANT POPULATION.
THEIR QUEEN, MEDUSA, TOOK IT UPON HERSELF TO **DESTROY** THE TERRIGEN MISTS ONCE AND FOR ALL.
THERE WOULD BE NO MORE NEW INHUMANS.

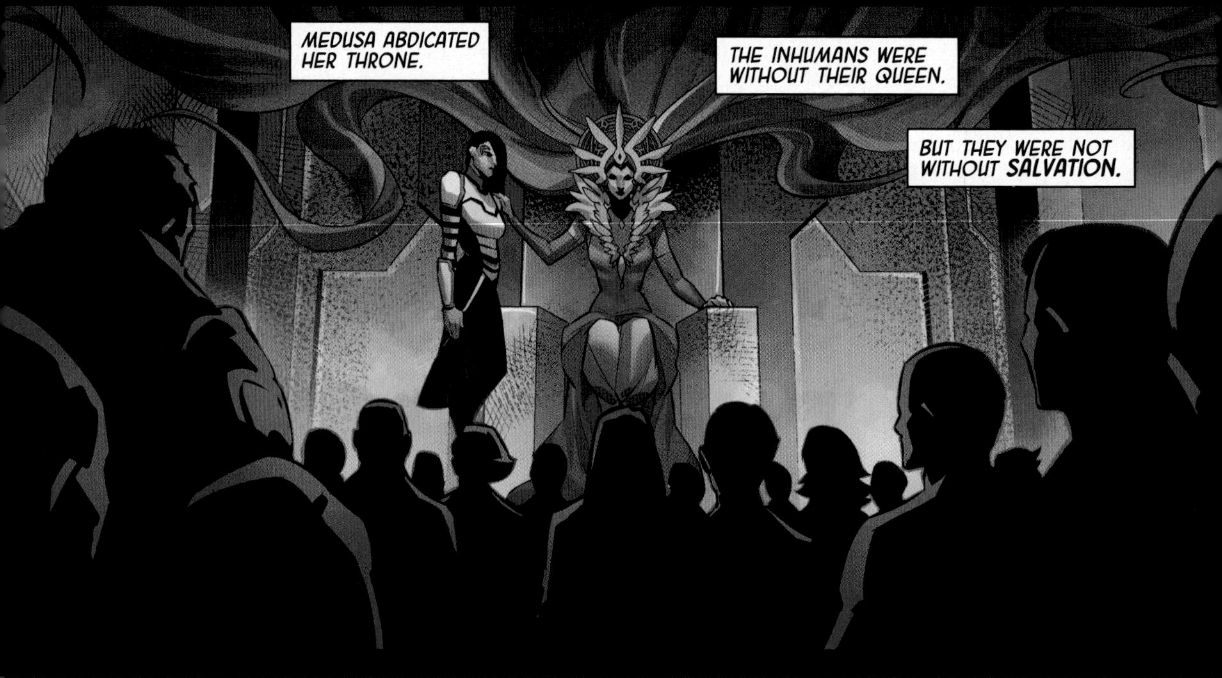
MEDUSA ABDICATED HER THRONE.
THE INHUMANS WERE WITHOUT THEIR QUEEN.
BUT THEY WERE NOT WITHOUT **SALVATION.**

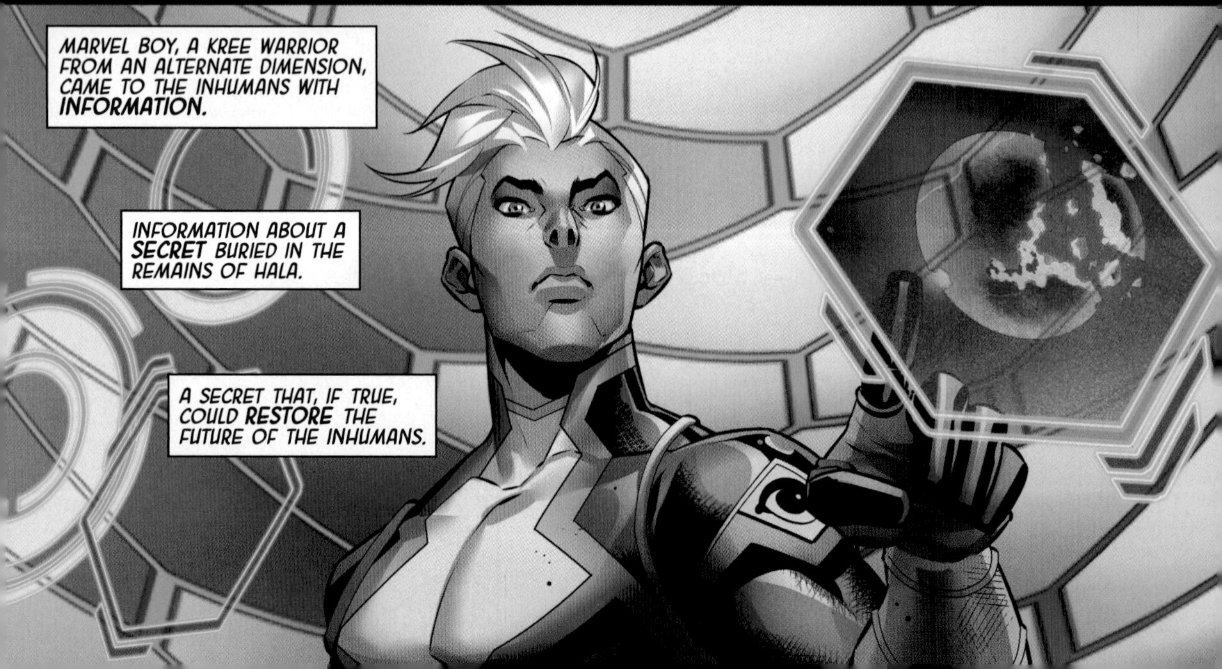
MARVEL BOY, A KREE WARRIOR FROM AN ALTERNATE DIMENSION, CAME TO THE INHUMANS WITH **INFORMATION.**
INFORMATION ABOUT A **SECRET** BURIED IN THE REMAINS OF HALA.
A SECRET THAT, IF TRUE, COULD **RESTORE** THE FUTURE OF THE INHUMANS.

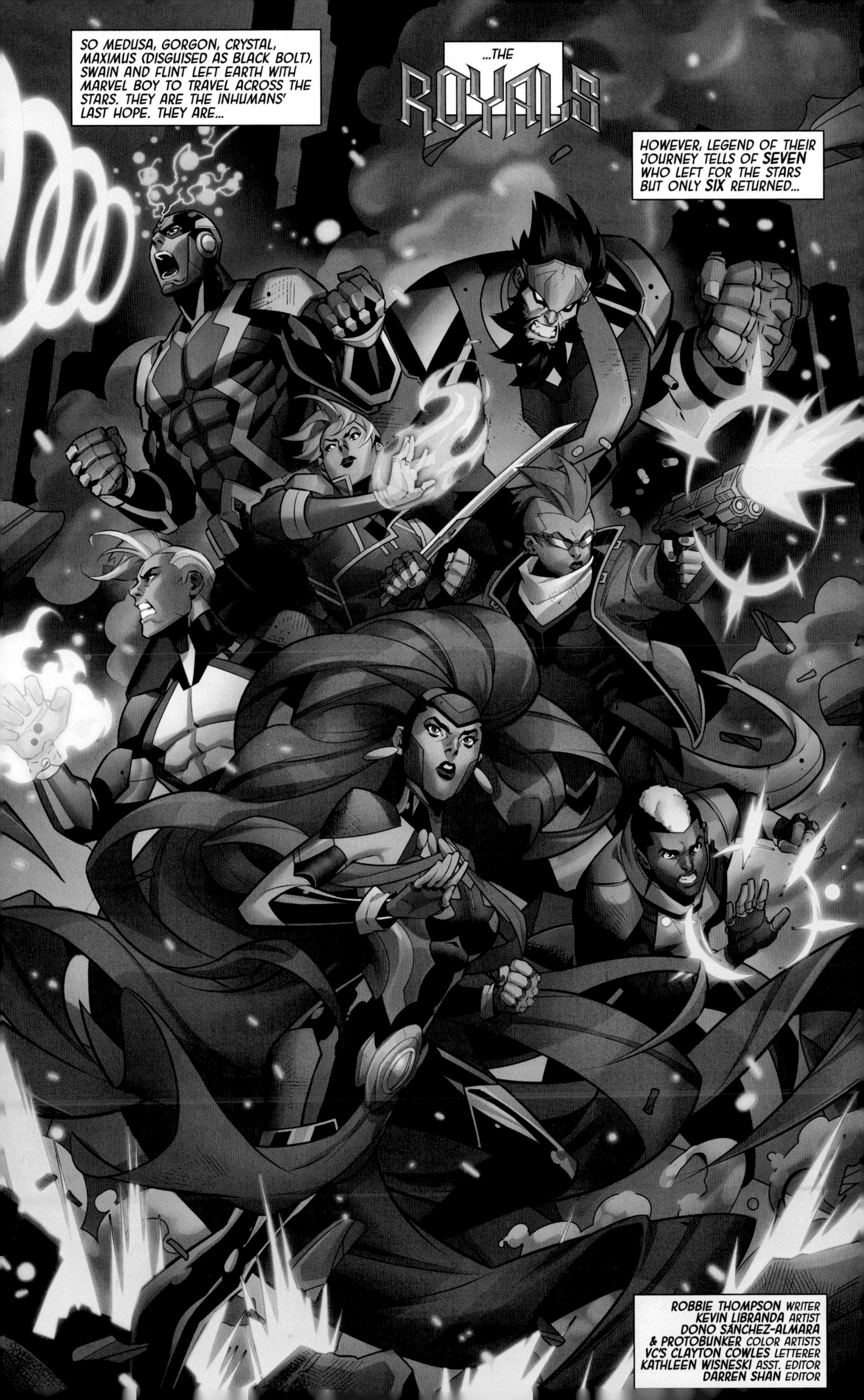

SO MEDUSA, GORGON, CRYSTAL, MAXIMUS (DISGUISED AS BLACK BOLT), SWAIN AND FLINT LEFT EARTH WITH MARVEL BOY TO TRAVEL ACROSS THE STARS. THEY ARE THE INHUMANS' LAST HOPE. THEY ARE...
...THE
ROYALS
HOWEVER, LEGEND OF THEIR JOURNEY TELLS OF **SEVEN** WHO LEFT FOR THE STARS BUT ONLY **SIX** RETURNED...
ROBBIE THOMPSON WRITER
KEVIN LIBRANDA ARTIST
DONO SÁNCHEZ-ALMARA
& PROTOBUNKER COLOR ARTISTS
VC'S CLAYTON COWLES LETTERER
KATHLEEN WISNESKI ASST. EDITOR
DARREN SHAN EDITOR

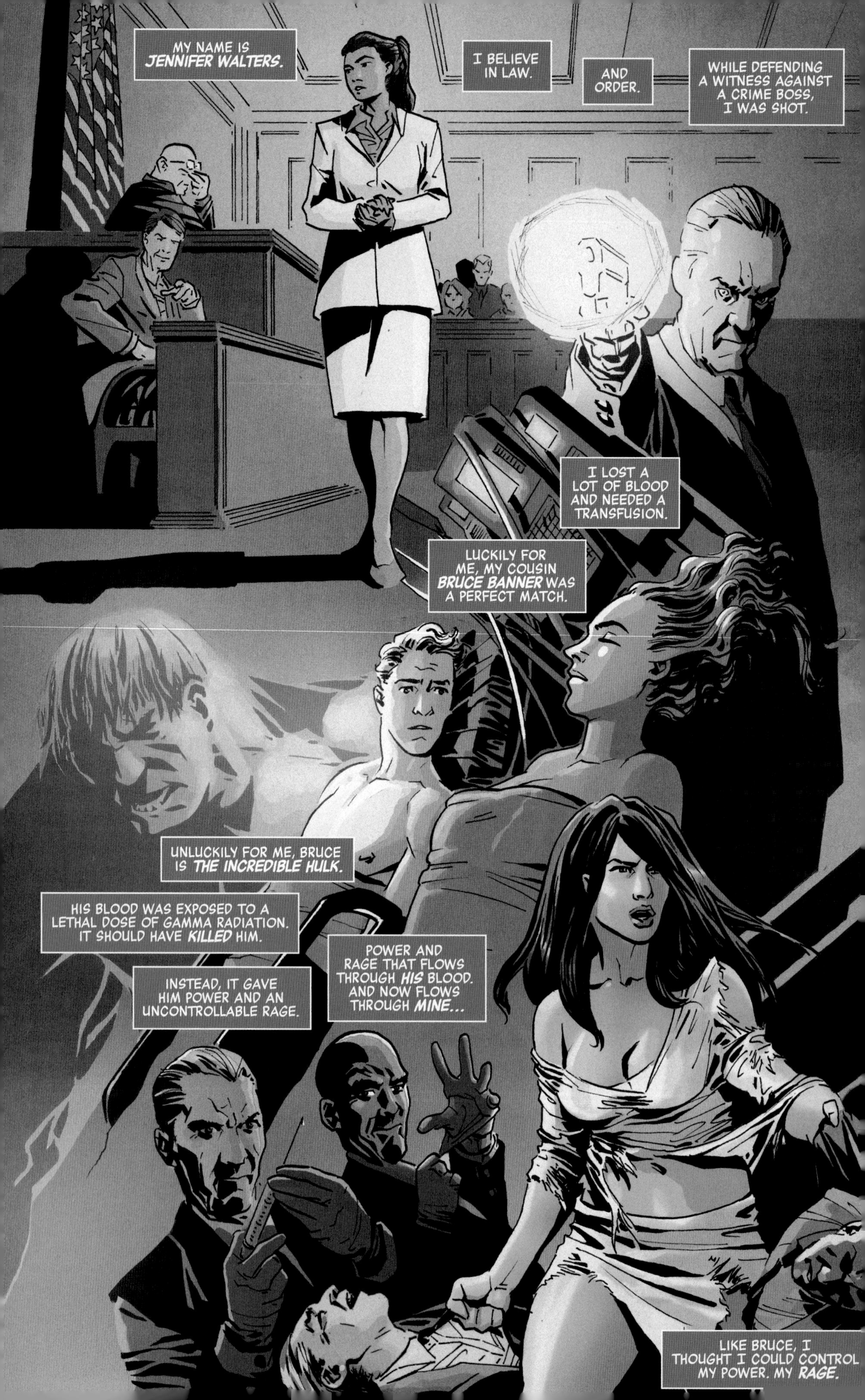
MY NAME IS JENNIFER WALTERS.
I BELIEVE IN LAW.
AND ORDER.
WHILE DEFENDING A WITNESS AGAINST A CRIME BOSS, I WAS SHOT.
I LOST A LOT OF BLOOD AND NEEDED A TRANSFUSION.
LUCKILY FOR ME, MY COUSIN BRUCE BANNER WAS A PERFECT MATCH.
UNLUCKILY FOR ME, BRUCE IS THE INCREDIBLE HULK.
HIS BLOOD WAS EXPOSED TO A LETHAL DOSE OF GAMMA RADIATION. IT SHOULD HAVE KILLED HIM.
INSTEAD, IT GAVE HIM POWER AND AN UNCONTROLLABLE RAGE.
POWER AND RAGE THAT FLOWS THROUGH HIS BLOOD. AND NOW FLOWS THROUGH MINE...
LIKE BRUCE, I THOUGHT I COULD CONTROL MY POWER. MY RAGE.

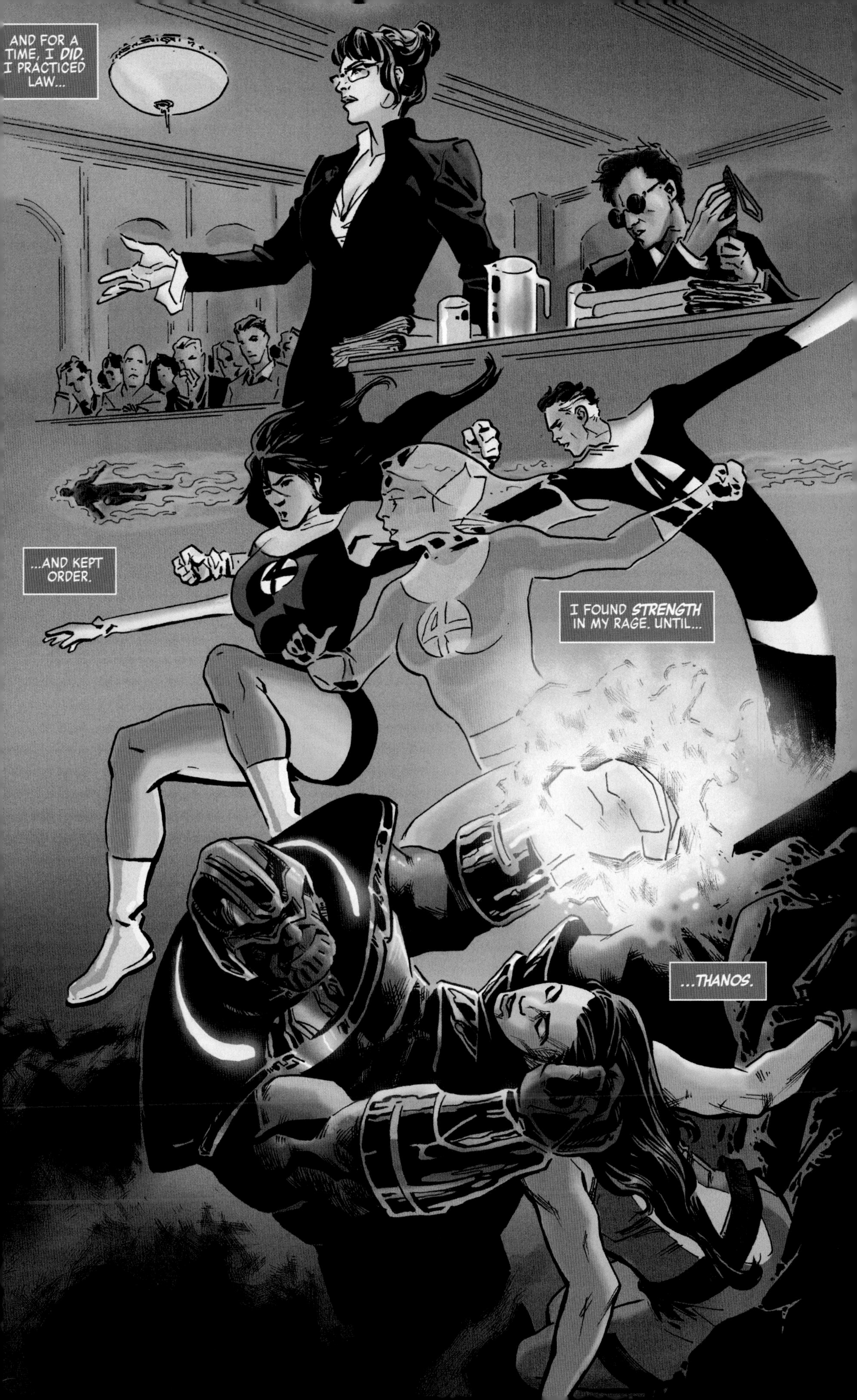
AND FOR A TIME, I DID. I PRACTICED LAW...
...AND KEPT ORDER.
I FOUND STRENGTH IN MY RAGE. UNTIL...
...THANOS.

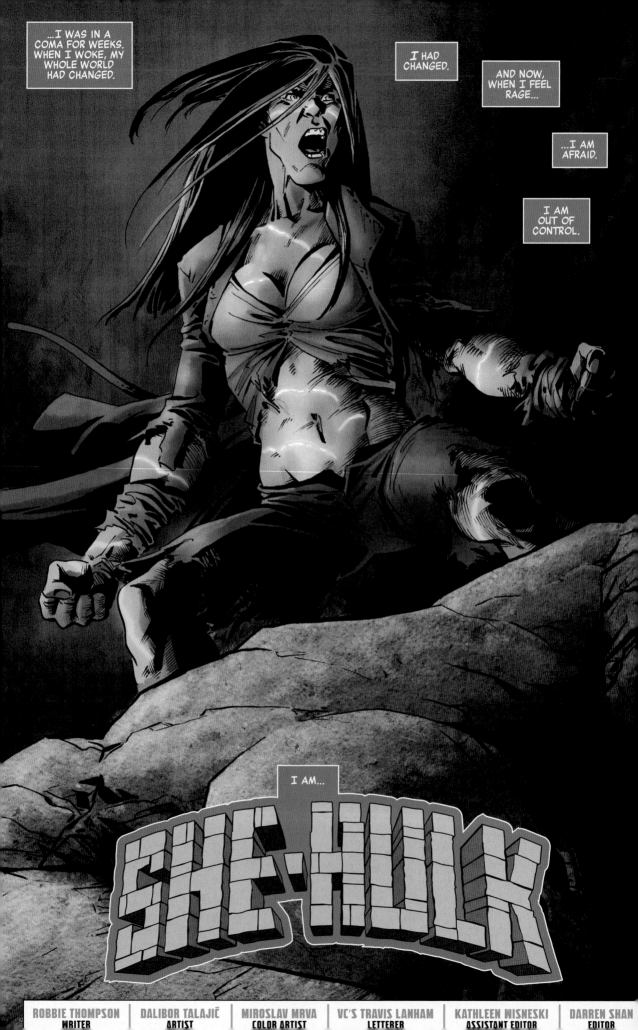

...I WAS IN A COMA FOR WEEKS. WHEN I WOKE, MY WHOLE WORLD HAD CHANGED.

I HAD CHANGED.

AND NOW, WHEN I FEEL RAGE...

...I AM AFRAID.

I AM OUT OF CONTROL.

I AM...

SHE-HULK

| ROBBIE THOMPSON | DALIBOR TALAJIĆ | MIROSLAV MRVA | VC'S TRAVIS LANHAM | KATHLEEN WISNESKI | DARREN SHAN |
| WRITER | ARTIST | COLOR ARTIST | LETTERER | ASSISTANT EDITOR | EDITOR |

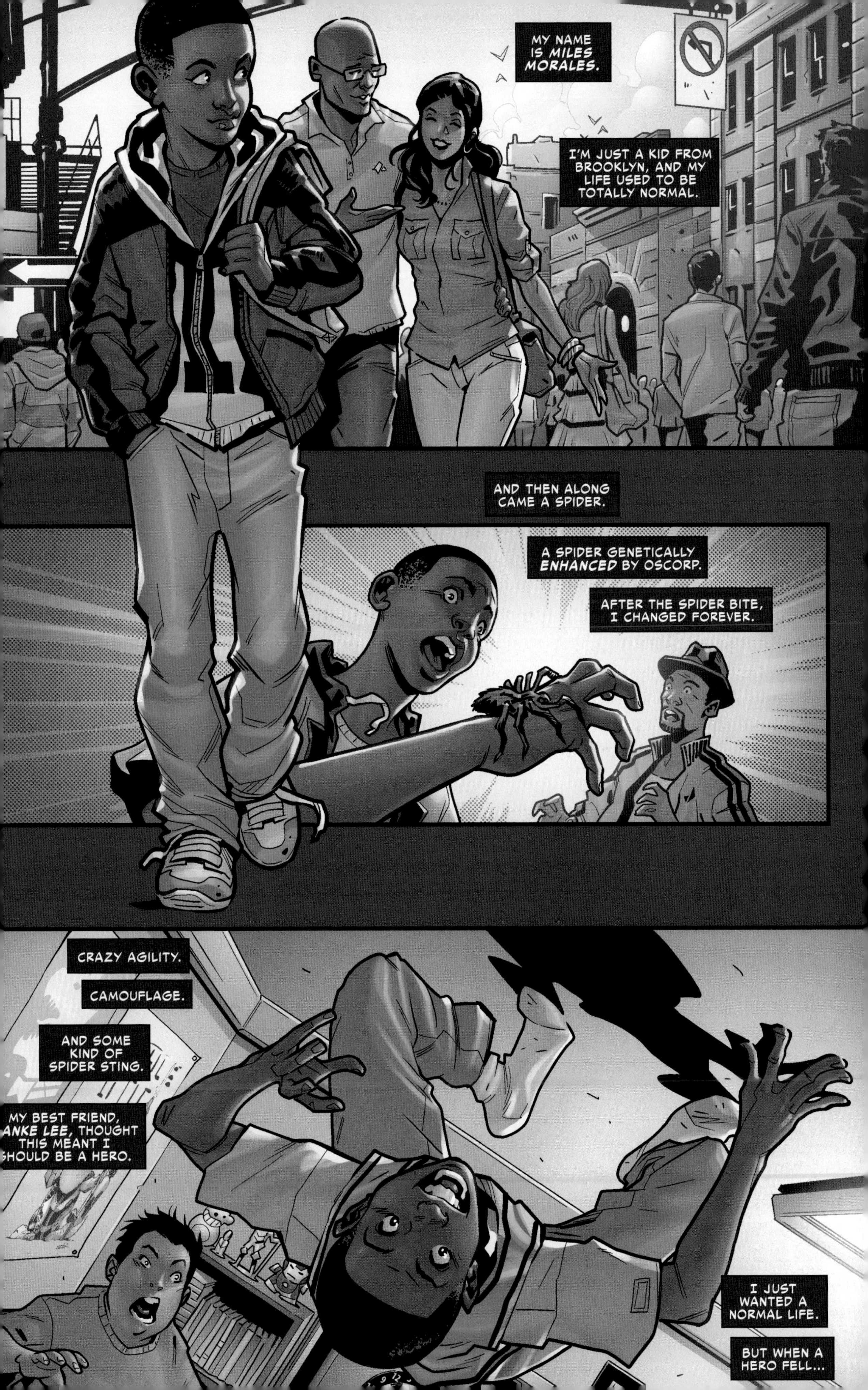
MY NAME IS MILES MORALES.
I'M JUST A KID FROM BROOKLYN, AND MY LIFE USED TO BE TOTALLY NORMAL.
AND THEN ALONG CAME A SPIDER.
A SPIDER GENETICALLY ENHANCED BY OSCORP.
AFTER THE SPIDER BITE, I CHANGED FOREVER.
CRAZY AGILITY.
CAMOUFLAGE.
AND SOME KIND OF SPIDER STING.
MY BEST FRIEND, ANKE LEE, THOUGHT THIS MEANT I HOULD BE A HERO.
I JUST WANTED A NORMAL LIFE.
BUT WHEN A HERO FELL...

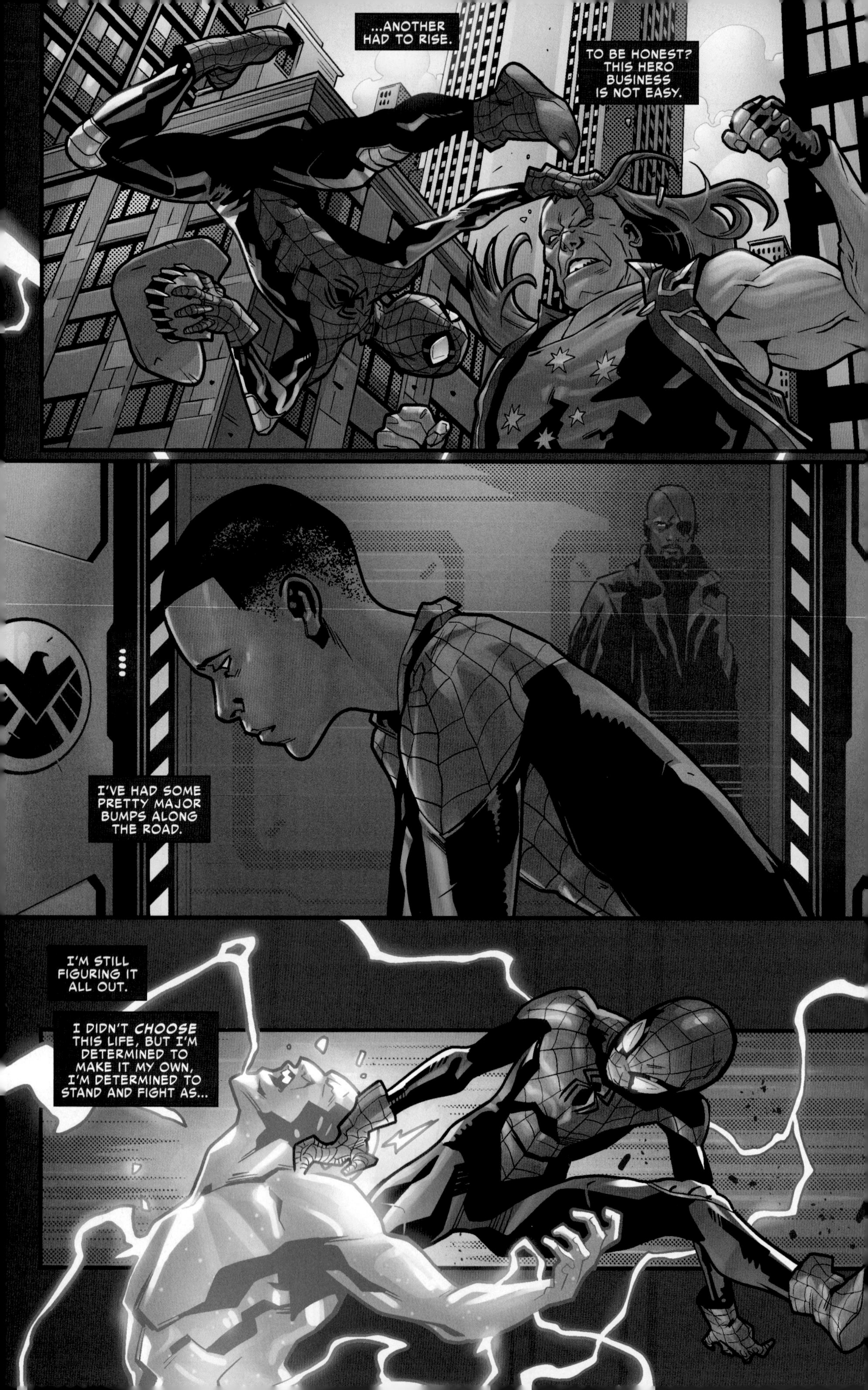
...ANOTHER HAD TO RISE.
TO BE HONEST? THIS HERO BUSINESS IS NOT EASY.
I'VE HAD SOME PRETTY MAJOR BUMPS ALONG THE ROAD.
I'M STILL FIGURING IT ALL OUT.
I DIDN'T *CHOOSE* THIS LIFE, BUT I'M DETERMINED TO MAKE IT MY OWN, I'M DETERMINED TO STAND AND FIGHT AS...

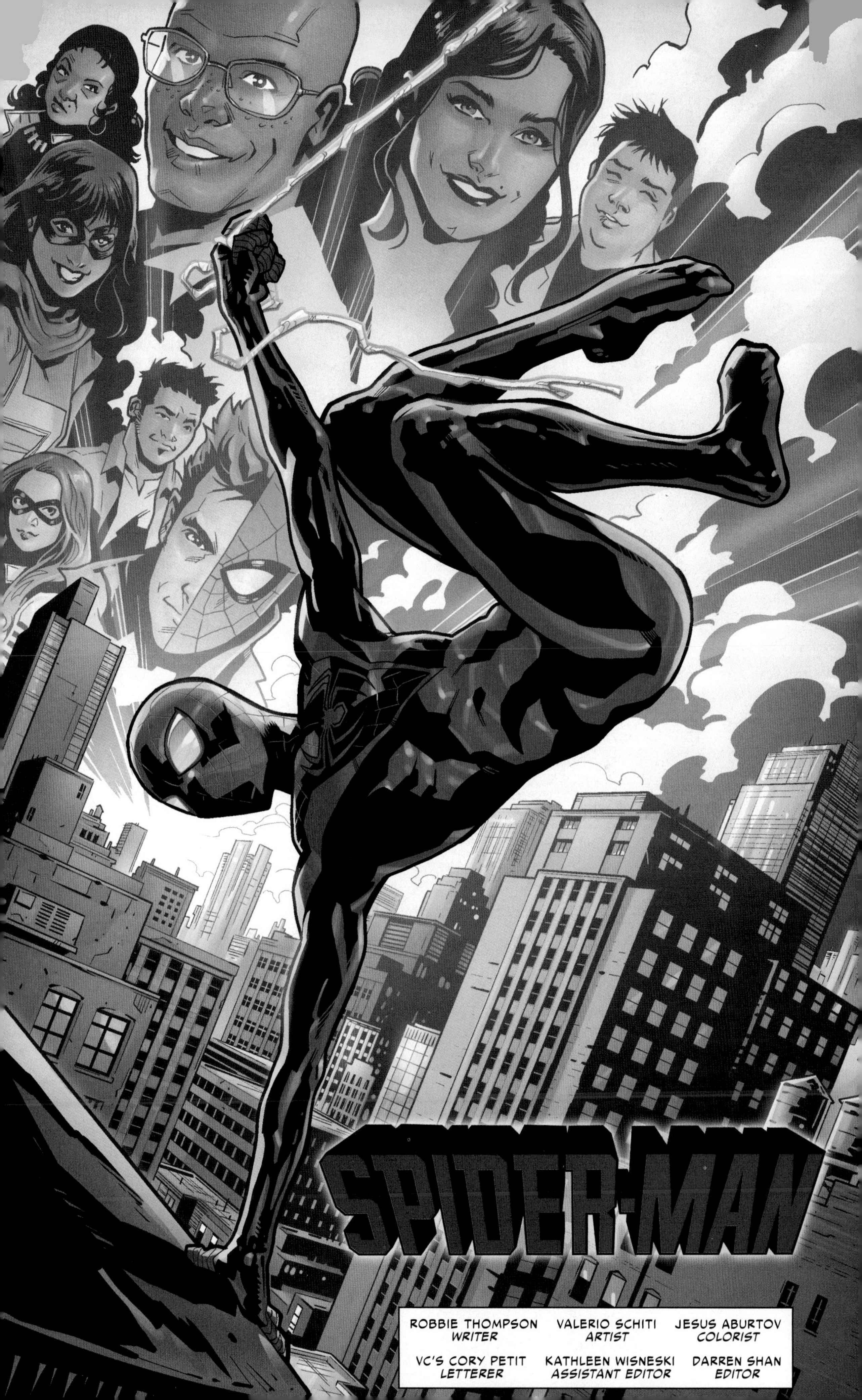
SPIDER-MAN
ROBBIE THOMPSON WRITER
VALERIO SCHITI ARTIST
JESUS ABURTOV COLORIST
VC'S CORY PETIT LETTERER
KATHLEEN WISNESKI ASSISTANT EDITOR
DARREN SHAN EDITOR

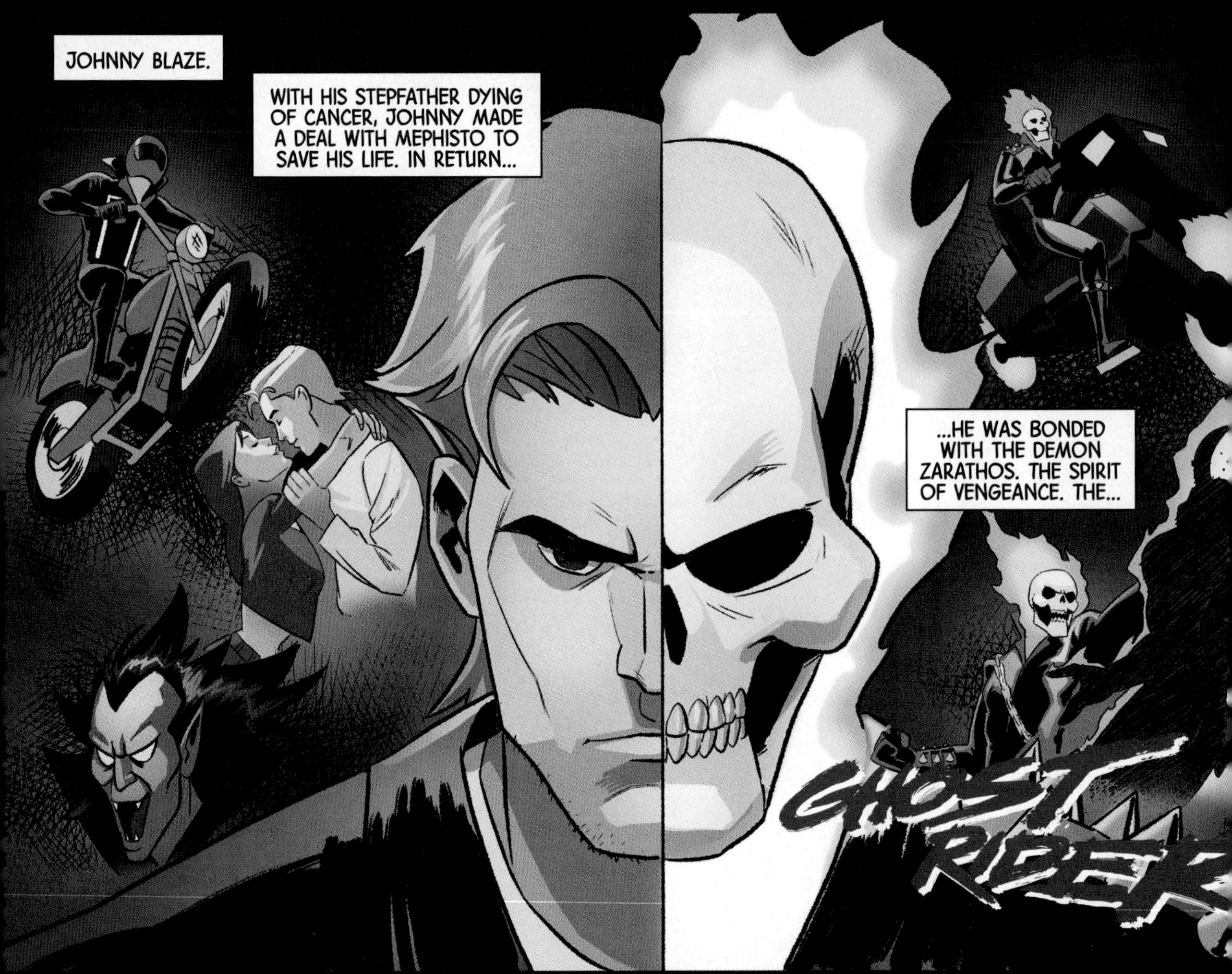
JOHNNY BLAZE.
WITH HIS STEPFATHER DYING OF CANCER, JOHNNY MADE A DEAL WITH MEPHISTO TO SAVE HIS LIFE. IN RETURN...
...HE WAS BONDED WITH THE DEMON ZARATHOS. THE SPIRIT OF VENGEANCE. THE...
GHOST RIDER

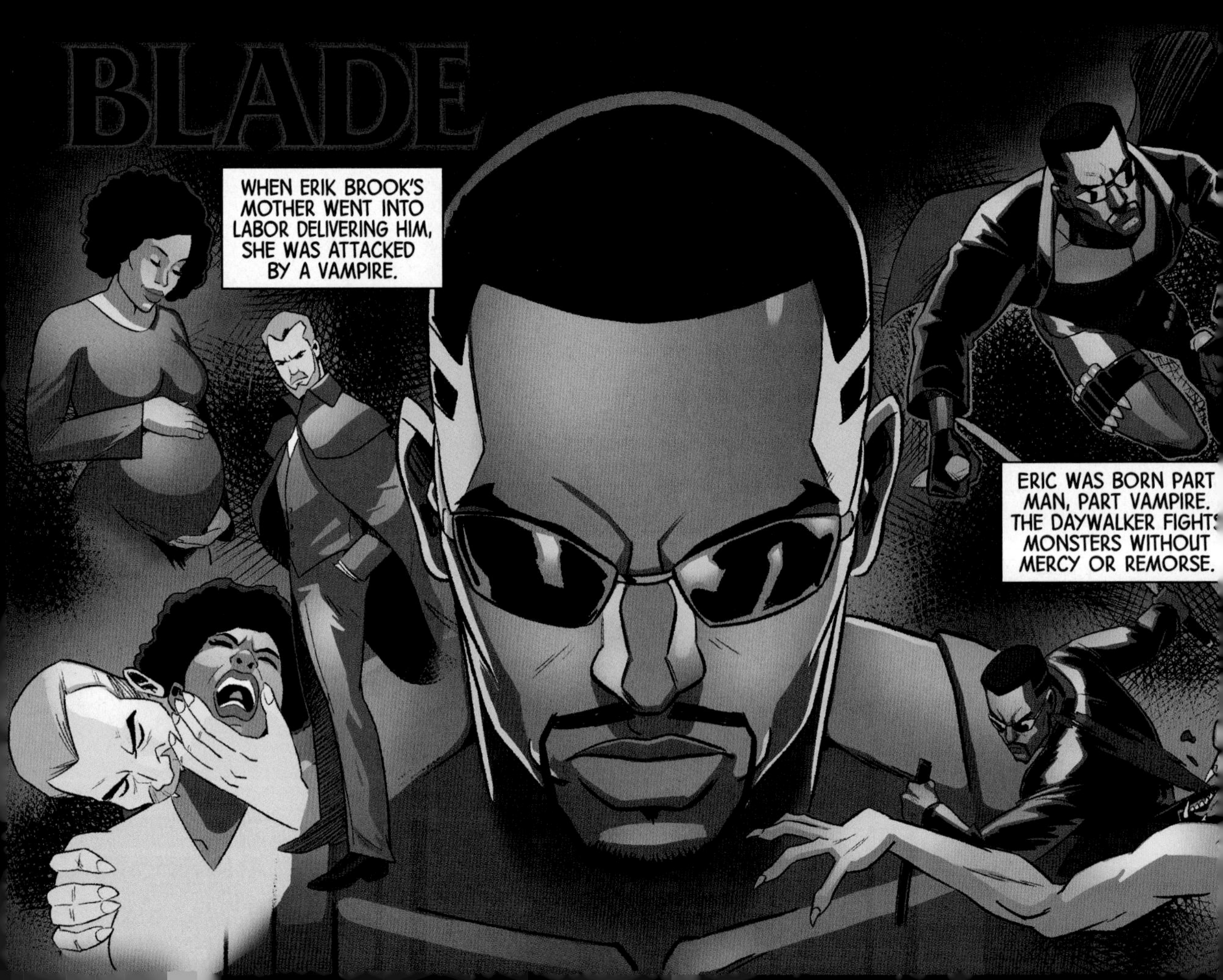
BLADE
WHEN ERIK BROOK'S MOTHER WENT INTO LABOR DELIVERING HIM, SHE WAS ATTACKED BY A VAMPIRE.
ERIC WAS BORN PART MAN, PART VAMPIRE. THE DAYWALKER FIGHTS MONSTERS WITHOUT MERCY OR REMORSE.

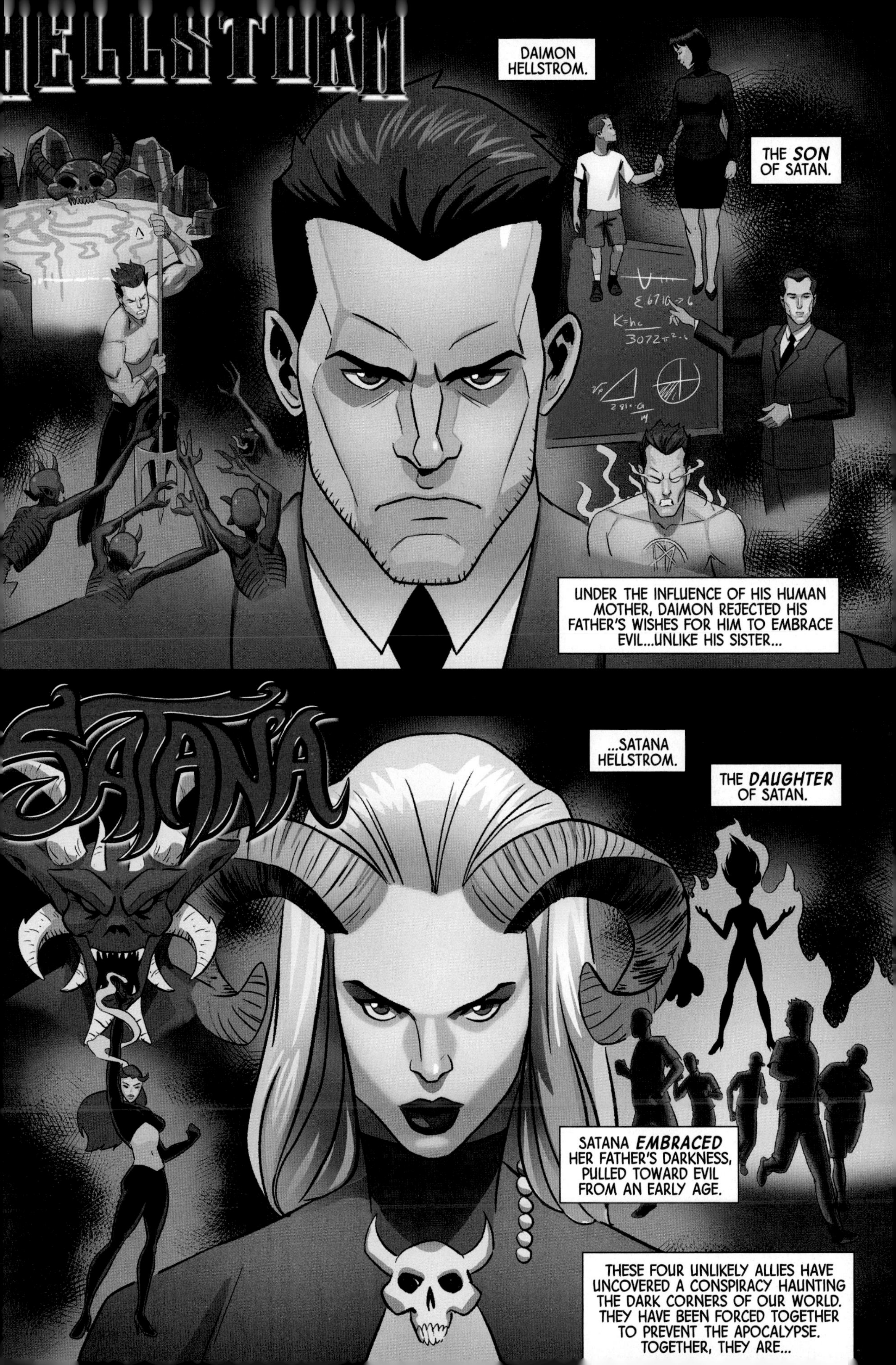
HELLSTORM
DAIMON HELLSTROM.
THE SON OF SATAN.
UNDER THE INFLUENCE OF HIS HUMAN MOTHER, DAIMON REJECTED HIS FATHER'S WISHES FOR HIM TO EMBRACE EVIL...UNLIKE HIS SISTER...
SATANA
...SATANA HELLSTROM.
THE DAUGHTER OF SATAN.
SATANA EMBRACED HER FATHER'S DARKNESS, PULLED TOWARD EVIL FROM AN EARLY AGE.
THESE FOUR UNLIKELY ALLIES HAVE UNCOVERED A CONSPIRACY HAUNTING THE DARK CORNERS OF OUR WORLD. THEY HAVE BEEN FORCED TOGETHER TO PREVENT THE APOCALYPSE. TOGETHER, THEY ARE...

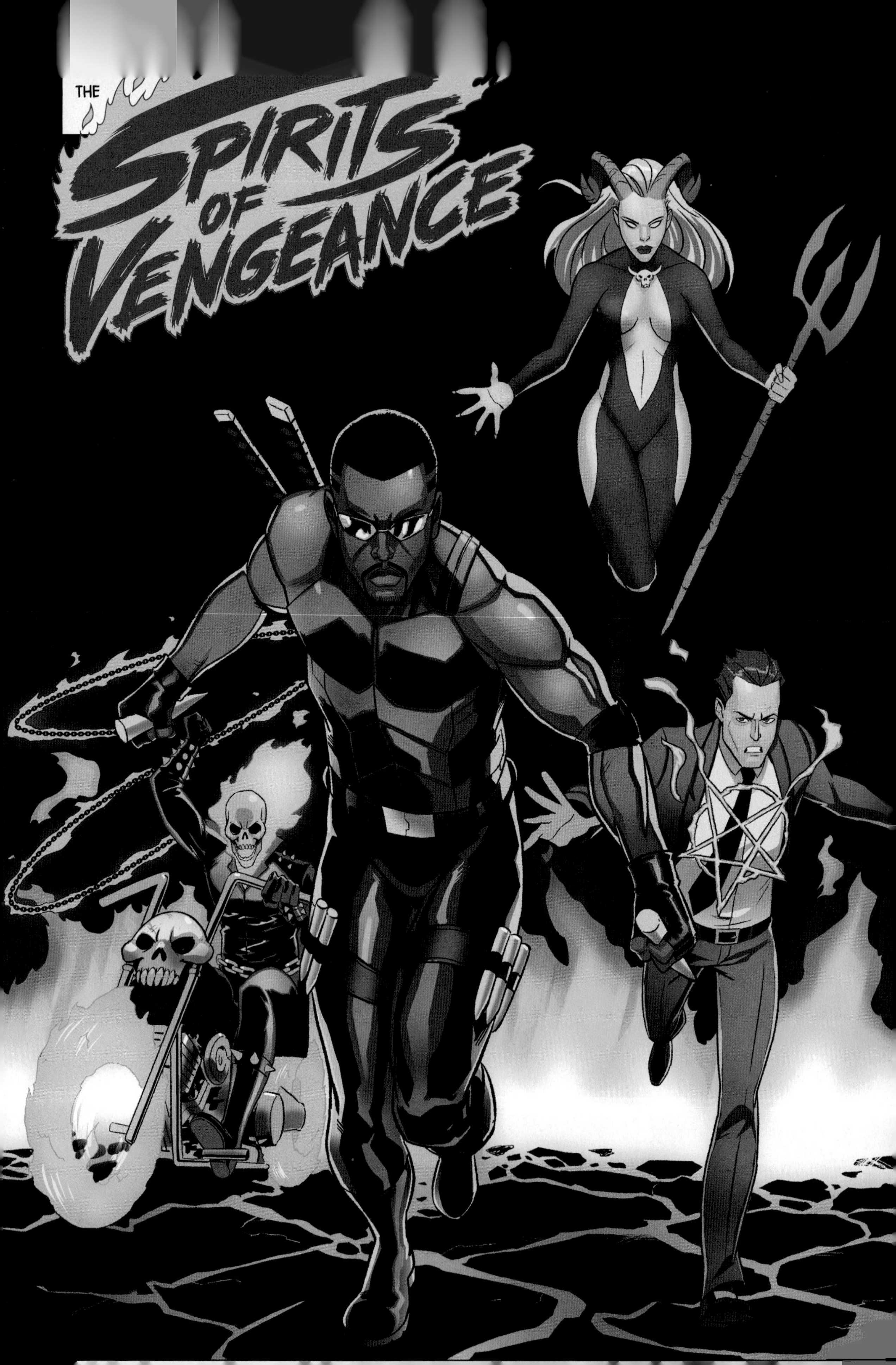
THE
SPIRITS OF VENGEANCE

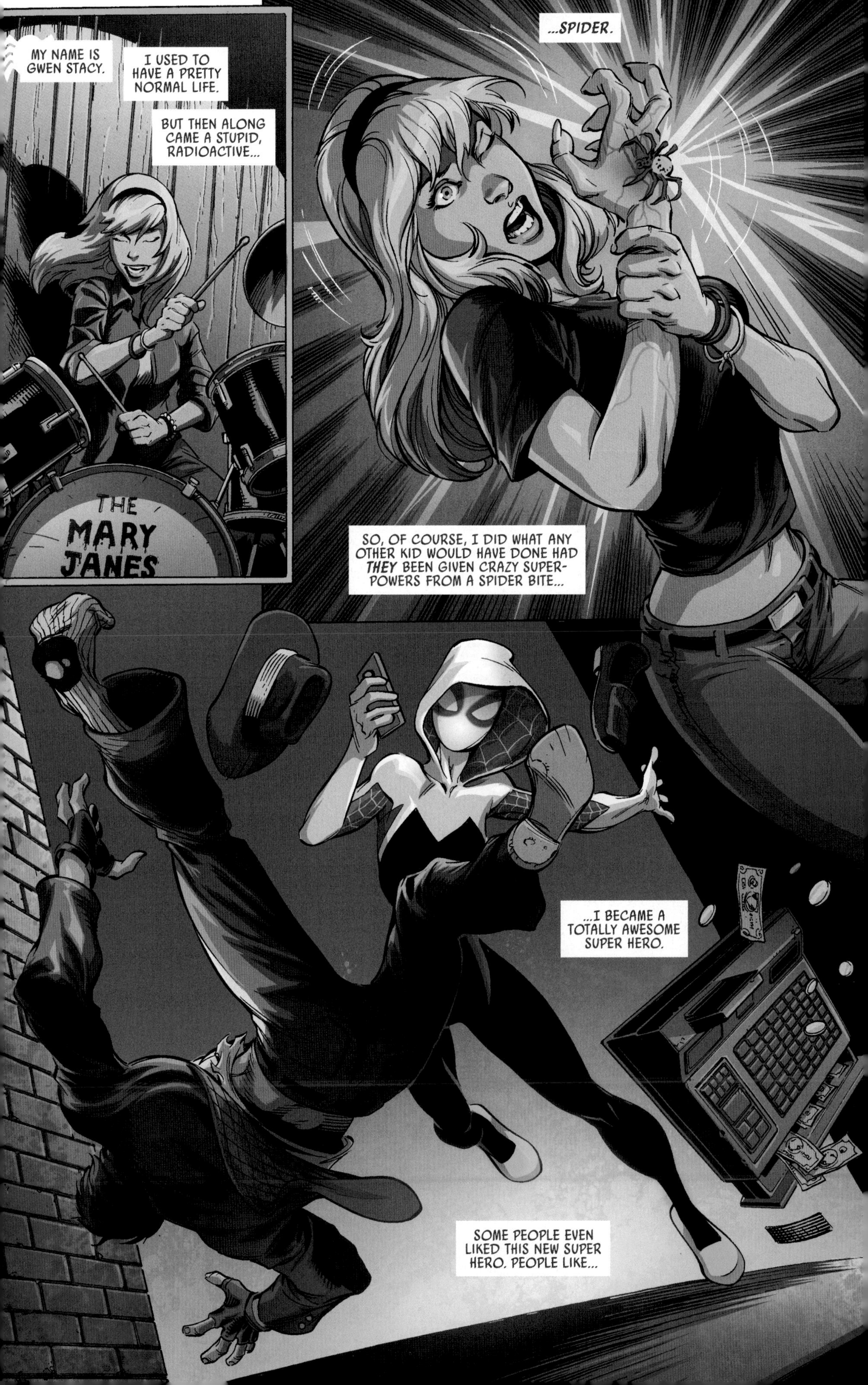
MY NAME IS GWEN STACY.
I USED TO HAVE A PRETTY NORMAL LIFE.
BUT THEN ALONG CAME A STUPID, RADIOACTIVE...
THE MARY JANES
...SPIDER.
SO, OF COURSE, I DID WHAT ANY OTHER KID WOULD HAVE DONE HAD *THEY* BEEN GIVEN CRAZY SUPER-POWERS FROM A SPIDER BITE...
...I BECAME A TOTALLY AWESOME SUPER HERO.
SOME PEOPLE EVEN LIKED THIS NEW SUPER HERO. PEOPLE LIKE...

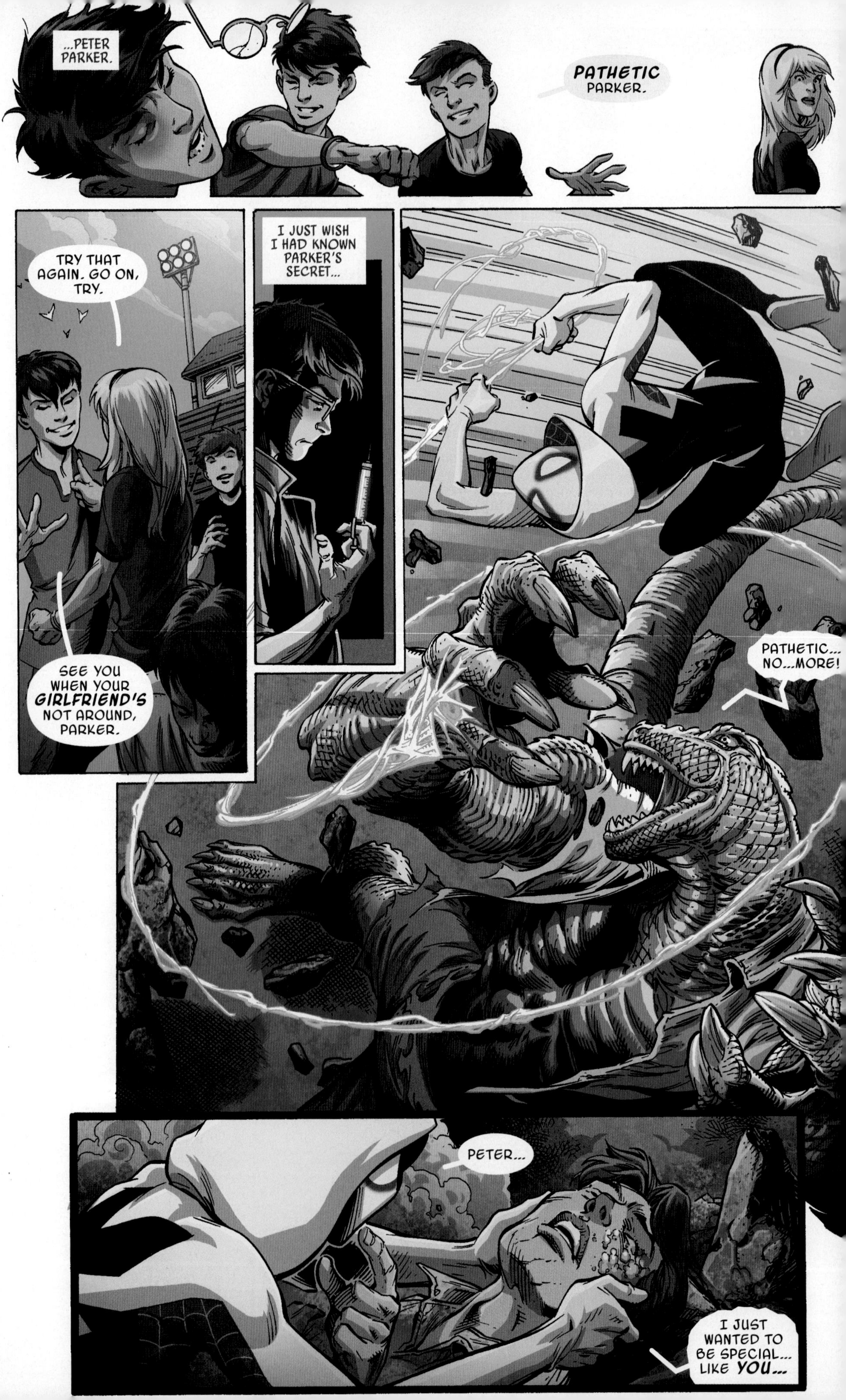
...PETER PARKER.
PATHETIC PARKER.
TRY THAT AGAIN. GO ON, TRY.
SEE YOU WHEN YOUR GIRLFRIEND'S NOT AROUND, PARKER.
I JUST WISH I HAD KNOWN PARKER'S SECRET...
PATHETIC... NO...MORE!
PETER...
I JUST WANTED TO BE SPECIAL... LIKE YOU...

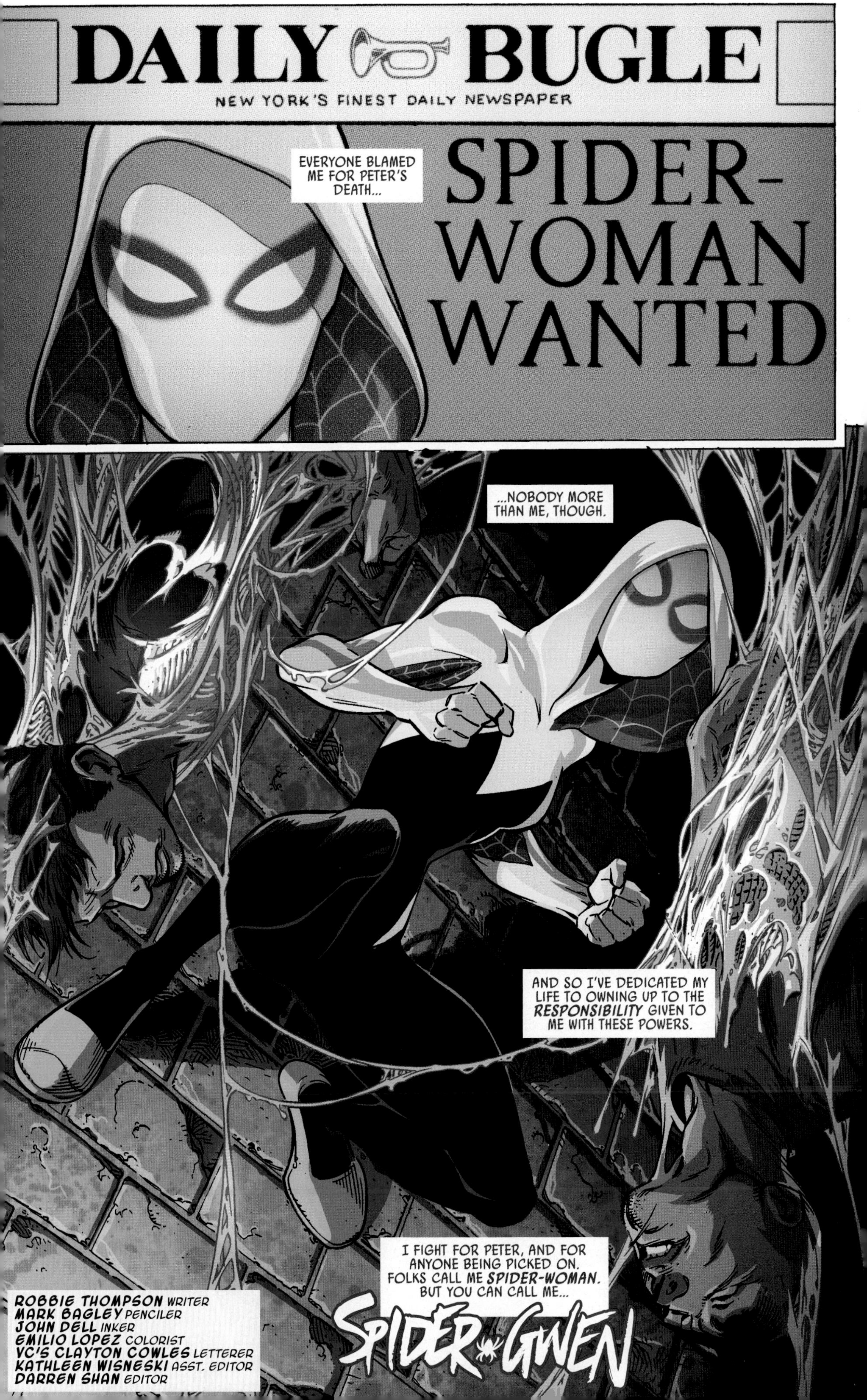
DAILY BUGLE
NEW YORK'S FINEST DAILY NEWSPAPER
EVERYONE BLAMED ME FOR PETER'S DEATH...
SPIDER-WOMAN WANTED
...NOBODY MORE THAN ME, THOUGH.
AND SO I'VE DEDICATED MY LIFE TO OWNING UP TO THE RESPONSIBILITY GIVEN TO ME WITH THESE POWERS.
I FIGHT FOR PETER, AND FOR ANYONE BEING PICKED ON. FOLKS CALL ME SPIDER-WOMAN. BUT YOU CAN CALL ME...
SPIDER-GWEN
ROBBIE THOMPSON WRITER
MARK BAGLEY PENCILER
JOHN DELL INKER
EMILIO LOPEZ COLORIST
VC'S CLAYTON COWLES LETTERER
KATHLEEN WISNESKI ASST. EDITOR
DARREN SHAN EDITOR

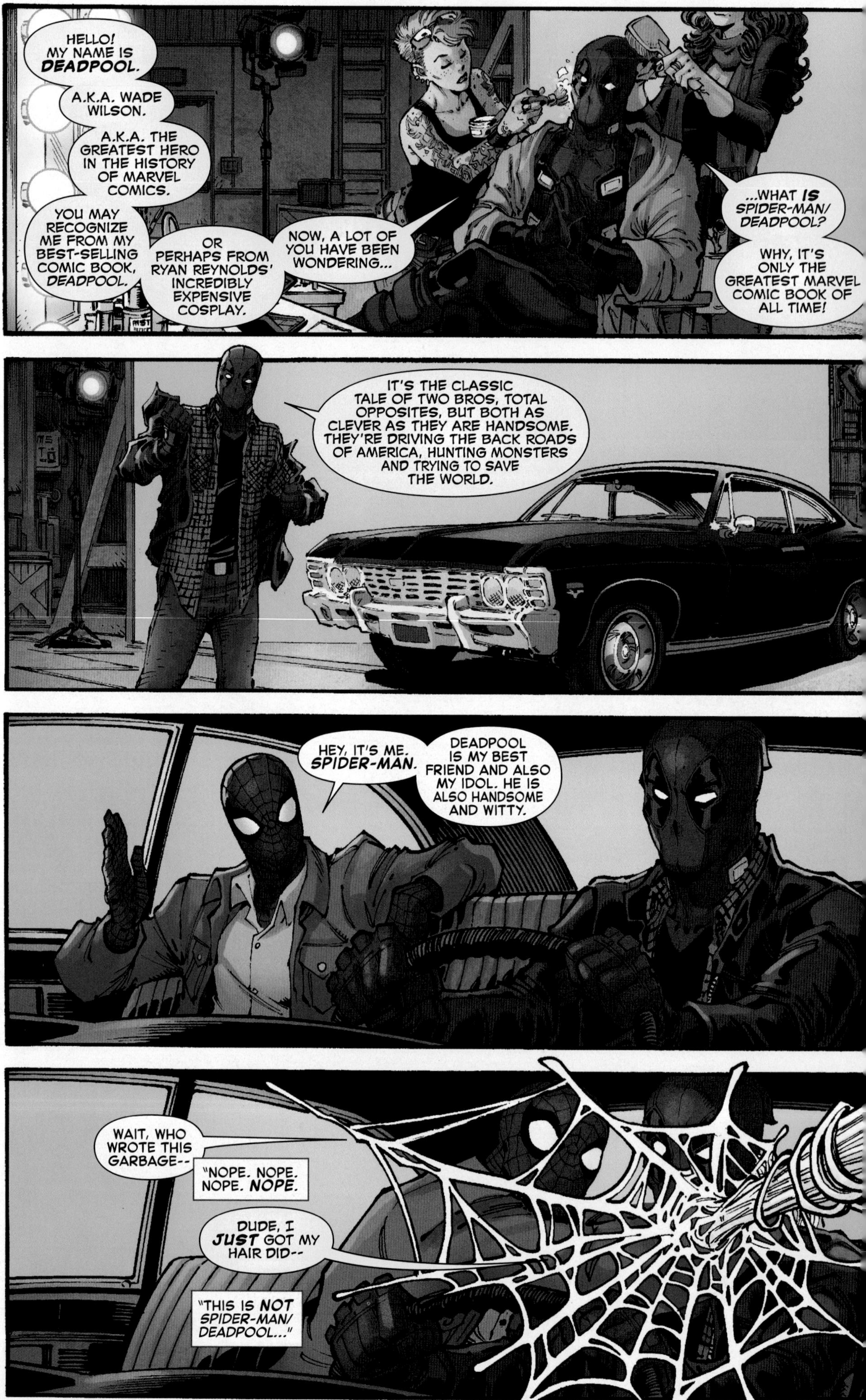

HELLO! MY NAME IS DEADPOOL.
A.K.A. WADE WILSON.
A.K.A. THE GREATEST HERO IN THE HISTORY OF MARVEL COMICS.
YOU MAY RECOGNIZE ME FROM MY BEST-SELLING COMIC BOOK, DEADPOOL.
OR PERHAPS FROM RYAN REYNOLDS' INCREDIBLY EXPENSIVE COSPLAY.
NOW, A LOT OF YOU HAVE BEEN WONDERING...
...WHAT IS SPIDER-MAN/ DEADPOOL?
WHY, IT'S ONLY THE GREATEST MARVEL COMIC BOOK OF ALL TIME!
IT'S THE CLASSIC TALE OF TWO BROS, TOTAL OPPOSITES, BUT BOTH AS CLEVER AS THEY ARE HANDSOME. THEY'RE DRIVING THE BACK ROADS OF AMERICA, HUNTING MONSTERS AND TRYING TO SAVE THE WORLD.
HEY, IT'S ME. SPIDER-MAN.
DEADPOOL IS MY BEST FRIEND AND ALSO MY IDOL. HE IS ALSO HANDSOME AND WITTY.
WAIT, WHO WROTE THIS GARBAGE--
"NOPE. NOPE. NOPE. NOPE.
DUDE, I JUST GOT MY HAIR DID--
"THIS IS NOT SPIDER-MAN/ DEADPOOL..."

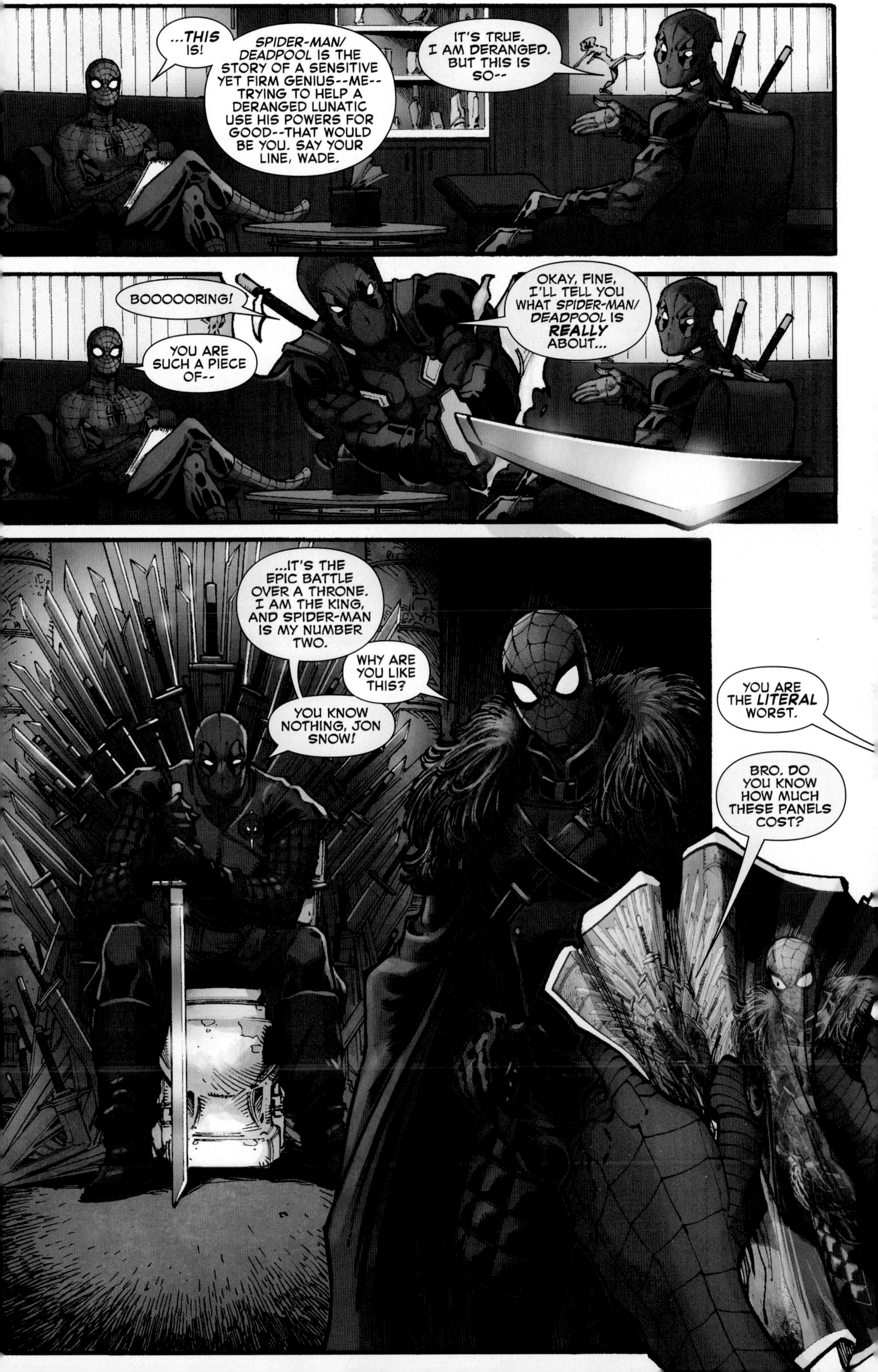

...THIS IS!
SPIDER-MAN/ DEADPOOL IS THE STORY OF A SENSITIVE YET FIRM GENIUS--ME--TRYING TO HELP A DERANGED LUNATIC USE HIS POWERS FOR GOOD--THAT WOULD BE YOU. SAY YOUR LINE, WADE.
IT'S TRUE. I AM DERANGED. BUT THIS IS SO--
BOOOOORING!
YOU ARE SUCH A PIECE OF--
OKAY, FINE, I'LL TELL YOU WHAT SPIDER-MAN/ DEADPOOL IS REALLY ABOUT...
...IT'S THE EPIC BATTLE OVER A THRONE. I AM THE KING, AND SPIDER-MAN IS MY NUMBER TWO.
WHY ARE YOU LIKE THIS?
YOU KNOW NOTHING, JON SNOW!
YOU ARE THE LITERAL WORST.
BRO. DO YOU KNOW HOW MUCH THESE PANELS COST?

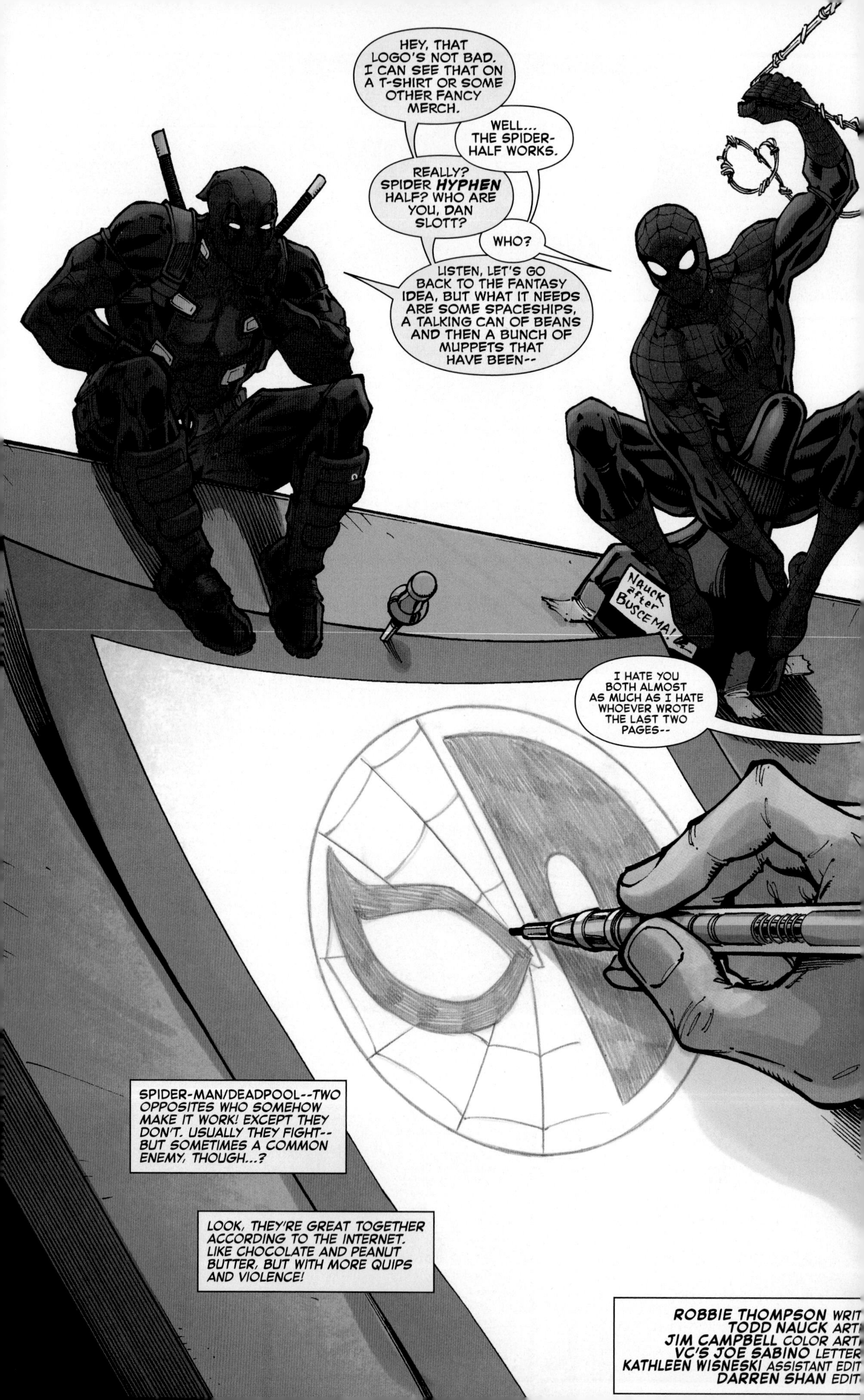

HEY, THAT LOGO'S NOT BAD. I CAN SEE THAT ON A T-SHIRT OR SOME OTHER FANCY MERCH.
WELL... THE SPIDER-HALF WORKS.
REALLY? SPIDER **HYPHEN** HALF? WHO ARE YOU, DAN SLOTT?
WHO?
LISTEN, LET'S GO BACK TO THE FANTASY IDEA, BUT WHAT IT NEEDS ARE SOME SPACESHIPS, A TALKING CAN OF BEANS AND THEN A BUNCH OF MUPPETS THAT HAVE BEEN--
Nauck after BUSCEMA!
I HATE YOU BOTH ALMOST AS MUCH AS I HATE WHOEVER WROTE THE LAST TWO PAGES--
SPIDER-MAN/DEADPOOL--TWO OPPOSITES WHO SOMEHOW MAKE IT WORK! EXCEPT THEY DON'T. USUALLY THEY FIGHT--BUT SOMETIMES A COMMON ENEMY, THOUGH...?
LOOK, THEY'RE GREAT TOGETHER ACCORDING TO THE INTERNET. LIKE CHOCOLATE AND PEANUT BUTTER, BUT WITH MORE QUIPS AND VIOLENCE!
ROBBIE THOMPSON WRIT
TODD NAUCK ARTI
JIM CAMPBELL COLOR ARTI
VC'S JOE SABINO LETTER
KATHLEEN WISNESKI ASSISTANT EDIT
DARREN SHAN EDIT

TIPPY-TOE'S GUIDE TO SQUIRREL GIRL

CARD 001 of ∞

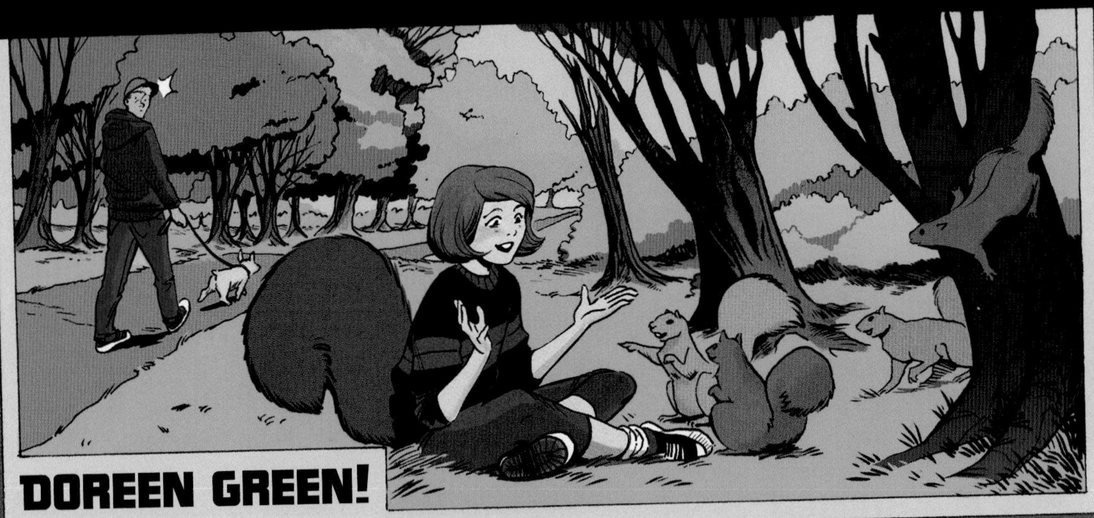
DOREEN GREEN!

Doreen was born with the ability to **communicate** with squirrels. How cool is that? What? You don't think it's cool? I mean, it's cooler than being born with the ability to communicate with sloths. Though I'd totally read an Unwakeable Sloth Girl comic. Any-old-who, the squirrels convinced Doreen to use her powers to help people! And you know what? She **did**! You're **welcome**!

Fun Fact: Did you know Squirrels are the smartest animals in the universe? Well, now you do. Because it's a fact. Also a fact? Nuts are all that matter in life. Nuts. You heard it here first. Tell your friends!

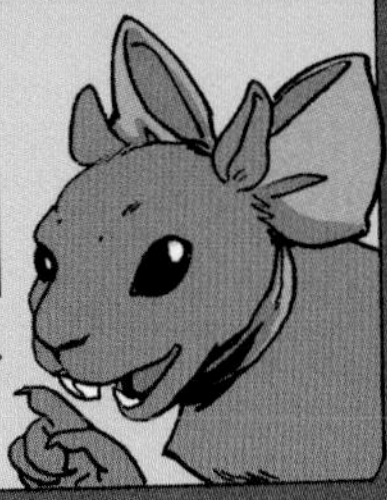

TIPPY-TOE'S GUIDE TO SQUIRREL GIRL

CARD 002 of ∞

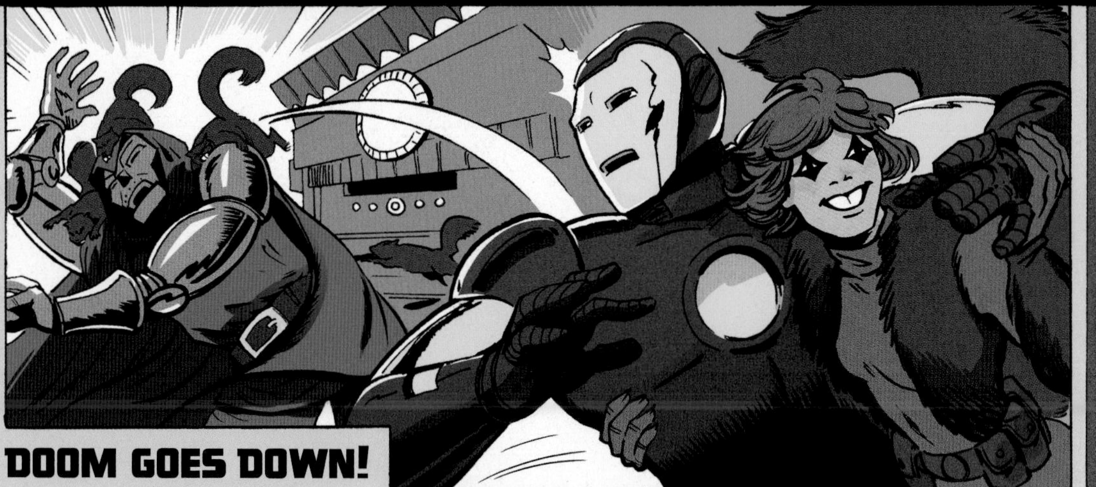
DOOM GOES DOWN!

In Squirrel Girl's first adventure, she totally **saved** her idol Iron Man from Dr. Doom and **proved** she belonged on the big stage! Look out, Avengers, here comes Squirrel Girl!

Fun Fact: Squirrel Girl never did make the Avengers. But she did make the Great Lake Avengers, the 8th or 16th best Avengers squad, where she met me, Tippy-Toe, her partner-in-justice. Also, the real hero of this comic. Seriously, check the wiki--I just updated it while you were reading this.

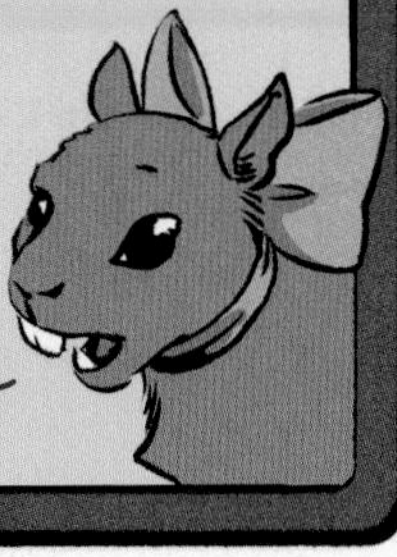

TIPPY-TOE'S GUIDE TO SQUIRREL GIRL

CARD 217 of ∞

HOMEWORK IS FUN
AND EDUCATIONAL!

Unlike most super heroes (for some reason), Doreen has actually grown **and** grown up...and also gone to college! She's a total genius and not just because she can talk to squirrels, but because she can do math and science stuff. So, when she's not busy saving the world from boredom and alien invasions, Doreen is a student of life **and** computer science!

Fun Fact: I'm still bummed she didn't major in squirrels, but maybe you will? Also, stay in school, kids! Like, seriously, when you're done reading this, do your homework. I'm not kidding. Go. Now.

TIPPY-TOE'S GUIDE TO SQUIRREL GIRL

CARD 237 of ∞

THUS FALLS GALACTUS!

It usually takes a whole bunch of heroes to take down Galactus, purple fanatic and part-time planet eater--but not Squirrel Girl. She crushed this menace with nothing more than her moxie and her adorable sidekick: me! You're welcome, Earth!

Fun Fact: Did you know Galactus is lactose intolerant? Dude can eat a planet but not a pizza. We all have our crosses to bear.

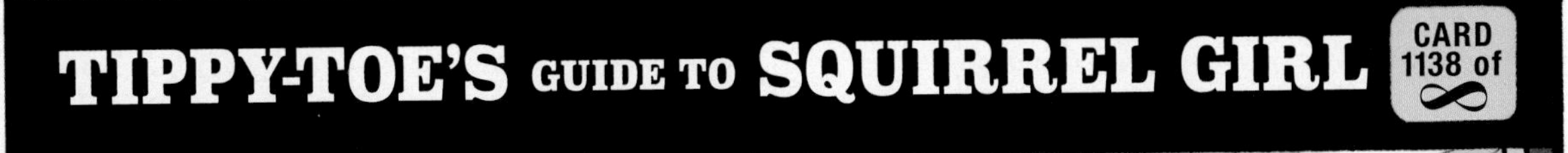

TIPPY-TOE'S GUIDE TO SQUIRREL GIRL

CARD 1138 of ∞

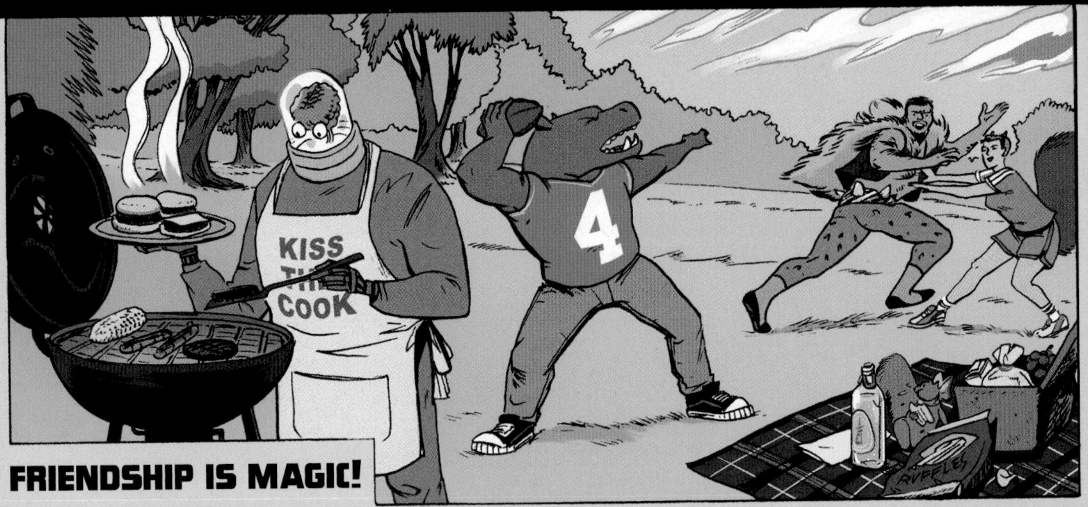

KISS THE COOK
4
FRIENDSHIP IS MAGIC!

It's not all punching, kicking and hoarding nuts, though--along the way Squirrel Girl has made friends. And enemies. She's so delightful, she sometimes turns enemies into friends. Because, c'mon, she's awesome. Who doesn't love Squirrel Girl? No really, who? Give me names.

Fun Fact: Despite being a former member of Hydra as well as a raging nihilist, Brain Drain makes a mean veggie burger.

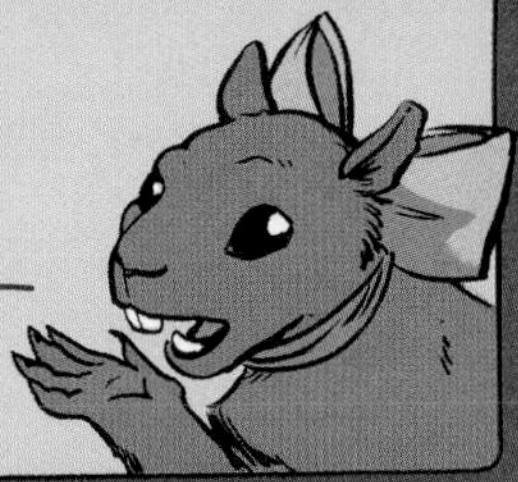

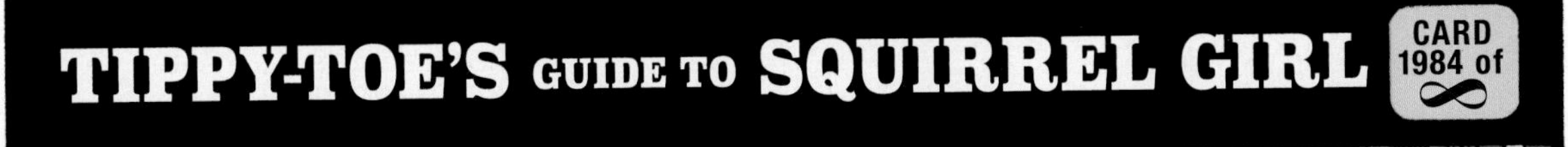

TIPPY-TOE'S GUIDE TO SQUIRREL GIRL

CARD 1984 of ∞

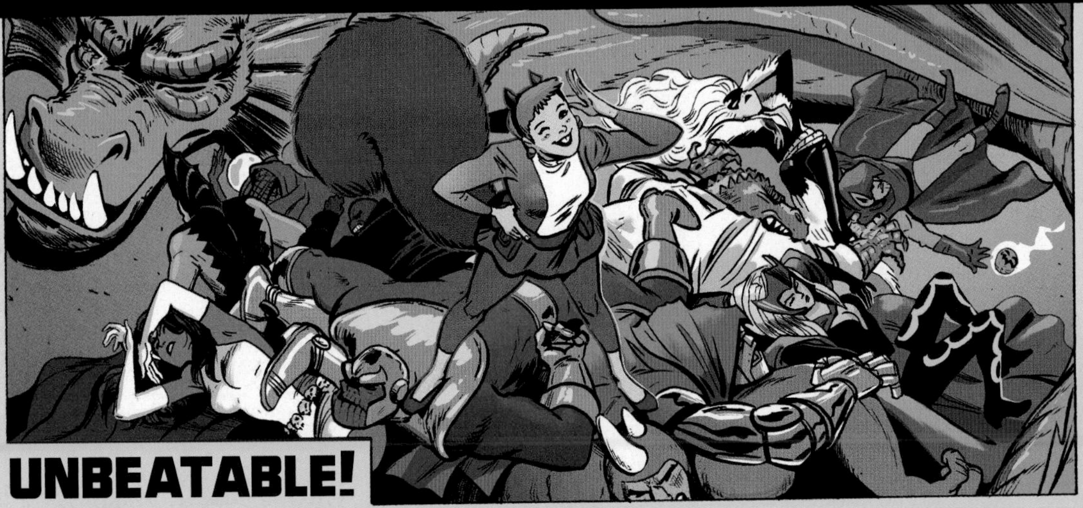

UNBEATABLE!

Squirrel Girl is unbeatable. No, like, for realsies. Look at this image! Do your eyes deceive you? Does this text lie to you? No! She beat all these fools by herself. Boom!

Fun Fact: She also beat them with *me*. And lots of squirrels. But yeah, she's totally unbeatable. And totally awesome! So, be like Squirrel Girl! Fight injustice! Be nice to strangers! And stay in school, fam!

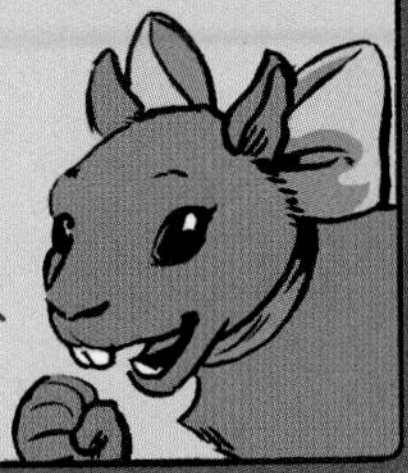

Robbie Thompson: Writer Veronica Fish: Artist VC's Travis Lanham: Letterer Kathleen Wisneski: Assistant Editor Darren Shan: Editor

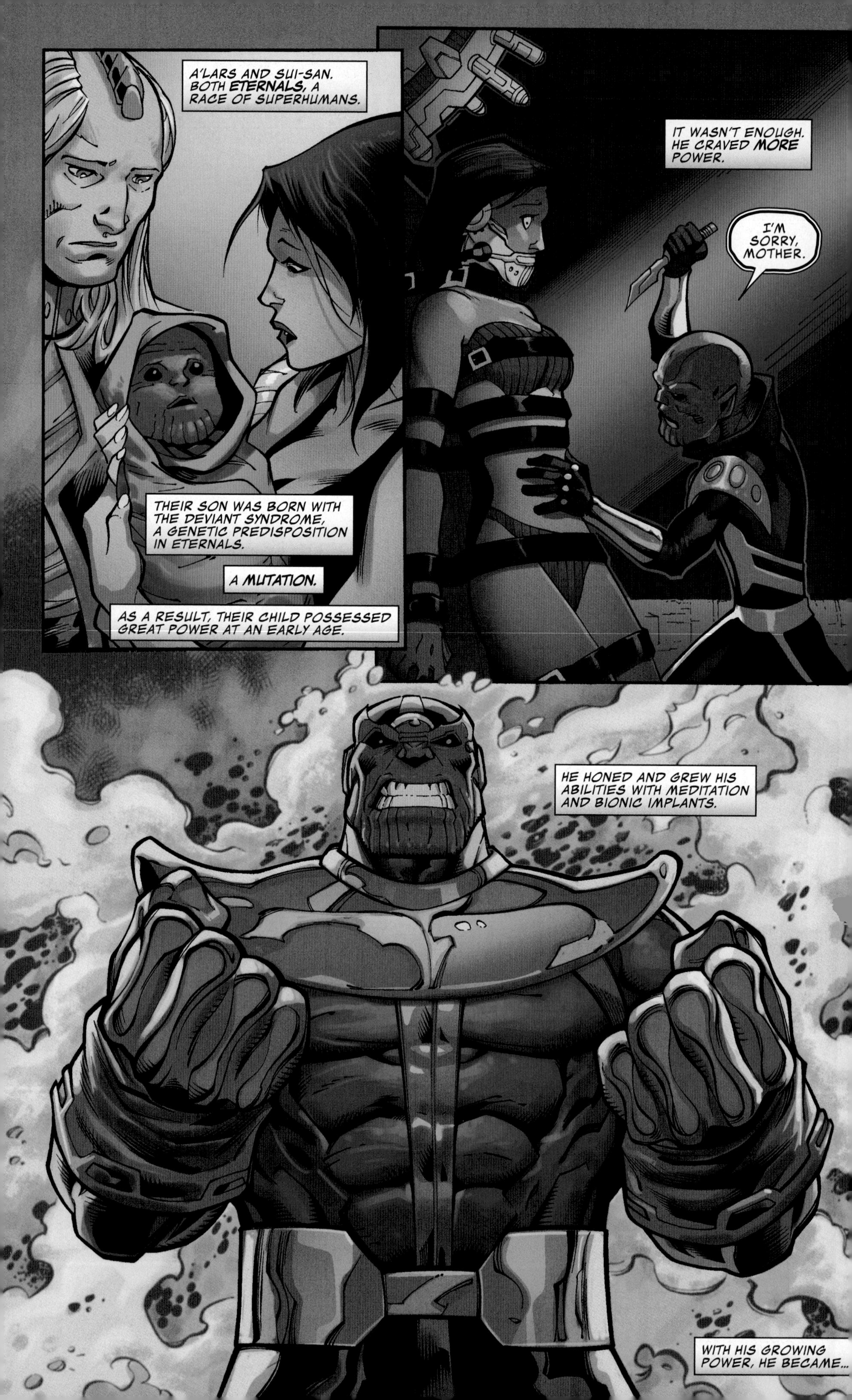
A'LARS AND SUI-SAN. BOTH ETERNALS, A RACE OF SUPERHUMANS.
THEIR SON WAS BORN WITH THE DEVIANT SYNDROME, A GENETIC PREDISPOSITION IN ETERNALS.
A MUTATION.
AS A RESULT, THEIR CHILD POSSESSED GREAT POWER AT AN EARLY AGE.
IT WASN'T ENOUGH. HE CRAVED MORE POWER.
I'M SORRY, MOTHER.
HE HONED AND GREW HIS ABILITIES WITH MEDITATION AND BIONIC IMPLANTS.
WITH HIS GROWING POWER, HE BECAME...

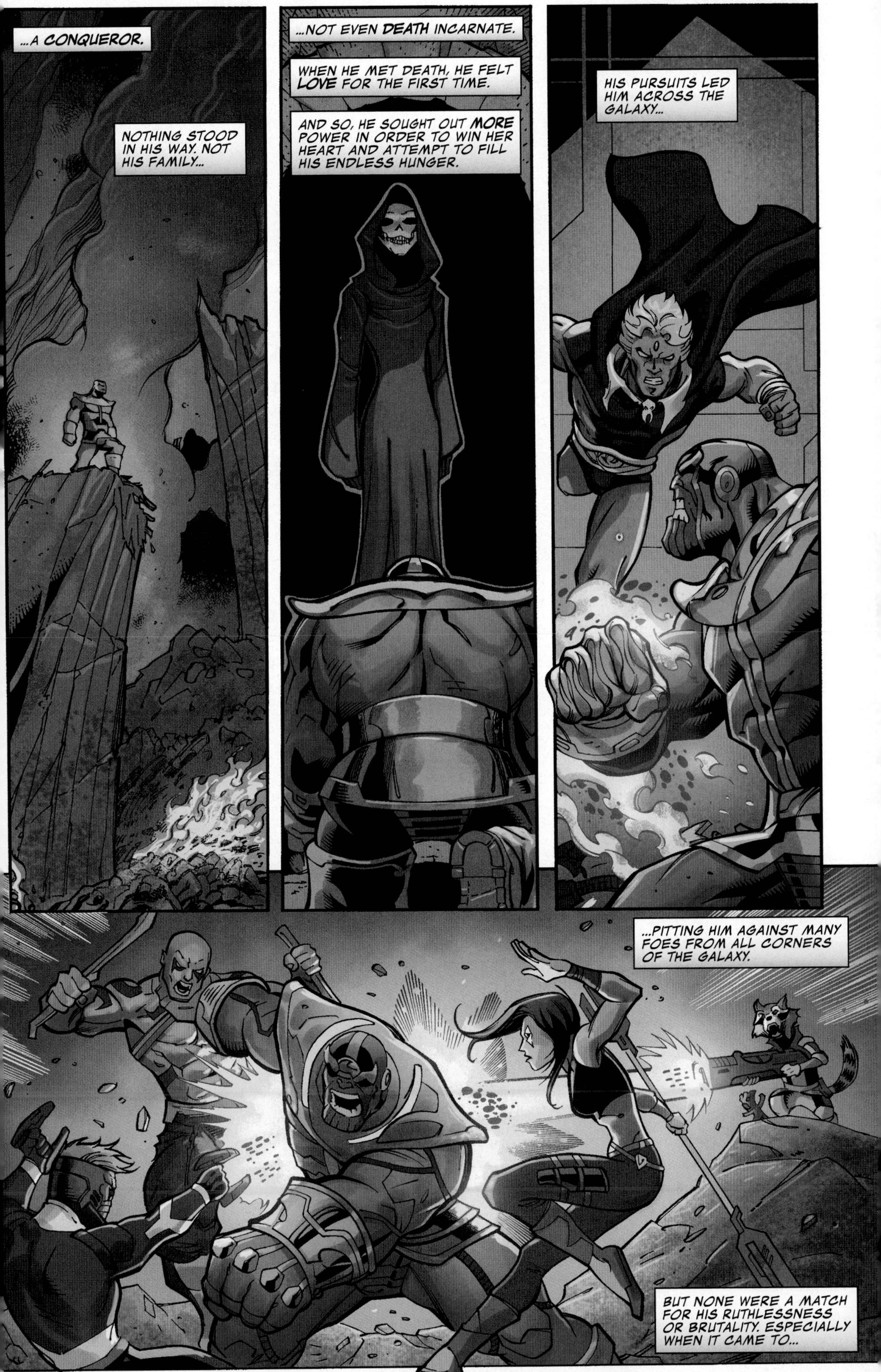
...A CONQUEROR.
NOTHING STOOD IN HIS WAY. NOT HIS FAMILY...
...NOT EVEN DEATH INCARNATE.
WHEN HE MET DEATH, HE FELT LOVE FOR THE FIRST TIME.
AND SO, HE SOUGHT OUT MORE POWER IN ORDER TO WIN HER HEART AND ATTEMPT TO FILL HIS ENDLESS HUNGER.
HIS PURSUITS LED HIM ACROSS THE GALAXY...
...PITTING HIM AGAINST MANY FOES FROM ALL CORNERS OF THE GALAXY.
BUT NONE WERE A MATCH FOR HIS RUTHLESSNESS OR BRUTALITY. ESPECIALLY WHEN IT CAME TO...

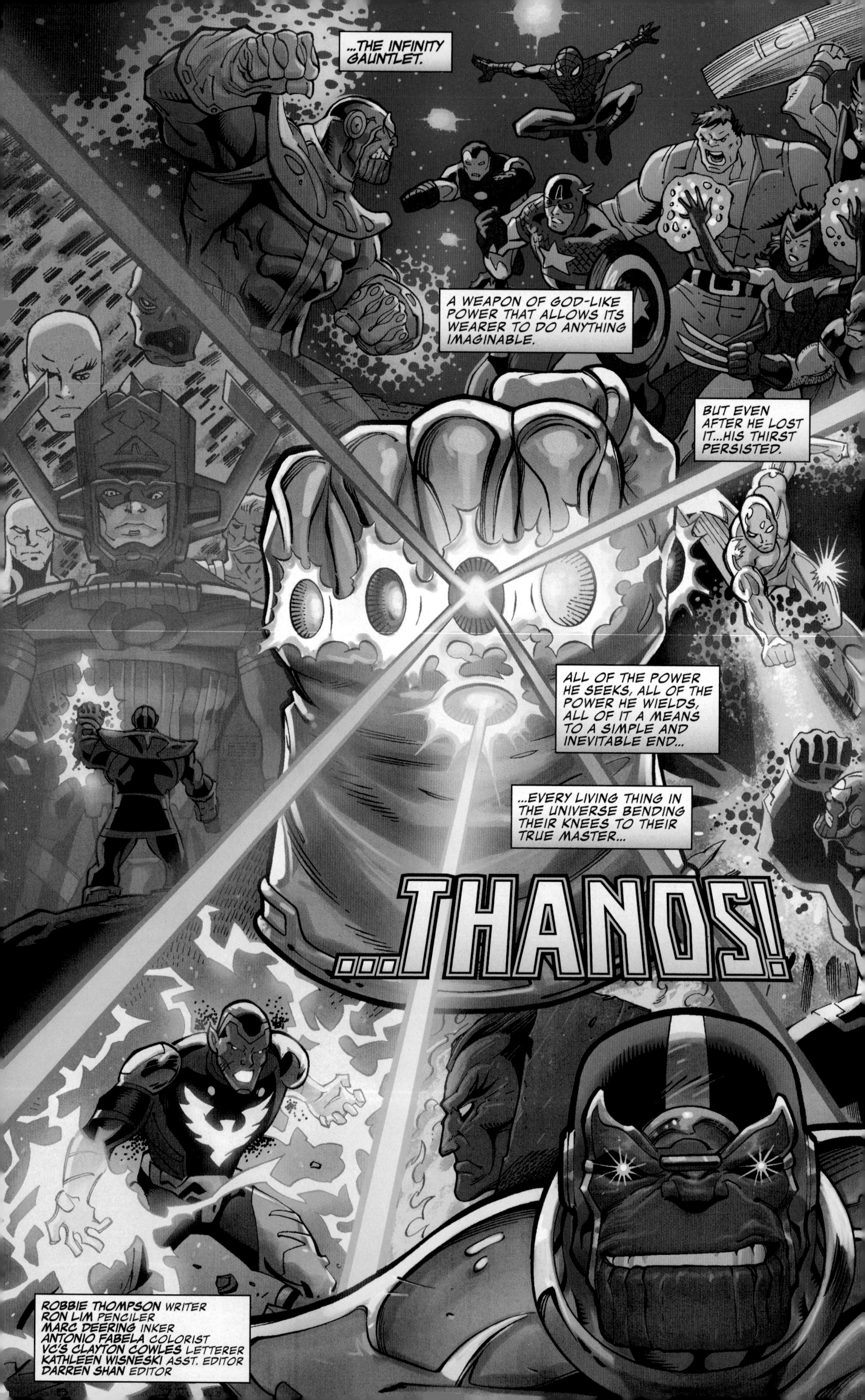
...THE INFINITY GAUNTLET.
A WEAPON OF GOD-LIKE POWER THAT ALLOWS ITS WEARER TO DO ANYTHING IMAGINABLE.
BUT EVEN AFTER HE LOST IT...HIS THIRST PERSISTED.
ALL OF THE POWER HE SEEKS, ALL OF THE POWER HE WIELDS, ALL OF IT A MEANS TO A SIMPLE AND INEVITABLE END...
...EVERY LIVING THING IN THE UNIVERSE BENDING THEIR KNEES TO THEIR TRUE MASTER...
...THANOS!
ROBBIE THOMPSON WRITER
RON LIM PENCILER
MARC DEERING INKER
ANTONIO FABELA COLORIST
VC'S CLAYTON COWLES LETTERER
KATHLEEN WISNESKI ASST. EDITOR
DARREN SHAN EDITOR

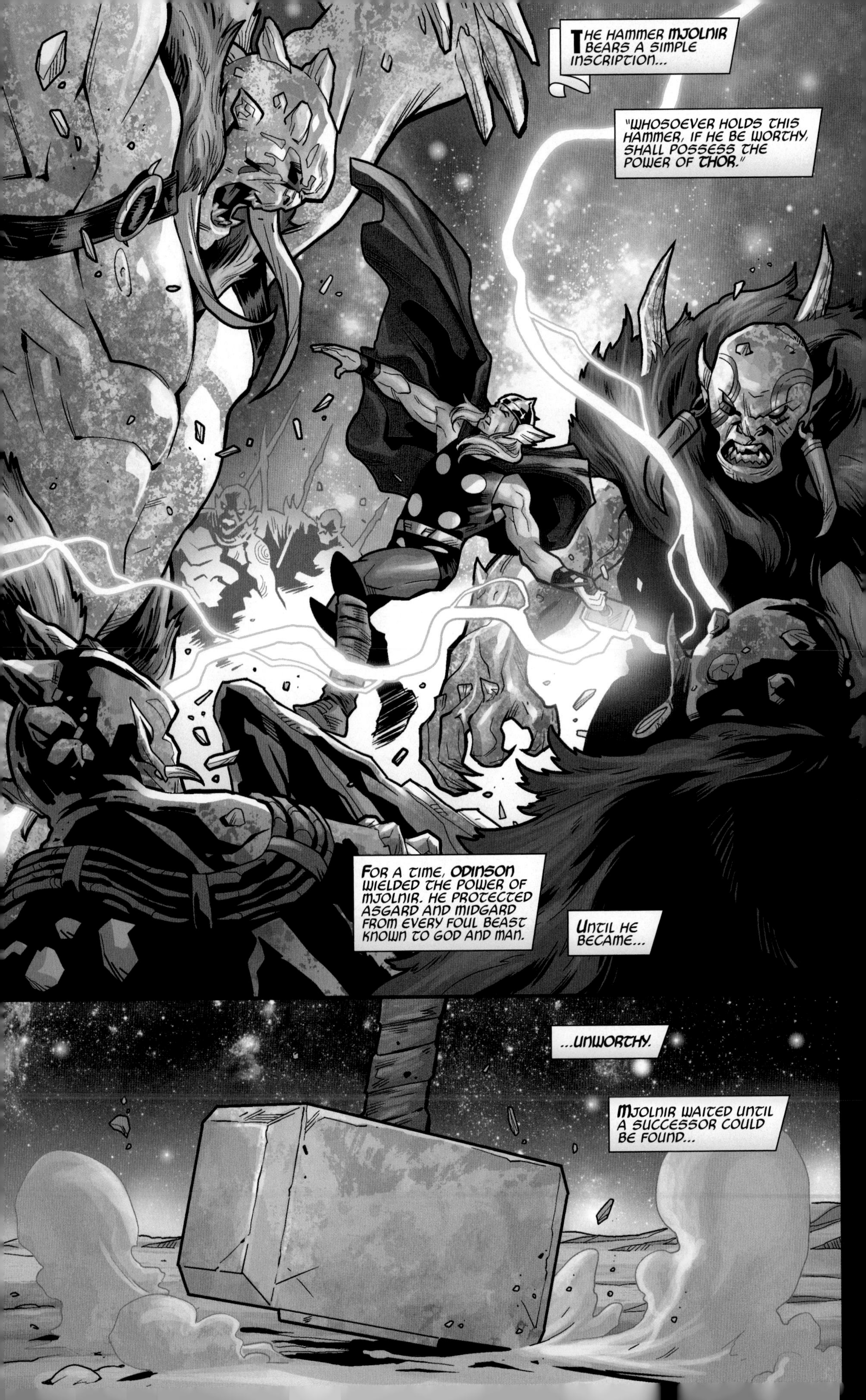
THE HAMMER MJOLNIR BEARS A SIMPLE INSCRIPTION...
"WHOSOEVER HOLDS THIS HAMMER, IF HE BE WORTHY, SHALL POSSESS THE POWER OF THOR."
FOR A TIME, ODINSON WIELDED THE POWER OF MJOLNIR. HE PROTECTED ASGARD AND MIDGARD FROM EVERY FOUL BEAST KNOWN TO GOD AND MAN.
UNTIL HE BECAME...
...UNWORTHY.
MJOLNIR WAITED UNTIL A SUCCESSOR COULD BE FOUND...

EMERGENCY

4

JANE FOSTER PURSUED A CAREER IN MEDICINE AFTER LOSING HER MOTHER TO CANCER AT AN EARLY AGE. THE SAME CANCER...

...THAT WOULD ONE DAY FIND JANE.

SHE BATTLED THE CANCER HEAD-ON, NEVER STOPPING.

UNTIL FATE INTERVENED.

CHEMOT
RO
Please Do

A LONGTIME FRIEND OF ODINSON, JANE ACCEPTED A POSITION IN THE...

...CONGRESS OF WORLDS, A CONGREGATION REPRESENTING THE TEN REALMS. IT WAS THERE THAT MJOLNIR FOUND ITS NEW OWNER.

GARD

THOUGH THE TRANSFORMATION CANCELS OUT HER CANCER TREATMENT, JANE HAS ACCEPTED HER NEW LIFE.

FOR NOW SHE KNOWS...

..."WHOSOEVER HOLDS THIS HAMMER, IF SHE BE WORTHY, SHALL POSSESS THE POWER OF..."

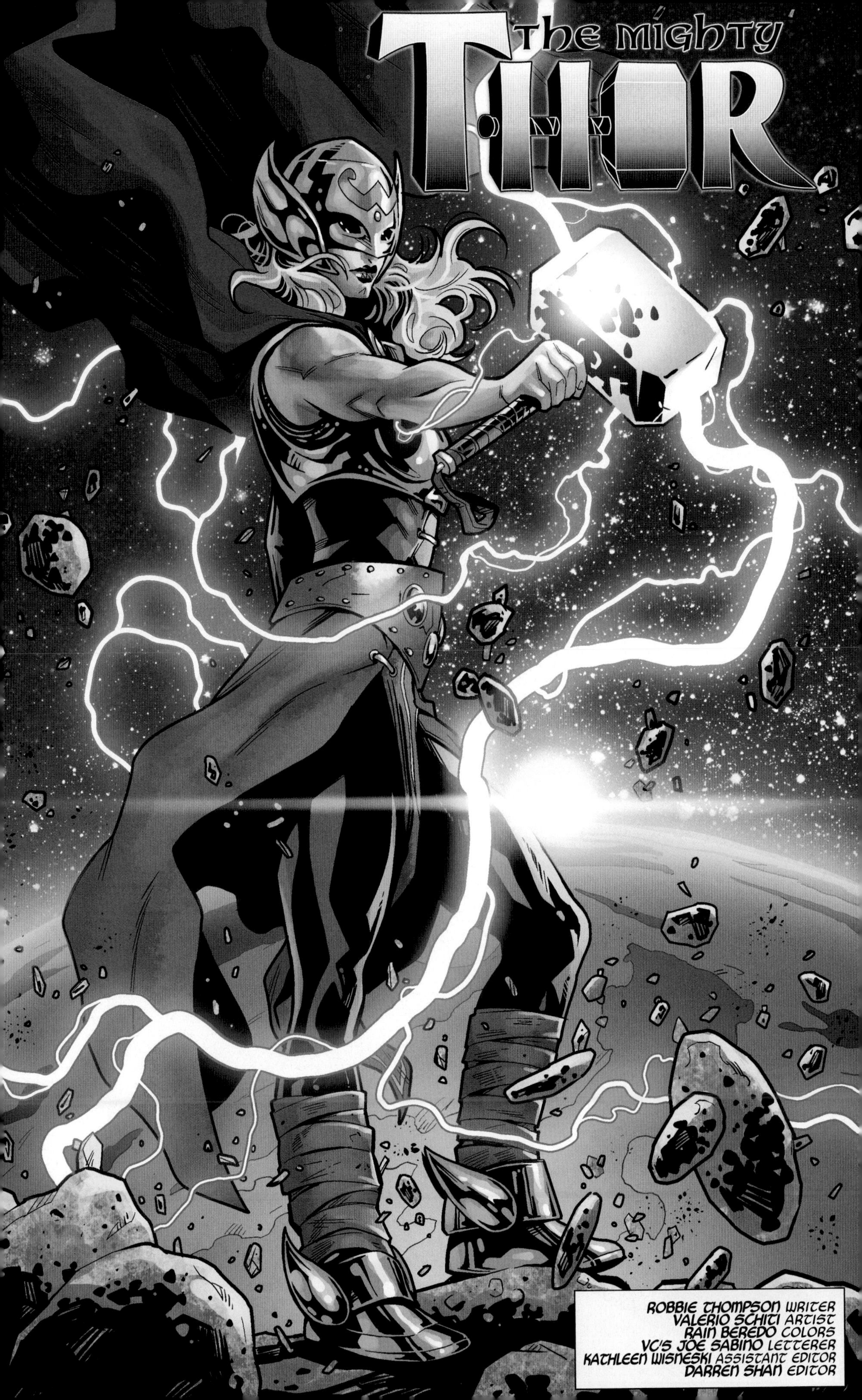
THE MIGHTY THOR
ROBBIE THOMPSON WRITER
VALERIO SCHITI ARTIST
RAIN BEREDO COLORS
VC'S JOE SABINO LETTERER
KATHLEEN WISNESKI ASSISTANT EDITOR
DARREN SHAN EDITOR

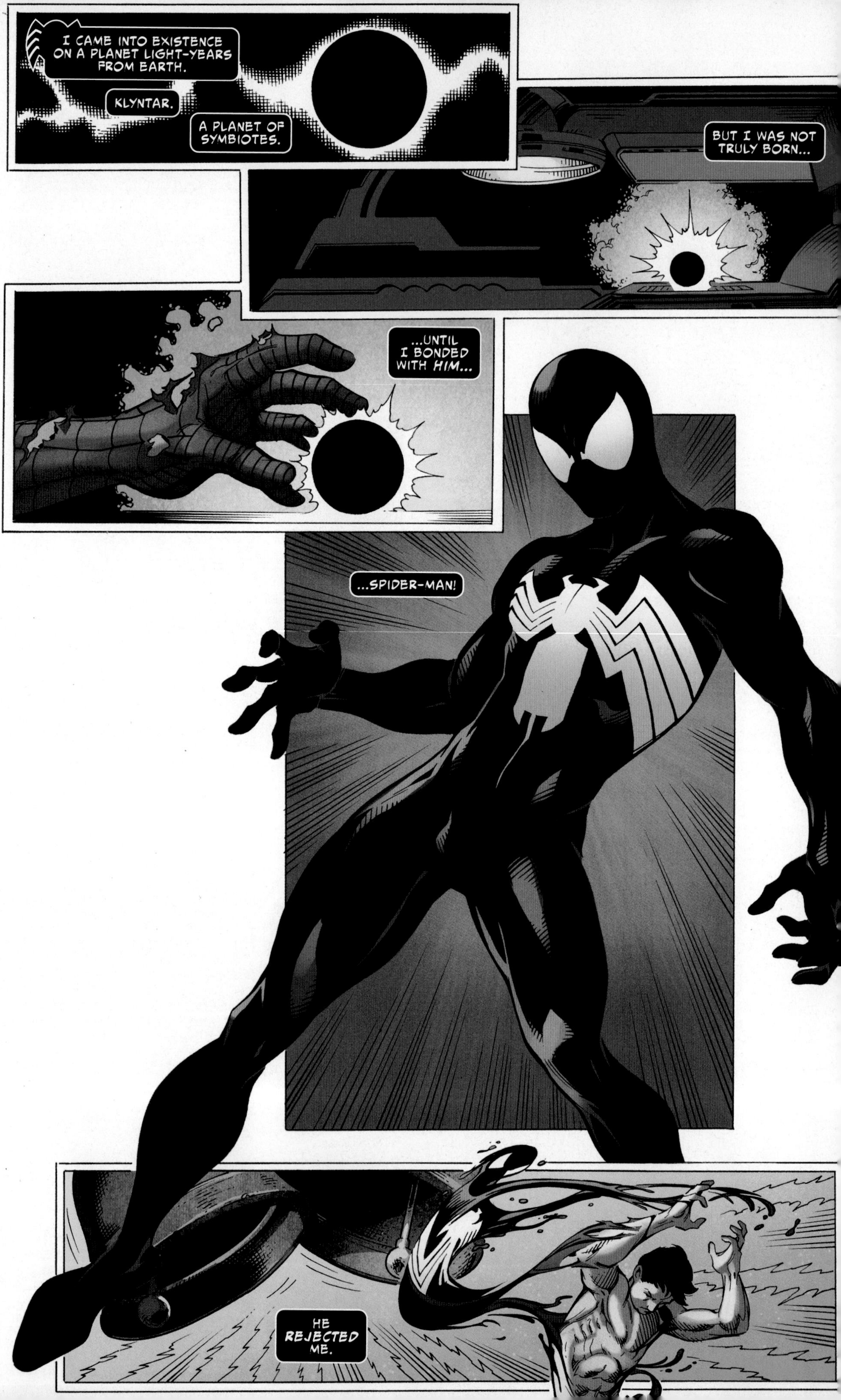
I CAME INTO EXISTENCE ON A PLANET LIGHT-YEARS FROM EARTH.
KLYNTAR.
A PLANET OF SYMBIOTES.
BUT I WAS NOT TRULY BORN...
...UNTIL I BONDED WITH *HIM*...
...SPIDER-MAN!
HE REJECTED ME.

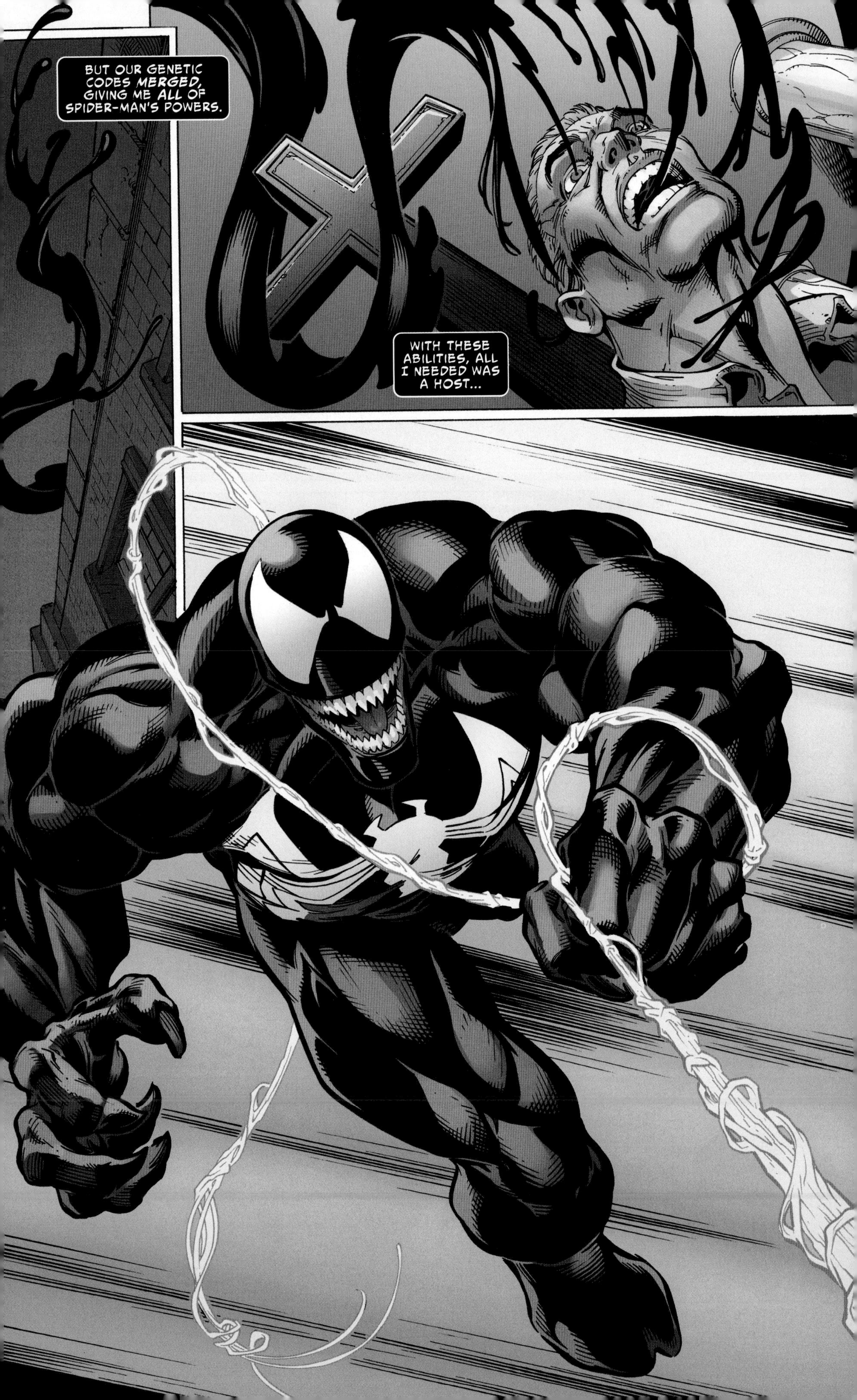
BUT OUR GENETIC CODES MERGED, GIVING ME ALL OF SPIDER-MAN'S POWERS.
WITH THESE ABILITIES, ALL I NEEDED WAS A HOST...

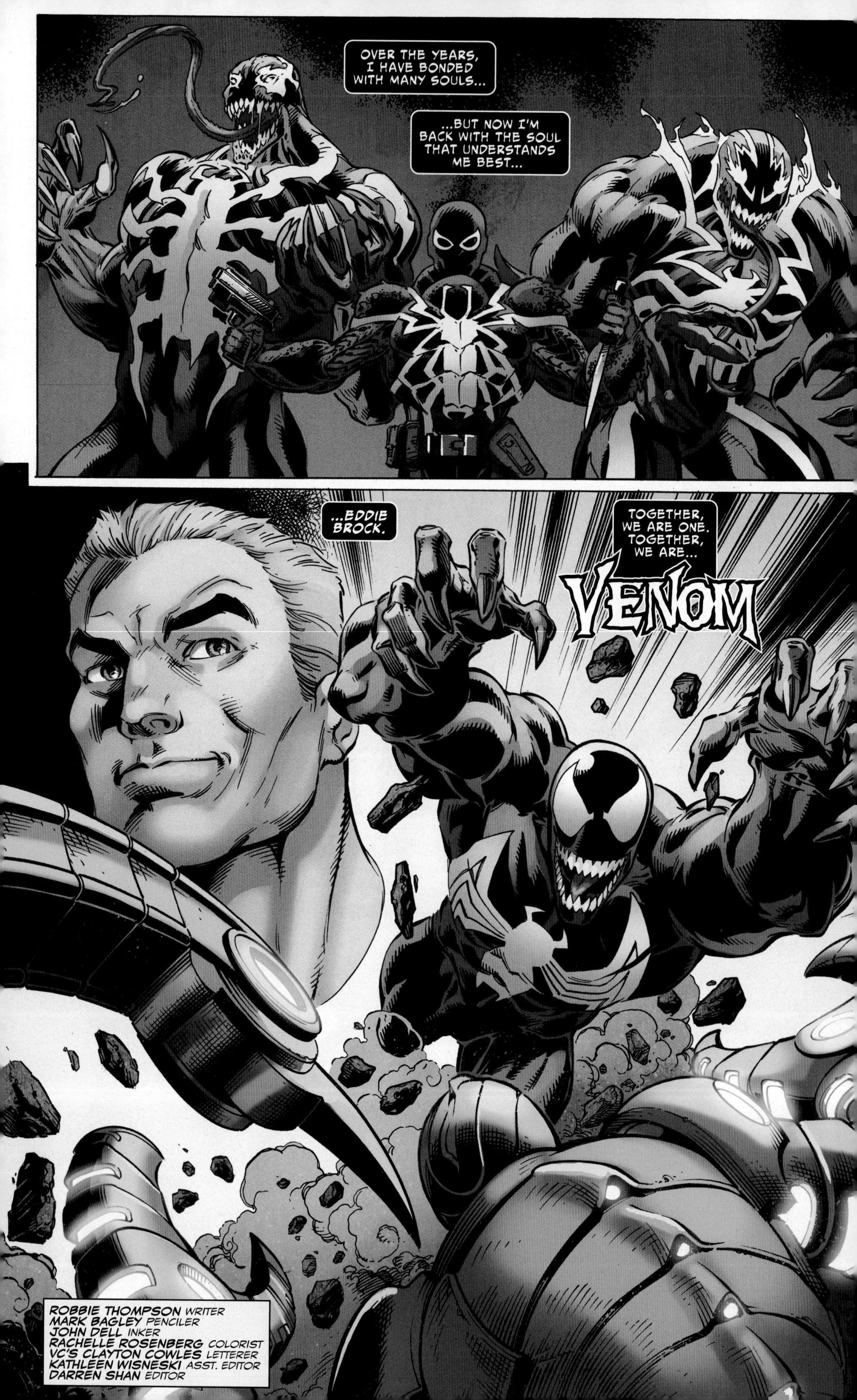
OVER THE YEARS, I HAVE BONDED WITH MANY SOULS...
...BUT NOW I'M BACK WITH THE SOUL THAT UNDERSTANDS ME BEST...
...EDDIE BROCK.
TOGETHER, WE ARE ONE. TOGETHER, WE ARE...
VENOM
ROBBIE THOMPSON WRITER
MARK BAGLEY PENCILER
JOHN DELL INKER
RACHELLE ROSENBERG COLORIST
VC'S CLAYTON COWLES LETTERER
KATHLEEN WISNESKI ASST. EDITOR
DARREN SHAN EDITOR

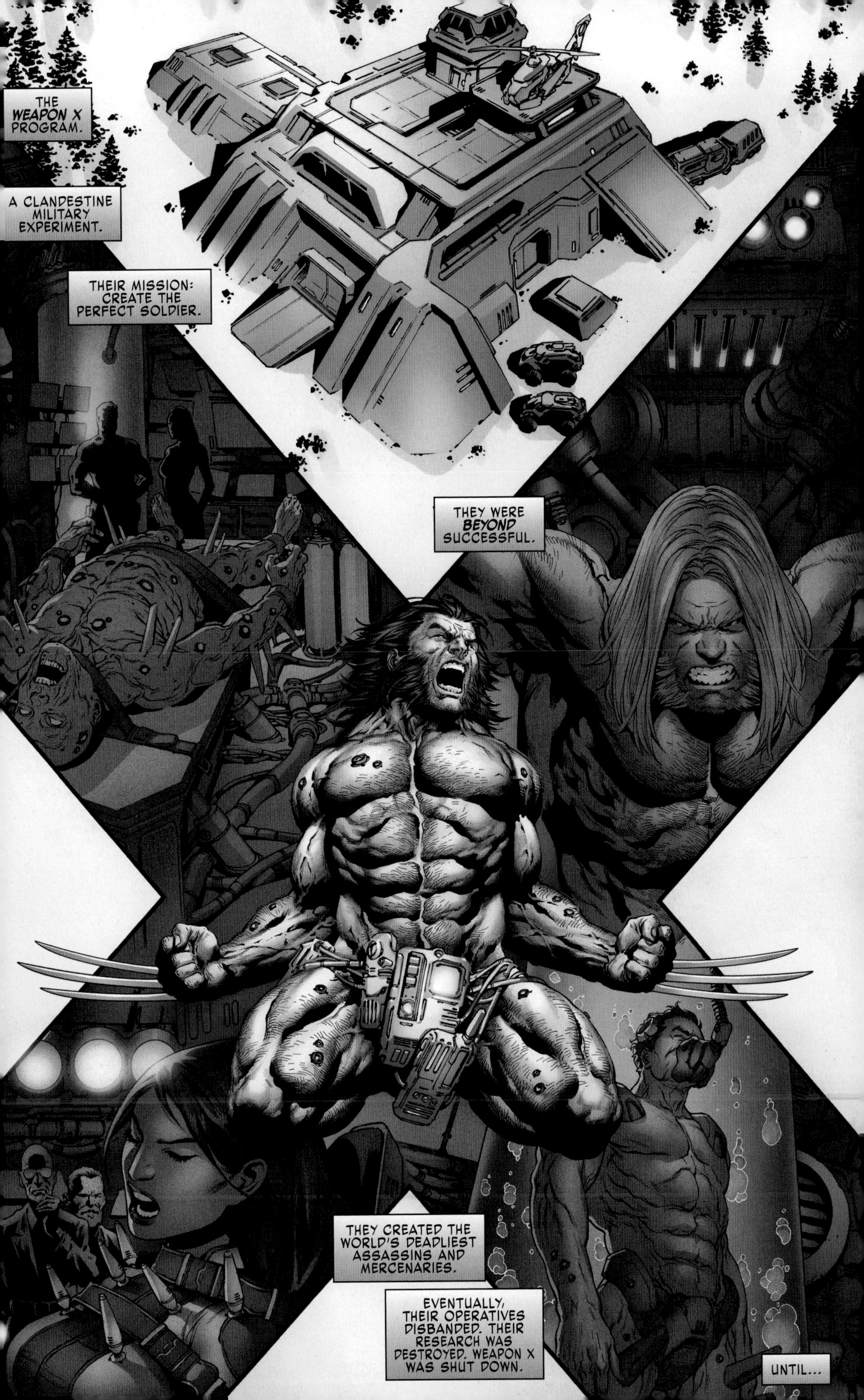
THE WEAPON X PROGRAM.
A CLANDESTINE MILITARY EXPERIMENT.
THEIR MISSION: CREATE THE PERFECT SOLDIER.
THEY WERE BEYOND SUCCESSFUL.
THEY CREATED THE WORLD'S DEADLIEST ASSASSINS AND MERCENARIES.
EVENTUALLY, THEIR OPERATIVES DISBANDED. THEIR RESEARCH WAS DESTROYED. WEAPON X WAS SHUT DOWN.
UNTIL...

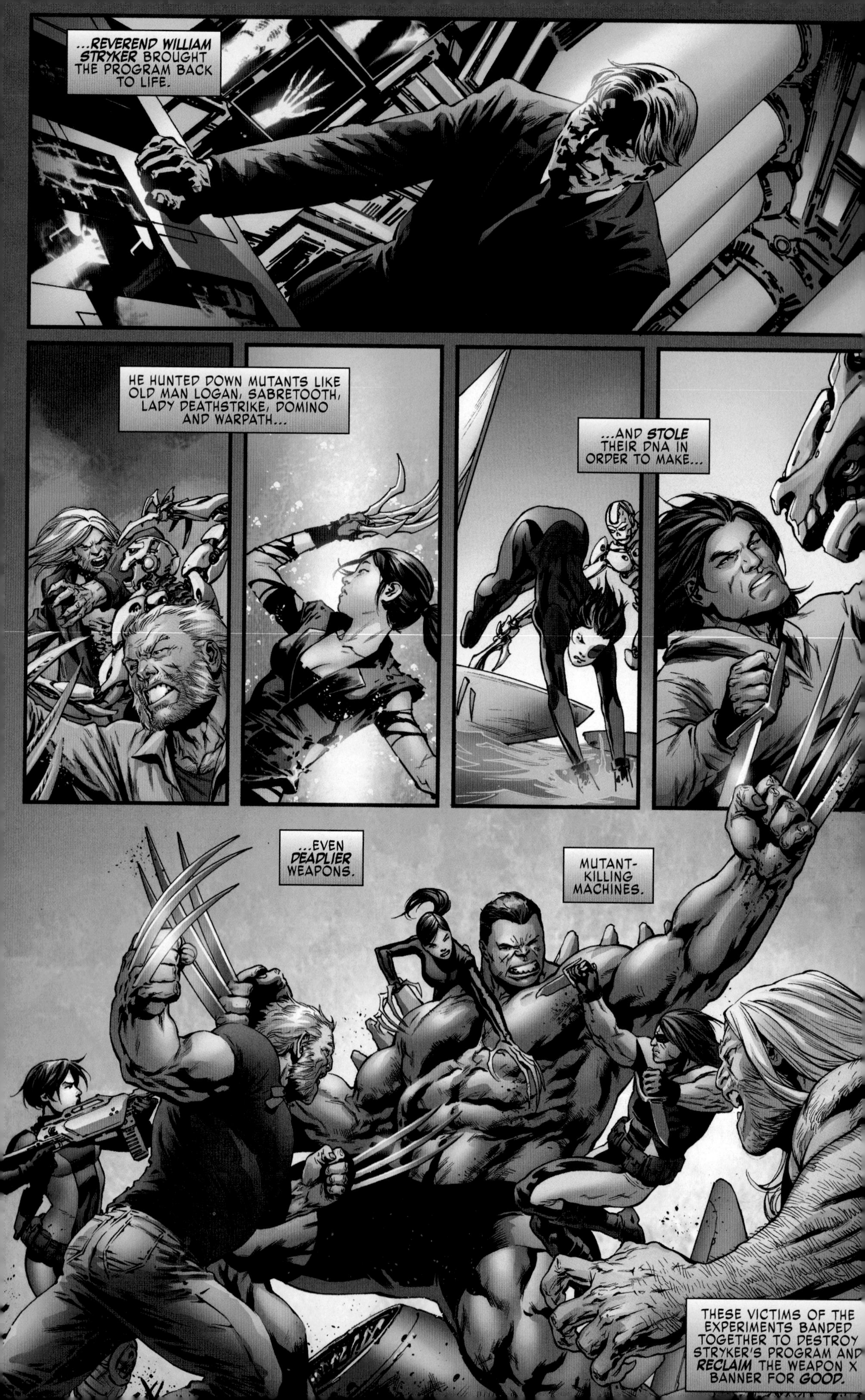
...REVEREND WILLIAM STRYKER BROUGHT THE PROGRAM BACK TO LIFE.
HE HUNTED DOWN MUTANTS LIKE OLD MAN LOGAN, SABRETOOTH, LADY DEATHSTRIKE, DOMINO AND WARPATH...
...AND STOLE THEIR DNA IN ORDER TO MAKE...
...EVEN DEADLIER WEAPONS.
MUTANT-KILLING MACHINES.
THESE VICTIMS OF THE EXPERIMENTS BANDED TOGETHER TO DESTROY STRYKER'S PROGRAM AND RECLAIM THE WEAPON X BANNER FOR GOOD.

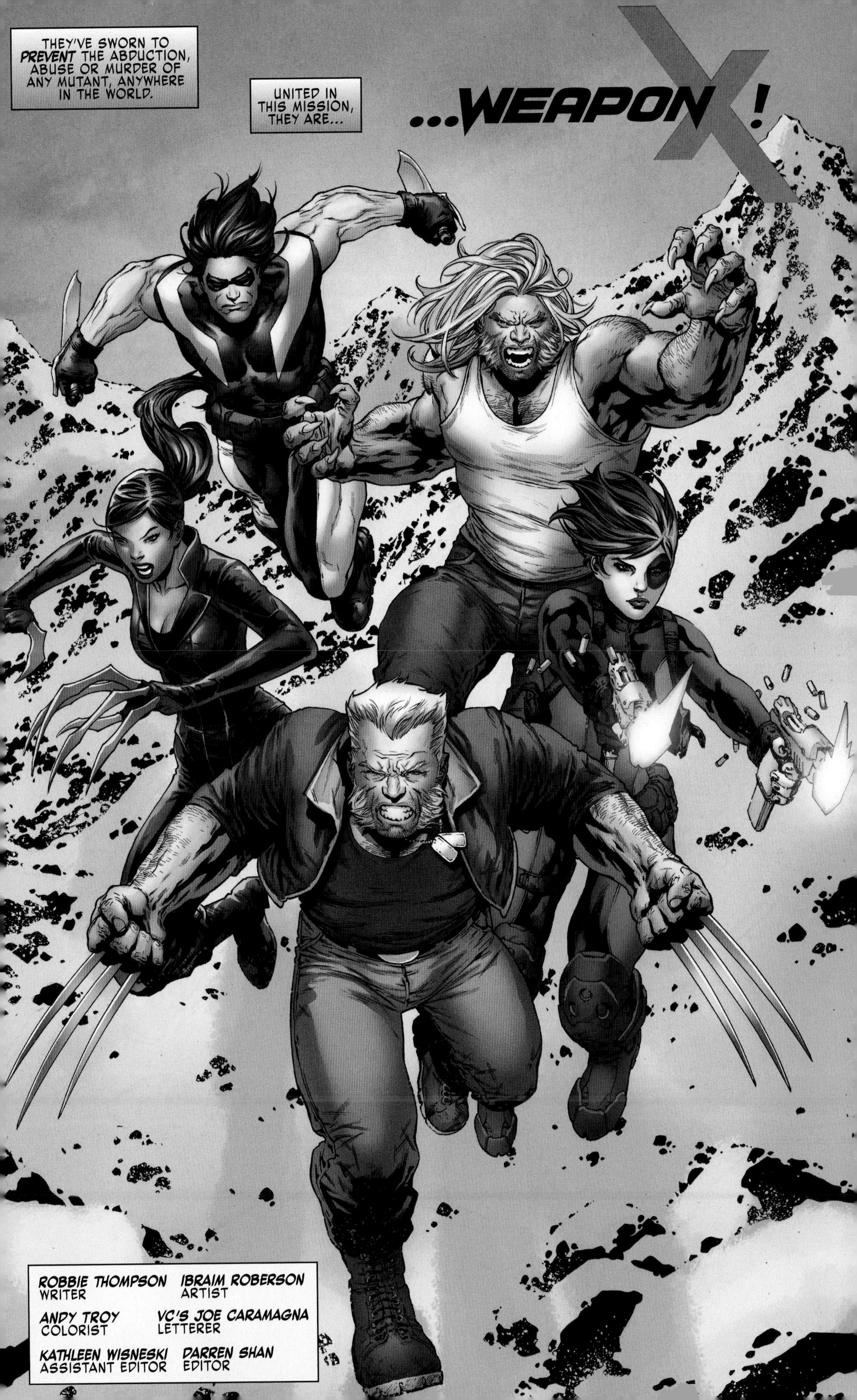

THEY'VE SWORN TO PREVENT THE ABDUCTION, ABUSE OR MURDER OF ANY MUTANT, ANYWHERE IN THE WORLD.
UNITED IN THIS MISSION, THEY ARE...
...WEAPON X!
ROBBIE THOMPSON WRITER
IBRAIM ROBERSON ARTIST
ANDY TROY COLORIST
VC'S JOE CARAMAGNA LETTERER
KATHLEEN WISNESKI ASSISTANT EDITOR
DARREN SHAN EDITOR

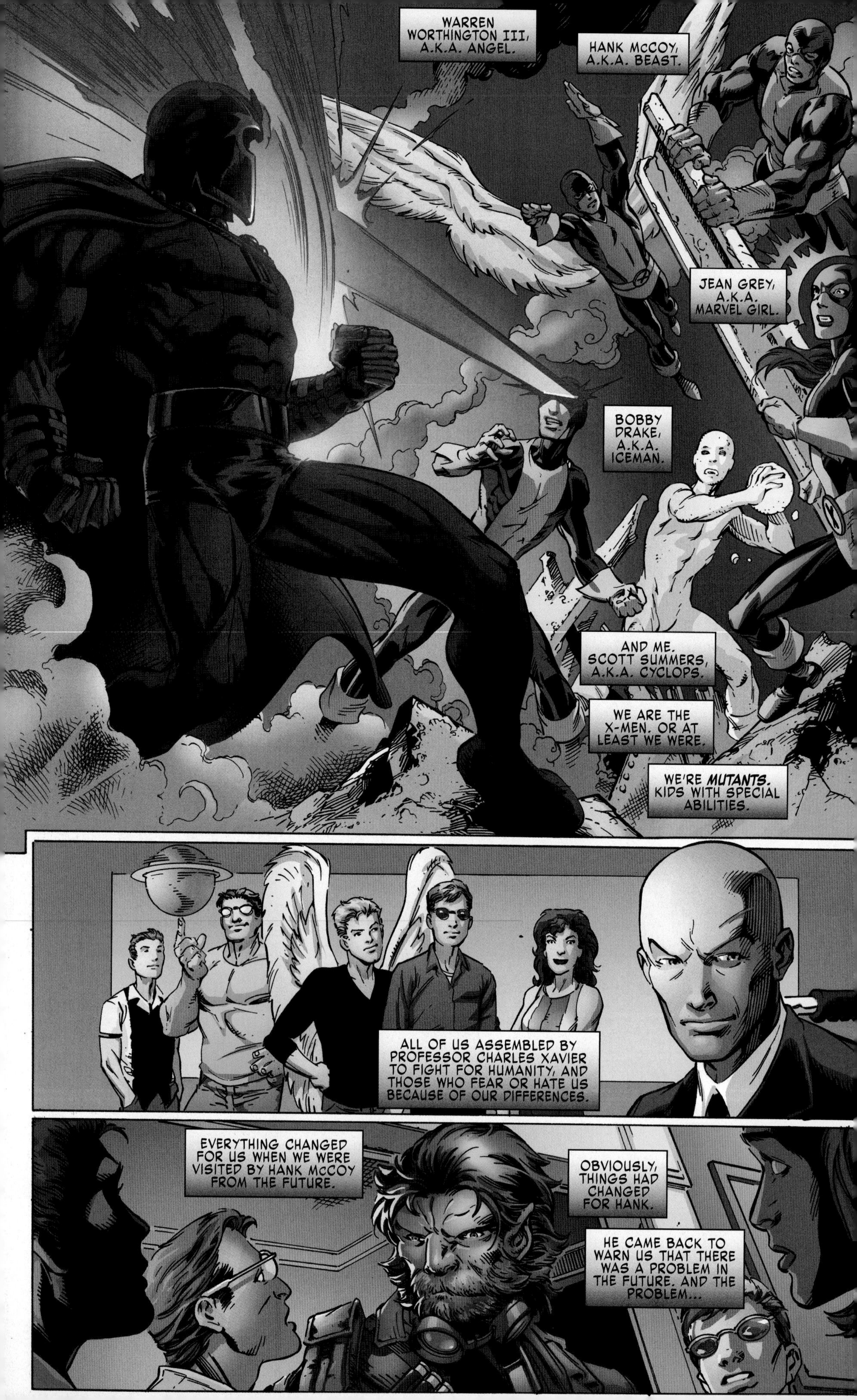
WARREN WORTHINGTON III, A.K.A. ANGEL.
HANK McCOY, A.K.A. BEAST.
JEAN GREY, A.K.A. MARVEL GIRL.
BOBBY DRAKE, A.K.A. ICEMAN.
AND ME. SCOTT SUMMERS, A.K.A. CYCLOPS.
WE ARE THE X-MEN. OR AT LEAST WE WERE.
WE'RE MUTANTS. KIDS WITH SPECIAL ABILITIES.
ALL OF US ASSEMBLED BY PROFESSOR CHARLES XAVIER TO FIGHT FOR HUMANITY, AND THOSE WHO FEAR OR HATE US BECAUSE OF OUR DIFFERENCES.
EVERYTHING CHANGED FOR US WHEN WE WERE VISITED BY HANK McCOY FROM THE FUTURE.
OBVIOUSLY, THINGS HAD CHANGED FOR HANK.
HE CAME BACK TO WARN US THAT THERE WAS A PROBLEM IN THE FUTURE. AND THE PROBLEM...

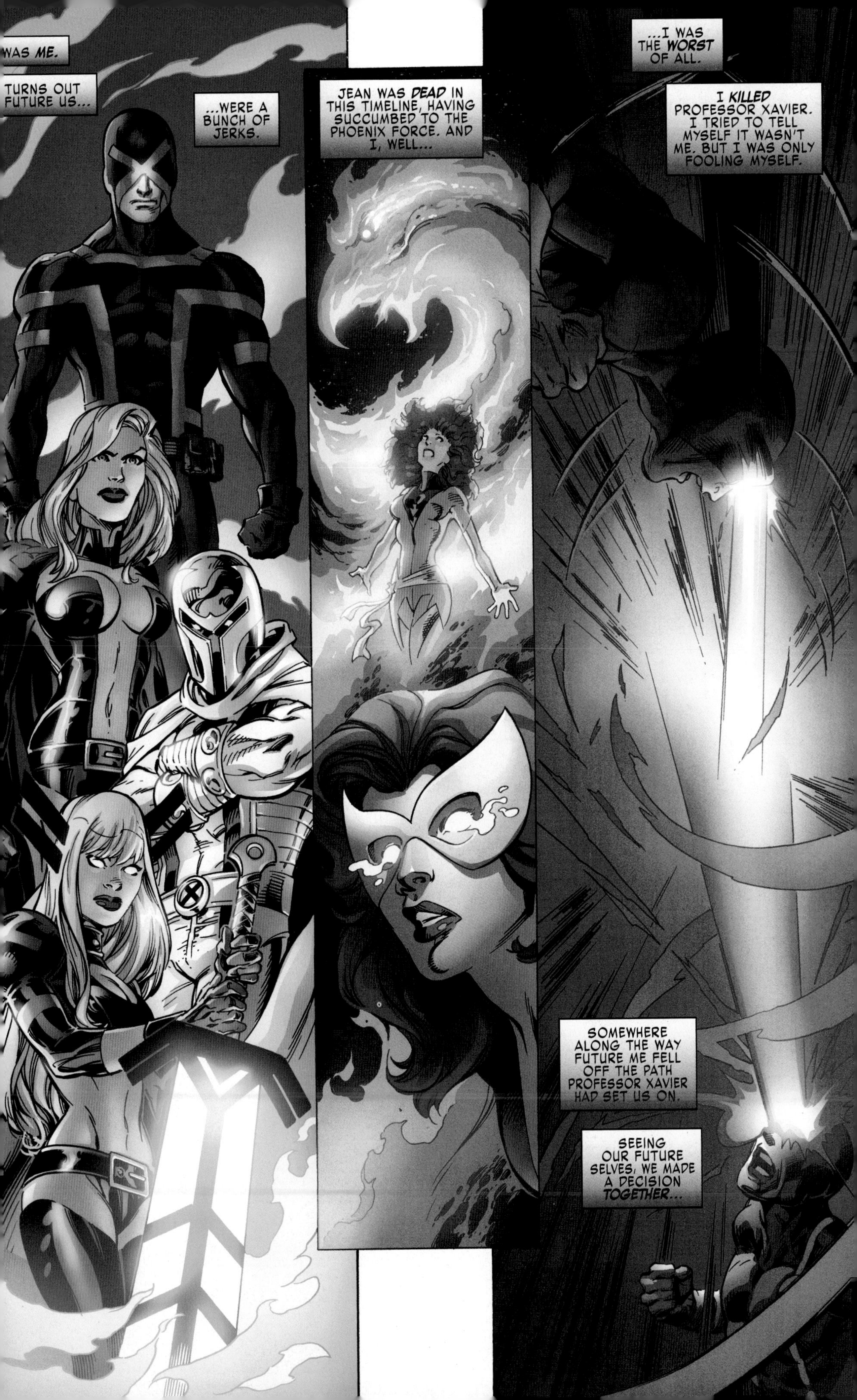
WAS ME.
TURNS OUT FUTURE US...
...WERE A BUNCH OF JERKS.
JEAN WAS DEAD IN THIS TIMELINE, HAVING SUCCUMBED TO THE PHOENIX FORCE. AND I, WELL...
...I WAS THE WORST OF ALL.
I KILLED PROFESSOR XAVIER. I TRIED TO TELL MYSELF IT WASN'T ME. BUT I WAS ONLY FOOLING MYSELF.
SOMEWHERE ALONG THE WAY FUTURE ME FELL OFF THE PATH PROFESSOR XAVIER HAD SET US ON.
SEEING OUR FUTURE SELVES, WE MADE A DECISION TOGETHER...

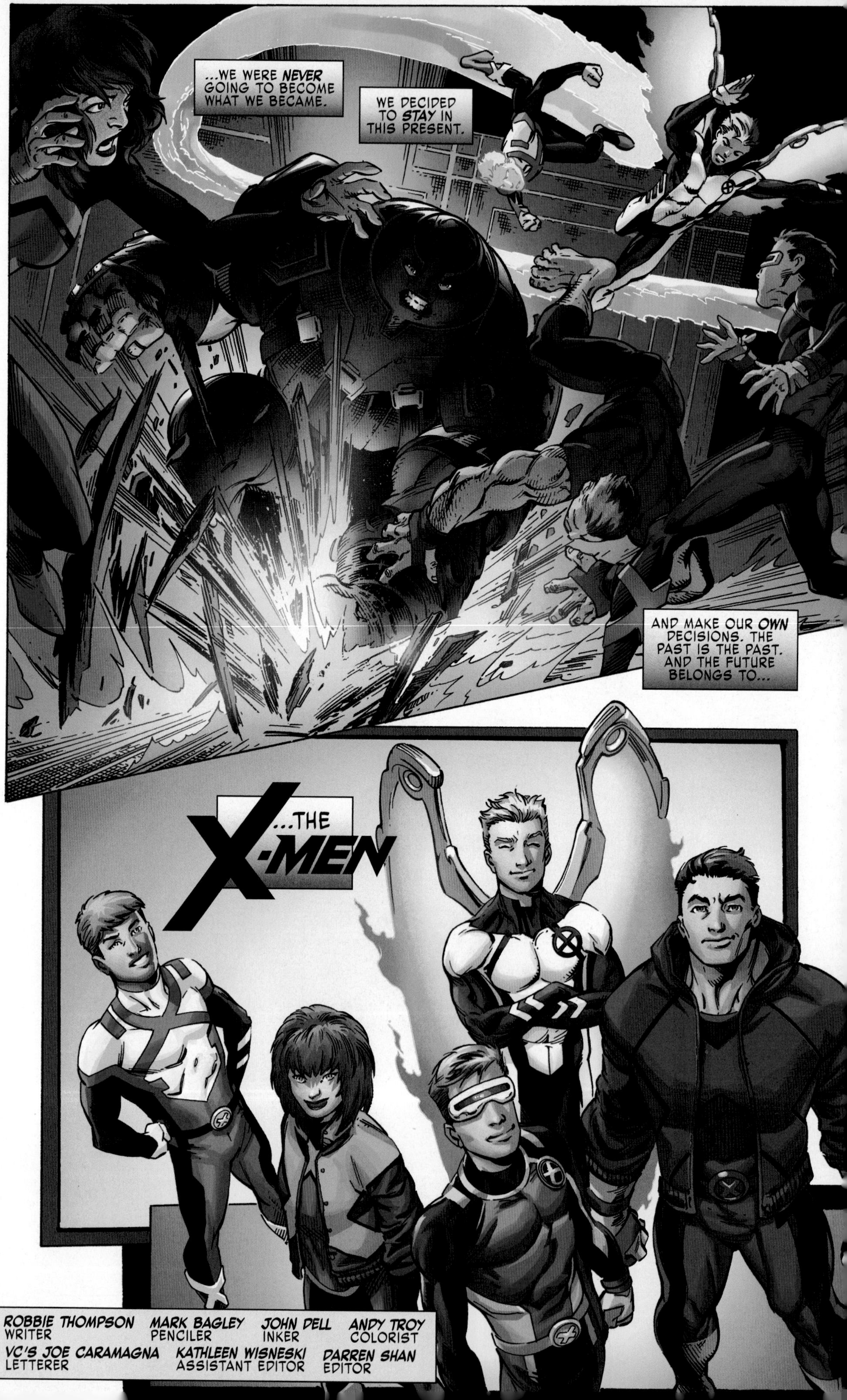

...WE WERE NEVER GOING TO BECOME WHAT WE BECAME.
WE DECIDED TO STAY IN THIS PRESENT.
AND MAKE OUR OWN DECISIONS. THE PAST IS THE PAST. AND THE FUTURE BELONGS TO...
...THE X-MEN
ROBBIE THOMPSON WRITER
MARK BAGLEY PENCILER
JOHN DELL INKER
ANDY TROY COLORIST
VC'S JOE CARAMAGNA LETTERER
KATHLEEN WISNESKI ASSISTANT EDITOR
DARREN SHAN EDITOR

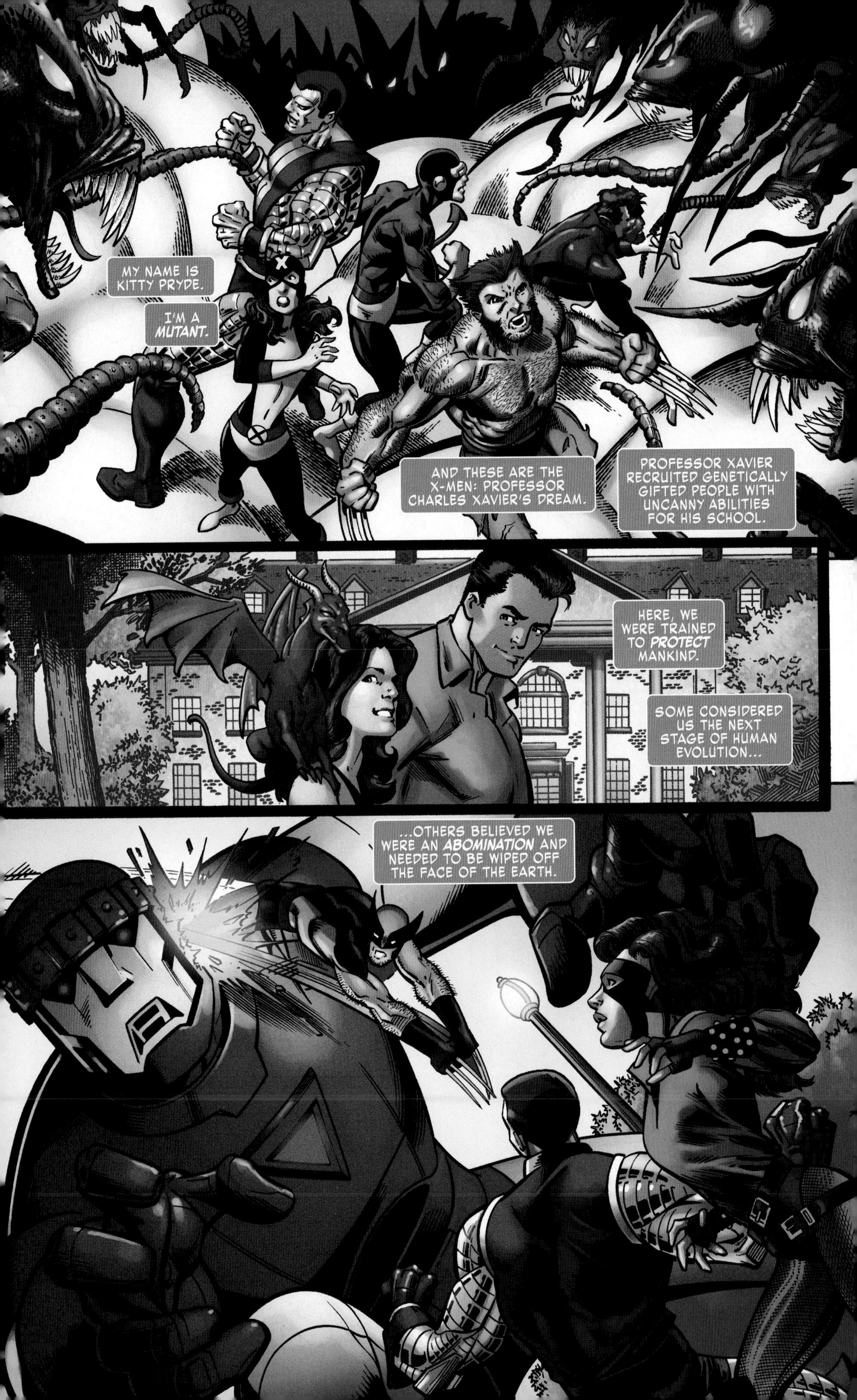

MY NAME IS KITTY PRYDE.
I'M A *MUTANT.*
AND THESE ARE THE X-MEN: PROFESSOR CHARLES XAVIER'S DREAM.
PROFESSOR XAVIER RECRUITED GENETICALLY GIFTED PEOPLE WITH UNCANNY ABILITIES FOR HIS SCHOOL.
HERE, WE WERE TRAINED TO *PROTECT* MANKIND.
SOME CONSIDERED US THE NEXT STAGE OF HUMAN EVOLUTION...
...OTHERS BELIEVED WE WERE AN *ABOMINATION* AND NEEDED TO BE WIPED OFF THE FACE OF THE EARTH.

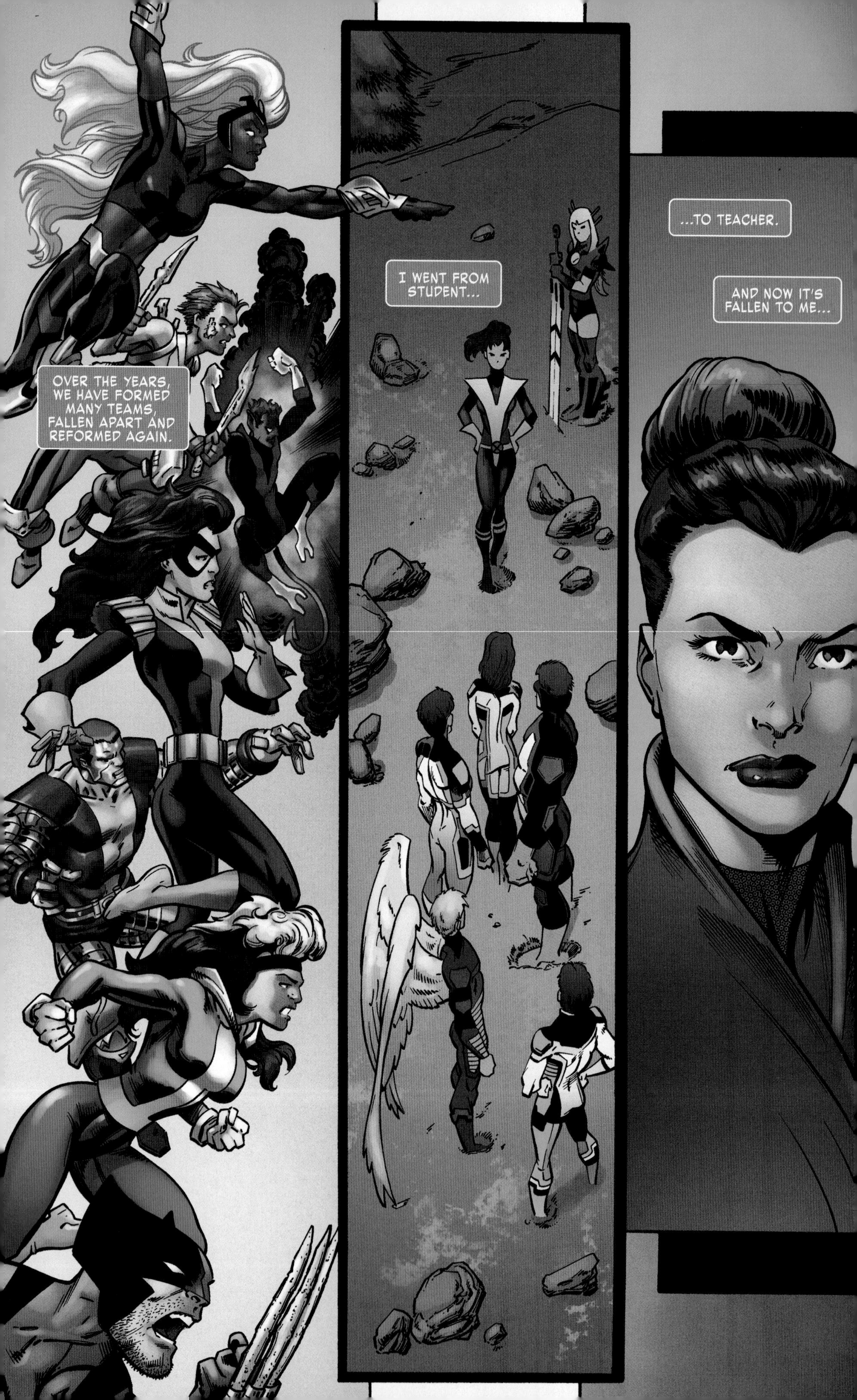
OVER THE YEARS, WE HAVE FORMED MANY TEAMS, FALLEN APART AND REFORMED AGAIN.
I WENT FROM STUDENT...
...TO TEACHER.
AND NOW IT'S FALLEN TO ME...

...TO KEEP XAVIER'S DREAM ALIVE, NO MATTER WHAT STANDS IN ITS WAY!

X-MEN
GOLD

ROBBIE THOMPSON	MARK BAGLEY	ANDREW HENNESSY	CHRIS SOTOMAYOR
WRITER	PENCILER	INKER	COLORIST

VC'S CORY PETIT	KATHLEEN WISNESKI	DARREN SHAN
LETTERER	ASSISTANT EDITOR	EDITOR

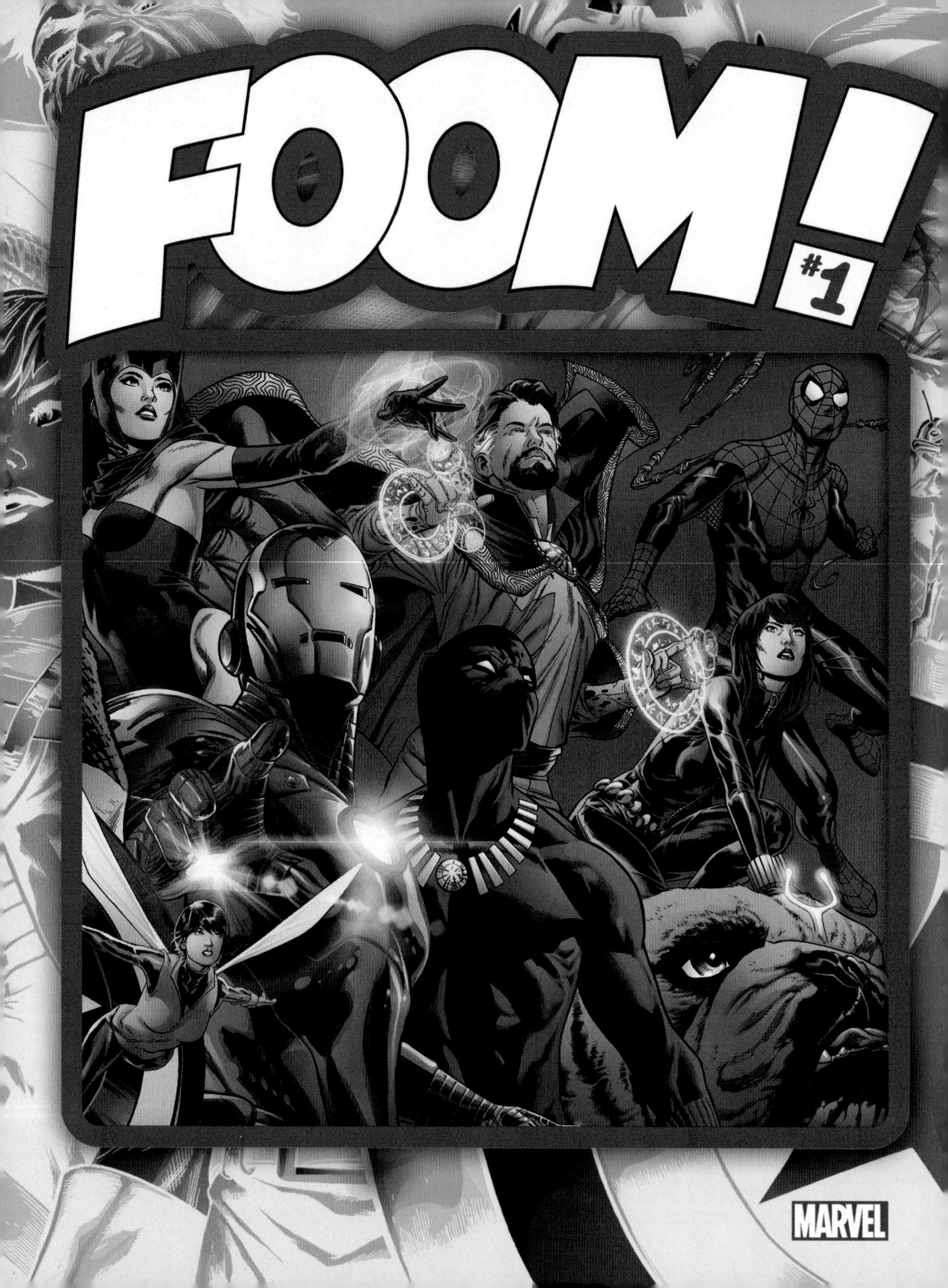
FOOM!
#1
MARVEL

Jeff Youngquist & **Brian Overton**
editors

Caitlin O'Connell
assistant editor

Joe Hochstein
associate manager, digital assets

Kateri Woody
associate managing editor

Mark D. Beazley
editor, special projects

Jennifer Grünwald
senior editor, special projects

Peter Charpentier
senior manager, merchandising & promotions

David Gabriel
svp print, sales & marketing

am Del Re, **Rodolfo Muraguchi**, **Joe Frontirre** & **Ashley Choy**
designers

Jacque Porte, **Avia Perez** & **Elissa Hunter**
proofreaders

Axel Alonso
editor in chief

Joe Quesada
chief creative officer

Dan Buckley
president

Alan Fine
executive producer

anks to the staff of the original FOOM for the inspiration!

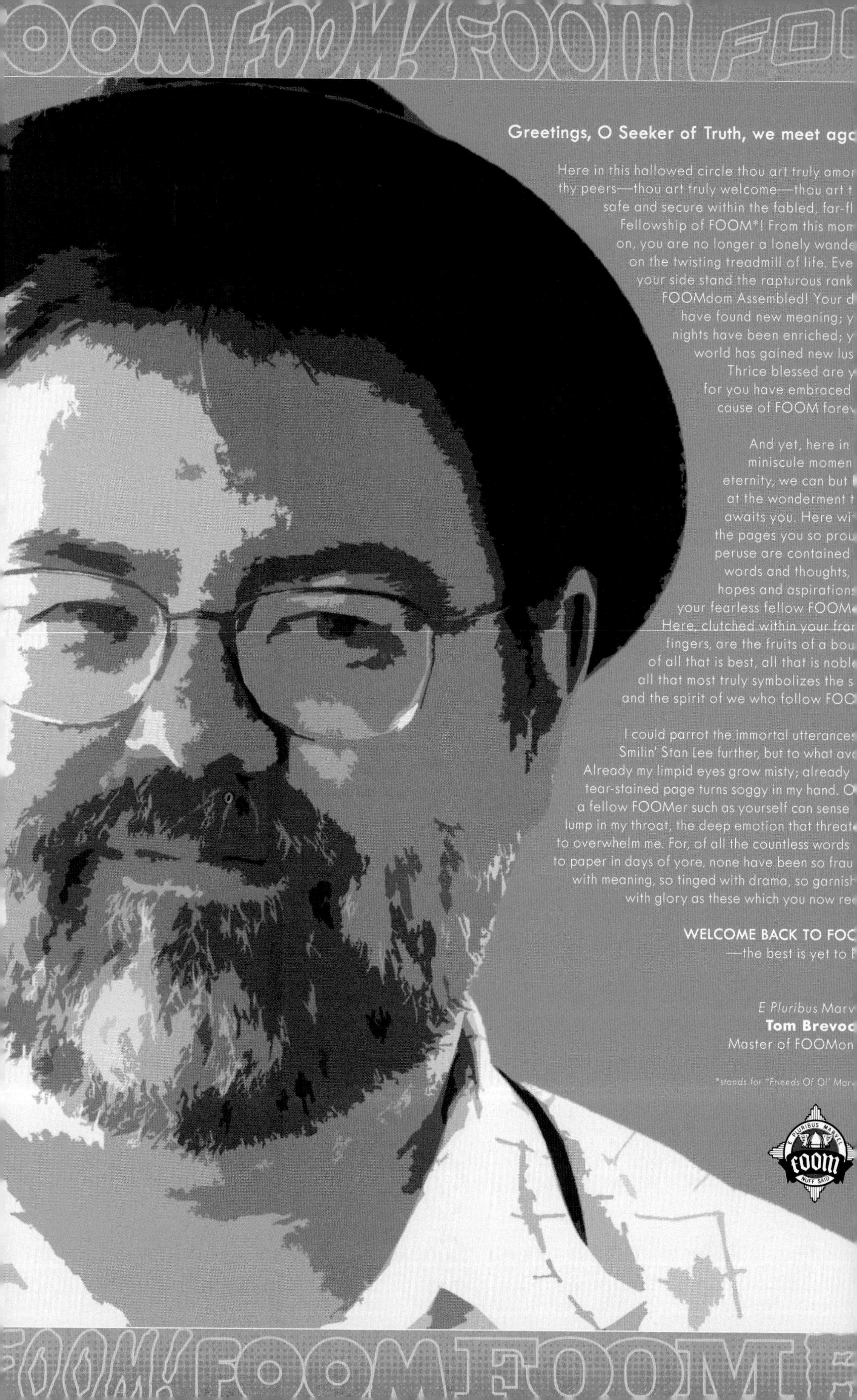

Greetings, O Seeker of Truth, we meet agc

Here in this hallowed circle thou art truly amor thy peers—thou art truly welcome—thou art t safe and secure within the fabled, far-fl Fellowship of FOOM*! From this mom on, you are no longer a lonely wande on the twisting treadmill of life. Eve your side stand the rapturous rank FOOMdom Assembled! Your d have found new meaning; y nights have been enriched; y world has gained new lus Thrice blessed are y for you have embraced cause of FOOM forev

And yet, here in miniscule momen eternity, we can but at the wonderment t awaits you. Here wi the pages you so prou peruse are contained words and thoughts, hopes and aspirations your fearless fellow FOOM Here, clutched within your fran fingers, are the fruits of a bou of all that is best, all that is noble all that most truly symbolizes the s and the spirit of we who follow FOC

I could parrot the immortal utterances Smilin' Stan Lee further, but to what avc Already my limpid eyes grow misty; already tear-stained page turns soggy in my hand. O a fellow FOOMer such as yourself can sense lump in my throat, the deep emotion that threat to overwhelm me. For, of all the countless words to paper in days of yore, none have been so frau with meaning, so tinged with drama, so garnish with glory as these which you now rec

WELCOME BACK TO FOC
—the best is yet to b

E Pluribus Marv
Tom Brevoc
Master of FOOMon

**stands for "Friends Of Ol' Marv*

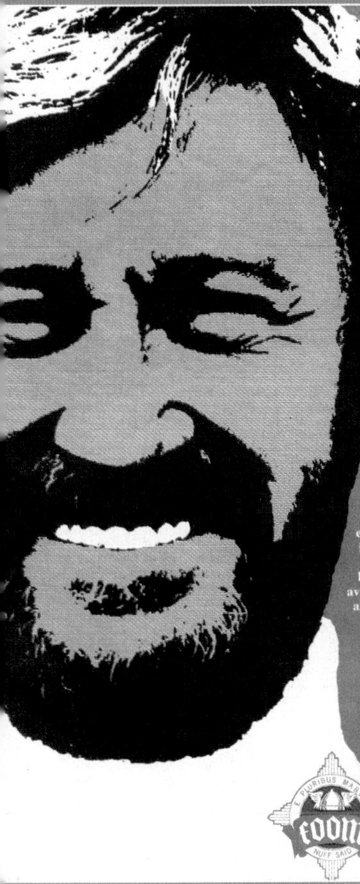

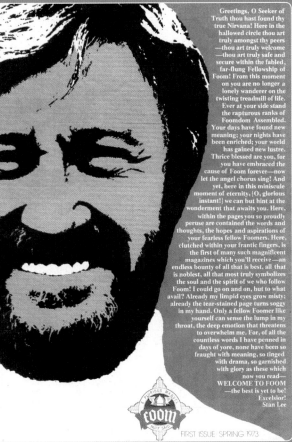

Greetings, O Seeker of Truth thou hast found thy true Nirvana! Here in the hallowed circle thou art truly amongst thy peers—thou art truly welcome—thou art truly safe and secure within the fabled, far-flung Fellowship of Foom! From this moment on you are no longer a lonely wanderer on the twisting treadmill of life. Ever at your side stand the rapturous ranks of Foomdom Assembled. Your days have found new meaning; your nights have been enriched; your world has gained new lustre. Thrice blessed are you, for you have embraced the cause of Foom forever—now let the angel chorus sing! And yet, here in this miniscule moment of eternity, {O, glorious instant!} we can but hint at the wonderment that awaits you. Here, within the pages you so proudly peruse are contained the words and thoughts, the hopes and aspirations of your fearless fellow Foomers. Here, clutched within your frantic fingers, is the first of many such magnificent magazines which you'll receive—an endless bounty of all that is best, all that is noblest, all that most truly symbolizes the soul and the spirit of we who follow Foom! I could go on and on, but to what avail? Already my limpid eyes grow misty; already the tear-stained page turns soggy in my hand. Only a fellow Foomer like yourself can sense the lump in my throat, the deep emotion that threatens to overwhelm me. For, of all the countless words I have penned in days of yore, none have been so fraught with meaning, so tinged with drama, so garnished with glory as these which now you read—WELCOME TO FOOM—the best is yet to be! Excelsior!

Stan Lee

E PLURIBUS MARVEL FOOM NUFF SAID

FIRST ISSUE: SPRING 1973

THE ORIGINAL FOOM

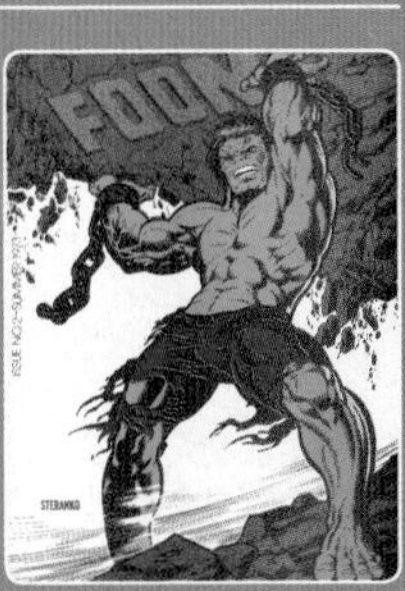
FOOM

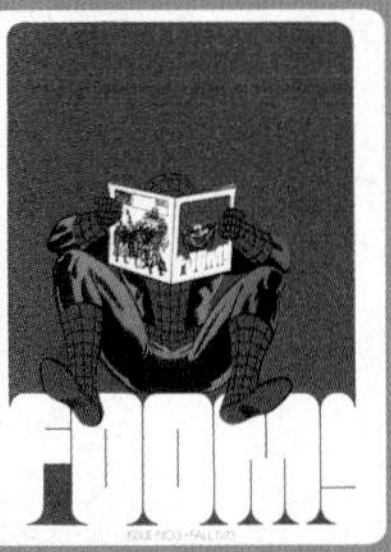
FOOM!

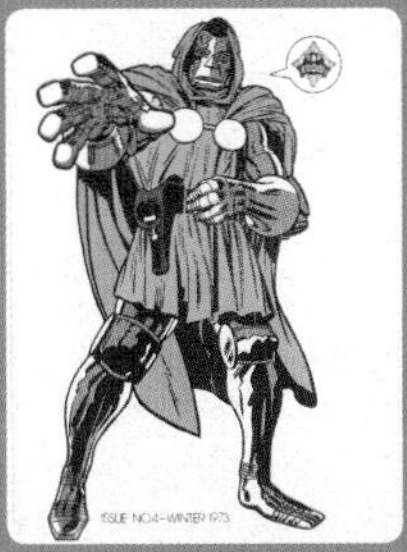
ISSUE NO.4—WINTER 1973

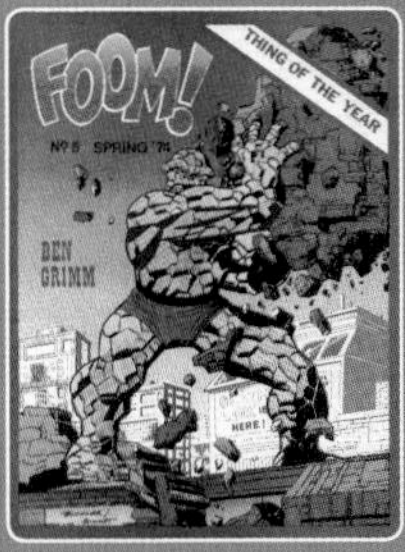
FOOM!
THING OF THE YEAR
No 5 SPRING '74
BEN GRIMM

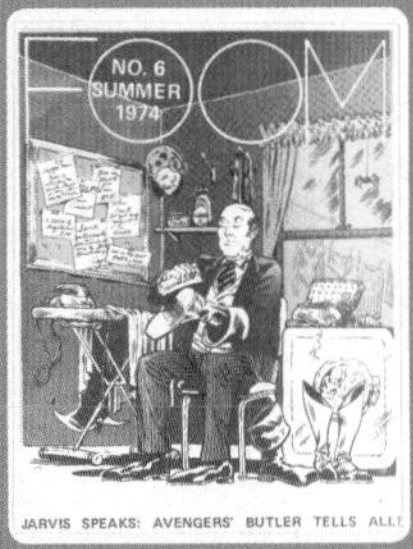
NO. 6 SUMMER 1974
FOOM
JARVIS SPEAKS: AVENGERS' BUTLER TELLS ALL!

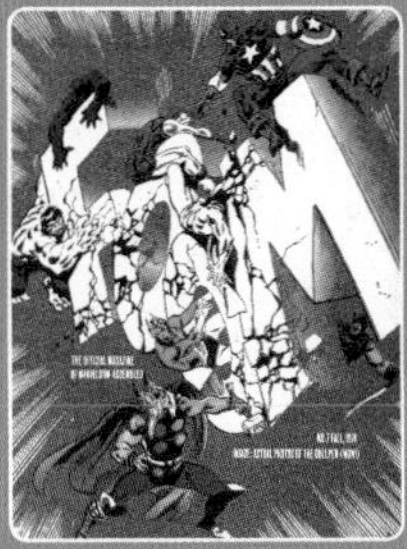
FOOM

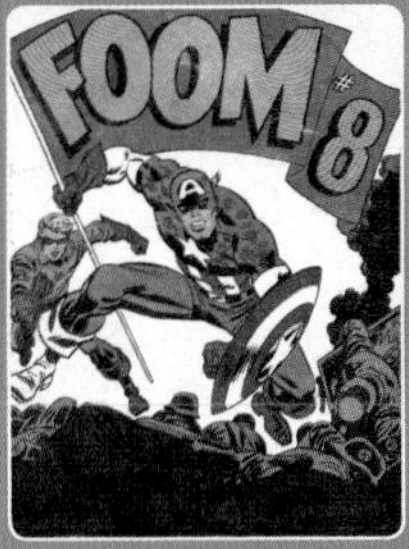
FOOM #8

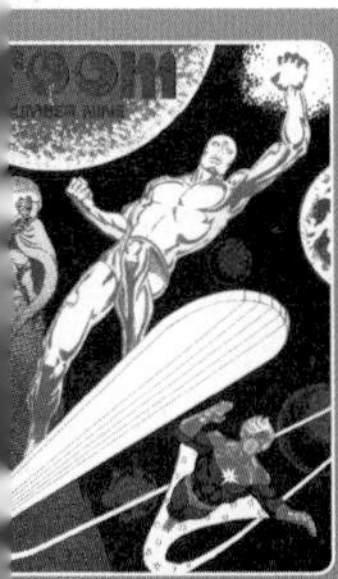
FOOM!!

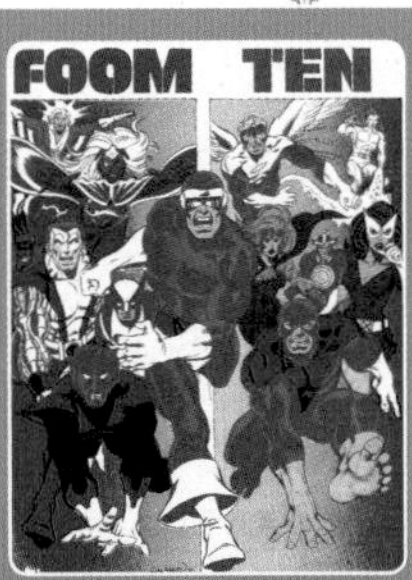
FOOM TEN

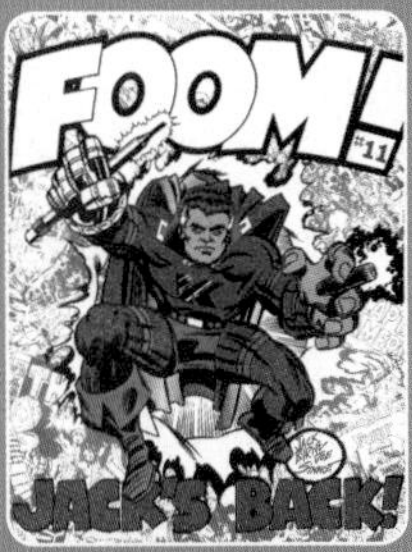
FOOM!
#11
JACK'S BACK!

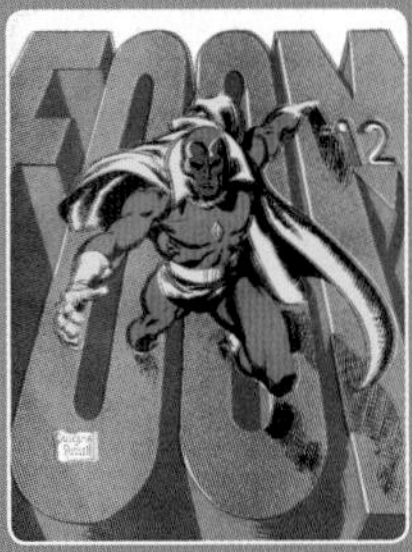
FOOM 12

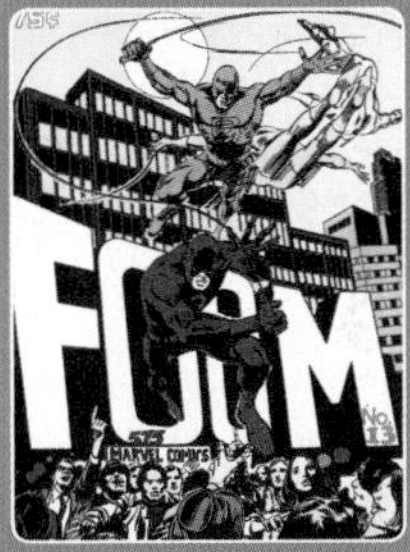
FOOM
No. 13
MARVEL COMICS

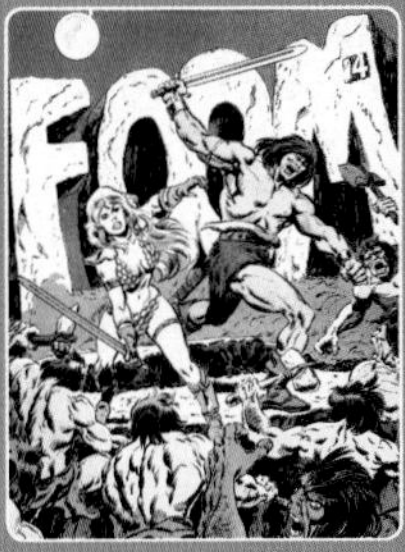
FOOM 14

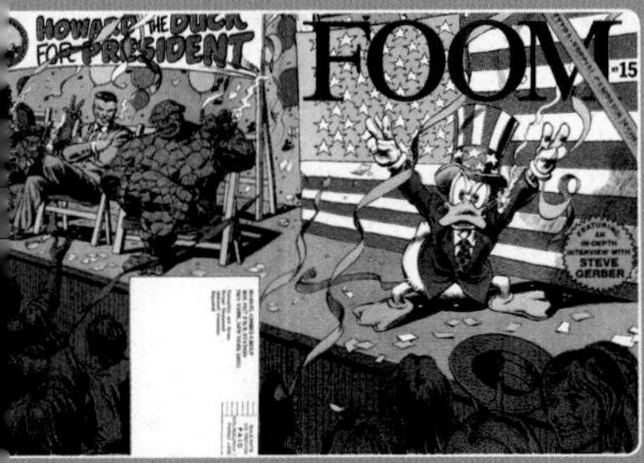
HOWARD THE DUCK FOR PRESIDENT
FOOM
#15
STEVE GERBER

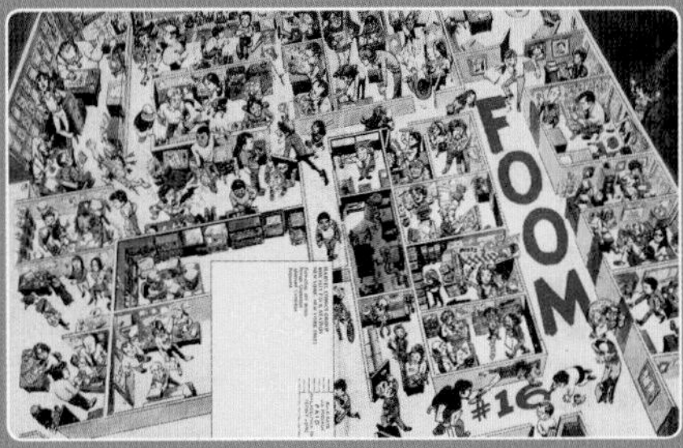
FOOM
#16

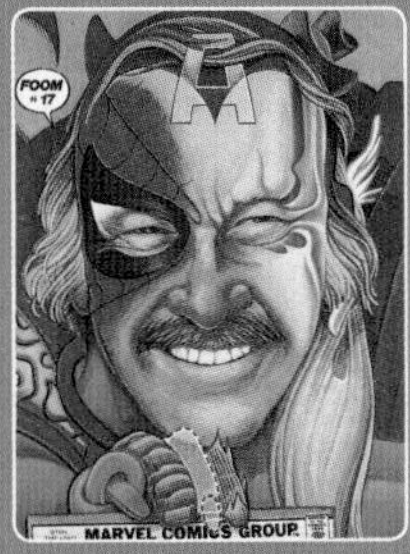
FOOM #17
MARVEL COMICS GROUP

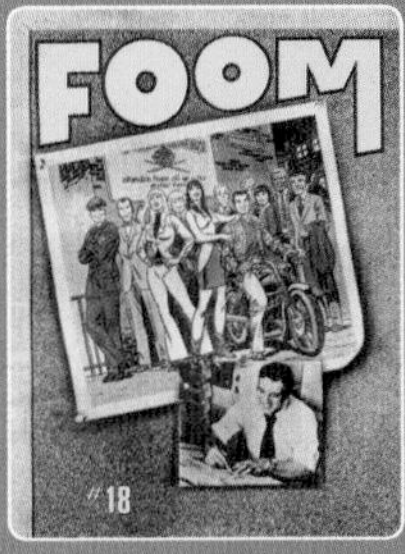
FOOM
#18

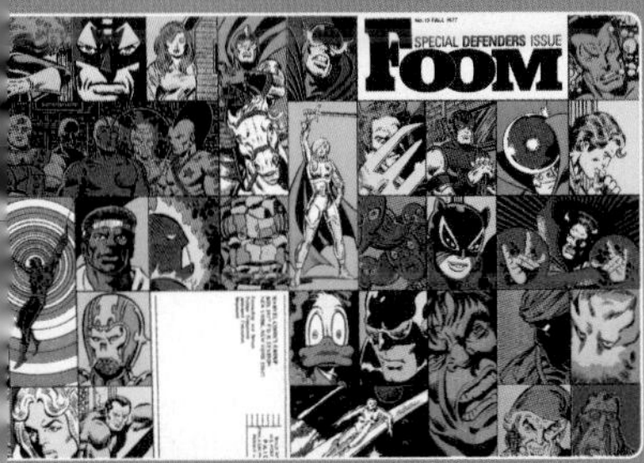
SPECIAL DEFENDERS ISSUE
FOOM

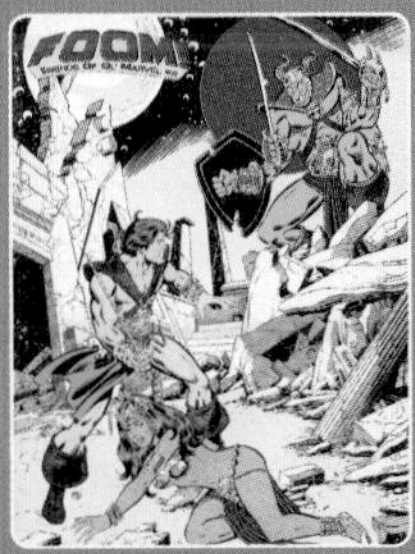
FOOM

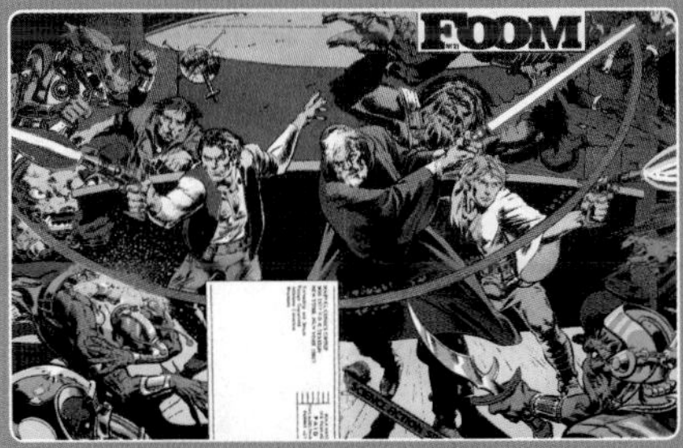
FOOM

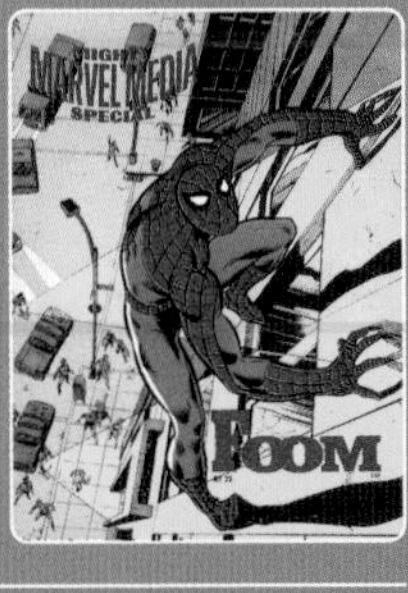
MARVEL MEGA SPECIAL
FOOM

JOE QUESADA, KEVIN NOWLAN & RICHARD ISA[...]

MARVEL LEGACY

BY **JESS HARROLD**

Want to know what's so exciting about Marvel Legacy? *FOOM* **spoke to Tom Brevoort and Jason Aaron to find out how their plans will push the Marvel Universe boldly forward, while paying due respect to the storied history of the House of Ideas.**

"Marvel Legacy is about touching base with the past as we build toward the future. It's about reminding people about the long history of the Marvel Universe and all of the great characters that have contributed to it over the years. And it's about telling the strongest stories that we can."

That's how Executive Editor Tom Brevoort sums up Marvel Legacy—a line-wide publishing initiative that's been taking shape in secret for months, and over the course of multiple creative retreats. Now, the time has finally arrived for every writer and artist to show readers what they can do.

"We challenged all of our creators to come up with the most exciting storylines that they could, drawing on the history of our characters," Brevoort says. "Stories that would tap into the mythology of the Marvel Universe without just being backwards-looking, which is sometimes the trap. Everybody was encouraged and challenged to bring their A-material to the table and really step things up, to take advantage of this moment to push their storylines forward and do

some remarkable things. So it should be a pretty great period to be a Marvel reader."

Anyone fearing Marvel Legacy is rooted solely in the past can rest assured that isn't the case. "There's nothing wrong with nostalgia," Brevoort says. "But you need to have more than just that in your tank, or it isn't going to carry you very far. So, yes, we're drawing inspiration from some great

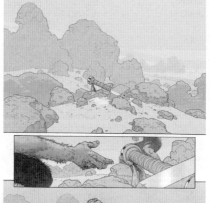

ESAD RIBIĆ

storylines and moments of the past— even hearkening back with things like old issue numbers and the trade dress so forth—but we're doing so in the ser of telling new stories, stories that propel the Marvel Universe and its her forward. We're embracing the past focused on tomorrow."

And that's good news for fans of Kan Khan, Miles Morales, Kate Bishop, J Foster, and other heroes who have m their mark in recent years. Brevo admits he finds it "baffling" to be as so often whether Legacy will put focus on "classic" heroes, at the expe of the more diverse cast of moc adventurers. "The Marvel Universe is and complex," he says. "There is more t enough room in it for the classic her and the newer Marvel icons that we introduced in recent years. I really d see how that's even a concern. But th not to say that absolutely every chara is going to be safe—these are Ma super-hero adventures, and that me there's going to be danger and jeopa at every turn. And I'd think no differe about the demise of a modern characte that's where the story took us, than I did killing the Hulk."

Brevoort is excited to welcome r creators to the House of Ideas, "great hopes" for Rodney Barnes, v is writing *Falcon*, and Ed Brisson, wh taking on *Cable* and *Iron Fist*. On the front, both Stefano Caselli (*Invincible*

) and David Marquez (*Defenders*) are g "next-level stuff," while Juann Cabal All-New *Wolverine* "looks to be an ting new member of our roster."

aring a thought for a Marvel vart, Brevoort adds: "He tends to get looked when you're talking about new tors breaking out, but I feel like Brian chael] Bendis is really stepping up ng Legacy on all of his titles, breathing energy and excitement into them."

ndis himself describes Marvel Legacy an opportunity for us to tell a story leaps the characters forward, but elements of the story are all classic vel"—and for more on his books, ck out page 12.

for the characters to watch, Brevoort *Marvel Legacy #1* will give readers he clues they need—but beyond that: fair to say that *Mighty Thor #700* is ıg to be a big book, even beyond its us as an anniversary issue."

ıyone who's been paying attention know that those two books have thing in common: They're both being ten by Jason Aaron, one of the finest oes around. Who better to plot the chapter of the future of the Marvel verse than a man who has left his siderable mark on iconic characters uding Wolverine, Doctor Strange, and, ourse, Thor?

ith *Marvel Legacy #1*—and indeed of his work—Aaron seeks to honor vel's rich history and the contributions he many creators who came before in a way that also moves the universe vard, telling stories that haven't been before. He describes the 50-page -shot as a "great primer" for everything ıg on in the Marvel Universe, adding: you haven't been reading Spider-Man or Captain America or Thor, or whatever, you can pick up this book and it will give you a tease of where all those characters are at. It kind of sets the stage: This is the Marvel Universe as we know it at this moment in time. And then at the same time, it introduces a couple of new major storylines into the midst of that, things that will begin here and will spread outwards throughout multiple books. This is a book about Marvel's past, present, and future."

As well as showcasing today's greatest heroes, including some who share costumed identities, and setting up a couple of "big dominoes" set to fall in the months to come, Aaron is going deeper into the past than ever, delving into the "unknown origins" of the Marvel Universe and introducing the prehistoric Avengers of 1,000,000 B.C. This primitive iteration of Earth's Mightiest Heroes is a concept he's been itching to explore for some time, and he's pleased with fan reaction to advance artwork showcasing the roster—particularly a certain flame-haired Spirit of Vengeance astride a woolly mammoth. "*Ghost Rider* was one of the first things I did at Marvel," he says. "And over the course of that run, I introduced a lot of different versions of Ghost Rider—so this is very much in keeping with that. Ghost Rider's a big part of this *Legacy* one-shot. And not just this prehistoric Ghost Rider—Robbie

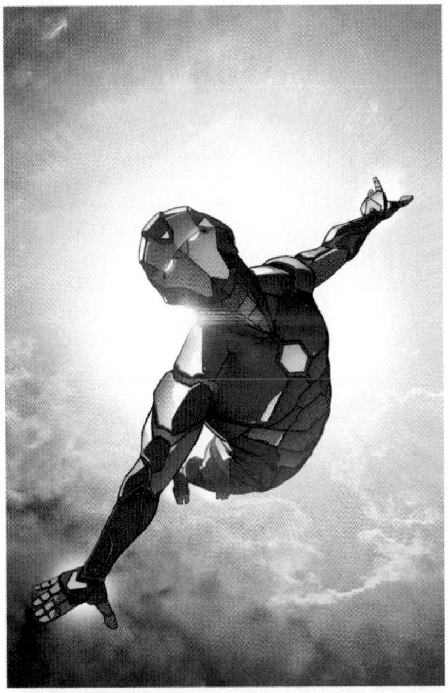

▲STEFANO CASELLI & MARTE GRACIA

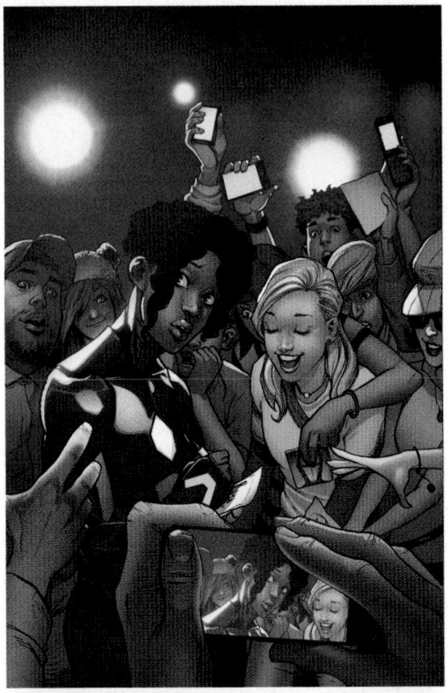

▲STEFANO CASELLI & MARTE GRACIA

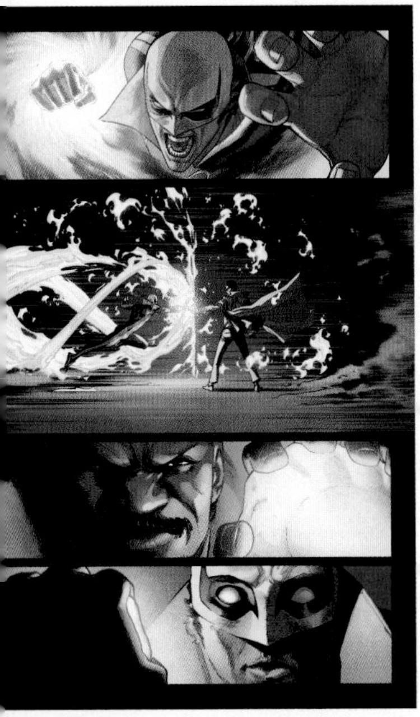

D MARQUEZ & JUSTIN PONSOR

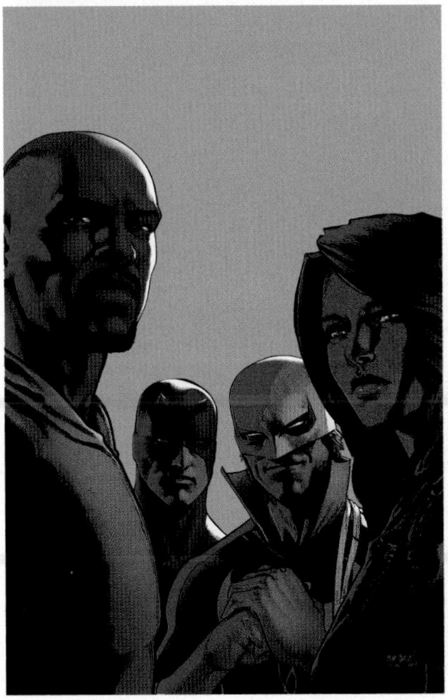

▲DAVID MARQUEZ & JUSTIN PONSOR

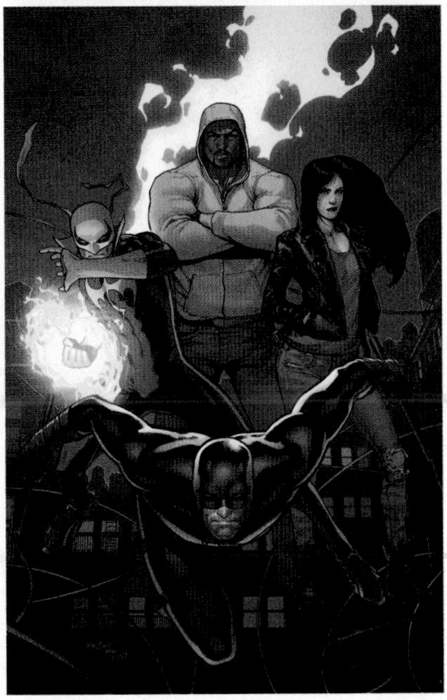

▲DAVID MARQUEZ & JUSTIN PONSOR

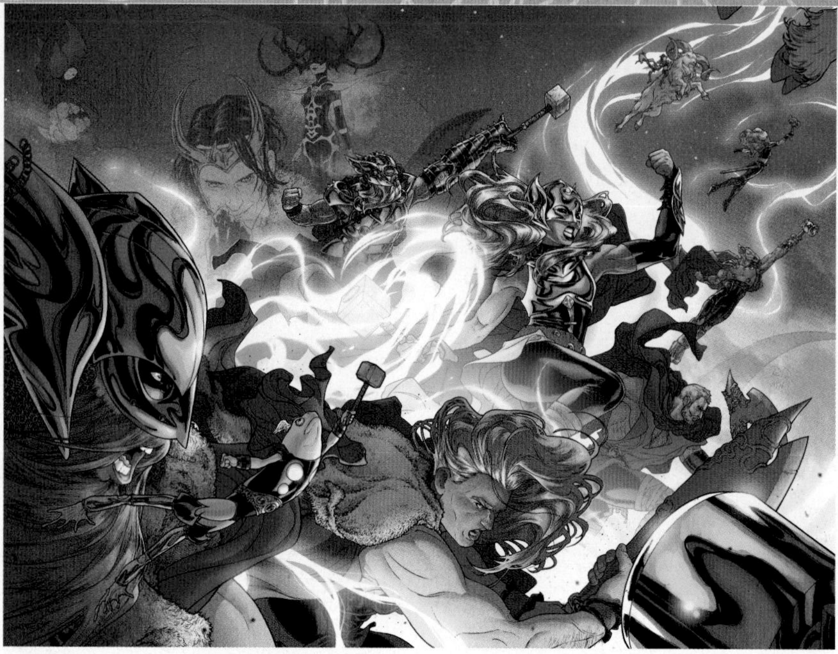

RUSSELL DAUTERMAN & MATTHEW WILSON ▲

Reyes also plays a major role here. It's fun to be writing Ghost Rider again, basically!"

No matter the era the story visits, the writer knew he could go "as big and crazy, dark and weird and fantastic as possible" because the book's artist—his *Thor: God of Thunder* collaborator, Esad Ribić—"can nail all of that." He adds: "This one-shot has a really ridiculous, epic scope to it with so many characters, and we zig and zag to so many different parts of the Marvel Universe that there was never any question of what Esad could bring to the table for all that. Plus, there are pages here and there that cut away to different characters, and those are drawn by, for the most part, the artists who are drawing those ongoing series—so it all adds up to being a pretty sweet murderers' row of artists for one book."

But he says it's a "neck and neck race" between *Marvel Legacy #1* and *Thor #700* as to which has the most imposing collection of illustrators. In addition to *Thor* regular Russell Dauterman, the 50-page issue features various versions of the Thunder God, as depicted by talents including Olivier Coipel and the legendary Walter Simonson. It is, as Aaron puts it, an "oversized celebration of all things Thor."

A celebration, but perhaps also a wake. The ominous title above Stephanie Hans' homage variant cover reads: "The Death of the Mighty Thor." But if the end is indeed

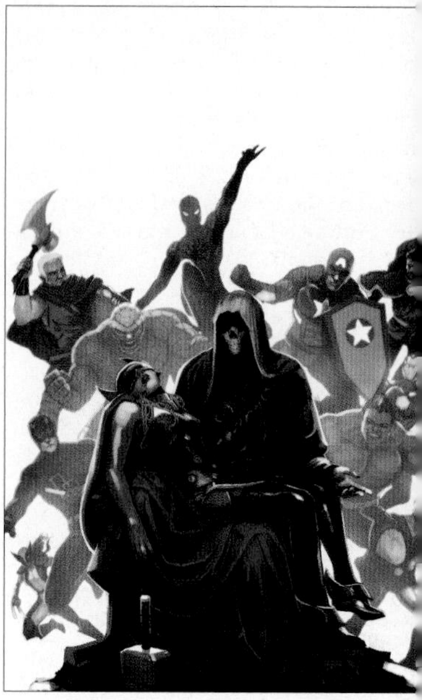

▲ STEPHANIE HANS

coming for one of Marvel's most pop
new heroes, it shouldn't be a surprise. "V
you know, this is not a new developr
for Jane," Aaron says. "For a while, s
been facing multiple battles—figh
against the forces of evil throughou
the Ten Realms as war spreads, but
fighting a very personal, human bo
against cancer. Now we see she's star
to lose one of those battles. That's on
the reasons that she's so worthy to be
with—she knows that being Thor is ki
her, but she doesn't slouch. She still g
and picks up that hammer when she ne
to. That storyline has always been buil
toward a culmination, and issue #70
the beginning of that."

To make matters worse for Jane
her allies, Aaron is also unleashing on
Thor's most fearsome enemies—and
of his favorite Jack Kirby creations-
the Mangog. With Malekith contin
to foment the War of Realms, this
chapter of Aaron's Asgardian epi
which began back in late 2012 with *T
God of Thunder*—threatens to be the r
explosive yet. "This is maybe the bigg
Thor story I've done, the one I've b
waiting to write for years," he says. "I t
it has the chance to be the best one
ever been part of."

For Aaron, *Marvel Legacy #1* and
#700 are two of the books he is prou
of during his Marvel career—and a platf
from which he can swing for ever gre
heights. "Together, they set the stage
what I'll be doing going forward,"
promises. "The seeds are planted in *Leg*
for my next series, and Thor isn't an endin
it's the next chapter. So if you want to k
what I'll be doing come next year for Mar
your answers are in the pages of these
books." True Believers old and new woul
wise to pay attention.

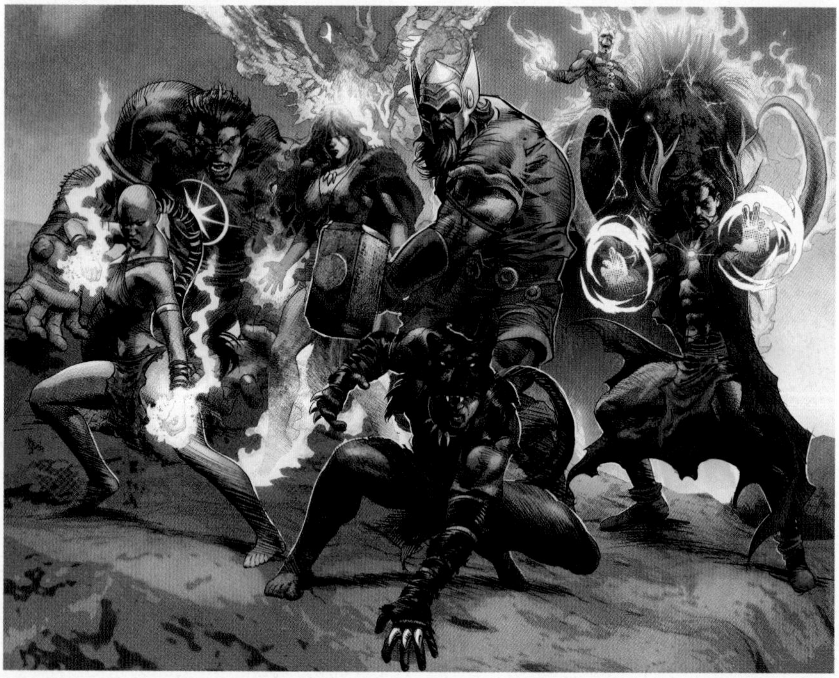

MIKE DEODATO JR. ▲

MARVEL LEGACY *Checklist*

ISSUE/NUMBER	STORY/ARC TITLE	WRITER	PENCILER
EMBER 2017			
Marvel Legacy #1		Jason Aaron	Esad Ribić
OBER 2017			
All-New Wolverine #25	Orphans of X	Tom Taylor	Juann Cabal
Amazing Spider-Man #789	Fall of Parker	Dan Slott	Stuart Immonen
America #8	Exterminatrix	Gabby Rivera	Joe Quinones
Avengers #672	Worlds Collide Part 1	Mark Waid	Jesús Saiz
Black Panther #165	Klaw Stands Supreme	Ta-Nehisi Coates	Leonard Kirk
Cable #150	The Newer Mutants	Ed Brisson	Jon Malin
Captain Marvel #125	Dark Origin	Margaret Stohl	Michele Bandini
Champions #13	Worlds Collide Part 2	Mark Waid	Humberto Ramos
Defenders #6	Kingpins of New York	Brian Michael Bendis	David Marquez
Despicable Deadpool #287	Deadpool Kills Cable	Gerry Duggan	Scott Koblish
Falcon #1	Take Flight	Rodney Barnes	Joshua Cassara
Iceman #6	Champions Reassembled	Sina Grace	Robert Gill
Incredible Hulk #708	Return to Planet Hulk	Greg Pak	Greg Land
Invincible Iron Man #593	The Search for Tony Stark	Brian Michael Bendis	Stefano Caselli
Iron Fist #72	Sabretooth: Round Two	Ed Brisson	Mike Perkins
Jean Grey #8	Psych War	Dennis Hopeless	Victor Ibáñez
Jessica Jones #13	Return of the Purple Man	Brian Michael Bendis	Michael Gaydos
Luke Cage #166	Caged!	David F. Walker	Nelson Blake II
Mighty Thor #700	The Death of Mighty Thor	Jason Aaron	Russell Dauterman
Monsters Unleashed #7	And Lo There Came… A Poison!	Cullen Bunn	R.B. Silva
Royals #9	Fire from Heaven	Al Ewing	Javier Rodriguez
Spider-Gwen #25	Gwenom	Jason Latour	Robbi Rodriguez
Spirits of Vengeance #1	War at the Gates of Hell	Victor Gischler	David Baldeón
The Unbelievable Gwenpool #21	Doom Sees You	Christopher Hastings	Irene Strychalski
U.S.Avengers #11	Cannonball Run	Al Ewing	Paco Diaz
Uncanny Avengers #28	Stars and Garters	Jim Zub	Sean Izaakse
Venom #155	Lethal Protector	Michael Costa	Mark Bagley
X-Men Blue #13	Mojo Worldwide Part 2	Cullen Bunn	Jorge Molina
X-Men Gold #13	Mojo Worldwide Part 1	Marc Guggenheim	Mike Mayhew
VEMBER 2017			
Amazing Spider-Man: Renew Your Vows #13	Eight Years Later	Jody Houser	Nick Roche
Ben Reilly: Scarlet Spider #10	The Slingers Return	Peter David	Will Sliney
Captain America #695	Home of the Brave	Mark Waid	Chris Samnee
Daredevil #595	Mayor Fisk	Charles Soule	Stefano Landini
Darkhawk #51	The Return	Chad Bowers, Chris Sims	Kev Walker
Doctor Strange #381	Loki: Sorcerer Supreme	Donny Cates	Gabriel Hernandez Walta
Generation X #9	OG Gen X	Christina Strain	Amilcar Pinna
Guardians of the Galaxy #146	Infinity Quest	Gerry Duggan	Marcus To
Master of Kung Fu #126	Shang-Chi's Day Off	CM Punk	Dalibor Talajić
Moon Girl and Devil Dinosaur #25	Fantastic Three	Brandon Montclare	Natacha Bustos
Moon Knight #188	Crazy Runs in the Family	Max Bemis	Jacen Burrows
Not Brand Echh #14	Forbush Man Returns!	Nick Spencer, Christopher Hastings, Jay Fosgitt, and more	Jay Fosgitt, Gurihiru, and more
Old Man Logan #31	The Scarlet Samurai	Ed Brisson	Mike Deodato Jr.
Peter Parker: The Spectacular Spider-Man #297	Most Wanted	Chip Zdarsky	Adam Kubert
Power Pack #64	Rarely Pure and Never Simple	Devin Grayson	Marika Cresta
The Punisher #218	Frank Castle: War Machine	Matthew Rosenberg	Guiu Vilanova
Secret Warriors #8	VS Mister Sinister	Matthew Rosenberg	Javier Garrón
She-Hulk #159	Jen Walters Must Die	Mariko Tamaki	Jahnoy Lindsay
Silver Sable and the Wild Pack #36	Silver and Bold	Christa Faust	Matteo Buffagni
Spider-Man #234	Sinister Six Reborn	Brian Michael Bendis	Oscar Bazaldua
Spider-Man/Deadpool #23	Spider-Man Versus Deadpool	Robbie Thompson	Chris Bachalo
Thanos #13	Thanos Wins	Donny Cates	Geoff Shaw
EMBER 2017			
Black Bolt #8	The Midnight King Returns to Earth	Saladin Ahmed	Christian Ward
Hawkeye #13	Family Reunion	Kelly Thompson	Leonardo Romero
Marvel Two-In-One #1	The Fate of the Four	Chip Zdarsky	Jim Cheung
Ms. Marvel #25	Teenage Wasteland	G. Willow Wilson	Takeshi Miyazawa
Tales of Suspense #100	Red Ledger	Matthew Rosenberg	Travel Foreman
The Unbeatable Squirrel Girl #27	The Forbidden Pla-Nut	Ryan North	Erica Henderson
Weapon X #12	Nuke-Clear War	Greg Pak	Yildiray Cinar

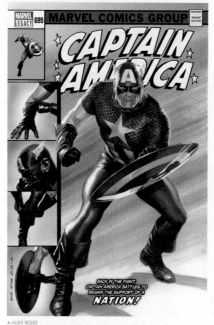

COVER TO COVER

BY **JESS HARROLD**

Legacy celebrates Marvel's glorious past—and limitless future! And what better way to illustrate that than with a series of lenticular homage covers that, with a flick of the wrist, transition between old and new. *FOOM* takes a good, long look at these modern masterpieces, together with some of the creators involved in bringing them to life!

Fun. That, pure and simple, is what the Marvel Legacy homage covers are all about, according to Executive Editor Tom Brevoort. "To us, it was really just a fun thing to do in the spirit of embracing our roots," he says. "And it's pretty cool to see the whole fleet of them spread out in front of you—like looking at Marvel history all in one go."

Brevoort is delighted to see some classic Marvel character logos back in play on the covers—particularly on *Invincible Iron Man* and *Captain America*—and has enjoyed how the extensive program has given artists the opportunity to "go deeper" into the Marvel catalogue to find covers to homage. "There have been maybe a dozen versions of that *Fantastic Four #1* cover homage over the years, but an homage to, say, *Fantastic Four #2* feels more novel, because it hasn't been done to death—and especially if the source cover bears some relevance to the story being told, you can find some hidden gold there."

And gold there has been, with Brevoort citing Alex Ross' *Captain America #695* cover as his favorite of the bunch—no surprise for a master painter with a flair for what the editor describes as "homages that are more than just homages." What others

MARVEL LEGACY
695
MARVEL COMICS GROUP
VARIANT EDITION
CAPTAIN AMERICA
BACK IN THE FIGHT, CAPTAIN AMERICA BATTLES TO REGAIN THE SUPPORT OF A NATION!

▲ALEX ROSS

#593
MARVEL COMICS GROUP
THE INVINCIBLE
IRON MAN
MARVEL LEGACY
TRAPPED IN A DUEL FOR THE LEGACY OF TONY STARK, IRONHEART FACES
DOCTOR DOOM!

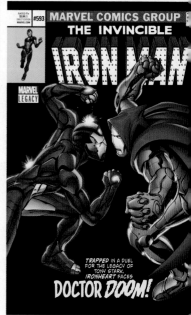

▲ALAN DAVIS, MARK FARMER & MATT YACKEY

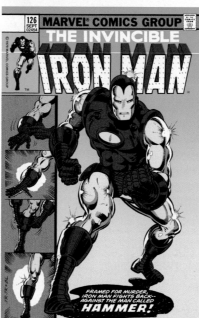

126 SEPT 02454
MARVEL COMICS GROUP
THE INVINCIBLE
IRON MAN
FRAMED FOR MURDER, IRON MAN FIGHTS BACK-- AGAINST THE MAN CALLED HAMMER!

▲JOHN ROMITA JR. & BOB LAYTON

150 SEPT 02454
MARVEL COMICS GROUP
SPECIAL DOUBLE-SIZED 150TH ANNIVERSARY ISSUE!
THE INVINCIBLE
IRON MAN
TRAPPED IN THE TIME-LOST LAND OF KING ARTHUR-- IRON MAN BATTLES
DOCTOR DOOM!

▲JOHN ROMITA JR. & BOB LAYTON

would Brevoort want on his wall? "I like the *Jean Grey* cover a lot, the red treatment there is striking, and the *Gwenpool* cover is a fun take on a memorable cover from my youth. I also like Dan Mora's pieces, the *Jessica Jones* cover and the *Champions* cover, both of which similarly go beyond being just a straight-up photocopy of the original."

And Brevoort was happy to share the joy, surprising Brian Michael Bendis with homages to some of the writer's all-time favorite covers on his books. "This is one of the things I love about working at Marvel," Bendis says. "I didn't actually pick any of my Legacy covers. Tom—who has such an encyclopedic knowledge of what

I loved and what influenced me and wh my heart lies in the classic stories—u them as my covers. The first being the *Man #150* cover [on *Invincible Iron M #593*] when Victor and Tony had the ti travel story where they went back to K Arthur's court. I love that story and h hearkened back to it a couple of tim And the *Marvel Team-Up Annual #4* Fr Miller cover [on *Jessica Jones #13*]— issue is the reason I did *Alias*. That co meant the world to me as a young m At the Marvel retreat where they w showing all the covers, mine came up a was like, 'Awww, Tom, I love you.'"

But most inspired of all by the program

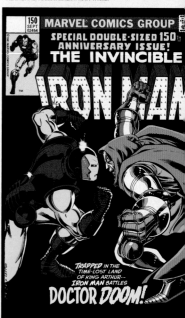

urse, Marvel's talented artists. Perhaps more so than Michael Allred, whose e style—a seamless marriage of classic nodern sensibilities—is an ideal fit for el Legacy. "It speaks to me in a very rful way," Allred says of Legacy. "I'm antly aware that my earliest memories in the roots of my deep affection for orytelling art form and characters who ike old friends. My goal is to always nto a timeless classicism while striving ogress and innovate." Seeing the line- series of homage covers really "lights ne fan in him, Allred says. "While I'm ys finding new art and creators to excited about, it's just as exciting to owledge the history that everything nues to build on."

Avengers #672, Allred followed in ootsteps of one of the all-time great ators of Earth's Mightiest Heroes, Buscema, paying tribute to his classic *gers #53* cover. Was Buscema one of g influences as an artist? "Absolutely!" d says. "'Big John' Buscema was right nere with Jack Kirby for my older er Lee and I—especially his work *vengers*. He drew some of our most ite stories with one iconic cover the other. Of all the great Marvel en artists, he understood as well as ne what made Kirby's work pop and fied the 'Marvel house style.'"

Allred, the secret to a great homage r is that it "needs to stand on its own," also bringing "something new, fun, y, or powerful to the party to justify

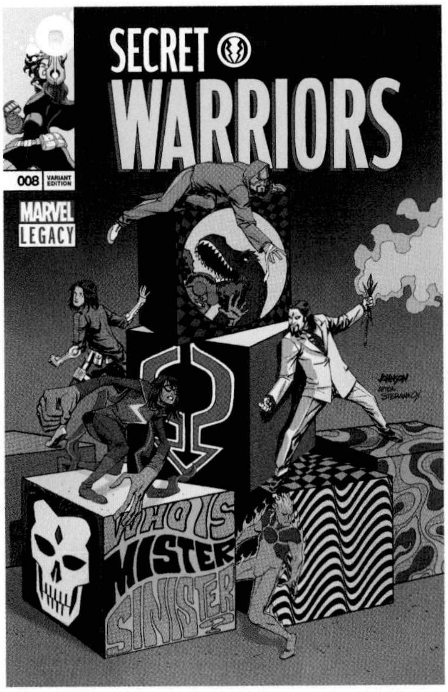
SECRET WARRIORS
008 VARIANT EDITION
MARVEL LEGACY
WHO IS MISTER SINISTER

DAVE JOHNSON ▲

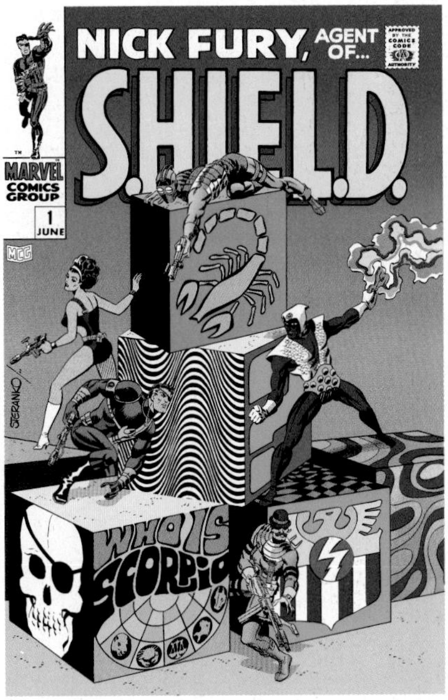
NICK FURY, AGENT OF... S.H.I.E.L.D.
MARVEL COMICS GROUP
1 JUNE
WHO IS SCORPIO

JIM STERANKO ▲

its existence." In his case, the new spin is pitting the Avengers against their youthful counterparts the Champions—but if Allred had any say, the outcome of that battle would be a swift victory for the old order. "That's one contest where the Champions wouldn't be the champs," he says. "Avengers Assemble!"

And assemble they do, alongside the rest of Marvel's greatest heroes across the Marvel Legacy homage covers. Here are just a few of them—together with the thoughts of some of today's finest talents who took inspiration from the legendary artists that came before them.

Secret Warriors #8 by Dave Johnson, based on *Nick Fury, Agent of S.H.I.E.L.D. #1* by Jim Steranko

Dave Johnson: "Homage covers are kind of fun. Especially when it's a great artist that you're paying tribute to—Kirby,

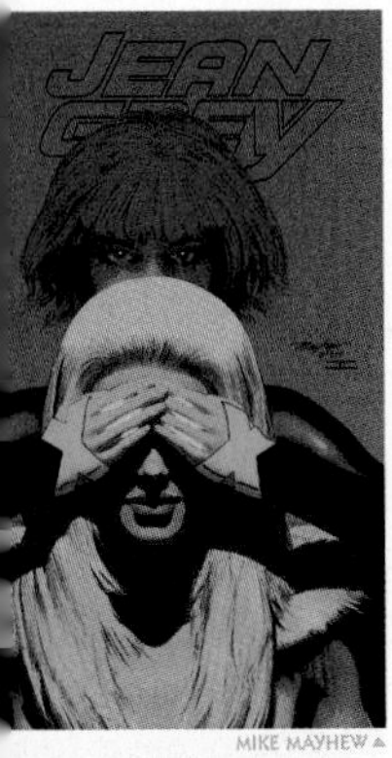
JEAN GREY

MIKE MAYHEW ▲

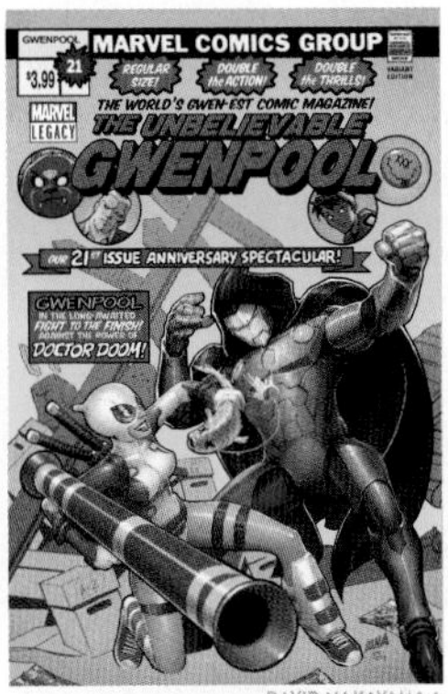
MARVEL COMICS GROUP
THE UNBELIEVABLE GWENPOOL
DOCTOR DOOM!

DAVID NAKAYAMA ▲

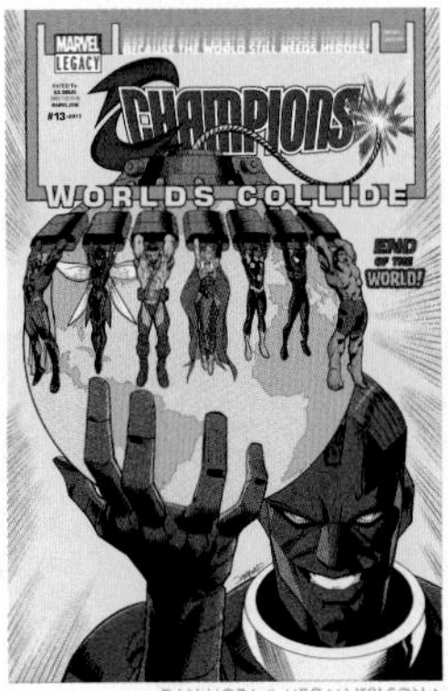
CHAMPIONS
WORLDS COLLIDE
END OF THE WORLD!

DAN MORA & MEGAN WILSON ▲

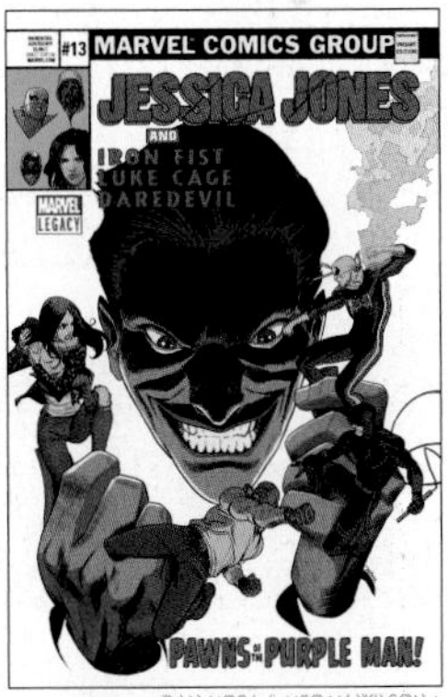
MARVEL COMICS GROUP
JESSICA JONES
IRON FIST
LUKE CAGE
DAREDEVIL
PAWNS OF THE PURPLE MAN!

DAN MORA & MEGAN WILSON ▲

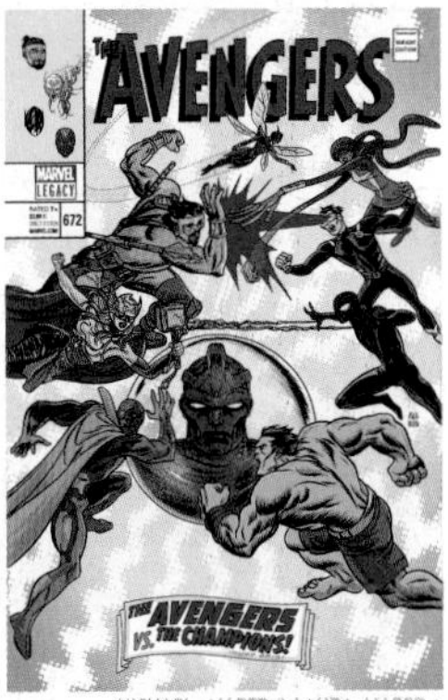
THE AVENGERS
THE AVENGERS VS. THE CHAMPIONS!

MICHAEL ALLRED & LAURA ALLRED ▲

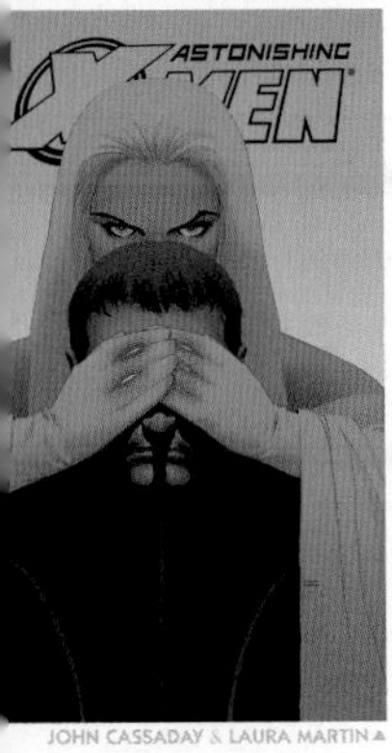
ASTONISHING X-MEN

JOHN CASSADAY & LAURA MARTIN ▲

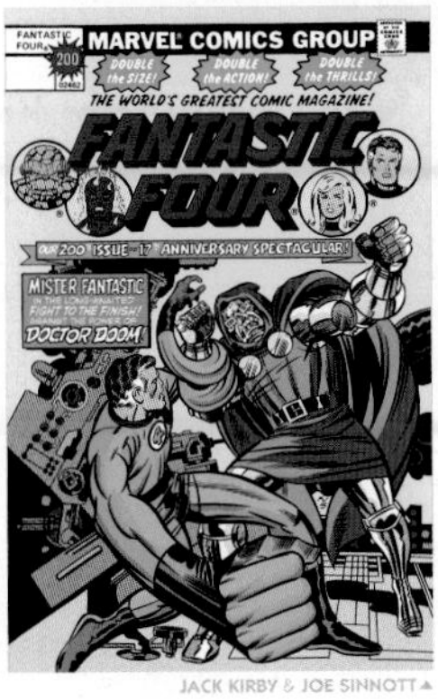
MARVEL COMICS GROUP
FANTASTIC FOUR
DOCTOR DOOM!

JACK KIRBY & JOE SINNOTT ▲

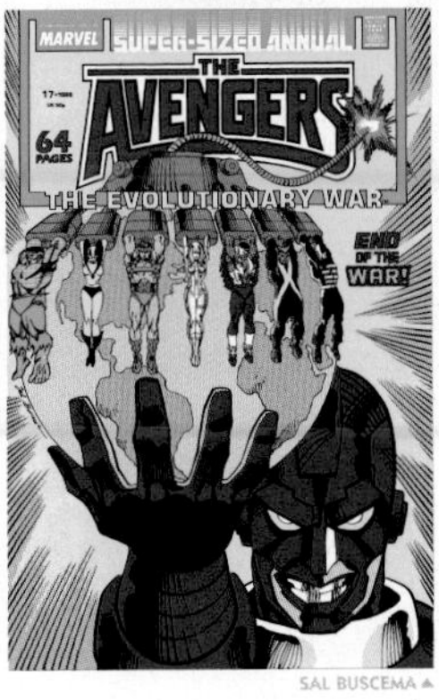
SUPER-SIZED ANNUAL
THE AVENGERS
64 PAGES
THE EVOLUTIONARY WAR
END OF THE WAR!

SAL BUSCEMA ▲

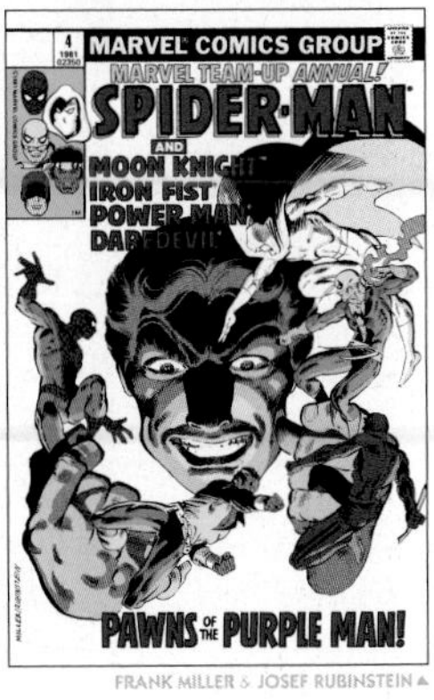
MARVEL COMICS GROUP
MARVEL TEAM-UP ANNUAL!
SPIDER-MAN
AND
MOON KNIGHT
IRON FIST
POWER MAN
DAREDEVIL
PAWNS OF THE PURPLE MAN!

FRANK MILLER & JOSEF RUBINSTEIN ▲

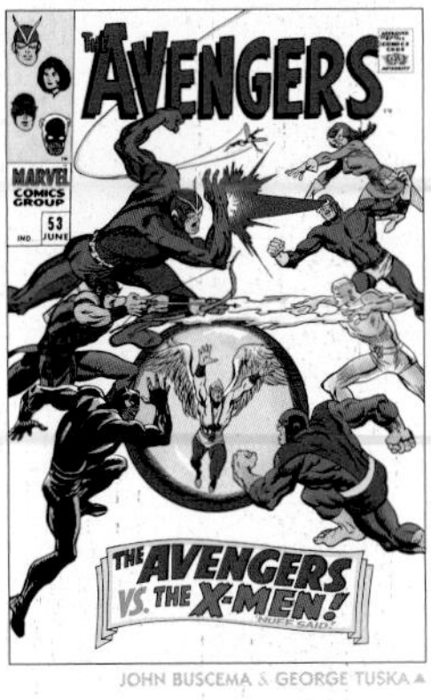
THE AVENGERS
MARVEL COMICS GROUP
53 JUNE
THE AVENGERS VS. THE X-MEN!

JOHN BUSCEMA & GEORGE TUSKA ▲

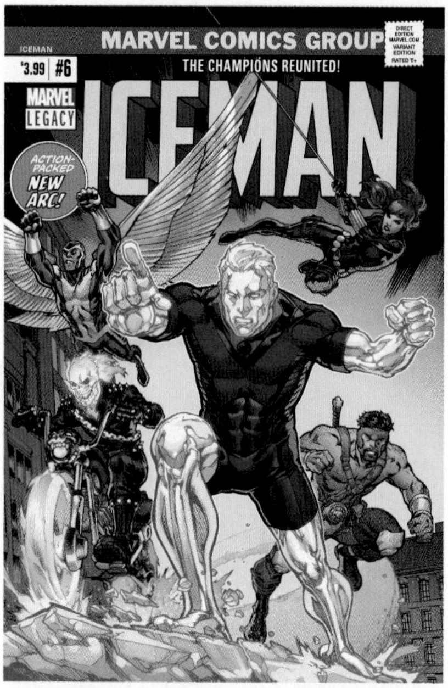
MARVEL COMICS GROUP
ICEMAN
$3.99 #6
THE CHAMPIONS REUNITED!
MARVEL LEGACY
ICEMAN
ACTION-PACKED NEW ARC!
▲MICHAEL RYAN & NOLAN WOODARD

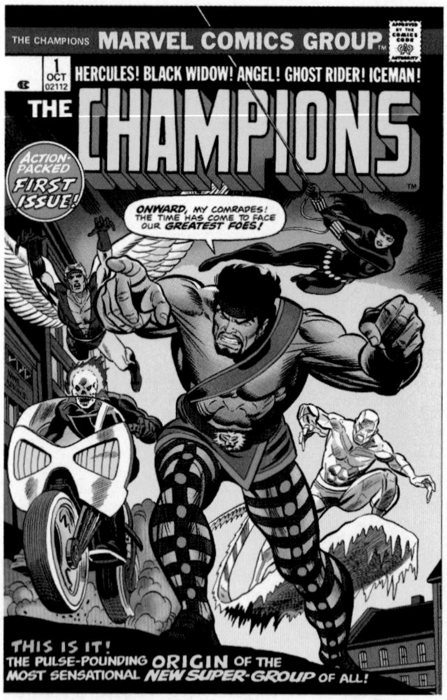
THE CHAMPIONS MARVEL COMICS GROUP
1 OCT 02112
HERCULES! BLACK WIDOW! ANGEL! GHOST RIDER! ICEMAN!
THE CHAMPIONS
ACTION-PACKED FIRST ISSUE!
ONWARD, MY COMRADES! THE TIME HAS COME TO FACE OUR GREATEST FOES!
THIS IS IT! THE PULSE-POUNDING ORIGIN OF THE MOST SENSATIONAL NEW SUPER-GROUP OF ALL!
▲GIL KANE & DAN ADKINS

Steranko, etc.—and when you get to include the original trade dress. Covers today just don't have that pop-art style that was all about bold action and trade dress and bold fonts. Of course Steranko is an influence. To be honest, I get that comparison a lot—but what most people don't get is that I would say that I was even more influenced by artists from a lot of different time periods, some that Steranko was also influenced by. There were a lot of artists from the sixties that were using trippy iconography. Steranko's genius was to bring current-at-the-time graphic-design ideas into the comics world and make them his own. And the world was better for it."

Iceman #6 by Michael Ryan, based on *Champions (1975) #1* by Gil Kane

Michael Ryan: "I had seen the original cover before in a friend's comic collection, but it was bagged and boarded, so I didn't get to read the issue until I found a reprint years later. My goal was really just to switch Hercules and Iceman, but there were unintended consequences that ended with me having to turn Herc's gaze to face out of frame rather than at Bobby—it seems like he might be unhappy having his spot stolen! In homages, the original image being awesome to start with is the main thing, but beyond that I think it's important to understand that you're not trying to copy that image—you're trying to re-create the image with your own set of skills and style."

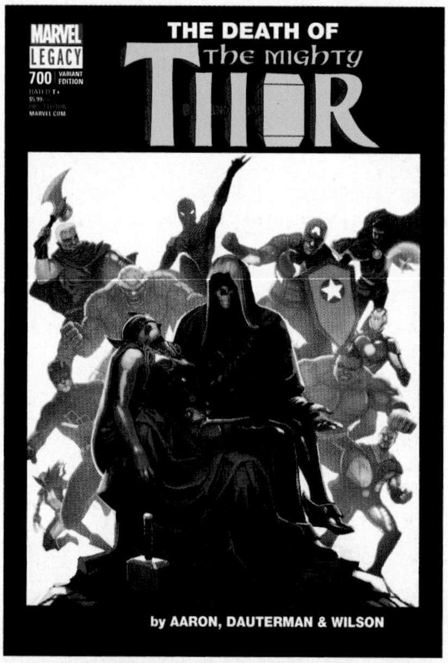
MARVEL LEGACY
700 VARIANT EDITION
THE DEATH OF The Mighty THOR
by AARON, DAUTERMAN & WILSON
▲STEPHANIE HANS

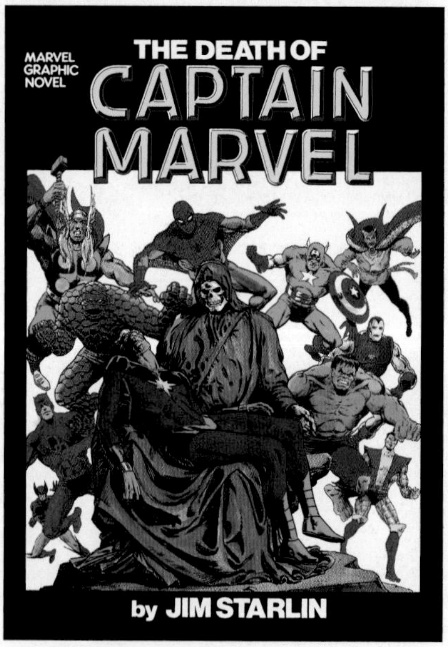
MARVEL GRAPHIC NOVEL
THE DEATH OF CAPTAIN MARVEL
by JIM STARLIN
▲JIM STARLIN

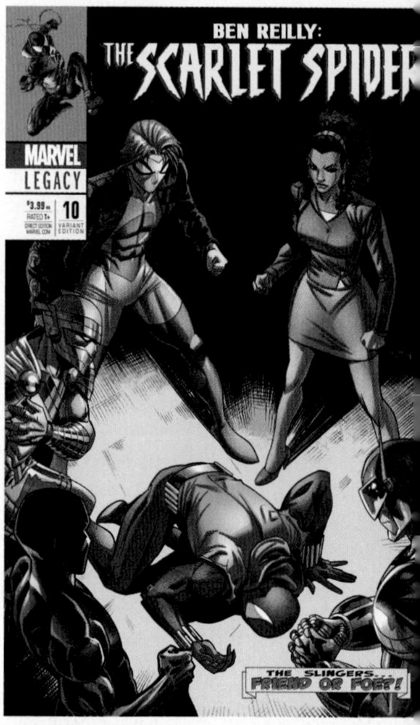
BEN REILLY: THE SCARLET SPIDER
MARVEL LEGACY
10
THE SLINGERS... FRIEND OR FOE?!
▲DAN MORA & ANDRES MOSSA

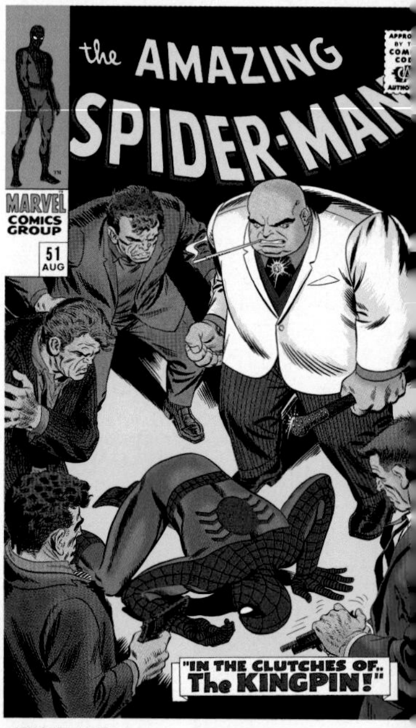
the AMAZING SPIDER-MAN
MARVEL COMICS GROUP
51 AUG
"IN THE CLUTCHES OF... The KINGPIN!"
▲JOHN ROMITA SR.

Mighty Thor #700 by Stephanie Hans based on *Marvel Graphic Novel #1* by Jim Starlin

Stephanie Hans: "Starlin's cover powerful image with an evident refer to Michelangelo's 'Pietà.' I love the a gothic vibe of this cover compare the other ones from that period—r symbolic, a bit less straightforw without leaving any doubt about wha the book. I often use fine art referenc comic art. This one is a double-refere one even, since I had both the ori cover and 'Pietà' pictures open at same time. For a traditional-art nerd me, it was extremely satisfying."

Reilly: Scarlet Spider #10** by Mora, based on *Amazing Spider-Man* 63) #51 by John Romita Sr.
sters Unleashed #7 by Dan Mora, ed on *Fantastic Four (1961) #1* ack Kirby
tain Marvel #125 by Dan Mora, ed on *Incredible Hulk (1962) #1* ack Kirby
Mora: "I'm very excited to be part of . The secret of a really good homage eeping the essence of the original er but also putting your own stamp on an artist. On *Ben Reilly: Scarlet Spider*), I love the classic cover composition the angle on John Romita Sr.'s original, just tried to put my mark on it and keep

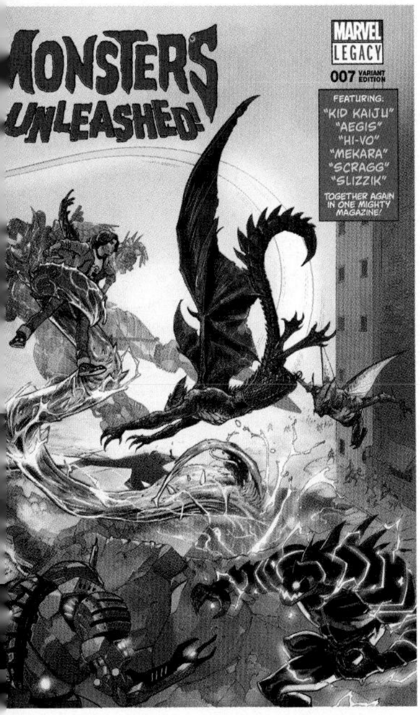
MONSTERS UNLEASHED!
MARVEL LEGACY
007 VARIANT EDITION
FEATURING:
"KID KAIJU"
"AEGIS"
"HI-VO"
"MEKARA"
"SCRAGG"
"SLIZZIK"
TOGETHER AGAIN IN ONE MIGHTY MAGAZINE!
DAN MORA & ROMULO FAJARDO JR. ▲

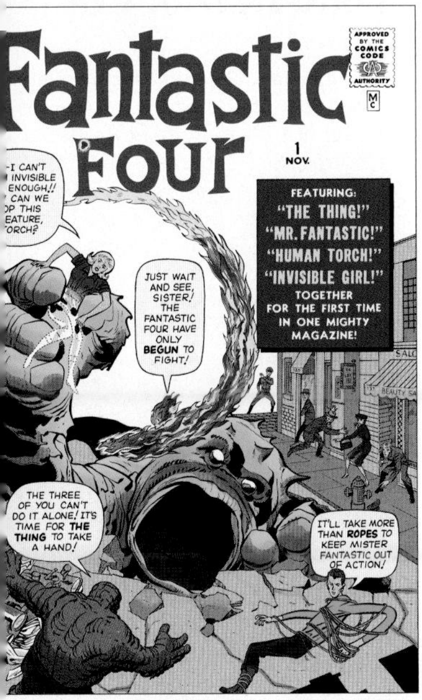
Fantastic Four
1 NOV.
FEATURING:
"THE THING!"
"MR. FANTASTIC!"
"HUMAN TORCH!"
"INVISIBLE GIRL!"
TOGETHER FOR THE FIRST TIME IN ONE MIGHTY MAGAZINE!
JUST WAIT AND SEE, SISTER! THE FANTASTIC FOUR HAVE ONLY BEGUN TO FIGHT!
THE THREE OF YOU CAN'T DO IT ALONE! IT'S TIME FOR THE THING TO TAKE A HAND!
IT'LL TAKE MORE THAN ROPES TO KEEP MISTER FANTASTIC OUT OF ACTION!
JACK KIRBY, GEORGE KLEIN & STAN GOLDBERG ▲

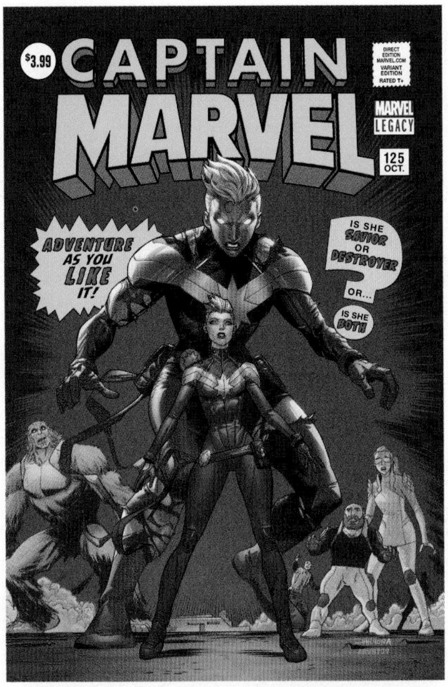
$3.99
CAPTAIN MARVEL
MARVEL LEGACY
125 OCT.
ADVENTURE AS YOU LIKE IT!
IS SHE SAVIOR OR DESTROYER
OR...
IS SHE BOTH
DAN MORA & JESUS ABURTOV ▲

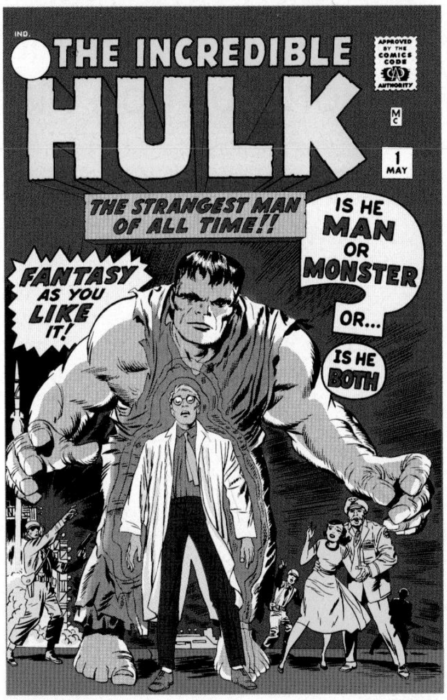
THE INCREDIBLE HULK
1 MAY
THE STRANGEST MAN OF ALL TIME!!
IS HE MAN OR MONSTER
OR...
IS HE BOTH
FANTASY AS YOU LIKE IT!
JACK KIRBY ▲

the retro feeling. It was an honor to do the *Monsters Unleashed* #7 cover in particular, and the hard part was to maintain the proportions of each hero, given that the new characters are very different in scale. *Captain Marvel #125* was a lot of fun, because Carol Danvers' physique is very different from the Hulk's—that one is my favorite, it is very different from the original but still feels retro."

America #8 by Ben Caldwell, based on *Amazing Spider-Man (1963)* #39 by John Romita Sr.
Ben Caldwell: "My favorite super hero was always Spider-Man, so for my 12th birthday a friend who was a serious collector gave me a mint copy of *Amazing Spider-Man* #39. It was a princely gift, but at the time I didn't fully appreciate it. So a few months later, when a dealer at a convention offered to trade it for a handful of random modern comics, I agreed. The second the deal was done, I regretted it and asked if I could undo it, but no luck. That lost comic has haunted me for the last three decades! Of course I can still read reprints, but it's not quite the same thing. When Wil Moss asked me to do an updated version of that cover for America, it was not only a great chance to ape Romita's singular style, but also a bit of self-redemption!"

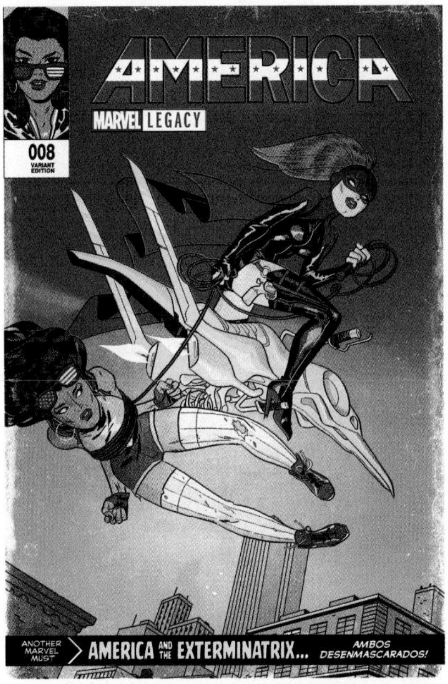
AMERICA
MARVEL LEGACY
008 VARIANT EDITION
ANOTHER MARVEL MUST
AMERICA AND THE EXTERMINATRIX... AMBOS DESENMASCARADOS!
BEN CALDWELL ▲

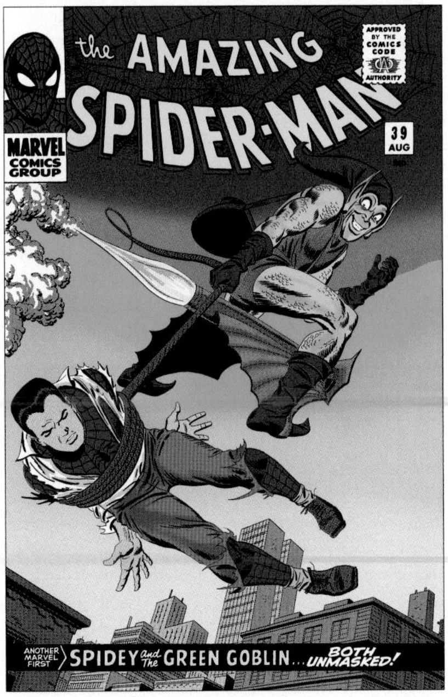
the AMAZING SPIDER-MAN
MARVEL COMICS GROUP
39 AUG
ANOTHER MARVEL FIRST
SPIDEY and the GREEN GOBLIN... BOTH UNMASKED!
JOHN ROMITA SR. ▲

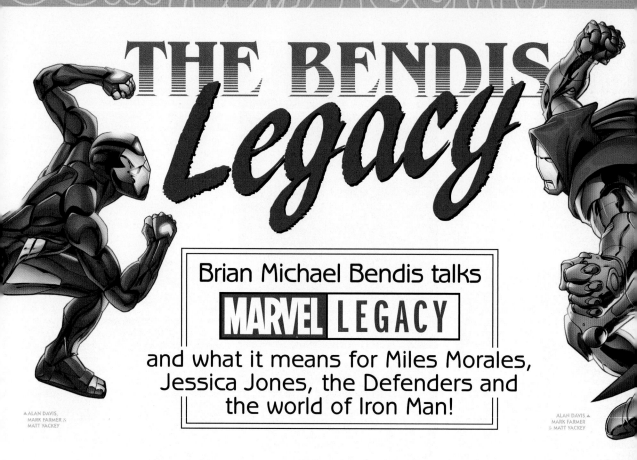

THE BENDIS *Legacy*

Brian Michael Bendis talks
MARVEL LEGACY
and what it means for Miles Morales, Jessica Jones, the Defenders and the world of Iron Man!

▲ ALAN DAVIS,
MARK FARMER &
MATT YACKEY

ALAN DAVIS ▲
MARK FARMER
& MATT YACKEY

BY **JESS HARROLD**

"Marvel Legacy is an opportunity for us to tell a story that speaks to the vast history of these characters—we get an opportunity to dive in and tell a brand-new story that leaps the characters forward, but the elements of the story are all classic Marvel." That's how an enthusiastic Brian Michael Bendis describes the core philosophy of Marvel Legacy—one that fits him like a glove. In his long career at Marvel, he has always been equally at home delivering revolutionary stories featuring classic characters, such as Daredevil and the Avengers, as he is introducing his own heroes—including Miles Morales, Jessica Jones, and, most recently, Riri Williams. For Bendis, the Marvel Universe is a big place, and Legacy is an opportunity to celebrate both the old and the new. "Just because we're adding new things to the toy box doesn't mean our love for the classic toys is diminished," he says. "In fact, it's the opposite. I see a lot of these newer characters as an extension of our love for Tony or Thor or Hulk—it's a crazy valentine, if anything."

While Marvel Legacy doesn't see Bendis launching a new title, it will majorly influence his four ongoing series (*Invincible Iron Man*, *Spider-Man*, *Jessica Jones*, and *Defenders*), but it will do so in tales he was already planning to tell. "I'm really happy about Marvel Legacy because it was where my books were headed," he

says. "For different reasons, because of the story I was telling with Riri and Victor and Tony, 'legacy' is all *Iron Man* was about. Because of Miles and Peter's unique relationship, 'legacy' is what that book is about—Miles' relationship to his parents, his uncle and all that made him who he is. Literally everything I am writing about is about legacy, so it just felt right. When you talk about my long time at Marvel, that

▲ ADI GRANOV

is what it's about. It's amazing how m[...] and the editorial team have always [...] the same goals in mind, whether we dis[...] it or not."

As the new initiative begins, Be[...] promises that every single one of his b[...] has "a major Legacy moment"—so [...] take a look at them in turn.

INVINCIBLE IRON MAN

With *Invincible Iron Man* #[...] Bendis begins the next stage of his [...] exploration of the world of Iron M[...] one that has already taken Tony Stark [...] the board, and seen two characters [...] their respective armors and take on [...] mantle. Now, as the saga continues [...] single title, Riri Williams and Victor [...] Doom are on a collision course. "[...] at *Invincible Iron Man* as an Iron [...] event," Bendis says. "All of the story[...] we have been telling about Riri, Vi[...] and obviously the search for Tony S[...] are slammed together in the very [...] issue of our Legacy storyline—so [...] that there's really no other place to [...] the story. Everything is converging on [...] and it's all going to lead up to a very [...] page count on #600—it's a runaway t[...] heading toward that issue. It is the [...] unique Iron Man story, it is the big[...] Iron Man story, and every single chara[...] involved in it will see a giant chang[...] the status quo coming out of it." For

SANFORD GREENE ▲

"It was that rare occasion where a writer earned his Legacy number all by himself," he says. "I've written every issue that has landed Miles here, so I was happy to own that number because it's a number I'm very proud of." It's an incredible achievement by any standard, even more so when one considers that the title no longer features the same star, and doesn't even take place in the same universe it started in. "We've taken as many bold choices as you can take in the course of the book," Bendis says. "It's amazing that people have stood by it." One reason they have is that Miles Morales is a fascinating character—it's hard not to root for him. "I'm writing a lot of characters that are just figuring out their place in the Marvel Universe," Bendis says. "Riri and Miles particularly are characters that are on a growth-and-discovery arc that is so intense and unique. And that is absolutely what the book is about."

Marvel Legacy follows hot on the heels of another story focusing on, well, legacy: the blockbuster sequel *Spider-Men II* reuniting Miles and his super-hero namesake, Peter Parker. "In that book, Ganke positions Miles to think that maybe some of his troubles are that he's living someone else's legacy," Bendis says. "Like, you're Spider-Man, you kick ass as Spider-Man, even Spider-Man said you can be Spider-Man, but you've been struggling and maybe it's because you're a cover band instead of an original. You're an excellent cover band, you can do 'Stairway to Heaven' as well as Led Zeppelin, but maybe you're not being true to you. And so this idea is out there—and it's a big one, one a lot of people can relate to: artists and writers and anybody who's growing up and doing something because they looked up to someone else who inspired them. You get to a place where you go, 'Now I have to stand on my own two feet.' Is that the story that's happening with Miles? It very well may be. At the same time, Miles and Peter are stars of their *Generations* special, and that's a massive storyline between the two of them. So when we're ready to go on Legacy, huge things will have happened to Miles and Peter that will make Miles' choices going forward just enormous and surprising."

And while Miles is dealing with all that, he'll also have his hands full with a new iteration of a classic Spidey staple: the Sinister Six. "Each one of the Sinister Six has a unique place in Spider-Man history, in the Spider-Man legacy," Bendis says. "And their joining together and their plan is unique to what is going on at Marvel right now. Who the Iron Spider is is a big question, and all will be revealed in the very first issue of the storyline! We've been planning this for literally years, and this Sinister Six story—who these villains are in relation to Miles, what they want from him—is the one that is going to change Miles' life forever, for real, no hype."

Bendis promises that there is more fallout to come from the destruction of the Ultimate Universe that brought Miles to his new home in the Marvel Universe. "One hundred percent," he says. "First of all, he remembers all of it. But how he's handling that, how do you process that? That has a lot to do with this story. A lot of these super-hero kids go through some pretty traumatic things, and they don't deal with them. With Miles it feels more real-world than a lot of super heroes, more intimate—we're in his dorm room, y'know? That gives us the opportunity to delve into what it really feels like to be part of these world-changing events."

JESSICA JONES

No stranger to life-altering super-hero madness herself, Jessica Jones will once again face Zebediah Killgrave—the Purple Man—in Marvel Legacy. "The first Jessica Jones series, which was called *Alias*, all came to a head with the reveal that has been haunting Jessica all her life has been the fact that the Purple Man, this super villain with the power to make you do anything he wants, took over her life," Bendis says. "Not only did he do that, but no one really noticed. It's one of the worst things that's ever happened to a super hero. Now, the only thing scarier than the Purple Man returning is the Purple Man returning when Jessica has healed herself to a place where she can be her version of happily married and have a child. So she has a lot to lose—and the Purple Man doesn't care about any of it. So his return to her life at this time is just about the scariest thing you can think of. On top of that, Jessica as a character is always about the Marvel Legacy—she's looking at the fabric of the Marvel Universe through the gritty reality of the cases that she gets. Jessica in a way embodies everything about Legacy in how she perceives the Marvel Universe."

In *Jessica Jones*, Bendis strives to portray the series star and her husband, Luke

[...] have complained about comic-book [eve]nts not taking place in the main title, he [say]s, this is what they've been waiting for: [...] looking at Legacy, every single title is [an] event in the main book. For those fans [who]'ve been preaching 'event in the main [boo]k,' and I actually agree with them, this [is y]our time to support it with your wallet." [Ben]dis' story will answer the question [of w]ho wields the armor?" as Riri and Victor [go] head-to-head. The writer adds: "Who's [goi]ng to be responsible for the legacy if [the]re is no Tony Stark? Who really has to [be] Iron Man? One person had permission; [one] person just took it. We'll see where it [en]ds." In the lead-up to the story, Bendis [pro]mises that the climactic issue of Victor's [boo]k, *Infamous Iron Man #12*, is "gigantic" [as t]he villains behind the scenes and the [nat]ure of the former Doctor Doom's goals [all] come to a head. Stefano Caselli, Alex [Mal]eev and Mike Deodato Jr. will all join [...] on the path to #600—"everyone [who] touched the *Iron Man* book with me [will] be part of this"—and the anniversary [issu]e will astound fans. "I can tell you that," [Ben]dis says, "because when I told the [Mar]vel creative retreat two of the ideas [for] *Iron Man #600*, the room gasped— [and] that's not an easy room to get a gasp [out] of."

[SP]IDER-MAN

[W]hile many titles are being renumbered [dur]ing Marvel Legacy, Miles Morales' book [has] a unique distinction: Every single one [of] the issues counted toward *Spider-Man [#]234* has been written by one man: Bendis. [Wit]h *Invincible Iron Man*, the scribe played [a] part in the calculation. But with *Spider-[Ma]n*, he wanted it to reflect the full history [of] the ongoing narrative that began with [*Ulti*]*mate Spider-Man #1* way back in 2000.

▼ DAVID MACK

Cage, as a real and believable couple, albeit with super-powers: "One of my goals with Jessica and Luke is to write a complicated, happy adult marriage—about two people who genuinely like each other, and genuinely love each other. It just so happens I'm in a relationship like that—I'm in a very happy marriage—and when I'm reading about marriages or seeing them on TV, I rarely ever see that, that the characters like each other. So I've put it upon myself to make Luke and Jessica teammates in this world, because it's a feeling I can relate to. When we see Luke and Jessica at the beginning of #13, they are actually in a very good place. Getting through the first storylines in this series made them both go: 'No, I want to be married to you. I could have walked away, but I want this.'" Clearly passionate about the book starring one of his signature co-creations, Bendis is also excited that he gets to worth with the same creative team that introduced the character in *Alias*: Michael Gaydos and Matt Hollingsworth on art, with David Mack on covers. As he puts it: "I'll exclude myself from this, but David Mack is a better painter, Mike is a better storyteller and illustrator, and Matt is one of the best colorists of all time. The legacy of the book is that it's the same people making it, but the book is actually better. Fourteen years have gone by since the original—that's an amazing thing that everyone's still alive!"

DEFENDERS

Daredevil and Iron Fist join Jessica and Luke in the pages of Bendis' newest book, *Defenders*—which remains at #6 as Legacy hits, despite being a famous name from Marvel's past. "I could have slapped a big, chunky number on *Defenders*," Bendis says, "but everyone involved went, you know, 'The other *Defenders* book was not this book. It's not the same legacy, so let's just stick to our numbering and focus more on what this Defenders legacy is—which is to defend the streets of the city.'" They may just be starting out doing that together as a team, but things are going to get harder than ever for Luke, Jessica, Matt, and Danny with what Bendis has planned. "The storyline for Legacy is: Who will be the new Kingpin?" he says. "That gives us the chance to just blow the book up. We're going for like a *Godfather* landscape of crime and street-level drama, and we can really open the floodgates in a way that no other book can. The basic fight is Black Cat versus Diamondback. That comes to a big head in #6—from there, what Diamondback has done will wake up a few more candidates who will see that there is serious money to be had. They are going to go for it, so the Defenders, in their attempts to

▲ DAVID MARQUEZ & JUSTIN PONSOR

defeat Diamondback, will cause, not a gang war, but a bloody and scary grab for the Kingpin title. What's really cool, and I think will get people excited, is that not all the good guys stay good guys, and not all the bad guys stay bad guys. There's going to be some serious soul-searching and switching going on, and I think people will be quite startled by who goes where and why, because we're going to see it and their argument is going to be very strong."

The four core Defenders won't be the only ones drawn into the fray, and Bendis teases that the book will have a close connection with *Spider-Man*, where Miles Morales has recently crossed the Black Cat's path. "You're gonna see Miles, Old Man Logan, so many street-level characters," he says. "Blade's already appeared, Elektra. I love this book, it is literally a pile of all my favorite things." And with #6, one of Marvel's highest-profile heroes drops by: a certain Merc whose Mouth seems ideally suited for Bendis to put words into. "It's the first time I have written Deadpool in the sense of 'Let me show everybody how I can write Deadpool,'" he says. "He is a character I have a lot of affection for. I love Gerry Duggan so much that I never even thought to write Deadpool. Now I wanted to do something, and *Defenders* is certainly the place to do it." Bendis pledges to build off the shared history that Duggan has established among Deadpool, Luke, and Iron Fist, but what will Jessica make of Wade Wilson? "Once you become a parent, nonsense—you have no time for it," Bendis says. "Any parent will tell you that. I have four kids, so I have no time for nonsense, but my day is filled with it. So I'm very excited for the scenes between

Jessica and Deadpool, because on [...] just a big pile of nonsense and the o[...] is like, 'I've got no time for this.'"

Defenders continues Bendis' crea[...] partnership with David Marquez, [...] pair having worked closely toge[...] since the artist arrived at Marvel. [...] came to Marvel with just killer v[...] and I jumped on the Marquez train v[...] early with *Spider-Man*," Bendis s[...] "David and I have become real frien[...] he actually moved here to Portl[...] and our families became very cl[...] Why is *Defenders* such next-level st[...] Because we're at the next level of [...] creative relationship. This is a book [...] really want to land and make a uni[...] statement with. Not just David and I, [...] Justin Ponsor, too. The script is wri[...] as much for Justin as for David— [...] one of the greatest colorists in com[...] like a cinematographer."

LEGACY THINKING

For anyone who has followed Ben[...] career, it's no surprise to hear him sp[...] warmly of his collaborators. He se[...] to have a knack for building partners[...] with his artists that are both creativ[...] successful and personally reward[...] "In my life, this is where I am inarguc[...] most spoiled," he says. "Mark Bag[...] Alex Maleev, David Mack, Sara Pich[...] David Marquez... I just adore th[...] people, and my legacy at Marvel [...] be these collaborations. Not only [...] immensely proud of the quality of th[...] collaborations, I am also immens[...] proud of those friendships behind [...] scenes. Comic books are the most [...] exciting, scariest collaboration you [...] have, and Marvel Comics just all[...] these collaborations to thrive, from [...] early days of Stan and Jack to now. [...] the opportunity to discover things ab[...] ourselves as creators having met th[...] other creators—things we would ne[...] have found out without meeting them[...]

So has all the talk of Marvel Leg[...] had him considering the scale of [...] own contribution to comics? "I try [...] to involve myself too much," he s[...] "But the fact of the matter is I do hav[...] legacy birthday in 2017, and it's hard [...] to take stock when you're at a dec[...] marker." Bendis turned 50 in Aug[...] "There we are writing 'Legacy' [...] everything, and it's hard not to conn[...] the dots. There's *Jessica Jones* Sea[...] Two; there's an animated Spider-M[...] movie that Miles is a part of that [...] helping with any way I can. So the[...] a lot going on connected to things [...] I've done at the company that I [...] very warm and tingly about. So [...] nice to be faced with your legac[...] and at the same time feel a lot be[...] about my place in the world than all [...] characters I write about do!"

...TAKE ...TWO -IN- ...ONE!

...ip **Zdarsky** is bringing back ...rious comic-book title from the ...t in ***Marvel Two-In-One***! But ...s doing it with a twist. Instead ...' teaming up with a different ...aracter each month, now the ...**ng** is permanently sharing the ...elight with his Fantastic Four ...buddy, the **Human Torch**. ...OM spoke with Zdarsky about ... plans to honor the marvelous ...gacy of *Two-In-One* and the ... FF with Ben and Johnny!

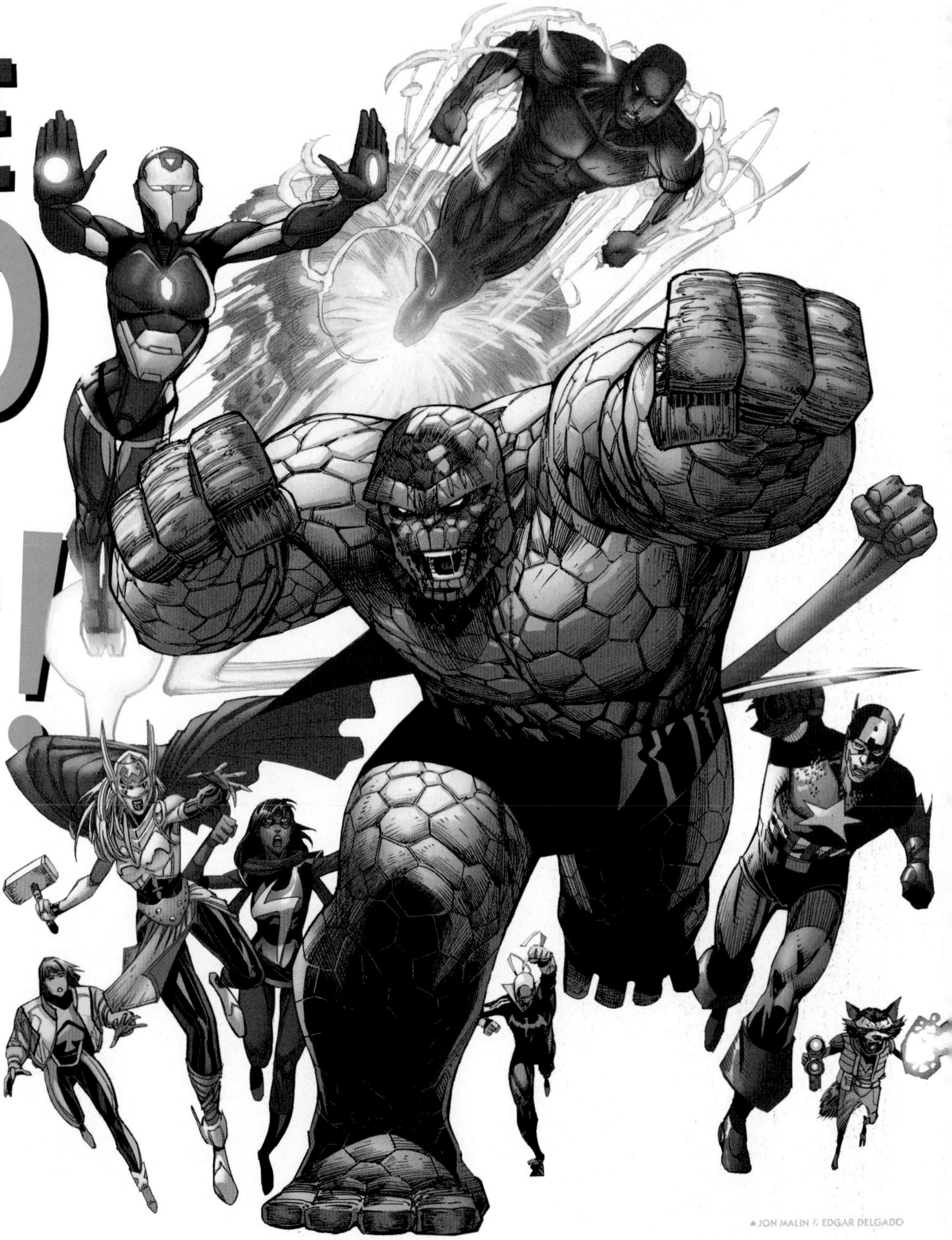

▲JON MALIN & EDGAR DELGADO

...SS HARROLD

...OM: *Marvel Two-In-One* recalls fond ...ories of the 1970s and 1980s, but ...isn't anyone's daddy's *Two-In-One*, is ...What's the premise of your book?

...RSKY: Yeah, it felt like a good time to ...g back the title! Obviously it was originally ...ceived as a team-up book featuring the ...g and other Marvel characters, but now ...Two-In-One* is more about the Thing and ...Torch coming together again to form a ... After spending time apart following ...et *Wars*, they're the Fantastic Two now, ...g to look toward the future.

...OM: It's been a volatile few years for ... of Marvel's true A-list super heroes. Where are they at right now? What, if anything, is their mission statement?

ZDARSKY: Both of them have tried to move on—with the Guardians, S.H.I.E.L.D., the Inhumans, the Avengers. Part of it is finding usefulness after a life of inherent structure. Part of it is distraction from their belief that Reed, Sue, and the kids have died. It's a huge weight that doesn't go away just from being busy. So I think their mission statement right now is to help each other finally deal with their reality: a world without their family. And where that world can take them.

FOOM: As part of the FF, the two have a small army of iconic villains in their rogues' gallery. Will we be seeing any of them rear their heads, or perhaps some new rivals for Ben and Johnny to go up against?

ZDARSKY: Yes. Of course! Even though it's not called "Fantastic Four," this is the book that will deal with their villains and allies. And, of course, their main villain turned "ally"—DOOM! Brian Michael Bendis and Alex Maleev have been doing amazing things with him in *Infamous Iron Man*, so it's been a lot of fun writing him here.

FOOM: Even without the rotating guest-star concept, the Thing and the Torch are among the more sociable of Marvel's heroes. Ben's been an Avenger, a Guardian, and the main man of Marvel poker parties. Meanwhile, Johnny's been hanging with the Uncanny Avengers and Inhumans. Surely we'll be seeing a few fellow inhabitants of the MU in this book?

ZDARSKY: Yeah, I mean, I tend to utilize guest stars in my books, and Johnny and Ben make that really easy! This book is about the Marvel Universe and the Marvel MULTIverse, so we'll see some twists on other characters as we go. Both Ben and Johnny are such distinct characters that it's always fun to see them interact with the other heroes. Which is probably why they've ended up on so many teams over the past couple of years!

FOOM: We have to talk about something that fans must be wondering about this book. With Ben and Johnny back together, thoughts inevitably turn to Reed and Sue. What stage have Ben and Johnny reached in the grieving process? Have they accepted they will never see the rest of their family again, or (such is the nature of loss in their world) do they hold out hope? If so, are they on the hunt for answers?

ZDARSKY: Yeah, there's always hope. I mean, they live in a world where both Ben AND Johnny have "died," so that has to mess with your concept of death. But between the two of them, Johnny is the one who most can't let go. He's tried distracting himself, but the weight of what he's lost is catching up to him. He definitely wants answers.

FOOM: As if *MTIO* coming back and you writing it isn't already too much excitement to withstand, you have pretty much the perfect artist on board for this book: Jim Cheung! Is he planning to stick around, and how has it been so far working with a modern-day Marvel legend?

ZDARSKY: Oh, man, I'm hoping we have him for a while! He's one of the best comics artists ever! The detail in his work is breathtaking, but it's never at the expense of story and emotion. The art coming in is blowing me away. I think it's the best work he's done. I think there's a very small handful of people who draw the Thing well, and Jim is on that list.

FOOM: He definitely is! But since you've recently treated fans to some "how to draw" variant covers, how's about you tell us the secret to drawing the Thing and the Human Torch?

ZDARSKY: Look, you think I'm just going to GIVE that kind of info away? Petition Marvel to get me to do one of these covers for *MTIO*!

FOOM: Folks, get writing in! Assuming that, at some point, you have typed or will get to type both of these phrases in a script, which one gives you the biggest tingle of excitement: "It's clobberin' time!" or "Flame on!"?

ZDARSKY: Ha! Catchphrases don't give me that tingle. But being able to Ben and Johnny as brothers really do one of the greatest relationships in c and I feel pretty lucky to get to write t

FOOM: Clobberin' aside, Thing has c the most distinctive "voices" in comics- that, when written well, makes him o Marvel's greatest characters, yet on comes with the danger of him desce into parody if it's overdone. How ar finding it so far?

ZDARSKY: I think, as long as Ben has h story, an inner problem that needs sc that saves you from making him a caric of himself. So, basically, you write h Ben, not the Thing. I hope I manage t the voice!

FOOM: Johnny has quite the d history. And for a guy covered in Ben is no slouch in that department, e Do you have any plans to introduce loves for either of our heroes?

ZDARSKY: Oh man, with what happe them in the first arc? There won't be an for romance!

FOOM: No new flame for Johnn Ben? What a revoltin' developmen is! Can you tease what else is comi five words?

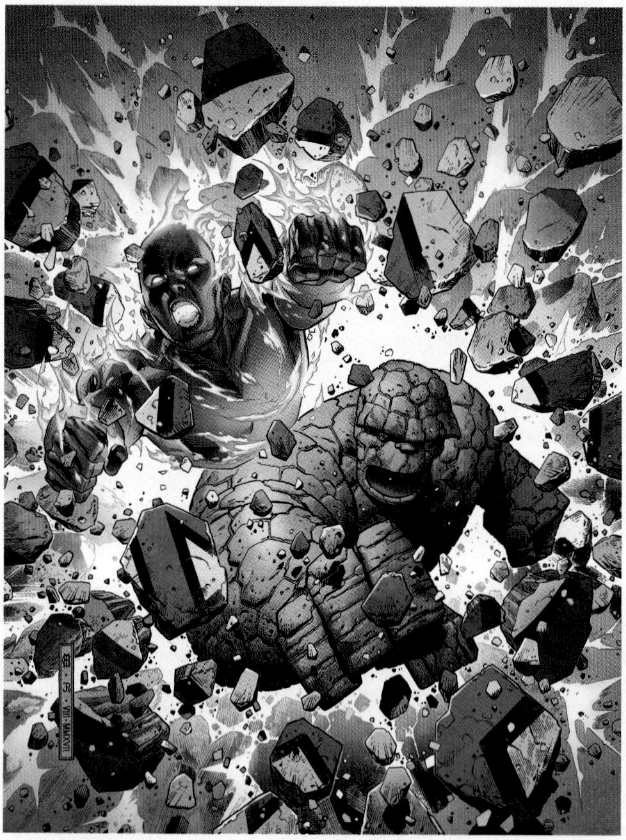

▲JIM CHUNG & JUSTIN PONSOR

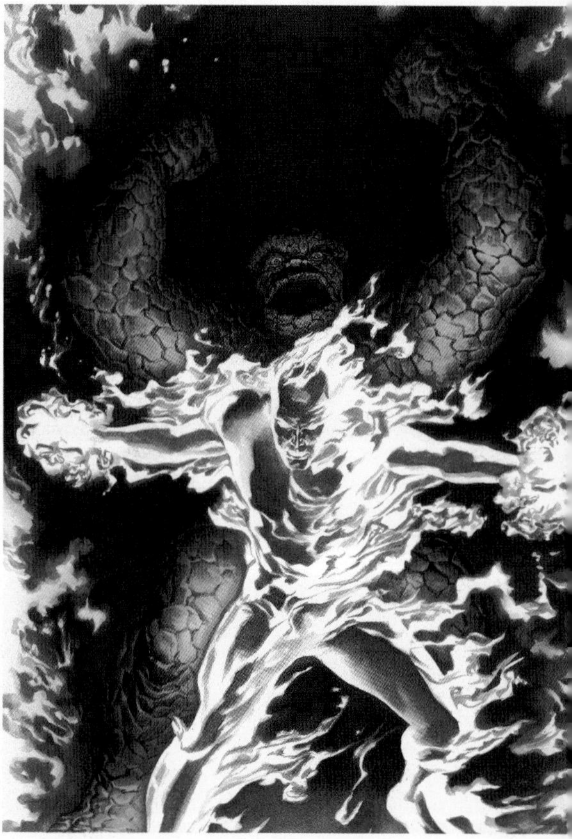

AL

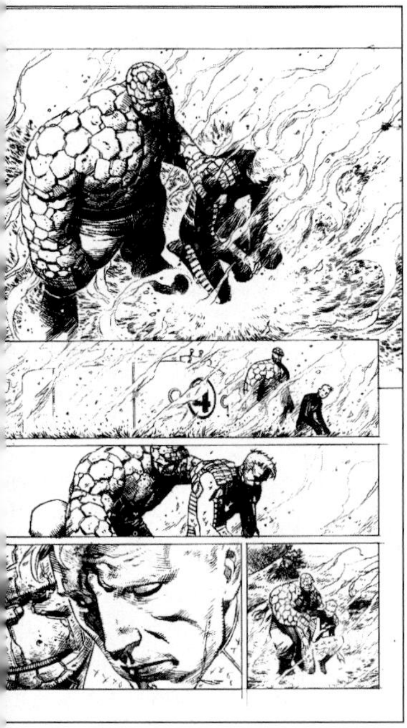

JIM CHEUNG

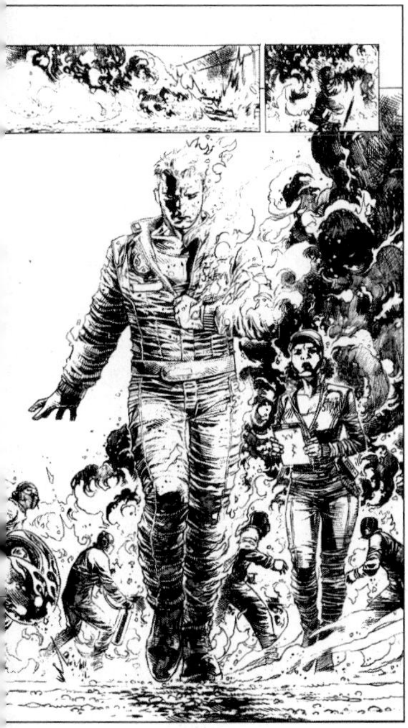

RSKY: Secrets. Adventure. Doom. ayal. Mole.

OM: So let's cut to the chase, then. *vel Two-In-One* is the new World's atest Comics Magazine, right?

RSKY: Look, far be it from me to weigh n matters that are, ultimately, to be ded on by the World Comics Magazine eme Court, but I think we have a strong here.

your verdict when ***Marvel Two-In-*** returns this December!

TWO GOOD TO BE TRUE

Four Fantastic *Marvel Two-In-One* Classics

The original *Marvel Two-In-One* ran for 100 issues between 1974 and 1983 as the Thing stomped his way across the Marvel Universe, making friends with everybody from Man-Thing to...Ben Grimm?! But these four *Two-In-One* team-ups are some of bashful, blue-eyed Benjy's best!

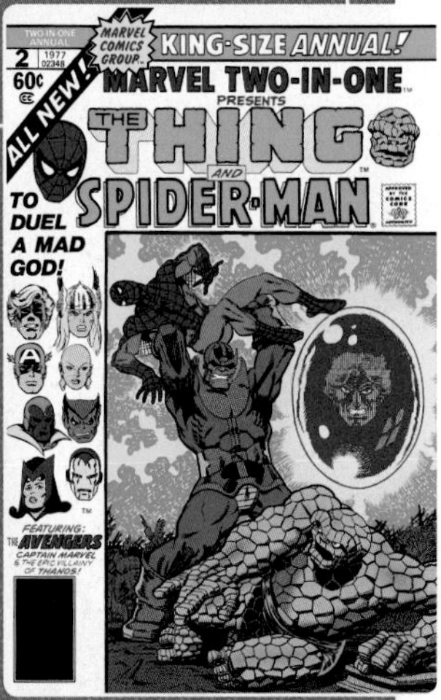
KING-SIZE ANNUAL!
MARVEL TWO-IN-ONE
PRESENTS
THE THING AND SPIDER-MAN
ALL NEW!
TO DUEL A MAD GOD!
FEATURING: THE AVENGERS
CAPTAIN MARVEL & THE EPIC VILLAINY OF THANOS!

"Death Watch!"

Marvel Two-In-One Annual #2

A key part of Jim Starlin's epic "Thanos War," this action-packed annual paired Marvel's two titans of the team-up, the Thing and Spider-Man, against a literal Titan—and a Mad one, at that! The Thing and Spidey vs. Thanos, drawn by Starlin? If that isn't a collector's item classic, we don't know what is!

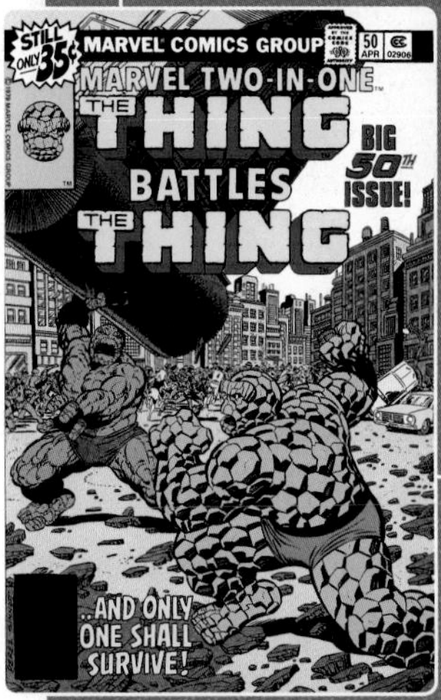
STILL ONLY 35¢
MARVEL COMICS GROUP
50 APR
MARVEL TWO-IN-ONE
THE THING BATTLES THE THING
BIG 50TH ISSUE!
...AND ONLY ONE SHALL SURVIVE!

"Remembrance of Things Past!"

Marvel Two-In-One #50

Thanks to the magic of Doctor Doom's time machine, Ben heads back to the early days of the Fantastic Four in the hope of finally curing his condition. But his old self isn't too happy to see him, resulting in the clobberin' time to end all clobberin' times. It's rocky Thing vs. original lumpy Thing—as only *FF* legend John Byrne could draw it!

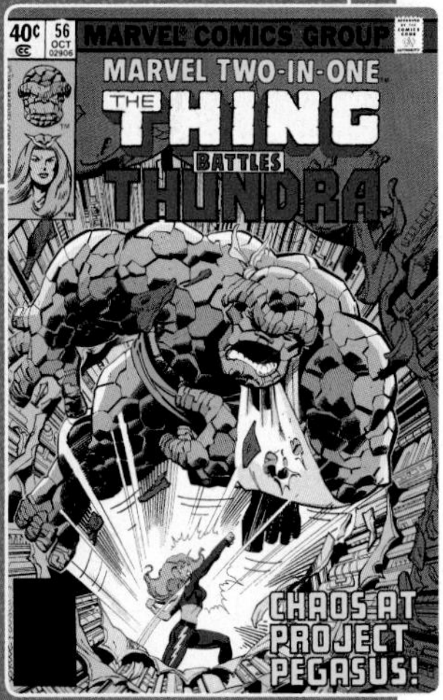
40¢ 56 OCT
MARVEL COMICS GROUP
MARVEL TWO-IN-ONE
THE THING BATTLES THUNDRA
CHAOS AT PROJECT PEGASUS!

The Project PEGASUS Saga

Marvel Two-In-One #53–58

Who do you ask to work security at a government research center/super villain prison? Why, the Thing, of course! But everything turns to chaos when Deathlok strikes, the deadly Nuklo gets loose, and Thundra leads a group of powerful lady wrestlers in an assault on the facility! Ben will need to call on some of his best *MTIO* buds, including Quasar, Bill "Giant-Man" Foster, and the wonderful Wundarr! Peril at Project PEGASUS means punches, power players—and poker!

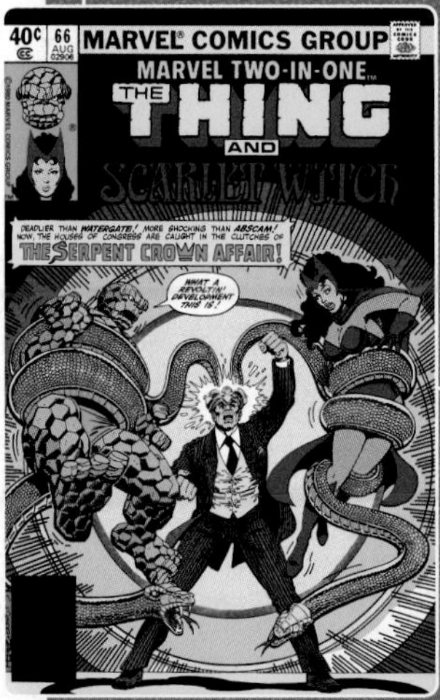
40¢ 66 AUG
MARVEL COMICS GROUP
MARVEL TWO-IN-ONE
THE THING AND SCARLET WITCH
THE SERPENT CROWN AFFAIR!

The Serpent Crown Affair

Marvel Two-In-One #64–67 and *Marvel Team-Up Annual #5*

Does the power of the Serpent Crown corrupt? Absolutely! So when a fiendish foe gets his hands on two Crowns and threatens to unleash the Serpent-God on Earth, life gets really interesting for the Thing, Stingray, Triton, and Scarlet Witch—culminating in a *Two-In-One Team-Up* with Spider-Man that also draws in Doctor Strange and Quasar! Snakes...why'd it have to be snakes?

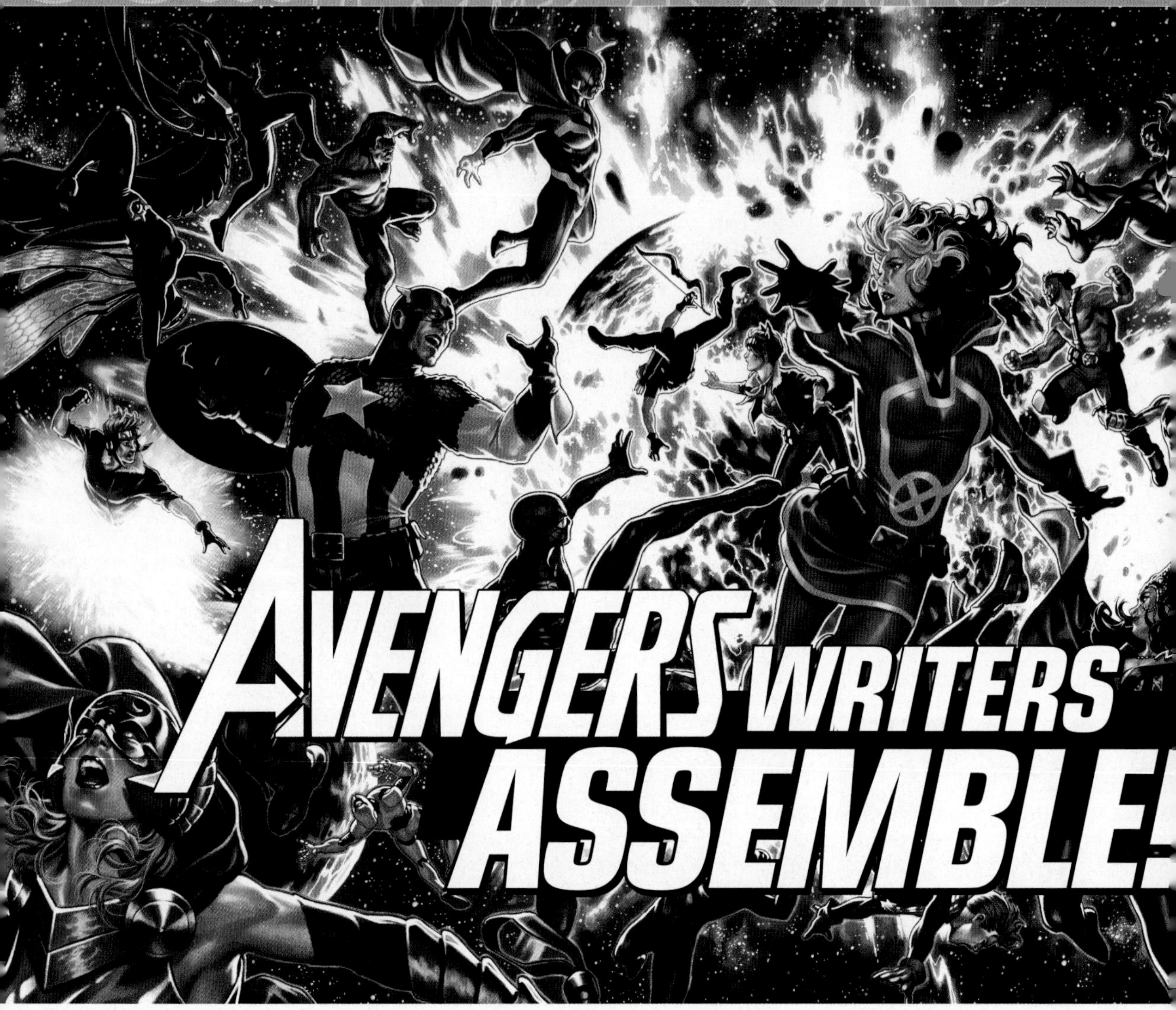

AVENGERS WRITERS ASSEMBLE!

MARK B

BY **JESS HARROLD**

Mark Waid, Jim Zub, and Al Ewing share their plans to take *Avengers, Uncanny Avengers,* and *U.S.Avengers* into Marvel Legacy, before combining all three titles into one weekly book starting with the landmark *Avengers* #675—and the epic "No Surrender"!

FOOM: Beginning with Mark, Marvel Legacy sees a crossover between your Avengers and Champions teams. It looks like they're going up against the High Evolutionary, but will the two teams be fighting for the same thing? Or in classic comic-book fashion, will there be some disagreement?

MARK WAID: The team-up encapsulates everything legacy means to Marvel. The classic generation and the younger generation have to put their differences aside, yes—but more than that, the Champions have to work hard not to be unconsciously marginalized by the Avengers. The center of all the friction is the Vision/Viv relationship, which as we see from the very first pages is in a rocky, ugly place. Whatever's happening between them seems to transcend a normal "father/teenage daughter" clash, and that tension spills out over both teams.

FOOM: Jim, with *Uncanny Avengers*, you're putting the focus on a classic Marvel bromance that unites the worlds of Avengers and X-Men: Wonder Man and the Beast. A lot has changed for both of them since their Avengers glory days—how's their friendship doing?

JIM ZUB: Hank and Simon have been through a lot since they had any time to hang out and commiserate. The fact that Simon has been away (lost as ionic energy absorbed by Rogue) for quite a while allows him a different perspective compared to Hank, who has been in the trenches for some of the biggest recent events of the Marvel Universe (the return of the original X-Men from the past, the M-Pox and battle with the Inhumans for mutant survival in *IvX*, and war between the Hydra Nation and New Tian in *Secret Empire*). In short, Beast has made some big mistakes and is trying to figure himself Simon thought he had his life sorted but was pulled away, and the world move without him. They're both looking for c and redemption in their own ways. Seein friends and taking stock of where your at and what you need to do next echoe other stories happening with the Unc Avengers and Marvel Legacy as a whol

FOOM: And what's going on with rest of the Uncanny team?

ZUB: The Unity Squad were offic disbanded by Steve Rogers in the buil to *Secret Empire*, but they kept operatir their own with shared purpose and a s of loyalty to each other. No charte membership IDs, no home base. Now need to decide if they formalize that structure once again or go their sepc ways. Rogue, Wasp, Synapse, Dc Voodoo, Quicksilver, and the Sc Witch will all be in the mix here, rebui after *Secret Empire* and planning fo future while dealing with the unexpe arrival of villains from their past. T

EL LEGACY CANNONBALL RUN PART 1
AMERICA'S FUNNIEST FIGHTERS!
U.S.Avengers

GEE, MISTER!
WHAT'S YOUR
STORY?

WHATEVER
IT IS, TELL
ME
FIRST!

DAVID NAKAYAMA ▲

...e plenty of love and loss, conflict and
...nity in the months to come.

...M: Al, where do recent developments
...e the U.S.Avengers?

...WING: They are heading out of *Secret*
...re and the aftermath issue in a state
...x—between Hydra machinations and
...banal evils, the team has been put
...gh the wringer, and one or two of
...won't ever be the same again. Also,
...ers can expect a new Supreme Leader
....I.M.—but what does that mean for
...rto Da Costa? You'll find out.

...M: Your first Legacy cover promises
...earch for Cannonball. And it looks
...hat's going to include a trip to a
...et that evokes a certain other comic
...k world beloved of Mark Waid...

...G: We are veering toward a certain
...cal Teenager," yes—it's one of those
...s that just fell together as the story
...esced out of the ether. It's not meant
...parody, exactly—I dig what the Archie
...s are doing right now—but I am finding
...riffing on that classical Americana, and
...ng it with sinister and alien undertones
...y beneath the surface, can make for
...enjoyably creepy moments. I've only
...en a little bit of "Ritchie Redwood," but
...urned out to be an oddly magnetic and
...ying presence so far.

D: WHAT? I need to catch up on my
...ing.

...M: And when Mark does that, Al,
...will he encounter with the rest of
...J.S.A. squad?

...G: There are a few changes to our

merry gang of misfits. One member's powers
aren't fully under control, one member's
powers are much more under control, and
one member has given up their super-hero
identity entirely. Also, fans of solicits will
have noticed the Shi'ar Superguardian
Smasher (her name is Smasher; she doesn't
smash Superguardians) is joining the team
during the search for Cannonball. Something
for readers who like mom-and-pop super-
hero pairings there, as well as big spaceships.

FOOM: So how many issues do you all
have before we get to the big one—
Avengers #675—and Earth's Mightiest
Heroes go weekly?

WAID: *Avengers* #674 is a finale for the
current team as it exists—Falcon, Spider-
Man, Hercules, Wasp, Thor, and Vision—
because, as is a staple of *Avengers*
storytelling since #16, the old order is
about to changeth...

ZUB: *Uncanny Avengers* #30 is our final
issue before the weekly format of "No
Surrender" launches. We cover a lot of
ground between now and then, tying up
old threads, rebuilding old bonds, and
setting the stage for our epic adventure in
Avengers #675 and beyond.

EWING: Issue #12 is going to be the last
issue of *U.S.Avengers*, then we're taking a
month break, and after that the team has a
very big role to play in "No Surrender"—
but will it be their last? Who will survive, and
what will be left of them? Kill your darlings,
they say...

FOOM: Uh-oh! How are you all ap-
proaching the collaboration on the new
"No Surrender" era?

TERRY DODSON & RACHEL DODSON ▲

ZUB: Mark, Al, and I have been planning this
massive weekly storyline since the start of
the year. We met up with Tom Brevoort and
Alanna Smith in New York for an Avengers
summit in February, and things quickly went
from concept to execution. It really is an
"all hands on deck" collaborative effort
between the writers, artists, and editorial
team with spreadsheets showing where
characters are at and where they're going
throughout the story, diagrams and new
character designs, location floor plans,
references from dozens of past Avengers
stories—you name it. It's been a wild ride
but also a ton of fun contributing to such an
important new chapter in Avengers history.

EWING: We're all working together—
some issues, one of us has more pages,
some issues that same person will have
less—but it's all essentially an equal share,
and we're all bringing our own particular
skill sets into the mix. I'm finding it fairly
reminiscent of previous collaborations—
"Trifecta," the Judge Dredd crossover
story in 2000 *AD* in particular, as that was
another weekly, three-person job with a
lot of connecting parts.

WAID: I was brought aboard as a key
player in the very first successful American
weekly comic, albeit from another
company, so I'm very comfortable with co-
plotting and divvying up sub-assignments
within the overall work. We do all tend to
"land" on certain characters, shepherding
certain ones—Al tends to handle the
Red Wolf beats, for example, and I lean
toward the Jarvis beats—but everyone
gets a say in everything, and everyone's
voice is heard. Even Brevoort's.

FOOM: What can you tell us about "No
Surrender"?

ZUB: "No Surrender" marks the final hurrah
for this era of Earth's Mightiest Heroes.
Beyond that, you'll just have to wait and see.

WAID: It's half celebration, half wake.

EWING: Some endings are also beginnings.
Mind you, some are just endings...

FOOM: Sounds ominous. Will the three
squads continue to operate separately,
or are we seeing a transition back to the
days of one true Avengers team?

ZUB: I don't think it's too much of a spoiler to
say that the teams start the story independent
and quickly realize their combined efforts
will be needed to tackle the Earth-shaking
threat at the core of our story.

FOOM: The classic statue of the founders
is central to the teaser image—is it fair
to say that this story resonates with the
history (indeed, the legacy) of the
Avengers?

ZUB: Absolutely. "No Surrender" is being built as a milestone that reflects on the past even as it looks toward the future. Old Avengers fans and new will find a lot to love here.

WAID: You can't tell a story of this scope and with this impact without considering all the eras of the Avengers past and present. Certain clues as to what's going on can be found in the past as well as in the present day, so it's critical that we give context.

EWING: And in terms of the legacy, we're adding some big, beautiful new pieces to the Marvel Universe with this series. I could definitely see a couple of these new creations being part of Avengers stories in the future—although that might depend if the Avengers have one.

FOOM: What can you tell us about some of the key Avengers in the story, and why they're major players?

ZUB: Quicksilver is in a dark place at the start of "No Surrender." He's looking for a way to prove himself in the days ahead.

WAID: Also, I have an affinity for writing super-speed characters. Go figure.

ZUB: Rogue thinks she's focused and ready for the challenges to come, but this battle is going to take something special from her. Beast is trying to reconnect to a time in his life when he knew who he was and what he stood for. The Avengers are a big part of that journey.

WAID: In a giant Avengers team this powerful, Beast quickly realizes that he serves best as a scientist, not a super hero—and the discoveries he makes alongside the Wasp will be crucial to the team's survival.

EWING: Vision gets some interesting beats over the course of the story. He's deeply connected to the history of the Avengers—not to mention that as the android Avenger, he can be a living communications hub between the three very different active teams. Which might put him in the firing line for some dark forces...

FOOM: Is that Living Lightning we can see, too?

EWING: That is Living Lightning—or just "Lightning," these days. He's someone who was an Avenger, but drifted away from the team, and is now re-examining that decision. I felt like it was a good idea to have someone coming back to prove the whole "once an Avenger, always an Avenger" thing—plus he's got some pretty cool powers, so it's a crime he's not used more often. He's joining us in #675 with his own supporting cast and even a little bit of romance. He hasn't just been sitting in a green room waiting to get the call all this time, he's been off having exciting adventures—and filling out suits really well.

FOOM: Are any other characters primed to make a big splash in "No Surrender"?

WAID: Jarvis. If you look at all of Avengers history as one long story, Jarvis is the through-line. He's been involved in every incarnation of the team, observing from the sidelines, and his knowledge of Avengers history will, at a key point, be critical to Earth's very survival.

EWING: Everyone gets their moment in the sun in this book—any reader coming into this from one of the current Avengers books will get to see their favorite characters from those books doing some cool things at some point in the story. For instance, Mark mentioned some Red Wolf beats earlier—in one of the issues, he gets a particular moment to shine that I'm hoping fans of his will enjoy. And we have a whole crew of bad guys, too—some old faves and some new faces I think you'll love.

ZUB: We have some new characters, both heroic and villainous, that we're really excited to unveil. Beyond that, the crew you see in the Alex Ross piece is central to the story, as well as at least two Avengers founders—but not necessarily the ones you'd expect.

FOOM: Who are the artists assembled to bring this story to life?

ZUB: Pepe Larraz is drawing month one of the story, bringing the same incredible storytelling and dynamic action fans have grown to love in *Uncanny Avengers*. Some of the scenes we've given him to draw to get this story underway have been staggeringly difficult, and he's delivered on them with style and grace beyond our wildest expectations. Seriously, this is career-making work for Pepe. Readers are going to freak out.

WAID: Kim Jacinto is drawing month two. He's my personal hero for bringing both the humanity and the bombast to a cast of roughly one billion characters. His eye is amazing when it comes to picking just the right split seconds to illustrate, and the way he handles action is remarkable. Couldn't be happier to have him aboard.

EWING: Paco Medina joins us for month three, making it a particularly favorite month for me personally. Fans of his immaculate art style will very much dig the big action beats of his issues—but there are also some chilling moments verging on horror mixed in, which is a little new for us, so I'm looking forward to what he does with that. *U.S.Avengers* fans will be d
satisfied, I think—as will everyone e

**FOOM: It all sounds great, but im
you're talking to one person who
the movies but has never rea
Avengers comic, and another who
loved the title but hasn't read an is
years. Why should they buy this b**

WAID: To the movie-lover, as big c
Avengers stories have been on the sc
this one's even more epic. We're al
soned storytellers, so we promise
that you'll never be lost or confused
thrilled. And to the returning fans, if t
a former Avenger you ever loved,
going to have an active role, whoeve

EWING: This is a big-budget Ave
spectacular, filled to bursting with
and cool characters as well as a
bunch of your cinematic favorites
if we're doing our jobs, you'll be a
pick it up from page one and dive ri
To Avengers fans of old, there have
some developments since you wer
with us, but the basics haven't cha
There has come a day—a day unlik
other—and Earth's Mightiest Heroe
answer the call, assemble and do
they do best in the face of overwhe
odds. Join us for the faces you kn
we'll make you fall in love with the
you don't. That's a *promise*.

ZUB: Al and Mark have said it all right
At this point in the collaborative pr
we've become a hive mind, so they
what I would say before it ever reach
mouth. By the time you read this, Mar
Al have written my weekly to-do lis
reminded me about my upcoming c
appointments. Go Team Avengers.

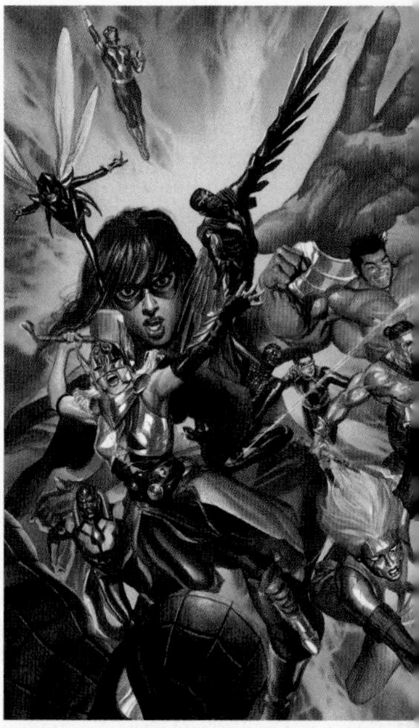

ALE

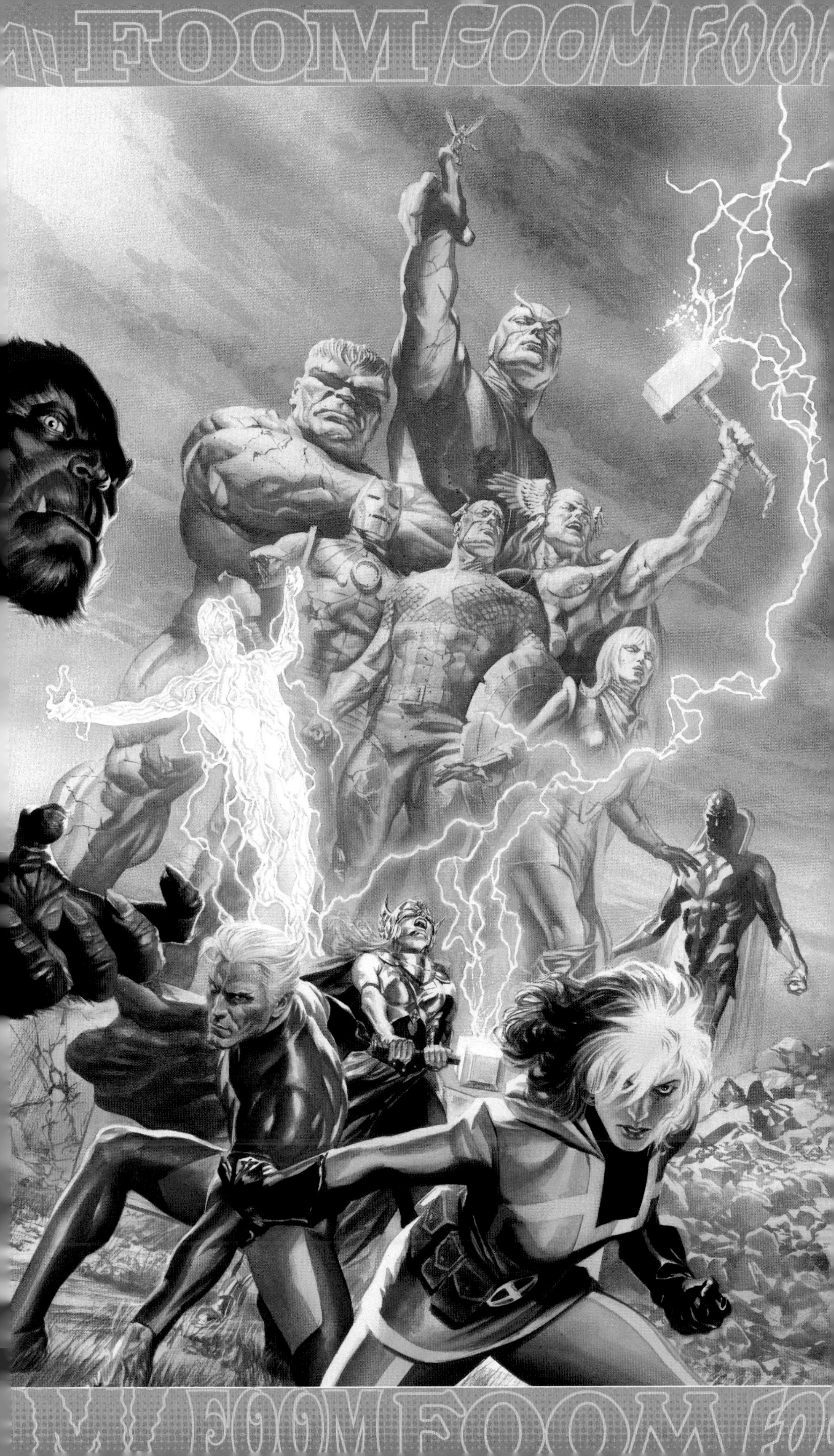
FOOM FOOM
FOOM FOOM

KELLY THOMPSON HITS THE BULLSEYE WITH HAWKEYE

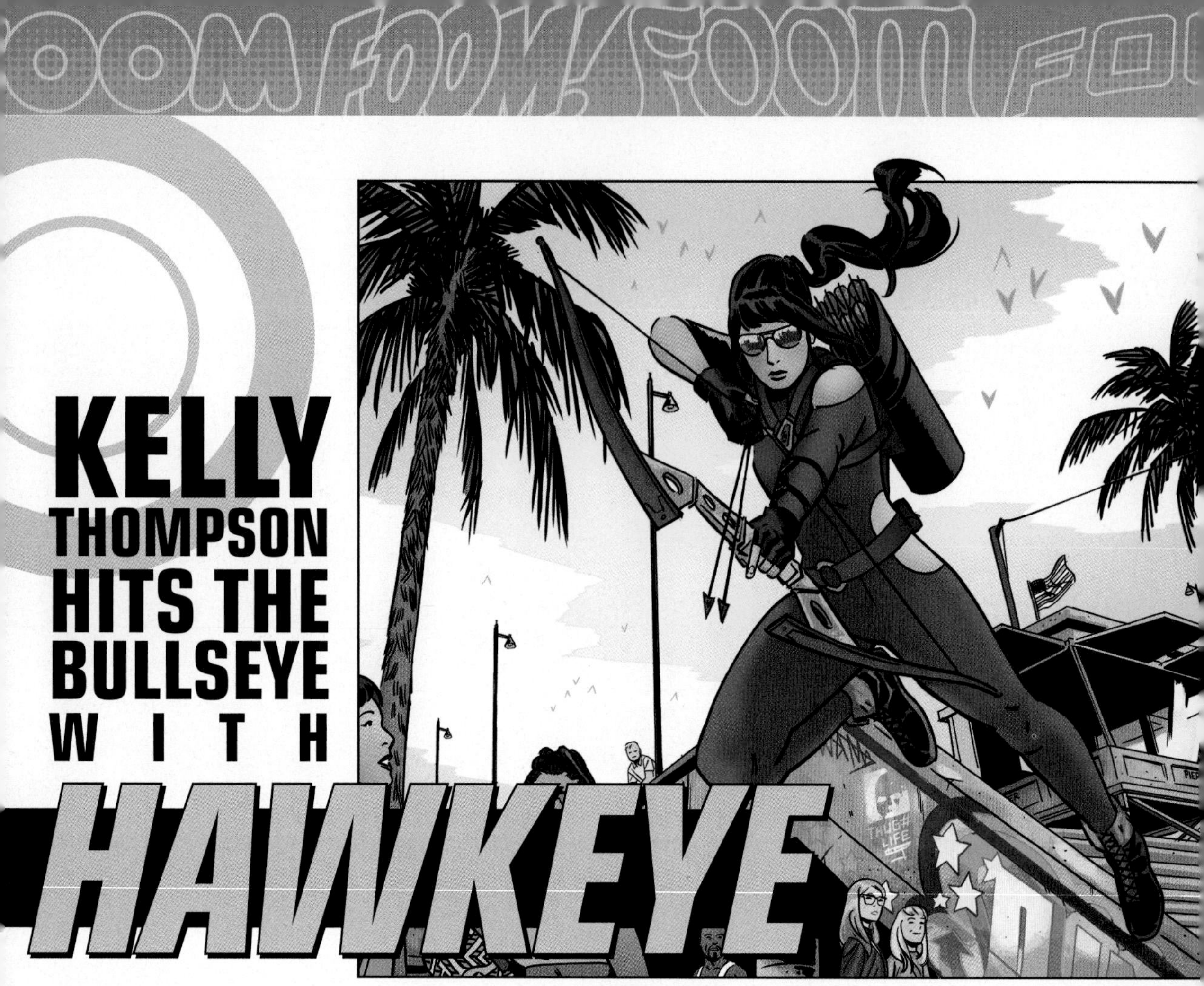
THUG LIFE

LEONARDO ROMERO & JORDIE BE

BY **JOHN RHETT THOMAS**

As the Kate Bishop–starring *Hawkeye* aims for its Legacy launch, *FOOM* decided it was perfect timing to check in with the series' writer, Kelly Thompson. Want my opinion? *Hawkeye* is one of Marvel's best series, and Thompson is one of its rising stars. Building on the success of Matt Fraction and David Aja's Eisner Award–winning series that matched Hawkeye (Clint Barton) with Hawkeye (the aforementioned Kate), Thompson and her creative partners maintained a similar vibe in what I find to be, as the writer puts it in our interview, an "eminently readable and lovable series." We talk about all that and more, including her comic-nerd bonafides (hint: she's a bigger fan of Rogue and Gambit than you are!), her background as a writer, and, of course, Hawkeye.

FOOM: What were some of your favorite comics/characters when you started reading as a teenager?

KELLY: I was hardcore for the X-Men as a teenager. And Rogue and Gambit were especially close to my teen heart. I had not only a copy of *X-Men* #24 framed in my room, but I had bought extra copies of both *X-Men* #24 and *Gambit* #1 and cut them up and made a framed collage as well. Can you say...SUPERFAN?!

FOOM: What about those characters clicked with you?

KELLY: I think—broadly—the X-Men connected with me then for the same reasons they click with people now: They're outcasts and misfits (something we all feel, but we feel especially as teens, I

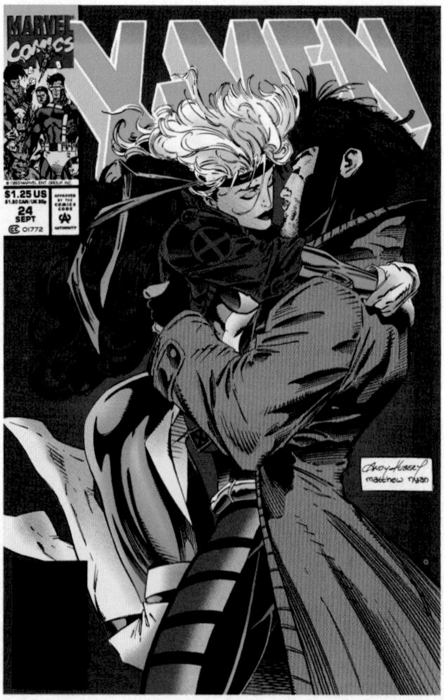
MARVEL COMICS
X-MEN
$1.25 US
24
SEPT

ANDY KUBERT & MATTHEW RYAN ▲

suspect), and they built their own ama powerful family together. Specifically Rogue and Gambit? I NEEDED THEM KISS. I NEEDED IT SO BAD!

FOOM: Your blog bio says you wer Savannah College of Art & Design to a degree in sequential art. Were intent on being an artist? Do you h any art skills under your belt that yo used in comics at all? Or wish to use?

KELLY: When I first discovered co as a teen, I was elated because I always wanted to be a writer, and co was such a fascinating merging of w and pictures that I became really exc about the idea of that specific art for made me think perhaps I could do it. I'm not a terribly talented artist, and w with practice I'm sure I could have go better, I doubt I ever could have reac the heights I aspired to. However, lots of writing practice, I do have h that I can achieve those equivalent wri heights. And yes, everything I lear about art (and in trying to be an ar helps make me a better writer—especi as it comes to breaking and pacing a st

FOOM: It has been five years since self-published your debut novel *Girl Who Would Be King*. Looking b what do you make of the success of

l, and how much longer 'til you think ll have a sequel complete?**

LY: Oof! You're not pulling any punches! ık *TGWWBK* first and foremost taught a lot about both writing and about ishing. The success of that book also ıed some doors for me and helped me ıcially make some progress in becoming l-time writer. I put off the sequel for a time as the book was in different stages eing optioned to be a movie or a TV v (as these things sometimes do), and in neantime I moved on to another series *ykiller*), but I have recently decided to rn to the sequel (*The God Slayer*). I hope 'l be out in 2018 with *Storykiller 2*, early at the latest. Fingers crossed!

)M: How did working at Marvel fit your plans as a writer? Was this even ething you'd dreamed of doing?

LY: Absolutely. I think from the first I saw Rogue in the '90s animated series :hing that Sentinel in a mall I knew I connecting to something powerful in me. And when I found comics (thanks y younger brother, Scott) a few weeks r, I knew I wanted comics to be my life. vel comics were my first loves. I even e a letter to Marvel when I was a . Comics is a very fast-paced industry, have struggled in these first years with ng time for novels in between comic-k deadlines, but I'm optimistic that I'm ing better at it.

)M: Of the Marvel Legacy books 've heard news of, which are you t excited about?

LY: I mean, *Hawkeye*, obviously! Just ing. I've been loving Tom Taylor's *New Wolverine*, so I'm really excited what's going to happen over there. I am always here for *Jessica Jones*. *Ms. vel* is always powerful, and the new *rdians* book has been excellent so I'm rested in checking that out, too.

)M: *Hawkeye* has been in excellent ds since Matt Fraction and David Aja : it to crazy heights of critical acclaim. r series seems to be a continuation hat storytelling excellence.

LY: What we're doing is definitely irect spiritual descendent from the :tion/Aja/Wu/Hollingsworth stuff—ecially the Kate in L.A. stuff. Their *vkeye* book is one of my favorite ic books of all time. I think it brilliantly vents itself (and super-hero books). smart and funny and emotional all at e, and it plays with (and breaks in half) ative and structure and visuals and ectations in a way that seems effortless ough I'm sure it was not). Stepping into

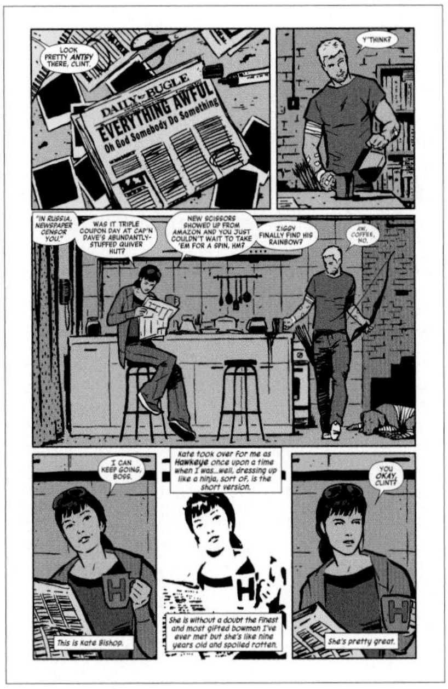

LOOK PRETTY ANTSY THERE, CLINT.
DAILY BUGLE
EVERYTHING AWFUL
Oh God Somebody Do Something
Y'THINK?
"IN RUSSIA, NEWSPAPER CENSOR YOU."
WAS IT TRIPLE COUPON DAY AT CAP'N DAVE'S ABUNDANTLY-STUFFED QUIVER HUT?
NEW SCISSORS SHOWED UP FROM AMAZON AND YOU JUST COULDN'T WAIT TO TAKE 'EM FOR A SPIN, HM?
ZIGGY FINALLY FIND HIS RAINBOW?
AW, COFFEE, NO.
I CAN KEEP GOING, BOSS.
This is Kate Bishop.
Kate took over for me as Hawkeye once upon a time when I was...well, dressing up like a ninja, sort of, is the short version.
She is without a doubt the finest and most gifted bowman I've ever met but she's like nine years old and spoiled rotten.
YOU OKAY, CLINT?
She's pretty great.

▲DAVID AJA & MATT HOLLINGSWORTH

that shadow is scary—it's a very deep shadow. But you just try not to think about it too much. You try your best to honor what came before while doing your own thing as much as you can. I am very lucky to have an incredible team to help me do that, creatively and editorially. I feel like we all came together with a really beautiful cohesive vision, and I couldn't be prouder of what we've done, despite very big shoes to fill.

FOOM: Leonardo Romero seems a perfect fit as the artist for your stories. It's plainly a super-hero book, but he also manages to convey the humor (sometimes subtle, sometimes slapstick) of your stories.

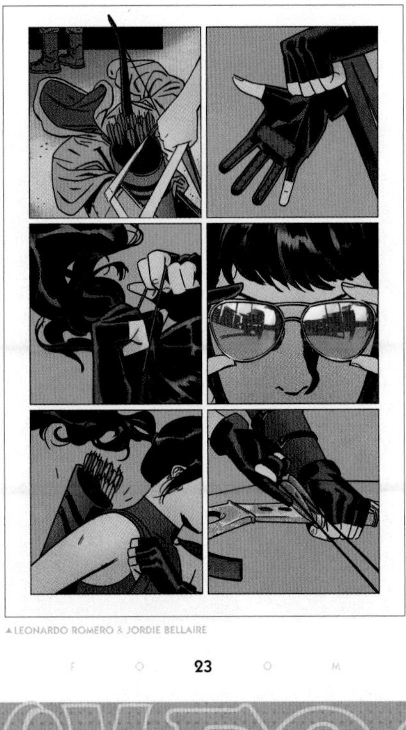

▲LEONARDO ROMERO & JORDIE BELLAIRE

KELLY: I am insanely lucky to have my team. Leo is a magnificent artist—a true talent—and he's a very good match for both *Hawkeye* and for me as a writer. He is the rare comic-book artist that can handle big super-hero stuff with the same ease as more street-level stuff, and since Kate's book is both, she needed that kind of artist. And I knew that from the beginning—that he was that kind of artist—but what I didn't know when we first began was how much Leo would "get me" and the sense of humor and fun I was trying to bring to Kate. But he gets it SO MUCH. And he makes everything I try to do about a hundred times better than it has any right to be.

FOOM: And let's not forget colorist Jordie Bellaire. What's your sense of what she brings to the table artistically?

KELLY: Ah, Jordie. My kingdom for a million Jordie Bellaires. She's a dream. When we were all first talking about the look of the book, and I was describing the tone and ideas behind the book, she goes (paraphrasing here), "So...Hollywood neo-noir meets *Miami Vice*," and we all went "YESSSSSS." She never disappoints, and much like Leo, just when you think she's done the best work she can do, she one-ups herself.

FOOM: Those covers by Julian Totino Tedesco are amazing. A really great sense of design style. Do you have a favorite (or three)?

KELLY: Oh man, Julian! Like everyone on our team, he's just totally bringing his A game to every cover. He has so nailed that perfect pulp-detective look for our book, and I adore it. If I had to pick a few favorites—probably *Hawkeye #1*, *Hawkeye #2*, *Hawkeye #7* (also my favorite issue, period), and the upcoming *Hawkeye #10*.

FOOM: How would you sum up Kate Bishop, her personality and her hero skills, to someone that's never read *Hawkeye*?

KELLY: Kate Bishop is all sass and never-give-up moxie. She's an extremely gifted bowman, and has a boatload of other talents, too—but she's also extremely flawed and relatable. She's a hero through and through, and she doesn't give up until she wins. Thus, she always wins. (*Laughter.*)

FOOM: Kate has a "go get 'em" attitude that routinely places her into sticky situations—but she also has a resolve and resourcefulness that serves her well in getting out of them. She's up for the challenge, in other words, even if she's

Kelly Thompson - Leonardo Romero
hawkeye
399¢
The adorable archer takes aim--
ON DANGER!
JULIAN TOTINO TEDESCO ▲

still learning, and that's endearing about her character.

KELLY: I like to think this "go get 'em" aspect of Kate is something that she and Clint share so deeply that it's basically become a quintessential Hawkeye trait. It's part of how they can survive considering they're often the (technically!) least powerful people in any super-hero scenario. They hold their own against the biggest bads in the universe, and alongside some of the most jaw-droppingly powerful heroes—and they do it with a shrug and the confidence of twenty heroes.

FOOM: The comic is set in Venice Beach, Los Angeles. Have you spent much time there? Any comments on what the setting/locale brings to the stories you tell?

KELLY: Yeah, I'm from California originally, and I lived in L.A. after college for about five years before moving to Manhattan. I love it there. I haven't been back in a while, so my version of L.A./Venice is likely a bit dated, but I think I still have a good grasp on what makes it such a special place, and I try my best to bring that unique California energy to the scripts. However, Leo and Jordie are the ones that really capture it so perfectly.

FOOM: The two-part Jessica Jones run shows a real kinship between the two characters. Definitely some hero worship there. How much of Jessica Jones' past did you model Kate's P.I. pursuits after?

KELLY: Well, I think Kate and Jessica are very different people, and thus they're very different P.I.s, but Kate absolutely looks up to Jess and knows that not only does she (Kate) have a lot to learn, but Jess has a lot to teach. They were magic together. I loved every minute of it, a real perfect chemistry in how they played off one another.

FOOM: One of the themes of your *Hawkeye* run is what are called "anchor points." In Kate's usage, it means the people who keep her grounded and focused on taking on life as it comes. When the book takes on its Legacy branding, what are the anchor points going to be? The dynamics of the supporting cast have been pleasingly slow simmering.

KELLY: Clint is and always will be one of Kate's primary anchor points, which is to both good and ill effect. Clint is a good man, mentor, and hero, but he's also a bit of an irresponsible and unpredictable wild card, and it's hard for that to be a point of stability for someone. Some of Kate's other anchor points (that have been breaking) are her family, and we'll be dealing with that in a big way for Legacy. It's hard to share a book with Kate—she shines so bright!—but she's built up a good little base of friends as her "L.A. family," and they have absolutely become new anchor points for her—she'll go to extreme lengths to protect them.

FOOM: Can you tease some of the guest-stars or bad guys we'll see as Kate's Legacy adventures unfold? Will Hawkguy make the scene? Any of her Yo Avengers pals? More Jessica Jones?

KELLY: I think at this point I'm allo to say that for *Hawkeye #12*, which standalone issue before we launch our Legacy storyline, we'll be ha Wolverine (Laura Kinney) and Gabb teaming up with Kate in L.A. for a c mission. It was really fun to write, anc have our Jessica Jones guest-arc c Michael Walsh coming back, so that really exciting for us. After that, for Legacy arc, we've got Clint coming onto the book—and I'm so excited a that. They have such a magic chem together. I'd love to have America an some of her Young Avengers crew po but we'll have to see what happens c the Legacy arc.

FOOM: Returning to the sense of hu in your writing style, it seems to have perfect amount for a super-hero b that doesn't take itself too serio but is still serious about the super-h stuff—if that makes sense! What kin sense of humor do you think Kate re on? She's at times goofy/sardo sarcastic/whimsical...

KELLY: One of my favorite things w been doing in this latest arc is that Ka "off"—because she's going through s big emotional things, she's not quite usual self, and her friends/colleagues h noticed. And yet, even with her being she never stops being the indefatig Kate. She has an almost absurdly bounc optimism and "can do" attitude, and e at her worst, it gets her through. In fo think it's when she's at her worst that attitude and approach to life actu propels her, helps her survive. Jes Jones said in *Hawkeye #6* that Kate to "make her own fun," and it's re true. And that aspect makes her emine readable and lovable.

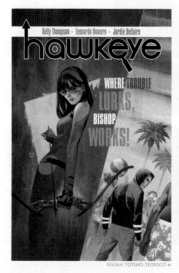

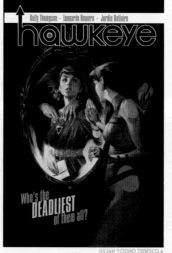

Kelly Thompson - Leonardo Romero - Jordie Bellaire
hawkeye
WHERE TROUBLE LURKS, BISHOP WORKS!
JULIAN TOTINO TEDESCO ▲

Kelly Thompson - Leonardo Romero - Jordie Bellaire
hawkeye
Who's the DEADLIEST of them all?
JULIAN TOTINO TEDESCO ▲

Kelly Thompson - Leonardo Romero - Jordie Bellaire
JULIAN TOTINO TE

)EADPOOL'S GUIDE TO DEADPOOL!

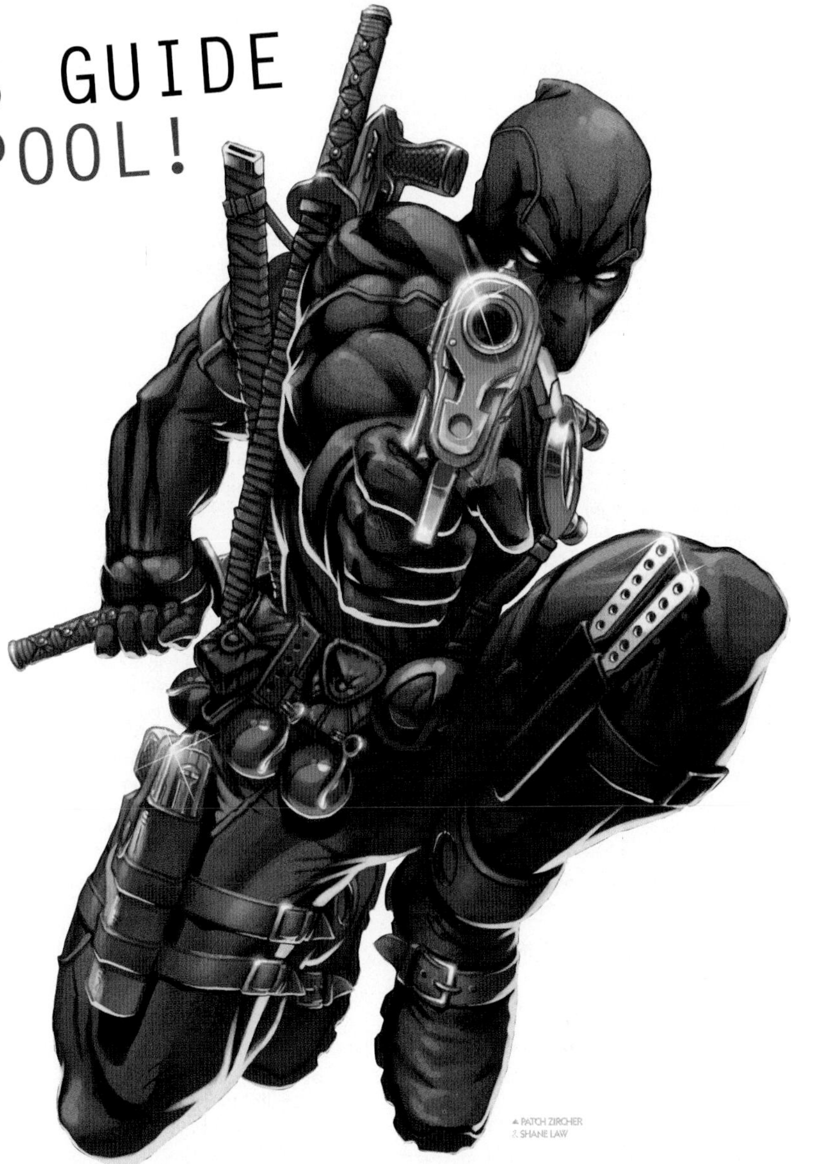
▲ PATCH ZIRCHER & SHANE LAW

t to read Deadpool comics but don't where to begin? Well, who better to ut the man himself! And the good thing 's his own favorite subject. Exclusively OOM, Wade Wilson selects some e tomes from his personal library— ot that personal library, we're talking llected-editions stash! (As told to Jess old.)

some reason, these last couple of , more and more people are stopping n the street to say: "Deadpool, we you! Where can we find more of zany adventures?" They also shout mum effort" at me like it's some sort of phrase. People are weird. But anyway, FOOM called asking me to pick my avorite Deadpool collected editions, I ed, hey, that's a great way to answer all doring fans in one go—so maybe I can ome peace. Maximum reward, minimum . Now there's a catchphrase. Without er a-doo-doo, on with the books!

DEADPOOL: BEGINNINGS OMNIBUS HC
New Mutants (1983) #98, Deadpool: The Circle Chase #1-4, Deadpool (1994) #1-4, and more!

start at the very beginning, which a ng nun once told me is a very good to start. This book kicks off with collector's classic *New Mutants #98,* nich Rob Liefeld and Fabian Nicieza how took my life and put it on the ed page, changing the course of comics ry—forever! Rob did an awesome of capturing my glorious image, though uld have used more pouches. The s dig pouches. Across this volume, see I went from standing on Cable's (not nsiderable) shoulders, to stealing the in his red-hot *X-Force* and other books, king my own fledgling steps into solo stardom in my first two limited series.

DEADPOOL BY JOE KELLY OMNIBUS HC
Deadpool (1997) #1-33 and more!

is where I really found my voice—and extra-strength yellow word balloons it s to contain it. Comic-book historians 're the ones who flunked out of history llege) speak of certain creators' runs in ently hushed tones. Miller on Daredevil. nson on Thor. Ditko on Speedball. n it comes to Kelly on Deadpool, they k in giddy excitement, stifling guffaws. Ed McGuinness on art sure could capture my good side, while Joe had a way of bringing it out, setting me on my heroic path to glory.

3 DEADPOOL & CABLE OMNIBUS HC
Cable & Deadpool #1-50 and more!

Back when this series first came out, would you believe top billing went to ol' Nathan Christopher Charles Dayspring Askani'son Stormborn of the House Summers, First of His Name, the Unburnt, Breaker of Chains, Mother of Dragons... Wait, I might have gotten distracted there. Let's just call him Cable. Well, it's Deadpool first on the Omnibus, one-eye! As for the contents, who better than Fabian Nicieza to reunite two great tastes that explode things great together—and recapture the volatile chemistry that made me and Cable icons of the nineties. If they remade *The Odd Couple* with, say, Ryan Reynolds and Josh Brolin, and threw in lots of guns, time travel and Bea Arthur jokes, they'd end up with something a little like this.

4 DEADPOOL BY DANIEL WAY OMNIBUS VOL. 1 HC
Wolverine: Origins #21-25, Deadpool (2008) #1-26, and more, on sale in February 2018!

When it comes to writing my adventures, there's no right way, and there's no wrong way. But there is a Daniel Way—and that involves not one, but two voices in my head. With my thoughts more confused than ever, and whacked-out hallucinations making matters even worse, Way picked a great time to slam me up against Wolverine in a knock-down, drag-out battle of guns, claws, swords, bazookas, bombs, and...a piano. Seriously, "X" on the floor, falling piano, the whole bit. Hilarious. That was the springboard from

which I dived back into my own book—which was bad news for the Skrulls, Norman Osborn, the Thunderbolts, and the simian assassin (assassimian?) Hit-Monkey. Plus, if you've ever asked, "Hey, why isn't Deadpool an X-Man?"—and believe me, many have—the answer is here.

5 DEADPOOL MINIBUS HC
Deadpool Kills the Marvel Universe #1-4, Deadpool Killustrated #1-4, Deadpool Kills Deadpool #1-4, Night of the Living Deadpool #1-4, and *Deadpool vs. Carnage #1-4*

One Deadpool book on the stands just isn't enough. A guy like me needs room to breathe. Only a seemingly endless supply of shorter stories could possibly capture every facet of my winning personality—not to mention all those other Wade Wilsons across the Multiverse. That's why I had no option but to become Marvel's king of the limited series—with no small help from Cullen Bunn, who took the wheel for all the tales in this "Minibus." Sometimes, when Spidey says "no killing" for the 37th time that day, or when I look in the mirror and don't see Danny Rand's handsome mug smiling back, I fantasize about murderizing every last one of the oh-so-perfect cape-and-tights brigade. In this book, I do. Or a version of me does, at least. There's plenty of other carnage, too—and also Carnage—as only Cullen could capture it. Hail to the bus driver, bus driver, Bunn!

6 DEADPOOL BY POSEHN & DUGGAN OMNIBUS HC
Deadpool (2012) #1-45 and more!

I'm the wisecracking, smart-talking Merc with the Mouth who just won't quit. So putting my words on the page is the work of two men. Surprising it took so long, then, for Marvel to hand my title to a comedy-writing team. But when they finally did, Brian Posehn and Gerry Duggan stepped forward to turn my world upside down. A secret daughter? A succubus queen for a wife? The darkest Deadpool tale ever told? These guys were supposed to be funny! Oh, wait, they were that, too. Not least in thinking they could turn in old inventory issues of Deadpool from the 1970s and '80s as their own work and get paid for it. What a pair of jokers!

9

7 DEADPOOL: BAD BLOOD OGN-HC

If you want to be taken seriously in the comics biz, you need to have a graphic novel. And my main man, Rob Liefeld, was just the guy to take me into the prestige format at long last (with help from Chris Sims and Chad Bowers). Thanks to the magic of flashbacks, Cable and his mutant Mouseketeers (you might remember them as X-Force) put in an appearance in an adventure that pits us against a new foe from my ever-murky past: Thumper. No, not the rabbit. Along the way, I jump rainbows on a freakin' unicorn. And you know how much I dig unicorns.

8 SPIDER-MAN/DEADPOOL BY JOE KELLY & ED McGUINNESS HC
Spider-Man/Deadpool #1-5, #8-10, #13-14 and *#17-18*, on sale in March 2018!

Never go back, they say. Screw that, say Joe Kelly and Ed McGuinness. The duo who cemented my place as one of the greatest characters in comics returned to do the same thing for Spider-Man—and I was only too happy to help out a friend. If you like your action with a heaping helping of bromance, this is the one for you. Spidey and I make for one hell of a double act—with Webs as the straight man, obvs. But prepare to be freaked out when our psycho "daughter," Itsy Bitsy, crawls up the water spout—she has the daddy issues to end all daddy issues. Whole long boxes full of 'em!

9 DESPICABLE DEADPOOL
Beginning with *Despicable Deadpool #287* in October 2017!

Which brings us all the way up to Marvel Legacy—and if anyone's the physical embodiment of that, then it's Deadpool! Let's take a little look-see at that checklist on page 7 and see what they have planned for my book... Wait a minute. "Despicable"—me? I'm loving the old-school alliteration, sure. And I dig the big number. But why not "Delightful Deadpool"? Or "Debonair Deadpool"? Or "Don't Give A @#$% What You Think Deadpool"? Anyway, sneaking a peek at Gerry Duggan's notes, it's gonna have old foes returning and "just wanting to get the hell out of Wade's orbit," while I'm my "own worst enemy." Well, maybe apart from Cable. Then there are these five words at the bottom that just sound like completely unrelated-yet-useful advice: "Don't co wounded animal." Well, that's it from good luck building your very own Dea library. And if you want me to cut the r when it's open, my rates are very reaso

1
DEADPOOL
BEGINNINGS
2
DEADPOOL
BY JOE KELLY
3
DEADPOOL & CABLE
4
5
DEADPOOL
MINIBUS
BUNN • TALAJIC • ESPIN
LOLLI • ROSANAS
6
DEADPOOL
BY POSEHN & DUG
7
DEADPOOL
BAD BLOOD
LIEFELD
SIMS
BOWERS
FAJARDO JR.
8

© BY MARYANN BATES

BY DUGAN TRODGLEN

After the industry-wide '90s bubble burst and Marvel filed for bankruptcy protection, the publisher's future appeared grim. One of the keys to emerging from bankruptcy was through innovations led by new President Bill Jemas and **Editor in Chief Joe Quesada**. Quesada was hired in 2000 after his own company, Event Comics (co-run by Jimmy Palmiotti), headed the well-received Marvel Knights imprint. Marvel Knights' approach and aesthetic was slowly adapted line-wide, and the publisher experienced a major resurgence. Quesada's tenure as EIC ended in 2011; he remains with the company as chief creative officer, with a hand not only in publishing, but other media as well—such as Marvel TV, the lineup of which includes his beloved Daredevil, the character with which he first made his mark at Marvel as editor and artist.

FOOM: You started at Marvel by editing small, tight line of comics with the Marvel Knights imprint. Were you surprised to get that call, and by how much creative freedom you were given?

QUESADA: Yes and no. It was a surprise to get a call from Marvel President Joe Calamari ("Joey Squid") out of the blue. We weren't quite sure what he wanted to talk about, but he started by saying that Marvel was in dire straits. He said he really admired the way Jimmy and I ran our own publishing company, Event Comics. We were a three-person company with no money and managed to really get our stuff out there using sheer energy and guerilla tactics. The questions he left us with were, "If you could do anything at Marvel, what would you do? How would you see Marvel going forward with you guys involved that might help improve our business?"

I ran to my apartment and put together a plan that was pretty much exactly what happened. We knew we wanted *Daredevil* and didn't think that would be a problem: The book was on the verge of being canceled.

The Punisher had been canceled, and the Inhumans and Black Panther didn't have books. But my idea was to go back to Joey Squid and say, "Give us the whole line. Let us be co-editors in chief." I knew if we asked for four books, he might give us one or two—but if we asked for more than we wanted, we'd get what we did want. So we went in and said, "Give us the whole line." And Joe said, "How about four books?" [*Laughs.*]

FOOM: After a couple of years at Marvel Knights, you were promoted to editor in chief.

QUESADA: You can't really call it a promotion, because Event Comics was hired on a contract to do Marvel Knights. In essence, when I was offered the job, I was hired away from my own company.

FOOM: What did that move—hiring the co-editor of its most forward-looking line—tell you about Marvel's vision of itself?

QUESADA: That they were desperate! [*Laughs.*]

We often talk about the time period. It really was the Wild West. With the exception of MK and some scattered projects here and there, everything was going down, and it was a struggle to sell anything. But those are the ebbs and flows of the comic-book industry that have been going on for decades. But this was probably the worst period we've ever, ever had.

So Marvel had this idea that they really wanted to shake things up. They had a guy in charge, Bill Jemas, who was a great risk-taker and in many ways a visionary. He took great chances—and the chances he took, part of which was making a change at EIC, seemed to work out. We teamed up to do some crazy stuff. Suddenly, sales started to tick up, and conventions that used to be ghost towns were full of people of all walks and sizes. So little by little, success started to come back.

FOOM: Aside from the ups and downs of the industry, another cycle seems to be between looking forward, trying new things, and looking back, drawing more on nostalgia and traditionalism. Right now, we seem to be in a cycle that does

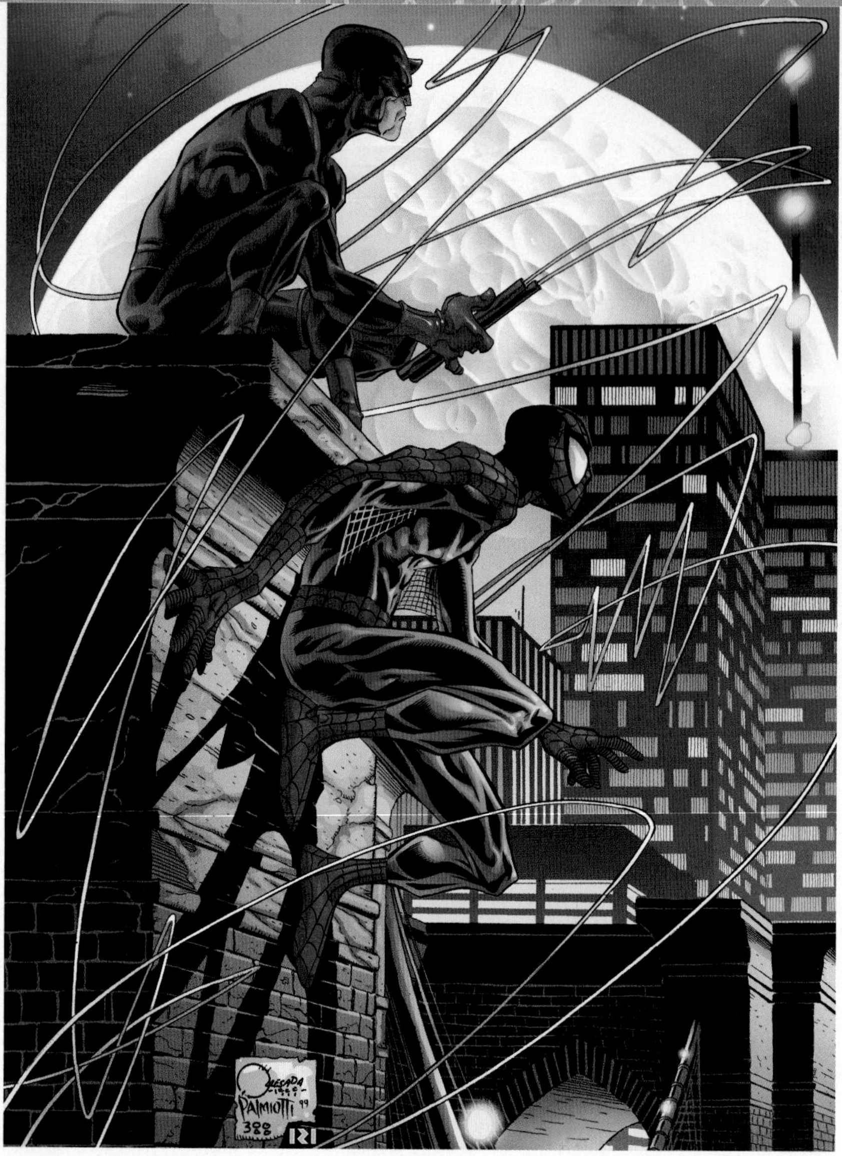

JOE QUESADA, JIMMY PALMIOTTI & RICHARD ISANOVE▲

incorporate nostalgia. What was it about the forward-looking approach that was so important at that time?

QUESADA: First, let me say that, as an industry, we have a very bad habit of always pointing at our own demise. Even when we're doing well, we wonder, "How much longer until it all collapses?"

Our goal at the start—mine, Bill's, all of the great writers and artists we worked with—was to bring in new readers and get them excited about comics, and to bring back lapsed readers. We did that by simplifying. When we came on board, Marvel was very continuity-driven. I remember reading one book in particular—I won't mention the title—but it was a 22-page comic, and 16 pages were flashbacks to previous things that happened to this character over the years. That was the world we were living in.

Now, probably the best comic of that period was Kurt Busiek and Alex Ross' *Marvels* [*A must-read look at the history of the Marvel Universe through the lens of photojournalist Phil Sheldon. -Ed.*]. It's an absolute work of art, but it also tapped into a theme that was going on in comics at the time: It took you back to that classic time period. It gave a warm, glowing feeling to the older fan, like myself at the time, so I loved *Marvels*. What happened, though, is that the industry started doing a lot of books like that: books that looked backward instead of forward. And that's death, because you are sacrificing the new reader who might be coming in for the sake of the reader you already have, who will probably cycle out one day. Then you have neither reader. That is why it was so important to get away from telling stories that kept new readers at arm's length.

FOOM: Once you laid the foundation—making the books accessible, using continuity as a tool and not a crutch, keeping the titles fairly independent of one another—eventually you felt comfortable once again cohering the Marvel Universe into something that co but didn't have to, move as a unit. Th was greater interaction among titles, eventually the crossover-event con returned—first with *House of M*, culminating with the watershed succes *Civil War*. How did you know the time right to make this move?

QUESADA: It was organic. When decided to do the crossovers, we wante make sure that the main series itself was contained, and if we were going to h ancillary titles, that they are not neces for the reader to grasp the main story. should be satellite stories that play o the core event, and hopefully deepe *Civil War* was, to me, the perfect const for the kind of crossover we wanted to from that point on. The smaller stories could be told within that event really exc us and excited the creators. And when creators are excited, they are going to their absolute best work.

FOOM: Your tenure was also marked the establishment of several publis lines, none more significant than Ultimate line. Was that in the works bef you were EIC?

QUESADA: The timing was that Bill Je came on as VP while we were doing Ma Knights, and he had this idea for this thing l called the Ultimate Universe. It was to b separate universe geared toward youn readers, with a Ground Zero approac our heroes. Then Bill started to meet editors to put together sort of off- beaten-path creative teams to launch *Sp Man* and *X-Men*, but the writers offerec were the same writers who were already the regular books. So he came into my of and asked if we knew any newer wri that could fill these slots. At that time, I just received a pack of independent co from Brian Michael Bendis, who was not known at the time. I had hired Brian to w *Daredevil*, so I showed his stuff to Bill said, "This guy has a tremendous voice, he might be your *X-Men* guy."

The next day he came in and said, "Love guy. I want him on *Spider-Man*. Who do have for *X-Men*?" [*Laughs.*] I told him ab this guy Mark Millar and gave him sc issues of the Wildstorm Comics series *Authority* that featured some pretty out-th Avengers analogues in them. I knew h either be really offended or realize h amazingly talented this guy is. The next he came in just over the moon, saying we to get this guy for *X-Men*. At that point, started bringing me in more and more the Ultimate Universe meetings, and it shortly after that that I was hired as EIC. away we went.

FOOM: It goes without saying that tra paperbacks and other collected editi

a major component of comic-book lishing. How did you know that ected editions were the future?

ESADA: All you had to do was do the ı, but for some reason Marvel just didn't it as a business model. All you had to was look across town—not just at our ls, but at Image, at Dark Horse. We e leaving money on the table. I guess fear was that having trades would make ple not want to buy the individual issues, I guess that kind of made some sort of hematical sense, but it didn't make sense ill and me.

ce the industry was driven by the ect market, the newsstand became the der that eventually got people into comic shop. That was going the way he dinosaur, and we needed a new der system. We figured that getting product into other venues would only ve the direct market better by helping g in new readers. And it did. It served rvel tremendously. Look, this was not a ius move—it was an obvious move— for some reason it was not obvious to rvel at that time.

a similar way, Marvel's coloring and duction on their books, before Marvel ghts, was abysmal. Image was doing utiful full-on computer coloring, as was ittle company Event Comics. Marvel was doing this old-school color that looked rible next to the new techniques. One of other stipulations I gave Bill when I was d was that we had to go to computer oring and better production.

OM: In 2001, Marvel abandoned Comics Code Authority—the archaic -regulation device created by the nics industry in the 1950s to appease government. Eventually, the other blishers followed, and the CCA "stamp approval" was replaced by ratings tems similar to video games or movies. sure the decision to get out from under CCA was easy, but was it difficult to ke happen?

ESADA: No! [*Laughs.*] Surprisingly not. ld Bill that we had to get out of it, and at the time I had no idea what would be involved with doing so. I only knew I hated seeing that stamp. First of all, its history is an insidious one. Not only does it represent the government's attempt to censor creativity based on false information, but it also represented the industry just taking it. I mean, I didn't live in that time period, and they were trying to save the industry, but I hated everything about it every time I looked at it. And not only that, but we paid for the pleasure of being censored! We paid to have our books sent out and scoured, and sent back with notes to fix the most ridiculous things.

When I told Bill we had to get out of it, he just said, "Okay!" Mind you, this did not go down well with other publishers. DC contacted us, Archie Comics contacted us. Everyone was in a panic. So we had a fateful meeting in Marvel's conference room with the heads of Archie and DC. They were giving us a history lesson, and the Archie guys had a portfolio with yellowed newspaper clippings from the period. [*Laughs.*] I remember one of them pointed to one of the clippings and said, "See? If we don't stay with the Comics Code, senators will come after us!" While I was stifling a laugh, Bill looked at him and said, "Frankly, I'm more scared of Sentinels than I am of senators." [*Laughs.*] That was the end of the meeting. So we left the CCA, eventually DC and Archie did as well, and you know what happened? Nothing!

FOOM: Without tooting your own horn more than you are comfortable doing, what can you say about the difference between Marvel from the day you sat down in the EIC chair and the day you turned it over to Axel Alonso?

QUESADA: There are interviews from my early days on the job where I said my goal as editor in chief is to tell some great stories, not break anything, and hopefully leave things right where I found them, hopefully in better shape than when I found them. My other hope was that I would know when it was time to leave on my own. I was lucky enough for that to happen. I was given the position of chief creative officer while I was still EIC. And shortly after that, I talked to then-Publisher Dan Buckley and told him

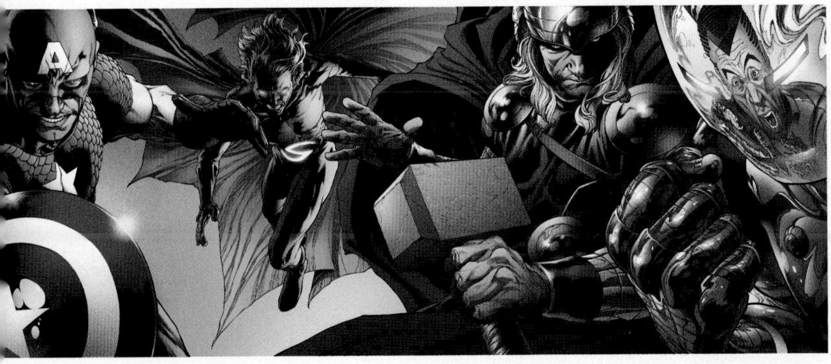

QUESADA, DANNY MIKI & RICHARD ISANOVE

HAIL TO THE CHIEFS

by John Rhett Thomas

Keeping the Marvel Universe together is a demanding job. This list includes everyone who oversaw the company's line of comics—spanning the Timely, Atlas, and Marvel eras. Most were called simply "editor," until Jim Shooter took the title "editor in chief."

1940–1941, Joe Simon
Martin Goodman's first hire as editor, Simon oversaw the company's comic-book expansion, including the launch of his and Jack Kirby's *Captain America Comics*.

1941–1942, Stan Lee
As a teenager, Lee oversaw Goodman's burgeoning comics empire until World War II service called.

1942–1945, Vince Fago
Fago, a Timely humor artist/writer, kept Timely going while Stan served.

1946–1972, Stan Lee
Lee guided the company through the ups and downs of the '40s and '50s until lightning struck in 1961 with *Fantastic Four* and the Marvel Age of Comics began.

1972–1974, Roy Thomas
Stan's right-hand man took over after his boss's promotion to president and publisher. Thomas oversaw Marvel's expansion into horror comics, licensed material, and black-and-white magazines.

1974–1975, Len Wein
1975–1976, Marv Wolfman
Comics fans turned pros, "LenMarv" arrived at Marvel together and picked up where Thomas had left off. Wein's tenure saw the creation of the All-New, All-Different X-Men, while Wolfman managed the publisher's line of black-and-white magazines before taking control of all of Marvel's publications.

1976, Gerry Conway
Amazing Spider-Man writer Conway's tenure lasted only a couple months.

1976–1978, Archie Goodwin
Star Wars came to Marvel during Goodwin's run, and female super heroes Spider-Woman and Ms. Marvel got their first titles.

1978–1987, Jim Shooter
Shooter launched the age of the limited series and the multicharacter crossover event, and created the New Universe.

1987–1994, Tom DeFalco
DeFalco saw the X-Men and Spider-Man universes expand, and new talent such as Todd McFarlane, Rob Liefeld, and Jim Lee flourish.

1994–1995, Mark Gruenwald/Bob Harras/ Bob Budiansky/Bobbie Chase/Carl Potts
For a brief period, Marvel split editor-in-chief duties among its group editors.

1995–2000, Bob Harras
Harras saw Marvel through its bankruptcy years, which included the years-long Spider-Man Clone Saga.

2000–2011, Joe Quesada
Quesada helped revitalize the company with storytelling innovations and new approaches to characters.

2011–Present, Axel Alonso
As Marvel has become a worldwide entertainment powerhouse, Alonso guides the company's fortunes through Marvel Legacy and beyond.

HOW "THE BOY" FOLLOWED "THE MAN"
ROY THOMAS LOOKS BACK ON HIS TIME AS EDITOR IN CHIEF
by Dugan Trodglen

When Stan Lee stepped aside as editor in chief in 1972, his natural successor was Roy Thomas, Marvel's most active writer at the time. Thomas was the first of his kind: a superfan turned creator, who grew up on comics and then turned that love into a profession. This provided him with an entirely different perspective than those who had come before—not only as a writer, but as an editor.

Thomas guided Marvel through the dawn of the "Bronze Age"—an era marked by line expansion; the acquisition of licensed titles such as *Star Wars* and *Conan the Barbarian* (the latter of which Thomas himself wrote for decades); the emergence of the All-New, All-Different X-Men; the introduction of new concepts including the Defenders, the Invaders, Ghost Rider, and *What If?*; the broadening of genres within publishing; and the influx of young, fresh blood into the Bullpen, which led to comics that were maturing with their audience.

• •

FOOM: Before you were EIC, you led the wave of younger creators joining the Marvel Bullpen in the latter half of the '60s. How do you think that infusion of youth affected Marvel going forward?

Thomas: It gave Marvel (and DC, which also began to hire young artists and writers) a new lease on life, as the people who'd entered the field in the '40s (there'd been relatively few new guys since) were aging and new blood was needed. But then, it always is, isn't it?

FOOM: Replacing Stan, you didn't just have to fill the shoes of an iconic editor, but also the only EIC Marvel had had up to that point. What was the transition like?

Thomas: Stan just told me about the change, appointed me story editor (the EIC came a week or three later), and we got back to work. There were changes, but they didn't happen all at once. Stan was still in charge, still acting like the head editor, though as time went by his publishing duties grew and he came to leave more and more to me.

FOOM: Although you grew up the world's greatest super hero fan, you had a hand in expanding the concept to include horror characters such as Ghost Rider and the martial artist Iron Fist. What led to the diversification?

Thomas: We knew that we needed to appeal to more readers than just those of super hero comics. Of course, many super hero fans also liked Ghost Rider, Iron Fist, et al.—but we thought we might grab a few readers who were more interested in horror/supernatural or martial arts than in super heroes, and to some extent that worked. But they were still super hero comics, in their way.

FOOM: You engineered the incorporation of the *Star Wars* comic book into Marvel's publishing line. Much like today, it was a boon for the publisher, and Jim Shooter is quoted as saying Marvel "would have gone out of business" without the *Star Wars* license. Hyperbole aside, how did that affect Marvel?

Thomas: Jim probably meant what he said. I thought *Star Wars* might be a fun project to do when George Lucas' media projects director, Charles Lippincott, brought it to me in February 1976 (more than a year before the movie opened—it was only then beginning filming in North Africa). It turned out to make the company so much money in 1977–78 that it bought time for Marvel to make some moves to adjust to the changing realities of the comic-book marketplace amid high inflation, etc. Marvel's then president, James Galton, said of me to a mutual friend about a decade and a half ago: "He made me rich." So I assume that Jim's statement was not meant as hyperbole.

FOOM: Unlike today, editors and EICs were very active as writers as well during the '60s and '70s. How did that affect your role as EIC?

Thomas: It left me less time for it than I should have had, because I had to write on evenings and weekends. Small wonder I gave up after a bit over two years... and that none of my next four successors lasted as long as I had!

it was time for me to cycle out. It was [...] for someone new. We took a year to gr[...] Axel, and I think that worked out great.

But as for my tenure, look, I was part [...] tremendous team, a tremendous crea[...] community. I was also lucky enough [...] be part of a very rare American suc[...] story: a company that went from noth[...] to exploding into popular culture [...] enormous success from the time of Stan [...] to the point when the company went pu[...] with its stock offerings, to then total collo[...] in the '90s. I was there as part of an incred[...] team to see it from collapse to resurgenc[...] not just to where it was, but beyond, all [...] way to merging with a company like Dis[...] So I was very lucky to have been the [...] sitting in the chair, and to be able to m[...] on within the company and hand the r[...] over to Axel of a company that I think w[...] better shape than when I started.

There is one thing that I think I can sor[...] toot my own horn about. When Stan Lee [...] in charge of the company, there was a [...] prominent, and vocal, face to the comp[...] He gave the creators a face and a voice [...] well. We lost that after Stan. We didn't h[...] someone who was really out there. That [...] something I wanted to bring back. I was re[...] happy to be able to do that, to put a f[...] on Marvel. And not just me, but the crea[...] and editors as well. We really got out th[...] and talked to fandom and helped create [...] kind of buzz that contributed to our succ[...]

FOOM: Speaking of Stan, he is argua[...] the only EIC that had a greater imp[...] than you on Marvel. Did you ever speak [...] Stan about the job or get advice?

QUESADA: Yes, absolutely. I would talk [...] Stan about Marvel and about our charact[...] before I was editor in chief. I would c[...] call Stan from the Marvel Knights office, [...] Marvel would be furious with me. "Wh[...] this guy who's calling Stan?" [*Laughs*.] But [...] one else was calling him. I sent the outli[...] of the first four Marvel Knights books [...] Stan, and he gave me some notes on the[...] which was fantastic. And he was so happy [...] get them because he said that no one w[...] sending him Marvel stuff. We would t[...] about how to create and build a perf[...] Marvel character. It was invaluable.

We talked sometimes about his EIC tenu[...] but it was such a different time. There we[...] similarities in terms of plugging creators, [...] positive outlook, and keeping a cheery f[...] regardless of what was happening, and [...] keeping in touch with fandom. But it was a [...] different, because Stan was also writing [...] of those books! My job was a bit differe[...] We were bailing water out of the ship. I h[...] been a writer/artist before my tenure, so [...] were both creators—but to me Stan, alo[...] with Jack Kirby, is the greatest comic crea[...] of all time.

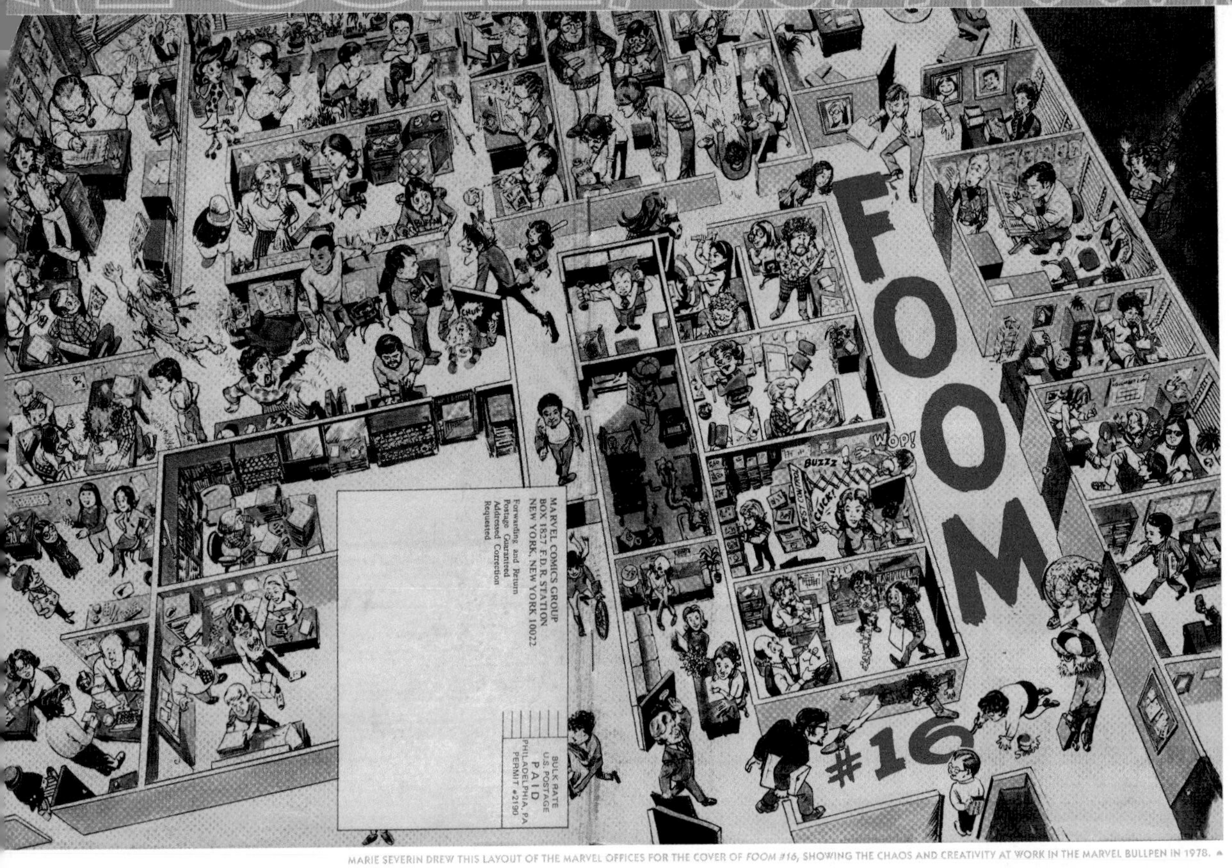
FOOM
#16
WOP!
BUZZ
MARVEL COMICS GROUP
BOX 1827 F.D.R. STATION
NEW YORK, NEW YORK 10022
Forwarding and Return
Postage Guaranteed
Address Correction
Requested
BULK RATE
US POSTAGE
PAID
PHILADELPHIA, PA
PERMIT #2190

MARIE SEVERIN DREW THIS LAYOUT OF THE MARVEL OFFICES FOR THE COVER OF *FOOM #16*, SHOWING THE CHAOS AND CREATIVITY AT WORK IN THE MARVEL BULLPEN IN 1978. ▲

A STRETCH IN THE PEN

\ (VERY) BRIEF HISTORY OF THE MARVEL BULLPEN

\ BEARD

ın Lee's penchant for distilling the cal from the mundane included the ologizing of not only his writers and ts, but also the office staff responsible he production of Marvel's comic books. e so-called Marvel Bullpen was born of necessity to conduct the business ublishing comics—though to Marvel's itude of fans, eagerly devouring Lee's pen Bulletins" on the books' letters es, one might think it sprang forth from head not unlike the goddess Athena Zeus' enlightened noggin.

e term "bullpen" is most notably ciated with baseball, denoting the ı in which relief pitchers warm up ɔre entering the game. But in Stan s "Bullpen Bulletins," he conjured up image of artists and writers banding ether to produce the best stories sible from their blood, sweat, and s.

the beginning, Lee *was* the Bullpen, for most part. Next came Flo Steinberg, "Gal Friday." Steinberg's standing not be diminished: The very idea of vel's office staff did not exist before —and while she didn't write *Amazing der-Man* or draw *Avengers*, her spirit work ethic set the tone for Bullpens to e, and persists to this day.

In the earliest days of Marvel, circa 1963, the Bullpen basically existed as a two-person operation: Lee was writer, editor, and art director; Steinberg was secretary and gatekeeper. Sol Brodsky would come into the cramped Marvel digs at 655 Madison Ave. to help with production, corrections, printing—the works—but was not yet a regular employee. That happy day came with a move up the street to 635 Madison Ave. and a bigger space—large enough for the two-person business to welcome a third cog into the machine. With Brodsky on staff, the three flew through their days at a frantic pace while other offices around them marveled at their efficiency and energy. It happened in one room—with a separate office for the editor, natch—and it shouldn't have worked. But somehow, it did.

As the Marvel line of titles grew, so did its Bullpen. Lee hired artist Marie Severin to assist Brodsky in production—she soon started on art chores as well—and from there the little company expanded to match the universe of super heroes within its publications. Before long, Lee, Brodsky, Steinberg and Severin welcomed letterers such as Art Simek and Sam Rosen into the furious fold, and they too were elevated into a kind of superstardom through Lee's perilous presentations of their personalities—artfully accentuated—in his "Bullpen Bulletins."

The end of the 1960s brought more change. Marvel switched printers, raised its 12-cent cover price to 15, and increased its output due to company owner Martin Goodman's deal with a new distributor. Despite the happy news behind the scenes, a note of sadness pervaded the Bullpen Bulletins when Lee announced the departure of stalwart Jack Kirby in early 1970.

Throughout the 1960s, Marvel saw even more new employees cross its threshold.

Artist John Romita Sr., who had worked for Lee in the 1950s, had thought he was done with comics, but Lee persuaded him to come aboard anyway. Most famously, he took over *Amazing Spider-Man* after Steve Ditko's departure. But he had a role behind the scenes as well.

"I asked Stan if I could work in the Bullpen a couple of days a week because I couldn't get my work done at home with two kids," Romita recalls. "That quickly became four, then five days, and then Stan began using me as a correction artist, which shortly led to me becoming a sort of 'art director.' Gradually, I began giving young artists Stan's take on the Marvel Way to tell a story with pictures... Thirty years slipped by. Sounds impossible."

As the Swingin' Seventies came around, the Bullpen became a training ground for new recruits at Marvel's new digs at 575 Madison Ave., and the production team found room there to spread out and perhaps discover desks of their own.

In 1972, when "The Man" finally accepted a somewhat-higher office as president and publisher, Marvel's then-40 books fell under the ever-watchful eye of Romita, its first art director beyond Lee himself.

Romita made it a family affair roughly 10 years into his tenure when his wife, Virginia, started helping him with filing and correspondence. Like many at Marvel, the part-time position grew into full-time work, and the Romita duo saw another 20 years pass working together.

"The time flew by, and it led to great times and innovations like Romita's Raiders," the artist notes, pointing out his personal team of production assistants who ran "raids" on aspects of the art that needed either a gentle nudge or sometimes a big push to fall into line. "We gave young artists a chance to learn how to tell stories the Marvel Way. One of those with talent stood out: John Romita Jr. I was also there to do many promotional projects like the Macy's Thanksgiving Day Parade balloon, coloring books, etc."

Luminaries such as John Verpoorten—who later became production manager—Morrie Kuramoto, Frank Giacoia, and Mike Esposito worked side by side in the office with the Romitas to keep the Marvel engine chugging along, and ensuring a look and style to the titles that Lee had inaugurated years before.

Many longtime Marvel Bullpenners can trace the lineage of their comic-book careers back to the Romitas' tutelage among the "Raiders."

Severin somehow captured the zeitgeist of those days in one amazing drawing. In 1976, for the sixteenth issue of FOOM, she laid out what was basically a caricature of the Marvel offices and its denizens. In the sprawling, somewhat irreverent view of the House of Ideas' rooms and hallways, nearly every employee could be seen creating the chaos that all Marvel fans knew went on each day there. Now fans had a visual document to cement the fantasy life of the Bullpen in their fevered brains.

In 1978, after a steady profusion of editors in chief following Lee's departure, Marvel promoted editor Jim Shooter to the position, and the Marvel Universe would never be the same as it headed

into another new decade. Lee moved to Los Angeles in 1980 to work on larger projects such as Marvel films and TV shows. Business continued, but not always as usual. Shooter reinstated a throwback Bullpen Bulletins in the comics in 1981, a column more like Lee's with mentions of weddings and promotions, births and deaths. One of those passings was that of longtime Bullpenner Kuramoto in 1985.

New World Pictures purchased Marvel in 1986; by the next year, Shooter was out as editor in chief, and Tom DeFalco was in. Together with new Executive Editor Mark Gruenwald, DeFalco oversaw another increase in the number of Marvel books on the stands, as well as maintaining the Bullpen Bulletins page to ensure that Marvel's personalities would continue to receive their due.

Among those Bullpen personalities was Dan Crespi, a letterer and inker who went on to become production manager until his death in 1985. His daughter, Susan, cites her father as the reason she has "comics in my blood."

"Growing up, he would always tell stories of Bullpen life, and it sounded like a fun place to work," Crespi says. "After college, I worked as a calligrapher in a scroll studio until I was let go in the early '90s. That fateful day I ran into my cousin, Nel Yomtov, on the subway platform. He was working as an editor at Marvel. I told him what had transpired, and he set up an introduction with one of the letterers, Jim Novak, who then trained me. When Jim felt I was ready, I was able to get my first

freelance gig. A few months later, the was an opening in the Bullpen for a letterer—and 25 years later, I'm still h

"During office hours, I did lette corrections, cover copy, and desi logos, all by hand as it was before digital age. Once computers came the picture, my role changed to di compositor. I worked my way up supervising the Bullpen and the freel letterers as the production manager job these days is more administrative anything else. I work closely with c departments to make sure that sys are running smoothly, and that files g press and are print-ready. I troubles problems that arise at the eleventh ho

Crespi says her greatest joy a Bullpenner comes from being in a pos to give others the chance to break into business. "I feel like in some small wa able to give back the opportunity that given to me," she says.

The dawn of the 1990s offered up a Marvel president, Ron Perelman, and happy occasion of a sales spike.

Another 1990s entrant into the hallo halls of the House of Ideas and the c call of the Bullpen was artist Scott Kc After receiving a referral from fe artist Bob Layton for an interview John Romita, Kolins was offered a spo the corrections team once its head viewed his portfolio.

"Besides the advantage of being in Marvel offices every day and being to ask the John Romita questions and tips," Kolins says of his Bullpen time, "

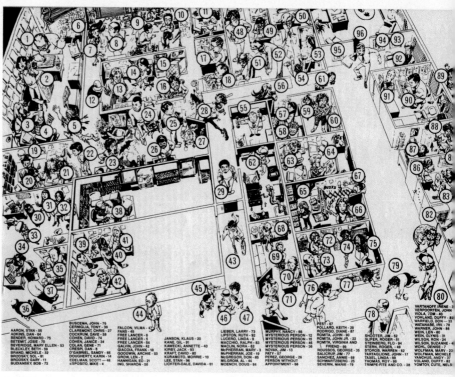

AARON, STAN - 55	BUSCEMA, JOHN - 76	FALCON, VILMA - 42	LIEBER, LARRY - 73	MURPHY, NANCY - 66	PEST - 67	SHOOTER, JIM - 52

AARON, STAN - 55
ADKINS, DAN - 64
BENDER, HOWARD - 75
BETEMIT, JOSIE - 70
BEVERIDGE, MARY ELLEN - 53
BLECKLEY, BETH - 55
BRAND, MICHELE - 32
BRODSKY, SOL - 81
BRODSKY, GARY - 11
BUDIANSKY, BOB - 72

BUSCEMA, JOHN - 76
CERNIGLIA, TONY - 39
CLAREMONT, CHRIS - 27
COCKRUM, DAVE - 58
COHEN, DAVID - 74
COHEN, JANICE - 34
COLAN, GENE - 71
CRESPI, JAN - 9
D'GABRIEL, SANDY - 65
DOUGHERTY, KARIN - 14
EDELMAN, SCOTT - 46
eSPOSITO, MIKE - 4

FALCON, VILMA - 42
FANS - 45
FREE LANCER - 6
FREE LANCER - 8
FREE LANCER - 54
GALVIN, JOHN - 42
GIACOIA, FRANK - 19
GOODWIN, ARCHIE - 50
GROW, LEN - 2
HANNIGAN, ED - 21
ING, SHARON - 56

JANSON, KLAUS - 20
KANE, GIL - 91
KAWECKI, ANNETTE - 43
KIRBY, JACK - 93
KRAFT, DAVID - 80
KURAMOTO, MORRIE - 19
LEE, STAN - 84
LICHTER-DALE, DAVIDA - 61

LIEBER, LARRY - 73
LIPSTON, RUTH - 92
LUCERO, LARRY - 5
MACCHIO, RALPH - 83
MACLIN, NORA - 63
McPHERRAN, MARY - 3
McPHERRAN, JOE - 59
McGREGOR, DON - 85
MILGROM, AL - 44
MOENCH, DOUG - 84

MURPHY, NANCY - 66
MYSTERIOUS PERSON - 12
MYSTERIOUS PERSON - 15
MYSTERIOUS PERSON - 35
NOVAK, JIM - 13
PATY - 57
PEREZ, GEORGE - 26
PERSON WITHOUT APPOINTMENT - 68

PEST - 67
POLLARD, KEITH - 29
RODRIGO, DIANE - 87
ROMITA, JOHN - 90
ROMITA, JOHN JR - 22
ROMITA, VIRGINIA AND FRIEND - 89
ROUSSOS, GEORGE - 35
SALICRUP, JIM - 77
SANCHEZ, ANNE - 68
SCHWARTZBERG - 25
SEVERIN, MARIE - 79

SHOOTER, JIM - 52
SLIFER, ROGER - 51
STERNBERG, FLO - 34
STERN, ROGER - 49
STOPJD, WARREN - 62
TARTAGLIONE, JOHN - 17
TAXEL, LINDA - 58
THOMAS, ROY - 95
TRIMPE-FITE AND CO. - 28

VARTANOFF, IRENE - 3
VERPOORTEN, JOHN
VIOLA, TOM - 40
VOHLAND, DON - 3
WARFIELD, DON - 33
WATANABE, IRV - 78
WARNER, JOHN - 44
WEIN, LEN - 60
WEIN, GLYNIS - 31
WILSON, RON - 3
WILSON, SUZANNE - 4
WOHL, DENISE - 7
WOLFMAN, MARY - 23
WOLFMAN, MICHELE
YANCHUS, ANDY - 37
VOLAND, DUFFY - 82
YOMTOV, CUTE, NELS

truly one of the nicest guys in comics."
hile much of the work could be spiring—minor corrections to larger es of art—Kolins relished the moments n he could do bigger work.
here are two pieces of art I happily ember working on... a couple of Michael den *Doctor Strange* and *Ghost Rider* ers that needed the empty old corner box filled in [with art] because Marvel making a poster book from them, and ing white dotted Zip-A-Tone over an n Davis–Mark Farmer *Excalibur* cover."
olins found that while his position ntially consisted of support work, e were times when he could fight for stic integrity.
One Michael Golden piece was ecially cool for me because the editor nted a whole leg redrawn as he thought den had drawn it poorly," Kolins s. "I went up the chain of command to plete the leg and its boot as Michael intended—to the best of my ability— how the junior editor wanted it. You 't 'fix' Michael Golden!"
he times were definitely a-changin'. rvel declared bankruptcy in 1996, but a kind of white knight charge up in the n of new owner ToyBiz in 1998. In-house, old ways of T-squares, paste-ups, and te correction fluid were giving way to e-of-the-art computer software, which course prompted the Marvel Bullpen to its game to stay current and increase ciency.
an Carr recalls those times as exciting, en new technology meant new ways to better work.
Longtime friend and colleague is Eliopoulos was able to get me an rview on April Fool's Day, 1991," Carr s. "I was hired by Virginia Romita as nighttime typesetter that day. And I came a full-time staffer on September d. I had the first Macintosh computer in publishing department—the desktop-blishing era had recently begun—and spearheaded all digital processes for nufacturing a comic, from scanning and coloring, to lettering and printing, etc. I was eventually promoted from production manager to production director."

Carr says one of the real joys of his position was being able to create the production workflows that the company uses to this day. "There are many talented individuals in the comics industry, and I was able to give many their start in the Marvel Bullpen," he says proudly. "I continue to watch in awe the talent in this industry, and I am grateful that Marvel has allowed me to do so for so long."

Today, Carr is Marvel's executive director of publishing technology, which sounds like a far cry from the days of a single room crammed with production assistants. Eliopoulos now runs Virtual Calligraphy, the company that letters the majority of Marvel's books, another change from a time when all lettering was done by hand and in-house. Chief among those who developed that in-house lettering system was Dave Sharpe.

"I came on staff under Virginia Romita in 1990 into the lettering section of the Bullpen," Sharpe says. "Everything was still being done by hand, and my job was to mimic lettering styles and do corrections on the lettering, which would be on overlays, or the actual art—back when lettering was actually done on the art boards! Around the year 2000, computers and fonts were introduced to comics, and I helped develop a lettering department. A few years later, lettering became fully outsourced.

"Learning the lettering-by-hand skill, and then evolving to computer lettering, and then continuing to letter in this business is a huge deal to me. And working alongside *legends* like John Romita Sr. and Michael Golden was a dream come true."

The new millennium brought even more fresh faces to the Bullpen as Marvel merrily marched into yet another exciting era with new Editor in Chief Joe Quesada and new President Bill Jemas. Among the those fresh faces of 2001 was writer, editor, and novelist Bob Greenberger, who felt the weight of history in the position he'd taken on, despite the stretch of years between him and those nascent days of Stan and Flo and Sol.

"One of the thrills about being hired at Marvel was that I would be tasked with overseeing the fabled Bullpen," he says. "Back in the 1960s, it was a tiny operation since there were just a few titles. When I got there, the company was putting out something like 60 titles, and the Bullpen had about a dozen people plus an in-house lettering department, which I would eventually come to oversee as well. It was also a time of transition as digital corrections and receipt of digital art files was becoming more commonplace.

"I was hired as director of publishing operations, and production was part of my initial portfolio. Many of the faces around me were young and incredibly enthusiastic, hardworking people who grew up as comics fans, as thrilled as I was to be working there. Anchoring the department's history was Assistant Production Manager Susan Crespi, whose father, Danny, was Marvel's art/production supervisor.

"Once I gained the lettering team, we began designing a digital workflow to make it easier for pages to go from editorial to proofreading—the lovely, late Flo Steinberg—to production to the printer."

Today, the Marvel Bullpen operates in a world perhaps undreamt of by its founders nearly 60 years ago. Writers and artists who ply their trade almost solely within the realm of computers, and those who receive their work and move it into production and publication do the same.

The Bullpen rolled with the times and worked according to the technology and the limitations of each decade. The end result is the same: Comics are comics, and the reader enjoys them whether or not they are aware of the men and women behind the scenes who make them happen.

However, thanks to Stan Lee's myth-making magic and the spirit of its denizens, the Bullpen will always retain an air of chaos and creativity in the Hallowed Halls of the House of Ideas.

BECAUSE YOU DEMANDED IT!
HERE'S A VERITABLE ROGUES' GALLERY OF CANDID PHOTOS, FEATURING JUST ABOUT EVERYBODY IN THE WHOLE BLAMED BULLPEN! IN CASE YOU'RE WONDERING HOW TO FIND YOUR FAVORITE, THEY'RE ALL IN ALPHABETICAL ORDER! AND SO, WITHOUT FURTHER ADO, HERE ARE THE MUG SHOTS! CAUTION!.. THESE PHOTOS MAY SELF-DESTRUCT!
STAN LEE
NEAL ADAMS
DAN ADKINS
DICK AYERS
SOL BRODSKY
JOHN BUSCEMA
SAL BUSCEMA
SHARON COHEN
GENE COLAN
JOHNNY CRAIG
BILL EVERETT
GARY FRIEDRICH
STAN G.
ARCHIE GOODWIN
SAM GRAINGER
DON HECK
AL HEWETSON
JEAN SIMEK IZZO
GIL KANE
JACK "KING" KIRBY
MORRIE KURAMOTO
SUZAN LANE
LARRY LIEBER
TONY MORTELLARO
TOM PALMER
PAUL REINMAN
JOHN ROMITA
SAM ROSEN
STU SCHWARTZBERG
JOHN SEVERIN
MARIE SEVERIN
SYD SHORES
ARTIE SIMEK
JOE SINNOTT
JIM STERANKO
JOHN TARTAGLIONE
JEAN THOMAS
ROY THOMAS
HERB TRIMPE
GEORGE TUSKA
JOHN VERPOORTEN
From left to right: Stan, Marie, John R., and Unidentified Friend.
THAT'S ENOUGH EYESTRAIN FOR NOW, BELIEVER. BY THE WAY, IF WE ACCIDENTALLY MISSED ANYBODY BECAUSE THEY FORGOT TO SEND IN A PIC, OR BECAUSE THEY DIDN'T DROP BY THE OFFICE IN TIME FOR US TO SNAP 'EM, WE'LL TRY TO MAKE UP FOR IT NEXT GO-ROUND! WHO KNOWS... NEXT TIME, WE MAY EVEN CAPTURE HONEST IRV! (HOLLYWOOD TALENT SCOUTS, TAKE NOTE... THE BULLPEN BELONGS TO US! NONE ARE AVAILABLE FOR HORROR MOVIES... UNTIL THEY ASK FOR A RAISE!)

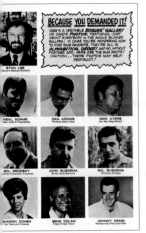

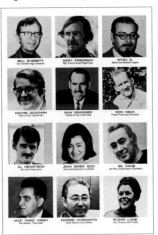

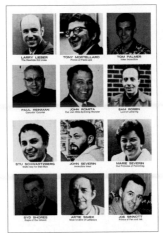

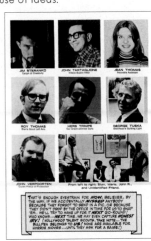

E BULLPEN AS IT EXISTED IN MARVEL'S EARLY DAYS, AS SEEN IN THIS LAYOUT FROM 1969'S *FANTASTIC FOUR ANNUAL #7.*

■ FLO STEINBERG'S FRIENDLY FACE GREETED A LEGION OF FANS IN THE 1960s AS STAN LEE'S "GIRL FRIDAY." ABOVE. FLO AS SHE WAS KNOWN BEST IN THE MARVEL OFFICES IN THE 1960S, CENTER, FLO SHOWING HER SPORTY SIDE IN 1974, TOP RIGHT, WITH WRITER DAVE KALLER AT 1965'S NEW YORK COMIC CON. AND BELOW RIGHT, IN COSTUME FOR A HOLIDAY GIG.

THE INSPIRATION OF THE OFFICE

*Flo served as a proofreader upon her return to Marvel in the 1990s, a job she held until she passed away this July. Along the way, she served as a coworker, friend, and mentor to countless Bullpenners. **Jacque Porte**, who joined Marvel as a proofreader in December 2014, was one of them.*

Fabulous Flo arrived at the end of my exhausting first week at Marvel, gave me a hug and a big wet kiss, and told me how excited she was to work with me. Imagine that! As if I were the one with the storied career and myriad accomplishments! She set herself up behind me with her giant headphones, her oversized sweatshirt and glasses, and an egg sandwich, and murmured away while she proofed the fantastical adventures of characters she had watched come to life decades before.

Her presence had a marked effect on the office. Even passing in the hallway, she could be depended upon for a humorous comment or a kind word, and her ability to remember even the most subtle detail made her an amazing proofreader and an even better friend. I don't think she realized just how broad her reach extended. She inspired me, helped foster my frustration into something productive, and encouraged my efforts to create an atmosphere of friendly teamwork with the other departments.

She made proofreading into a team sport. We argued over points of grammar, giggled over amusing errors (she'd underline your/you're errors at least five times), and mooned over the Punisher (she was quite fond of Frank's strong jawline, and the fact that his books were more sound effects than text didn't hurt his appeal either).

Now she sits behind me in memory, bent over the latest proof, and I can only hope to carry on her legacy of making every book a little bit better, every soul a little bit brighter.

BY **JOHN RHETT THOMAS**

In the Marvel Universe, there was a galaxy. And in that galaxy was a planet. And on that planet was a city. And in that city was a comic-book publisher. And in that comic-book publisher's office were three people: one editing, one in charge of production, and one so fabulous they capitalized the word whenever they affixed it to her name. And that woman was one of the most important women in Marvel Comics history, which—let's be honest—makes her one of the most important women in comics history. That woman's name was Flo Steinberg—and that's *Fabulous* Flo to you and everyone who ever had the pleasure of meeting her.

In the spring of 1963, the Marvel Comics office at 625 Madison Ave. was hardly the center of any kind of grand, interconnected universe. That would come later. It was a two-person operation run by Stan Lee, the editor in chief, and Sol Brodsky, the man who could do it all in production—and *had to* because he was the only one around to do it! The pair often played host to a gaggle of talented artists (at that time, legendary names such as Kirby, Ditko, and Heck, among others) who mostly worked from home, only visiting the office to turn in pages, review plotlines

with Stan, and maybe do a little draw[ing] as needed.

But Stan was having problems. M[ind] you, they were the kinds of probl[ems] that were born of success: *Fanto[stic] Four #1* had appeared in comics r[acks in] the summer of 1961 and been the kin[d of] hit that pumped new life into the fa[ding] company. The FF was soon followe[d by] a host of new super heroes: Ant-M[an], Thor, Hulk, Spider-Man, and Iron M[an,] all with titles that needed to be wri[tten] and drawn and delivered to the prin[ter] on time. And each new charac[ter] brought in a boatload of enthusia[stic] new fan mail Stan felt compelled [to] reply to in person. Marvel's fortu[nes] were on a steep upward curve, [and] Stan needed someone to help manage the office so he could focus [on] the creative side of things.

And that's when Florence Steinb[erg] walked through the door. An employm[ent] agency sent her over to interview w[ith] Stan, who had solicited a position [as] a "girl Friday," a term popularized [by] the 1940 film *His Girl Friday* starr[ing] Cary Grant and Rosalind Russell. [At] age 25, Flo could scarcely guess w[hat] she was walking into. Born and rais[ed] in Boston, and schooled at Univer[sity] of Massachusetts in Amherst, she ha[d a] history degree under her belt when s[he] ded to move to the Big Apple and ›blish her future. She didn't know :isely what she wanted to do with life, only that like so many "career " of the time she wanted to do it in v York City.

ɜr immediate concerns on the job e secretarial in nature: answering nes, reaching out to printers, sulting with engravers, and checking vith freelancers on their deadlines. ɜly, her charm and perky sensibility ɔed smooth over any rough edges he daily grind of putting out comic ›ks on time. It also helped in the kind ecretarial duties nobody could have pared her for: dealing with the fans! ıe deluge of fan mail needed wering, and every day it seemed be increasing. Stan couldn't keep with the amount of correspondence had been doing; he also felt connecting with readers of expanding universe of comic ɔks was of key importance to the npany's future. So that responsibility ted over to Flo, who would go on to wer thousands (tens of thousands?) etters that arrived in the office on a y basis. Stan hit pay dirt with Flo's ıble, fandom-friendly personality. truly was a mirror image of his own husiasm and ability for reaching out ans in the Marvel Age way. No stuffy, ch-the-clock secretary was she! hrough Stan and Flo's efforts, small three-man office was thologized into a hustling, bustling lpen of madcap creativity. The kind office environment that enlivened imaginations of readers already ıt into far-out realms by the cutting-ge adventures of their Marvel oes. It was indeed all part of Stan's n: to create a passionate, personal ationship between readers and the e of comics they had embraced. And helped steer the ship.

Meanwhile, some of her duties truly re of the "Batty Bullpen" variety, one nous example being her facility with ashtray whenever artist Wallace ood visited Stan's office. The chain-oker routinely—and some would y passive-aggressively—ignored e ashtrays available to him and opped ashes on the carpeting in an's office. Flo would be right there inconspicuously set an ashtray der his cigarette whenever the ash as getting long and droopy. She so had to run interference on fans no called to talk to Stan, or arrived the office unannounced to get a ord in with Stan, or lurked around e elevators to just *please, please, let tell Stan how much I love Marvel!* ot to mention fielding phone calls om fans who simply fell in love with r and wanted to yak it up with the

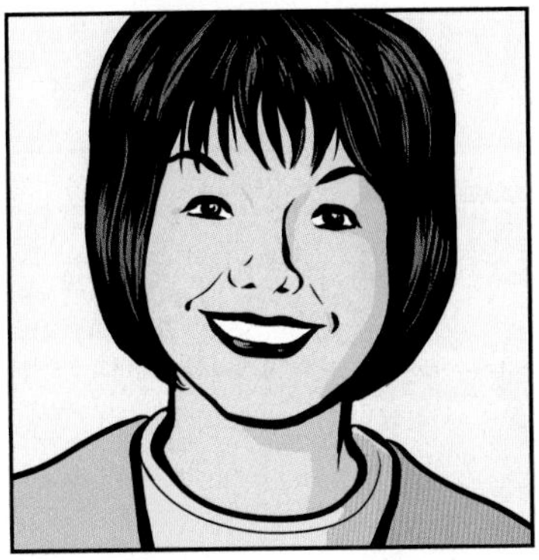

▲COLLEEN COOVER

Fabulous gal who was at the center of their beloved Bullpen.

And in 1965, two years after her arrival, when Stan formed the Mighty Marvel Marching Society (MMMS) to harness the fandom that had reached critical mass, it was Flo who made sure all the club's goodies—from membership cards to a vinyl flexi disc record of the Bullpen talking and singing to their legions of fans—got in the mail and out to everyone who had ordered one. Membership of the MMMS reportedly grew to 50,000, each one considering Flo a superstar of the Bullpen firmament.

Stan once came up with a description of Flo in one of the credits boxes in a Marvel annual: "Flo Steinberg—Exasperated Example of Secretarial Suffering." Later in the decade, Fabulous Flo left the job she'd held for five years. Sure, her position had been "secretary," but that was only because "Center of Gravity of the Marvel Universe" hadn't existed before her arrival.

After Marvel, Flo held various jobs inside and outside the comics and publishing industries. She even developed her own underground comic magazine, *Big Apple Comix* (which featured cover art from the ash-dropping Wood). She lived on in Marvel Comics through various cameos, the most famous being a role as the Invisible Woman in a Kirby-written-and-drawn issue of *What If?* She returned to Marvel in the '90s to serve as a proofreader, a position she held for the rest of her life.

Sadly, we write this article as a eulogy. Flo passed away on July 23, 2017, from complications from a brain aneurysm and metastatic lung cancer. Tributes flowed in from all corners of the comic-book industry and fandom. Perhaps the most fitting thing one could say of Fabulous Flo comes from the mouth of her boss and fandom mentor, Stan Lee. When someone would bring up her name, the first thing out of Stan's mouth would often be: "Flo...what a gal!"

She was all that and plenty more. Rest in peace, Flo Steinberg.

THE STEALTH PHILOSOPHER

***Linda Fite** arrived at Marvel in the late 1960s to perform various tasks in the Bullpen, but was soon writing stories that appeared in various Western titles, X-Men, and* The Cat. *She also contributed to Flo's* Big Apple Comix. *Fite married longtime* Incredible Hulk *and* G.I. Joe *artist Herb Trimpe, and started a family with him while also working for 20 years as a staff writer for the* Times Herald-Record *in Middletown, New York. Through it all, she remained the closest of friends with Flo.*

"Fabulous Flo" is right.

I was hired, at Flo's behest, to help her with the increasing influx of fan mail, as well as all sorts of other "editorial/production" assistance I could offer. She reached out to me (by letter, then by phone) after I wrote to Marvel asking for a job. (I still have a copy of that letter, as well as Flo's response, encouraging me to come talk to Stan after I moved to New York City, without a promise of a job, but with plenty of hope thereof.) One thing that cracks me up, in retrospect, is that Stan had circled the sentence "I can type" in my letter!

As anyone who ever spent more than a minute with her knows, Flo was incredibly kind, incredibly "nice" to everyone. And that made my first post-college job so easy (that and the genial atmosphere of the Bullpen).

We were close friends ever since that time. She was my son's godmother! And she loved and showered affection on all three of the kids born to me and Herb.

I have scads of anecdotes, of course, but most of them are...I dunno... not very "pithy" and maybe not so appropriate for print! But after going through her effects as her executor, I came across a small, cloth-bound notebook in which she had written or photocopied dozens and dozens of quotes or passages, short and long, from authors, wits, and wags—people whose thoughts tickled her or impressed her or made her say (to herself, presumably), "Damn right!"

A rather telling number of these quotations had to do with mortality or solitude or courage. Here are a few:

"The cherry blossom falls from the tree with the first strong breeze, but we do not say that it has never lived. A bloom that lasts only a day is no less beautiful for that."
– *Shike: Last of the Zinja* by Robert Shea

"Time is the random wind that blows down the long corridor, slamming all the doors."
– *A Tan and Sandy Silence* by John D. MacDonald

"To see what is right and not to do it is want of courage."
– Confucius

"Love consists in this—that two solitudes protect and touch and greet one another."
– Rilke

"Do not desire that everything happen as you wish, but desire that everything happen as in fact it does happen, and you will be free."
– Epictetus

"To be attached to the subdivision, to love the little platoon we belong to in society, is the first principle (the germ as it were) of public affections. It is the first link in the series by which we proceed toward a love to our country, and to mankind."
– Edmund Burke

"...Life is hard and getting no easier. But there are exceptions, moments of, if not hope, at least relief. A child is born healthy. A book absorbs us. A friend laughs. Unwanted guests depart and never return."
– Spoken by the character Rostnikov in *Death of a Russian Priest* by Stuart M. Kaminsky

All these quotes were very much Flo: the ponderer, the thinker, the stealth philosopher. Wise, funny, intelligent, fun, loyal, considerate—fabulous.

MIGHTY MARVEL MINI-ITEMS

VALUE STAMPS CAN'T BE LICKED!

Break out your scissors, Marvel Mavens! A brand-new array of Marvel Value Stamps are coming your way courtesy of Marvel Legacy! For those of you asking, "What the heck is a 'Marvel Value Stamp'?"—the small, stamp-shaped curiosities, emblazoned with portraits of Marvel's most famous heroes and villains, appeared in select Marvel comics from 1974–1976. Just over 30 years later, *Marvel Spotlight* revived the concept, publishing a new slate of Value Stamps. And now comes Marvel Legacy, bringing with it 53 stamps illustrated by Mike McKone! Be sure to ask your local comic store for a copy of the free Marvel Stamp Collector Album, available Nov. 1st—then get clipping, True Believer!

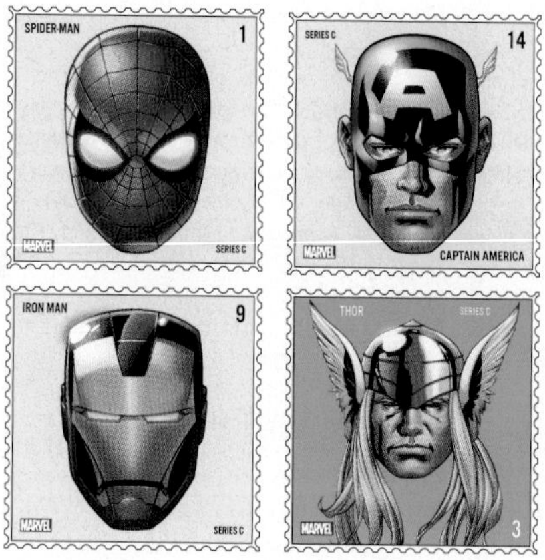
SPIDER-MAN 1
SERIES C
SERIES C 14
CAPTAIN AMERICA
IRON MAN 9
SERIES C
THOR SERIES C
3

MIKE McKONE & RACHELLE ROSENBERG

AN ISSUE OF CLOSURE

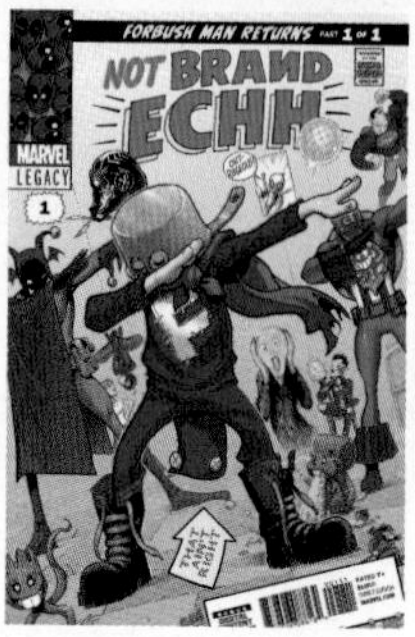
FORBUSH MAN RETURNS PART 1 OF 1
NOT BRAND ECHH
MARVEL LEGACY

DAVID NAKAYAMA

Think your beloved *Not Brand Echh* collection is complete? Guess again! A mere 48 years after issue #13—how's that for a shipping delay?—the unforgettable Forbush Man makes his triumphant return as issue #14 finally sees print! It's one of a number of dearly departed titles from yesteryear returning as part of Marvel Legacy for one final issue—for now, at least! Say goodbye all over again with *Silver Sable & the Wild Pack #36*, *Power Pack #63*, *Darkhawk #51*, *Master of Kung Fu #126*—and, of course, *Not Brand Echh #14*.

THE LEGACY PITCH

FOOM grabbed hold of a handful of writers passing through the batty Bullpen and urged them to hit us with the quick pitch for their upcoming Marvel Legacy storylines—and this is what they threw our way!

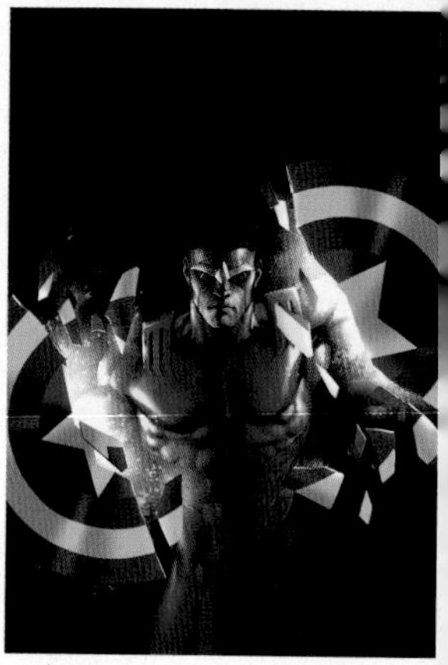

JESÚS SAIZ

Max Bemis on *Moon Knight*: "If Moon Knight is a Batman for the unhinged, who would his Joker be? Moon Knight fights his new archnemesis for the fate of creativity and freedom itself."

Victor Gischler on *Spirits of Vengeance*: "When a third-rate sorcerer looks to make a name for himself, he discovers how to weaponize the 30 pieces of silver paid to Judas for betraying Jesus. What is the only answer for the ultimate betrayal? The ultimate vengeance, of course."

Margaret Stohl on *Captain Marvel*: "When Captain Marvel discovers an Upside-Down Earth—where she is a super villain called the Private, and the Zeta are her criminal crew—she finds herself caught in the crosshairs of a deadly intergalactic assassin: Peter Quill, also known as Lord Starkill!"

Rodney Barnes on *Falcon*: "In the aftermath of Secret Empire, Sam Wilson seeks to reconnect with grassroots America—only to find Blackheart standing in his way!"

OPTIMUM PRIMERS

Want a refresher course in the history of Marvel's colorful cast of costumed characters? We have you covered! The first issue of each Legacy title will feature three page "Primers," written by Robbie Thompson and—in many cases—drawn by the incomparable Mark Bagley. "When I first approached Robbie and Mark to do these Primer stories, I gave them only one edict," editor Darren Shan said. "To remind all readers both who these characters are and what they're about in three all-new pages. What we got back has been some of the most fun art I've ever seen from Mark! And we couldn't be luckier to have someone like Robbie to cherry-pick the most classic moments in Marvel history. The two of them tie this all up into one perfect package." Speaking of perfect packages, there's a good chance all the Marvel Legacy Primer pages will be collected in a single trade paperback in the near future—so keep your eyes peeled!

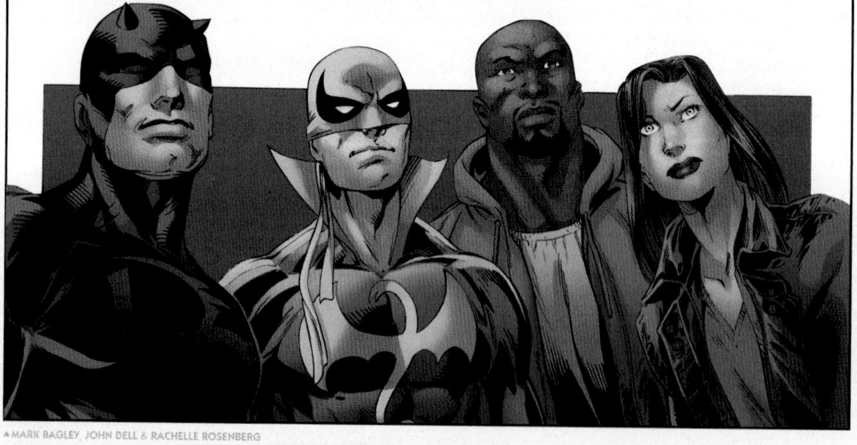

MARK BAGLEY, JOHN DELL & RACHELLE ROSENBERG

PERIODICALS OF TERROR!

Did you know Marvel once graced the newsstands as well as the comics racks? *Marvel Horror: The Magazine Collection TPB* collects the most horrifying stories of the 1970s magazines. Blade, Satana, and Gabriel, Devil Hunter, join a selection of scary stories for the Halloween season. Pick it up in stores everywhere Oct. 11th.

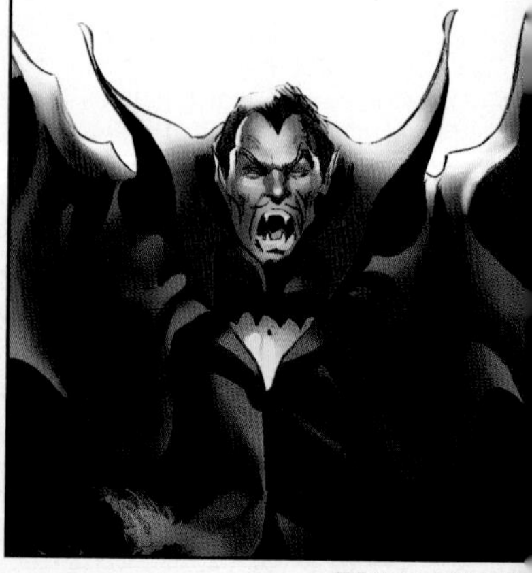

GENE COLAN & JUSTIN PONSOR

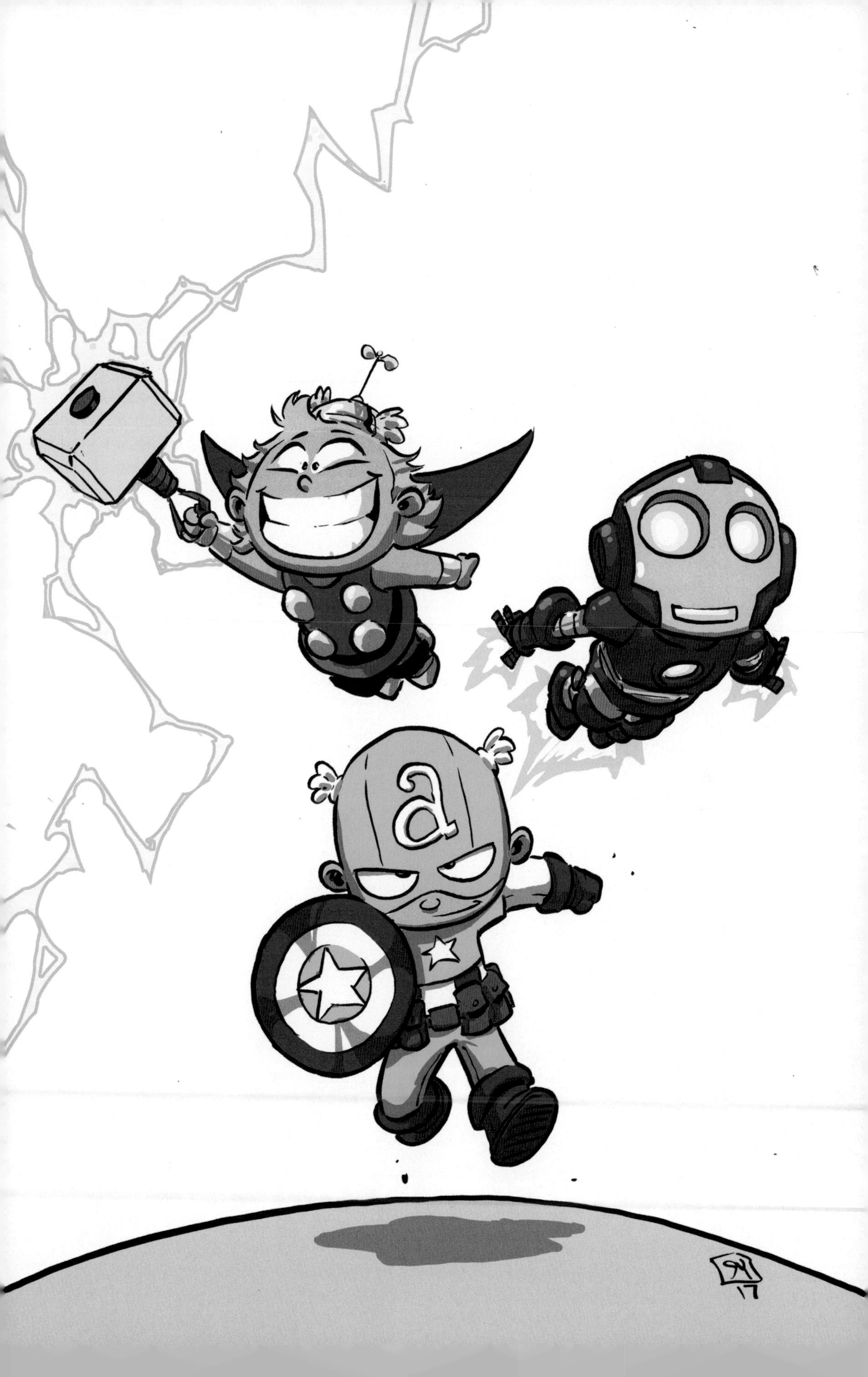

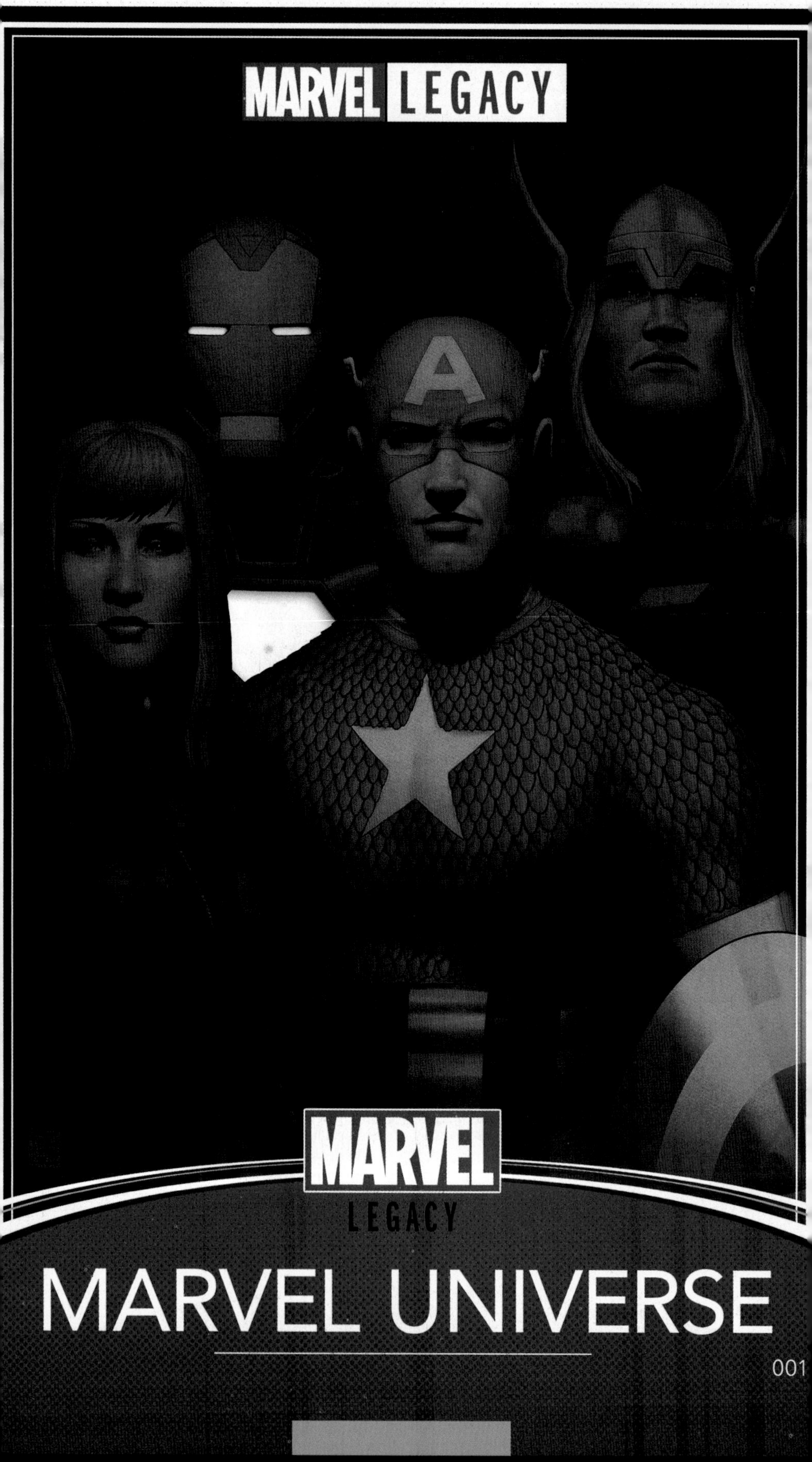
MARVEL LEGACY
MARVEL
LEGACY
MARVEL UNIVERSE
001

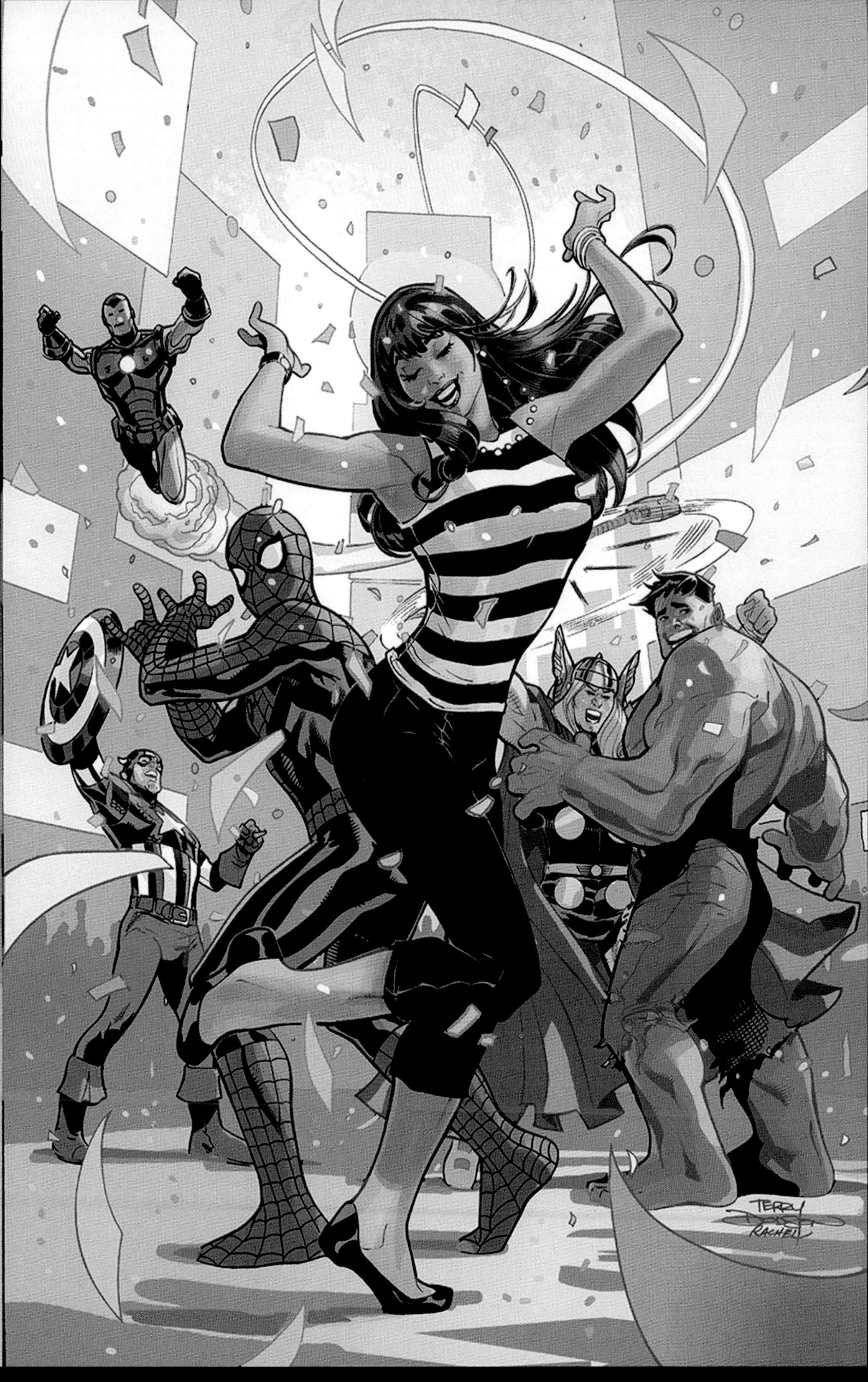
TERRY
DODSON
RACHEL

MARVEL LEGACY #1 PARTY VARIANT BY TERRY DODSON & RACHEL DODSON

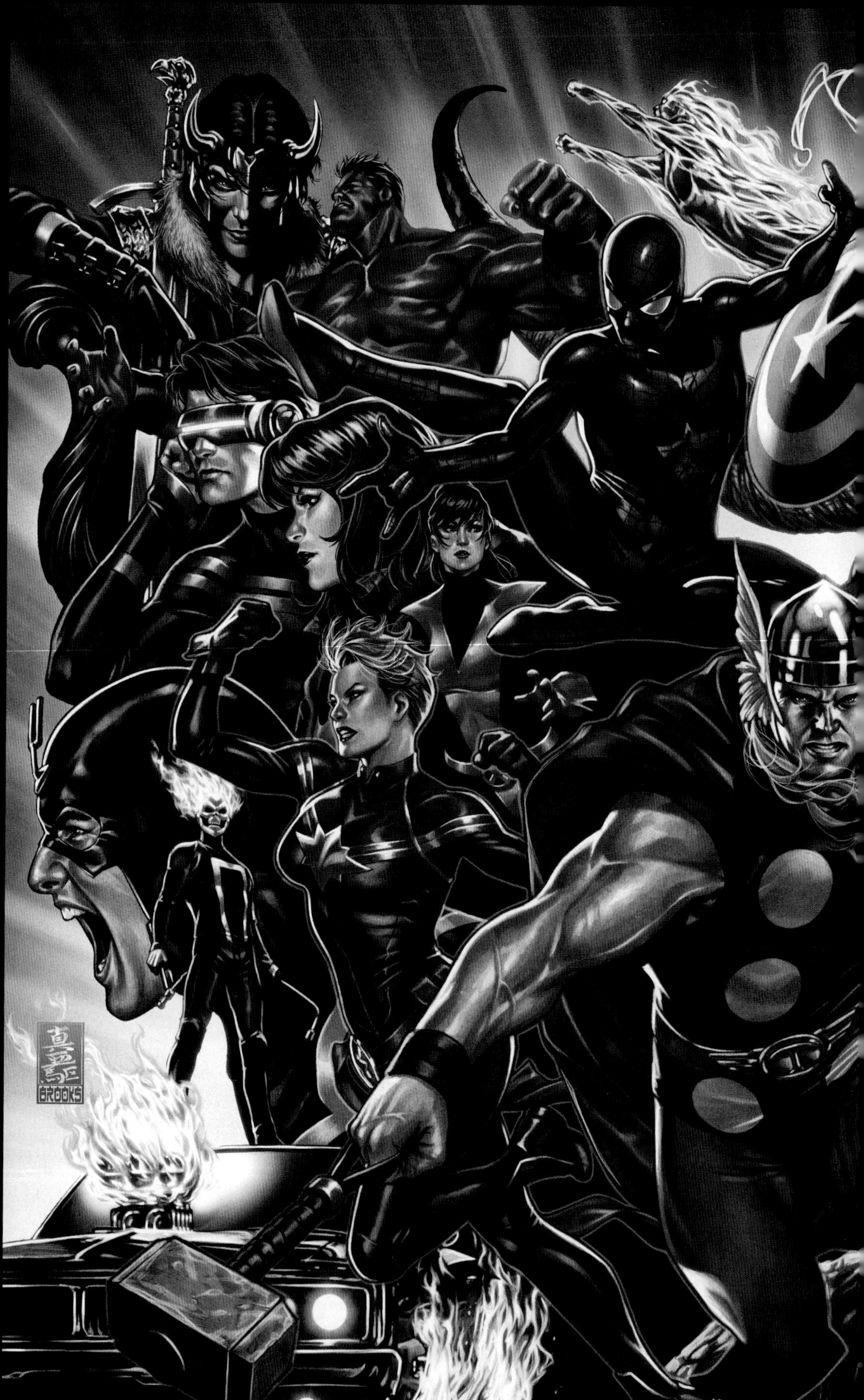
BROOKS

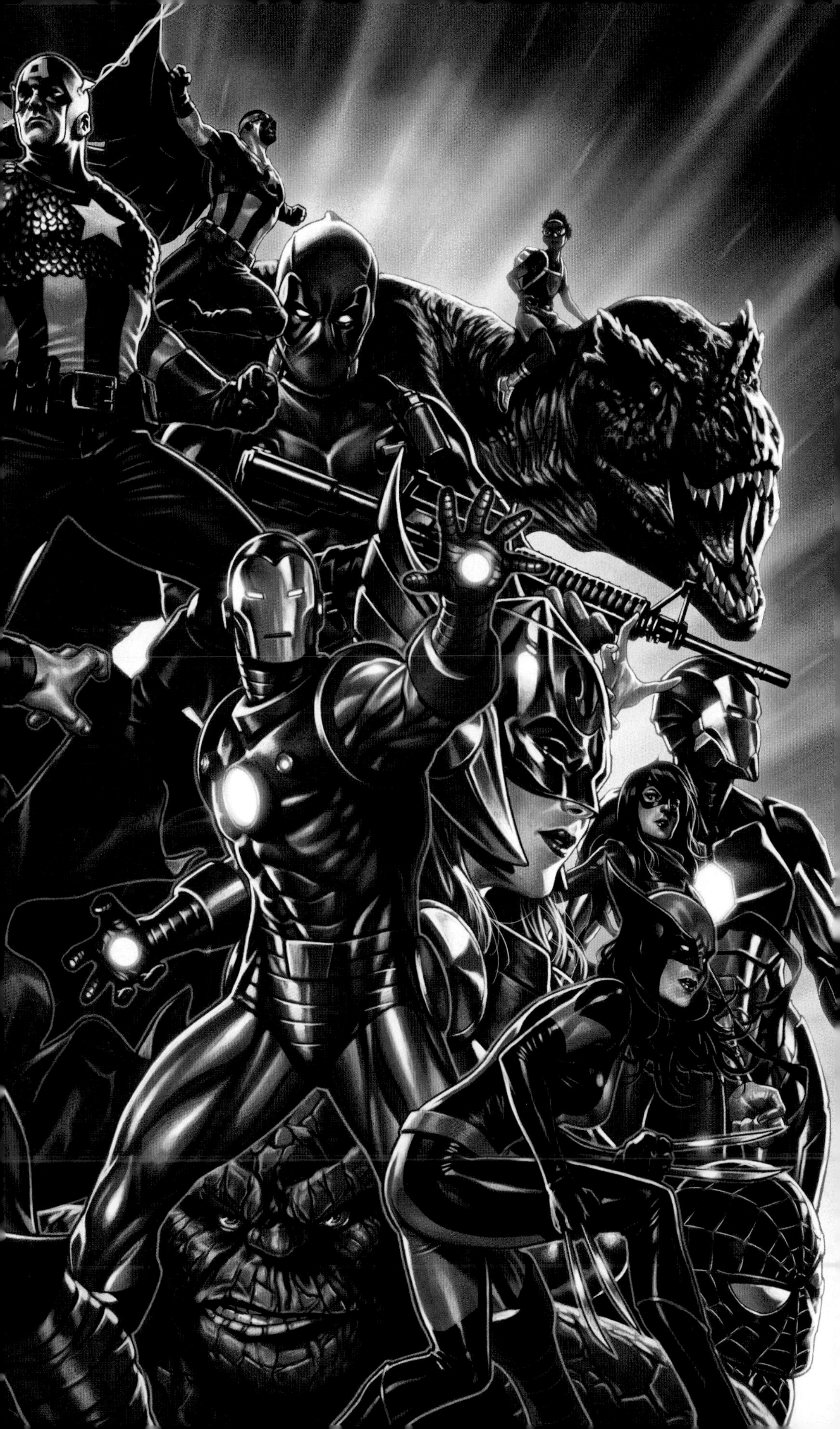

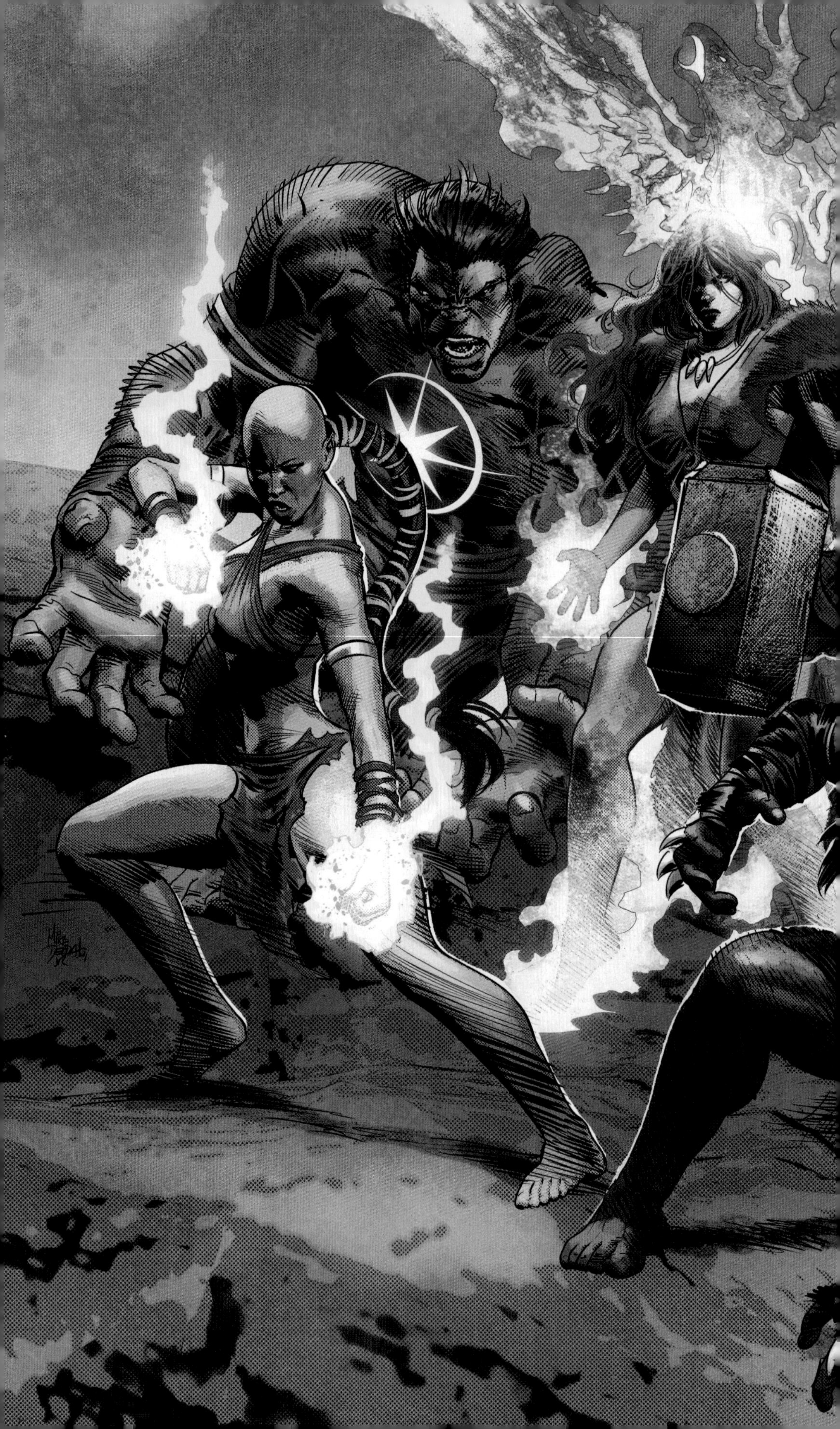

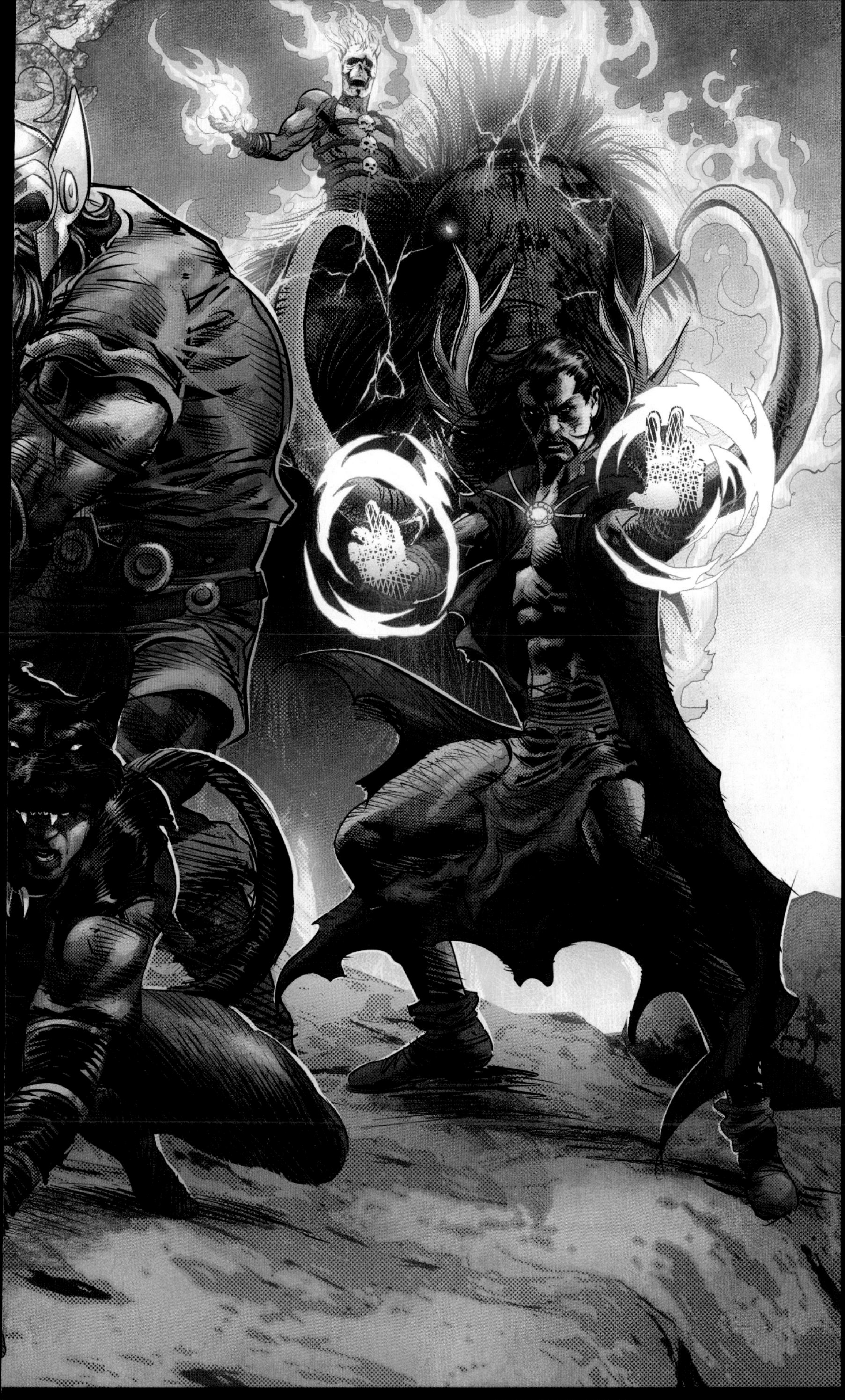

MARVEL LEGACY #1 VARIANT BY **MIKE DEODATO JR.**

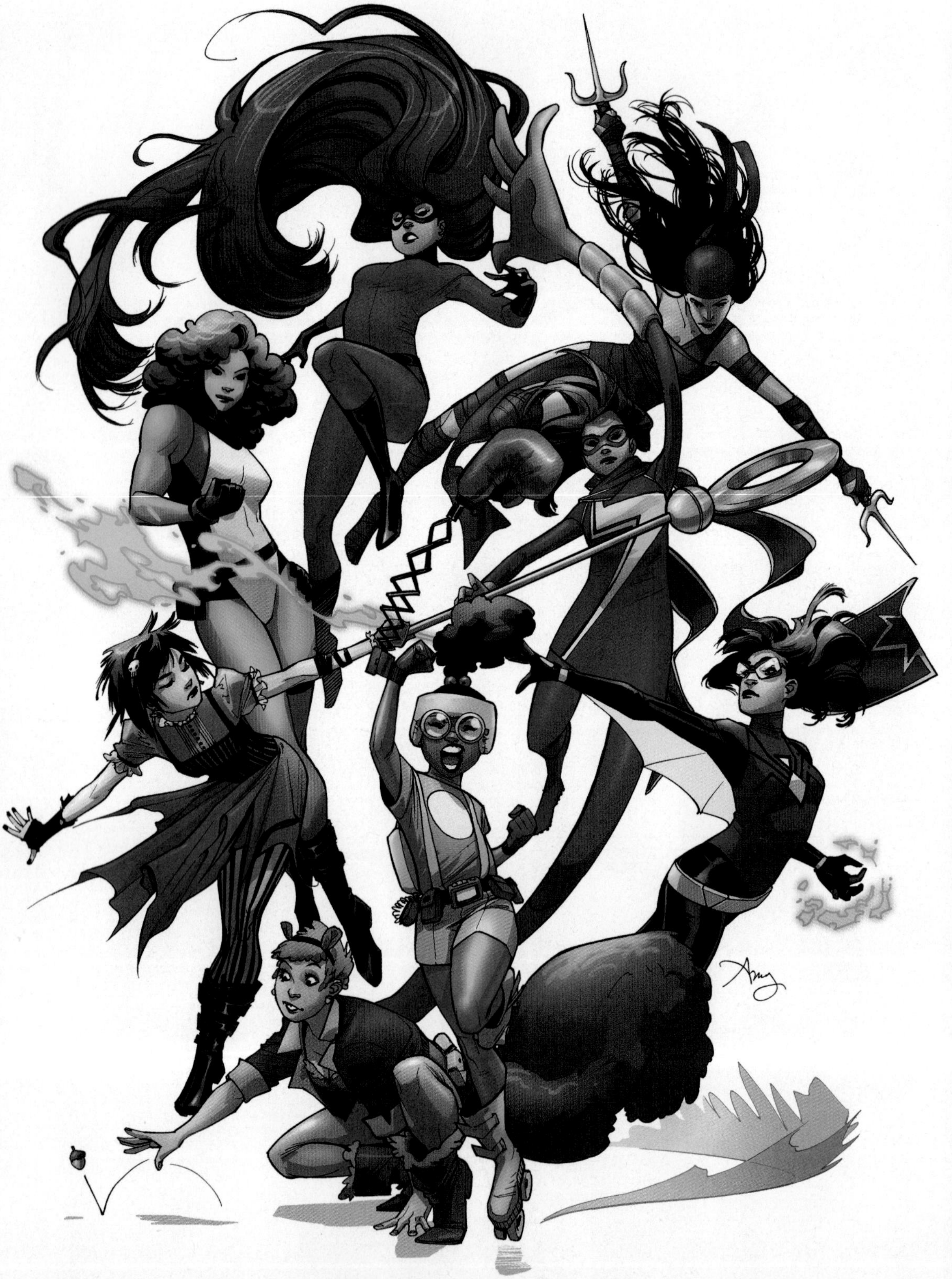
Amy

MARVEL LEGACY #1 WOMEN OF MARVEL VARIANT BY AMY REEDER

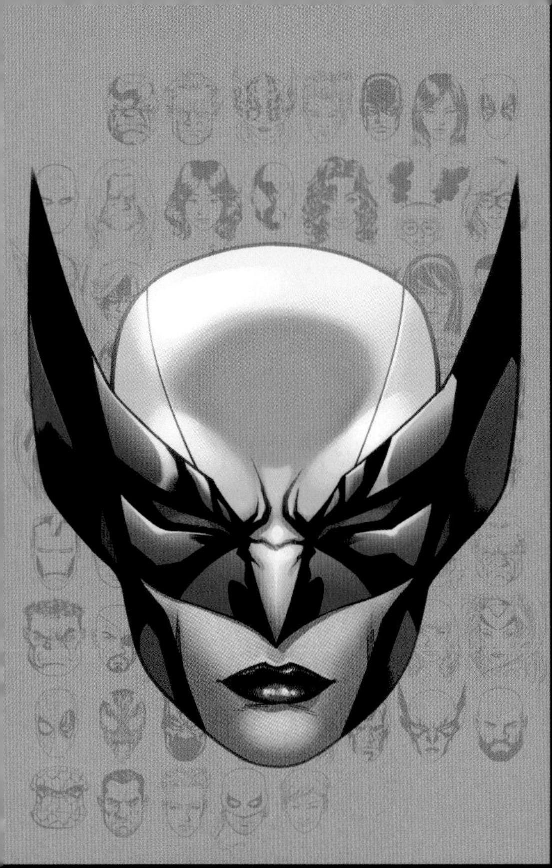

ALL-NEW WOLVERINE #25
LEGACY HEADSHOT VARIANT BY
MIKE McKONE & RACHELLE ROSENBERG

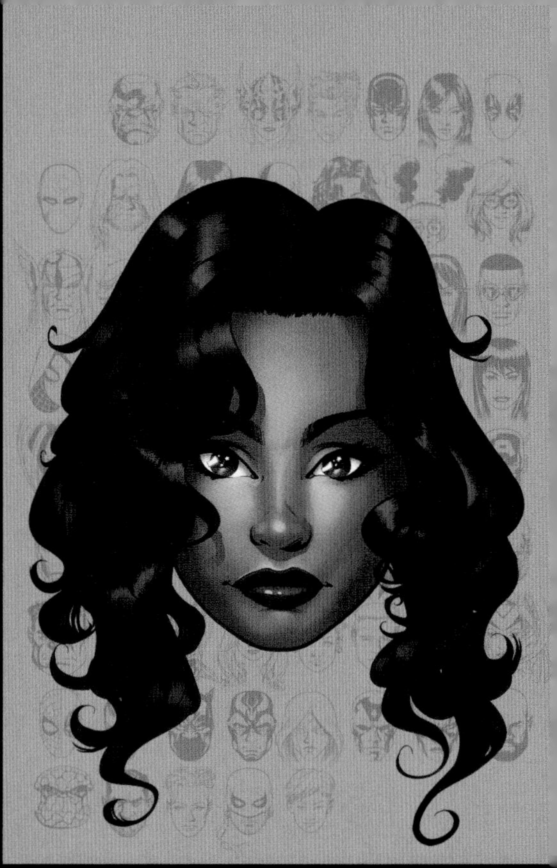

AMERICA #8
LEGACY HEADSHOT VARIANT BY
MIKE McKONE & ANDY TROY

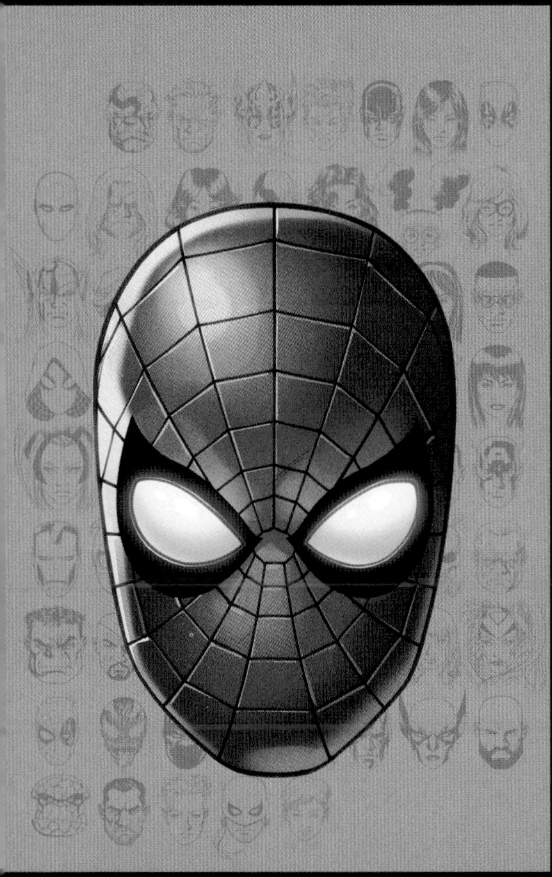

AMAZING SPIDER-MAN #789
LEGACY HEADSHOT VARIANT BY
MIKE McKONE & RACHELLE ROSENBERG

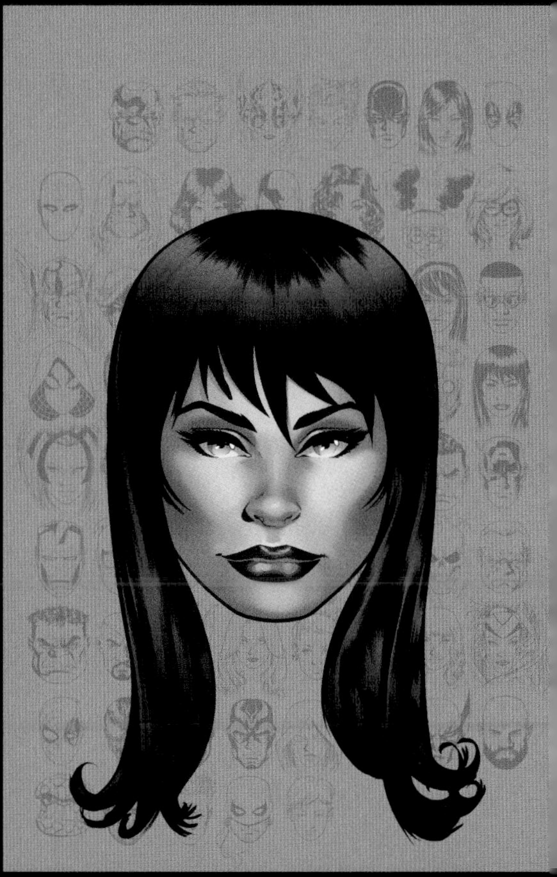

AMAZING SPIDER-MAN: RENEW YOUR VOWS #13
LEGACY HEADSHOT VARIANT BY
MIKE McKONE & RACHELLE ROSENBERG

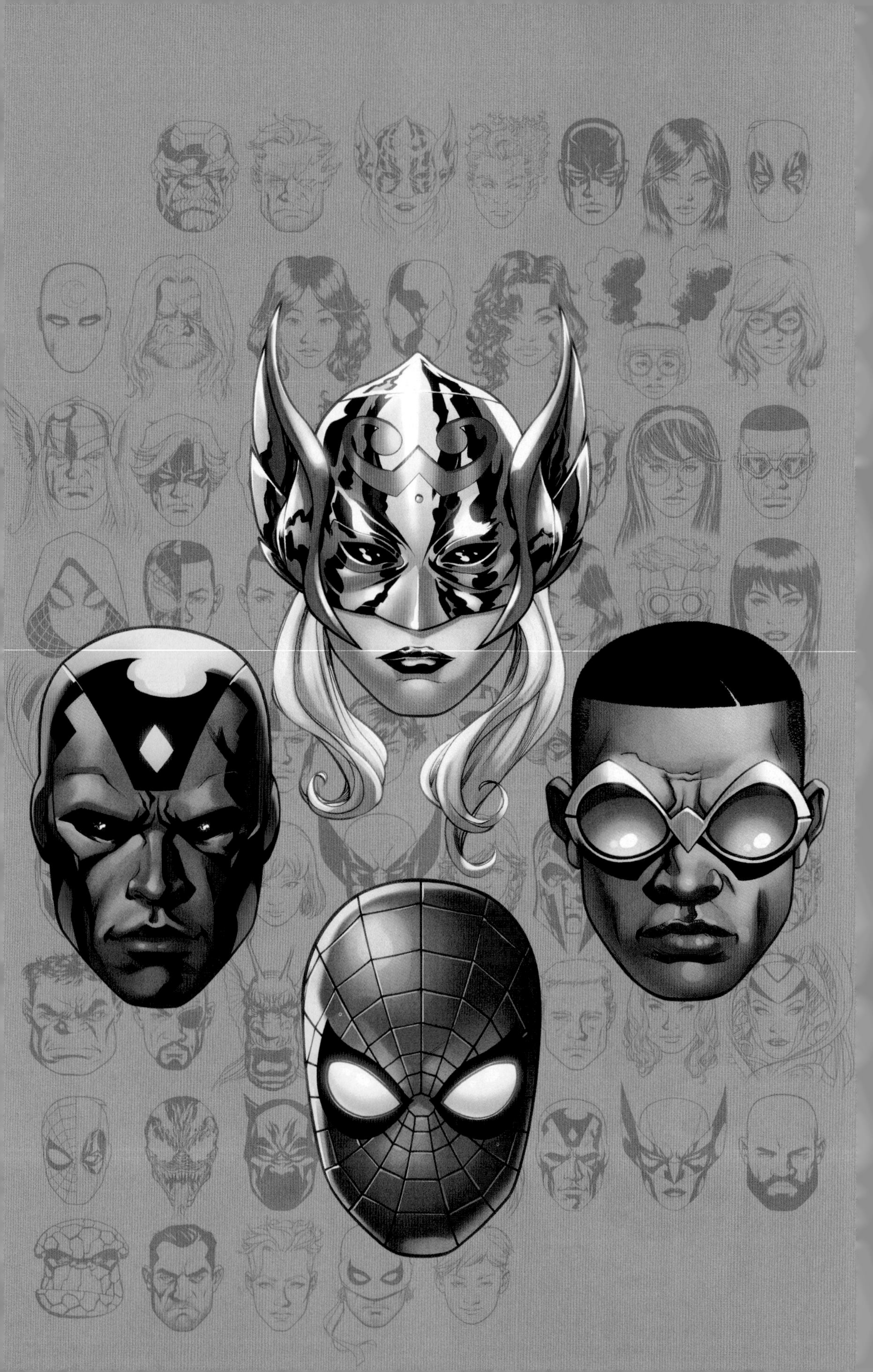

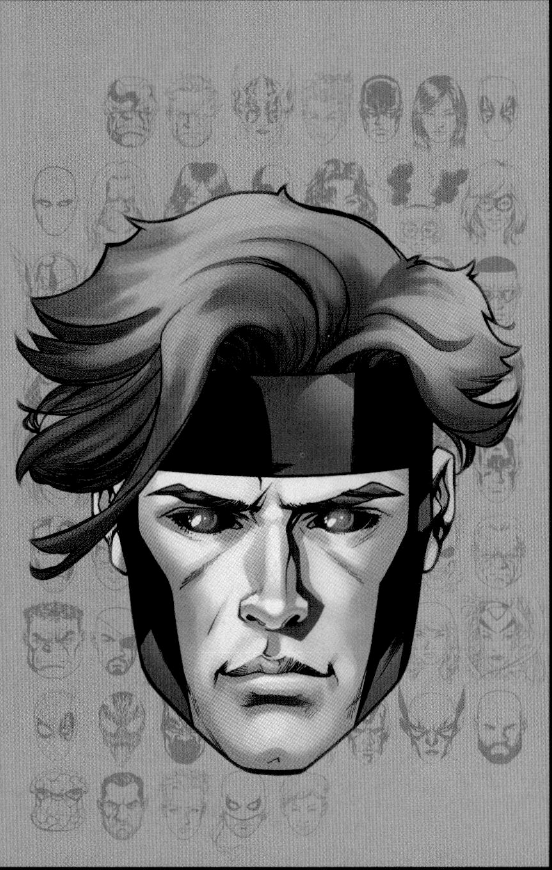

ASTONISHING X-MEN #7
LEGACY HEADSHOT VARIANT BY
MIKE McKONE & RACHELLE ROSENBERG

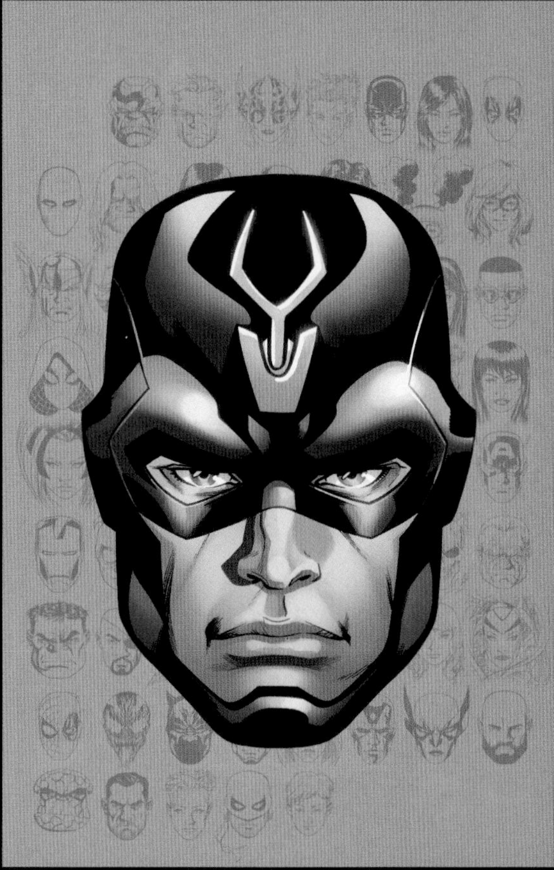

BLACK BOLT #8
LEGACY HEADSHOT VARIANT BY
MIKE McKONE & RACHELLE ROSENBERG

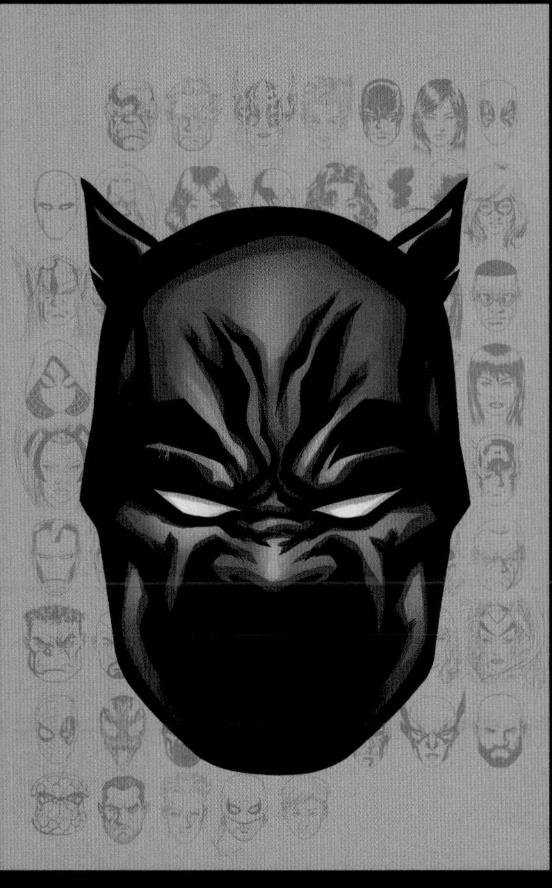

BLACK PANTHER #166
LEGACY HEADSHOT VARIANT BY

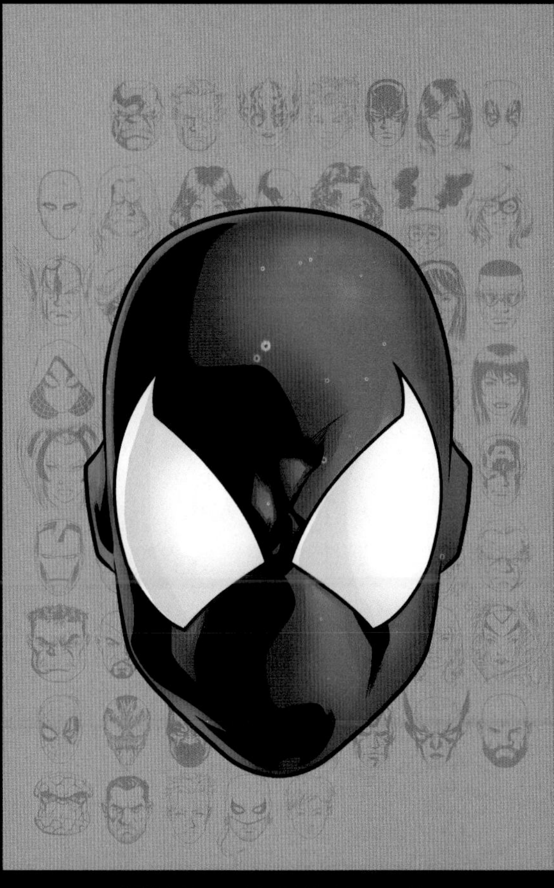

BEN REILLY: SCARLET SPIDER #10
LEGACY HEADSHOT VARIANT BY

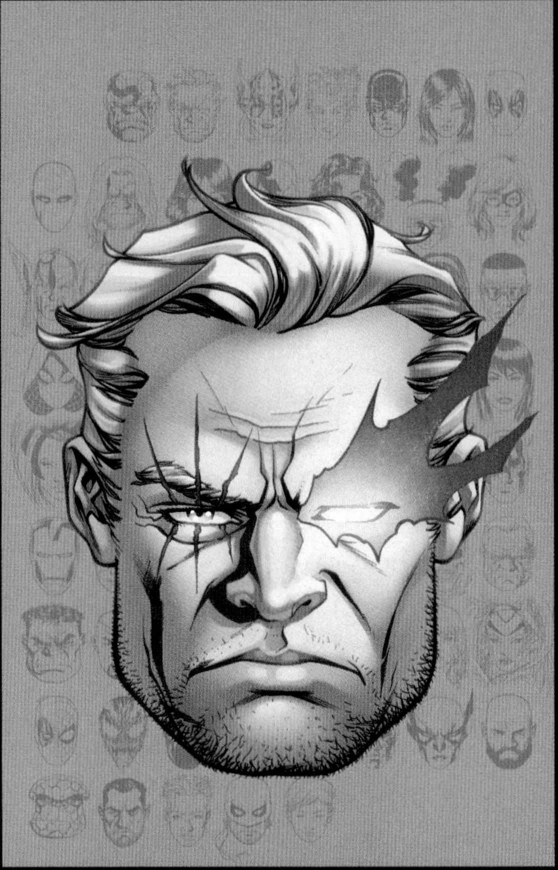

CABLE #150
LEGACY HEADSHOT VARIANT BY
MIKE McKONE & RACHELLE ROSENBERG

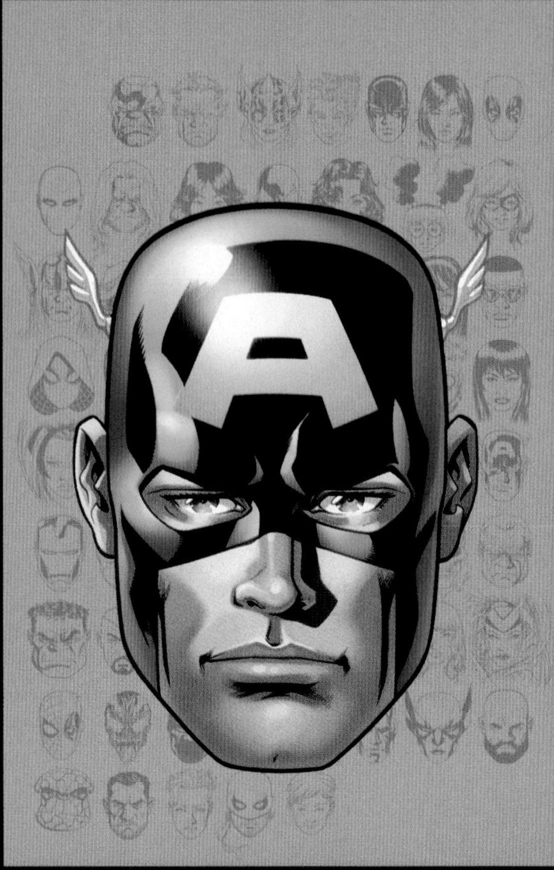

CAPTAIN AMERICA #695
LEGACY HEADSHOT VARIANT BY
MIKE McKONE & RACHELLE ROSENBERG

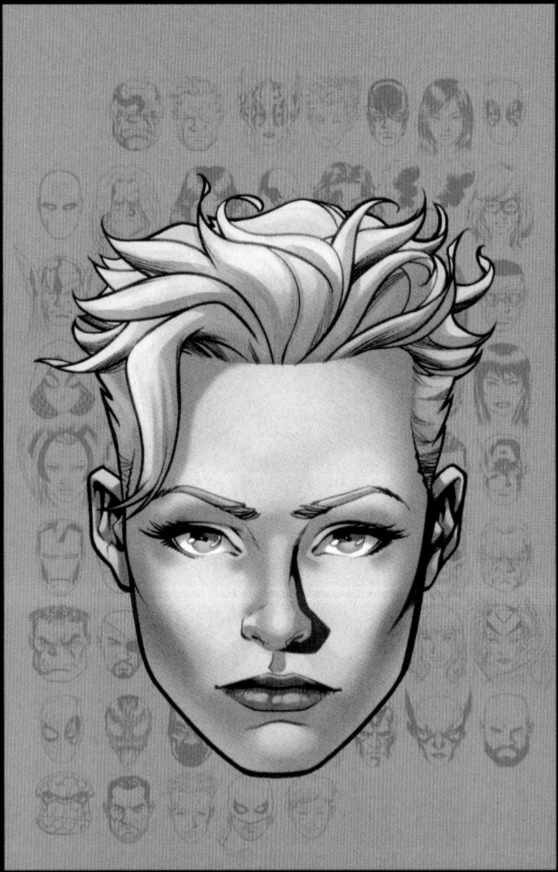

CAPTAIN MARVEL #125
LEGACY HEADSHOT VARIANT BY
MIKE McKONE & RACHELLE ROSENBERG

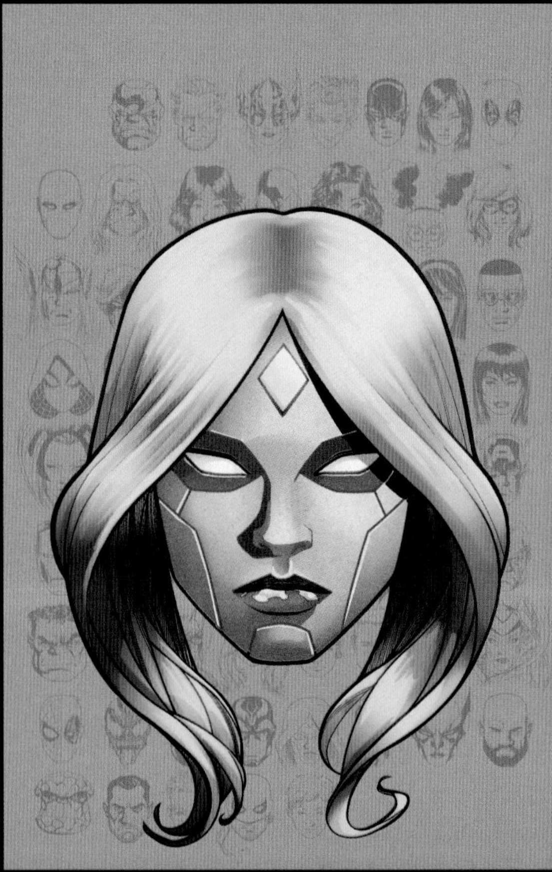

CHAMPIONS #13
LEGACY HEADSHOT VARIANT BY
MIKE McKONE & RACHELLE ROSENBERG

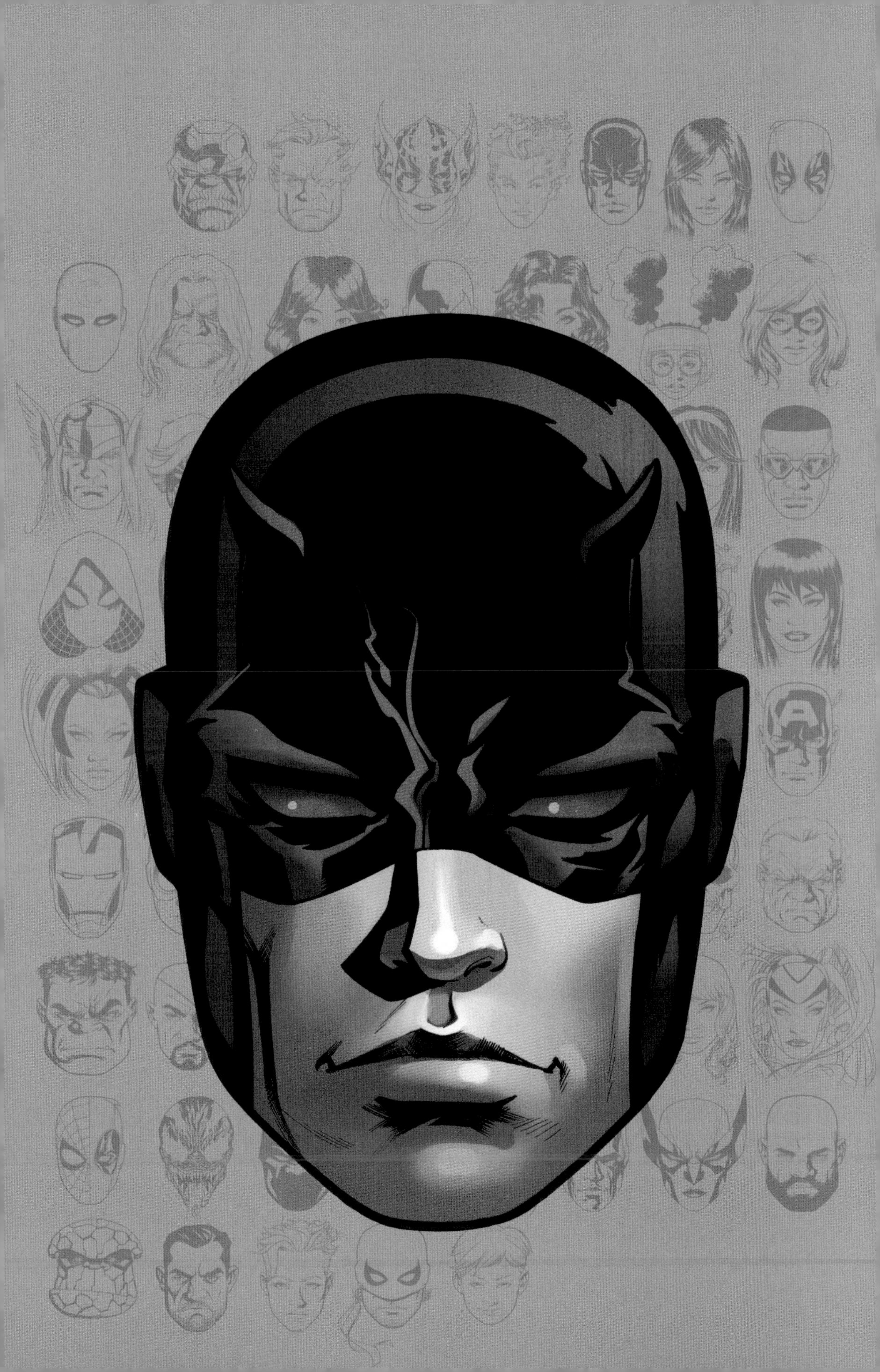

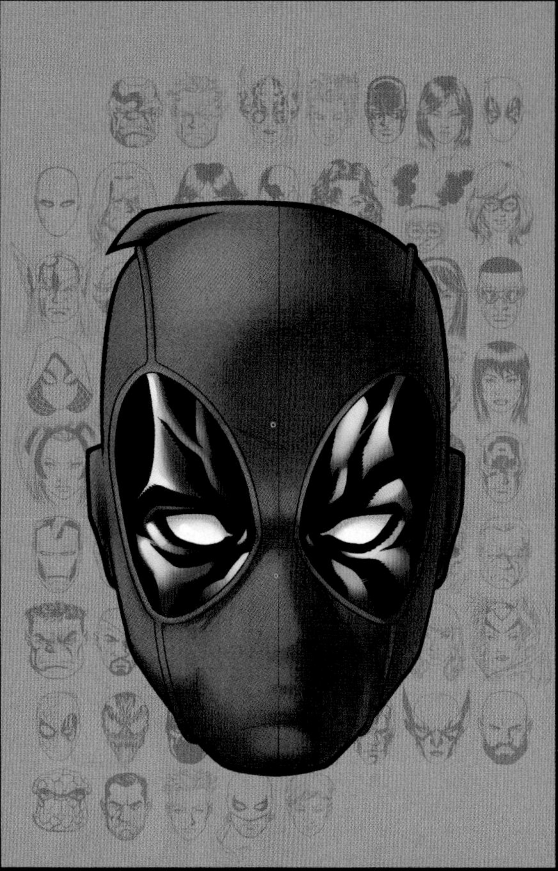

DESPICABLE DEADPOOL #287
LEGACY HEADSHOT VARIANT BY
MIKE McKONE & RACHELLE ROSENBERG

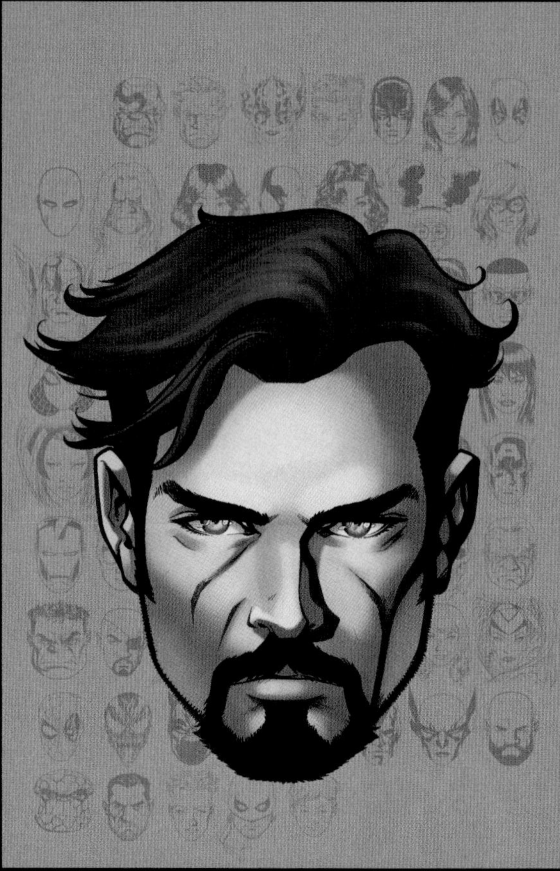

DOCTOR STRANGE #381
LEGACY HEADSHOT VARIANT BY
MIKE McKONE & RACHELLE ROSENBERG

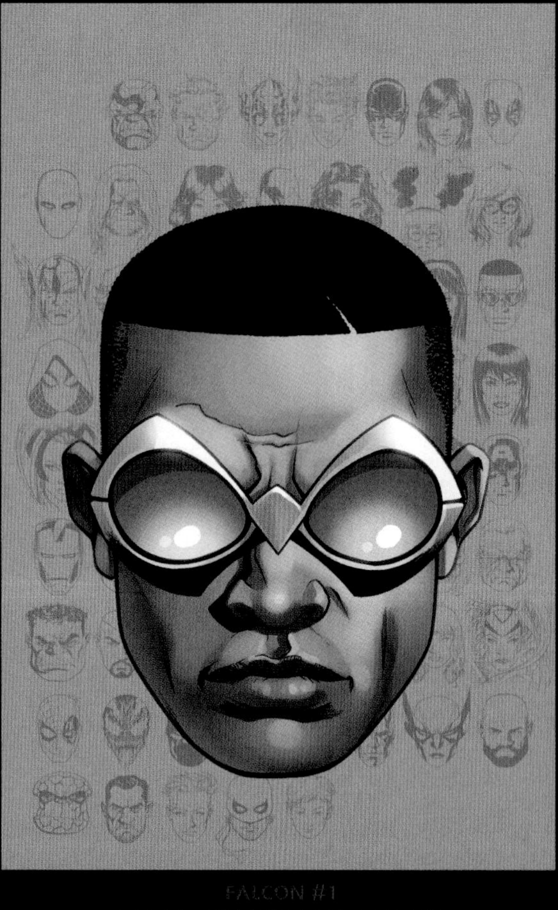

FALCON #1
LEGACY HEADSHOT VARIANT BY
MIKE McKONE & RACHELLE ROSENBERG

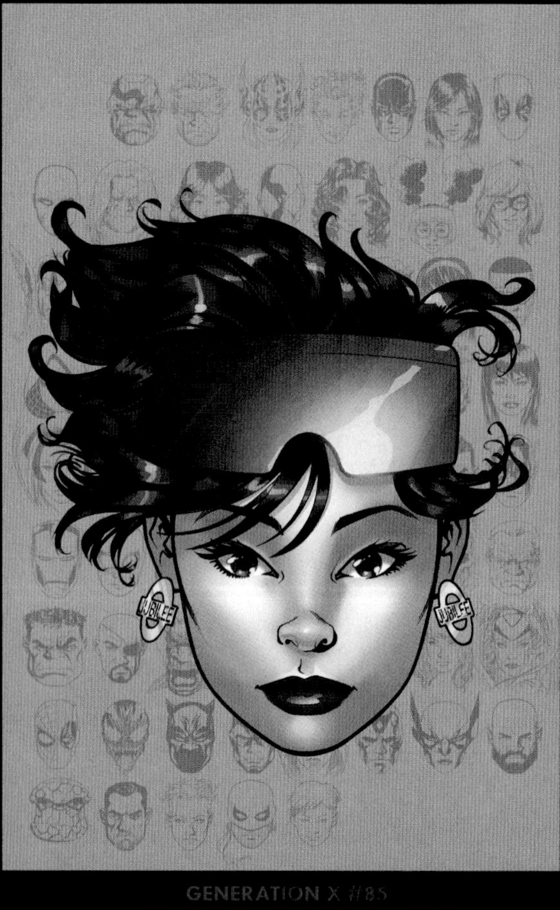
JUBILEE
JUBILEE

GENERATION X #85
LEGACY HEADSHOT VARIANT BY
MIKE McKONE & ANDY TROY

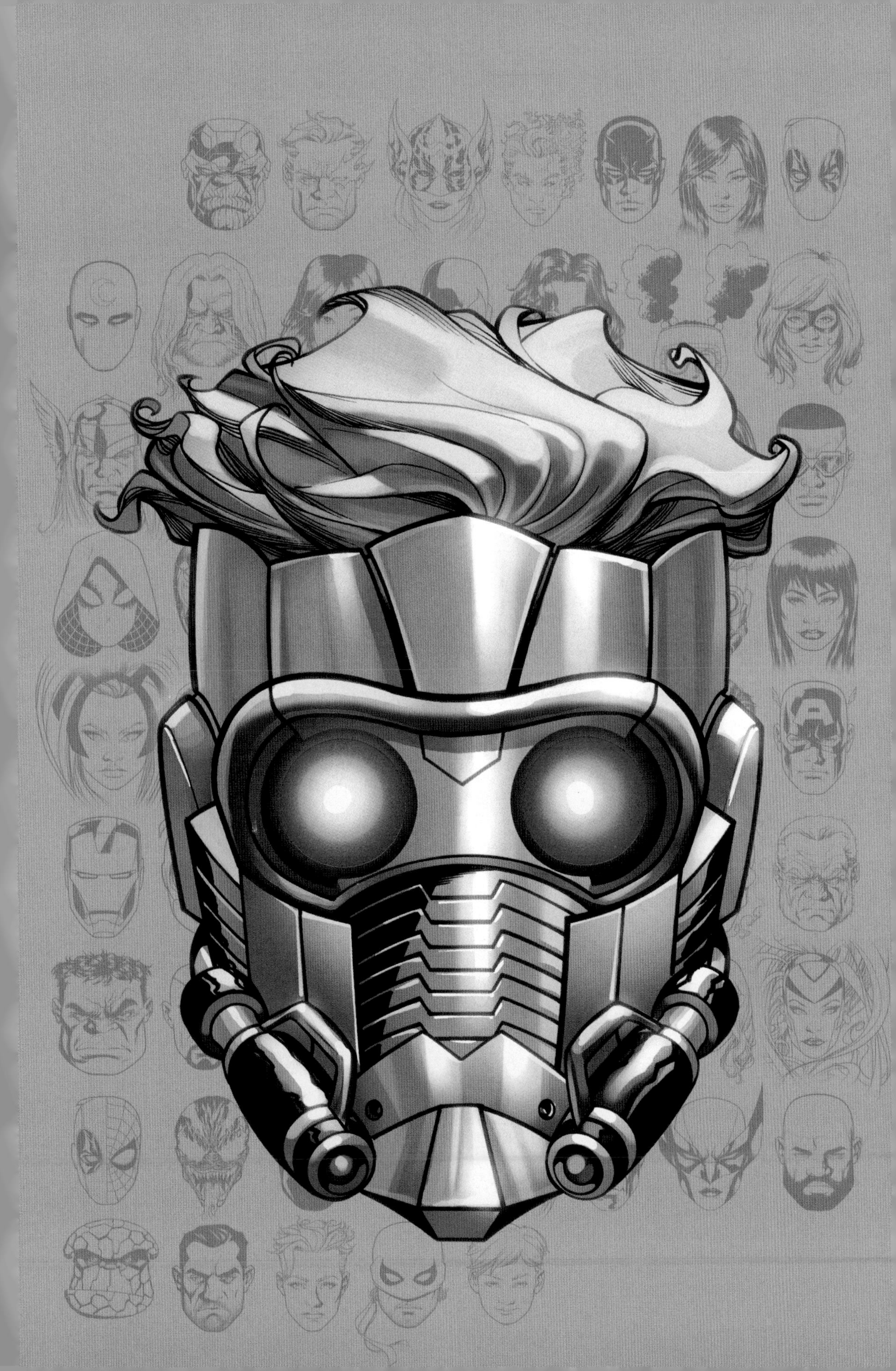

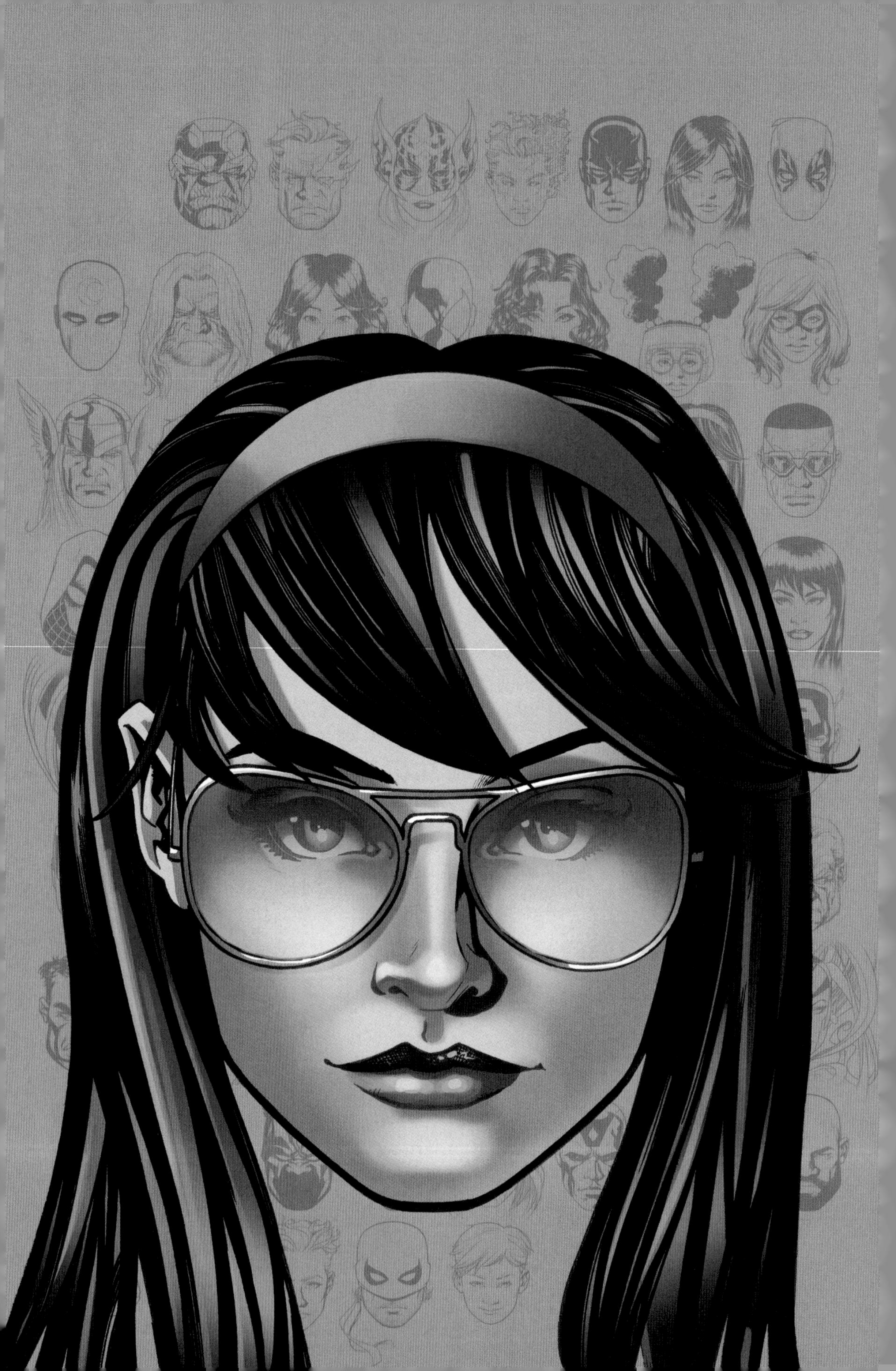

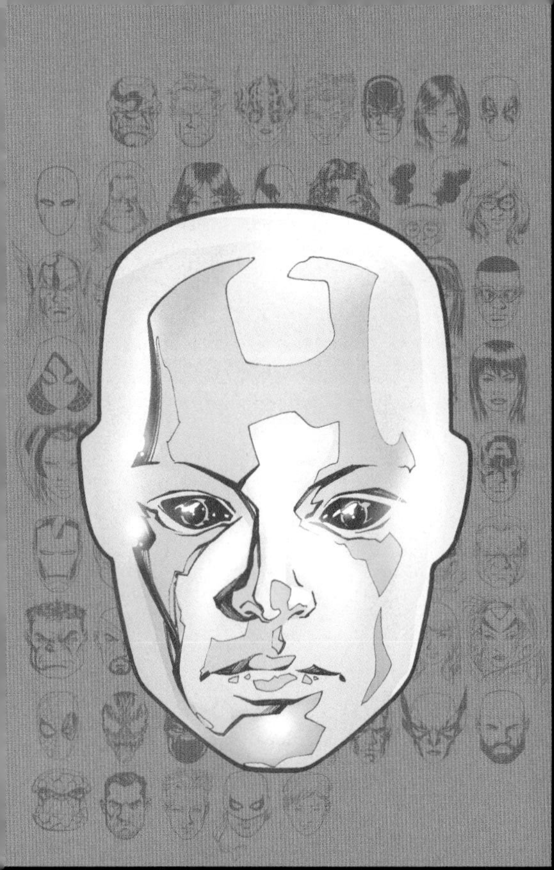

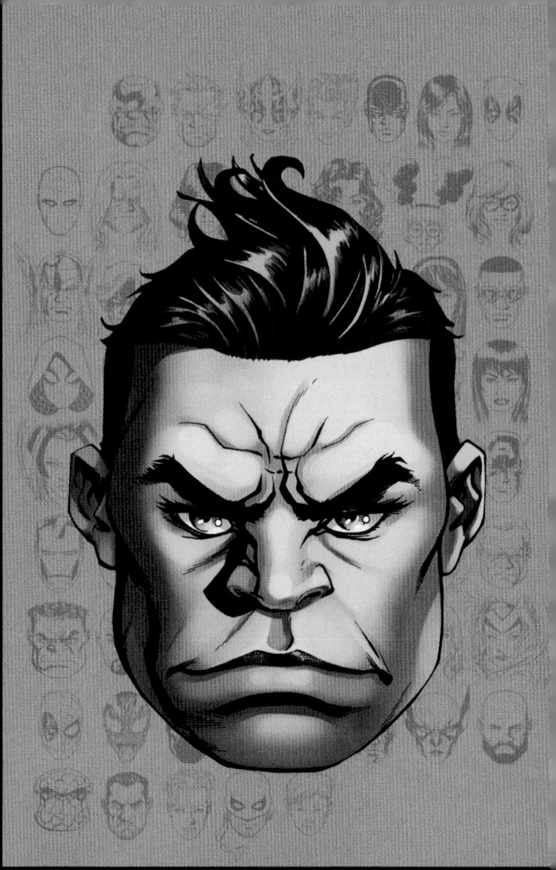

INCREDIBLE HULK #709
LEGACY HEADSHOT VARIANT BY
MIKE McKONE & RACHELLE ROSENBERG

INCREDIBLE HULK #709
LEGACY HEADSHOT VARIANT BY
MIKE McKONE & RACHELLE ROSENBERG

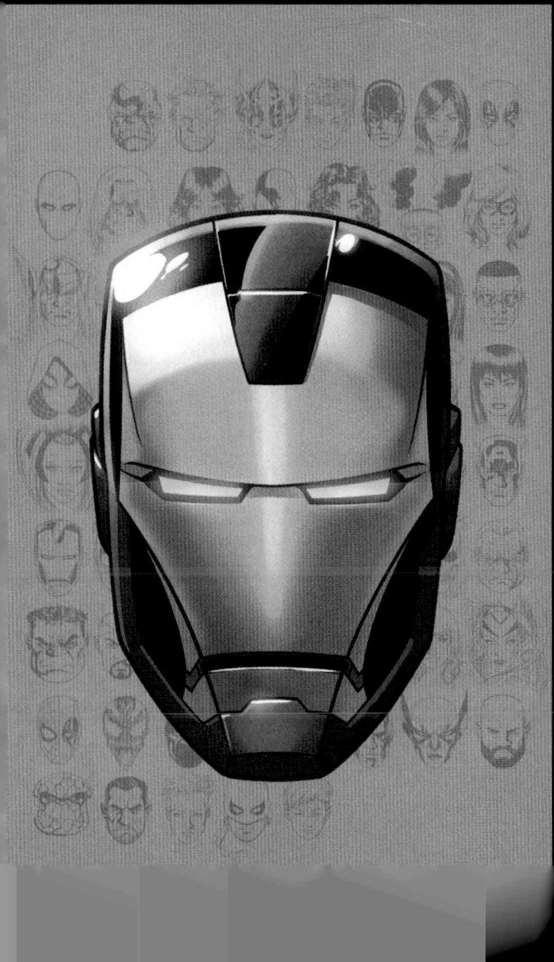

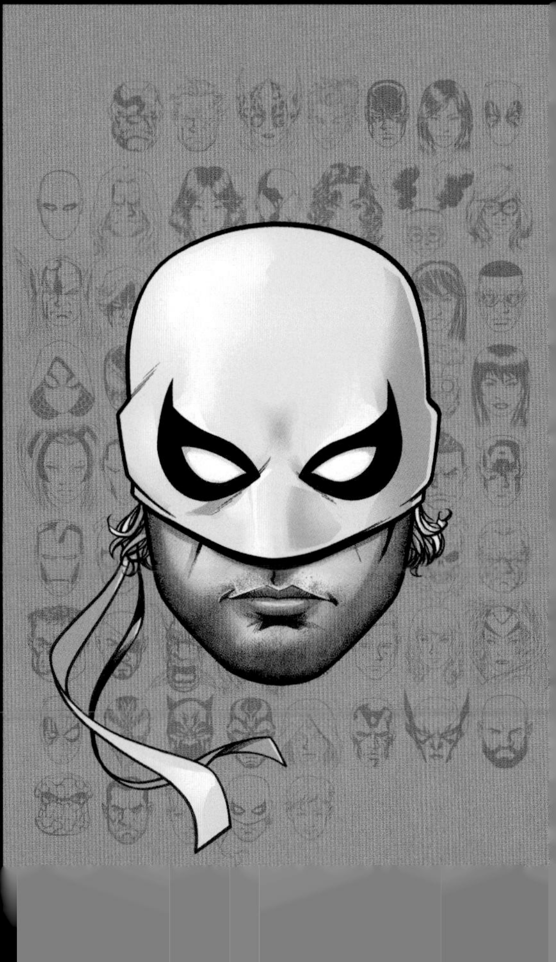

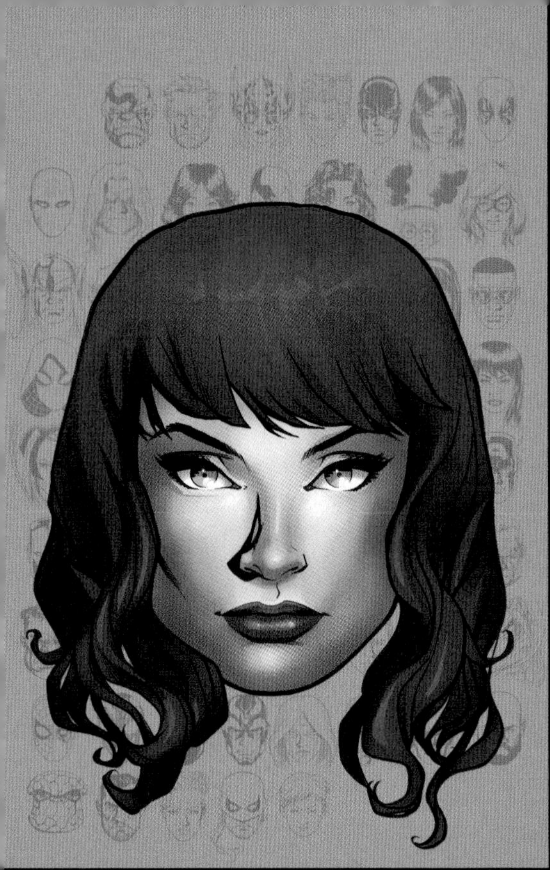

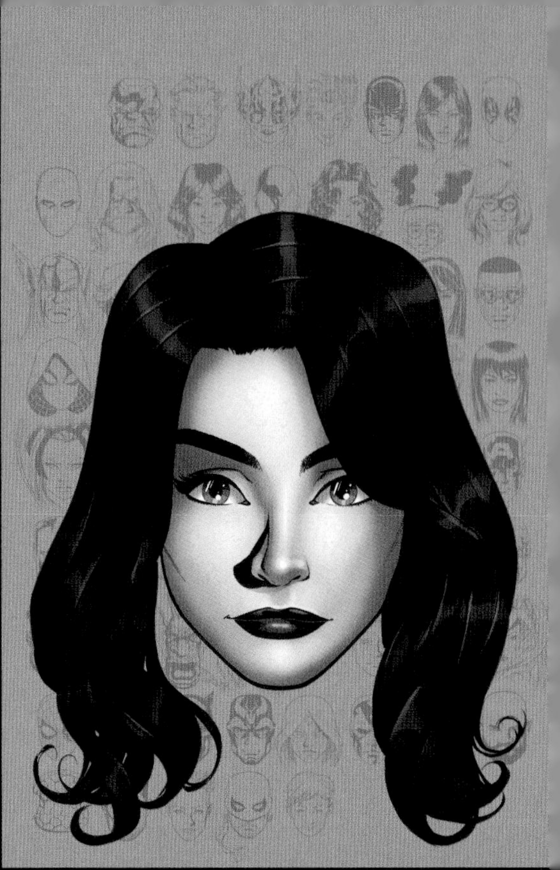

JEAN GREY #8
LEGACY HEADSHOT VARIANT BY
MIKE McKONE & ANDY TROY

JESSICA JONES #13
LEGACY HEADSHOT VARIANT BY
MIKE McKONE & ANDY TROY

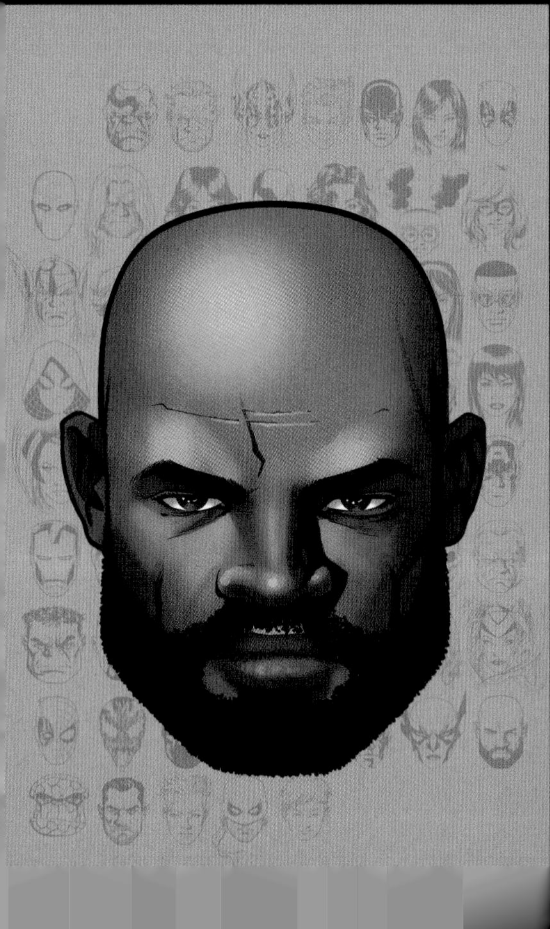

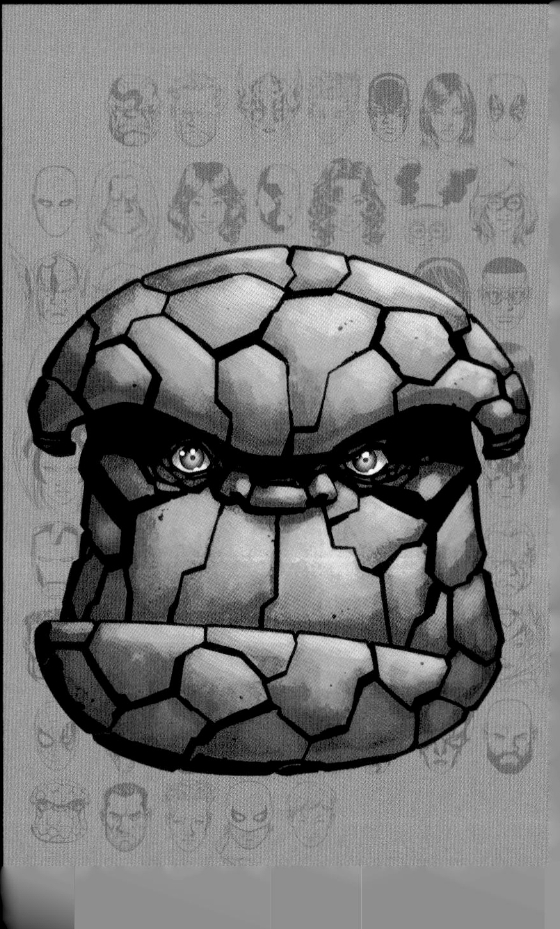

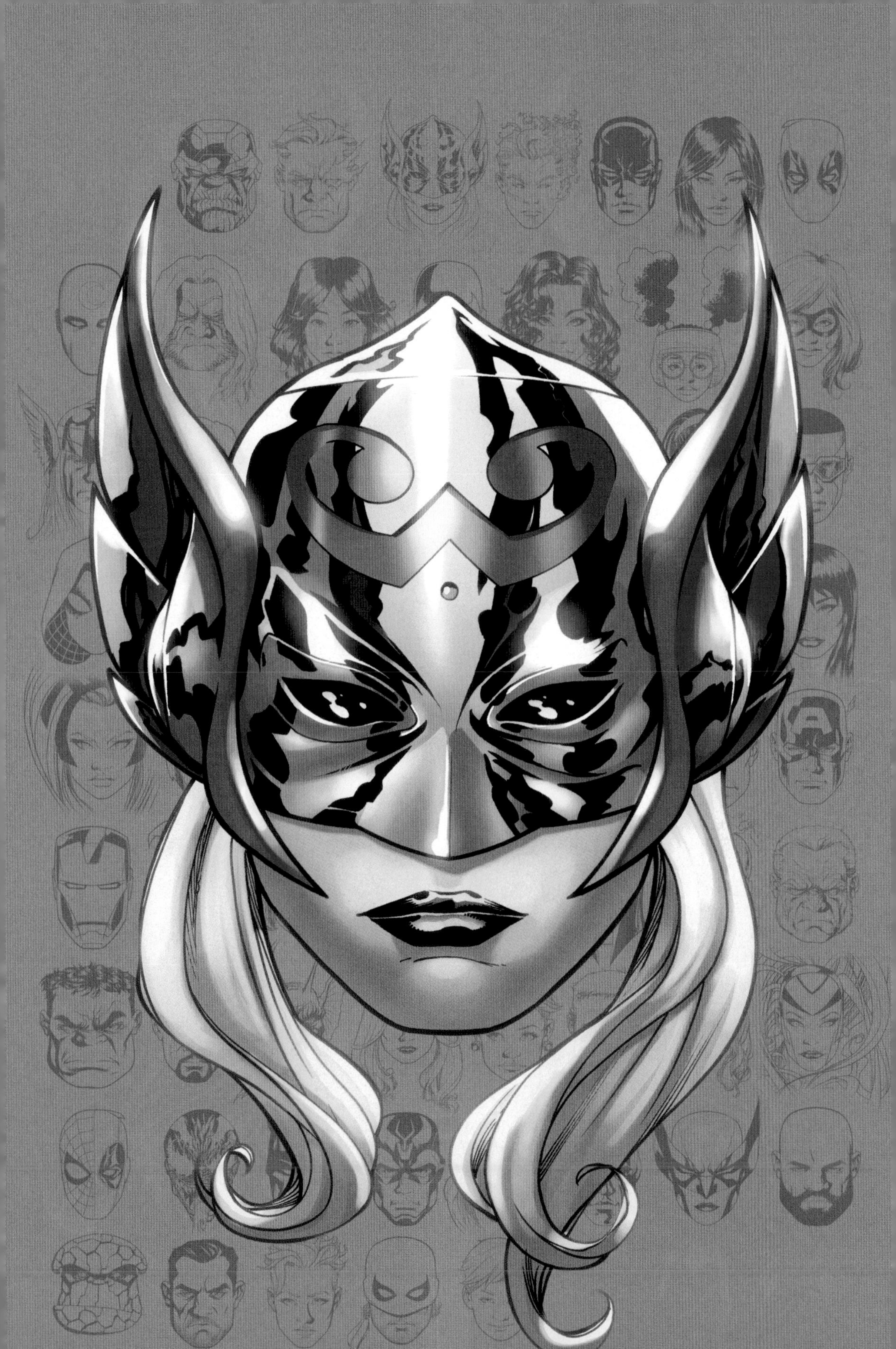

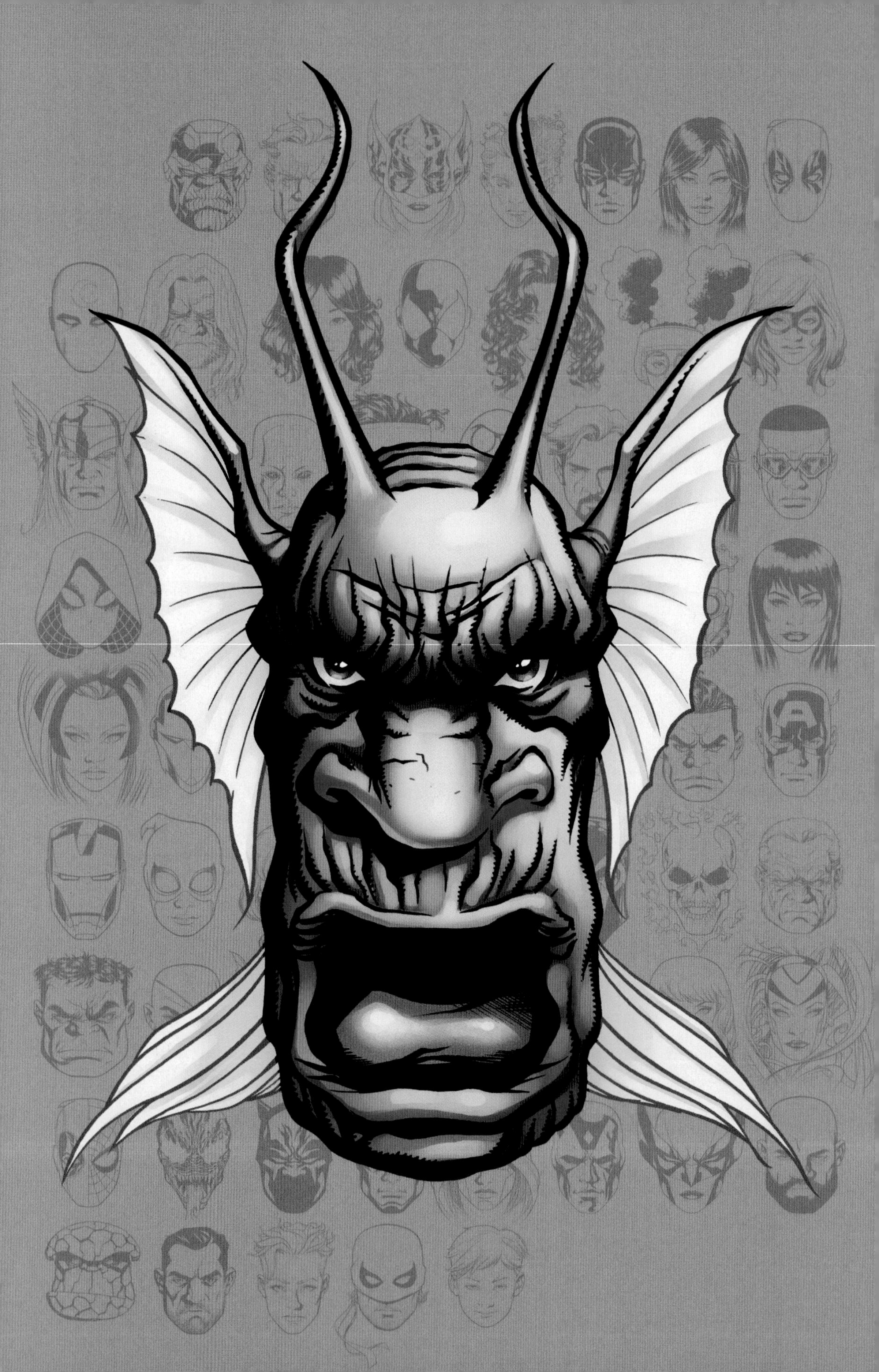

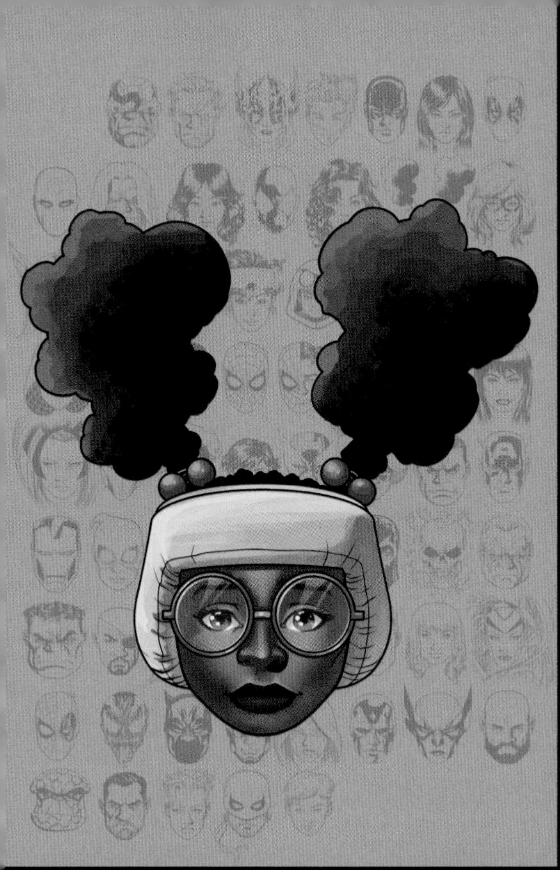

MOON GIRL AND DEVIL DINOSAUR #25
LEGACY HEADSHOT VARIANT BY
MIKE McKONE & ANDY TROY

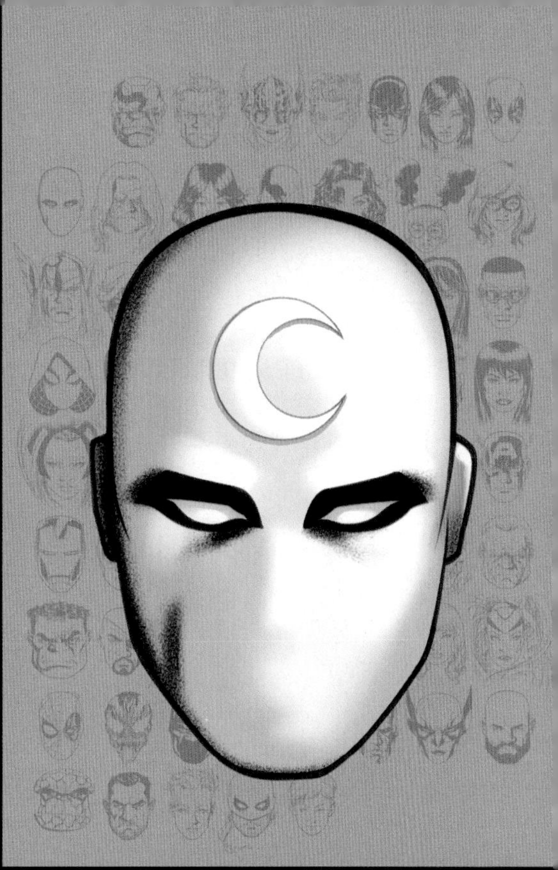

MOON KNIGHT #188
LEGACY HEADSHOT VARIANT BY
MIKE McKONE & RACHELLE ROSENBERG

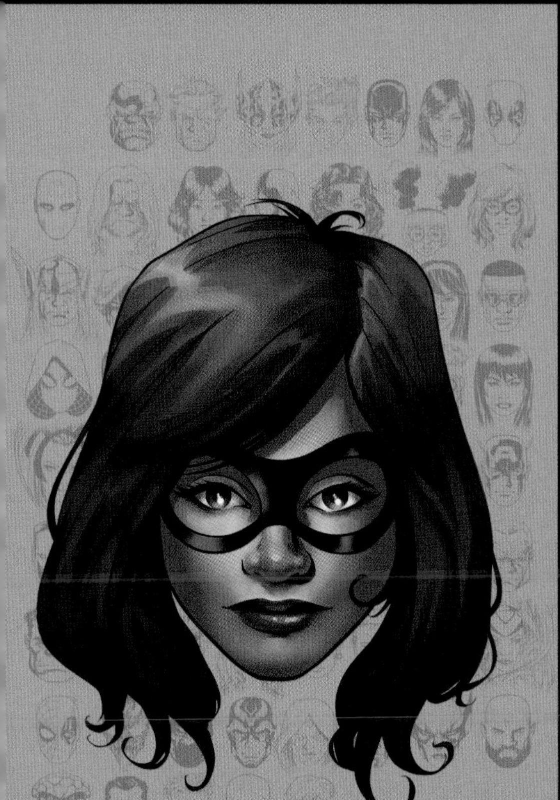

MS. MARVEL #25
LEGACY HEADSHOT VARIANT BY
MIKE McKONE & ANDY TROY

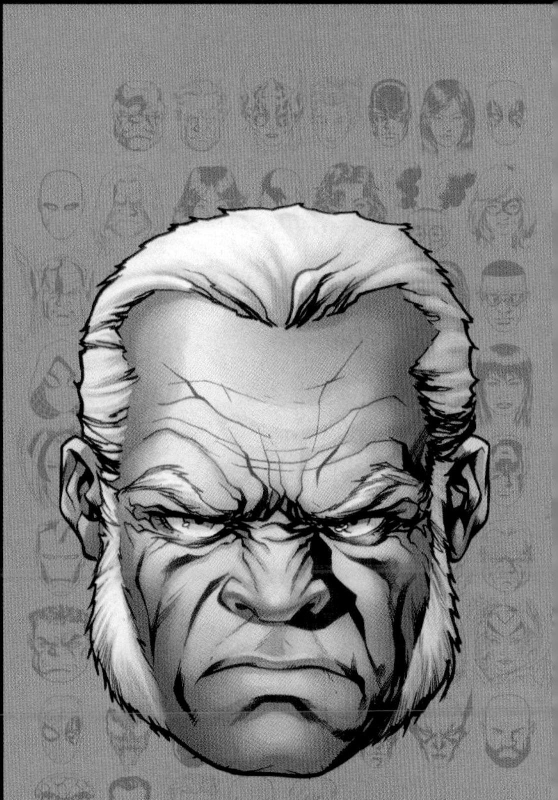

OLD MAN LOGAN #31
LEGACY HEADSHOT VARIANT BY
MIKE McKONE & RACHELLE ROSENBERG

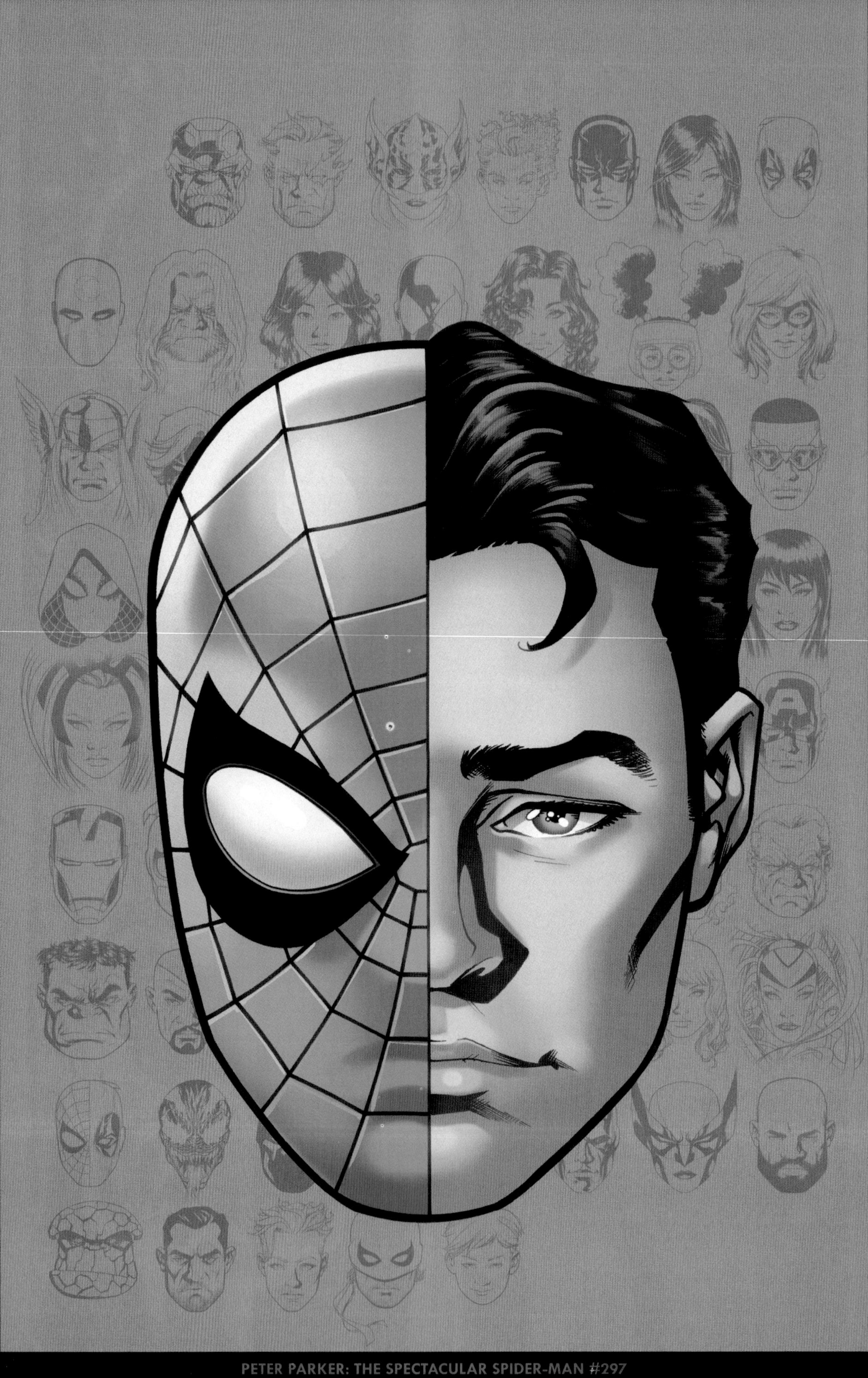

PETER PARKER: THE SPECTACULAR SPIDER-MAN #297
LEGACY HEADSHOT VARIANT BY
MIKE McKONE & RACHELLE ROSENBERG

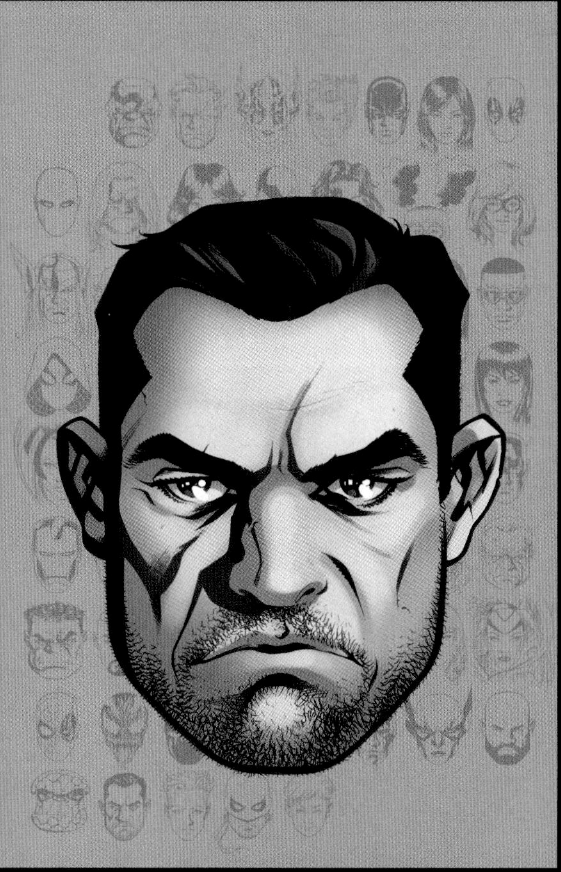

PUNISHER #218
LEGACY HEADSHOT VARIANT BY
MIKE McKONE & RACHELLE ROSENBERG

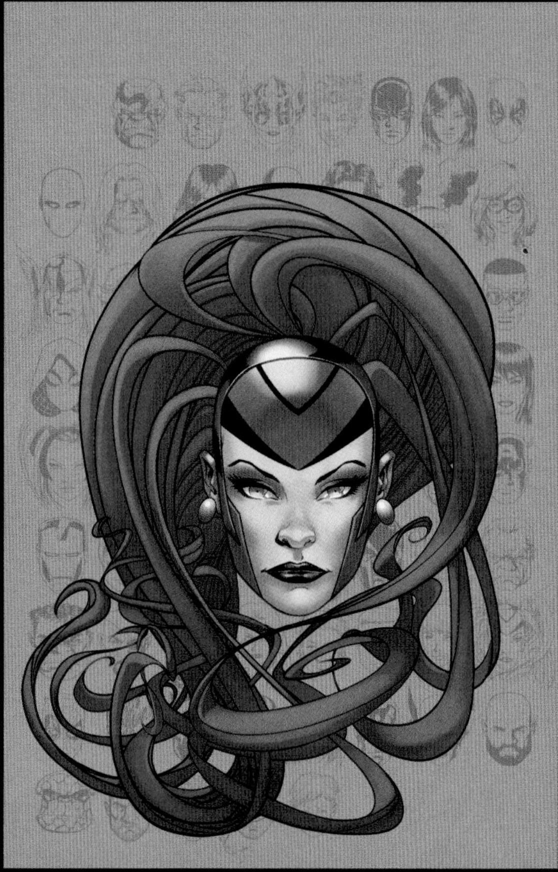

ROYALS #9
LEGACY HEADSHOT VARIANT BY
MIKE McKONE & RACHELLE ROSENBERG

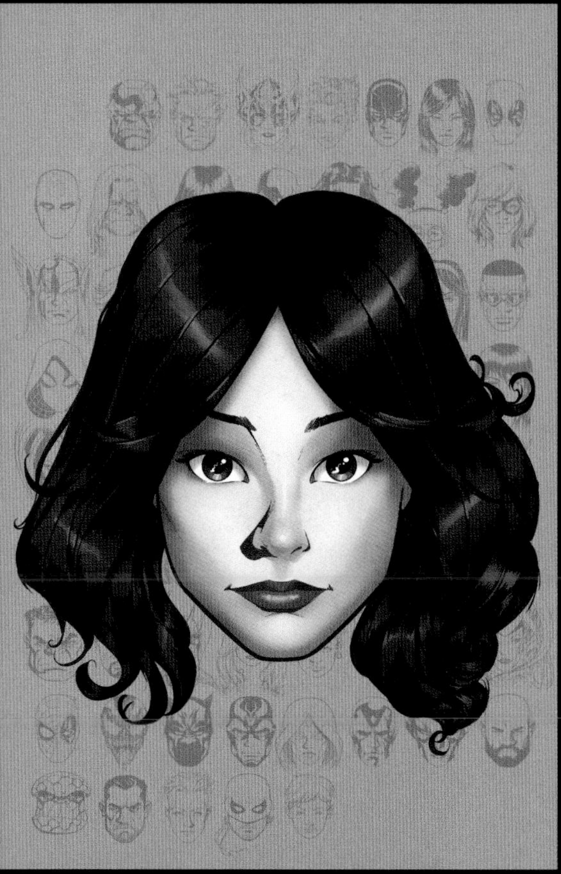

SECRET WARRIORS #8
LEGACY HEADSHOT VARIANT BY
MIKE McKONE & ANDY TROY

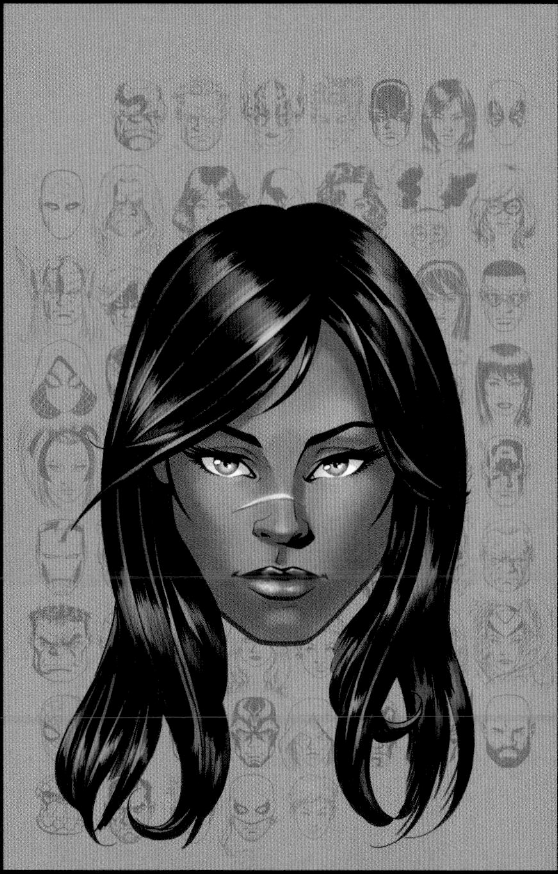

SHE-HULK #159
LEGACY HEADSHOT VARIANT BY
MIKE McKONE & RACHELLE ROSENBERG

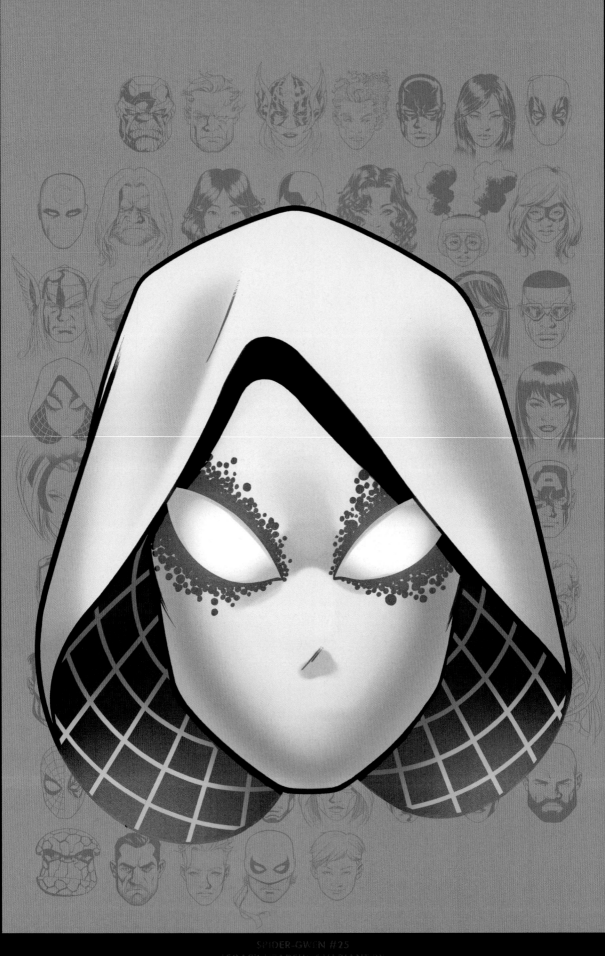

SPIDER-GWEN #25
LEGACY HEADSHOT VARIANT BY
MIKE McKONE & RACHELLE ROSENBERG

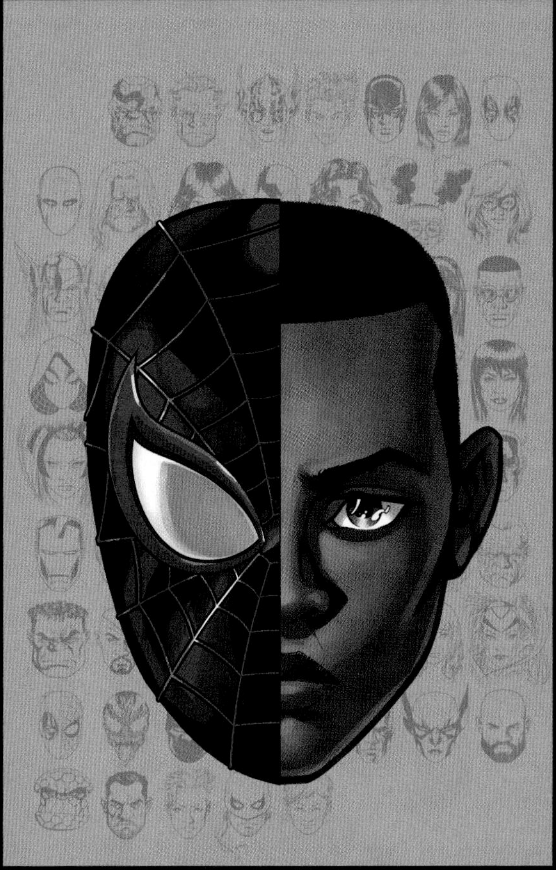

SPIDER-MAN #234
LEGACY HEADSHOT VARIANT BY
MIKE McKONE & ANDY TROY

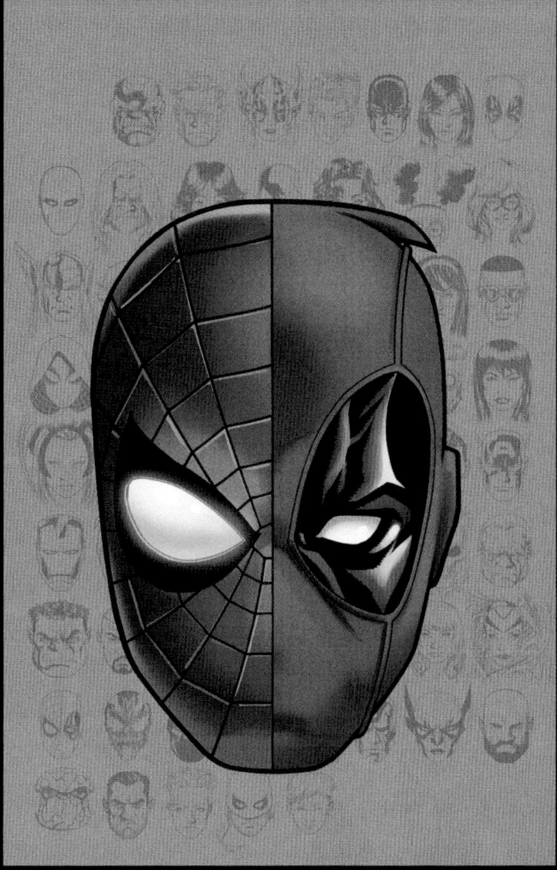

SPIDER-MAN/DEADPOOL #23
LEGACY HEADSHOT VARIANT BY
MIKE McKONE & RACHELLE ROSENBERG

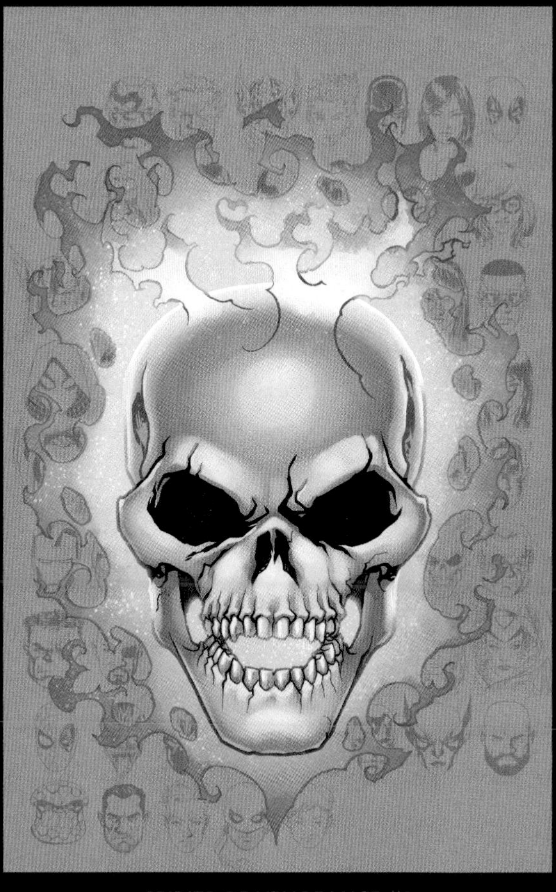

SPIRITS OF VENGEANCE #1
LEGACY HEADSHOT VARIANT BY
MIKE McKONE & RACHELLE ROSENBERG

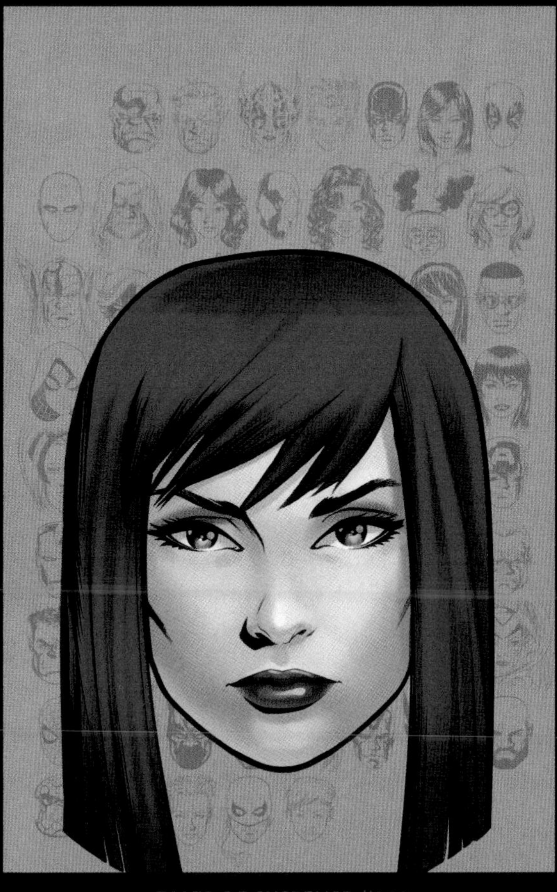

TALES OF SUSPENSE #100
LEGACY HEADSHOT VARIANT BY
MIKE McKONE & RACHELLE ROSENBERG

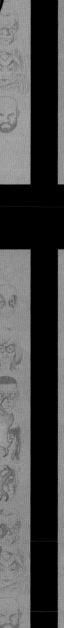

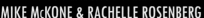

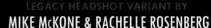

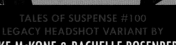

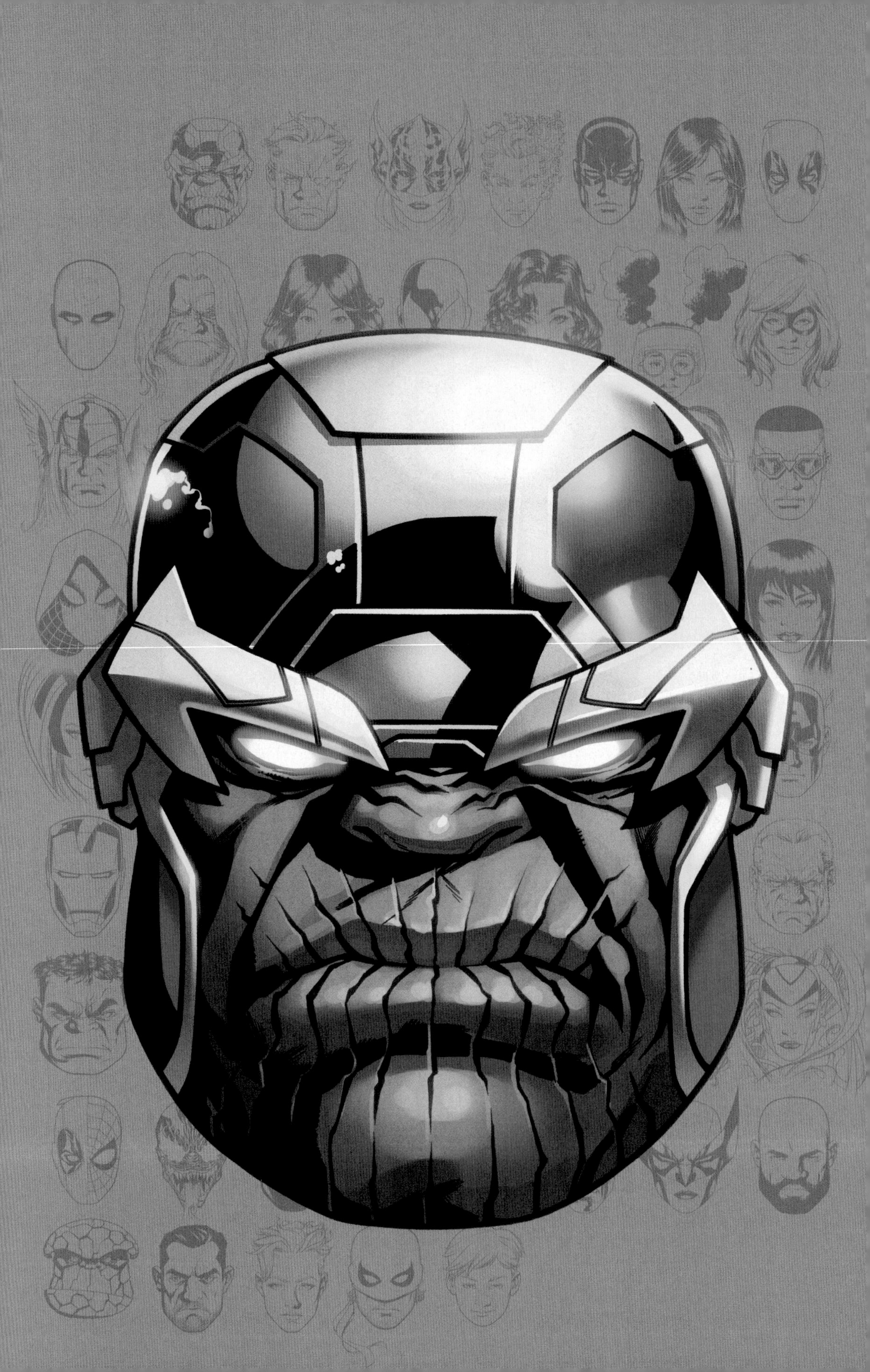

UNBEATABLE SQUIRREL GIRL #27
LEGACY HEADSHOT VARIANT BY
MIKE McKONE & ANDY TROY

UNBELIEVABLE GWENPOOL #21
LEGACY HEADSHOT VARIANT BY
MIKE McKONE & RACHELLE ROSENBERG

UNCANNY AVENGERS #28
LEGACY HEADSHOT
MIKE McKONE &

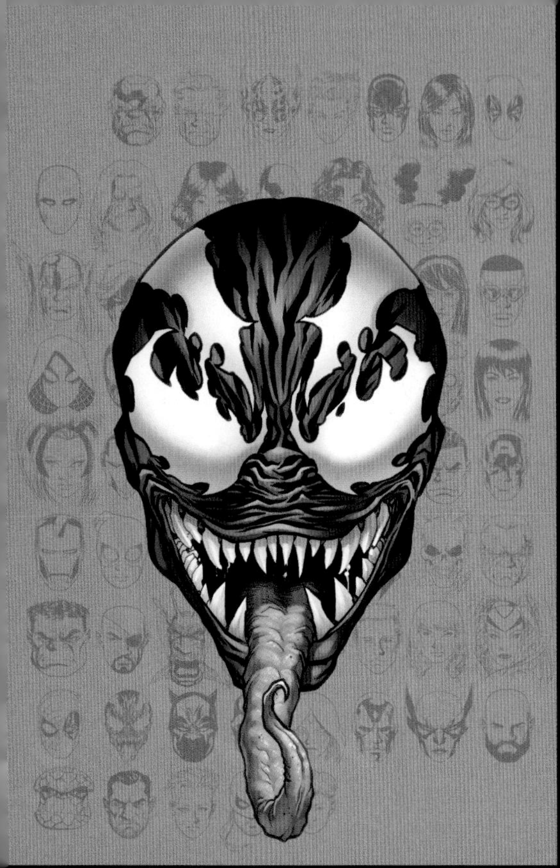

VENOM #155
LEGACY HEADSHOT VARIANT BY
MIKE McKONE & RACHELLE ROSENBERG

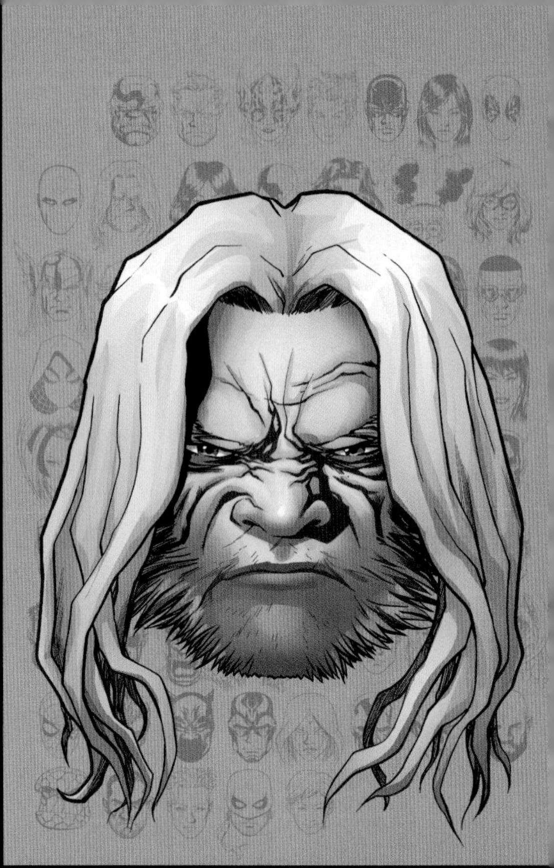

WEAPON X #12
LEGACY HEADSHOT VARIANT BY
MIKE McKONE & ANDY TROY

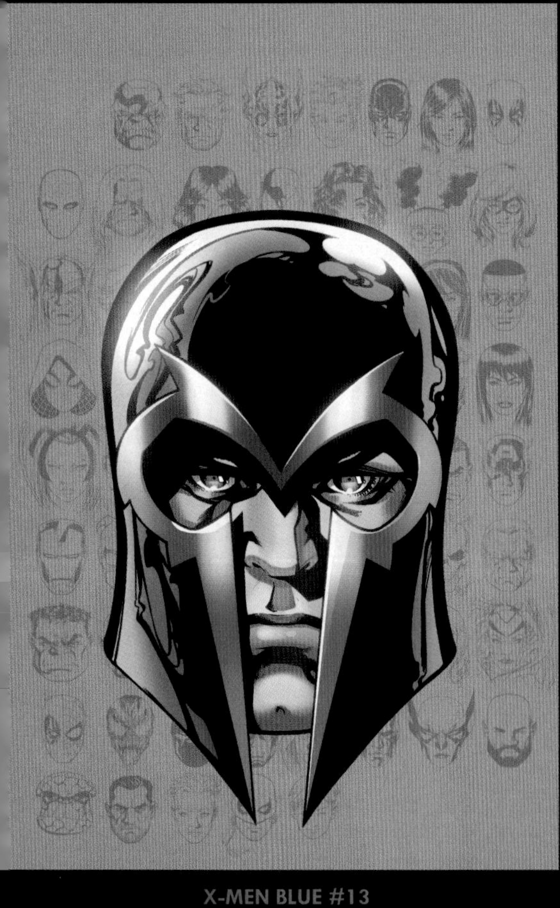

X-MEN BLUE #13
LEGACY HEADSHOT VARIANT BY
MIKE McKONE & RACHELLE ROSENBERG

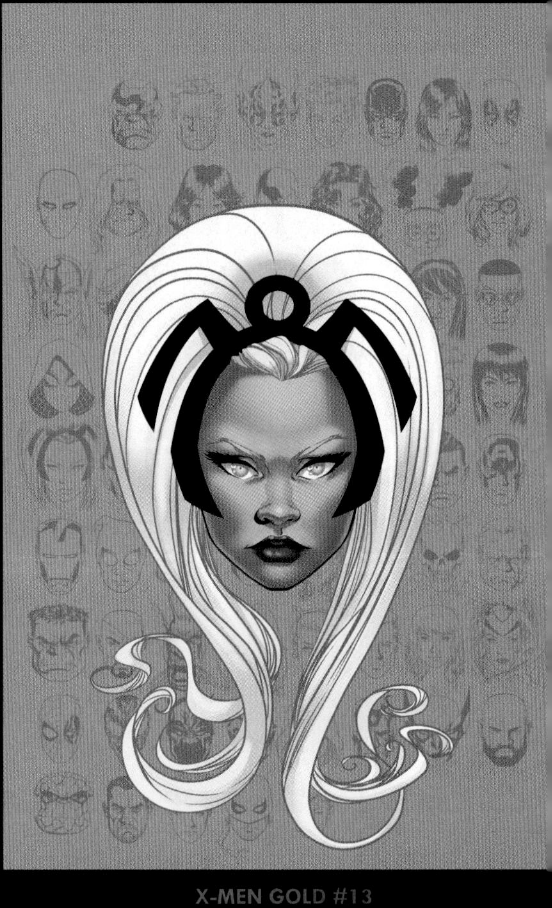

X-MEN GOLD #13
LEGACY HEADSHOT VARIANT BY
MIKE McKONE & RACHELLE ROSENBERG